OPEN SOURCE SOLUTIONS FOR
SMALL BUSINESS PROBLEMS

Open Source Solutions for Small Business Problems

John Locke

CHARLES RIVER MEDIA, INC.
Hingham, Massachusetts

-04

Acquisitions Editor: James Walsh
Production: Datapage Technologies
Cover Design: The Printed Image

CHARLES RIVER MEDIA, INC.
10 Downer Avenue
Hingham, Massachusetts 02043
781-740-0400
781-740-8816 (FAX)
info@charlesriver.com
www.charlesriver.com

This book is printed on acid-free paper.

John Locke. *Open Source Solutions for Small Business Problems*.
ISBN: 1-58450-320-3

Library of Congress Cataloging-in-Publication Data
Locke, John, 1968-
  Open source solutions for small business problems / John Locke.
    p. cm.
  ISBN 1-58450-320-3 (pbk. with cd-rom : alk. paper)
  1. Small business—Computer programs. 2. Open source software. I. Title.
  HF5548.38.O64L63 2004
  005.3—dc22

                              2004005015

Printed in the United States of America
04 7 6 5 4 3 2 First Edition

CHARLES RIVER MEDIA titles are available for site license or bulk purchase by institutions, user groups, corporations, etc. For additional information, please contact the Special Sales Department at 781-740-0400.

Contents

Introduction

Computers have revolutionized business at all levels. The smallest businesses regularly use computers to create mailings to their customers. Email and the Internet have provided whole new media for communicating information. Accounting software has greatly eased tasks for the bookkeepers of the world. However, few small businesses have done anything more with their computers than these basic tasks.

Large businesses have spent millions of dollars developing and implementing powerful computer systems to support their operations. In many cases, this software makes managing their businesses possible—but for a large business to remain competitive, it needs to reinvent itself at regular intervals, driving ever more costs in software development, or forcing them to work around software that doesn't fit them anymore.

Many of these systems can tremendously cut business costs, if chosen wisely and implemented well. Some of them even make new types of business possible. Most of them have been financially out of reach of small business—until now.

A revolution in software is happening all around us, and it's called Open Source. Many people feel open source software development is a better way of making software. The open source process rewards technical excellence, decimates cost, and prevents vendor lock-in, but sometimes at the expense of usability.

The purpose of this book is to take a sweeping view of everything computers do that can help a business, and identify how you can do it with open source software. Many businesses are curious about implementing open source software, but are hesitant to try. The single biggest reason? Belief that changing to open source is an all-or-nothing proposition. It's not. One of the best ways to get started with open source is to install it one bit at a time. Try an open source office suite on your Microsoft Windows computer. Install Linux on a server somewhere in your company. Use an open source Web browser to block pop-up advertising, make searching easier, and improve the security of your system.

Most of this book discusses open source server solutions that run on a Linux server, and client software that runs on Windows, Linux, or an Apple Macintosh. You do not need to be a Linux person to get something out of this book. You can almost always continue to use your Windows PC, or a Mac, to connect and interact with the server applications—you generally won't see any difference. This book can help you understand what systems are available to you, along with many of the limitations.

This is not a Linux guide. It will not teach you how to administer a Unix-based computer, or very much about switching entirely to open source software. You will need other resources to implement these solutions—a working knowledge of Unix permissions, users and groups, file editing, and command line basics. Other Linux books can get you started in these areas. This book is also not meant to be a comprehensive resource for each of the topics—it's an overview, an introduction, and a starting point for the topic. But this book provides many solutions that require a Linux server, and points out Linux desktop solutions wherever they're available.

NOTE

When providing Linux examples, the author has described how to install and use software based on a Mandrake distribution. All of the server software described in the book will work with any Linux distribution, and most of the software works with other Unix systems as well, but may involve different installation and configuration steps. The Apple Mac OS X operating system is considered a Unix system.

Desktop software for Windows in the book will work with Windows 2000, any flavor of Windows XP, or later, unless otherwise noted. Some, but not all, of the software runs in Windows 98 and Windows ME. Desktop software for the Apple Mac runs only on OS X or later. The only applications in this book that can run in OS 9 or earlier are browser-based applications.

Chapters in the book are grouped into four major parts. Part I describes the fundamentals of open source, servers, networks, and desktops, along with the core technology most of the solutions in the rest of the book depend upon. Part II takes a look at basic business operational needs, and how they can be met with open source software. Part III contains more specific solutions, ways that computers and open source software can make things possible that were impossible before. Part IV is all about dealing with the downsides of computers: the extra security needed, dependence on your data, and bombardment with the annoyances of spam and viruses.

There are many thousands of open source projects in various stages of development, and no author could possibly discover them all. This book attempts to identify some of the best solutions of each category for small business use. Because hundreds of new open source projects appear daily, this book focuses on what businesses need, instead of what individual software does. Every chapter attempts to provide insight into what to look for in a software project, how to go about finding one that best suits your needs, and where to go for more information. This is a book about computer strategy, with enough tactical information to get practical solutions implemented. Each chapter provides a quick-start guide on what you need to know about a broad topic, and could easily be expanded to be a book by itself.

Because the details of installing software packages change from project to project, and even from month to month within an active project, implementation details are kept light in this book. You can find more step-by-step help on the Web site that accompanies this book, *http://www.opensourcesmall.biz*, or on the Web pages for the corresponding projects.

One goal of this book is to bridge the communication gap between business people and information technology (IT) people. If you're a business person, you should be able to find many helpful hints in the pages of this book, to help you streamline your business operations using open source software. Some parts of the book are quite technical. The idea here is that you should be able to get a sense of what a particular type of software can do for your business, and then hand this book to an IT consultant to get it implemented. Feel free to skip the technical parts—though if you read through them you may be in a better position to evaluate a proposal from a consultant.

If you're an IT consultant, or IT manager within a company, this book should help you make a business case for installing a particular type of software. It should also give you a head start on finding open source projects to actually deploy, along with some tips, hints, and pitfalls to avoid. There's a big opportunity here for small business-oriented IT consultants. You can set up many systems in this book yourself, and then host services for your clients.

Students may also find this book useful. This book is designed to be good for a business class within a technical computer science track, or for a technology class within a business track.

So now you might ask: How big is a small business? The United States Small Business Administration defines a small business as a firm that employs between 1 and 500 people. That's quite a big range, and includes many businesses most people would consider to be medium-sized. Businesses with 5 to 50 computers will probably find every solution in this book to be useful. Businesses with more than 50 computers should still find most of the information in this book helpful, especially for deciding an IT strategy, but the size may dictate choosing a project optimized for greater use. Businesses with fewer than five computers will still find much of this book useful, though some of the chapters may not be as relevant.

Software engineers, like engineers in most other fields, are fond of jargon and obscure acronyms. The author has made every attempt to define these words and acronyms at least once in the book, though it's not always at their first mention. If you find yourself lost in unfamiliar terms, you can always check the glossary at the back of the book—most of the jargon and acronyms used in the book have been defined there.

This book only scratches the surface of the open source world. If you know of a great open source program I've overlooked, or find cool business uses for software I've discussed, I'd love to hear about it. Write me at john@opensourcesmall.biz, and I'll consider it for future versions of the book or Web site.

Finally, I would like to thank everybody who made this book possible. To all the open source developers who have devoted time and energy to making top quality software available to everyone, the computer users of the world, not to mention this book, owe you a great debt. To my friends, family, and customers who have supported my efforts writing this book, your insights, comments, and advice are very much appreciated. I'd like to thank Zoka Cafe, Caffe Zingaro, and El Diablo Coffee Company, three coffee shops in Seattle that provided me with many hours of wireless access in exchange for purchasing a steady stream of caffeine. And this book could not have been written without my lovely wife, Jill, who has had to put up with incessant talk about open source and small business for the better part of a year.

Enjoy!

— *John Locke*

Seattle, WA, February 2004

Small Business Computing Infrastructure

This part of the book contains core information to help you set up a computing infrastructure for your business. If you have much IT experience, you'll probably find much of this material to be a review, though you may find a few hints to help you along. If you're starting out, these chapters cover what you need to know, and need to have in place, before you'll be able to implement the solutions in the rest of the book.

Chapter 1 introduces open source software, defining what it is, who makes it, and what you need to know about how viable it is for business.

Chapter 2 discusses server hardware and software, giving guidance for choosing an operating system and installing Linux successfully.

Chapter 3 covers choosing an Internet connection, sharing files in a network, setting up a firewall, and getting an office network to run smoothly.

Chapter 4 is the only chapter in the book that focuses exclusively on desktop applications, surveying the current state of open source on the desktop.

Chapter 5 provides background to help you get a mail server running on your network.

Chapter 6 helps you set up a Web server, an essential server for the solutions in this book.

1 Open Source Software in Your Small Business

INTRODUCTION

For decades, sophisticated computer systems have helped large enterprises manage finances, schedules, systems, and data. These enterprise systems have long been out of reach of the budget of small business owners. A new type of software, called Open Source software, promises to bring enterprise-class computer systems to the small business.

Many people with small businesses have never heard of open source software. Ask a manufacturer of carpentry tools if he knows what Linux is and you'll most likely hear "Isn't that some kind of china?"

Simply put, open source software is software that is freely distributed, complete with the original code that makes it possible to easily change it. There are no restrictions placed on your specifying how you use it, and you can usually obtain and install it with no licensing charges. Furthermore, you may freely distribute open source software to others, as long as you observe the terms of the license. In contrast, proprietary software is software sold by a company or vendor without the source code, or with licensing restrictions.

Why should you care? Consider that open source software can save small businesses a lot of money, and make it possible to manage more projects than you could before. With it you can run enterprise-level software on a small business budget. If you don't, your competitor surely will, and will be able to do more work with less overhead.

One of the problems with open source software is that there are an overwhelming number of choices. For every type of system, there are at least a couple, if not dozens, of specific open source projects to choose from. This book can help you make good choices for your business, recommending one particular program or set of programs for each type of system, and pointing out its shortcomings so you can choose another one that better suits your particular needs.

The plethora of choices means you can build a system that exactly suits your needs, your processes, and your preferences, rather than having to adapt your processes to fit the way a particular program works. A big idea behind open source is that software should be a service set up to help your business, rather than a product your business consumes.

The list of free software grows longer every day. Already most of the Web servers in the world run on free software. There's free software for email, graphics manipulation, financial software, authentication and encryption, remote access, customer resource management (CRM), content management, scheduling, and even entire office suites.

In this chapter, we discuss what you need to know about open source software, how to get help when you need it, and how to be a responsible member of the open source community. We'll dispel many myths about open source software along the way.

WHAT IS OPEN SOURCE?

To fully answer the question of what open source is, we need to understand at a basic level how computers work. Computer programs are simply a series of yes/no decisions, combined with actions to go with them. Has the user pressed a key? Put the code corresponding to that key into the file. Then draw the character on the screen. Then wait for the user to press another key.

At the most fundamental level, computers handle information as *bits*—a simple switch that can be on or off. A bit can be either one or zero. String a bunch of bits together and you have a *binary* system—a number comprised of powers of two, also called *base two*. If you remember any algebra from high school, you may recall that base 10 is the decimal system, where each digit has 10 possible states: the numerals 0 through 9. In most cases, when you view binary data, the computer shows it to you in groups of eight bits, in a system called *hexadecimal* or base 16. In addition to the numerals 0 to 9, the values of 10 through 15 are represented by the letters *a* to *f*.

Programmers build up libraries of little programs to handle ever more complicated actions, with an increasing sophistication in the decisions being made. For example, did the user fill out the tax form correctly and confirm that he's ready to file?

Compress the contents of their tax return into the standard format, open a network connection to the IRS, and send the return in a stream of ones and zeros to the server at the other end.

For any of these actions, the computer is doing the same thing—making a yes/no decision and changing the state of something else. It's just doing this several hundred million times a second.

There are many different computer languages, but they all have one thing in common—they're for people, not for computers. Computers only understand machine language. C, C++, Perl, Visual Basic, Python, Lisp, Cobol®, Fortran, and Java® are a few of the many computer languages out there that provide metaphors such as algebra, photographs, windows, buttons, music tracks, and tax returns. All programs need to be translated from the human language into the native machine language for the individual type of processor before they can be run. These, and other languages, are what computer programmers use to write programs. What they actually write is the *source code* of a program. Listing 1.1 is an example of some source code, straight from the Linux kernel (the program that controls all of the hardware, and manages all other programs):

LISTING 1.1　A Look at Some Source Code

```
unsigned long mem_total, sav_total;
unsigned int mem_unit, bitcount;

/* If the sum of all the available memory (i.e. ram + swap)
 * is less than can be stored in a 32 bit unsigned long then
 * we can be binary compatible with 2.2.x kernels.  If not,
 * well, in that case 2.2.x was broken anyways...
 *
 *   -Erik Andersen <andersee@debian.org> */

mem_total = val.totalram + val.totalswap;
if (mem_total < val.totalram || mem_total < val.totalswap)
  goto out;
bitcount = 0;
mem_unit = val.mem_unit;
while (mem_unit > 1) {
  bitcount++;
  mem_unit >= 1;
  sav_total = mem_total;
  mem_total <<= 1;
  if (mem_total < sav_total)
    goto out;
}
```

Notice that the source code has some explanatory text describing what the software is doing. There are statements, variables, and numbers, each with a specific meaning. When you learn the conventions of the computer language, it's not too hard to figure out what a section of source code does.

Now let's see what the computer runs. Listing 1.2 is a chunk of *object code*:

LISTING 1.2 Object Code Is Mostly Impenetrable

```
0000000 c0b8 8e07 b8d8 9000 c08e 00b9 2901 29f6
0000010 fcff a5f3 19ea 0000 bf90 3ff4 d88e d08e
0000020 fc89 e18e 78bb 1e00 c564 b137 5706 a5f3
0000030 1f5f 45c6 2404 8964 643f 478c be02 01c5
0000040 98ac c3a3 8101 c9fe 7301 910d d231 00bb
0000050 b802 0201 13cd e872 03b4 ff30 10cd 09b9
0000060 b300 bd07 01c9 01b8 cd13 b810 0001 d4be
0000070 8900 3104 30c0 cdd2 bb13 0200 f1a0 8b01
0000080 c30e 2b01 380c 76c8 a105 01c3 042b 7ce8
0000090 5000 a3e8 5800 0628 01f1 e075 0068 0710
00000a0 37e8 e800 0116 f0e8 a100 01fc c009 1c75
00000b0 1e8b 01c3 08b8 8302 0ffb 1074 1cb0 fb83
00000c0 7412 b009 8320 24fb 0274 00b0 fca3 ea01
00000d0 0000 9020 0000 0000 0000 c08c ffa9 750f
00000e0 31fe ffdb 201e 3b02 f406 7601 c301 c3a1
00000f0 2b01 8904 c1c1 09e1 d901 0973 0774 c031
0000100 d829 e8c1 e809 0005 2de8 eb00 60d6 b860
```

Even programmers have a difficult time understanding that. There are tools to help decode object code, but all of the comments, variable names, and hints about what each step represents are no longer available at all.

Most proprietary programs are sold as object code—the actual instructions for the specific processor describing which bits to flip when. Each microprocessor can only execute its own specific flavor of machine language represented at the lowest level as something called *assembler code*. Assembler code and the corresponding machine language are completely different between a Mac, a PC, or a mainframe.

Again, the computer at its most basic level doesn't know or care about source code—it just sits there flipping switches, crunching bits. There are two ways to do this: a program called an *interpreter* can interpret the source code on the fly and translate it into machine language as the program runs, or a program called a *compiler* can translate the human language into machine language all at once, before the program ever gets used. The compiler translates the source code into object code for a particular microprocessor.

Computer languages are divided into two different groups, based on this distinction—they're either compiled or interpreted languages. Interpreted languages are easy to learn, because you can play with them and get immediate results. But most serious development is done with compiled languages, because they end up being much faster—and for proprietary software companies, have the added benefit of hiding how you made the program work.

Which brings us back to the definition of open source software: software that freely distributes the source code along with the object code, so that any programmer familiar with the language can tweak, improve, modify, or customize it without needing to ask anyone for permission or wait for a vendor to do it for them.

DIFFERENCES BETWEEN OPEN SOURCE AND PROPRIETARY

The opposite of open source software is proprietary software. Proprietary software is usually developed by a commercial software company that is specifically in business to sell that software. Sometimes proprietary software is just software developed internally by a company and not released to the outside world—but you can't get hold of this software, so it doesn't really come into discussion in this book.

The primary goal of most open source projects is technical excellence. The primary goal of most commercial software companies is to make money. This fundamental motivation illustrates the primary difference.

In many cases, money is essential to software. Money buys marketing, making a software product well known. Money pays for people to provide the finishing touches to software, making it easier to use, prettier to look at, and more dominant in the marketplace. Money can bring a critical mass of developers together in one place, making it possible to develop large, powerful software systems.

Before the widespread use of the Internet, it took a large budget to be able to get a lot of programmers working together on a project. With the advent of cheap communications and powerful collaboration tools, hundreds or thousands of developers can easily work together on an open source project without the overhead of a company and its management. Some of the implications of the different motivations behind open source software and proprietary software are listed in Table 1.1.

Several points in this table bear more explanation. The financial stake of the company, for one. Software companies have gotten into the habit of continually releasing new versions of their software to fix shortcomings in the previous version. Some growth and change in software is inevitable and is great for improving the software—but if you're a software company, you have the added incentive of being able to sell upgrades to existing customers to maintain your bottom line.

TABLE 1.1 Characteristics of Open Source and Proprietary Software Development

	Proprietary Software	*Open Source Software*
Software is fundamentally ...	A product Intellectual property	A service An expression of technique
Programmers ...	Are assigned to particular parts of a project	Choose which parts of the project they want to work on
Installing a copy of the software on more computers without paying for it ...	Is piracy	Makes the software more valuable because of the network effect
Security is ensured because ...	Nobody on the outside knows how it works	Anybody in the world can look for flaws and propose solutions
Marketing message	You don't need to understand how it works, it just does (usually without fail)	You need to understand the basics of the system, just as you need to know how to use any other tool
Hardware requirements	Runs better on newer, more powerful, more expensive computers	Runs well on older, cheaper computers
Programs are	Big, monolithic, multi-purpose systems that attempt to do everything for everyone	Small, single-purpose units that can be chained together to build a custom system that exactly meets your needs
Profits are generated by ...	Selling new versions of the software product Support contracts	Selling additional services, or reducing costs in the core businesses Support contracts

One of the most valid criticisms of open source software is that it can be hard to use. Most of it was developed by software engineers, for other engineers. Once the software works well enough to accomplish a task, often that's as far as the software develops. User interface design may be poor, documentation is usually plentiful but poorly written and hard to find. You, as the user, are expected to have enough background knowledge to be able to use the software in spite of its poor interface.

The good news about open source software is that most participants are fully aware of this shortcoming, and it's only a matter of time (and enough squeaky wheels, or better yet, volunteers) before quirky designs are improved and documentation written. In most open source software projects, the priority is on getting it to work reliably—most programmers don't care what it looks like.

For software companies, on the other hand, the look, feel, usability, and documentation of their products is a much higher priority, because that's what the customer sees and works with.

An interesting result of this different focus is the reliability of pre-release software. Most software follows a similar release numbering system: early, partially working versions have numbers less than 1. As the program nears release, the project releases an *alpha* version that is meant to go out to a wider audience for testing purposes and to get feedback about features that may need improvement before release. Next comes the *beta* release, which generally has all of the features of the final release, but may still have a lot of bugs. Then comes a series of *release candidates*, often referred to as RC1, RC2, etc. Finally, when enough bugs have been resolved and the decision-makers of the project are satisfied that the program is ready, it's declared a release.

Open source software projects and software companies both use this same release cycle. The difference is what gets done first. Many alpha releases by proprietary software companies have pretty interfaces, but crucial functions may not work. On the other hand, open source alpha releases are generally rock-solid with months of active use in production—but the user interface may be poor or entirely missing.

Open Source Is Not Shareware

Many people confuse open source software with shareware. Shareware has a long history on the Internet, and wide visibility. Shareware is inexpensive proprietary software, usually developed by a single programmer. You don't get the source code when you download shareware. And while you may be able to get it for free, shareware doesn't usually have the same quality as open source software, for most of the reasons listed in the previous section.

Open Source Licenses

We've learned what source code is, and how open source software differs from proprietary software. But we still haven't looked at what makes it open source. The Open Source Initiative (OSI) is a non-profit corporation that exists to promote the concept of open source to businesses. OSI manages something they call "The Open Source Definition," which is used to definitively identify whether a software license can be considered open source. The Open Source Definition is reprinted in Appendix A. Wherever the term open source is used to describe software in this book, it means that the software uses a license that has been approved by or meets the standards of the Open Source Definition.

Basically, an open source license grants you the right to freely use and redistribute the software, modify it however you want, and distribute derivatives from the software, under the terms of the original license. There are other requirements of a license to meet the open source definition, but these are the defining characteristics.

Open source software is simply software released under a license that meets the Open Source Definition. It is not software placed in the public domain; the owners of a copyright have not given up any rights to the software. They have basically granted you the right to copy the software, modify it, and distribute it to other users, with restrictions. An example of a restriction might be that the copyright notice of the original author must be included in any derivative programs. The original copyright holder may offer the software under an open source license, and under a commercial license with different terms.

Open source software is usually, but not always, free of charge. A software company may charge you for an open source license—but they can't restrict you from giving the code away to somebody else. This provides incentive for the copyright holder to provide some additional service beyond just the code.

Just because you have the source-code for a program doesn't mean it's open source. Many commercial software companies are starting to realize the advantages of the open source development model, and have started to share their source code to help improve their product. While many of these programs provide the customizeability and several other benefits of open source software, if you're not allowed to redistribute it, it doesn't meet the Open Source Definition. Several programs of this nature are discussed in this book. In the discussion, we have noted where source code is available, but not under an open source license.

There are many different common open source licenses, each with slightly different terms. If you're not a software company, the differences in these licenses are not going to affect you—you're free to use and modify any open source software you receive, with no obligation to redistribute it. Here's a list of a few popular open source licenses:

- Gnu General Public License (GPL)
- Gnu Lesser General Public License (LGPL)
- Mozilla Public License (MPL)

- Apache Software License
- Apple Public Source License
- Artistic License
- BSD License

Take the time to read the licenses that come with your software. You may be surprised how liberating it is to read fine print that grants you rights, rather than taking them away.

COMMON BUSINESS QUESTIONS

So let's get down to business. Most business people have a lot of questions about open source when they first hear about it. Many of these are prompted by rumors or misinformation you'll find all over the place. There are a lot of myths surrounding open source software. Open source developers call these myths *FUD*, for the Fear, Uncertainty, and Doubt they spread. Nothing debunks myths like good information, and that's the purpose of this whole book.

Can I Use Open Source with My Current Systems?

One common misconception people have about using open source software is that it's an all-or-nothing proposition, that you have to convert everything or you can't use it. The reality is you already use open source software, without even knowing it.

One of the strengths of open source software is that the people developing it strive to make it available on as many different platforms as possible. Often it doesn't make sense for you to switch your desktop computer to Linux and open source software. For most of the systems in this book, there's no need to make a switch—you can simply add these services to your systems, and use your PCs and Macs to access them. Even if your business is so small that you don't need a server, this book provides the information you need to find somebody on the Internet to host some system you learn about in these pages.

You Already Use Open Source Software

If you've ever used a Web browser or sent an email across the Internet, you've used open source software. The Internet is built on open standards and runs on open source software. Over 60% of all Web sites use the open source Apache Web server. The open source Sendmail™ program has dominated the Internet email landscape until very recently. At an even lower level of networking, the BIND program, which associates domain names with Internet Protocol (IP) addresses, is another open source program. This is the program that tells your browser that *http://www.google.com* can be found at the IP address of 216.239.51.99, and that mail for somebody@yahoo.com should go to the server at 64.156.215.5.

The Internet in its current form exists because of open source software. Even Microsoft has based the networking part of its operating systems on an open source package called the Berkeley Software Distribution (BSD) network stack. The Internet is the global system it is today because a large number of diverse people agreed upon a set of open standards and wrote programs adhering to those standards.

Open Source Is Widely Used in Business

Many large companies use open source software without management realizing it—a handful of IT personnel install a Linux server to handle mundane file sharing, and nobody is the wiser. The list of companies using Linux is growing longer every day, and already includes many Fortune 500 companies and governments, along with many of the major companies that still exist that formerly sold software. A few examples include:

- IBM
- HP
- Oracle
- The city of Munich, Germany
- Amazon.com
- Yahoo!

The list is much longer than this. The list of Fortune 1000 companies that use open source software might be longer than the list of those that don't.

Can I Get Help for Open Source Software?

If anything, support for open source software exceeds that of proprietary software. True, there is no software company obligated to help you just because you paid for a product, but there are many service-oriented companies that provide support for a fee. Many proprietary software companies charge extra for support, with various types of support plans.

In addition to telephone support, however, most open source projects have their own mailing list of users and developers who freely help each other solve problems. By subscribing to the mailing list and asking a question, you'll likely get a response within an hour or two, if not sooner. And quite often, you get an answer directly from a programmer who knows the software intimately. Furthermore, if your problem is related to a limitation of the software, you might find someone willing to implement a solution for you on the spot.

Inconsistent Help Documentation

A common complaint about open source software is that it lacks documentation. For some projects, this is certainly the case, but others have documentation that rivals the best anywhere. Some projects emphasize the importance of documentation while others have yet to become enlightened to the need. You could say the same thing about proprietary software. This book, and many others you can find in the computer section of your local bookstore, attempts to alleviate this problem.

Is Open Source Secure?

Security is a big concern, especially if you need to keep data private. Several industries are mandated by law to keep personal data confidential. Some open source projects have a poor security record, while others are very strong. Again, the same thing can be said about proprietary software.

Security is a big topic, and the main focus of Part IV of this book. It's important to understand that no computer system is secure by itself—security is a process you need to go through no matter what operating system or server programs you choose. Having said that, there are a few characteristics of open source software and Unix-based systems that make for better security out of the box.

Users Don't Have Administrative Permissions

Microsoft® Windows® NT-based systems (including Windows 2000, Windows XP, Windows 2003, and later) have a security model similar to that in Unix, in that accounts have different levels of privilege, and only administrators have unrestricted access to the entire system. The problem is, in these Windows operating systems, normal user accounts are set up with administrative rights automatically, unless you specifically restrict them. In Unix-based systems, including Linux and Mac OS X, normal users do not have access to critical system files at all. You have to change to an administrator account (called the *root* account) to do any real damage to the operating system.

This simple problem makes Windows computers vulnerable to attack through any network-related program a user chooses to run. Without a savvy, security-conscious network administrator, most users are left wide open to system compromises, especially if they don't keep things like their Web browsers or email programs up to date.

Many Small Programs Instead of Few Big Ones

Open source software tends to be built as a collection of tiny, special-purpose programs, each doing a particular function, together acting as a coherent system; proprietary software tends to be gigantic collections of code attempting to do everything for everyone. Under the hood, the differences aren't that great—proprietary software builds more sophisticated functions on top of libraries of special purpose programs—but because of the need to sell the product to as many people as possible, software companies bundle everything together, and sell the software as one-size-fits-all.

Is it easier to buy a big program and strip out what you don't need, or build a system up from a bunch of small programs to suit your needs? The answer depends on your needs—if you are a large company and need most of the features offered by a big software package, you may be better off installing it and then turning off the unnecessary parts. Chances are, if you're part of a small business, you don't need the kitchen sink and can do just fine with a streamlined collection of programs that do exactly the tasks you need.

One problem with using the large software package is that it's very easy to overlook parts of the program that may provide an open door to crackers looking for a vulnerable system or a virus that exploits a flaw in software you didn't even know you had. In January 2003, the Slammer worm infected more than 75,000 vulnerable installations of Microsoft SQL Server in less than 10 minutes. The worm propagated throughout the Internet, around the world, grinding all traffic to a crawl. As is often the case, Microsoft had released a patch that blocked this particular vulnerability in the server months before the worm hit—but it turns out that the SQL server engine was installed in a lot of other software packages sold by Microsoft, and these installations were also vulnerable to the worm, and people who used these other software products had no idea they were even at risk.

Software Diversity

One more factor makes open source software a more compelling option for security: diversity. In the physical world, diversity ensures survival of a species, providing at least some of the population with resistance to a virus. The computer world works the same way. Viruses have had such great impact in the last few years because so many people use the same operating system—Microsoft Windows. Whatever its security strengths and weaknesses, the sheer dominance of the Windows operating system, and of the Microsoft email programs Outlook and Outlook Express, has created an environment where one worm can take out millions of machines.

Unix-based systems aren't one single operating system. There are literally hundreds of variations of Unix and Linux-based operating systems, with particular critical system files in completely different places. Having a greater diversity of operating systems and applications in the world would make us all a little less susceptible to worms and viruses.

Is Open Source Reliable?

As mentioned earlier, technical excellence is the primary goal of many, if not most open source projects. Open source projects are guided by engineers, not managers. Programs that have been developed in an open source environment tend to be extremely stable and reliable. Engineers tend to focus on each individual detail of a problem, working at it over and over again, until they have it working just right. Without a manager to veto the effort on what may seem like a small program to work around a problem, the lead programmers of a project work out the most technically sound solution to an architecture problem, instead of the most cost-effective.

While mature proprietary projects eventually reach the same levels of stability, adding new features tends to capture more of the development focus than fixing the underlying architecture.

The flip side of having engineers running the project is that it can take a lot longer to make a software package work. With no deadlines, and no fixed budgets, projects can stretch out far longer than necessary before they're declared stable.

Is Open Source Easy to Install?

Sometimes open source can be installed effortlessly. Most open source software that runs in Windows installs like any other Windows software. With a few Linux distributions, downloading and installing open source software applications is a one-step process. The Mandrake Install Software program has to be about the easiest way to find and install packages anywhere—you can search for software that matches a description, select it, and click Install. The tool downloads the program and everything the program depends upon, installs it, and adds it to your menu.

But not all software is available through these easy installation systems, and there are many different ways to install software packages. Windows definitely has an edge in consistency—you can pretty much count on relatively easy software installation. In Linux, some server programs require many arduous steps, sometimes from a command line, to put all the pieces together in the right place.

For the operating system itself, many Linux distributions are every bit as easy to install as Windows. The Mandrake installation has about eight steps, and can be done in about 15 minutes on a reasonably recent computer.

Is Open Source Easy to Use?

Now here is one area where commercial software is often better, especially for sophisticated programs. Because most open source software is developed by engineers, for engineers, there is a strong tendency to make a program work, make it work well, but then ignore the quirks that might stymie a user unfamiliar with the program.

In general, proprietary software provides more hand-holding, and designs interfaces that help people through complex tasks. With open source, you generally need a better understanding of what the program is trying to do, to be able to accomplish the task successfully. Perhaps one of the best examples of the way proprietary software can help people accomplish a task is tax software. Most commercial tax software interviews you, asking you questions about your finances, and fills in the underlying forms. At this writing, there isn't any good open source tax software, but if there were, it would likely be limited to a form-only mode for a long time.

On the other hand, sometimes when a fancy program doesn't allow you to make changes you know you want to make, these wizard-types of interfaces can lead to more problems, changing values in unexpected places. In general, the more familiar you are with a task, the more likely you'll want direct access to the data. Along with extra knowledge about tasks comes a better ability to identify and fix the source of a problem.

Even this assessment may be misleading. The world of open source software is fast catching up to commercial user interface quality, even in areas like usability. Many projects have caught the attention of people who aren't software engineers, and these people contribute designs and feedback to make the user interface better. For the vast majority of open source software, usability lags only a couple years behind the leading edge of proprietary software.

Using a Command Shell

In the early days of Linux, you had to type commands in a *shell*, which is basically a powerful equivalent of a DOS prompt, to perform most tasks. Now there are graphic interfaces for almost all server software, and you can control many programs extensively by using any Web browser.

A lot of experienced administrators still favor the command line, however. It takes some time to learn the available commands, but once you've learned a few, you can perform an amazing number of tasks much more quickly. And often it's much easier to run a single command in a shell than to find the graphical interface that you need to accomplish the task.

Choosing from Too Many Options

Perhaps the worst part about using open source is that you have too many choices. There are thousands of programs included with every distribution, and dozens of them are text editors that do exactly the same thing: edit text. There are four major open source mail servers, and, again, all of them do the same thing: send email. How do you choose?

There are a lot of different ways of accomplishing the task of sending email. It can be very hard to determine which way is best. You might have trouble figuring out what one system administrator did to build your particular system, making it more expensive to fix when you integrate new software.

The key to addressing this situation is insisting on good documentation—anyone installing software should document exactly what they installed and how it's configured. This book can help you choose what to install and how to configure it among the major business applications. To use a simple text editor, you're on your own.

Will Open Source Meet My Needs?

Obviously, the answer to the topic question depends on what your needs are. For most businesses, the answer is a qualified yes. Read the rest of the book for more specific detail. There are some definite reasons to stick with proprietary software. Like any major purchase, you need to do some research before installing a major system. But it can be difficult to compare the features and performance of an open source project to those of proprietary software. Almost invariably, the only place you can find accurate information about an open source project is from the project's Web site, and from the people who use it.

Read through the Lines of Product Reviews

Take published feature comparisons and benchmarks from any source with a large grain of salt. Performance benchmarks are often heavily skewed towards one particular solution, often unbeknownst to the group doing the testing. One often-cited study compared file serving performance between a Windows file server and an open source Samba file server. The results were favorable to Microsoft, but it turned out that the Windows version had been tuned with suggestions from internal Microsoft personnel, using settings that had not been previously published anywhere. Meanwhile the Samba server had been set up with no optimization for the hardware it was running on, with a couple of well-known settings misconfigured, making its performance in the test poor.

Likewise, white papers comparing a proprietary server with an open source equivalent often fail to take into account what we learned earlier in this chapter: that open source software is generally a collection of single purpose programs built into a customized system, rather than a big monolithic program. Of course a single-purpose program doesn't have all the features of the more sizeable proprietary one—but that doesn't mean the feature is unavailable. You just have to install the software that performs the function or has the performance you need.

Reasons to Use Proprietary Software

There are some good reasons to use proprietary software. The most obvious reason, very much in keeping with small business practice, is "If it ain't broke, don't fix it!"

You may already use and are comfortable with a Windows or Mac system and don't care to change.

This book is about enhancing your business with open source software, and almost all of these enhancements happen on a server somewhere. We will discuss installing open source software on servers, and for most of the chapters, we'll include instructions for accessing these servers from Windows. Switching desktop computers to any new operating system will consume many hours of learning, cause grumbling by employees, and create unforeseeable problems you may need to hire professionals to solve.

Another reason to use proprietary software is that there is no open source software that does a particular task you need to do. You can either use an existing package, hire a programmer to develop the software, or sponsor the addition of features to an existing open source project that can be modified to suit your needs. If a proprietary product exists, and you need the functionality immediately, go with the proprietary solution.

Along the same lines, proprietary software tends to be at the forefront of software development. While there are already some open source projects that do things no proprietary software can match, many good software innovations come out of proprietary software companies that will take several years to be developed by the open source community. As of Fall 2003, current examples of proprietary software innovations not yet fully available in open source versions include the Tablet PC and the .NET framework for Web application development. Often brand-new hardware initially works only with proprietary software.

The only other reason to use proprietary software is so that you can interoperate with existing systems, perhaps belonging to your clients, or old legacy systems of your own. As more and more companies use open standards like XML, this issue becomes much smaller—already for basic networking, open source systems can communicate with any other operating system out there.

Who Pays for Open Source?

Okay. This all sounds suspicious. Who are all these programmers, writing programs for free? How do they pay their bills? What happens when something goes wrong with the software—how can you rely on a volunteer toiling away during the middle of the night to solve a problem when the software you've installed quits working?

It is comforting to have a company standing behind a product. You buy a product, and expect it to work. If it doesn't, you call the company's technical support and get your problem solved. If there's no software company, who do you call? Who can you hold responsible?

The whole idea behind open source software is that it is an exchange of ideas and techniques among professionals. By sharing knowledge, everyone who participates benefits. If you stop thinking about software as a product and start thinking of it as a service provided by professionals, open source software begins to make a lot more sense.

The amazing thing about software is that it keeps getting better over time. It's now possible for a single Web developer to roll out a sophisticated authentication system using free software for a client extranet at a cost of a few thousand dollars. In 1997, building a site with equivalent functionality might have cost well over $100,000 and taken a team of developers to create. Software is continuing to build upon a foundation of a few decades. Most of the software that provides the infrastructure of the Internet has been free for a long time—it was paid for by the pioneering companies and government agencies who needed it. Once the software is built, what do the software developers do? They turn to new projects, solve new problems.

Most personal computer software is easy to see as a product. You have an accounting program, a word processing program, a spreadsheet, an email program, a presentation program, and a browser. Get beyond these programs, however, and it becomes much harder to draw boxes around individual software products—the system itself begins to be more important than the individual programs used by it.

Let's take a closer look at one of these: email. Your email program is but one tiny part of a large system of programs that make email possible. When you send an email to your friend Joe across the country, your email program contacts a program called a *Message Transfer Agent* (MTA) that handles mail for your location. This MTA contacts a program called a DNS server to find out the address of another MTA that receives mail for the destination you specified, and then transfers the mail to that MTA. The receiving MTA may run the email through a virus scan and check to see whether it can be identified as spam, before dropping it into a file somewhere on the server. Now when Joe wants to get his email, he fires up his email program, which connects to still another type of server program called a *Post Office Protocol* (POP) server. This POP server finds the email in the file where the MTA left it and delivers it to Joe's email client. To send a simple email to your friend involved eight different programs.

Even if you buy these programs from a software company, you still have to spend time and money getting them set up right for your location. As soon as you have a network, you need somebody to administer it. This is true no matter what type of software you use—somebody needs to get it set up in the first place, monitor it for problems, and help other people access what they need. If you buy a software product, first you pay the software company, and then you pay your IT person to set everything up.

More and more businesses have found that they can save a lot of money by skipping the software company part of their expenses. Instead of paying for a one-size-fits-all product, companies of all kinds are finding it more economical to pay someone to install free software that already exists and to develop specific customizations for their particular needs.

Many companies have built businesses around open source. None of these companies are software companies, per se—they don't sell software. Instead, they sell support for the software they give away, making them service companies. None of them have skyrocketed to the heady profits of Microsoft—but service companies never do. Open source businesses are thriving, because instead of selling a big fancy product, they focus on solving the problem of the customer. The open source movement is a group of professionals connected by the Internet, working on common problems, sharing their efforts, and providing much-needed perspective on solutions.

Instead of being concentrated in software companies, open source programmers are spread out across all sorts of industries and all kinds of companies, wherever there are computers. The Internet allows them to work as a virtual team, sharing the benefits of that work with everyone in the team, along with their employers. It's estimated that only 5% of software programmers work for proprietary software companies. The other 95% work for other types of businesses, often in financial services and manufacturing sectors. These businesses stand to gain far more value from the use of free software than they pay in the salaries of their open source programmers.

Why Should I Use Open Source Software?

Open source software is a great fit for small business. Computers are capable of helping your business in ways you probably haven't even thought of. Until recently, only expensive proprietary software packages addressed these needs, and only large enterprises could afford these solutions. With the latest open source software, suddenly you have access to high quality, stable, excellent software at an affordable price—the cost of implementing changes to suit your needs.

All software costs money. You either have to pay somebody to implement and maintain the server systems, or you have to take the time out of your income-producing activities to implement them yourself. But with open source software, that's your only cost—you can avoid the thousands of dollars of licensing costs of proprietary software.

We've discussed at length many of the other benefits of open source software. It tends to be more stable, meaning it almost never crashes. It tends to be more secure—the worst worm to infect an open source application to date has been the Slapper worm, which in September of 2002 infected some 13,000 SSL-enabled Apache Web servers. Due to the architecture of Unix servers, cleaning an infected machine involved turning off one option, stopping the Web server program, deleting a few files, and starting the Web server again. No reboot was necessary. The record of Windows-based Web servers is far worse. Security is not something to be taken for granted, however, and the last part of this book will discuss security issues small business owners should consider when running any type of server.

Another huge advantage to open source software is that it makes old hardware useful. Open source software can be installed on almost any computer system ever made. The longer a particular hardware item has been around, the more likely there's a reliable Linux driver to use with it. Finding Linux drivers for brand new computers can be a problem, though. Most proprietary software companies only support one or two previous generations of hardware—anything older gets dropped from the software product. This condition reflects the overall position of open source software on the curve of innovation—in some areas it trails behind proprietary software, but gains from the benefit of experience. When a new type of software is implemented in open source, the programmers can design around the flaws uncovered by the first generation proprietary software.

Finally, when creating a system for your business, you can tailor the software to exactly fit your needs, instead of trying to shoe-horn your process into a one-size-fits-all product filled with features you'll never use.

No Vendor Lock-in

One concern many people have about buying proprietary software is getting *locked in*, so that after investing so much time and money into putting data into a system, it costs too much to change to another. This puts you at the mercy of the vendor for future releases and maintenance of already purchased systems.

Good open source software neatly sidesteps this issue. Should the original vendor disappear, you can hire your own programmer to maintain the software, or add improvements if you need them. If you find a different program that better meets your needs, you can usually export and import your data with minimal hassle, because most open software tends to adhere to published standards, rather than locking data into proprietary file formats.

No Need for Piracy

Furthermore, once you have a basic installation of the software, you can replicate it on as many computers as you like without incurring more licensing fees. Several companies have been audited or threatened by an audit of their software licenses by the Business Software Alliance, a coalition of software companies dedicated to stopping software piracy. Sterling Ball, a guitar string maker in California, was fined $90,000 for having eight unlicensed copies of Microsoft® Office® installed on its computers. After the audit, the company eliminated all Microsoft software from every computer in their 80-computer company, and saved $80,000 in the first two years alone. A similar story comes out of Oregon, where a small school district replaced all proprietary software on its computers with open source software, and the full-time systems administrator for the school district was able to return to teaching three-quarter time because he had so little to do.

BEING A GOOD OPEN SOURCE COMMUNITY CITIZEN

Open source software is built by a large community of like-minded individuals. Many companies directly support the open source community by employing software developers, contributing to projects, paying for the development of specific features they need, or filling other needs. These companies provide support in the form of enlightened self interest, believing they can gain more in return from the open source community than the dollars they spend to support it. And everybody benefits from the contribution.

If you implement and use open source software, you are under no obligation to contribute anything. However, you will find that if you do contribute, you may gain rewards in unexpected ways. Perhaps a mention of your company's name on a project sponsorship page will tip a new deal in your direction. Perhaps the open source programmer you hire to get your system working together will think of a new software solution specifically for your business, saving you thousands of dollars. Even if you never see the result of your contribution, you can still be one of many who have contributed to its development, making the software itself more valuable to yourself and others.

Many small open source software projects work on a similar model as National Public Radio (NPR). If you're unfamiliar with NPR, it's a national network of public radio stations supported by donations from the community. It's a thriving example of a business that exists to serve its customers, instead of stockholders. If you make a living out of installing open source software for your customers, consider budgeting a percentage of your receipts directly back into the projects you benefit from—it's really in your own best interest.

SUMMARY

In this chapter, we learned what open source software is, how it differs from proprietary software and shareware, and took a look at open source licensing. We answered a variety of questions many businesses have about open source software: is it secure, reliable, easy to use, easy to install, and will it meet your needs? We took a look at the economics of open source, and how you can keep the open source community working for you.

In the next chapter, we'll take a close look at setting up and administering a Linux server, which lies at the heart of most of the solutions in this book.

OTHER OPEN SOURCE RESOURCES

An updated list of resources for this chapter is on the Web site for the book at *http://opensourcesmall.biz/opensource.*

Books

The Business and Economics of Linux and Open Source, by Martin Fink, Pearson Education, Inc., 2003.

The Cathedral and the Bazaar: Musings on Linux and Open Source by an Accidental Revolutionary, by Eric Raymond, O'Reilly & Associates, 2001.

The Joy of Linux, by Michael Hall and Brian Proffitt, Prima Publishing, 2001.

Open Sources: Voices from the Open Source Revolution, edited by Chris DiBona, Sam Ockman, and Mark Stone, O'Reilly & Associates, 1999.

Articles

"Is Windows 2003 Server really faster than Linux/Samba?" by Joe Barr, Linux-World. Available online at *http://www.linuxworld.com/story/32673.htm,* May 9, 2003.

"Market Share for Top Servers Across All Domains August 1995–May 2003," by Netcraft, Inc. Available online at *http://news.netcraft.com/archives/web_server_survey.html*

"Rivals chip away at Microsoft's dominance," by Byron Acohido, *USA Today*. Available online at *http://www.usatoday.com/tech/news/2003-02-26-desktop_x.htm*, February 26, 2003.

"The Spread of the Sapphire/Slammer Worm," by David Moore, Vern Paxson, Stefan Savage, Colleen Shannon, Stuart Staniford, and Nicholas Weaver. Available online at *http://www.cs.berkeley.edu/~nweaver/sapphire/*, 2003.

Web Sites

http://www.npr.org National Public Radio

http://www.opensource.org The Open Source Initiative

2 Why You Need a Server

Inside This Chapter

- Introduction
- Choosing a Server
- Choosing a Server Operating System—Types of Operating Systems
- Small Business Linux: Mandrake
- Summary
- Other Server Resources

INTRODUCTION

Most people who use computers know how to run desktop applications. Word processors, spreadsheets, graphics programs, accounting programs, and many games are all different types of applications you can run on a single computer. These programs are workstation-based: you don't need to be connected to any other computer or network to get them to work.

A different type of application is a *server application*. Server applications are programs that have functions broken into *server* and *client* parts. For example, a Web browser such as Internet Explorer is a client application that accesses content on a Web server, and an email program such as Eudora or Microsoft® Outlook® Express is a client for a mail server. These applications depend on your computer being connected to the Internet, or at least to a computer that provides these services.

To make things more confusing, the term *server* is used to describe several different things:

- A program that provides a service used by other client applications
- Any computer running one or more server applications
- A specific type of computer built with hardware optimized for providing specific server applications

In this chapter, we'll first take a closer look at these meanings for the term server. Then we'll discuss choosing a computer to use as a server. After that, we will take a brief foray into server operating systems, and finally set up and explore the basics of server administration.

This chapter is meant to help non-technical users understand the different meanings of a server, and provide an evaluation of how Linux compares to other operating systems for use as a server. When we get to actual implementation of the server, the information becomes a bit more technical, and you will need a basic understanding of computer hardware for it all to make sense.

Server Applications

The first definition listed earlier is often used with the name of the type of service it provides. A server application is a program that runs continuously, waiting for a *request* from a client application. When it receives a request, it performs whatever action it needs to fulfill it, and returns the result as a *response*. The rules for exchanging requests and responses are called a *protocol*.

A server application is often called a *service* on Windows® platforms, or a *daemon* on Unix platforms, both of which mean the same thing. Systems that use client applications to interact with server applications are said to use a *client/server architecture*. It's also possible to set up systems that have multiple layers of clients and servers—one server is a client for another server. Figure 2.1 illustrates a client/server architecture.

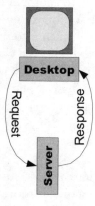

FIGURE 2.1   Client/server architecture.

Just about everything you use on the Internet has a client/server architecture. You use the client application on your computer to interact with the server application somewhere else.

As soon as you have more than one computer that needs to access the same data, you'll want to set up some sort of server. There are many other types of server applications, some of which are covered in Chapter 3:

- File & Print
- Web
- Email
- FTP
- Databases
- Domain
- Authentication

These are but a few of the many services you can set up.

A client/server architecture provides many advantages. First of all, the server provides a central location for storing data, permissions, security, or whatever you use the server for. If you store everything of value on a server, you don't need to back up data stored on client computers. Secondly, if the protocol a particular server provides is well defined, you can use many different types of client applications to access it. This often means you can access the same information from Windows PCs, Macs, or Linux.

In this book, we're going to explore primarily different server applications, and discuss some of the client applications you can use with them. In most cases, the server applications will be on a Linux computer, but often you can use Windows clients with them. You don't have to abandon your current system to gain the benefits of open source software—because most of the applications are server applications, you can simply add the functionality you need to your current systems.

Server Computers

The second way the term server is used is to describe a computer that provides one or more services. This is the meaning we most commonly use in this book. You can set up nearly any physical computer as a server, simply by running server software on it and making it available to other computers. Quite often, you will hear people talk about this type of server with the name of the primary service: "Post it to the Web server," "Connect to the email server," or "Open up a share on the file server."

There's no reason that a single computer can't fill several roles. In most small businesses, all you need is a single server to provide most of the services you need. As your business and computing needs grow, you may find that putting specific services on dedicated computers improves performance—or adds a layer of security, in the case of services exposed to the Internet.

Server Hardware

The third definition of a server is a computer with hardware optimized to run server applications. There are many variations of servers, but generally, compared with workstations, servers have more memory, more processors, more hard drive space, and more efficient ways of transferring data throughout the internal system. Servers generally don't need a sound card, however, or much of a video card.

CHOOSING A SERVER

One of the big benefits of open source is that it tends to run great on older hardware. You can convert old hardware to provide basic services such as sharing an Internet connection or a printer—it's possible to recycle an old PC without even a hard drive to act as a firewall.

If your business needs a server, but you can't afford to get a full blown server, you can install Linux on a workstation, add some RAM, and have a fully functional server by the time you're done.

Servers used to cost a lot of money, but you can now buy one with plenty of power for under $2,000. When shopping for a server, here are some questions you may want to ask:

- Can you add additional Central Processing Units (CPUs)? Servers with more than one CPU can handle more tasks at once, which can make them respond faster for processor-heavy applications.
- How much memory can you install? Adding more Random Access Memory (RAM) is usually the best way to solve performance issues with any computer. If a computer doesn't have enough RAM, the operating system "swaps" memory out to the hard drive, which is much slower. As more people use your server, the load on it increases, and if there's not enough memory to handle all the requests, the hard drive starts "thrashing," and performance grinds to a halt. For a file or print server, you don't need much memory at all. For a Web server, you'll likely run out of bandwidth in your connection before you run out of memory. But if you run some sophisticated Web applications that are heavily used, you can quickly consume all of the available RAM and grind your system to a halt. One GB of RAM is a good place to start.
- What sort of redundancy can you build into your hard drive system? Hard drives are one of the most common pieces of hardware to fail. A technology

called a Redundant Array of Inexpensive Disks (RAID) provides a way of duplicating data across multiple hard disks in a way that is totally transparent to the operating system. Different types, or "levels," of RAID provide different features in terms of performance and redundancy. RAID 5 is perhaps the best level of RAID to put in an office server, providing a system where any single drive can fail and be replaced without losing any data. With RAID 5, you need at least four hard drives of identical size. If you use 40 GB drives, you'll end up with an array that acts like a single 120 GB hard drive—with fault tolerance.

■   How will you back up your server? RAID provides a great way of ensuring that you don't lose any data due to hard drive failure—but does nothing to recover from a virus, hacker, human error, or other disasters such as fire. Tape drives are the traditional way to back up servers, but today you might consider a DVD writer. For comparable cost, you get more reliable backups on much cheaper media. We will discuss backups more fully in Chapter 18.

These are the main features you need to consider when buying a server. Other features you might consider are their shapes: you can buy towers, big boxes, rack mounted servers, or tiny cubes. One layer of security is physical security—protecting a computer from being logged into by somebody on your premises. To prevent someone from resetting a password at boot-time, most servers come with a lock for the cover. We will go into more detail about different types of security in Chapter 16.

CHOOSING A SERVER OPERATING SYSTEM—
TYPES OF OPERATING SYSTEMS

Now that you have a computer ready to go as a server, what do you put on it? There are dozens of operating systems you can install on a computer, but for business use, there are pretty much only two types to consider: Windows NT-based systems, or Unix-based systems. The following table illustrates some of the differentiating features between these groups.

There used to be several other operating systems worthy of consideration in a business environment, the most widely used being the Netware operating system. Netware is still in use at many companies, but doesn't have any compelling advantages over Windows NT or Unix-based systems.

Table 2.1 shows some of the differences between Unix and Windows NT systems, but doesn't necessarily show a compelling benefit in either one. The fact is, for a server operating system, either type will probably meet your needs very well. Most desktop users in your company will never know the difference. You can install a Unix-based server that interoperates with all of the Windows desktops you already use.

TABLE 2.1   Major Operating System Types for Servers Currently Being Installed

	Windows NT Systems	Unix-Based Systems
Example Operating Systems	Windows NT Windows NT Server Windows 2000 Advanced Server Windows XP Windows .NET Server 2003	Linux Mac OS X BSD Sun Solaris HP-UX AIX

Advantages	Easier to install software
	Graphical administration
	Packages sold with what seems like
	  every imaginable feature
		Less expensive
		History of better stability
		One administrator can
		  handle more computers
		History of better security

Where to get help	Help system Microsoft Web site Newsgroups User groups Dedicated Web sites	Manual pages Dedicated Web sites Mailing lists User groups Newsgroups

Who has expertise?	Many small consulting businesses
	Employees of Microsoft-based
	  IT businesses
		People who have worked in the
		  telecommunications industry
		Many government employees
		Students from major universities

TABLE 2.1 Major Operating System Types for Servers Currently Being Installed *(continued)*

	Windows NT Systems	*Unix-Based Systems*
Major email servers	Microsoft Exchange	Sendmail Postfix Q-mail Exim
Major Web servers	Microsoft Internet Information Services (IIS) Apache	Apache Sun Web Server Netscape Web Server
Network File Sharing	Windows Networking (SMB) WebDAV	Windows Networking (Samba) AppleTalk® Network File System (NFS) WebDAV
Domain authentication system	Active Directory	Various Pluggable Authentication Modules (PAM)
Databases	Microsoft SQL Server Microsoft Access Filemaker® Pro DB/2	Oracle DB/2 MySQL PostgreSQL Filemaker Pro (Mac only)

Microsoft server systems provide a few features that are more developed than Unix-based systems. Of particular note are Active Directory® and IntelliMirror®. Active Directory is a complete implementation of Lightweight Directory Access Protocol (LDAP) to manage users, computers, software, settings, printers, organizational units, and other objects, providing a context for security and management of an IT infrastructure. While LDAP is available and in growing use on Unix-based systems, Active Directory is tightly integrated with many areas of the newer Microsoft operating systems, and easier to use out of the box.

In Unix, the Network Information Service (NIS) provided similar authentication functionality, but NIS doesn't interoperate with Windows systems, and only manages users—not computers, software, or other objects.

The other Microsoft feature that is very nicely done is something called IntelliMirror, which makes installing software over your network very easy. IntelliMirror manages software installations and licenses from a server. With IntelliMirror, software is installed as soon as it's needed. For example, you could send a Page-Maker®file to another user in your company, and if the user didn't have Page-Maker installed, he could still attempt to open the file. With IntelliMirror, his operating system automatically downloads PageMaker from the server, installs it, and opens the file.

While IntelliMirror makes opening files and installing software very easy for the user, it's at the expense of the administrator. The administrator has to set up custom installation routines for each software package, track licenses, and set up Group Policies for each software package. Some Unix-based systems are fast developing equivalent features, such as urpmi in Mandrake Linux, or apt-get in Debian Linux.

Unix-Based Operating Systems

This book, however, is about open source solutions, so now that we've seen where Microsoft has the lead, let's turn our attention to Unix-based systems. In the 1980s, Unix splintered into many different variations, leading to incompatibilities and software that only works on the platform it was compiled for. This makes delivering proprietary software to Unix-based systems difficult—if you don't want to release your source code, you have to compile a different version of your program for every different variation of Unix.

To overcome this limitation, software developers came up with sophisticated configuration tools that allowed them to quickly reconfigure the source code of a program to compile on multiple platforms. For open source software, these tools mean you can install most server applications on any Unix-based system.

Table 2.2 lists some of the major Unix-based operating systems.

TABLE 2.2   Major Unix-based Operating Systems

	Linux	BSD	Solaris	Mac OS X
Distributions	Red Hat® Linux Mandrake Linux Debian Linux SUSE Caldera Yellow Dog Red Star Linux … and many others	OpenBSD FreeBSD NetBSD	Solaris	Mac OS X
Open Source?	Yes (GNU License)	Yes (BSD License)	No	Partial
Advantages	Wide use International support Greatest compatibility/ availability	Best security	High Performance Good security Easy to administer large numbers of computers	User oriented— very easy to use Most refined desktop applications
Disadvantages	Confusing number of choices for many things	Under-developed GUI applications	Relies on proprietary hardware for performance advantages Poor compatibility with some software	Expensive Newcomer— relatively untested

You may be surprised to learn that the Apple Macintosh now uses a Unix-based system. Up until the Mac OS version 9, the Mac used a proprietary operating system, completely developed by Apple. With OS X, Apple ported their graphical user interface to run on top of a version of BSD. This means that most of the server applications mentioned in this book will compile and run in Mac OS X, sometimes with a little tweaking here and there.

The Solaris operating system, from Sun Microsystems, is one of the few remaining operating systems that is officially Unix, rather than a rewritten derivation of it. There are several other proprietary versions of Unix, but Solaris is perhaps the main one that still has widespread use, and is still being installed on new systems. Like Apple, Sun is both a hardware and software company, and has a history of making high performance workstations for scientific and technical uses. The Solaris operating system is designed to run on Sun's SPARC™ line of workstations and servers, but Sun has also released a version that runs on Intel-based computers.

Solaris is a popular choice for large enterprises, engineering firms, and telecommunications companies that need to do vast amounts of processing. However, one of the drawbacks of being a true Unix variety is that it comes with the original tools; the GNU set of tools have been rewritten to include many options that make them more consistent and easier to use. For most small businesses, SPARC workstations don't provide any compelling advantages to the much cheaper Intel computers, and Linux is generally easier to install and use.

BSD is perhaps the first true open source operating system. It has branched into three varieties: OpenBSD, NetBSD, and FreeBSD. OpenBSD in particular is developed with high security in mind, and has the best security record of any operating system available. The BSD systems were derived from the original AT&T Unix, but have been completely written to eliminate any proprietary code, and have been released under a license that allows anyone to do anything with the code. The BSD varieties are extremely popular among universities, and have been installed in many businesses, particularly to support the services on the Internet where security is a concern.

All of the server applications in this book work with BSD. While BSD does not use the Linux kernel, it is very similar to Linux, and can be considered alongside the Linux distributions.

Linux Distributions

Linux is the runaway success of the Unix world. It's easy to obtain, install, and administer. It has an enormous body of software available. It costs nothing in licensing fees. It runs on nearly any computer hardware available. Newer distributions rival Windows in terms of usability on the desktop. And, most importantly, it has a large number of active developers participating in making Linux better.

So what is Linux? Technically, it's just the *kernel* of the operating system, the core program that mediates input and output between all of the hardware devices on the system, and decides which other programs to execute and when. By itself, the Linux kernel is useless—you need a host of other programs to make up the operating system. A Linux *distribution* is a collection of programs, combined with the Linux kernel and an installation routine and perhaps some custom programs to go with it.

There are hundreds of different Linux distributions, each providing a different set of software programs; Table 2.3 shows some comparisons. The first step of installing Linux is choosing a distribution.

Debian

There are many other distributions available, but these four seem to have the biggest followings in Europe and the English-speaking world. Debian is considered the most "pure"—it's maintained by a community, rather than a company, and strictly adheres to the tenets of the open source movement. Debian has a reputation for stability—its stable releases use software several releases older than other distributions, including versions that have been proven to work well.

Debian is a bit hard to install and configure, but it has a package management tool that is considered the best available, called apt-get, which downloads software packages and all their dependencies, and configures, compiles, and installs all in one step.

Overall, the main reason you might choose to use Debian is if the IT professional you hire insists on it. Debian is top-notch quality, but takes a thorough understanding of Linux to administer successfully. If you have such a person available, Debian is a good choice.

The other three distributions listed—Red Hat, SuSE, and Mandrake—are much easier for a non-technical person to install and use. They can all be installed from a bootable CD, and each provides a graphical installation procedure that walks you through the important steps using their own tools to help with system administration.

Red Hat

Red Hat is probably used more in business than any other Linux distribution, mainly because Red Hat, Inc. was able to gain a lot of public exposure in the late 1990s. Red Hat created the first software package management tool for Linux, called Red Hat Package Manager (RPM). RPM is a packaging system much like the various installers for Microsoft systems. It bundles all the necessary files into a single *.rpm file. Each .rpm file includes a list of other packages it depends upon, so when you go to install the file, it will either work or tell you what other packages you need to install first.

TABLE 2.3 Comparison of Major Linux Distributions

	Mandrake	Red Hat	SuSE	Debian
Advantages	Great hardware support Great software installation system Good security tools User focus	Enterprise focus Great remote management/ deployment tools Good security tools Widely used in business Premium support options	Good administration tools Now owned by Novell, being widely installed in large enterprises, especially in Europe Corporate desktop focus	Adherence to open source ideals Great software installation system Very stable
Drawbacks	Less used in larger businesses	Non-standard file system arrangement	Some distribution/ licensing issues	Difficult to install User groups less tolerant of inexperienced users Few GUI administration tools
Software Package system	RPM URPMI	RPM Up2date	RPM	Apt-get

As of January 2004, Red Hat now sells an enterprise version only. The old standard Red Hat distribution has been completely released from the Red Hat company, and is now a community-managed distribution called Fedora Core.

RPMs store object code, so when a package is installed, the RPM program simply copies the files to appropriate locations on the system after checking for dependencies. But the main innovation of Red Hat, Inc., is their business model. Their main income comes from providing paid support. They developed a distribution containing a number of tools like RPM to make it possible to quickly set up systems, and then for a fee, provide telephone support for their distribution. Many other open source software companies have copied this business model.

Red Hat has developed or acquired many other tools, all of which they distribute freely. These include Cygwin, which makes it possible to run Unix programs on Windows systems, and Redboot, which provides tools for embedding and interacting with Linux on tiny systems such as media players, security systems, and other special function hardware devices.

The main reason you might choose a Red Hat distribution is to have access to Red Hat support. You get accountability similar to Microsoft—when you run into a problem, you have somebody to call for help.

SuSE

SuSE is another business-oriented Linux company. In 2003, SuSE was purchased by the networking giant Novell, Inc., which has also purchased Ximian, a leading open source programming company of the GNOME desktop. SuSE has been the dominant Linux distribution in Europe for years, and due to extensive backing by Novell and IBM, is likely to take a greater role in large enterprises in North America, too.

In contrast to Debian, SuSE includes some proprietary software without releasing the source code. SuSE straddles the line between proprietary software and open source. By doing so, they can charge for their innovations, and create a platform that other proprietary software companies can use to develop and sell software easily, while not releasing source code.

SuSE also uses RPM to install software, but since files are arranged differently in the separate distributions, an RPM for Red Hat often won't work in SuSE.

You might choose SuSE if you need to use some proprietary software package developed for it and not available for other platforms. Also, you can buy some servers from HP or other hardware manufacturers with SuSE bundled and pre-installed, with a support contract.

SMALL BUSINESS LINUX: MANDRAKE

For this book, the author has chosen to use Mandrake. Originally a spin-off of Red Hat, Mandrake has distinguished itself by providing a great software updating/

installation utility, superior hardware detection and support, attention to security, and the best support for using Linux on the desktop. Mandrake has long had the reputation of being "Linux for your grandma," the easiest distribution to install, learn, and use. Its reputation is justified—but ease of use is hardly a limitation.

 All of the software in this book that runs on Mandrake Linux will run on any other Linux distribution just as well. However, installation and configuration details may be different.

Mandrake has taken great pains to provide security-conscious features and is a compelling server environment for small businesses. Besides its excellent software updating utility, it creates server packages pre-compiled to take advantage of newer hardware, including features that most businesses will want to use. Three particular projects come to mind:

■ Advanced Extranet Server, the standard Apache server pre-compiled with the OpenSSL libraries, mod_perl, support for multiple domains, and hardened with some security enhancements
■ Shorewall Firewall, a set of scripts that make it easier to manage the firewall built into the Linux kernel
■ Prelude Intrusion Detection System, an advanced tool used by security administrators to detect, analyze, and block network attacks

All of these projects are open source, freely available to install in any Linux distribution—but they come with Mandrake.

The exact choice of Linux distribution ultimately is an arbitrary one. In the open source software world, there are often a multitude of choices, each with slightly different ways of accomplishing the same thing. Choosing a different distribution, or installing BSD instead of Linux, may change the exact steps or commands to get something to work correctly, but the overall concepts are the same, and you should find the information in this book to apply equally well, whichever choice you make.

Now that we've discussed the specific options for operating systems and distributions, let's take a look at some of the basics of using Linux on a server.

Obtaining Mandrake Linux

If you already have a high speed connection to the Internet, and a computer that can burn CD-ROMs, the easiest way to get Mandrake Linux is to go to *http://www.mandrakelinux.com*, follow the Download links, and download the CD images for your computer type. If you have a typical Intel-based PC, look for the

ISO images for i586 or higher. With Mandrake 10.0 there are three CD images to download to get the basic distribution.

To prevent the main Mandrake servers from overloading, the images are available on many different mirror sites scattered around the world. Pick one in your region, download the three files with the *.iso extension, and save them to your hard disk. On a DSL connection, each download can take over an hour—over a dial-up connection, the download could take days.

ISO stands for International Organization for Standardization (ISO is actually the abbreviation in French), the same organization that standardizes weights and measures. The ISO 9660 standard defines how data is stored on a CD-ROM. When working with recordable CDs, the entire CD image can be stored in an ISO file. Windows uses the *.iso extension to identify CD image files, and so the term ISO image has come to refer to a single file containing a CD image. Most CD writing packages can transfer an ISO image directly to a blank CD. ISO images have a couple of advantages for working with operating systems. The resulting CDs can be understood by most operating systems, and you can directly create bootable CDs from an image.

Once you have the ISO images for your processor type, burn the CDs using whatever CD burning software you have on your operating system. Make sure you burn the CD from the image—if you copy the image file as a file to the CD, it won't work.

If you don't have a high-speed connection, you can buy the Mandrake CDs online from *http://www.mandrakelinux.com*, or get them from a variety of computer stores, resellers, and computer consultants. Like other Linux distributions, downloading Mandrake is free, but there's usually a charge for buying the CDs.

Installing Mandrake Linux

Now that you have the Mandrake CDs, the next step is to install Mandrake on your server. If your server can boot from the CD-ROM drive, installation is simple—but there are a couple of things to plan out before doing the install.

Set Up RAID/Other Hardware

If you have a RAID array, you'll need to configure that first. Linux can tell that you're using a RAID array, but treats it as a single disk. Use whatever configuration tools that came with the RAID controller to get it set up properly.

Partition Your Hard Drive

The other thing you must do before installing Linux is to decide upon a partitioning strategy. Most Windows computers are set up with a single partition on each hard drive. The entire hard drive is set up as the C:\ drive. If you add a second hard drive, it's mounted in Windows as the D:\ drive. But you can also divide a single hard drive into multiple *partitions*, each of which can be formatted independently of the others. In Windows, a hard drive with multiple partitions looks to the user like multiple drives.

The main reason to have multiple partitions is that if something goes wrong with your system, you can (hopefully) reinstall the operating system without losing your data. In fact, you can set up multiple operating systems, each in their own partition, and choose which one to boot into when you start up.

Unix was developed in the days of much smaller, much more expensive hard drives, and tradition has led to using different partitions on a disk for different types of data. Ask 10 Unix or Linux experts how to partition your hard drive, and you'll get 10 different answers. A lot depends on how you'll use the server. The main consideration is that however you partition your system, you should never run out of space on the partition containing the temporary files. If you run out of space on this partition, it can bring down the entire operating system. To prevent this, system administrators tend to put user files, log files, and other things that can grow to fill all available space on a separate partition so a user can't (intentionally or accidentally) crash the server. It's also possible to set up disk quotas to prevent particular users from taking too much space.

In Unix-based systems, a partition is mounted as a *file system* somewhere within the *root file system*. A file system consists of all the files and directories on a partition of a hard drive. There are other types of file systems, but for the most part, they act in a similar way to a file system based on a disk partition. The root file system is simply the partition mounted at the highest level of the directory tree: /. The root file system can be compared to My Computer in Windows—you can descend through the directories to see everything on your computer.

An *absolute path* in Unix-based systems always starts at the root file system, with the forward slash. At the top of the root file system are a number of directories. To refer to a file within a directory, you can use an absolute path starting with the forward slash, then the name of a directory, then another forward slash, and any other directories separated with forward slashes, until you descend in the hierarchy to the name of the file.

You can mount a file system on any directory in the root file system—or on other file systems. If My Computer is the root file system in Windows, the drive letters are the mount points for each of the drives. But instead of using drive letters, Unix-based systems provide a name. If you look at the root directory of any Unix-based system, like the one shown in Figure 2.2, you will find the following top level directories: `boot`, `dev`, `etc`, `home`, `lib`, `opt`, `proc`, `root`, `sbin`, `tmp`, `usr`, and `var`, and probably a few others. `/proc` is a special file system that contains all sorts of information about what's currently going on in the kernel and doesn't actually exist on disk, but the rest of these directories may simply be descendents of the root file system. Or, they could be a different partition mounted in the root file system at that directory.

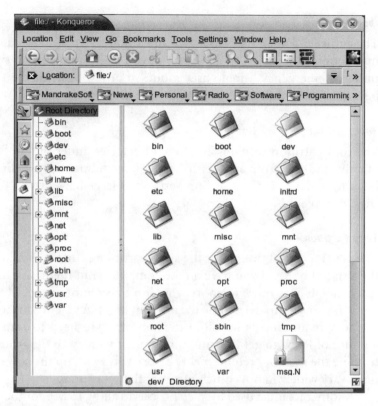

FIGURE 2.2   The root file system.

When discussing partitions, it's common to refer to the partition by the name of the directory where you plan to mount it. Each partition can have any number of different types, depending on the operating system you want to use to access it. Linux can read and write to a variety of different partition types, but the standard type is called ext3. If you plan to access the same drive using both Windows and Linux directly (not through a network), you might want to set up a FAT32 partition, which both can use, though it doesn't offer the same reliability or security as other file systems. You also need to create a swap partition, a special area of the hard drive used by the kernel when the computer runs out of Random Access Memory (RAM) to perform its tasks.

There's a lot more to partitioning a hard drive, and any Linux system administration book will provide many more details. It's much harder to change the partitions on your hard drive after you've installed an operating system though, so here are some of the file systems you may want to create special partitions for, along with recommended sizes.

/boot Partition

The kernel and memory map for the operating system are stored in /boot. By keeping /boot on a separate, small partition, you make it possible to start up your computer in emergency "single user mode" if any (or all) of the other file systems become damaged. It only needs to be 10 MB or so.

Root Partition (/)

The root partition contains all of the directories under the root directory not explicitly mounted from another file system, including the /tmp directory. If you follow the guidelines in this section and have a large hard drive, 10 GB of disk space should be plenty.

Swap Partition

The general rule of thumb for the swap partition is that it should be twice as big as the amount of RAM you have on the computer. But there isn't much basis for this rule—if you have more memory, you don't need more swap.

A better way to determine the amount of swap you need is to add up all of the memory requirements for all of the software you need to run, and subtract the amount of RAM to get the minimum size of your swap file—but how do you determine the memory requirements before you've set up the server? Server applications vary widely in how much memory they consume.

Another formula used by Web hosts is to allow 16 MB for the basic system, plus 2 MB per user—if you have 50 users, your swap partition should be at least 116 MB. With the low cost of hard drives, allocating 512 MB to swap should provide enough room to start—you can add swap files later if you need to—or better yet, add more RAM.

/home Partition

Each user on a Unix system has a "home" directory on the system, much like the My Documents folder in Windows. Many system preferences are stored in hidden files in this directory. All of the user home directories are stored in the /home file system. By putting /home on its own partition, you isolate user files from the rest of the system. You can easily upgrade the system without touching user files—and also easily back up the entire file system. If a server is going to store a lot of user files, you'll want to make this one of the largest partitions.

/var Partition

Most data stored on a Unix-based system not associated with a specific user ends up in /var. This includes system logs, Web sites, databases, LDAP directories, and email. Data in this file system changes quickly, and should be backed up often. On most servers, this should be the largest partition, unless most of the data is going to be kept in user home directories.

/usr Partition

Most of the programs on your server are stored in /usr. There isn't much need to split /usr out of the root file system, but some people like to do so to add a level of protection from viruses or hackers—you can mount the entire /usr file system as read-only, and then nobody can over-write any programs kept there. This practice makes it more difficult to install or upgrade software, however—to do so you'll have to take the server offline and re-mount the file system as writable.

Some people also create a separate partition for /usr/local so that they can completely update the system but leave programs installed for the computer itself (local programs, as opposed to server programs) unchanged.

Files on the /usr file system generally only need to be backed up when you install or upgrade software, and if you don't have this file system backed up at all, you can almost always reinstall the software from other locations. Depending on how much server software you plan to install, two to eight GB of space is sufficient.

/opt Partition

/opt is traditionally where you put "optional software." After a default installation of Mandrake, this directory exists, but is empty. It's a good place to put copies of things you already have backed up on CDs or other permanent media.

For example, you can put a copy of the Mandrake installation CDs into /opt, and actually mount them in the file system as if they were in the CD drive. Doing so makes installing additional software very easy—you don't need to swap the CDs in and out of the CD drive (or find them if you've taken them to another computer). Since you already have the CDs, using this strategy means you don't need to back up the /opt file system at all.

Partitioning Strategy

Unless you have a specific need to keep separate partitions, keep your partition system simple. At a minimum, you can get by with three partitions: root, swap, and /var. If you allow users to store data in their own directories on the server, you should also have a separate /home partition. You can make partitioning as complex as you want, but this is as simple as you should go. Give the root partition 10 or 15 GB of space, swap about 500 MB of space, and divide the rest of the drive between /var and /home, depending on how much individual data will be on the server, as opposed to shared data.

Run the Mandrake Installer

To install Mandrake Linux, configure the BIOS of the server to boot from the CD-ROM, put disk one of the CD-ROM set in the drive, and start up the computer. The Mandrake installer should launch, and give you a series of installation options. Among the first is partitioning the hard drive.

The longest step of the installation is choosing the type of installation and the software packages to install. Don't worry about getting everything installed now—you can always add packages you missed later, or remove packages you don't need. Choose the option for doing a server installation.

The other crucial step of the installation is setting up user accounts. You need a user account to log into the computer. When you create a user account, you get the ability to log into the computer, read, write, and execute programs that you have the correct permissions for, and change the permissions and attributes of files you are the owner of.

One user account, called the superuser, has the ability to change the ownership of files, change passwords for any user, and override the permissions on any file in the system. The superuser account is named root, and you must choose a secure password for this account—if anyone gains access to the root account, he can do anything he wants on your computer. In day-to-day use, log in under a normal user account, and switch the root user only when you need to do something that requires root permissions. During the installation, choose a secure password for root, and set up at least one user account.

Linux Server Administration

If you have a background using Windows computers, administering a Linux server may seem intimidating at first. Most Unix administrators use command line tools instead of graphical interfaces. Linux computers don't have a c:\ drive, or any other drive letter for that matter. Installing a new software program often involves compiling source code. Let's go over some of the basics of using Linux computers.

Using the Command Line: A Thousand Words Are Worth a Picture

When you first log into a graphical interface on Linux, you may be surprised by how similar it is to Windows. There's an equivalent to the Start button, which provides access to many programs and control panel functionality. There's a desktop. There's a task bar, with a notification area.

Open a program, and you'll find that menus, toolbars, and everything else seem equivalent. The mouse works the same way, and you can minimize windows and open a window that lets you configure nearly anything on the computer. Right?

Not quite. Spend any time around people who use Linux regularly, and you'll notice that they all have a command line window open, and they spend a lot of time typing things in it. Isn't this a throwback to the days of DOS? Didn't the Macintosh prove that Graphical User Interfaces are much easier to use ? Why don't people use the menus?

Two reasons: speed and power. If you use computers day in and day out, you'll quickly realize that mice are slow—typing is much faster. If you learn the keystrokes to perform a certain task, you'll find them much quicker to use.

Take the example of cutting and pasting. In Windows, you can cut, copy, or paste text by selecting it, right-clicking on the selection, and left-clicking on the action you want. Or click the toolbar icon. Or click the Edit menu, and then click the action you want. All of these steps take moving your mouse to at least one precise point and then clicking, often more than once.

In contrast, using the keyboard, you can select text by holding down the shift key while you press an arrow key, then CTRL-C to copy, CTRL-X to cut, and CTRL-V to paste. They're all right at the bottom of your keyboard, in a row. Alt-TAB takes you to another application where you can quickly paste that item you just copied.

In Linux, the command line may at first seem daunting—a white square after your name, computer name, and current directory. No indication of what you can do. But learn the language of the command line, and you'll be amazed at how quickly you can get around.

Power? Why is the command line more powerful? Simply because you have access to every program on your system. Take a look at the most sophisticated graphical user interfaces (GUI) for a program you use every day. Look at how cluttered Microsoft Word is, for example—toolbar after toolbar, nine different menus, flyout sub-menus and everything arranged to cascade into view.

How much time have you spent searching the menus for the action you're looking for? You know it's there somewhere. You hunt and peek into all the options, looking for something you may even know the name of. And even in the most sophisticated applications, you only have access to maybe two or three hundred commands at the most.

The DOS command line is a pitiful shadow of a Unix shell. Most Linux distributions, including Mandrake, provide a shell named Bash as the default command line environment. A shell is a program that provides interaction with the system by allowing the user to type commands and presenting the output. The Bash shell provides a huge number of shortcuts that make using the command line easy. For example, you can start typing a command, and press the tab key to get all the possible commands Bash recognizes that begin with the letters you typed. Type nothing and press tab, and you'll get the number of commands (programs) available from the current prompt.

On the system illustrated in Figure 2.3, a normal user account has access to 2,592 programs, and the root user has access to 3,054 programs. Try fitting that onto your start menu.

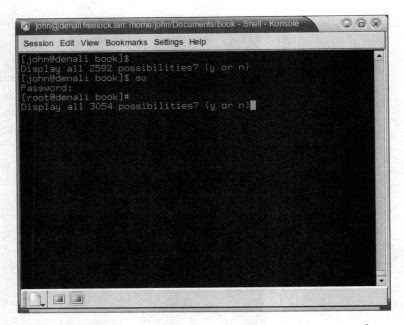

FIGURE 2.3   Number of commands available from the command line on a typical Linux workstation.

But what can you possibly do with over 3,000 programs, when you only use half a dozen or so? This question goes back to one of the characteristics of Unix-based systems we discussed in Chapter 1: lots of little single-purpose programs instead of few do-everything programs.

GUI interfaces work well if you're manipulating some object: a text file, a newsletter in a page layout program, or a digital photograph. But for performing actions, nothing beats a command line—it's hard to draw a picture of a verb.

For example, most open-source software is distributed in a compressed archive, very similar to a Zip file in Windows. Once you've downloaded the archive with GUI-based tools, you have to double-click the archive, find the extract command, and choose a location to put the unpacked files. This takes opening up three or four different windows, and moving the mouse to the proper buttons.

If you know the command line version, you simply change to the directory in which you saved the file, type `tar -xzf`, the first couple characters of the filename, press the tab key to have the shell automatically complete the filename, and press the enter key. The archive is extracted to the current directory—but you can also specify any other directory to put the extracted files. Command lines are all about shortcuts. The main drawback is figuring out what command to give.

We're not going to get into the details of using Linux, or interacting with the command line. There are many excellent books and online tutorials that can help you get up to speed, a few of which are listed in the references at the end of this chapter. The main point here is that people use command lines because once they've learned a basic set of commands, they can accomplish their tasks much more quickly and more accurately than through a GUI. But in most cases, there is a GUI available to do what you need to do if you still want to take that route.

Help for the Command Line

So how do you learn to use the command line? One or two commands at a time. First off, by far the easiest way to figure out the command you need is to do a quick search on Google. Type a few words describing the task you're trying to accomplish, and you'll find a bunch of resources describing how to do it. You can also search the manual pages by typing `man -k` followed by a word or words to search for.

Once you have the command you want to use, there are a couple of places (besides the Web) where you can get additional help. You can access usage help for most programs by simply adding `--help` to the end of the command. For example, `tar --help` reveals the following (actually, this is only part of what it reveals—several pages of help have been omitted):

```
GNU 'tar' saves many files together into a single tape or disk archive,
and can restore individual files from the archive.

Usage: tar [OPTION]... [FILE]...

Examples:
tar -cf archive.tar foo bar       # Create archive.tar from files foo
                                    and bar.
tar -tvf archive.tar              # List all files in archive.tar
                                    verbosely.
tar -xf archive.tar               # Extract all files from archive.tar.

If a long option shows an argument as mandatory, then it is mandatory
for the equivalent short option also. Similarly for optional arguments.

Main operation mode:
-t, --list                list the contents of an archive
-x, --extract, --get      extract files from an archive
-c, --create              create a new archive
-d, --diff, --compare     find differences between archive and file system
-r, --append              append files to the end of an archive
-u, --update              only append files newer than copy in archive
```

```
-A, --catenate           append tar files to an archive
    --concatenate        same as -A
    --delete             delete from the archive (not on mag tapes!)
-z, --gzip, --ungzip     filter the archive through gzip
-Z, --compress, --uncompress       filter the archive through compress
    --use-compress-program=PROG    filter through PROG
                                   (must accept -d)
Report bugs to <bug-tar@gnu.org>.
```

For even more help, you can consult the manual. Most command-line programs include a page inserted into a system manual on your computer. You read the help for a program by using the man command. To get the manual page for tar, you simply type man tar.

Install Software

Installing software is one of the major drawbacks in Linux—there are many different ways to do it, and few standards. To get started, always read the Web site for software you download to install and look for tips. Quite often, the help you need is in a file called INSTALL or README, bundled into the software package. Some software packages have unique installation steps, so you have to read the directions provided.

In general, though, you'll find that most of the software you want to install is available in one or both of two ways: as a source tarball or an RPM package.

Installing from a Source Tarball

As we discussed in Chapter 1, the very definition of open source software is that the source code is available along with the object code. You can download the source code for any open source program, and compile it on your system. It may sound intimidating, but it's really not all that hard.

One advantage of compiling from source code is that the same source code is used to build the software for any system. As long as you have the prerequisite software on your system, you end up with a program that works. Also, if there are some custom patches you want to apply to the software (to add specific features you want to use, for example), you need to patch the source files and recompile the software.

A *tarball* is a slang expression for a single file archive containing multiple files. The tar command was originally an acronym for "Tape Archive," and provided a method for backing up a bunch of files to a single stream you could store on a tape. Now it's more often used simply to bundle a bunch of files to a single archive, with a filename ending in *.tar. By itself, a tar file isn't compressed. To make downloads much quicker, the tar file is compressed, usually with a program called gzip, and stored as a *.tar.gz file (or sometimes a *.tgz file).

First, download the source tarball of the program you want to install from its Web site using your Web browser. Save it to some directory on the disk—you might want to create a src/ directory in your home directory to store all the tarballs and related source files.

Then, open a shell window, change to the source directory, and untar the file. The following commands accomplish this for a software package called weather.tgz:

```
[john@denali john]$ cd src
[john@denali src]$ tar -xvzf weather.tgz
```

At this point, you'll see a list of all of the files in the archive as they get unpacked.

```
[john@denali src]$ ls -l
total 7464
drwxr-xr-x    9 john    john    4096 Mar 27 10:54 weather_1.3.2/
-rwxr--r--    1 john    john    472381 May 20 07:28 weather_1.3.2.tgz
```

Unpacking the archive created a directory called "Weather" and put all of the files in it. You can then change into the Weather directory, where you should find a README or INSTALL file. The more command will show them to you, one screen at a time.

```
[john@denali src]$ cd weather_1.3.2
[john@denali weather_1.3.2]$ more README
```

The instructions should tell you what you need to know to get this software installed and working.

Many open source programs use a package called autoconf to create configuration scripts for the compiler. There is one set of commands that most software packages use, and if you ever install software from source, you'll find yourself typing these commands over and over again. You start by running the configure script:

```
[john@denali weather_1.3.2]$ ./configure
```

The configure script checks to see if you have a compatible compiler, and sets up another file with the exact location of various files and programs on your system. You'll see a bunch of text fly by the screen as it does these checks. If it can't find something it needs, the text will stop and the last line or two will tell you the problem. You can then search the README or other notes in the source directory to get more explanation. If you end up back at the prompt, with nothing that sounds like an error, you can continue building the software.

The next step actually compiles the software, creating the object code for the program:

```
[john@denali weather_1.3.2]$ make
```

Again, you'll see a bunch of lines of text scroll by, way too fast to read or understand. This step can take anywhere from seconds to hours, depending on the size of the program you're installing (and the speed of your computer). If there's a problem, the compilation will interrupt, and you'll have to track down the source of the problem. Reread the README to see if the software requires you to do something unusual before compiling it.

If the software has been compiled successfully, the last few lines will indicate that it's done, and you'll find yourself back at the prompt. For most software, you need to become the superuser to install it. You should do all the configuring and compiling as a normal user, but you can't install programs system-wide without becoming the root user. The su command (short for Switch User) allows you to become the superuser after you type the root password. Then, as root, you install the software:

```
[john@denali weather_1.3.2]$ su
[root@denali weather_1.3.2]# make install
```

Again, you'll see many lines of text scroll by as the install script puts all the files where they need to go in the system. When it's finished, type exit to leave the superuser account, and your software is installed.

Installing from source files is definitely laborious, but the result nearly always works. If it doesn't, you are left with all kinds of hints to help you track what went wrong. You can take this information and send an email to the mailing list for the community that uses and supports the software, and often get an answer within a couple of hours, regardless of the time of day you post.

Install a Mandrake Package

The package system was developed to make installing software a quick one-step process, instead of four-step (unpack, configure, compile, install). The problem is, packages only work if the package was created for the exact layout of the computer you're installing it on. A package created for Red Hat likely won't work for SuSE or Mandrake. A package for Red Hat 7.2 probably won't work for Red Hat 9.0, either. You need to get the package for the exact version and distribution you're using—and if nobody has created one, you're stuck installing from the source.

Mandrake has developed a fantastic tool to make software installation easy. It's called urpmi, and it has a graphical interface version. Not only can it download and install the latest version of a software package for your version of Mandrake, it also downloads and installs any packages it depends upon. To use the GUI version, open the Mandrake Control Center (Figure 2.4). You'll get asked to type the root password. In the control center, go to the Software Management page. The four options you see here are all part of Mandrake's software installation system. It's all based on RPM, which was developed by Red Hat, but Mandrake's system integrates with online repositories of packages built particularly for Mandrake, as well as giving you access to all of the packages on your CD.

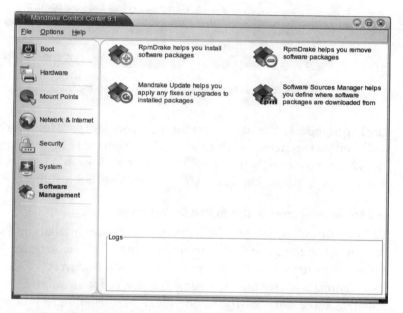

FIGURE 2.4 Mandrake Software Management.

The Software Sources Manager configures the location of online repositories. You can even set up your own software repository if you want. This provides most of the benefits of the Microsoft IntelliMirror feature, publishing all of the software available to install by package.

There are thousands of software packages available through this system, especially if you add some publicly available sources to the list.

The RpmDrake item (Figure 2.5) provides a list of all the software available on all the sources your system knows about. You can search for words in the description, search for specific packages, or browse software by category.

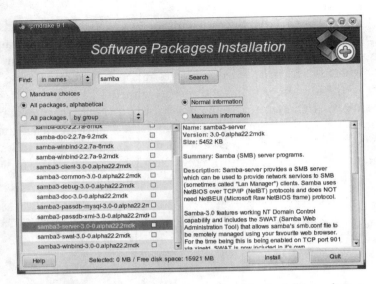

FIGURE 2.5 Mandrake's `RpmDrake` wizard for installing software.

The Mandrake Update feature lists only software packages you have already installed on your system, for which updated versions have been released. This feature provides almost exactly the same benefits as Microsoft Windows Update, only it searches for all packages installed on your system (not just those from Mandrake).

Add Software Sources to Use in RpmDrake/urpmi

Adding software sources to the Mandrake software installation system is one task that's much easier to do from a command line. Search Google for "mandrake software sources urpmi" and you'll get a list of good resources for adding online software repositories so that the software they contain appear in the Mandrake installer. At the time of writing, one site in particular had a little tool that lets you choose the location of the mirrors you want to use, and generates the command line for you to copy and paste to set up your software sources in one fell swoop. It's called Easy URPMI, and it's at *http://urpmi.org/easyurpmi/*.

Install a Web-Based Administration Tool

Finally, the last thing we're going to do in this chapter is install a package for managing many of the services we will discuss later in the book. The software package is called Webmin, and it's a set of scripts that run as a Web server on your new server.

If you're using Mandrake, you can install it using the Install Software screen we discussed above. If you can't find it on a search, it may already be installed. The following command will tell you whether Webmin is installed:

```
[john@denali john]$ rpm -q Webmin
```

Instead of using the install screen, you can use the command line to install it (after you've become the superuser) by typing:

```
[root@denali john]# urpmi Webmin
```

You'll get prompted to insert the specific installation CD containing the Webmin package, and it will be automatically installed and started up.

Using Webmin

To use Webmin (Figure 2.6), you open a browser and point it to the SSL version of port 10000. We'll cover ports in Chapter 3, but for now, the address you would type from the server is `https://localhost:10000`. This will first give you a security warning, because a part of SSL-encrypted connections is verification of the identity of the server. Since nobody has certified that your server is who it says it is, you will always see this warning. Go ahead and accept the certificate.

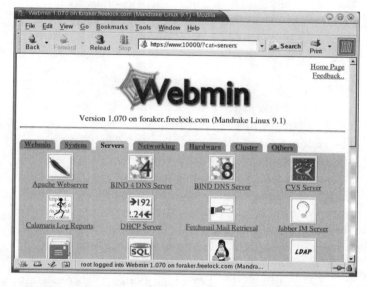

FIGURE 2.6 Webmin, a Web-based server administration tool.

You will then get a log-in screen, where you can type "root" as the user, and your root password to get in.

With Webmin installed, once you have the server set up on your network, you can remove the monitor and never connect it to this server again, unless you run into a hardware problem.

SUMMARY

In this chapter, we've discussed what a server is, how to choose hardware and software to run on one, looked at some major Linux distributions, and gone over some of the things you need to know to successfully install Mandrake Linux on a server. We've also explored the benefits of using the command line to administer a server, along with graphical alternatives. In the next chapter, we'll dig into the details of setting up and managing a local area network.

OTHER SERVER RESOURCES

An updated list of resources for this chapter is on the Web site for the book at *http://opensourcesmall.biz/server.*

Books

Linux For Dummies, by Dee-Ann LeBlanc, John Wiley & Sons, 5th Edition, 2003
Red Hat Linux 9, by Michael Jang, Sybex, 2003
Running Linux, by Matt Welsh, Matthias Kalle Alheimer, and Lar Kaufman, O'Reilly & Associates Inc., 4th edition, 2002

Software

Mandrake Linux *http://www.mandrakesoft.com*
Red Hat Linux *http://www.redhat.com*
The Fedora Project *http://fedora.redhat.com/*
SuSE Linux *http://www.suse.com/us/*
Debian Linux *http://www.debian.org*
Microsoft Windows *http://www.microsoft.com*
Apple Mac OS X *http://www.apple.com*
Sun Solaris *http://www.sun.com*
Advanced Extranet Server *http://www.advx.org*
Shorewall Firewall *http://www.shorewall.net*
Prelude Intrusion Detection System *http://www.prelude-ids.org*
Webmin *http://www.webmin.com*

Web Sites

Easy URPMI, configure media sources for Mandrake *http://urpmi.org/easyurpmi/*

3

Setting Up Your Office Network

In This Chapter

- Introduction
- File and Printer Sharing
- Choosing An Internet Connection Type
- Setting Up Your LAN
- Summary
- Other Local Area Networking References

INTRODUCTION

In Chapter 2 we discussed choosing and setting up a server. But there are a bunch of unanswered questions to consider: How do you use the server once it's set up? How do you set up a Local Area Network (LAN) and get the computers on your network to see each other? What services should you host on your server, and how do you make them visible to the Internet? What kind of Internet connection should you get to support these services?

The first half of this chapter is non-technical, showing you how to use files over a network and choose connection types. The second half of this chapter gets fairly technical, dealing with network configuration. For more background, read the Networking primer in Appendix B.

FILE AND PRINTER SHARING

The biggest reason to set up a server on a local network is to provide central access to your files. If you have files scattered across half a dozen workstations, it can be difficult to find them, ensure that backups are being made, keep track of who's working on what, and move to another workstation.

Basics of File Sharing

Since Windows 98, Microsoft systems have had basic file sharing built into the operating system, but you generally need to turn it on. File sharing works by making one computer a server, and the other computers clients. In this case, the server can be any computer that provides file sharing services. You can make any of your Windows computers a file sharing server, with a couple of steps:

1. In the property page for your network adapter, turn on File and Printer sharing. This makes your computer visible on your network, and shares any printers installed on it.
2. In the Properties for the directory you want to share, go to the Sharing tab, click the radio button labeled "Share this folder," and choose an appropriate name for the share.

This *publishes* the share to your network. One of the huge vulnerabilities of doing this is that if your computer is connected directly to the Internet without a firewall, other people on the Internet can get to your files. For this reason, you should never turn on File and Printer sharing on a laptop—if you ever use a dialup network, or a wireless connection in a public place, your file shares will be available to others on the public network.

There are a couple of layers of security you can enable to mitigate (somewhat) the security risks. You can, on the Sharing tab, designate what users or groups may access the share. This layer of security is generally considered insecure, however, because savvy users can trick the system to bypass the security it provides. On Windows 95/98/ME, this is the only layer you have available, and for this reason, you probably shouldn't publish from these machines at all.

The next layer of security is related to NTFS-formatted drive partitions. NTFS stands for "NT File System," and is a particular way of formatting a hard drive that has security restrictions built in. It's available in Windows NT, Windows 2000, Windows XP, and later. With these systems, you also have a Security tab on the Properties page for a folder. You can define much more granular types of access using NTFS permissions, and the file system enforces them much better.

But the best way to prevent insecure file shares is not to publish them on your workstations at all. Create some file shares on your server, and use them as a single central place for storing and transferring data.

Using File Sharing in Windows

If you use Windows networking, every computer on your network needs to have a unique name. The steps to set the name of a computer vary by the version of Windows, but in general you can find it in the System control panel, under Computer

Name or Network ID. With Windows networking, each computer is also either a member of a *domain* or of a *workgroup*. In a Windows domain, a server handles authentication, user accounts, and security for all computers. In a workgroup, each computer is on its own, and can browse other computers in the same workgroup.

For now, set each of your computers to the same workgroup. Windows networking takes a few minutes to discover all the computers on your network, but if you have them all plugged in, you should be able to open the Network Neighborhood or Entire Network (the names are different in different versions of Windows), and see the workgroup you chose. Inside the workgroup you'll find all of the computers that belong to that workgroup that have File and Printer Sharing enabled (including all Windows NT-based computers). You can then browse into each computer to see all of the published *shares*, and if the user account and password match one that exists on the other computer, copy files back and forth using Windows Explorer.

Often browsing your network doesn't work. Windows networking can be a flaky thing—it takes time for the network to discover all the computers on it, and often conflicts arise that block browsing. You can usually access computers directly by name, however, and bypass browsing.

In Windows, you refer to a computer on a Windows network using what is called a Universal Naming Convention (UNC) path. It's not universal—most paths use a different standard, called a Uniform Resource Locator (URL). The difference between a UNC path and a URL is that a UNC path uses backslashes (\), whereas URLs specify a protocol and use forward slashes (/). If this seems confusing, it is. Windows networking is the main service that uses UNC paths. Most other services use a URL.

The general form of a UNC path is:

```
\\COMPUTER\SHARE
```

You access shared folders using Windows Explorer, or in most Windows programs that have Open and Save As menu items. You can type a UNC path into any address bar in Windows Explorer or Internet Explorer. A particularly convenient way to open an Explorer window on a share is to click Start, click Run, and then type in the UNC path (with back slashes).

A very common way to use a network share is by mapping it to a drive letter. To do this, open any Windows Explorer window, and on the Tools menu, click Map Network Drive. Select whatever letter you want to associate with the share, and type a UNC path containing at least the computer name and share name. With a drive letter mapped to a UNC path, you can treat the network share exactly like another drive.

You can also connect to a printer on the other computer. By opening a UNC path to the computer, you can select a printer attached to that computer and install it on your workstation. You can then print to that printer.

Creating Windows File Shares in Linux

Windows Networking uses a protocol called Server Message Block (SMB). One of the most successful open source projects added a couple vowels to SMB to become Samba. Samba has both server and client components, and can interact seamlessly with Windows networks.

On your server, check to see if you have Samba already installed. In Red Hat or Mandrake systems, you can find out if the package is installed by typing the following command:

```
[john@denali john]$ rpm -q samba-server
```

If the package is not already installed, you can use the URPMI command (as the superuser) in Mandrake to install it, as we discussed in the previous chapter. In case you haven't figured it out yet, the su command is short for Switch User (or Superuser!):

```
[john@denali john]$ su
[root@denali john]# urpmi samba-server
```

Once you have the Samba server installed, you can use the Webmin package to set up shares on the server. Open a browser on the server and point it to the URL *https://localhost:10000*. On the Servers tab, click Samba Windows File Sharing. From this page, you can poke around into different settings, and create shares for the users. There are two special shares already set up: homes and printers. Neither one is visible directly from Windows computers. The printers share publishes all of the printers installed on the server, just like in Windows. The homes share publishes the Unix home directory of each user if the username and password provided by the client computer matches a Unix account.

To make the Samba server appear on your Windows network, click the Windows Networking icon, and provide a few values: the same workgroup you set your workstations up in, and an appropriate name for your server. For WINS mode, select None (unless you set up your own DHCP server—if so, read the section about DNS and DHCP at the end of this chapter and set WINS to the Be WINS server option), and for Security, choose User level.

The next thing to do is set up all of your users. On the main Samba page, follow the link to configure automatic Unix and Samba user synchronization, and select all three options (Add, Change, and Delete). Normally, Samba users are associated with a particular Unix user, but are completely independent accounts, and can have different passwords. If you use Webmin to manage your server you can keep these passwords synchronized. Go back to the main Webmin index page, and you'll find the Users and

Groups control on the Systems tab. Add a user for each of the employees who need to work with any type of files (generally those who have their own computers).

The one tricky issue with setting up users is you need to provide a password for each one. If it's inconvenient to get each user to type in a password as you set them up, one strategy is to create a generic password for each user, such as "ChangeMe." Users will have to log into the server and change both the Unix and the Samba passwords later.

Finally, go back to the Samba configuration tool in Webmin. In the Authentication section, you can map Windows user names to Unix usernames if they're not the same. For example, a Unix username can't have spaces, and is case sensitive (generally lowercase). If a Windows account uses a full name, you can map the full name to the shorter single name in Unix. For example, you can map "John Locke" and "John" to the Unix user account "johnl," and the server will then recognize both of these variations as the correct user.

Click the Restart Samba Servers button to apply the changes you've made.

Using Windows Networking in Linux

With the release of KDE 3.0, you can now browse Windows Network shares, using Konqueror (the KDE version of Internet/Windows Explorer). In KDE-based programs, you can use the same method in Open and Save As dialog boxes, as well. We'll discuss what KDE is in Chapter 4, but for now we'll point out that KDE uses a URL scheme to refer to Windows shares, and it looks like this:

```
smb:/computername/sharename
```

Instead of using a UNC path, the Linux version provides a protocol ('smb:'), and then a normal path to the resource.

There are a number of other graphical tools you can use to browse and mount file shares on a directory in Linux. Check out the LinNeighborhood program on the installation CD of most Linux distributions.

The traditional way to use Windows Networking in Linux is to mount a file share on a directory. In Unix, you can't use UNC paths because the backslash character is actually used to escape other characters. Instead, replace the backslashes with forward slashes, so they look like any other URL (without the protocol): `//servername/share`. The command to use is `smbmount`. In your home directory, create a directory to serve as the mount point, and then use the command to mount the share:

```
[john@denali john]$ mkdir mountpoint
[john@denali john]$ smbmount //foraker/john mountpoint
```

Samba interoperates seamlessly between Linux and Windows, as well as between Windows and Linux, and Linux and Linux. As a Unix-based system, it even works with Mac OS X. For Mac OS 9 and earlier, check out the Netatalk package to add AppleTalk functionality to the server.

Until recently, `smbmount` was the main way to use Windows Networking from a Linux client. Once the share is mounted in the file system, you can use other tools to browse the share and copy to or from it.

CHOOSING AN INTERNET CONNECTION TYPE

To choose the best type of Internet connection for your business, you have to evaluate your needs. Here are some questions you'll need to answer to determine the best type of connection:

- Do people in your company need full-time access to the Internet?
- Do you need to transfer large amounts of data over the Internet during the course of business?
- Are you willing to have someone else host your public services—your public Web site, and your email?
- If you choose to host your own business Web site, do you anticipate it becoming overwhelmingly popular?
- What options are available in your location?

Let's take a closer look at each of these questions.

Full Time Access

By far, the cheapest type of access is a regular dial-up account. If you're not paying extra for the call to your ISP, you can get dial-up accounts for next to nothing. If anyone in your company needs to use the Internet regularly, though, you can waste a lot of time waiting for the connection to get made. If you have several people in your office using the Internet simultaneously, you want some sort of permanent connection.

High Bandwidth

Bandwidth is a term for the quantity of data that can pass through a given connection. For network connections, it's measured in some multiple of bits per second—Kilobits (Kbps) or Megabits (Mbps) for most network connections. If you have to download large photographs, or have many people using the Internet at the same time, having a large amount of bandwidth is a good thing. For example, downloading a CD-ROM image for a new version of Linux can take about five hours on a 640 Kbps connection. On a dialup connection, at 53 Kbps, it could take 10 times as long.

The surprising thing about bandwidth is you may not need as much as you think. Even if you have a lot of users on your LAN, downloading an email or a Web page only takes a few seconds for each item, and most people don't tend to use the full bandwidth capacity at the same time. If you have to transfer large files, however, you'll quickly notice your network grinding to a halt.

Public Services

The previous items discussed downloading bandwidth, how many files you download, and how big they can be. As a business, it can be even more important to make sure your potential customers always see your Web site when they visit it. Wherever your Web site is hosted, it should respond quickly, and always be available. If you plan to host your business Web site on your own server, you need to pay for a reliable connection.

High Traffic Events

There's something on the Internet called the Slashdot effect. A Web site will go along unnoticed for months or years. At some point, something on the site catches the public eye—the site owner posts something funny or insightful, or perhaps the Web site is about some obscure topic that suddenly becomes the center of news. The amount of traffic on the Web site explodes, with millions of visitors checking it out in the space of a few hours. Often, the Web server can't handle the load. Other times, there may not be enough bandwidth to accommodate the requests. In either case, suddenly your Web site is down.

It's called the Slashdot effect, because one of the most popular technology news sites on the Internet is *www.slashdot.com*, and sites that get a link from Slashdot are very often incapacitated from the load.

You need to consider the possibility that someone will find your Web site interesting enough to share with a few million of their closest friends. If you host the site yourself, you won't be able to keep up with the traffic. If you have someone else host it, you might get hit by a hefty surcharge when the traffic exceeds your allotment.

Types of Connections

Now that we've considered some of the deciding issues, let's see what types of connections are available. Table 3.1 lists the basic types of Internet connections that make sense for business use.

TABLE 3.1   Internet Connection Types

Type of Connection	Download Speed	Upload Speed	Full Time	Response Time	Connection	Available	Cost
Dial-up	53 Kbps (max)	28.8 Kbps	No	Slow	Simplex	Everywhere there's a phone	Cheap (< $20 per month)
ISDN	128–256 Kbps	128–256 Kbps	Yes—can get disconnected	Okay	Simplex	Everywhere there's a phone	Expensive to install
Cable	Up to 3 Mbps	Up to 750 Kbps	Yes, mostly (not guaranteed)	Fast	Simplex	Requires digital cable system	Inexpensive (~$50 per month)
ADSL	Up to 1.5 Mbps	Up to 750 Kbps	Yes, mostly (not guaranteed, but more reliable than cable)	Fast	Simplex	Must be very close to telephone exchange	Medium ($50–$150 per month, depending on speed)
SDSL	Up to 1.5 Mbps	Up to 1.5 Mbps	Yes, guaranteed	Fast	Simplex	Must be near a telephone exchange, but can be further than ADSL	Medium ($100–$300 per month, depending on speed)
T1	1.5 Mbps	1.5 Mbps	Yes, guaranteed	Fast	Duplex	Anywhere they can lay wire	Expensive ($300–$400 per month, depending on location)
Satellite	Up to 1.5 Mbps	Up to 384 Kbps	Mostly	Very slow	Duplex	Anywhere on the planet	Expensive

Dial-up Connections

Dial-up connections only make sense for tiny businesses with a handful (or fewer) of regular computer users, if the business is trying to keep the overhead down, or is located in a place where other options are unavailable.

ISDN

ISDN is an older connection type that provides a more reliable, faster connection than dial-up. Compared to newer connections like DSL and cable, it's expensive and slow. The main reason to choose an ISDN connection is if you're in a remote location and can't get a DSL connection, and don't have enough need for a T1 line.

Cable

In most of the United States and Canada, cable has emerged as an excellent, inexpensive way to get a high bandwidth, always available connection. The cost of cable can be less than the cost of a dial-up connection combined with a second phone line. For very small businesses in areas where cable Internet connections are available, it's an excellent way to go.

The downside of cable is that it's not good for hosting public Internet services. Cable is optimized to provide extremely fast download speeds, but the bandwidth is shared by other cable users, so speed can fluctuate significantly with the amount of use by others in your neighborhood. Upload speed is much slower than download speed, and while uploading can still be fast, it reaches the capacity limits of the service much quicker. For this reason, most cable companies do not allow you to run a server connected to the Internet, and can cancel your connection if they discover one.

Cable is generally targeted towards consumers rather than businesses, but if you're a small business and willing to host your Web site and email with an external provider, it can be an inexpensive way to get a good connection.

ADSL

Asymmetric Digital Subscriber Line (ADSL) is another newer way to connect to the Internet. ADSL runs over traditional telephone lines, at slower speeds, and costs about the same as cable. Unlike cable, you have a dedicated connection, not shared with your neighbors or affected by their use. ADSL can be more reliable than cable, and is much better for businesses who plan to host their own Web site and email.

Asymmetric refers to the fact that upload speeds are different from download speeds. You can generally choose from several different options of upload and download speeds, depending on what you're willing to pay. If you're hosting public services, you'll probably want more upload speed.

The drawback to ADSL is that the signal over ordinary telephone lines degrades quickly over distance. The wires between your business and the local exchange for the telephone company need to be less than 5,000 feet or so, or the signal becomes unusable. The further away you are, the lower the quality of the signal, and the slower your connection. If you happen to be too far, you can't get this type of service at all.

SDSL

The other type of DSL connection is Symmetric Digital Subscriber Line (SDSL). It's symmetric in that the upload speeds and download speeds are the same. SDSL runs over a dedicated set of wires, which must be installed running from the telephone exchange directly to your business.

Because you get a new set of wires, you get a higher quality connection with guaranteed speeds. SDSL costs a bit more, especially for installation, but by using fiber optics instead of the existing copper lines, it can be installed at greater distances than ADSL.

T1

A T1 line is an older type of connection that provides 1.5 Mbps of bandwidth in both directions. T1 is the smallest classification of bandwidth for lines that run between telephone exchanges.

The main reason to choose a T1 line is to get a high bandwidth connection in a location where other options aren't available. You can run a T1 line to any location if you're willing to spend the dollars to get the wire installed.

The main benefit of a T1 over an SDSL connection is that the connection is *full duplex*, instead of *simplex*. What this means is you get the full speed of the connection in both directions at the same time. With a simplex connection, network traffic works like a walkie-talkie or a ham radio—you have to stop talking to hear anything. The data either sends or receives, and does so with a packet of data called a *window*. What this means is that even if your Web server has been slashdotted, you'll still be able to browse the Internet unaffected. With DSL and other types of connections, your bandwidth in both directions can be affected by an onslaught of traffic to one service.

If you're in a high profile business, or need reliable, high bandwidth in a remote location, T1 is probably your best choice. Otherwise, a DSL connection is more economical and sufficient for most businesses.

Satellite Connections

Finally, if you're in an extremely remote area, without reliable telephone connections, you can get a satellite connection from anywhere on the planet. This type of connection is expensive, and while the transfer of information is fast, there is a noticeable delay before you get any response. Satellite connections work well for transferring large amounts of data, but every request takes a large fraction of a second just to go from your computer to a server and back again. Satellite works if you want to run your business from your yacht, or dispatch reporters to the wilds of Africa, but it's not a realistic option for most businesses.

SETTING UP YOUR LAN

For small business use, an ADSL or SDSL connection is probably the best type of connection to get, if they're available in your area. A T1 connection, cable, or ISDN connection are not quite as good (in the case of T1, mainly because of the cost), but they are still viable connection types. All of these are considered broadband connections.

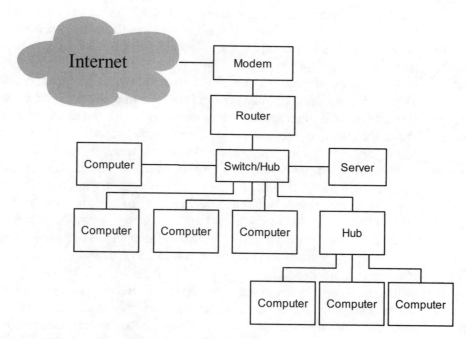

FIGURE 3.1 Example of a simple LAN.

All types of Internet connections use some type of modem to translate the electronic signals coming over the wire into digital packets of information. You can purchase a modem for the type of connection you use, or may be able to lease one from your ISP.

This section gets a bit technical. Appendix B has a primer about networking, putting all of these terms in context. If you want to get a better idea of how all of this works, read Appendix B and come back later to finish the chapter.

Between your modem and the rest of your LAN is a *router*. A router is a device that transfers packets of information from one network to another. In this case, it transfers packets between the Internet (via the modem) and your LAN. There are several different types of routers, but they all need to have some sort of computing power to evaluate the contents of a packet, determine its destination, and send it there. We'll discuss routers shortly.

In an Ethernet-based network, each computer uses a network card as its interface with the network. You plug an Ethernet cable into the network card, and plug the other end into a switch or a hub.

Switches and hubs serve the same purpose—they provide a way of combining signals from multiple network cards. The difference is the level of sophistication of the device. A hub is very simple. It essentially connects all of its ports to each other. When network traffic comes from one port on the hub, it is sent to all of the others. Hubs are very cheap, but are slow and not good for more than two or three devices.

A switch is slightly more sophisticated. It doesn't understand a thing about TCP/IP, but it does recognize MAC addresses and the lower-level Ethernet protocols that allow it to remember which device is connected to which port, and send the traffic only to the correct device. This means that traffic can pass from one network device to another without affecting any others attached to the device.

Setting up the hardware for a LAN is simple. Use a standard Ethernet cable to connect each computer to a switch or hub (switches are not much more expensive than hubs, and provide noticeably better performance, even on a small LAN). Use other Ethernet cables to connect your router to the switch or hub, and to the modem. If you want to simplify wiring to different areas of your building, you can run a single wire from one switch or hub to another, and put it closer to another cluster of computers. One thing to be aware of, when connecting two hubs or switches together, is that some older hubs or switches need to be connected using a special *crossover* cable—an Ethernet cable designed to connect two devices of the same kind. Most newer network hardware devices do not have this limitation— they can auto-sense the correct configuration, so you can use any Ethernet cable to connect them.

Provide power to all of the devices, and the physical work of setting up your LAN is done. Next, you need to set up TCP/IP and get all of your devices to see each other on the network. The best way to do this depends a lot on what you need to do on your network, and is also affected by the type of router you use. Let's take a closer look at routers.

Choose a Router

As mentioned before, a router is simply a device that transfers packets from one network to another. But because of its position straddling networks, it's a convenient place to provide a few other features, often including:

- Network Address Translation (NAT), allowing computers in the private IP address space to access services on the Internet
- Firewalling, filtering traffic in one or both directions
- Dynamic Host Configuration (DHCP), automatically assigning IP addresses to the computers on your network
- Port forwarding, accepting connections to particular ports and forwarding them to specific computers on the LAN
- Built-in switches, providing several LAN ports and eliminating the need for a separate switch
- Wireless Access Point, providing routing and other services to computers with wireless network cards

You need to have some sort of router to be able to share your Internet connection with more than one computer. At the simplest level, you can use a regular computer with two network cards as a router. All versions of Windows since Windows 98 provide some sort of Internet connection sharing using NAT, and Linux provides both NAT and a sophisticated firewall built into an entire distribution on a CD-ROM. Two examples are Smoothwall (*http://www.smoothwall.org*) and Mandrake MNF (*http://www.mandrakesecure.net*). You can also use your server as a router.

As a general rule, however, whatever you use as a router should be a dedicated computer or device. Because a router sits on two different networks, it is permanently exposed to the Internet, and if it is running services that have known vulnerabilities, will inevitably get hacked. The best thing to do is buy a dedicated router that runs no other services, and has nothing extra running that might provide a door for a hacker to break in.

You can buy a consumer NAT router for less than $50. For a little more, you can get one that provides wireless access—but read Chapter 17 first, to make sure you understand the security issues.

Consumer Routers versus "Real" Routers

Shop around for a router and you'll find a big price gap between the bottom-end consumer routers, and regular commercial routers. What's the difference, and why would you want to spend more for a real router?

For the smallest of businesses, a consumer router is fine. The main difference is in how configurable, and how reliable the router is. Consumer routers are all NAT routers—they have a single Wide Area Network (WAN) interface, which can only be set to one IP address. They translate all network traffic from the LAN side, rewriting the packets to come from the public IP address. They can forward specific ports to any designated private IP address on the LAN side, and usually provide the ability to designate one internal IP address as a default computer to handle all incoming requests. Many of these consumer routers call this a Demilitarized Zone (DMZ), but network professionals don't consider this type of feature a real DMZ. Some units provide firewall capabilities built in. They also provide DHCP, which can automatically configure the network settings of computers on your LAN.

There are several drawbacks to these NAT routers, however. Most of them cannot handle multiple subnets. A real DMZ involves creating a separate subnet for servers available to the Internet, and putting a second firewall between the DMZ and your LAN. Consumer routers generally cannot support a DMZ of this nature. They cannot handle multiple IP addresses on the WAN side. The process of doing NAT can break some types of Virtual Private Networking (VPN) connections, and while some of these routers create special tunnels for these connections, the firmware that drives most of these routers can be flaky.

If you need some of these features and have an older computer you're not using, you can drop a couple of network cards in it and set up a Linux firewall. Check out the Smoothwall open source project at *http://www.smoothwall.org* for a good way to do this.

On the other hand, if your business involves moving a lot of data around between your partners, you need a real router for its reliability. A Cisco router is optimized for the task of routing, and has its own operating system built around doing that one task and doing it well.

What Is NAT?

Network Address Translation (NAT) is a way of rewriting TCP/IP packets so that they appear to come from the router as they leave your private network. The router remembers which address on the LAN sent the package, and when the response comes back, rewrites it and routes it back to the original computer.

In the earlier IP discussion, we learned that there are three IP address ranges set aside for private networks. These network ranges are ideal for setting up a LAN, because you do not have to reserve (and pay for) a block of public IP addresses—you only need a single IP address for your entire business. NAT is the mechanism that allows computers on your private network to use services on the Internet.

Besides making Web use possible, NAT provides a layer of security. On the Internet side, computers on your LAN are completely hidden behind your router. As long as your router is secure, it's difficult for an attacker to get past it to break into your computers. It's still possible for a hacker to attack your network and find a way to get in, but it's much more difficult a target than the average computer attached directly to a modem.

Firewalls

A firewall is something that monitors traffic into and out of a computer or network, allowing or blocking it according to a set of configurable rules. The best firewalls monitor traffic going in both directions. A basic rule set for a firewall might consist of the following rules:

1. Drop outgoing traffic for any protocol going to ports 137–139 (the insecure Windows networking ports)
2. Drop incoming packets that are a fake response to a non-existent earlier request
3. Forward incoming traffic going to port 80 to the Web server
4. Forward incoming traffic going to port 25 to the email server
5. Forward incoming traffic going to port 22 to the SSH server
6. Forward all outgoing traffic
7. Drop all other traffic

It's possible to create all sorts of secondary rule sets to handle services like FTP that use multiple ports to set up a file transfer based on a trigger port, but this simple set of rules provides a fair amount of security.

Many routers, including consumer NAT routers, have configurable firewalls built in. You can also buy stand-alone firewalls and segment your network to set up a true DMZ. To set up a DMZ, you actually configure three sets of firewall rules: one between the Internet and the DMZ, one between the LAN and the DMZ, and one between the LAN and the Internet. The main purpose of doing this is to isolate the computers that host your public services so that even if they are hacked into, your LAN remains intact. It's another layer of security we'll discuss in more detail in Chapter 17. Standalone firewalls provide the greatest amount of flexibility to set up these segmented networks, and some provide more advanced Intrusion Detection systems.

It's also possible to run software firewalls on individual computers. One particularly popular software firewall for Windows PCs is ZoneAlarm, which only blocks outgoing traffic. Most other Windows firewalls only block incoming traffic. One good reason to block outgoing traffic on a PC is that you may be able to detect a Trojan horse, a type of virus that connects back to some other service where an attacker can gain control of your computer. However, good firewall protection at the router, along with safe email/Web browsing habits, greatly reduce the need for such software.

Assigning IP Addresses

The remaining issue we need to discuss in this chapter is how to configure individual computers on your network so that they can use the Internet and see the servers. You basically have three options:

- Assign network settings manually on each computer.
- Use the DHCP service on the NAT router to automatically configure your network, and set up your servers manually.
- Set up a DHCP and DNS server.

For any of these options, the first thing to do is choose a subnet to use. Most consumer routers automatically use one of the subnets in the 192.168.x.x range, which can handle up to 253 computers per subnet. If your business has more than one office, make sure you use different subnets for each location, so that you can set up private tunnels between them without using overlapping addresses. For example, you might use the 192.168.34.x subnet in one location, and 192.168.35.x in another.

Manual Configuration

You generally want to configure the network settings on your server manually, so that you can forward the appropriate ports on the router to it without having it change after a power outage or other reboot.

You can configure all of your computers manually, but there really isn't much need to do so, and it makes maintaining your network difficult because whenever you add a new computer, you have to figure out which IP addresses are still available and potentially make changes to files on every other computer. But understanding the manual configuration process helps you make the correct choices when setting up automatic configuration using DHCP.

When you use manual configuration, you need to manually set up each computer with a unique IP address, and provide the appropriate subnet mask, DNS server address(es), and the router address. For the 192.168.x.x address space, the usual subnet mask is 255.255.255.0. If you set the IP address for a computer to

192.168.34.23, for example, this subnet mask makes your network card treat all addresses from 192.168.34.1 through 192.168.34.255 as being on the same local network, and it will try to send any traffic going to any of these addresses directly, rather than going through the router. To find the correct Ethernet address for another IP address in this range, your computer will broadcast to 192.168.34.255, and give its Ethernet address out if it hears a request for 192.168.34.23.

It is absolutely essential that all computers on your network have an identical subnet mask, and have a unique IP address in the same subnet, for your LAN to work. To be able to connect to the Internet, you also need to give the computer the internal IP address of your router as the default gateway. The router IP address must also be on the same subnet, and use the same subnet mask (typically you would set the router's internal IP address to 192.168.34.1, in this example). Finally, to be able to browse the Internet, you need to add the IP address of a caching name server in the list of DNS servers for the connection. This can be the DNS server provided by your ISP. Most NAT routers also forward DNS requests, so you can usually set the DNS server setting to be the same as the default gateway—your router.

In Windows computers, you'll find these settings on a properties page for a particular network connection associated with your network adapter. On Linux computers, the IP address and subnet are set using the `ifconfig` command, the default gateway is set using the `route` command, and DNS servers are listed in the `/etc/resolv.conf` file.

Both Windows and Linux operating systems have wizards to make it easy to set these values up. The main problem is, you have to do this on every computer on your network. If you only have a few, this isn't a big problem, but as your network grows, the time you'll spend increases exponentially.

If you have set up Windows Networking as described at the beginning of this chapter, from a Windows computer you should be able to reach other Windows computers and Linux computers running a Samba server by the name of the computer, once your TCP/IP settings are correct. Linux computers, on the other hand, do not use Windows Networking natively. You may be able to browse your network using some of the programs in KDE (see Chapter 4), but generally, to see other computers on your network from Linux, they either need to be listed on the DNS server (which is not likely) or added manually to the `/etc/hosts` file. This file is a two-column list, with an IP address on the left side, and a computer name on the right side. You can add any computers you want to this list, and by default, the computer will resolve these names to the IP address listed before looking it up at the DNS server.

Windows machines also have a hosts file, and it does exactly the same thing. It's in different places on different machines. Try looking in C:\Windows\System32\drivers\etc.

Using a NAT Router for DHCP

By far the easiest way to get your LAN up and running is to turn on the DHCP server in a consumer NAT router. The router will come with instructions for configuration—most of them involve simply typing in the private IP address of the router into the address bar of a browser. NAT routers almost always come with DHCP turned on, so when you plug everything in and reboot, you should have network access automatically, without having to do a thing.

You might want to change the subnet used by the router. Choosing a valid private IP address range that is not the default range provided by the router can provide yet another layer of difficulty for a hacker trying to explore your network—they have to guess what subnet you're using. You also want to make sure that your router does not assign an IP address you've manually configured on a server to another computer, or you might be mystified when your server disappears. Whatever subnet you put your LAN on, remember that the entire network must be on the same subnet and use the same subnet mask. For example, you might change the internal IP address of your router to 192.168.34.1, tell it to allocate DHCP addresses from a pool of addresses between 192.168.34.32 and 192.168.34.253, and then set up servers and other network devices with static IP addresses between 192.168.34.2 and 192.168.34.31.

To set up the Internet side of the router, use the settings and instructions provided by your ISP. To set up the client computers, just make sure they all are set to automatically configure their network settings.

When you change the internal IP address of the router, it may move to a different subnet, and suddenly your computer can no longer communicate with it. When this happens, you can either reboot to have your computer get a new IP address on the new subnet, or you can release and renew it using a command that quickly becomes habitual when you work with networks.

On Windows computers, the command is `ipconfig`, and the exact syntax varies by the version of Windows. Open a command prompt window (you can generally find the command prompt in the Accessories menu, or click Start | Run and type `cmd`. In the command prompt window, type `ipconfig /release` to release the IP address, and `ipconfig /renew` to renew it.

On Linux computers, the command is `ifconfig`, and the syntax is `ifconfig eth0 down` to release and `ifconfig eth0 up` to renew the address on the first Ethernet card. You must run these commands as root. Running `ipconfig` or `ifconfig` alone will show you the current network settings.

The main problem with using DHCP provided by your router is that you can't use DNS to locate computers on your LAN. Since Linux uses DNS to resolve names, this means that from a Unix computer, you can't open any TCP/IP services on any other computer on the LAN—which can defeat one of the main purposes of having a LAN.

You can add each computer to the /etc/hosts file on every Linux computer, but then when the IP address of any computer changes, the file becomes out of date. And since addresses are allocated dynamically as computers log into the network, the address for any computer you don't manually configure is subject to change at any time.

Windows networking still works, however. From Windows computers, you can browse to any computer on your LAN that is providing Windows services—Windows computers with File and Printer sharing turned on, or Linux computers running Samba service.

In a small business, as long as your primary workstations are Windows based, DHCP configuration from a consumer NAT router is sufficient.

Running a DHCP and DNS Server

If you start using Linux workstations, or if you have more than one location and want computers in other subnets available, you'll have to set up your own DNS server. Since DHCP makes client configuration so simple, it's highly desirable to use. If you set up your own DHCP server, it can automatically update your DNS server as it assigns IP addresses to clients.

DNS is divided up into zones. When you set up your own DNS server, it needs to be the authoritative name server for your domain. The problem is, in most cases you want your computers to be able to see both the Internet and other computers on your LAN. There are two types of name servers for DNS: authoritative name servers, which define the names and IP addresses in terms of zones of authority; and caching name servers, which connect to the authoritative name servers for each request, return and cache each result. A caching name server finds the authoritative name servers by contacting the root name servers on the Internet.

To get DNS to work for both public and private IP addresses, you have basically three options:

■ Set up fake root servers that point to the authoritative name servers for your domain, and forward all other requests to the real root servers.
■ Register a real domain, and run an authoritative name server that provides both public and private IP addresses.
■ Run a single name server that acts as a caching name server and is authoritative for a fake domain for your LAN.

Setting up fake root servers used to be a common way to deal with the issue of keeping your private IP addresses private, while still allowing access to everything from the LAN. With a newer feature of name server software called *views*, this has become a clumsy way of addressing the problem, requiring you to run two different servers and do some dirty tricks.

Registering a real domain is the "correct" way to handle the situation, but for a small business, it means you have to host your own name servers for both your public and your private services. To register a domain, you are required to have not only a primary, but also a secondary, authoritative name server for your domain. The secondary is used as a backup. Furthermore, the secondary name server is supposed to be on an entirely different subnet as the primary, in case there are routing problems on the Internet. Meeting these requirements can be challenging for a small business, especially on something less than a full T1 connection.

Still, if you're hosting everything else yourself, you should host your own name servers. Often your ISP can provide a secondary name server for a small fee, and there are a few third party service companies that provide nothing but DNS services.

A program called BIND is the granddaddy of DNS software. Version 9 of BIND introduced the views feature, which allows you to return different views of DNS records to different subnets. Whatever you do, you don't want to have a map of your internal LAN published somewhere accessible on the Internet. Views allow you to publish only your public services (Web and email, usually) to the Internet, and use a different view to provide a full map of your network to computers on your LAN.

If you host other services such as a Web site with a service provider, you might be able to get them to delegate authority for a particular zone to your name server. For example, if you already own the domain example.com, you might be able to get whoever is hosting it for you to delegate the `lan.example.com` zone to your name server. Then you can run a name server that is authoritative only for the `lan.example.com` domain, and each computer on your LAN will be a part of this domain: `computer1.lan.example.com, computer2.lan.example.com`. You can then firewall this server off from the rest of the Internet, and it will only show up on your LAN.

The other way to set up your DNS is to run a single server as both a caching and authoritative name server. In this configuration, you set up some arbitrary domain name for your LAN. If you use a real TLD (Top Level Domain), you make any Web sites that use the domain you chose unavailable from your LAN, so it's best to invent your own, such as `*.lan`. In this configuration, all of the computers on your LAN might be in the `example.lan` domain, and computers would have hostnames like `computer1.example.lan` and `computer2.example.lan`.

Apple's Rendezvous network system reserves a .local TLD. If you have any Macs on your network, do not use .local!

For small businesses, running a single name server that caches and forwards DNS requests to the Internet, but is authoritative for an arbitrary fake domain, is often the best solution. You can keep your public name servers on the Internet and never have to be concerned that mail or Web traffic might get lost if you lose your network connection.

The final piece of the DNS and DHCP puzzle is getting the DHCP server to update DNS. To do this, you specify a forward and reverse zone in the DNS server for your LAN, and mark it to allow client updates. You then generate a key and add it to the configuration file.

A forward zone takes a domain name and looks up the IP address associated with it. A reverse zone takes an IP address and looks up the name associated with it.

In the DHCP server configuration, you specify that the DHCP server is authoritative for a zone, create a pool of IP addresses for it to use that are in the reverse zone for your LAN, specify the domain to add new computers to (for the forward zone), and provide the same key as you added to the DNS server.

In the DHCP configuration, you also list the IP address for the caching name server you set up on your network, as well as for the router. One other thing you can add here is the name of a Samba server that can act as a WINS server. WINS is a service that supports Windows networking across subnets, but it seems to make Windows networking more reliable when you use it on the smallest networks. Make sure you enable WINS in the Samba settings, too.

Also make sure you add the servers to which you've assigned static IP addresses to the appropriate forward and reverse DNS zones, as well as your router. Finally, turn DHCP off in your router, and either release and renew or reboot all the client computers on your network.

Webmin, the Web-based administration program described at the end of Chapter 2, can help you configure and administer DHCP and DNS servers.

Entire books have been devoted to DNS and BIND. It's a complicated subject, and takes a fairly savvy person to implement. The hints in this chapter will hopefully get you going, should you find it necessary to set one up.

SUMMARY

In this chapter, we've covered how to set up an office LAN. It is easy to set up an old unused computer with a couple of Ethernet cards to be a router or firewall using a Linux firewall distribution. We covered file servers and printer servers, along with the many different options you might have for connecting to the Internet. Finally, we discussed choosing a router, and setting up automatic network configuration for your workstations.

In the next chapter, we'll take a look at open source on the desktop, and how you can save a lot of money on office software by choosing an open source version.

OTHER LOCAL AREA NETWORKING REFERENCES

An updated list of resources for this chapter is on the Web site for the book at *http://opensourcesmall.biz/lan.*

Books

DNS and BIND, by Paul Albitz and Cricket Liu, O'Reilly and Associates Inc., 4th edition, 2001

Networking: A Beginner's Guide, by Bruce A. Hallberg, McGraw-Hill, 2001

Software

ISC BIND, the leading DNS server *http://www.isc.org/products/BIND/*

ISC DHCP, the leading DHCP server *http://www.isc.org/products/DHCP/*

Djbdns, a free (but not open source) DNS server *http://cr.yp.to/djbdns.html*

Samba project *http://www.samba.org*

Smoothwall Firewall *http://www.smoothwall.org*

Mandrake MNF *http://www.mandrakesoft.com/products/mnf*

4 Open Source on the Desktop

In This Chapter

- Introduction
- Open Source Windows Applications
- Switching to Linux
- Open Source on the Mac
- Summary
- Open Source Desktop References

INTRODUCTION

One reality of using computers in small business is that it's rarely a good idea to move wholesale to a new technology. In most cases, business systems have grown organically over time, and only merit replacement when the business needs exceed the capabilities of what you have available.

This chapter is non-technical, and should be easy to follow for most people with experience using computers.

Most of this book is predicated on the assumption that you can add open source technologies to your business, without abandoning the investment in software, hardware, and hands-on experience of what you have. You can supplement your existing Windows desktops with a Linux server, adding substantial benefit without everybody having to learn their basic computer applications all over again. Server applications are where open source software is most mature—but desktop applications have become compelling alternatives to proprietary software.

Why would you want to start using open source software on the desktop?

- It saves money over licensing proprietary desktop applications.
- You can copy software to any computer on your network, without incurring the risk of a software audit, or a fine for "pirating software."
- You have access to a wider range of software applications than you could otherwise afford.
- The latest generation of open source software has matured to have 90% (or more) of the features offered by their proprietary counterparts, and can usually read or convert files generated by them.

Many small businesses, when they add a computer to their network, install software from other copies they've already purchased. Another reality of small businesses is that paying for every copy of Microsoft Office or Adobe Photoshop they install is prohibitively expensive. Many small businesses install multiple copies of these software packages, and hope they never get audited. The software industry calls this practice piracy, and imposes huge fines if you get caught—and with the various product activation technologies being developed and used, it's more and more likely you'll get caught, or perhaps be unable to install that second copy in the first place. Open source software finally provides a great option, avoiding all of these issues.

In this chapter, we'll take a look at open source applications for the desktop. First, we'll explore open source projects that run on Windows-based computers. Then we'll look at Linux on the desktop, surveying the array of applications you can run on a Linux desktop and showing how you can even run Windows applications in Linux. Finally, we'll take a brief look at open source Mac software.

OPEN SOURCE WINDOWS APPLICATIONS

Most businesses have some flavor of Microsoft Windows on their computers. Microsoft Office has become the standard for documents, spreadsheets, and presentations—when you email somebody a document, it's a Word document. You got a spreadsheet in email? It's probably an Excel spreadsheet. And PowerPoint is *the* name for a computer presentation. How much did you spend to install that Office package on every computer in your organization? If you didn't spend a few hundred dollars on Microsoft Office for each computer, how big a fine might you be risking by not paying for those copies?

 Be sure to check out The Open CD, on the CD-ROM included with this book. **ON THE CD** It's packed full of open source software for Windows.

Did you know there's a free Office suite that offers the same basic applications as Microsoft Office, that reads and writes Word documents, Excel spreadsheets, and PowerPoint presentations? That also includes a vector-based drawing program and an HTML editor? It's called OpenOffice.org, and you can download and install it for free, in either Windows or Linux.

OpenOffice.org versus Microsoft Office

OpenOffice.org has its roots in a much older office suite, StarOffice. StarOffice was developed in Germany in the middle 1980s, and had several major releases but was eclipsed in popularity by Microsoft Office. In 1999, Sun Microsystems bought StarOffice, and released the source code to the public as OpenOffice.org. Sun continues to maintain and fund the OpenOffice.org project, but basically has given the product away for free. The irony of this business tactic is that Microsoft used the same in the Web browser market by releasing Internet Explorer for free, a move that severely impacted the previous market leader, Netscape.

ON THE CD
OpenOffice.org is part of TheOpenCD, on the CD-ROM included with this book.

So how does OpenOffice.org compare to Microsoft Office? Quite well, actually. Each product has its strengths, but for the most part, both Microsoft Office and OpenOffice.org provide all the features most people need and use. It's surprising how close the feature set of the two compare.

Table 4.1 lists some of the differences between OpenOffice.org Writer and Microsoft Word. While the two programs look quite a bit different, and the commands are on different menus, for the most part the only differences are in the advanced features, and even there they are both relatively even.

TABLE 4.1   OpenOffice.org Writer versus Microsoft Word

Feature	*OpenOffice.org Writer*	*Microsoft Word*
Most general word processing features: spell-checking mail-merges grammar-checking change-tracking headers and footers tables font options	Provides all these features, has no trouble handling these features when editing a Word document	Provides all these features

TABLE 4.1   OpenOffice.org Writer versus Microsoft Word *(continued)*

Feature	OpenOffice.org Writer	Microsoft Word
character and paragraph styles multiple columns embedding images/ objects automatic tables of content Search and Replace Autocorrect Wizards for creating letters, memos, etc.		
Bullets and Numbering	More consistent than Word. If you use OpenOffice.org exclusively, bullets and numbering tend to work better. However, conversion to/from Word documents is not clean.	This is one of the problems with Word. It's common to have lists break when opened in a different version of Word.
Macros	Uses its own Macro language (a version of Basic). There is no macro recorder—you have to write macros step by step. On the plus side, the language is different enough that it's immune to Word macro viruses.	Macro recording provides a great way to automate particular tasks. Powerful macro language (Visual Basic for Applications) provides access to all sorts of Windows objects. Downside is security—Word macro viruses are common on the Internet.
Master Documents	Available, but relatively untested. The purpose of this feature is to have a single document that includes multiple sub-documents—like the chapters of a book.	Difficult to use. Master documents are a feature that has been broken in many versions of Word. If you don't follow a particular, undocumented sequence of steps, your document can become completely corrupted.

TABLE 4.1 OpenOffice.org Writer versus Microsoft Word *(continued)*

Feature	OpenOffice.org Writer	Microsoft Word
Outlining view	Has a simple outline view showing the headings in your document	Has a sophisticated, powerful outlining view. This is perhaps the one feature where Microsoft Word is clearly superior to OpenOffice.org Writer.
Page styles	Provides the ability to create page templates, and more easily manage headers and footers for similar pages in long documents	You must use sections to get this type of functionality, and every section is completely separate from others, even if in the same layout.

In practice, most Word documents open flawlessly in OpenOffice.org (see Figure 4.1). The biggest conversion issues generally have to do with embedded pictures, bullets, and numbering. The better the shape of the Word document, the fewer problems you'll encounter opening it in OpenOffice.org. If you don't need to be 100% compatible with Word, you can switch to OpenOffice.org without sacrificing a thing.

The other applications in the suites also compare very evenly. The spreadsheet programs are very evenly matched—there isn't much difference between them at all, other than the macro language, and some workflow features Microsoft has added to Excel.

Microsoft PowerPoint has some clear advantages over OpenOffice.org Impress, including a more usable layout. The drawing tools are similar, and the basic presentation functions you need are there, but some of the extra bells and whistles are nowhere to be found. Drawing tools in OpenOffice.org seem to be very similar to use, though there aren't as many pre-made shapes available.

There isn't a standalone desktop database to compare against Microsoft Access, but there is substantial integration with a variety of data sources, including address books or virtually any server database that you can connect with ODBC or JDBC. Finally, OpenOffice.org includes a basic HTML editor, and you can save any OpenOffice.org file in HTML format.

Table 4.2 compares some of the features of the other major office programs.

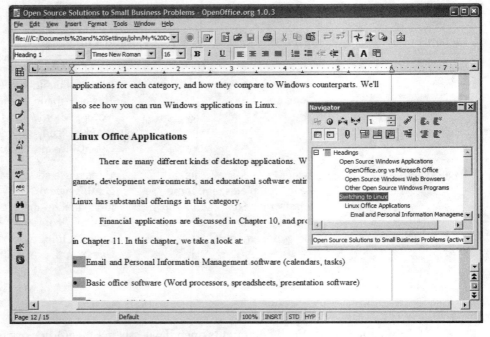

FIGURE 4.1   OpenOffice.org in action.

TABLE 4.2   OpenOffice.org versus Microsoft Office

Spreadsheets	*OpenOffice.org Calc*	*Microsoft Excel*
Most general spreadsheet features: 　Auto-fill cells 　Basic formulas 　Statistics 　Financial equations 　Matrices 　Charts 　Filtering 　Sorting	Provides all these features, has no trouble handling these features when editing a Excel spreadsheet	Provides all these features
Multiple views of data	Provided by DataPilot feature, very similar to PivotTables.	Provided by PivotTable feature

TABLE 4.2   OpenOffice.org versus Microsoft Office *(continued)*

Spreadsheets	*OpenOffice.org Calc*	*Microsoft Excel*
Manipulating data from other data sources	Integrates with any ODBC database connection, or other OpenOffice.org Calc documents	Integrates with Access or any ODBC database connection
Summary	No compelling advantage to either product—both provide an almost identical feature set	

Presentations	*OpenOffice.org Impress*	*Microsoft PowerPoint*
Overall:	Basic presentation needs. Few extras. Best advantage: connectors that "glue" to shapes, providing lines that stay connected to objects as you move them around	Many extras. Best advantage: Excellent multi-monitor support when giving presentations—you can have the main presentation on the projected image, and a note view with previews of the next slide
Most general presentation features: - drawing - outlining - font controls - insert from other programs	Better support for connecting shapes	More pre-formatted shapes
Export to Web	Exports several formats of Web pages, Java-based slide show	Exports several formats of Web pages, ASP-based slide shows
Create self-contained presentation	No	Yes
Track changes in presentations	No	Yes
Show presentation on one monitor and notes on laptop screen	No	Yes
Record voice-overs	No	Yes

The notable missing component of OpenOffice.org is that there is no Personal Information Management tool to compare to Microsoft Outlook. You can get the email and address-book functionality from Mozilla, or any of a variety of other programs, but the calendar, to-do lists, and journal features are not available in OpenOffice.org. There are some compelling alternatives that run in Linux, and some Web-based groupware tools we will explore in Chapter 8.

The bottom line is that thanks to open source, you now have a compelling free option to Microsoft Office. You can install it on all the computers in your company, without having to worry about compatibility, licensing charges, or features.

Open Source Windows Web Browsers

Why would you want to use an open source Web browser in Windows, when Microsoft Internet Explorer is free and already installed? One big reason: viruses. In 2003, Explorer was an extremely popular browser. This made it the favorite target of all kinds of malicious exploits. That fact, coupled with tight integration with the operating system and the increasing number of security-related patches that keep coming out, and an alternative Web browser starts to become a more attractive option.

ON THE CD
Mozilla 1.5 is part of TheOpenCD, on the CD-ROM included with this book. Mozilla Firefox is also included on the CD-ROM.

One of the biggest open source projects around is the Mozilla Web browser. Mozilla is a direct descendant of the Netscape browser that used to be the dominant Web browser before Internet Explorer knocked it off its perch.

Mozilla is a full-featured Web browser, and also includes an email client, an HTML editor, a chat client, and an address book. You can download the latest version from *http://www.mozilla.org*, or you can install from the CD-ROM provided with this book.

Mozilla has some nice features built in, such as a tabbed browser window (Figure 4.2) and the ability to block pop-up windows. You can also quickly find text on a page by simply pressing the forward slash (/) key and typing the text.

Mozilla also has a satisfactory email client that does a fine job working with both IMAP and POP servers, and connects to LDAP address books as well.

Other Open Source Windows Programs

The open source movement has not ignored Windows entirely. Many server applications are available for Windows—a majority of the software discussed in this book can be installed and run in Windows instead of Linux, although some of it takes a substantial amount of tweaking and adding additional software to get it to work right.

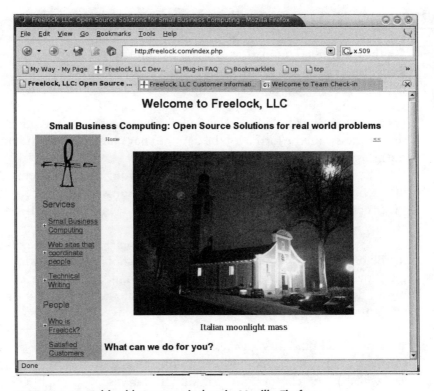

FIGURE 4.2 Tabbed browser window in Mozilla Firefox.

One package in particular, the Cygwin environment, is designed to bring many Unix tools, including the basic GNU compiler (which allows you to build open source software on whatever computer you're running) into the Windows platform. Cygwin is an open source software project managed by Red Hat, the company behind Red Hat Linux. You can find it at *http://www.cygwin.com*. Cygwin doesn't provide much benefit for most small business users, but can provide a way for an experienced system administrator to install a Linux application on a Windows server.

Most of the chapters in this book cover applications that have a client/server architecture: the client runs on your workstation and connects to software running on a Linux server. Because most small businesses use Windows computers extensively, rather than trying to persuade you to abandon what you already have and know, we'll set up the Linux back-end systems and discuss Windows clients when they are available, along with the Linux counterparts.

SWITCHING TO LINUX

On the other hand, Linux is becoming a completely viable option on the desktop. There isn't much you can do in Windows that you can't do in Linux. The biggest reason not to use Linux on a desktop computer is that you already have a substantial investment in proprietary software running in Windows—which can be an investment in training, the skills developed over time by you and other employees in the business, and the format of the data you have built up over the course of doing business.

These are compelling reasons to stay with your current systems. And, because of the client/server architecture of most of the software in this book, you can gain the benefits of open source software without throwing away the investments you've already made.

Any time you have to learn a new system, you're going to lose some productivity. Before changing any computer system, you should evaluate why you're making the move. Perhaps the fundamental tenet to think about is the saying "If it ain't broke, don't fix it!" So in the context of this statement, what is broken enough to warrant switching your desktop to Linux?

- You are a brand new business, without any existing computer systems.
- You need to do some new computing task, and a good application for it is available and cheaper under Linux. In this case, you might consider keeping your Windows machines intact, and start using Linux in a limited way.
- You've been fined by the Business Software Alliance for installing unlicensed software on some of your computers, and you want to install free software instead of paying for proprietary software.
- You haven't been caught, but you are using software on more computers than the licenses you've agreed to allow. This is called piracy, and is one of the central motivations of free software: to provide alternative software that gives you the right to install and use it on any computer you want.
- Your existing systems have reached their capacity, and you need to move to more robust systems. Examples of this might be an Access database that is starting to be used by too many people at once, systems that have to be rebooted several times a day, or corrupted email stores that cause loss of data.

Switching your workstations to Linux has a few downsides to consider, as well:

- Using something as simple as a floppy disk, or a CD-ROM, can sometimes entail cryptic commands to get them to mount correctly in the operating system, and these commands can vary by the flavor of Linux.

■ Power management on laptops (as of 2003) is still not completely polished. A great many laptops cannot use hibernation or standby features reliably under Linux. Similar issues plagued Windows systems until the release of Windows 2000—hopefully these issues will be resolved soon. It's possible that by the time this book is published, power management will be working.

■ Solving problems in Linux tends to require more familiarity with the basics of Unix. It's beneficial if somebody on your staff has used Linux for a few months before you try converting your entire office—you should have some people who have developed a good Linux troubleshooting mindset, along with a good understanding of Unix file permissions, ownerships, file systems, and other basics on hand to help others get started.

Ready to take the plunge? In the remainder of this section, we'll take a look a brief survey of some of the major categories of desktop applications, some leading Linux-based open source applications for each category, and how they compare to proprietary Windows counterparts. Many of these open source programs also have Windows versions, a few of which are included on the CD-ROM for the book. We'll also see how you can run Windows applications in Linux.

ON THE CD

Linux Office Applications

There are many different kinds of desktop applications. We're going to entirely ignore games, development environments, and educational software in this book, though Linux has substantial offerings in these categories.

Financial applications are discussed in Chapter 10, and project management tools in Chapter 11. In this chapter, we take a look at:

■ Email and Personal Information Management software (calendars, tasks)
■ Basic office software (Word processors, spreadsheets, presentation software)
■ Desktop publishing software
■ Image editing software
■ Multimedia software

There are also a multitude of utilities available for Linux. You can find Linux software for managing computers, hardware, networks, files, preferences, and just about anything related to computers. You can run programs that show you the current area of the earth that is lit by sunlight, get the current temperature, barometric pressure and wind on your task bar, see the current state of the moon at a glance, or add a set of electronic eyes that follow your cursor across the desktop. For manipulating things on computers, or for the wide range of programming utilities available, no operating system beats Linux.

For using your desktop to accomplish some business task otherwise unrelated to computers, you'll probably find the Linux applications to lag somewhat behind Windows applications in completeness of features, and often usability. But more Linux applications are reaching stable release points every month, and the gap is diminishing.

The software discussed in this section reflects some of the leading software packages for each category. One of the downsides of open source software is the sheer number of programs available—it can be hard to find and identify the best software for a category. Source Forge, one of the leading Web sites that hosts open source projects, had over 65,000 individual open source projects in July 2003, and was adding new projects at the rate of 70 per day, according to an email they sent to their subscribers.

Another thing to keep in mind is that there are two major Linux graphical environments, and many more smaller ones. The major graphical environments are called KDE and GNOME. These two environments are developed by two competing communities, both vying to become *the* Linux desktop environment. These environments provide libraries that other programs use to draw graphical user interfaces. They provide different ways of drawing a menu, or panel, or button, or any of the myriad interface elements. The reason you need to understand this is that many desktop applications are built around one or the other set of libraries. (There are a couple other graphical environments that a few programs use—wxWindows is one, designed to be a cross-platform window solution, as it can be installed and run in Windows. The Mac OS X provides another.)

When you install Linux, the best practice is to install both KDE and GNOME. You can run either one as your primary desktop. GNOME programs run in KDE, as long as you have the GNOME libraries installed on the computer, and vice versa.

KDE (the 'K' Desktop Environment) was developed to be an open source replacement for the Common Desktop Environment (CDE), the standard graphical interface used by Sun Solaris and other Unix systems. It relied on some code that was not released as free software, which irked some of the Free Software fundamentalists, who decided to start their own desktop environment. The GNU Network Object Model Environment (GNOME) project was started to provide an environment completely free of proprietary software. As GNOME became popular, the developers of KDE released the remaining proprietary toolkits with an open source license.

Many programs that use the libraries provided by KDE have a name beginning with the letter "K": konqueror, korganizer, koffice, kghostview, kivio, etc. Likewise, many GNOME-based programs begin with "G" or "gno" or "gnu"—but far from all of them.

Email and Personal Information Management

Personal Information Management (PIM) refers to software that manages addresses, schedules, task lists, and memos—the basic functions you find on any Personal Digital Assistant (PDA) such as a Palm Pilot. In the Windows world, Microsoft Outlook is a program that combines PIM with email.

Evolution is an Outlook clone that uses the GNOME libraries. It provides many of the same features as Outlook, and even looks quite similar (see Figure 4.3). It can also connect to Microsoft Exchange, a proprietary mail server that also provides scheduling and shared address books.

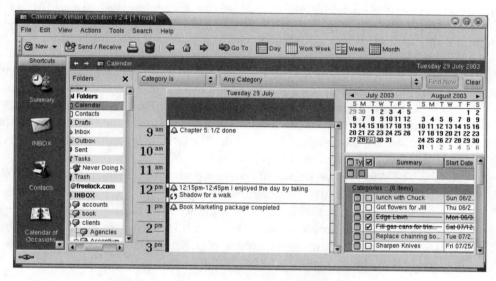

FIGURE 4.3 Personal Information Management with Evolution.

If you're willing to use different programs for PIM and email, you have hundreds of options to choose from. The KDE project has an email client called Kmail, which has great support for encrypted emails (see Chapter 17). For PIM, there's KOrganizer, KPilot, and JPilot, all of which synchronize with Palm devices (as does Evolution).

Mozilla works the same way in Linux as it does in Windows, providing email, an address book, and also newsgroup access. You can also use KNode or Pan to access Internet newsgroups.

You can actually do a few things with Palm devices you can't easily do in Windows. The Pilot-link package provides command-line access that allows you to directly interact with Palm databases. One common problem with Palm devices if you synchronize to a new program is that all of your address book or calendar entries get duplicated. The *pilot-dedupe* command deletes all of the extra copies of your addresses (or whatever database you point it to).

Office Software

We already looked at OpenOffice.org, the most comparable office package to Microsoft Office. It's available for Linux, Windows, and Mac OS X, and several other operating systems as well. There are two other suites of office software—one for KDE, and one for GNOME.

The KDE package is called KOffice, and is comprised of a drawing program (Karbon14), a presentation program (KPresenter), a chart program (KChart), a spreadsheet (KSpread), a word processor (KWord), a formula editor (KFormula), and a diagram program (Kivio). These programs will open most basic files from the Microsoft Office counterparts, though their feature set is limited and many find that the compatibility is not as good as OpenOffice.org.

Still more spartan in features are the GNOME office applications. AbiWord is the most basic of word processors. Gnumeric is a trimmed-down spreadsheet application. Unlike the KDE applications, the GNOME versions often don't read files from their Microsoft counterparts at all.

on the cd The Windows version of AbiWord is part of TheOpenCD, on the CD-ROM included with this book.

In general, OpenOffice.org is the choice for users who need full-fledged features in an office program suite. The other office program suites are fine for newer computer users, or any user who doesn't need advanced features and just wants to create some basic documents.

Image Editing

Image editing programs can be put into three broad categories: pixel-based editors, vector-based drawing programs, and diagramming tools. Pixel-based editors are programs for manipulating photographs, and include most painting programs. One of the most popular pixel-based editors is Adobe® Photoshop®. Think of these editors as working dot by dot. If you enlarge a pixel-based picture, you make the dots bigger—the picture usually ends up looking jagged and rough.

A vector-based drawing program, instead of tracking the individual pixels in a drawing, keeps track of the length and direction of lines (vectors, in mathematical terms). Vector-based drawings can be enlarged to any size without losing detail—a curved line in a vector drawing is curved at any resolution, whereas a curved line in a pixel-based drawing becomes jagged as you enlarge it. Examples of vector-based drawing tools are Adobe® Illustrator®, Freehand®, and CorelDRAW®.

Diagramming tools are a type of vector-based tool that provides pre-drawn stencils of shapes you can use to quickly create a diagram, along with connectors that "glue" shapes together, staying connected to shapes as you move them around your diagram. One of the most popular diagramming tools is Microsoft Visio®.

As software has matured, many high-end image editing tools have grown to include capabilities that cross these categories. Photoshop now has limited vector-based tools, and you can include pixel-based images in most vector-based editors.

For Linux, the GNU Image Manipulation Program (the GIMP) is the primary professional level image editing tool. The GIMP is another old, powerful open source project. It provides most of the features and capabilities as Photoshop, but it also provides quite a few of the vector-based tools of Illustrator. The GIMP is primarily a pixel-based editor, and if you're used to Photoshop, it will take some getting accustomed to. But there are few image editing tasks you can't do in the GIMP.

ON THE CD The Windows version of the GIMP is part of TheOpenCD, on the CD-ROM included with this book.

There isn't a strong contender in the pure vector-editing application category, though there is a decent Computer Aided Design (CAD) program called QCad, and Karbon14 provides basic vector drawing.

Two programs aim to be Visio replacements as diagramming tools: Dia and Kivio. Dia has a very similar interface to the GIMP—many floating toolbars without a containing window. You perform most actions either by selecting a tool and using your mouse in the workspace, or right-clicking the image to get to the full menu of options.

Kivio, like other programs in the KOffice suite, is easy to learn and figure out, but there aren't many stencils available at this writing, so using it for much beyond a simple flowchart involves creating your own stencils.

Desktop Publishing

Desktop Publishing tools have become very sophisticated in the Windows world. For publishing brochures and small newsletters, Adobe PageMaker, has long been one of the standard applications.

Open source desktop publishing tools are fairly scarce, but the Scribus project provides all of the basic functionality you need for small projects. It handles a wide range of image formats, provides basic text placement and font control, handles the CMYK color model (Cyan, Magenta, Yellow, and blacK), a standard color model used in professional printing) properly, and is fairly stable. It has a strong community of printing professionals, so the support is good and files you create are easy to take to a professional printing house to get good results.

Microsoft Publisher is another program in this space. Publisher has more samples and templates, but poor compatibility if you plan to take the result to a print house. PageMaker has a few more features, such as support for Pantone colors, and a few other wizards for generating tables of content and converting pages to booklets, for example. Scribus compares to both of these products very well—it's easy to use, and you can find a way to do most small projects.

For longer publications, like magazines or catalogs, QuarkXpress™ and Adobe InDesign® are among the market leaders. If you need to lay out longer publications, as of this writing, there is no good open source equivalent.

For books, Adobe FrameMaker® seems to be one of the last remaining desktop publishing applications in wide use. FrameMaker used to be available in a Unix version, but Adobe seems to have dropped support for it.

There are a few publishing standards that many Linux programs support. These standards describe how to place any text, graphics, images, formulas, or other items exactly where you want them, and involve marking up text using special codes. People have been using these standards for decades in technical publications—but few editing programs hide this markup from you. You spend more time creating a description of each item on the page, and then have to print the page to see the result.

The standards include:

- TeX
- LaTeX
- Docbook SGML
- Docbook XML

FrameMaker supports both of the Docbook standards. TeX was very popular long before there were good graphical user interfaces and layout programs that hid the complexity from you. LaTeX is basically a set of extensions to TeX that provide more features, or make it easier to do common layout tasks. All of these require substantial learning to use effectively.

If you need to do professional publishing of anything longer than a short newsletter, it's worth finding a professional technical communicator well versed in the standards and software to assist with the task.

Multimedia

Multimedia includes both video and audio, and in software, programs for playing, producing, and serving multimedia files or streams. Excellent open source multimedia players abound, including MPlayer, XMMS, Noatun, Xine, and many others. You can play most media formats, other than the latest Microsoft Windows Media® formats, with one or more of these players.

For producing audio, there are many visual tools to help you work with wave forms. Audacity is one that allows you to slice and manipulate audio files graphically. The SoX library performs all kinds of filtering of audio files on a command line.

RealNetworks®, a popular streaming media company, has released their players, production tools, and server software under an open source license as the Helix project. RealNetworks provides a great example of a company that formerly specialized in proprietary software. Now, however, RealNetworks has changed its business model to be a content company, trying to sell subscriptions to exclusive content such as Major League Baseball broadcasts.

Apple has also released open source versions of its QuickTime® broadcasting software, and there are a number of open source production tools you can use to make video.

Many high-end movie-creation programs run on Linux—DreamWorks studios did most of the image processing for the animated film "Spirit: Stallion of the Cimmaron" using Linux workstations and a mix of proprietary and open source software.

You can also install many proprietary multimedia software packages in Linux, other than those made by Microsoft. SHOUTcast makes a streaming audio server that streams files in MP3 format. The QuickTime® player and an older Real Player® are available.

What is notably missing from the Linux multimedia scene are the latest Windows Media formats—older ones have been reverse-engineered and are supported by most of the open source players.

Running Windows Programs in Linux

If you find some Linux-based software you want to use in your business, but still rely on Windows software, you're not entirely out of luck. Besides getting a second computer, you basically have three options:

- Create a dual-boot machine, and boot into the operating system you need at the moment.
- Install the software in Linux using the Wine libraries.
- Run a Virtual Machine that hosts the other operating system.

Dual-Booting Windows and Linux

Most people who start using Linux on the desktop don't switch over all at once. It's possible to install both Linux and Windows on the same computer, and choose which one to launch when the computer boots.

The best way to set up a dual boot computer is to use empty disk space to create completely separate Linux partitions, or to add a blank disk drive. If you're going to repartition your hard drive, realize that it is a risky procedure—you could lose everything already on the computer. Make sure you have a good backup, and defragment your hard drive.

The Mandrake installer can change the size of the Windows partition to create enough room for your new Linux partitions (as long as you have enough free space). Simply boot the computer using the Mandrake installation CD, and when you get to the portioning part of the installation, choose to resize the Windows partition. Then follow the guidelines in Chapter 2 to choose a partitioning strategy and install the operating system.

You generally need to install Linux after installing Windows. When you boot a PC, the first thing that happens is a small program called the BIOS, installed in read-only memory on the motherboard, scans the hardware devices and checks memory. It then checks each boot device (floppy drive, CD-ROM, hard drives, network) for a *master boot record*. The master boot record is the very beginning of the hard drive, along with the partition table, and exists outside any disk partitions. A tiny program called a *boot loader* is installed in the master boot record, and contains instructions for loading the actual operating system.

When you install Windows, it overwrites the master boot record, installing its own boot loader. The Linux boot loader is a bit more sophisticated—it can boot into either Windows or Linux. For this reason, if you install multiple operating systems, you should install Linux last.

Wine and CrossOver Office

The Wine project is an open source project that aims to make Windows programming libraries available in Linux, so you can install and run Windows programs. To date, these libraries provide most of the publicized interfaces of Windows 95/98/ME, meaning that software you install thinks it's running under one of these operating systems, and not Windows NT/2000/XP.

CodeWeavers is a commercial software company that works to update the Wine libraries, and adds convenient software for installing and managing Windows software in Linux. You can download a trial version of their CrossOver Office® from *http://codeweavers.com*. With CrossOver Office, you can install and run many Windows programs with few problems, including Microsoft Office, Adobe Photoshop, Intuit® Quicken®, and many others.

Create a Virtual Machine with VMware

VMware® is a proprietary program that completely simulates the environment of a PC, creating a virtual PC. You can install another operating system inside this virtual PC, and run both Linux and Windows at the same time, on the same computer.

Obviously, you need to have a fast computer and a lot of RAM, or performance of one or both operating systems is poor. But it's quite an amazing way of getting the best of both worlds. If you have enough RAM, you can even run more than one virtual machine at the same time.

VMware is available in both Windows and Linux versions. Get the version to go with your base operating system. The main operating system on your computer is called the host operating system, and the virtual operating systems are called guests.

When you start up the program, you can install a guest operating system on a different partition or disk, or in a single (very large) file. You go through a normal operating system installation, except that the guest operating system sees the generic hardware provided by VMware, instead of the real hardware on your computer. You can run the guest operating system in its own window, and also expand the window to full-screen, making the host operating system invisible.

VMware is especially useful for testing software, Web sites, or other things that would ordinarily require a bunch of computers. It's the most expensive of these solutions, however—less expensive than a new computer, but not cheap, or open source.

Desktop Linux Hints

So now we've seen some examples of software available in Linux, and ways of continuing to use your business-critical software after moving to Linux on your desktop. Here's a couple of nifty tricks you'll quickly become accustomed to, and find missing when you go back to Windows.

Copy/Paste with the Mouse

The Mac mouse has one button. The Windows mouse has two buttons. The Unix mouse has three. What's the third button for? Usually for pasting.

Unix people, having lived at the command line for so long, strive for efficiency of design. Since copying and pasting text is such a universal computing task, it got its own button when they finally added a mouse to their workstations.

Your PC was probably designed for Windows, however, and only has two buttons on the mouse. If you have a mouse wheel, you can usually click it to have it act as the third mouse button. If not, if you're coordinated enough to click both mice buttons at once, the X-Windows system (the program that controls the mouse) will interpret it as a third mouse button click.

So what do you do with it? Using your left mouse button, you click and drag to select text, just as you would in Windows. Then you click with the wheel button to paste.

This basic technique works in most Linux programs, but exactly what happens can vary. If you select a URL and middle-click in any browser window, the browser will go to that URL. If you middle-click in a terminal window, the text is pasted at the command line, even if you scrolled back to select the text.

In KDE, a program called Klipper sits in the task bar, and remembers the last few items you selected. You can quickly pop open its little window to select a previous item for the next paste. It also provides some custom actions, such as offering to open up a browser when you select a URL—these can be disabled if you find them annoying.

One problem with copying and pasting in Linux is that there are actually several different clipboards. Consistency between programs for all kinds of things is one of the biggest problems of Linux, and clipboards are a prime example. Many newer programs provide the same keyboard shortcuts for cutting, copying, and pasting as Windows: Ctrl-X to cut, Ctrl-C to copy, and Ctrl-V to paste. When you copy or paste using these commands, the result isn't often available to paste with the mouse button. Sometimes you can copy and paste these items between programs, but not always.

The bottom line is that copying and pasting text is extremely fast and easy in Unix, but copying other items, like pictures or formatted text, doesn't always work as you'd expect. These are the quirks you'll find when switching to Linux. Along with this, dragging and dropping is mostly unavailable. Both KDE and GNOME have built ways of supporting dragging and dropping, but they're not compatible with each other. You'll find you can usually drag and drop within an application, sometimes drag and drop between KDE applications when you're running KDE, and usually not be able to drag and drop anything else.

Use Multiple Desktops

Another cool feature of Linux on the desktop is that both GNOME and KDE provide multiple desktops. The default is four, but you can change this to have up to 16 desktops. A little section of the task bar shows a thumbnail of each desktop, and you can click on the one you want to get to. The idea is you can have a few applications open on one desktop, then instantly switch to another to have a fresh, clean work area. You might have your email open in one, your accounting software in another, and a spreadsheet in a third. You can also "pin" any window to all of the desktops, move the window among the desktops, or make it stay on top of other windows.

OPEN SOURCE ON THE MAC

With all the discussion of PCs, you might think that Macs are completely isolated from the solutions in this book. The reverse is true—when Apple developed Mac OS X, it chose a BSD kernel, and many of the same tools as Linux. What this means is that almost everything that runs in Linux is now available for Mac OS X.

Choosing to run Unix under the hood was a good strategy for Apple. A lot of open source software developers have switched to Macs so that they can use their favorite Linux software on a polished and user-friendly desktop. OS X is not Linux but it is Unix, and so most Linux software compiles on it, often with little hitches here and there.

The graphical part of OS X is all Apple, though, combining the ease of use Apple is known for with the wide and growing range of open source software.

SUMMARY

People keep asking, "Is Linux ready for the desktop?" The answer is a resounding yes. You can do just about everything you need to do in a small business without booting into Windows. You can even run Windows programs in Linux.

On the other hand, the newest Microsoft Windows releases provide brand new features such as handwriting recognition that aren't available yet in Linux. And Apple continues to do an impressive job of making creative work a breeze. In short, Linux is a completely viable environment for doing business, but if you choose to stick with your current operating system, you can find powerful open source software to augment your office capabilities.

In this chapter, we explored some open source Windows applications, and then checked out Linux on the desktop. We looked at native Linux business applications, and two different ways to run Windows software in Linux. Finally, we looked at how the Mac platform can run many programs developed for Linux.

In the next chapter, we'll take a close look at email.

OPEN SOURCE DESKTOP REFERENCES

An updated list of resources for this chapter is on the Web site for the book at *http://opensourcesmall.biz/desktop*.

Books

Moving From Windows To Linux, by Chuck Easttom, Charles River Media, 2003.
Moving to Linux: Kiss the Blue Screen of Death Goodbye! by Marcel Gagne, Addison-Wesley, 2003

Articles

Jaques, Robert, "Worm mutants spoof Internet Explorer," January 28, 2004. Available online at *http://www.vnunet.com/News/1152347*.
Shankland, Stephen, "HP, Linux snag DreamWorks deal," C|Net News.com, January 30, 2002. Available online at *http://news.com.com/2100-1001-825967.html*.
"SourceForge Sitewide update," email sent to SourceForge.net subscribers, July 24, 2003.

Software

Microsoft Office, commercial office suite *http://www.microsoft.com*

Sun StarOffice, commercial office suite *http://www.sun.com*

OpenOffice.org, open source office suite based on StarOffice *http://www.openoffice.org*

Mozilla, open source Web browsers and email readers *http://www.mozilla.org*

Cygwin, open source Unix environment for Windows *http://www.cygwin.com*

Knoppix, bootable Linux distribution *http://www.knoppix.org*

KDE, graphical desktop for Linux *http://www.kde.org*

GNOME, graphical desktop for Linux *http://www.gnome.org*

Evolution, personal information management email program like Outlook, *http://www.ximian.com/products/evolution/*

Koffice, KDE-based office suite *http://www.koffice.org/*

Pan, Newsgroup reader for GNOME *http://pan.rebelbase.com/*

Adobe Photoshop, premier commercial graphic editor *http://www.adobe.com*

The GIMP, open source graphic editor similar to Photoshop *http://www.gimp.org*

Qcad, open source CAD program *http://www.ribbonsoft.com/qcad.html*

Dia, open source diagram tool *http://www.lysator.liu.se/~alla/dia/*

Kivio, open source diagram tool for KDE *http://www.thekompany.com/projects/kivio/*

Scribus, open source desktop publishing tool *http://web2.altmuehlnet.de/fschmid/*

LaTeX, document publishing language *http://www.latex-project.org/*

Docbook, document publishing language *http://docbook.sourceforge.net/*

Helix, an open source media player and server from Real Networks *http://www.helixcommunity.org*

Mplayer, an open source multimedia player for Linux *http://www.mplayerhq.hu*

Wine, Windows program libraries that allow Windows software to run in Linux *http://www.winehq.org*

CrossOver Office, commercial software built on Wine that installs Windows software in Linux *http://codeweavers.com*

VMware, commercial emulation software that allows you to run Windows within Linux, or vice-versa *http://www.vmware.com*

Web Sites

Business Software Alliance, organization of commercial software vendors *http://www.bsa.org/usa/antipiracy/*

Source Forge, leading repository for open source projects *http://www.sourceforge.net*

5 Setting Up an Email Server

In This Chapter

INTRODUCTION

As people have become more comfortable with email, a reliable email address has become a business necessity as important as a telephone or fax number. You need to have a reliable way to send and receive email.

The first part of this chapter discusses the business decisions involved with getting a domain for email, and choosing whether to host an email server in house, or outsource it to someone else. Later on in the chapter, the discussion gets much more technical.

Many small businesses start out with a basic ISP account, using an email address at their provider, such as AOL.com, EarthLink.net, Comcast.net, or any number of others. The biggest problem with having an email address at your ISP is that you don't own or control it. In 1999, the users of Excite@Home, the largest cable Internet provider in the country at the time, suddenly lost not only their Internet access, but also their email. Their access was restored in a matter of days, but any email sent to their @home.com email address was lost forever.

In 2003, millions of users of AT&T Broadband had to change their email address to Comcast.net when Comcast bought AT&T's cable division. This time the changeover was less painful—no email was lost, and there was a healthy transition period when both email addresses worked—but think about all of the business cards, brochures, and other marketing material that had to be changed through no fault of the individual business.

You need to have your own domain. When you own a domain, you can move it to another provider anywhere in the world, without your customers ever knowing anything changed. You can host your own email, allow your ISP to host it, or have a third party hosting provider handle it for you. Most Web hosts also host a limited number of email accounts as part of the hosting package (see Chapter 6 for more about choosing a Web host). For the smallest of businesses, with a need for only a handful of email addresses, using your Web host is the simplest option. There are several reasons a Web host may not meet your needs, however. Here are a few:

- You connect to the same email account from more than one computer.
- You want to be able to access your email (including archived messages) from anywhere using a Web-based mail program.
- You want to keep internal company business private, rather than sent through the Internet.
- You want to use capabilities not offered by the Web host.
- You have a large enough number of people to make outsourcing your email more expensive.
- You send large files, and don't want to be constrained by the space limitations of your host.

Besides Web hosts, there are companies that specialize in email hosting. For smaller businesses, going with some type of host that provides good email services is probably the most cost-effective way of having more advanced email services.

Why Email Isn't Easy

You can host your own email, and do it very cheaply. However, setting up an email server is not for the faint of heart. In spite of email's apparent simplicity, it takes a lot of programs to make email work. Make a mistake in the configuration, and soon your computer will be hijacked by spammers, and used to spew messages to millions. Let this happen once, and you won't even be able to send messages to the people you're trying to email, as your server will get blacklisted.

Ask any group of network administrators what their biggest headache is, and the consensus will likely be spam. We will discuss specific strategies for dealing with spam and viruses in Chapter 19, but the first fundamental step is having an email server that won't relay it. One of the worst characteristics about spam is that most of it comes from forged addresses. Spammers take advantage of a weakness of email— that nothing about an email positively identifies who sent it. This "feature" makes it extremely hard to determine where an email actually came from, or take any steps to block it. There's a huge battle going on right now on the Internet between the spammers and those who try to stop it. This battle causes several problems:

- Your Inbox gets filled with email you don't want, making it harder recognize email you do want.
- Software that filters for spam sometimes generates "false positives"—it marks a legitimate message as spam, and the intended recipient never receives it.
- Server administrators, in an attempt to reduce spam, configure rules to not accept connections from other poorly configured mail servers, causing messages to or from you to bounce.
- Individual users delete mail from people they don't recognize, out of a general fear of viruses and spam.

As a result, email has become an unreliable way to communicate. It can be forged, lost, forwarded to unknown people, and misunderstood. Still, it's a critical business communication medium, and you need it.

Benefits of IMAP

Most small businesses start out with a type of email called POP (Post Office Protocol). With POP, you connect to your mail server with some type of email client software and download your mail. Once you've downloaded the mail, your client usually deletes the mail from the server, but it can be configured to leave it there for other email clients.

POP works fine if you only check your email from a single computer. If you want to check it from any other computer, you can only see new messages, or messages you left on the server. For example, if you have a computer at work you use during the day, but want to check your email from your home computer, you can only see emails your work computer hasn't removed from the server. If you tell your work computer to leave messages on the server, you'll then download another copy of messages you may have already read and handled. In short, as soon as you try to use POP mail from a second computer, you either can't access old messages, or have to deal with the same mail twice. Not only that, if you decide to change email software, you'll have to import or copy it from one program to the other.

Web mail services, such as Hotmail or Yahoo, keep all mail on the server. This type of email solves the problem of using multiple computers to access a single account, but has its own set of drawbacks. You're limited to a particular allocation of disk space, and if you exceed it, you have no choice but to delete mail. Using a Web browser is simple, but specialized mail programs are easier to use, especially for moving messages into different mail folders. If you use one of the free services, you have to put up with advertising from other companies attached to your outgoing messages—not a very business-like impression to make to your customers. If you have a dial-up connection, or if you travel, you have no access to your mail while you're disconnected. If you use Web mail provided by your Web host, it has the same limitations as checking your email from a second computer.

Another type of email server addresses these issues. Internet Message Access Protocol (IMAP) is an alternative to POP. It provides much better support for storing all mail on the server. Like the Web mail services, you're limited by disk space. But most email client programs handle IMAP as well as POP. With IMAP, you see the same mail folders no matter what client computer or program you use. You can use IMAP-compatible Web mail and see the folders you created in Outlook Express or Thunderbird. Any email you saved becomes available from any computer you log in from.

Because your email folders are on a server, you can also add special processing rules to sort incoming mail into folders automatically, keeping newsletters or mailing lists out of your Inbox. Unlike Web mail, IMAP provides a way to read and manage email when you're disconnected, in *offline* mode. To go offline, your email client software downloads a local copy and caches it so you can access it. When you connect, the email software synchronizes your changes with the server. Some email clients handle this better than others.

Most email clients handle IMAP. A partial list includes: Microsoft Outlook and Outlook Express, Mozilla Mail, Mozilla Thunderbird, Netscape Communicator, Pegasus Mail, Eudora, The Bat!, Ximian Evolution, KMail, Pine, Sylpheed, Mulberry, and Mutt.

Setting up your email client is almost identical to setting up a POP mail account—just select IMAP instead of POP when you set up the new account. However, you'll quickly notice a few differences. In most email software, you have some set of local folders, which are in one or more files on your hard drive somewhere. All POP mail is downloaded first to your Inbox. In some programs, you can configure sorting rules to have mail moved from your Inbox to somewhere else.

With an IMAP account, your program may still show your local folders, but it adds a completely new set of folders that represent the IMAP folders on your server. Messages appear in the IMAP Inbox, instead of the Inbox in your personal folders. Often, mail sorting rules don't work for IMAP accounts, because the mail software doesn't necessarily get the opportunity to see the messages as they arrive. You can almost always copy messages back and forth between your local mail folders and the IMAP folders.

IMAP is designed to provide a great many useful features. Support for these features varies a lot. For example, with IMAP it's possible to delete messages from the server without ever downloading them. But getting your email client to do this may be a different story. Some email clients say they support offline IMAP access, but only download new messages in folders you specify. With good offline IMAP support, you can move, copy, and do most activities with your email whether you're online or offline. Your changes get synchronized back to the IMAP server when you reconnect.

Microsoft Outlook supports most of the features of IMAP, but many find Outlook Express easier to use—Outlook 2000 sometimes crashes often when accessing IMAP folders, and Outlook XP requires you to go through a bunch of menus to first mark messages to download, and then download them. Outlook Express, on the other hand, seems to be as easy to use with IMAP as with POP, and its offline support is reasonably good.

There is one other email client protocol in fairly wide use: Messaging Application Programming Interface (MAPI). It's a Microsoft-proprietary mail protocol, and only works on Windows operating systems. A number of Windows programs have been developed that support it. MAPI is the primary difference between Outlook and Outlook Express.

The Microsoft Exchange Server is the primary mail server that uses MAPI, though Lotus supports it as well. Both of these servers add calendaring, address books, task lists, and journals to the email capabilities. The biggest advantages of MAPI over IMAP are that these groupware features are built into the system, and everything works together relatively well. The biggest noticeable disadvantage is that if you connect to a MAPI store over a slow connection, you often can't do anything else in the mail program—it really works best when connected on a fast LAN. Other disadvantages are the lack of choices of client software, dependence on Windows, and the prevalence of viruses that specifically target Microsoft Outlook. Because there are no open source MAPI applications, we won't discuss them further.

Hosted Email

If all you need is POP mail, whatever you use as a Web host will almost certainly provide it for your domain. Many Web hosts also provide IMAP, sometimes with a small extra fee depending on the amount of disk space and the number of mailboxes (email accounts).

Extra features to look for in an IMAP host include:

- Spam filtering
- Virus filtering
- User configurable email sorting rules
- SSL-encrypted connections
- A good Web mail interface
- Authenticated outgoing mail

If you need these features, and your Web host doesn't provide them, there are many providers on the Internet that can provide them for you, often for as low as $10 per month per mailbox. Changing your email provider usually just involves signing up for an account, changing the email DNS record for your domain to point to the new host, and adding the new account to your email client software.

EMAIL SECURITY CONSIDERATIONS

Email, by its very nature, is very insecure. Once you send an email, you have no reliable way of preventing it from falling into someone else's hands—the recipients can do whatever they want after they receive it. Even if you trust your recipients, your email may get intercepted as it travels from you to them. When you receive an ordinary email, there is no easy way to prove it came from who you think it came from. Finally, if you store your mail on a shared server (using an email host, for example), it's possible for other users of the server to read your email.

There's no technical solution to the first problem, preventing your recipients from redistributing your message. The other problems can be addressed by controlling the server and public key encryption.

Controlling the Server

You should treat ordinary unencrypted email sent through the Internet like a postcard. Anyone who handles the postcard can see your message. Whether they choose to read it or not is out of your control. However, only people handling your postcard (or email) can read its contents—it's not necessarily broadcast to everyone. If you don't control every server between you and the eventual destination, you can't be certain who can read your email.

On a hosted system, your mail can be read by:

- Any administrator on the email server you use to send the message
- Any administrator on any server the email passes through on its way to the destination
- Any administrator, and sometimes malicious users, who can log into the server that receives your email

On the Internet, controlling all these servers is just not possible. However, for mail you send within a company, the sending and receiving email server is usually the same, as long as you use your company's domain. If you host your own email server, email you send within your company never reaches the Internet. If someone else hosts your email server, and you care about keeping internal company email private, get a list of everyone who might be able to access your email, and keep that list in mind before sending.

To get the most privacy for internal company email, look for an email provider that encrypts both IMAP and SMTP connections, and either provides a dedicated server for your use, or does not allow user logins to the server.

Public Key Encryption

There is one way to ensure the privacy of your messages—using encryption. Public key encryption actually provides two different benefits: encrypting the content of your message so that only your intended recipient can read it; and positively identifying a message as coming from you and nobody else.

The problem with encrypted email is that it's a pain to use. You need to have the public key of the recipient before you can encrypt an email to them. They need to have your public key to be able to verify the digital signature you add to your email. To further complicate the issue, there are several different methods to encrypt emails, and different email clients use different standards.

All public key encryption uses similar principles. Each person has a pair of keys, one public and one private. Anyone can use your public key to encrypt a message that can only be decrypted with your private key. You can *digitally sign* a message using your private key, and anybody can use your public key to verify the signature. These are two different, complementary features of public key encryption: encrypting data, and authentication.

For public key encryption to work, you need to distribute your public key widely, but keep your private key completely secret. Different ways of distributing keys and actually applying encryption and signatures to messages have emerged—unfortunately, these standards do not work with each other.

The two leading standards are OpenPGP and S/MIME, compared in Table 5.1. Few mail clients understand them both. Furthermore, there is an older Inline PGP standard that encrypts message contents inline rather than as a separate attachment. The end result is usually a mess. You cannot decrypt an S/MIME-encrypted message using a mail client that supports only OpenPGP. You cannot verify the signature of an OpenPGP-signed message using a client that only uses S/MIME.

In general, S/MIME has greater support among large companies. It uses the same Certificate Authorities that identify Web sites to certify public keys for individuals. Generally, S/MIME integrates better with other authentication systems (such as Windows domains and directory servers), and is more likely to become an official Internet standard.

But OpenPGP and the older Inline PGP standard are still very popular, having more grass-roots support. We will discuss these standards and how they work in greater detail in Chapter 16. Encryption and digital signing happens at the end clients—messages are encrypted or signed in one client, can travel through any type of email servers regardless of the standard used, and decrypted or verified at the recipient's client.

Another advantage of using an IMAP server over a POP server is that you can receive mail encrypted or signed with any of the standards, and open up whatever email client can handle it. So you can use whatever different encryption standards you need to communicate with other people.

TABLE 5.1 Email Clients That Have Support for Different Encryption Standards

S/MIME	OpenPGP	Inline PGP
Microsoft Outlook	Ximian Evolution	Eudora (with plugin)
Outlook Express	KMail	Outlook (with plugin)
Mozilla Mail	Pegasus Mail	Outlook Express (with plugin)
Netscape Communicator	Marlin	Lotus Notes (with plugin)
Mozilla Thunderbird	Mac OS X Mail	Novell Groupwise (with plugin)
KMail (with Aegypten plug-in)		
Lotus Notes•		
Novell Groupwise•		

HOW EMAIL WORKS

If your business is small enough to go with some sort of hosted solution, we've covered most of what you need to know about email. You configure your email clients using the instructions provided by your host.

The rest of this chapter covers concepts important to understand when you host your own email, and describes how to get a basic email server running and providing all the necessary services.

NOTE

The rest of this chapter contains very technical information, mainly necessary to get a basic email server configured and working. If your business only needs a handful of email addresses, stick with a host unless you have a pressing reason not to. You will need some good Unix skills to be able to complete the implementation steps in this chapter.

Email, despite its apparent simplicity, relies on a lot of different server programs, and travels through several different computers on its way to its destination. We will follow an email from your computer to a final recipient. But first, let's take a look at the structure of an email.

Anatomy of an Email

An email is made of a set of headers and the body of the message. The headers contain all kinds of details about the message: who it came from, who it's going to, which computers it went through on the way, the time and date it was sent, the subject, what program was used to write the email, and many other optional details. As noted earlier, however, there is nothing that prevents somebody from forging any or all of these headers. Various email server programs can add or change headers as they handle an email.

The body used to be plain text, but now it's often a set of Multipurpose Internet Mail Extensions (MIME). MIME provides a mechanism for sending more than plain text via email. It handles HTML-formatted mail, pictures, plain text, digital signatures, and any other type of attachment.

Finally, while all an email contains is a header and the body, the entire email is wrapped by an *envelope* that specifies the address to deliver the mail to, and the address it came from. These envelope addresses are independent of the To and From headers. Blind Carbon Copies (BCCs) work by putting the destination of the mail in the envelope, but not in the header. These envelope addresses disappear as each mail server receives the mail, but many mail servers can be configured to copy them to other special headers. For example, Postfix inserts the envelope addresses as X-Original-To and Return-Path. The To address in the envelope is required, or the mail wouldn't get delivered anywhere. The From address in the envelope is where a properly configured server sends a bounce message if it can't deliver the message.

The path an email has traveled to reach the destination can be traced in the Received headers—each server that handles the email adds a Received header indicating which computer it received the message from, and at what time. The problem is, nothing prevents someone from forging any or all of this information. If you trust your mail server, then you can trust only that it received the email from the previous computer in the list. You cannot trust any further back than that.

A Trip in the Life of an Email

Let's see what happens when you send an email to your friend. You open up Thunderbird, since you're now using open source wherever possible. You create your email, address it to jane@example.com, and click Send. A diagram of the path an email takes through the Internet can be seen in Figure 5.1.

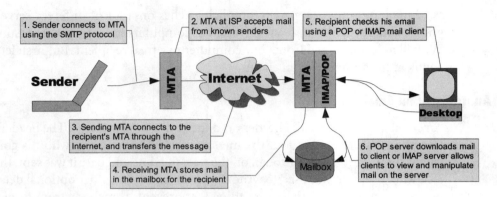

FIGURE 5.1   Sending an email through the Internet.

 The Windows version of Thunderbird is part of The Open CD, on the CD-ROM included with this book.

Because you've already configured Thunderbird with an outgoing Simple Mail Transport Protocol (SMTP) server, it knows what to do with it. It opens a connection to the SMTP server, passes your username and password if necessary for authorization, and sends the message.

Your message is now at your SMTP server, but where is that? There are basically four different SMTP servers you could use:

■ A mail gateway provided by your ISP
■ An outgoing server provided by your Web host
■ Your own mail server
■ Some random unprotected server on the Internet

There are advantages and disadvantages to all four. Providing an outgoing mail server is one of the core jobs of your ISP, and using this mail server is generally the best way to go. To prevent spam, your ISP's mail server will only accept mail that comes from an IP address belonging to the ISP. In other words, you can only send mail through Speakeasy® if you're connected to the Internet via Speakeasy. If you take your laptop and dial in to EarthLink®, however, you can't send your email through Speakeasy's mail server.

Using your Web or email host has the advantage of being accessible from anywhere. However, to prevent spam, your Web host needs to implement some sort of authentication mechanism so that it can trust you. This generally involves either *SMTP Auth,* or *Pop-Before-SMTP.* With SMTP Auth, you send authentication credentials—either a public key certificate, or a username and password. Pop-

Before-SMTP records your IP address when you download mail using POP or IMAP, and then accepts outgoing mail from that IP address for a limited time, usually 30 minutes.

If you don't have a Web host, if you're doing your own email hosting, you can set up your own SMTP service. Again, you can choose between SMTP Auth or Pop-Before-SMTP. Or, you can only relay mail coming from your internal network, and not allow anybody outside your network to send through your server. One potential disadvantage to running your own SMTP server is that if you don't have a static IP address, many mail servers won't accept your mail. Again, the reason is spam—there has been so much abuse by spammers logging into the Internet, getting a dynamic IP address, and sending mail directly using their own email servers, that many email administrators just reject anything that comes from any range of IP addresses used for dynamic connections. If you're on a consumer DSL or cable connection, you will run into this problem. If you want to host your own email server, the solution is to forward all outgoing mail to your ISP's mail server.

The other type of outgoing server you can use is called an *Open Relay*. Relaying mail is the act of transferring a message from one computer to another. An open relay is a mail server that doesn't check where a message came from, before forwarding it on to the destination. Open relays are what have allowed spam to become such a problem on the Internet. When email was developed, all mail servers were open relays, but now most servers fall into one of the first three categories . If you run an open relay, you're asking for trouble—spammers will discover you, send messages through your server, and then your IP address will get blacklisted by most legitimate mail servers.

So back to our email message: it's now sitting in a queue on the outgoing SMTP server. SMTP refers to the protocol used to send email, and because a lot of email programs call the outgoing server an SMTP server, that's the term we're using here. But the actual type of server that delivers mail with SMTP is called a Message Transfer Agent or Mail Transport Agent, depending on who you ask. Either way, it's known as an MTA. MTAs are what make emails possible on the Internet. They send, receive, and route email wherever it needs to go. So the MTA looks at your outgoing message to see where it's heading. For each address in the envelope To address, it first looks to see if the domain is one handled by this MTA. If not, it makes a DNS request for the MX (Mail eXchanger) record for the domain. The DNS server returns the IP address of the appropriate mail server, another MTA.

Your outgoing MTA connects to the receiving MTA, in pretty much the same way that your email client connected to it, using SMTP. The receiving MTA checks to make sure that it recognizes, and handles, the To address in the envelope—if not, it rejects the message. Many people configure their MTA to also check out the sending MTA to see if it's on a dynamic IP address, has been blacklisted for sending spam, or has a different domain name than the envelope sender. It's possible for this MTA to route to yet another MTA, for several reasons—but if it doesn't have a rule for specifically dealing with the domain in the envelope To address, it should reject the message.

All things being successful, your email is now sitting in yet another queue on the MTA for example.com. This MTA has accepted the mail for local delivery. Another server program on the same computer, called the Local Delivery Agent, takes the mail from the queue, processes it for any delivery rules set up by the recipient, and puts it in a file in the recipient's mailbox.

So far, your mail has been handled by four programs, and Jane hasn't even seen it yet!

Jane opens up her email client, and logs in. The email client uses either POP or IMAP to connect to yet another program on the mail server, a POP or IMAP daemon. This daemon looks in her mailbox, finds the new message, and notifies the email client. Finally, Jane sees the new message, clicks it, and the client goes back to the server to download it. A diagram for the process inside the receiving e-mail server can be seen in Figure 5.2.

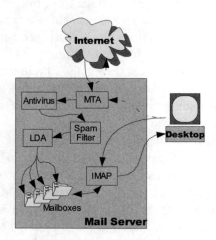

FIGURE 5.2   Inside the receiving email server.

The backbone of the entire email system is the MTA. When you set up an MTA, you must configure it for both outgoing and incoming email. For outgoing mail, you need to make sure you only allow known computers or users to relay mail through the MTA, or else you'll contribute to the overall spam problem and eventually not be able to send legitimate mail. For incoming mail, you have a lot of decisions to make about what to do with the mail after it has arrived—and then set up an IMAP or POP server to allow your users to get to it.

Email isn't easy. There are a lot of steps involved in the entire process, no matter what type of email service you provide. As described in Chapter 1, in the Unix philosophy, each task is broken down to small parts, so you end up with a different program to handle each task, rather than one big monolithic program that attempts to do it all. In the rest of this chapter, we'll show you how to set up an email server.

SMALL BUSINESS EMAIL: POSTFIX/IMAP SERVER

The two biggest parts of your email server are the MTA and the POP/IMAP programs. There are many options for both. In addition, not only do you have a choice of Local Delivery Agents, but you can also plug special purpose spam and virus filters and mail sorting rules into the LDA process.

For our small business email server, we're going to configure the Postfix MTA, several different LDAs, and the Courier-IMAP server. We will also set up the Squirrelmail Web mail package and SMTP Auth using Cyrus-SASL.

Choosing an MTA

There are many different MTAs available (see Table 5.2), and most of them do exactly the same thing. Table 5.2 lists some of the more common MTAs, though there are many others. Because the MTA is the heart of the email system, and email is such a complicated system, the most important thing to consider when choosing an MTA is the experience of the person who has to administer it. Regardless of the MTA, somebody needs to actively administer the mail server: add and remove accounts, monitor logs for attempts to relay messages or harvest email addresses, and deal with problem messages in the various queues. Each of the mail servers listed have at least one book devoted to them.

TABLE 5.2 Common MTAs

MTA	Characteristics	Reasons to Use
Sendmail™	The granddaddy of all MTAs. Big, cumbersome to configure, has reputation for not being secure—but runs on some 90% of all email servers.	You're already a Sendmail expert. Security issues have been resolved in recent versions.
Microsoft Exchange	Microsoft's MTA/MAPI server/LDA/ Webmail/do everything server. Can be difficult to configure and secure.	Runs on Windows. Uses Domain authentication so individual users don't need to log in.

TABLE 5.2 Common MTAs *(continued)*

MTA	Characteristics	Reasons to Use
QMail	Early alternative to Sendmail. Designed to be much simpler, faster, and better. Uses different configuration options than other MTAs, and has limited delivery options, but has a reputation for being fast.	Popular among a small group of email administrators. Performance and security.
Exim	Excellent open source MTA. Much easier to administer than Sendmail, has better security record.	Ease of use and security.
Postfix	Excellent open source MTA, with reputation for performance, security, and ease of administration.	Performance, security, and ease of administration.
Courier-MTA	Complete Mail Server package, including all major parts of the system. The MTA does not have widespread use, however, or any kind of reputation.	

Most MTAs that run in Unix are designed to be drop-in replacements for Sendmail, the original MTA. They usually install programs named `sendmail` and `newaliases`, so that other programs can interact with the MTA without knowing it's not really Sendmail. In this way, most MTAs provide pretty much the same features, as far as transferring messages is concerned. There are some performance differences that affect how quickly mail gets processed, and how much a server can handle in a given time period. There are also some design considerations that some MTAs use to reduce the amount of damage they can do if an attacker somehow compromises it.

We've chosen Postfix because it has a top-notch reputation for security and performance, and it comes with two useful Local Delivery Agents that integrate well with other parts of our small business mail server. It's also now the default MTA in Mandrake, and there are packages available for Red Hat, SuSE, and Debian.

Configuring Postfix

Installing Postfix on most Linux systems is very easy. In Mandrake, you can use the Mandrake Control Center's software installation page to find and install Postfix, or type `urpmi postfix` at the command line, as root.

Most configuration for postfix happens in one of two files. `/etc/postfix/main.cf` is the main configuration file, and it contains a list of directives. To set a directive, you must make sure there are no spaces, tabs, or any other characters before the directive name on any line within the file. Put an equals sign after the directive, and then zero or more values. Values can be separated by whitespace (tabs, space characters), and may continue on successive lines, as long as the line begins with whitespace. Values can be strings, network addresses, other directives, or the contents of external files of various types.

The most common type of external file is a Berkeley database file, also known as a hash. Hashes in Postfix are files that have two columns: a key and a value. You can create a hash by simply creating a new text file, putting all the keys on the left side, and separating them from values with any whitespace. There cannot be any spaces in the key, but spaces in the value are considered part of the value. Once you've edited the text file, you turn it into a hash by running the `postmap` command on it, which creates the actual hash in a file with a `*.db` suffix. In main.cf, where values represented by a hash start with `hash:/`, follow with the full path and filename, and omit the `*.db` at the end—the value in main.cf should point to the original text file.

There are several other protocols that you can use for a main.cf value. Which ones you can use depend upon the settings Postfix was compiled with. Other useful ones are `regexp:` for a regular expression, `pcre:` for Perl-compatible regular expressions, `mysql:` for information in a MySQL database, and `ldap:` for information in a Lightweight Directory Access Protocol (LDAP) database. The last two are particularly useful, because you can keep all the details for a single user in one place, rather than scattered around multiple hashes. But getting Postfix to work with either generally takes recompiling the RPMs with the appropriate development libraries.

The other configuration file for Postfix is `/etc/postfix/master.cf`. Postfix is actually comprised of several different programs, each with a distinct task. `master.cf` defines how each of these programs run: which user account, whether to isolate them in a *chroot jail* (an isolated part of the file system that limits the potential damage an attacker can do if the program is compromised), which LDA to use, what parameters to pass, what port to listen to, and several other details.

The default parameters for Postfix are designed to be mostly secure and to work with very little configuration at all. To get it up and running, edit the `main.cf` file and set the directives in. See Table 5.3.

TABLE 5.3   Basic Postfix Directives to Get the Server Up and Running

main.cf directive	Description	Set This Value
alias_maps	Lists where to find local users	alias_maps = hash:/etc/alias
Mydestination	Lists domains to accept mail for, when using the local transport for local delivery	If your computer's hostname is set correctly, you should be able to set this to: mydestination = $myhostname, localhost.$mydomain, $mydomain You can set these to your specific domain, if necessary.
Mynetworks	Determines what IP address range to accept mail from. Defaults to accepting mail from any computer on the same subnet.	As long as the mail server is on a LAN, you can leave this directive as is. If this computer is connected directly to the Internet, set it to specific IP addresses to always accept mail from: mynetworks = 127.0.0.0/8 12.228.122.48/32
Relayhost	Designates another SMTP server to relay all mail not delivered locally	By default, this is set to nothing, meaning this server attempts to connect directly to the receiving MTA. If you're on a dynamic IP address, set this to the name or IP address of the mail server for your ISP.
smtpd_recipient_ restrictions	Determines what to check for, before relaying the mail. You can add black hole lists here, check for forged Hotmail/Yahoo mail, and many other things.	Here's a basic list that blocks unauthorized relaying and connections that don't speak proper SMTP: smtpd_recipient_restrictions = reject_unauth_pipelining, reject_unknown_sender_domain, reject_unknown_recipient_domain, permit_mynetworks, reject_unauth_destination

The next thing to do is edit the /etc/aliases file to make sure all required aliases point to a valid local user. This file is another Berkeley DB hash, but the key values must all end with a colon, and you use the postalias command instead of postmap to generate the actual database file.

All mail servers are required to maintain a postmaster and abuse accounts. In this file, you can redirect mail going to these accounts to a particular user. In Mandrake, the default file maps abuse to postmaster, and postmaster to root. All other user accounts should also map to root. However, it's important to set root up to point to a regular user account—when Postfix runs in a secure mode, it cannot deliver mail to root. Edit the line beginning with `root:`, putting your local user account name in the second column, and then run `postalias`.

The `postfix` command starts, stops, and checks the Postfix configuration for errors. Before starting Postfix, run `postfix check` to see if there are any problems with the changes you made. If it indicates a problem, check to see if you have any typos in your configuration. If it indicates that two versions of a file differ (`/etc/hosts` and `/var/spool/postfix/etc/hosts`, for example), this indicates that Postfix is set up to run the main process in a chroot jail. This is a security precaution that basically protects the rest of your system if the main process is somehow compromised—it runs in a small section of your filesystem, with no access to anywhere else on your computer. To do this, it needs to have certain configuration files copied into the jail, which by default is `/var/spool/postfix`. If you get a message that the files do not match, copy the file from outside the jail into it.

Finally, if all checks out okay, start Postfix with `postfix start`. Your mail server should now allow you to send mail from any mail client using SMTP, as long as you're connected to the same subnet. It should also accept mail to any local user account listed in `/etc/passwd` or `/etc/aliases`, when mail arrives at the computer using a domain or host listed in the `mydestination` directive.

Configure DNS for Email

The next trick is getting mail for your domain to be sent to your server. You do this by adding a Mail eXchange (MX) record to the name servers for your domain (see Chapter 3). Many Web hosts have a tool that allows you to set your own MX records. If you have an option for setting a priority for the MX record, the server with the lowest priority number is the one that will be used. If you have one available, it's possible to add additional MX records that point to mail servers that provide backup email services for your domain. If you do this, make sure the backup servers have a bigger priority number than your main server.

Finally, changes you make to your DNS settings are cached for the length of time specified in the Time-To-Live (TTL) setting for your domain, which can be anywhere from an hour to several days. It's not uncommon for some services to cache these values for much longer—some mail servers may continue to send mail to the old mail server for your domain even months after you've changed the DNS. To force these servers to update their cache, get the administrator of the mail server that used to handle your mail to reject messages to your domain. The tardy mail servers will then do a DNS lookup and connect to your real mail server.

Email Ports

If you're running a firewall or a NAT router, you'll need to allow access to certain ports on your server to allow email traffic. To receive email, you need to forward TCP connections to the SMTP port, 25. To be able to check mail remotely, open up the appropriate port for the service you want to allow access to. Note that both IMAP and POP send passwords over the Internet in plain text, so it is recommended that you only open the SSL-encrypted versions. The various email ports are listed in Table 5.4.

TABLE 5.4 Email Ports

Protocol	Port	Description
SMTP	25	Open this port to receive email from the Internet.
POP3	110	Open this port to allow POP clients to connect from remote sites. Not recommended.
IMAP	143	Open this port to allow IMAP clients to connect from remote sites. Not recommended.
IMAPS	993	SSL-encrypted IMAP connection. If you want to connect to your email from remote locations using ordinary mail clients, open this port. Not necessary for Web mail.
POP3S	995	SSL-encrypted POP connection. If you want to be able to download POP mail from remote locations on the Internet. Generally IMAP is preferred.

Choosing an LDA

Local Delivery Agents are often included with other email servers. Postfix includes two delivery agents: `local` and `virtual`. `local` delivers mail to a local Unix user account. To create a new email account on a domain handled by `local`, you simply create a new Unix user. Local users are identified in the `/etc/aliases` file. When `local` delivers an email, it follows a series of Unix conventions: executing a `.forward` file in the user's home directory if it exists, running any notification scripts, and getting delivered to the system mailbox for the user.

In contrast, `virtual` can create mailboxes for arbitrary email addresses, independent of Unix users. A series of lookup tables indicate what filename and location to deliver to, along with the user and group identity that owns this file. The mail is delivered to the specified mailbox, with no other processing available. `virtual` provides a secure way to host mail for users for whom you don't want to provide login access to the server.

Another LDA is installed in most Linux and Unix systems: Procmail. Procmail is capable of applying all kinds of customizable rules to mail, automatically delivering mail to different mail folders, forwarding specific messages, running auto responders, or passing it to any arbitrary program on the computer. A savvy individual user can actually put a command in their `~/.forward` file to make Postfix hand the mail off to Procmail, and then define a bunch of Procmail *recipes* to sort their mail as it's delivered. Procmail recipes follow a very unusual, specific syntax that takes a bit of practice to figure out.

A new LDA gaining popularity is part of the Courier mail project, called Maildrop. It basically does the same things as Procmail, but has a syntax similar to scripting languages, so people unfamiliar with Procmail often find it easier to learn. It's still not easy for non-technical computer users, however.

For small businesses, the Postfix `local` LDA is a good choice—you don't have to do anything to configure it, and all of your users will most likely need to have local server accounts anyway. If you're going to host mail for other companies, or people who do not otherwise have access to your servers, the `virtual` LDA is the easiest secure way to provide them with email accounts. If you have some fairly technical users, point them to the Procmail FAQs or install Maildrop.

Postfix allows you to set up different LDAs for different domains. You define a transport to use, and a program that handles that transport. By default, the transport called local uses the `local` LDA, and the transport called virtual uses the `virtual` LDA. Since we're only going to set up local users, there's nothing you need to do to make this happen—the `local` LDA should already be actively delivering mail to your mailbox.

Where's the Mailbox?

So with Postfix up and running, and accepting mail for local users, where does the mail go? Unix systems have a built-in mailbox for each user. The location of this mailbox varies depending on the distribution. On many Linux systems, you'll find it in `/var/spool/mail` or `/var/mail`, as a single file with the same name as the user. If you start up a mail client application on the server, it will likely find this mail automatically. But you don't want everybody to have to log into the server to check their email. We're going to set up an IMAP server that also provides POP access, so users in the company can read their mail from other computers.

Some IMAP servers (notably the UW IMAP server) automatically use the Unix mailbox. The mailbox format is simply a single long text file, with new messages added to the end. The main issue with using a Unix mailbox is that only one process can write to the file at a time—if you delete messages while a message is being delivered, you need to set up some sort of locking system to prevent the mailbox from being corrupted. Also, if you have a lot of messages in your mailbox, the IMAP server or mail reader needs to scan through the entire file to extract the headers.

The developers of the QMail MTA created a directory-based mailbox format called a Maildir, providing a number of advantages over the file-based version:

- Each message is its own file, so new messages can be written without affecting processing of other messages.
- Getting a list of messages involves a simple directory listing, instead of having to parse through all of the messages to extract the headers.
- If something happens to corrupt a message, you only lose the message, not the entire mailbox.

There are several other mailbox formats supported by various LDAs and POP or IMAP servers, but Maildir is becoming the most widespread alternative, with many programs supporting it. Postfix can deliver to a Maildir mailbox, and Courier-IMAP only works with Maildirs, so that's what we're going to use.

To get Postfix to deliver to a Maildir, you simply add a slash to the end of the mailbox name, wherever it's specified. Of course, since we're using mostly default settings, we haven't specified. Adding the following directive to /etc/postfix/main.cf will change the delivery location to a Maildir-style mailbox in the user's home directory, named $HOME/Maildir, creating it if it doesn't already exist:

```
home_mailbox = Maildir/
```

To make Postfix recognize the change, type postfix reload as root.

Forward Mail to Another Email Address

To make things particularly confusing, Postfix has two completely different features, both named virtual. So far, we've discussed the virtual mailbox transport, an LDA used to provide a simple, secure way to host mail for users without a local user account. Postfix also provides virtual aliases. To get the documentation for virtual mailboxes, type man 8 virtual. To get the documentation for virtual aliases, type man 5 virtual.

Virtual aliases work similar to the alias_maps directive, in that they forward mail bound for one destination to another. The main difference is that alias_maps only handles local user accounts, and accounts sent to the domains listed in the my-destination directive. Virtual aliases can redirect from any valid email address accepted by the server to any other email address. You can use a virtual alias to forward mail to your pager, to a home email address, or to a group of email addresses. You can also use a virtual alias to support a "catchall" email account, sending all mail sent to a particular domain to a single email address.

To set up virtual aliases, you create a hash file to hold the aliases, and point the `virtual_alias_maps` directive to it. Here's an example. In `/etc/postfix/main.cf`:

```
virtual_alias_maps = hash:/etc/postfix/virtual
```

Create `/etc/postfix/virtual` as a text file. In the left column, type the email address you want to redirect. Add a space or a tab to make a second column, and then type one or more email addresses to send the mail to. If you want to send to more than one email address, separate the addresses with commas. If you want the original address to receive the email, and also forward it to additional addresses, list the original address in the second column. Add more lines for other addresses to redirect.

When you're done creating the file, run `postmap /etc/postfix/virtual` to create the hash, and get Postfix to re-read its configuration file with `postfix reload`.

Choosing an IMAP Server

You also have several choices of IMAP servers available. Table 5.5 lists some of the main contenders. The University of Washington maintains the definitive IMAP server, known as UW-IMAP. If you have an IMAP server installed, but don't have any indication of which one, it's probably UW-IMAP.

All of the IMAP servers discussed provide SSL encrypted connections. The authors of UW-IMAP pioneered the development of IMAP, and the UW IMAP code is incorporated into many IMAP clients, but in practice the UW-IMAP server is slow and a bit of a resource hog. The other IMAP servers provide sorting and threading, making it much more efficient to find and read messages in large mailboxes.

Cyrus makes a complete database-backed IMAP system, and is probably one of the better choices for extremely large numbers of users. However, it requires a bit more configuration than the others—you need to use its own LDA to deliver to the database, it's not very interoperable with other email systems, and it's overkill for most small and even medium-sized businesses.

Courier is a complete mail server project, with an MTA, an LDA (called Maildrop), an IMAP server, and a few other parts. The MTA is generally considered not ready for prime time, but Courier-IMAP seems to be the most complete, best implemented IMAP server for small installations. Maildrop is also highly regarded. Courier-IMAP only handles mail stored in Maildirs.

TABLE 5.5 IMAP Servers

IMAP Server	Mailbox Type	Strengths	Weaknesses
UW-IMAP	Unix Mailbox Mmdf Mbx Maildir (with 3rd party patch)	Simple to use. All configuration is done at compile time—there is nothing to configure once it's compiled—all you need to do is start up the daemon.	Slow. Uses lots of memory. Does no server-side sorting or threading.
Courier-IMAP	Maildir only	Reasonably simple to set up. Can be configured to use MySQL, LDAP, or PAM for authentication. Relatively fast, small memory footprint. Includes a POP server as well as IMAP.	Potential scalability limits for thousands of users.
Cyrus	Cyrus format only	The Cyrus mailbox format is a database, resulting in very efficient sorting and searching, and supporting the largest number of users.	Hard to configure. Not compatible with other filtering tools (such as Procmail), hard to import/export mail to other systems.
Microsoft Exchange	Proprietary database format	NTLM authentication (with Windows domains)	Can be hard to install and administer. Expensive.

Configuring Courier-IMAP

In Mandrake, if you have added the `contrib` media source to urpmi, installing and configuring Courier-IMAP is simple. As root, type:

```
# urpmi courier-imap
```

If this doesn't work, go back to the end of Chapter 2 to add media sources to URPMI.

If you want to add support for POP, or for storing virtual user accounts in MySQL, install the appropriate package:

```
# urpmi courier-imap-pop
# urpmi courier-imap-mysql
```

If you're not using Mandrake, download the source from *http://www.inter7. com/courierimap.html*, and follow the directions to compile and install it.

When you install from source, the configuration files for Courier-IMAP are in `/usr/lib/courier-imap/etc`. The Mandrake packages put them in `/etc/courier`. The configuration files are set to use the Pluggable Authentication Module (PAM) system by default, which is the same system Mandrake and Red Hat use to authenticate user logins. This means you don't have to configure anything to log into the IMAP server with a local user account. But you do need to start the IMAP server.

Courier provides a System V startup script. For most Linux configurations, this is used by the system to start and stop services. If you installed from source, you'll have to copy this script by hand into the appropriate directory, using the instructions provided with the source. It should get copied there automatically if you install a package.

Courier actually runs a separate daemon for each type of connection: normal IMAP, IMAP over SSL, POP, and POP over SSL. Each of these daemons has its own configuration file, named `imapd`, `imapd-ssl`, `pop3d`, and `pop3d-ssl` respectively. At the bottom of each of these files is a directive that indicates whether or not to start the daemon. So to start the IMAP daemon, simply edit the `IMAPDSTART` directive in `/etc/courier/imapd` to equal `YES`. If you want the SSL-encrypted daemon, do the equivalent in `imapd-ssl`. Once these flags are all in place, start or restart the Courier daemons by using one of the following:

```
# service courier-imap restart
# /etc/rc.d/init.d/courier-imap restart
```

The SSL-encrypted version of the daemon listens on TCP port 993. The installation script automatically generates a test certificate for this server. If you connect to the SSL-encrypted IMAP server, your client should give you an authentication warning, informing you that the authenticity of the certificate could not be verified. If you accept the certificate, all traffic will be properly encrypted—but in most clients, you'll have to accept it every time you connect. We will discuss setting up a Certificate Authority and signing certificates in Chapter 15.

Configuring Email Clients

With the IMAP server up and running, you should be able to set up any IMAP-capable email client that can see the server on the network. If you started the POP daemons, you can also use POP, if you want, though there are few reasons to do so with a working IMAP server. You generally do not want to use both for the same account—if you download mail to a POP client, you could easily (unintentionally) remove it from your IMAP mailbox.

One case where you might want to use POP is to have a secondary email account. A good strategy to help reduce spam is to have one email address to use for private email with colleagues, friends, and business associates, and a second email address for bulk mail. Use the secondary email address for mailing lists, signing up for services on Web sites, posting on your Web site, or anywhere where there's a chance it might get harvested by spammers. You can then configure your email client to check your secondary email account using POP, and move new messages to a specific IMAP folder so you don't have to deal with these messages in your mailbox.

Fetchmail is a tool that fetches mail from any POP mail account, and delivers it to the mail system. You can set it up to run at any interval. Type `man fetchmail` at the command line for instructions to set it up.

To configure email clients to use your new mail server, use whatever dialog they provide to add a new IMAP account. If you enabled Samba (as described in Chapter 3), you should be able to use the Samba computer name as the sending and receiving server name on Windows computers. If you're running a DNS server and have the mail server listed in DNS, you can use the DNS name from any mail client on your network. If you're trying to configure a mail client on a Linux or Mac computer, or do not have Samba running on the mail server, and do not have an internal DNS server, you'll need to either use the IP address of the server, or add the server name and IP address to the `hosts` file on each client.

If your LAN uses wires exclusively, and you don't need to provide remote access for mail clients over the Internet, there's no need for encryption. If you have a wireless LAN, you should use the SSL-encrypted IMAP connection to prevent people from sniffing out your passwords, as discussed in Chapter 17.

SUMMARY

At a certain size, a business is going to need to run its own mail server. Many content management tools and supply chain systems depend on email for one reason: it has an infrastructure that can more reliably send messages. With the Web, if a connection goes down, or the Web server goes offline, programs can't interact with each other. Email is designed to operate in a disconnected environment, so if you use Web applications that need to send messages, an email interface may be the simplest way to ensure it gets delivered.

In this chapter, we've discussed the issues of running your own email server, compared to having it hosted by another company. We've taken a brief look at encrypted email, and an in-depth look at how email works. Finally, we've looked at all of the parts of an email system, and open source software to fill each role.

This chapter intersects with several others. Chapter 15 discusses Certificate Authorities and encrypted email in greater depth. Remote access is discussed in Chapter 14. Setting up spam and virus filters is covered in Chapter 19. In the next chapter, we cover the other major Internet server, the Web server, providing the other half of your Internet infrastructure.

EMAIL REFERENCES

An updated list of resources for this chapter is on the Web site for the book at *http://opensourcesmall.biz/email.*

Articles

"Postfix SASL2 & TLS Configuration Guide," by SecuritySage Inc. Available online at *http://www.securitysage.com/guides/postfix_sasltls.html.*
"SMTP Authentication with Postfix and MySQL," by Craig Small. Available online at *http://small.dropbear.id.au/myscripts/postfixmysql.html.*

Software

Postfix, open source MTA *http://www.postfix.org*
Sendmail, original MTA *http://www.sendmail.org*
Exim, open source MTA *http://www.exim.org*
Qmail, free, non-open source MTA *http://www.qmail.org*
Microsoft Exchange, commercial MTA *http://www.microsoft.com*
Procmail, open source LDA *http://www.procmail.org*
Maildrop, open source LDA *http://www.flounder.net/~mrsam/maildrop/*

Courier-IMAP, open source IMAP/POP server *http://www.inter7.com/courier-imap.html*

Cyrus IMAP, open source IMAP server *http://asg.web.cmu.edu/cyrus/*

UW-IMAP, open source IMAP server *http://www.washington.edu/imap/*

Fetchmail, open source POP/IMAP client *http://www.catb.org/~esr/fetchmail/*

Web Sites

The IMAP Connection, comprehensive information about IMAP protocol *http://www.imap.org/*

6 Setting Up A Web Server

In This Chapter

- Introduction
- Why You Need an Internal Web Site
- Where to Put Your Public Site
- The World of Web Servers
- Small Business Web Server: Apache 2
- Summary
- Web Server References

INTRODUCTION

For most people, the World Wide Web is the Internet. Besides email, nearly everyone uses the Web at some point. While the Internet provides several other things, few are as universal as the Web.

The first part of this chapter discusses the business issues of running both a public and a private Web site, and is not technical. The implementation section of this chapter gets fairly technical.

For small businesses, it's important to have a public Web site of some sort. It doesn't have to be much—a single page with a description of your services and contact information is sufficient for many businesses. Adding more to your Web site, such as testimonials from customers, detailed descriptions of your products and services, or perhaps some sort of information request or online ordering system, can be valuable ways of marketing your company.

We'll be discussing public Web sites in greater detail in Chapter 13. In this chapter, we're going to take a look at the software that makes the Web possible: Web servers.

WHY YOU NEED AN INTERNAL WEB SITE

Besides hosting your public Web site, Web servers are becoming outstanding ways of managing computer systems and providing access to other services. Web servers sit behind accounting systems, revision control systems, content management systems, Web email systems, client/partner extranets, supply chain software, and groupware packages.

Close to half of the solutions in this book use a Web server somewhere along the way. A Web server on a server is one of the basic pieces of infrastructure that can add a lot of useful features. If you have a retail or some consumer-oriented business, you might post the employee schedule on an internal Web site where your employees can see it. You can post project schedules, timelines, a list of links to resources for new employees, and access to email.

In all likelihood you won't have many users going to an internal Web site at the same time. The users who do will be visiting most heavily during working hours—it's generally not a problem if an internal Web site goes down for an hour or two for maintenance. If you have set up a server on your network, you can easily add a Web server to it to host an internal company Web site.

WHERE TO PUT YOUR PUBLIC SITE

In contrast, your public Web site should be always available. If something happens to your server or your connection, you disappear off the Internet. You don't want potential customers to get a Server Not Found error when they're looking for your services—they'll just move on to your competitor. Your public Web site is like the Open sign in your window—if it's not there, people won't come in.

Unless you have an extremely reliable Internet connection, and a server already set up and running smoothly, it's worth paying a few dollars a month to a hosting company to host it for you. Choose a hosting company that has servers in a data center on or near one of the Internet backbones, and has 24-hour support. It then becomes their job to make sure your Web site is always available. Should something happen to the Web server, such as a power outage or a malicious hacker, their personnel will get paged and fix it, even in the middle of the night. Also, should your site get noticed by the national media, or *slashdotted*, your site is more likely to stay up and running despite a huge amount of traffic—though you might get hit by extra bandwidth charges.

Types of Web Hosting

Obviously, you generally don't want to keep sensitive data on a shared computer. There are several types of hosting packages you can use, summarized in Table 6.1.

TABLE 6.1 Types of Web Hosting

Type	Cost Range (monthly)	Who Can Access Data	Advantages	Drawbacks
Shared hosting	$2-$20	Potentially anyone you share the server with	Extremely cheap Reliable, high-speed	Very little security Limited disk space
Virtual Server	$75-$150	Only you and administrators of the host server	Very reliable, high speed, can install your own software, do anything with root access, easy for provider to back up, hardware can be replaced without affecting service	You must trust your hosting provider
Co-located (Dedicated) Server	$100-$400	Only you and people you authorize	Good security, all the advantages of running your own server, with extremely high speed, reliable access	Expensive
Self Host	N/A	Only you	Best security, total control over server and environment, no cost (other than that of your connection)	Generally not as good a connection, no network operations support

By far, the most common type of hosting is a simple shared hosting arrangement. Prices are very reasonable for this type of service. Your site is one of potentially hundreds of sites on a single server, in a data center with huge data pipes connecting to the Internet. Besides the basic disk space for the Web site, most hosting providers include DNS name servers and email as part of the package. This is by far the best way to go for your basic Web site. The biggest problems are related to installing special software to handle things like e-commerce, or other sensitive applications. You're also generally stuck with the software the hosting provider chooses to make available to you—you won't have root access to the computer, meaning there's not that much you can do with it. Another potential issue is that many providers allow users to log into the server to do basic tasks as a non-privileged user. Even though most providers have strong policies against looking at other users' data, there's always a chance someone can look over the fence. So never put anything confidential or proprietary on a shared server.

A newer option for hosting is something called a virtual server. In a normal shared server, each account is a non-privileged user account. In a virtual server, you have a root account, and a complete file system at your disposal. You can add users, whatever software you want (within the bounds of the terms of service), and basically do anything you can do with your own server. It's called a virtual server because it isn't a separate computer—it actually is a single instance of a program running on another computer. There can be several different computers running their own virtual environments on a single computer, as long as the host computer has enough RAM, disk space, and processing power. If you don't need all of the processing power of your own server, a virtual server can give you most of the benefits of one, without the full cost. The administrator of the host computer can still peer into the virtual server to see what's going on there, but otherwise only you have access. This type of solution works great if your company is geographically dispersed—you can set up secure types of services in a private way, with reliable, high-speed access, using the Internet as your LAN.

The highest level of hosting services is either co-locating a server or leasing a dedicated server. The difference is who owns the hardware. In either case, you're paying for somebody to host your computer and take care of all the hardware and connectivity issues. With this arrangement, only you have root access to the machine—though you will probably want to grant back-up privileges at least to the host. The main reason to do this over hosting your own server is that you likely don't have a data center sitting on an Internet backbone, or the capability to run multiple dedicated super-high bandwidth lines to your site. This is overkill for almost all small businesses—unless you're trying to start the next eBay or some other high-traffic Internet-related business.

For all of these hosting solutions, there are a number of benefits, besides the high bandwidth we already mentioned. By sharing a data center with many other companies, you're splitting the cost of maintaining a 24-hour staff that's available to make sure your server is always up and running, monitoring incoming traffic for viruses, hacking attempts, and other unsavory items, and generally there so you don't have to be.

Hosting your own Web server, on the other hand, is not all that difficult to do, and if you have a reliable connection and a relatively small amount of traffic, you can save yourself the cost of a Web host. For a connection, you should ideally have an SDSL or T1 for the reliability of the connection and high speed. See Chapter 3 for more about connection types.

Compared to hosting an email server, a Web server is much easier to administer. But because email traffic doesn't need to be instantaneous, you need a better connection. Usually the cost of a good connection is much higher than the cost of having your Web site hosted. The best way to go for most small businesses is to have your public Web site hosted, and host your own internal Web site. You can then keep control over confidential information, while maintaining a reliable, quick public Web site.

If you're too small a business to otherwise run a server, you might consider a virtual server to provide other services described in this book. There's also a growing market of independent Information Technology consultants who run their own virtual servers and provide services to their clients under a subscription basis at a very reasonable price.

THE WORLD OF WEB SERVERS

A Web server is a pretty simple program. It accepts a connection on a specific port, handles a request, and sends a response. At its simplest, it simply returns a file located at a specific location in the file system. Web servers have been developed to include many more features, including the ability to run scripts in various languages, interact with databases, provide authentication, encrypt connections, and perform all sorts of different tasks.

Apache is not only one of the dominant Web servers on the Internet, it's also one of the preeminent open source projects. In 2003, some version of Apache was used by approximately 60% of all Web sites. Another common Web server is Microsoft Internet Information Services. What is notable about both of these Web servers is that they provide a framework for many other special purpose modules to plug in and provide more complex functionality than simply returning a file at a specific location.

In nearly all respects, these Web servers are extremely comparable, especially with the latest versions. Most of the security, stability, and administration issues of IIS have made it effectively equivalent to Apache, while having a slight performance edge. On the other hand, like most open source projects, you have more choices of languages and tools with Apache, and the performance differences can be eliminated (if not surpassed) by using a second kernel-based Web server to handle static files (such as images), while still using Apache where needed to process complicated scripts. For those few sites that really need maximum performance, you can set up the TUX Web server to serve static files every bit as fast as any other Web server out there. Unless you are co-locating a server, or using a virtual server, you'll likely run out of bandwidth long before you exceed the performance of Apache.

The main reason you might choose to run IIS instead of Apache is if you want to run some Web application that only works with IIS. Microsoft keeps innovating new development platforms, such as the .NET framework, which provide an easy way for developers to quickly develop and deploy Web services.

There are many competing development platforms, though the .NET framework has gained a lot of popularity in a short time. Like most good ideas that begin in proprietary companies, there is a full blown open source project, called Mono, being developed to provide support for .NET-based Web applications on Apache. It lags behind Microsoft by several months, however.

The bottom line is there's not much reason to use any Web server other than Apache. It's free, it supports Perl, PHP, ASP, ISAPI, some .NET, and most other Web technologies, and it runs on most operating systems, including Windows and Mac OS X. It has a wide range of configuration tools, and many people who know how to support it.

Apache has been the dominant Web server since 1996. In July 2003, according to a Netcraft survey, Apache ran 63% of all Web sites. But in 2003, only a tiny fraction of these were running Apache 2, even though it's been recommended as the replacement since late 2001. There are several reasons for this:

- "If it ain't broke, don't fix it!" The Apache 1.3 series of servers has been extremely effective at doing what it needs to do, and for a great many Web sites, there has been no compelling reason to upgrade.
- Lack of support for major modules. Many features are added to Apache in the form of modules. Several of the most popular of these did not work reliably until early 2003.
- Not shipped in major distributions. The first major distribution to use Apache 2 instead of Apache 1. 3 was Red Hat 8, which was released in early 2003. Mandrake added it in 9.1, in spring 2003.

Now that the third party modules all support Apache 2, and it's been included in the major distributions, there is little reason to go back to Apache 1.3. Some of the software in this book depends on Apache 2, and will not run under older versions. Still, expect to see Apache 1.3 in commercial settings for many more years to come, because of its reliability and track record.

In the rest of this chapter, we'll take a look at how to administer Apache, specifically Virtual Hosts, authentication, and SSL encryption.

SMALL BUSINESS WEB SERVER: APACHE 2

First, a bit about Apache configuration. Apache comes with a great manual, which is installed on your server at *http://localhost/manual*. The manual details all of the standard directives you can use in Apache configuration files, and how to use many of the standard modules that come with Apache.

The rest of this chapter gets a fair bit more technical, and will be most useful to people trying to actually manage an Apache Web server.

If you have any questions or problems, the manual is the first place to go for help. Apache is configured using a set of files. The location of the main Apache configuration file is compiled into the server, although it can be overridden when the server is started. Different distributions put the configuration files in different places. It might be named `httpd.conf` or `httpd2.conf`, and there are many different places to find it:

- `/usr/local/httpd/conf`
- `/usr/lib/apache/conf`
- `/usr/local/apache2/conf`
- `/etc/httpd/conf`

Furthermore, in many systems, all configuration details for the server are in this file. But often package-based systems, such as Mandrake and Red Hat, make use of an Include directive to include other text files. In this arrangement, you can put any directive or set of directives in another file, and Apache treats the directives as if they were in the main file.

In Mandrake, the main configuration file is `/etc/httpd/conf/httpd2.conf`. This file is mostly empty, specifying a few Apache 2-specific directives and including any configuration file in the `/etc/httpd/conf.d` directory, which is where individual module packages add their configurations. This arrangement allows the Mandrake installer to drop entire configuration files in the conf.d directory and have them automatically included in the Apache directives. The `httpd2.conf` file also includes the `commonhttpd.conf` file in the same directory, which is where you specify directives related to logging, the *canonical* name of the computer, which ports and IP addresses to use, and other directives related to the main Web service. Finally, the `httpd2.conf` file includes the `vhosts/Vhosts.conf` file, where you can add configuration details for individual *virtual hosts*. We will discuss virtual hosts shortly.

Other distributions have different arrangements. When you install Apache from the source files, all the directives will be in the single `httpd.conf` file, wherever it's located.

However the configuration files are arranged, there are several different scopes you can use directives in. In the main configuration file, directives apply to the server itself, or everything. You can also create several different containers within a configuration file to make directives that only apply to the specified item. These containers look a lot like an HTML or XML tag—the name of the container is surrounded by angle brackets, followed by a list of directives, and finally a "closing" version of the container tag. Some of these containers are:

- `<Virtualhost></Virtualhost>`
- `<Location></Location>`
- `<Directory></Directory>`
- `<File></File>`
- `<Limit></Limit>`

`<Directory>` and `<File>` specify files and directories on the Unix file system, and apply restrictions to these areas. Most distributions define a `<Directory "/">` block with no permissions to lock down the root directory of the server, and then define more specific <Directory> blocks to provide necessary access only to particular directories.

`<Location>` blocks, on the other hand, refer to particular paths in the URL requested by a browser. As a general rule, you use `<Directory>` and `<File>` blocks to restrict access to the file system, and `<Location>` blocks to perform actions handled by alternative modules. `<VirtualHost>` blocks define how Apache responds to different domain names. `<Limit>` blocks are used to specify fine-grained access to particular types of requests—we'll discuss these later in the chapter, in the section about WebDAV.

All of these containers are stored in the Apache configuration files, and are only activated when the server is started or reloaded. To reload the server, type:

```
# apachectl graceful
```

This command starts up new Web server processes to handle new requests, while allowing those currently running to finish what they're doing, instead of cutting off existing connections. Check the log for Apache after applying any configuration changes to make sure the server didn't choke on a typo or an invalid directive.

There is one other type of container that can contain directives: the .htaccess file. This file is equivalent to a <Directory> block, except that it's an actual file put in the directory you want to configure, and its directives are read during every request, instead of only when the server starts. This file allows you to change things like password-protected areas of the site, without needing root access. Upload an .htaccess file with the rest of the files, and the server immediately starts following the instructions it carries.

.htaccess is the customary name for the override file. You can change it by specifying a different AccessFileName directive. Also, the AllowOverride directive associated with a <Directory> block identifies what types of directives are allowed in .htaccess files.

You can use the Webmin program we discussed in Chapter 2 to manage Apache, or you can edit the configuration files directly. There are many different directives you can configure, but for the most part, if you have the modules you need installed, there are few you'll need to change.

Basic Apache Configuration

By default, Apache runs in Linux as a non-privileged user. In Mandrake and Red Hat systems, Apache runs as a user named apache and a group named apache. In other systems, it runs as user nobody, group nobody. This user needs to have at least read permissions on a file to be able to serve it to a Web browser.

The basic things you'll need to do to get Apache running on a Web server are:

1. Make sure the root of your file system is not allowed access, using a <Directory /> block.
2. If this server is going to handle more than one host/domain name, turn UseCanonicalName off.
3. Check or choose a DocumentRoot, and set up a <Directory> block that allows access to files in the DocumentRoot. In Mandrake and Red Hat, the DocumentRoot is /var/www/html.
4. Put files into the directory specified by the DocumentRoot.

Remember that Apache runs as a non-privileged user—usually apache or nobody. Any files you put in the DocumentRoot need to be readable to this user. Usually you will just make the files world-readable.

Table 6.2 lists some useful directives you may want to set up on your server.

TABLE 6.2 Useful Apache Directives

Directive	Where You Can Use It	Description	Example
DirectoryIndex	Server, <Directory>, .htaccess	Specifies a list of files to load automatically when a directory is given as the URL. The first matching file in this list will be loaded.	DirectoryIndex index.php index.shtml index.html index.htm default.htm
Options +Indexes	<Directory>, .htaccess	If no DirectoryIndex file exists, shows a friendly listing of files in the directory.	Options +Indexes (turns it on) Options Indexes (turns on only Indexes, turns off other options) Options-Indexes (turns indexes off) Options All (turns all options on)
ServerAdmin	Server, <VirtualHost>	Email of the server administrator, listed on error pages.	ServerAdmin webmaster@example.com
ServerName	Server, <VirtualHost>	Host name of the computer. Usually obtained automatically from the system.	ServerName www.example.com
Redirect	<Location>, <Directory>, .htaccess	Sends a redirect back to the browser to indicate that a page has moved. You must specify an absolute path to the new location.	Redirect /moved.htm http://new.example.com/new.htm
Alias	Server, <VirtualHost>	Returns the content of a different location in the file system. Unlike Redirect, nothing changes in the browser. A <Document> block should allow the appropriate permssions for the location specified.	Alias /manual/ /usr/share/doc/apache2-manual-2.0.47/
ErrorDocument	Server, <VirtualHost>, <Directory>, .htaccess	Specifies a non-default error page or message to return. You must list the error code you want to specify, followed either by text in double quotes, a local URL path beginning with a forward slash, or an absolute URL beginning with http://.	ErrorDocument 404 /error/page_not_found.html ErrorDocument 403 "Can't let you in today" ErrorDocument 500 http://example.com/cgi-bin/tester

Posting Files: Samba, FTP, and WebDAV

For new Unix users, file permissions are one of the stickiest points about the operating system. By default, the Web root directory (specified by the DocumentRoot directive) is owned by root, and other users do not have write access to it. The file permissions and ownership to use depends on how you plan to get the files there. There are basically four ways to do it:

- Copy the files locally, doing all editing on the server.
- Use a network file system, such as Samba or NFS, to copy it directly from another computer on your LAN.
- Set up FTP or SFTP and transfer your files.
- Set up WebDAV and post your files through Apache.

Another consideration is how many people need to be able to update the files? For the first three options, the easy way to provide access is to change the ownership of all the files and directories from the Web root down to the Web developer. If you have multiple people who need access using these methods, set up a Unix group (www-devs, for example), turn on the Group sticky bit on directories, and change the Umask to allow group writes. You can use the Webmin tool to add a Unix group and add users to the group. Then, presuming you're using Samba, set up a share pointing to the /var/www directory, and change the default Umask setting for the share to 002. What this does is make it so files are automatically saved with group write access—normally they are only user-writable.

Finally, set the permissions on the files and directories themselves. As root, these commands should do it:

```
# chgrp www-devs -R /var/www/html
```
(changes the group ownership of all files to www-devs)
```
# # chmod g+w -R /var/www/html
```
(makes all files under the Web root group-writable)
```
# # find /var/www/html -type d -exec chmod 2775
```
(makes all the directories beneath the Web root user and group-writable, world readable, and makes it so that group ownership is preserved to any new files stored in this directory.)

See Chapter 3 for more about Samba. NFS is not covered in this book, as it does not work well with Windows or other computers commonly used by small businesses.

FTP is also not discussed in this book. It's possible to set up an FTP server and have it point to the Web directories, allowing designated users to post files.

However, FTP is not a secure system for transferring files, and WebDAV goes a long way towards removing the need.

WebDAV, short for Web-based Distributed Authoring and Versioning, is basically a way of posting files to the Web server. If you need to allow remote access to your server across the Internet, this is a much better way to do it than FTP, mainly because HTTP is more efficient than FTP, and you can take advantage of authentication and authorization provided by Apache, as well as SSL encrypted connections. Using WebDAV, you can effectively isolate access to a particular directory on the server, and you don't need to set up local Unix user accounts to grant that access. To set up WebDAV, you need to make sure the mod_dav module is installed and loaded in Apache, and then add the Dav On directive to a container for a particular URL. You also need to specify a directory that the Apache user can write to, to create a lock file for WebDAV.

Because you are granting write access to your server, you should set up authentication first, and either use an authentication system that encrypts passwords, or encrypt the whole connection with SSL.

Generally, you set up a dedicated WebDAV repository, but you can point it to some directory under the DocumentRoot. For example, you could set up a different virtual host for remote users who need full access to your document root by adding the Dav On directive to the virtual host. Unlike the other posting methods we've discussed, for WebDAV, the Apache user must be able to write to the files and directories, not just read. WebDAV users have no relationship to Unix users: all WebDAV user files are posted by the Apache user and group.

Here's an example Apache configuration to enable Dav on a particular directory:

```
Alias /dav /var/www/dav
<Location /dav>
  Dav On
  AuthUserFile /var/dav/htpasswd
  AuthType Basic
  AuthName "Simple WebDAV Repository"
  Require valid-user
  ForceType text/plain
</Location>
<Directory /var/www/dav>
  Order deny,allow
  Allow from all
</Directory>
```

In this code, the Alias line maps the /dav URL to a specific directory on the server. The Location block specifies what to do with this URL—handle it with the Dav module, use basic authorization, and override any mime-type specified by the file, allowing you to copy scripts that would normally be executed on the server. The Directory block allows access to this directory from any IP address. Note that you must create the /var/www/dav directory, change its ownership to the Apache user, and add the necessary users and passwords to /var/dav/htpasswd.

To use WebDAV, you open up a WebDAV client and copy or save files as you do to any other directory. In Windows, Internet Explorer has a built-in WebDAV client. To open a WebDAV directory, you use File | Open to get the Open window, and check the box "Open as a Web Folder." This opens the directory on your Web server as if it were a local directory. If the user is authorized, he can simply drag and drop to post files to the server. The KDE equivalent is to use the webdav:/ or webdavs:/ protocols (the latter for SSL-encrypted connections). The KDE version works best to copy or save files from within KDE applications—you need to enable indexes to browse, and you can't easily copy into Konqueror. There are many other applications that support WebDAV: Microsoft Office and Macromedia® DreamWeaver® to name a couple.

There is one other way to copy files to and from the server securely, and that is by using Secure FTP, part of the SSH package. SSH is discussed in Chapter 14. SSH is very secure, and provides a way for you to log into the server as a local user. You can then copy files back and forth, even across the Internet, through an encrypted tunnel. Using this from Windows requires a dedicated SFTP client, such as the free FileZilla program. In KDE, you can use the fish:/ protocol. SFTP is great for transferring files for trusted users, but difficult to set up in cases where you want to limit access to parts of the server. To grant SFTP access, you typically have to give a user a full Unix account, which can open your server up to all sorts of other problems. In other words, it's fine to use SFTP for your employees, but a bad idea for transferring files from other companies.

Authentication and Authorization

You don't want just anybody to save files to your server, however. You need to implement some sort of access control, authenticating the user before authorizing access.

In security terms, authentication and authorization are two completely different things. *Authentication* identifies who a user is, and provides some mechanism to prove it. The most common authentication method is a password, though there are many more complex ways: using certificates signed by an authority, smart cards, random number generators, fingerprints, and retinal scanners. *Authorization* identifies whether a given user has permission to perform some action on an object. This is really a two-step process—first, you identify the user, then you specify which users have access to which files, directories, and programs.

There are two types of authentication supported by Apache: Basic™ and Digest™. Both operate in a similar way. When a Web browser (the client) requests a URL that requires authentication, Apache returns a 401 error, which indicates that authorization is required. This prompts the Web browser to get a username and password from the user, and sends those credentials back to the same URL. Apache uses the specified authentication modules to determine whether the credentials are valid, and then either authorizes the user, or returns a 403 error, specifying that access was denied. The difference between Basic and Digest authentication is that with Digest, your credentials are encrypted instead of being passed in plain text.

The problem with using Digest encryption is that not very many clients support it. You can use it with newer versions of Internet Explorer, Mozilla, and Netscape, but it's a newer protocol, and due to lack of real-world implementations, has been considered experimental for many years now.

Instead, most organizations simply encrypt the entire connection using SSL. If you connect to a server using the https:// protocol, everything in the connection, including your user name and password, is encrypted.

There are several Apache modules that use Basic authentication. The most commonly used module is `mod_auth`, which uses plain text files to store user information. To set up this type of authentication, you add a section like the following to either a <Directory> block or an .htaccess file:

```
AuthType Basic
AuthName "Message to show user in Password dialog"
AuthUserFile /var/www/htpasswd
```

The `AuthName` directive specifies the *Realm* of the authorization. Browsers use realms to cache user credentials. If the browser gets an "Authorization Required" message from the server and if the host name and the realm match user credentials it has already collected, it sends them to the server instead of asking for a password again. By setting the same realm to all protected areas on your server, your users only need to log into the site once in each session (and the browser may have an option to cache usernames and passwords for future sessions).

The `AuthUserFile` directive points to a password file you need to create to contain usernames and passwords. The `htpasswd` program can be used to manage these files: creating them, adding users, and changing passwords. The first time you run `htpasswd`, use the `-c` switch to create the initial file. After that, omit it to add other users to the file (use the same command to change the password for a user):

```
# htpasswd -c /var/www/htpasswd user1
New password:
Re-type new password:
# htpasswd /var/www/htpasswd user2
```

```
New Password:
Re-type new password:
```

You can name the file to store passwords in anything you like—but it should not be under the Web root, or users may be able to download and crack it. The actual passwords are stored using a relatively simple encryption method.

We have now set up authorization, but we haven't directed Apache to use it. To actually make a directory password protected, add the Require directive to the <Directory> container or .htaccess file:

```
Require user user1 user2
Require valid-user
```

The first form of this statement specifies particular users to grant access. The valid-user statement allows access to any user (with the correct password) listed in the AuthUserFile.

You can also create groups, using an AuthGroupFile. There is no command to manage these files—just create a simple text file and add one group per line. The group name must start at the beginning of a line, end with a colon, and then have a list of all the users who belong to the group separated by spaces. The users must be specified in the password file.

```
/var/www/htgroups:
employees: user1 user2

.htaccess:
AuthGroupFile /var/www/htgroups
Require group employees
```

You still need to provide all of the other authorization directives already listed (AuthUserFile, AuthType, AuthName).

The users and groups you define for mod_auth have nothing to do with any other user accounts—they do not match mail accounts, Unix users, or anything else. This is a completely independent authentication system, and to change passwords, you have to change them with the htpasswd program. The other problem with basic authentication using mod_auth is that plain text files become very slow to search as they grow in length. This system works fine for up to a few dozen users. If you need to provide access to more, you can use other Apache authentication modules.

mod_auth_dbm provides a simple fast database format for storing users, groups, and passwords. mod_ldap allows you to connect to an LDAP server to look up user credentials, allowing you to store the same authentication credentials for a wide range of systems. See Chapter 7 for more about LDAP. Both of these modules are part of the basic Apache distribution. See the Apache documentation for specific instructions to set these up.

Another authentication module might prove useful: mod_auth_mysql. With this module, you can store user credentials in a MySQL database, which is extremely fast for very large numbers of users, and can be a very easy place to add and remove users using some Web scripts. It's fairly easy to set up a single MySQL account to provide a single username and password for sending and receiving email, including Web mail, and protecting Web directories. This module is not part of the core Apache distribution, but can be downloaded from *http://modauthmysql.sourceforge.net/*.

You can mix and match basic authentication modules, using more than one to find a valid user. Each has an "Authoritative" directive, and when a user enters a name and password, Apache goes through the modules in the order they were loaded. If it reaches a module with the Authoritative directive set to On, if it doesn't find valid user credentials, it rejects the authentication. So to use multiple modules, you need to set the last module to be Authoritative On, and all the rest to be Authoritative Off.

There is another authorization module, mod_access, which does not use authentication at all. mod_access uses the IP address of the computer making the request to determine whether to allow or deny the request. The Order directive specifies whether hosts you've specified in Allow override those in Deny, or vice versa. Order allow,deny with nothing else specified denies all hosts by default. Choose this order for directories you do not want to provide general access to, and then use an Allow directive to allow access from your LAN. The mod_access page of the Apache documentation provides some good examples.

Finally, the Satisfy directive specifies whether you want to allow access based on either authentication or the mod_access module, or both. This directive can be set to either:

```
Satisfy Any
Satisfy All
```

Satisfy Any is useful for directories you want to allow unrestricted access to any computer on your LAN, while forcing users from the Internet to authenticate with a valid username and password. Satisfy All, with the same access or authorization directives, only allows access to users on your LAN with a valid password.

Virtual Hosts

What's a virtual host? Think multiple personalities. Apache listens to particular ports on particular network cards for a request. The default Web port is 80, though you can configure Apache to listen on a different port, or multiple ports. When a request for a Web page comes in, the domain name is stripped, and everything from the first slash after the domain name is sent to Apache as the requested page. For example, when you type in a URL of *http://www.example.com/manual/index.html,* your browser attempts to connect to port 80 on whatever IP address www.example.com represents. On the server, the request looks something like this:

```
GET /manual/index.html HTTP/1.1.
Host: www.example.com.
User-Agent: Mozilla/5.0 (Windows; U; Windows NT 5.1; en-US; rv:1.5a)
Gecko/20030728 Mozilla Firebird/0.6.1.
Accept:
text/xml,application/xml,application/xhtml+xml,text/html;q=0.9,text/pla
in;q=0.8,video/x-mng,image/png,image/jpeg,image/gif;q=0.2,*/*;q=0.1.
Accept-Language: en-us,en;q=0.5.
Accept-Encoding: gzip,deflate.
Accept-Charset: ISO-8859-1,utf-8;q=0.7,*;q=0.7.
Keep-Alive: 300.
Connection: keep-alive.
```

The crucial lines here are the first two: the GET and the Host. The rest of the lines indicate various things about the browser, operating system, and language of the client computer. Apache, in response to this request, responds with:

```
HTTP/1.1 200 OK.
Date: Thu, 21 Aug 2003 03:52:59 GMT.
Server: Apache-AdvancedExtranetServer/2.0.47 (Mandrake Linux/1.1mdk)
mod_perl/1.99_08 Perl/v5.8.0 mod_ssl/2.0.47 OpenSSL/0.9.7a DAV/2
SVN/0.26.0+ PHP/4.3.1.
Last-Modified: Thu, 10 Jul 2003 03:30:28 GMT.
ETag: "98314-1b6a-13d41d00".
Accept-Ranges: bytes.
Content-Length: 7018.
Keep-Alive: timeout=15, max=99.
Connection: Keep-Alive.
Content-Type: text/html; charset=ISO-8859-1.
```

... followed immediately by the contents of the file. If the Web root is /var/www/html, it would return whatever is at /var/www/html/manual/index.html.

If you haven't defined any virtual hosts in Apache, you get the same content from this server, no matter what domain name or IP address you use, as long as the connection goes to this server. Because of this, you can point a bunch of domain names to the IP address of your server, and they will all see the same Web pages.

But say you want to provide a different Web site for different domain names. For example, you might want to have one Web site for your employee time scheduling system, a different one for your supply chain, another for a key product, and also run your main public Web site, all on the same server. You could put them on a single domain, and use subdirectories for the various sites. By defining virtual hosts, however, you can give them all a different name.

You might want *http://example.com* and *http://www.example.com* to first return your public Web site, and then provide a private site at *http://employees.example. com*. Your partners could log into *http://partners.example.com*. To get Apache to return a different Web site for different host names, you set up virtual hosts.

There are actually two different types of virtual hosts: Name-based virtual hosts, and IP-based virtual hosts. Name-based virtual hosts use the Host: header from the initial request to determine which virtual host to use. There are two problems with name-based virtual hosts:

1. Very old browsers do not send the Host: header—it was added to version 1.1 of the HTTP protocol.
2. Only one SSL certificate can be used per IP address—you cannot use SSL encryption with name-based virtual hosts.

IP-based virtual hosts solve these problems by using the IP address and/or the port the browser connected to to determine what virtual host to use. The problem with this arrangement is that you have to have additional IP addresses assigned to your server, and if these are public IP addresses, they won't work behind a NAT router. See Appendix B to brush up on these networking concepts if this doesn't make sense.

In practice, you'll use name-based virtual hosts far more often, because they cost nothing to add, and you can usually get by with a single encrypted domain.

To set up name-based virtual hosting, first add the NameVirtualHost directive somewhere in the Apache configuration files. In Mandrake, you'll find an example in /etc/httpd/conf/vhosts/Vhosts.conf. This directive is supposed to be set to the IP address and port that handles the name-based virtual hosts. Set it to the wildcard "*" to have Apache listen for virtual hosts on all network addresses:

```
NameVirtualHost *
```

Next, you define the actual virtual hosts using the <VirtualHost> container. Again, you specify a wildcard for the IP address. The ServerName directive provides the name to match in the Host: header in the request. If you want the same content to be returned for a different host name, you can add additional names to a Server- Alias directive. Finally, the DocumentRoot points to the directory containing the actual files for the Web site:

```
<VirtualHost *>
  DocumentRoot /var/www/html
  ServerName example.com
  ServerAlias www.example.com
<VirtualHost>

<VirtualHost *>
  DocumentRoot /var/www/html/partners
  ServerName partners.example.com
</VirtualHost>
```

When a request for a particular domain comes in, and there are name-based virtual hosts defined, Apache ignores any DocumentRoot and ServerName defined outside the virtual host blocks. It scans all the blocks, trying to match the Host: header to a ServerName or ServerHost inside a <VirtualHost> block. The first one it finds that matches, it uses. If it doesn't find a match, it uses the first <VirtualHost> block defined in the configuration file. For this reason, the first <VirtualHost> block is the default one, used for any request coming to this server that you don't otherwise define a host for. It's a good idea to use this as your public site, since it's probably the one you don't mind people reaching by accident.

You can put nearly any other directive inside a <VirtualHost> block, to set something specific to that host, such as the location of CGI scripts. Reload Apache, and your virtual hosts will start responding. The other thing you have to do, of course, is get your browser to connect to your server when it requests the host name. You do this by adding host records to the authoritative name server for your domains. See Chapter 3 for more about DNS.

CGI, Perl, PHP

For static pages, getting your Web site up and running is a breeze. Make a few simple entries in the configuration files, copy some HTML pages to the appropriate directory, configure DNS and forward appropriate ports through your firewall, start it all up and you're done. If you're going to do anything more sophisticated, however, you're probably going to need to add support for some sort of scripting language.

The original way to make your Web sites do something was by writing a script in a language called Perl, and using the Common Gateway Interface (CGI). Actually, you can use many different languages, limited only by what you choose to install on your server. Perl is common because it's particularly good at manipulating *strings*, variables containing text, which is what Web pages are made of.

You need to configure several things to get a CGI to run. First of all, the script must start with a line indicating what language it's in, with the path to the interpreter. All CGI scripts must begin with a pound sign, an exclamation point, and this path. Here are some examples:

```
#!/usr/bin/perl
#!/bin/bash
#!/usr/bin/php
```

Secondly, the script must be executable by the Apache user, which means the Apache user or group must own the file, or the file must be world-readable and executable. It is possible to use an Apache module to run the script as some other specific user—read the documentation for suEXEC in the Apache manual if you want to do this.

Thirdly, the script must have the correct line endings. This is one of the most puzzling causes of script failure, especially if you edit a script in Windows and then try to run it in Unix. Windows and Unix have different conventions for the characters that identify the end of a line. Generally files with Unix line endings run anywhere, but files with Windows line endings often do not run in Unix. To test the file, use the `file` command. In the directory containing your script, type `file test.pl` to find out what type of line endings test.pl has. If it has Unix line endings, the result should be "ASCII text." If it says "with CRLF line terminators," the file will need to be converted.

To convert the line endings, you can use a quick search and replace tool called `sed`. This command strips out the extra carriage returns of a file named `test.pl`, and saves it under a new name:

```
$ sed s/\\r// test.pl > test_unix.pl
```

Finally, you need to tell Apache where the scripts are, and how to run them. The `ScriptAlias` directive maps a URL to a directory of scripts. For example, Mandrake sets up this `ScriptAlias` by default:

```
ScriptAlias /cgi-bin/ /var/www/cgi-bin/
```

Any file in this directory will be treated as a script, and Apache will attempt to execute it when the URL is called. If the test.pl script is in this directory, Apache will run it if you visit `http://example.com/cgi-bin/test.pl`.

Alternatively, you can specify that files with particular extensions, such as *.cgi or *.pl located in the normal Web root are to be executed as CGI scripts by adding this directive:

```
AddHandler cgi-script cgi pl
```

CGI scripts are extremely flexible. You can program scripts in nearly any language. A drawback of scripts is that they are relatively inefficient—every time a script is requested, the server has to start up a new process, and load an entire environment to execute it. CGI scripts, for this reason, can be slow.

A newer way of providing dynamic content is to use a language handled directly by an Apache module. The supreme example is PHP. PHP stands for *PHP Hypertext Processor,* another fairly meaningless recursive acronym. But PHP is hardly a meaningless improvement—you can code some amazingly complex Web applications using relatively simple, straightforward scripting.

PHP is handled by the `mod_php` module, provided with most Linux distributions. Several of the Web applications used in this book rely on PHP, so it's a good module to install.

Apache 2 is designed to be highly modular. You can add new modules to it by simply compiling them on their own, putting them in a place where Apache can find them, and adding a `LoadModule` directive to the httpd.conf configuration file.

OpenSSL

The last thing we'll talk about in this section is enabling SSL connections. We'll cover encryption in greater detail in Chapter 15—here we'll show you the basic configuration for Apache. SSL stands for Secure Sockets Layer, which describes roughly how an encrypted connection is made. The Web server and the browser exchange public keys, and then each packet of data is encrypted by a new session key, which is in turn encrypted to the public key for the destination.

Why do you need encryption? Mainly to keep information private. SSL is an end-to-end encryption protocol—everything between the Web browser and the Web server is encrypted. Even if somebody were snooping and captured every packet, they would be unable to decrypt it to determine what information was transferred. All they can tell is what IP address and ports were used at each end, and roughly how big the transmission was.

Anytime you're using Basic authentication, you should be using encryption. A malicious snooper could not only read the password, but also whatever files or Web pages the user downloaded. About the only time this isn't much of a concern is when you completely control the network over which the traffic passes. You probably don't need to encrypt your internal company Web site for people browsing it on the LAN—but if you run a WEP-encrypted or unencrypted wireless network, or if people connect to the internal site over the Internet, you most definitely should be using SSL.

Apache 2 comes with `mod_ssl`, a module that interacts with a set of encryption libraries provided by yet another program called OpenSSL. Make sure you have both OpenSSL and `mod_ssl` installed.

The first step is to create a certificate for the server. This certificate is a public/private key pair. The public key will be sent to the browser, which will use it to encrypt its requests to the Web server. Only the private key can be used to decrypt the request.

When you create a certificate, the script asks for a passphrase for unscrambling the secret key. Usually for the Web server certificate, you want to skip this step (just press enter), because if you have a passphrase here, you'll have to enter it every time your Web server starts. If your server reboots for some reason when you're unavailable, the Web service will dutifully wait for somebody to type in the passphrase, and your site will be offline.

Apache provides a script for generating a test certificate. If you don't need to encrypt a Web page for customers, and can live with an authentication warning every time you go to your site, this script is acceptable. Otherwise, use the OpenSSL tools to create a real certificate.

The certificate itself (even a test certificate) provides the encryption part of SSL, but not the authentication part. Before you type your credit card number into an online merchant's Web page, you want to have some assurance that not only can nobody intercept the number as it travels across the Internet, you also want to be sure that the Web site you're visiting actually belongs to the merchant, and hasn't been hijacked by somebody else. A Certificate Authority is a centralized entity that signs a server certificate, providing a guarantee that this server is who you think it is. Web browsers come with the public keys for a few Certificate Authorities that are well known and accepted (by the browser programmers, anyway) as being trustworthy. These Certificate Authorities include VeriSign, TrustE, and several other companies that have achieved reputability. For SSL to work without an authentication warning, you need to get one of these universally recognized Certificate Authorities to sign your server certificate. This usually involves a fee, generally over $100 per year.

The OpenSSL key generation scripts can save you a step by creating both a certificate and a certificate signing request in one step. In Mandrake, the OpenSSL package, with its tools, gets installed in `/usr/lib/ssl`.

There are a number of good tutorials on the Web to help you create server certificates. The gist of it is to run the `misc/CA.pl` script with the `-newreq` command, give it all the appropriate details about your server name, location, and contact info, and then copy the certificate to some appropriate location such as `/etc/ssl/apache/server.key`. Then, send a copy of your key to the Certificate Authority to get it signed, which takes a few days. Alternatively, you can set up your own Certificate Authority, although people using it will have to install its public key as a trusted root authority or they will get authentication warnings. See Chapter 15 for more details.

Finally, set up Apache to handle the encryption. If you install the `mod_ssl` module package, most of these will already be set up for you—all you'll need to do is change the paths to the certificate and key. In Mandrake, these are in the `/etc/httpd/conf.d/41_mod_ssl.default-vhost.conf` file. The directives to change are `SSLCertificateFile` and `SSLCertificateKeyFile`.

Remember that you can only run one SSL server per IP address or you will get unpredictable results. So define a Virtual Host, add your certificate and key, make sure the SSLEngine is On, and you're good to go. Reboot and you should be able to connect your server using any SSL-encrypted browser.

SUMMARY

In this chapter, we have learned about installing, configuring, and managing the Apache Web server. We looked at the issues of hosting a public Web site, running an intranet server, transferring files, configuring authentication, and setting up virtual hosts. We also took a brief look at server scripting, and setting up SSL. Apache is one of the most popular Web browsers available. It provides a framework for modular extension, supports many standards and languages besides HTML, and is the platform for solutions in every chapter of the next part. Apache is available for any Unix-based operating systems and Windows, but it comes with almost every Linux distribution.

We've reached the end of Part I, having covered the fundamental computer infrastructure you need to be able to deploy business applications. In Part II, we'll take a look at business applications, beginning with Customer Relationship Management.

WEB SERVER REFERENCES

An updated list of resources for this chapter is on the Web site for the book at *http://opensourcesmall.biz/web*.

Software
Advanced Extranet Server *http://www.advx.org*
Apache Web Server *http://www.apache.org*
Internet Information Services, commercial Web server built into Windows
    http://www.microsoft.com
OpenSSL, open source Secure Sockets Layer libraries *http://www.openssl.org*
.NET, Web services framework *http://www.microsoft.com*

Mono, .NET framework for Linux *http://www.go-mono.com/*
Filezilla, SFTP client for Windows *http://filezilla.sourceforge.net/*
mod_auth_mysql, authentication module for MySQL *http://modauthmysql. sourceforge.net*

Web Sites

Apache Manual *http://httpd.apache.org/docs-project/*
Reference site for the PHP scripting language *http://www.php.net*
WebDAV information site http://www.webdav.org/

II
Computing Your Business Operations

In Part II, we change our focus to cover the core business operations common to every business. This part explores how computers can help manage all the little details of managing your business. In a couple of these areas, open source software has some way to go to catch up to the state of proprietary software, especially for the smallest of businesses. In others, open source software provides a more useful set of features.

Each chapter evaluates a whole spectrum of solutions for a wide range of businesses, helping you choose between not just open source, but proprietary, solutions if they offer compelling benefits. Many of the open source solutions run as Web applications on the Apache server we set up in Chapter 6. Most businesses should find all of these chapters useful, especially if the businesses are starting out.

Chapter 7 discusses managing your customers, using customer relationship management software.

Chapter 8 covers managing your schedule, using computers with calendars, appointments, meetings, and tasks.

Chapter 9 proposes a way to manage your business documents, applying a type of tool used by software developers for decades.

Chapter 10 compares different systems for managing your finances.

Chapter 11 provides help for managing everything else in your business.

7 Customer Relationship Management

In This Chapter

- Introduction
- Refining the Problem
- Small Business CRM: Retriever CRM
- Using a Directory
- Summary
- Customer Relationship Management References

INTRODUCTION

Everybody has an address book. Scraps of paper inserted into a shoebox. Little address books with pages worn thin from repeated eraser use. We keep our addresses scattered through our lives on bits of paper, envelopes teetering close to the recycling bin, special folders in our email, or on the refrigerator door.

This chapter contains mostly non-technical information.

NOTE

You'd think technology would have better answers for us. If you're disciplined in your use, in some ways it does—but there is no single system that automatically keeps your addresses in one place, up to date, without effort.

If you use email at all, you probably have a large and growing address book associated with your email software. Do you keep your contacts' physical addresses in the same place, or in a physical book somewhere? Or in a spreadsheet, ready for creating a mail merge to your customers? The problem is, we use different types of addresses in different contexts every day. The same person may be in several different address systems, and if that person's address changes, how do you know which entries you've already updated? In this chapter, we'll take a look at the various systems that use address information, and some strategies for managing them.

REFINING THE PROBLEM

The thing is, there's more than one problem here. Computers are good at solving specific problems. The key to getting a computer to solve your problem is to define it clearly. And when we discuss managing your address book, we're really talking about a rats' nest of problems:

■ Keeping your address book, whatever form it happens to be, available, easy to find when you need it
■ Keeping your address book up to date
■ Using email addresses in email
■ Using street addresses in direct mail
■ Having a phone list handy of people you need to call often
■ Keeping track of who you have called recently, and who you need to call
■ Getting your customer's address onto an invoice or statement
■ Managing lists of suppliers, vendors, customers, and employees
■ Providing a company directory to employees
■ Managing your password across different computers in your office
■ Managing your password across your business applications
■ Sharing contact lists and sales opportunities among your sales people

Where do you start?

Strategies for Managing Addresses

The first thing to do is to group these problems into categories. Then we can try to figure out the best approaches for each of these, keeping track of the bigger picture.

First of all, everybody needs to have some sort of address book, whether it's an old-fashioned little black book, a Palm® Pilot®, a Rolodex®, a spreadsheet, or something in a more formal computerized system. The big problem here is that we end up with several competing address books: we have the one built into our email software, a scratched-out updated list by the phone, and perhaps a spreadsheet we've made to do a Christmas mailing, all in addition to whatever we consider to be our primary book. And we haven't even gotten to the business systems yet. Is it feasible to keep all of these addresses in one place? Or is it better to not even try—just keep synchronizing changes among all of them?

For the business systems, we probably have a company directory we distribute to all employees, customer listings in our invoice-generation software, and whatever system we use to track sales calls, opportunities, and prospects. And then there are the computer systems. At first glance, these do not necessarily relate to addresses. But user accounts on a computer share one thing with people in your address book: each account is associated with a person. The correlation between people in a company directory and people who log into a computer in that company is one to one: each person with an email address on a system should be able to check their mail on that system. This is especially true in large organizations, such as governments, universities, and large enterprise corporations. In these settings, an organization-wide directory can be essential, and tying it to user accounts makes a lot of sense.

Small businesses tend to interact with a much higher percentage of people outside their business than inside. The roles people play in a small business can be a lot more fluid, changing from customer to partner to supplier depending on the context.

The bad news is, despite there being millions of small businesses, most of them have not demanded effective computer systems for managing their contacts, but have instead grown their own custom databases, or sets of spreadsheets.

So let's take a look at three basic strategies for managing your addresses across all the systems you use:

1. Keep a personal address book and use it for everything.
2. Add addresses to each of your systems, and synchronize as necessary.
3. Set up a centralized directory containing all your addresses, and configure systems to use it.

Use a Personal Address Book for Everything

By having one address book that you know contains the most current contact details, you can prevent mistakes of sending things to the wrong place. The drawback is you have to check this address book every time you make contact with somebody. To make this strategy most effective, you must have an address book you like, you keep available, and that you use. This will probably be a book or some sort of PDA—to keep it up to date, you probably need to carry it with you. Keeping your address book accurate requires discipline to actually use it.

When you write an email, first check the address against your address book to make sure it's correct. When you send an invoice, verify that the address is correct against your address book. Where this system might break down is when you go to do a direct marketing campaign, or mail your Christmas cards. If you can synchronize your PDA with a desktop program, you can probably export an up-to-date list to generate a mailing. The advantage is, you don't have to maintain any other address books. The drawback is, you do a lot more typing.

Synchronize Your Address Books across Systems

The second strategy is to not try to keep any one authoritative address book, but just keep each system as up to date as possible, and synchronize changes as necessary. The big risk of doing this is that address changes may not get made across all your systems—or you may find two different addresses for the same contact and not know which is correct.

There is a growing niche of software designed to help you manage multiple address books. These tools can copy addresses to and from multiple Personal Information Management programs on multiple computers and devices. Copy your contacts to a Web site, to your laptop, to a desktop, to your mobile phone, to your PDA. It may take more specialized scripts or macros to synchronize contacts in your invoicing software and your sales automation package, but it might be possible.

By using these tools, you may also be able to share contacts across your sales team, or keep a company address book that gets synchronized with all of your employees. The advantage is, it's easier and faster to use each system. The drawback is, you're going to make more mistakes.

Use a Centralized Directory System

Like keeping a personal address book, a centralized directory of addresses reduces mistakes—there is only one place you keep up to date with current addresses, and use that centralized information in all systems. The difference is, you can usually configure each software package to use this directory automatically, saving a lot of typing. The drawback: implementing a directory is expensive, and takes a lot of forethought.

As your business grows and technology improves, you will implement a directory. Sooner or later it becomes cost effective. What makes directories expensive is that no two organizations have exactly the same needs in a directory. Most directories have been implemented in large organizations, such as universities, government agencies, and large companies. These directories only include contacts within the organization. Sales and accounting systems tend to keep separate address books for their own contacts, or use something called *Enterprise Resource Planning* (ERP) software. We discuss ERP software a bit more in Chapter 12.

So while theoretically a centralized directory is the best option, it's fraught with all sorts of issues that make it difficult to get it in place:

- Different software applications support different external address systems
- Most software that uses directories cannot modify information they contain
- Applications define the same types of data in different ways, leading to conflicts

At this writing, in early 2004, all the technology exists to create powerful directories that can store address information for everything in your business, but nobody has put this technology together in a way that works well for a small business. Each implementation is custom and expensive.

Mixing Address Book Strategies

Obviously, you're probably going to need a mix of these strategies. As people develop good systems for managing addresses across small business systems, check them out. The rest of this chapter can give you some ideas on what to look for. Next, we're going to look at individual types of systems for managing addresses, and later we'll take a look at software that helps you manage these systems.

Address Book Systems

Computers are supposed to make it easier to do complicated tasks. The irony is that it often makes tasks more complicated, requiring their own use. Addresses are one such area.

Before email, most people kept an address book with the addresses of their friends and family. A telephone book might help you find the number of an acquaintance you wanted to contact. The Rolodex eventually became a popular solution for business people who needed to keep track of hundreds of addresses. Creating a mass mailing to customers was extremely expensive—first you might have to pay for the printing of your mailing, and then pay somebody to address each envelope by hand.

One of the first business uses of computers was to merge addresses automatically into letters, labels, or envelopes, saving the time and cost of having a secretary type each address individually onto an envelope. Of course, somebody still had to type the addresses into some sort of database. At this point, you had each address in your Rolodex, on your computer in a database or spreadsheet, and in your address book—with a phone list at your desk of your most frequently called contacts.

Now add email to the mix. Every email program has its own address book. Unless you are a supremely organized person, you probably don't have all of your addresses organized in your email software. If you do, are they current? So now we have email addresses that change frequently, often several for the same person. We have phone lists. We have mail merge databases. We have address books and Rolodexes.

If you're in sales (and what small business owner isn't?), it would be great to know the last time you followed up with a prospect, and what you discussed. If you get a lot of repeat business, wouldn't it be nice to know what each customer has purchased in the past, to be able to recommend or market your next product to them? Or remind them that it's time for a scheduled service?

Before computers, personal service involved a lot of effort to keep track of your customers. You simply couldn't provide a high level of service to everyone. Now, not only can computers help you provide better service to all of your customers, they also help your competitors. You can't afford to not provide personal service—your customers will go to a business that will.

In this brief discussion, we've touched upon the full range of address systems. In this chapter, we'll dig deeper into each one, building up to the most comprehensive systems:

- Paper address management
- Personal Digital Assistants (PDAs) and Personal Information Management (PIM) tools
- Spreadsheets and custom databases
- Customer Relationship Management (CRM) systems
- Directories

Address Books and the Rolodex

Once you've moved your address book online, you'll be hard pressed ever to go back to a paper address book. But paper address books have one major advantage over all the other solutions available: They don't need a power source. All the other address systems we discuss in this chapter need to be plugged into a wall, charged regularly, or have their batteries replaced.

The other main benefit of a paper address book is that it's easy to carry. If you're traveling, you can write somebody's address in your book during takeoff and landing, or in the midst of an African Safari. If you can still conduct your small business while you're on such a trip, drop the author a line, and tell him how!

Otherwise, paper address books have a list of obvious drawbacks:

- They're hard to keep up to date.
- They're hard to back up.
- Using an address or phone number requires you to create a manual copy—they don't integrate with other systems, such as email or promotional fliers, at all.

However, perhaps the most important thing about using any address system is that you keep it current. If you're strongly attached to your address book, by all means, use it. The point is, don't try to keep multiple address systems up to date. Make a commitment to updating one address book with all the changes, and then copy the addresses to other systems as necessary.

PDAs and PIMs

A Personal Digital Assistant (PDA) is the modern portable address book. There are dozens of different PDAs available, using a variety of operating systems. Some of the most common systems at this writing are:

- Palm Pilots and compatible (Palm Tungsten™, Sony Clie™, Handspring™, etc.)
- Microsoft Pocket PCs (Compaq Ipaq, others)
- Linux-based (Zaurus, some cell phones)
- Apple iPods

Each of these handheld computers provide the benefits of a small paper address book, without its limitations. You get automatic backups every time you synchronize with your desktop. It's remarkably easy to update somebody's address. You can often synchronize with your email software, and run mail merges from the same address book.

Personal Information Management (PIM) software is the desktop counterpart to your PDA. PIM software manages contacts, appointments, to-do lists, and notes. Many PIM packages manage much more—email, documents, journals of activities, and so on.

The Palm Desktop application is a good basic PIM tool for Windows, included with any Palm OS device. If you're running Linux, you can use Jpilot (Figure 7.1) to get exactly the same features (*http://www.jpilot.org*).

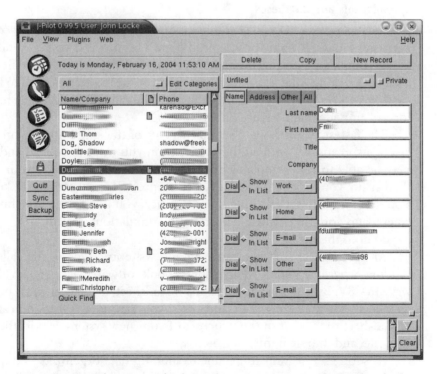

FIGURE 7.1   Jpilot Personal Information Management software for Linux.

There are hundreds of PIM programs, and you can find many choices for every operating system. The most successful integrate email with your address book. Arguably the most popular PIM for Windows is Microsoft Outlook. A very similar program for Linux is Ximian Evolution®. These programs synchronize with your PDA, allowing you to carry your address book with you, and giving you access to addresses you've collected offline. Both programs also make their addresses available for mail merging.

A *mail merge* involves taking a list of names and addresses and inserting each one into a letter or other document to generate a copy personalized for each recipient. Outlook integrates with Microsoft Word to provide mail merges. Evolution's address book is available to OpenOffice.org for doing a mail merge. We discuss a little more about how to do a mail merge in Chapter 13.

So if you have both a PDA and a favorite PIM, which one is the one to keep up to date? The advantage of using a PDA is that both can be—your changes automatically synchronize back and forth. As long as you've sufficiently tested your systems, you can consider both to be the same address book—you have access to it on both your PDA and your email program.

Spreadsheets and Databases

For most people, a PDA/PIM combination is all you'll ever need for contact management. However, some people need quite a bit more. If you create regular marketing campaigns, sending postcards or brochures to potential customers, you need a way of tracking what you've sent to whom. Some businesses need to know which customers have bought which products, so they can tailor additional marketing efforts or provide maintenance offers.

The fastest, easiest way to set up this type of tracking information is to simply create a spreadsheet with all the information you want to collect, and use it. You may be able to find templates or programs that closely match your needs—but then again, you may not. A spreadsheet is a great place to capture all kinds of data. You don't need to set anything up in advance, you don't need to define what goes where, and you can perform all sorts of manipulations directly in the spreadsheet as you need them.

All spreadsheet software can read and write to a type of file called CSV, for *Comma-Separated Values*. Many address book software packages can also read and write to CSV. By keeping your data in a spreadsheet, if you ever come up with a better system for managing your addresses, you can do a few modifications to the spreadsheet to make it fit the structure of your new system, export the data into a CSV file, and import it into your new system.

As soon as you want to be able to look up data organized a couple different ways, you've reached the limits of a spreadsheet. While you can build complex summary reports in a spreadsheet, and sort rows by any particular column, it's difficult to associate a customer with multiple products, or with a record of each time you've called them.

The next step in complexity beyond a spreadsheet is a *relational database*. A spreadsheet is a simple database, with rows, columns, and worksheets. With a spreadsheet, you can put different types of information on different worksheets, but you can't easily associate a row on one table with an arbitrary row on another.

A relational database uses a different table for each type of item, and defines relationships among these tables. You might have one table representing your customers, and another table for your products. A third table provides the relationships, listing each existing combination of customer and product. Using such a system, it becomes easy to get a list of all customers that have purchased a particular product, or all products an individual customer has purchased.

A database system can be a powerful tool for supporting your business. Managing data is what a computer does. Popular desktop databases include Microsoft Access and Filemaker Pro. Many small businesses have built custom systems using these databases, growing them as their needs change.

In the open source world, there are few desktop databases. But you can inexpensively run a database server capable of everything these other desktop databases can do, and are designed to do with disconnected clients. Like other open source systems, you have more options for server components than desktop. One option for setting up a completely free, powerful database system is to set up MySQL as a database server, and connect to it with OpenOffice. OpenOffice does not come with a database, but it can connect to external databases such as MySQL and Postgresql, and it has a graphical relationship view very much like the tools you find in Microsoft Access.

Many businesses use invoices, statements, and receipts to track payments from their customers. Most accounting packages have their own address books in some database format to simplify generating these documents.

CRM Systems

Customer Relationship Management (CRM) refers to a database system designed for keeping track of your interactions with your contacts. Sales people use CRM systems to remind them who they need to call. The traditional CRM system is a set of manila folders, one for every day of the month, and one for every month of the year. The sales person writes a note reminding her of someone she wants to follow up with, and drops it into the corresponding daily or monthly folder. At the end of the month, she takes some time to go through the next month's folder, sorting its contents into the appropriate daily folders.

With a computerized CRM system, you have your contact information all in one place, and the computer reminds you of the daily tasks you have assigned for yourself. Perhaps the most popular CRM software, other than homegrown database systems, is ACT!®. ACT! is an address book that provides a CRM system. You can add activities to your contacts, and be automatically reminded when it's time to give them a call. ACT! can integrate with Microsoft Outlook.

For some sales and agency related positions, ACT! isn't enough. Other systems have been built with the goal of providing you access to everything you need to get to, indexed in a variety of ways. GoldMine® is a more comprehensive CRM solution. It provides its own mail server and client software. In GoldMine, you can open up a contact and quickly see all email you sent to and received from that person, find any documents they have sent to you, or see other people in the same organization. If your job is presenting an applicant to many different clients, you can quickly find out when and where you sent the applicant's resume.

Obviously, this addresses a particular business need that most businesses probably don't have. A similar feature might allow a writer to keep track of which publications he's submitted a particular proposal to. Most CRM systems help you manage marketing commands, keeping track of what you've mailed to whom.

ACT! has been so successful because it addresses the business needs of sales people. More sophisticated packages often need to be customized to meet the particular needs of an individual business. And that's where open source comes into the discussion: nothing is easier to customize than an application you have all the source code for.

The author was unable to find any open source desktop contact management program that compared to ACT! or GoldMine. Like much of the open source software in this book, the solutions are all server-based. There are a number of Web-based open source CRM projects, and if you have unusual needs, it's easy to customize these to get a system that works for you.

The vast majority of open source CRM packages are designed for help desks. Managing trouble tickets, keeping track of support-related problems, and assigning and tracking incidents are tasks that employ a lot of computer technicians. When the telephones aren't ringing, many of them work on their own software projects. Naturally, many of these software projects exist to make their job easier—thus the plethora of help desk software.

Sales people, on the other hand, tend to spend more time trying to make sales, and less time refining their tools. At least, successful sales people do. Unless your product is some sophisticated technology-related product, you're much more likely to need software optimized for sales rather than another help desk management tool. Few of the latter exist. Later in this chapter, we'll take a closer look at CRM systems.

Directories

A completely different type of address management system is called a Directory. Large companies publish their own internal corporate directory, providing contact details for their employees and suppliers, along with other internal numbers and addresses. Telephone companies publish perhaps the most familiar directories.

Several different ways of managing directories on computers have developed over the years. Most have coalesced into an implementation of Lightweight Directory Access Protocol (LDAP), a smaller version of the original X.500 directory standard. LDAP describes a free-form object-based database system. Compared to a relational database, LDAP databases contain objects instead of records. Each object can have any number of characteristics. An LDAP entry for an employee, for example, might contain a home address, multiple telephone numbers, relationships to other people, a list of computers that person is allowed to log into, a picture, and multiple email addresses. You can't easily store the same type of information in a relational database—with a relational database, you have to figure out every type of information you're going to associate with a person ahead of time.

LDAP is primarily used to keep track of user accounts within a large company. Its overwhelming advantage is that the security information for each person is stored in one place for all systems. This means that when you change your password in one place, it changes it everywhere. Without some centralized user management, each computer will have its own login for each user. Your timesheet account password might be managed separately from your accounting system login, and it becomes nearly impossible to change your password regularly because you'll inevitably forget to change it on some system, out of potentially dozens you interact with.

LDAP unifies all of these user accounts. Its downside is complexity, the flip side of its flexibility. LDAP uses *schemas* to define the characteristics associated with each object. A schema is a definition of what data is stored in a database, and where. In a relational database, each table has one schema. In an LDAP database, each object can use multiple schemas. To make an object contain additional data, you just add a corresponding schema. The end result is that every system can use its own schema. So while all the information for a user ends up in a single object, defining what data each object needs to have is a daunting task.

LDAP objects can represent nearly any physical object you can think of, not just people. As you might imagine, the flexibility of data definition in an LDAP database can often provide a much better representation of real life than a row in a relational database. However, manipulating LDAP data in a way that makes sense, and actually getting software to use it correctly, challenges the cleverest software architects.

So at this writing, the only widespread implementations are for managing user accounts in large organizations. Most popular email clients can look up email addresses in a corporate LDAP directory. Most computers can be configured to look up user accounts from a centralized LDAP directory. You can use LDAP to authenticate your email account, log into a password protected Web page, and do many other things. Microsoft provides a slightly modified LDAP authentication system called Active Directory, which can be used to provide a security context to all kinds of programs. However, most of these LDAP-compatible programs only read data from LDAP—you cannot easily write to it. Network Administrators use special tools to add and manage user accounts.

What's the point? Why is LDAP important for small businesses? While deploying an LDAP system is out of reach for most small businesses, surely in the near future, perhaps even when you read this, there will be LDAP systems optimized for small business use.

Managing sales and customer contact information is an obvious use for LDAP. In 2003, you might have your contact information in a CRM system, on an email address book, in your accounting system for generating invoices, and on a Web site where your customers can track their orders. Without LDAP, you have the data repeated in several places—and if it changes somewhere, how do you know which system is most up to date? That's what LDAP is for. Unfortunately, there is no standard way of using LDAP across multiple business systems. The few systems that make use of LDAP for customer data are either very expensive to deploy and implement, or limited in functionality. If you find a better quote generation tool for your particular industry, for example, you can't necessarily access contact information you've already stored in your accounting system. Managing contacts in your client or partner businesses is a completely different problem than managing user accounts on your LAN.

Synchronizing Your Contact Information

Now that we've seen some of the different systems that use address books, let's take a look at how you can keep them synchronized. If you have a PDA, you probably received software with it that synchronizes it with a desktop PIM. Palm OS PDAs come with the Palm Desktop, and often conduits for synchronizing with Outlook. There are a lot of third party utilities that allow you to synchronize PDAs with all sorts of different programs. Some even synchronize your contacts with a directory on the Web.

PDAs rely on synchronization for their basic functionality, so the vast majority of synchronization programs are designed for them. A few programs are capable of synchronizing several devices at once, including multiple address book programs. A proprietary program that can do this in Windows is Intellisync®, from Pumatech (*http://www.pumatech.com/is_desktop_main.html*).

With the advent of address books in cell phones, it's quite convenient to be able to copy the phone numbers of your contacts onto your phone. Due to a proliferation of different devices with different software, a standard called SyncML has emerged for exchanging contact and calendar data. Pumatech is one of the leaders in creating synchronization tools based on SyncML, including a centralized server.

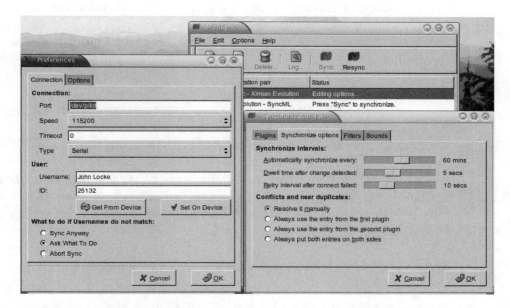

FIGURE 7.2 Configuring Multisync to synchronize Palm Pilot data with Ximian Evolution.

A new open source project called Multisync (*http://multisync.sourceforge.net/*) provides similar functionality on Linux systems (Figure 7.2). With Multisync, you can synchronize contacts, calendar events, and task lists between Ximian Evolution, Pocket PCs, Palm OS PDAs, a variety of cell phones, and other computers using SyncML. It can also synchronize with an LDAP directory, and, being open source, you can develop plug-ins for custom databases or other systems.

Managing Sales Calls

Most small businesses need a good CRM system. Sales are the life blood of any business, and paying attention to your customers can help improve your sales. A CRM system helps you remember details about each of your prospective customers, and reminds you when it's time to give them a call.

There are a lot of open source CRM programs, but most of them are designed to support a help desk in a reactive capacity—they keep track of open issues and customer incidents, helping you respond to something initiated by a customer. Few open source systems help you track prospective customers, mailings, and phone calls you initiate.

Of the few that exist, most of them are parts of much larger Enterprise Resource Planning software packages, which are used to integrate many different systems. We'll be looking at these tools more closely in Chapter 12. For a standalone open source CRM system, there are only a handful. Let's take a quick look at a few of them:

- Gnubis (*http://gnubis.sourceforge.net*)
- Customer Touch CRM (*http://sourceforge.net/projects/customer-touch/*)
- GuanxiCRM (*http://www.guanxicrm.com*)
- Anteil/Retriever CRM (*http://opensourcesmall.biz/crm/*)

All of these are Web-based systems, using the LAMP platform we talked about in Chapter 6 (Linux, Apache, MySQL, and PHP/Perl). Several promising CRM systems have disappeared since the tech bubble, but these are left. Let's take a closer look at each one.

Spartan Contact Management with Gnubis

Gnubis (*http://gnubis.sourceforge.net*) is basic and functional. It uses a template system that's very easy to customize and integrate into your existing internal Web sites. But it is perhaps too sparse. There is no easy way to see what calls you need to make, and using it seems a bit awkward.

Gnubis is a framework being developed by a Brazilian company, PHPerl. Contact management is one part of the system—there's also a project management component and a clipping tool. Its simplicity makes it extremely easy to customize if you have special needs.

Reach Out with Customer Touch CRM

Open source CRM software seems to have a big international following, and relatively light participation of North Americans. Perhaps tools like ACT! have gained such a strong foothold in North America that nobody has spent the time to get a good system working. In other parts of the world, where the costs of American proprietary software can put such systems financially out of reach, open source systems have a much stronger foothold.

One such system is Customer Touch CRM (*http://sourceforge.net/projects/ customer-touch/*). This appears to be a fairly complete sales management package, but even though it has an English version, and there are a number of other languages available, much of the text is in Italian, making it difficult for North American users to figure out. Once the language issues and a few browser compatibility issues have been worked out, Customer Touch CRM is worth trying out.

Saving Face with GuanxiCRM

Another reason basic packages like ACT! have not gained a foothold overseas, besides price, is culture. Business culture varies in different countries and regions. The Chinese concept of *guanxi* is perhaps the biggest difference between doing business in east Asia and North America. Guanxi essentially refers to a network of relationships. You build guanxi by doing favors for people and being trustworthy. There is an element of reciprocity associated with guanxi, an understanding that the more favors you do, the more you are owed, and the more ability you have to succeed in your business.

GuanxiCRM (*http://www.guanxicrm.com*) acknowledges the concept of guanxi, providing a tool to help you manage not just your customer contacts, but also your reputation. GuanxiCRM is a fork of the Relata project, an earlier open source CRM project that is no longer available. In true open source fashion, GuanxiCRM took an existing open source project and modified it to make it work for a different group of people. As a result, it's one of the most successful CRM projects available.

SMALL BUSINESS CRM: RETRIEVER CRM

For small business use, one of the biggest needs is to be able to quickly see who you need to call today. One open source package gives you your list of action items right when you log in. While trying out demos of all available open source CRM projects, the author was most impressed with a CRM system called Anteil.

Anteil (*http://www.anteil.com*) was released as an open source system under the GPL in 2001. Unlike most open source projects, however, there was no community supporting it. It's apparently a program developed by a single consulting company, who customizes and implements it for a variety of clients (see Figure 7.3).

However, development of the publicly available version of Anteil appears to have halted, and the company is unresponsive to requests for more information. Very little help is available, unless you're willing to pay for support.

Because Anteil seems like the most effective open source CRM system for small businesses available in early 2004, the author of this book has created a fork of the Anteil project, calling it Retriever CRM. It's available on the Web site for this book at *http://opensourcesmall.biz/crm*. So here's an example of open source in action—with a big void of available systems, the author is taking the best one available, and building a community around it.

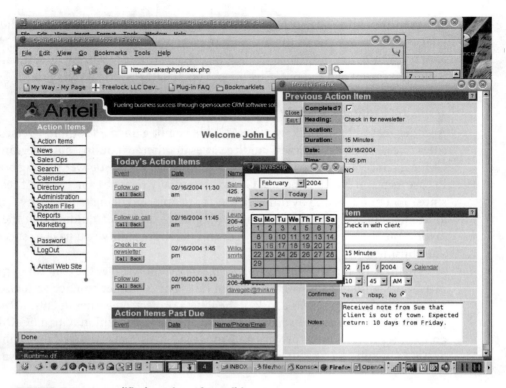

FIGURE 7.3 A modified version of Anteil in use.

At this writing, Retriever CRM provides a very basic contact management system, with a few nice features. You can easily see your action items and sales opportunities, quickly mark action items as completed and simultaneously schedule the next action item for the opportunity, and assign opportunities to other people in your business. Check the Web site for current versions, and to find out how to implement it on your system.

In the future, this project will support keeping address information in an LDAP directory, providing a universal interface for managing your sales contacts inside the directory. It will also integrate with some sort of calendaring service, allowing you to see your appointments in whatever PIM tool you choose to use.

USING A DIRECTORY

The stated goal of many CRM systems is to make your operations *customer-centric*. In other words, you have all the information about a particular client in a single place. LDAP directories are designed to store information about people, doing a particularly good job with data that is read often but written rarely. Most LDAP implementations are used for organizational directories, with a focus on authenticating users. So far only large companies or particularly tech-savvy companies have any centralized management of customer information that is used by CRM systems, billing systems, and email.

The problem is primarily that nobody has defined the problem in small business terms, or developed the tools to make it easy to use. There are a number of administration tools for LDAP, and a few Web applications. Many email programs can look up email addresses from an LDAP database, but, as of December 2003, only one writes contact information to an LDAP directory: Ximian Evolution. We took a brief look at Evolution in Chapter 4. It's an email program and PIM for Linux that provides very similar functionality to Microsoft Outlook.

An open source Web application designed for storing contact information in a Web database is the Rolodap project, at *http://rolodap.sourceforge.net/*. This program can provide access to the same customer data as Evolution.

SUMMARY

Most of the business systems discussed in this book are isolated, individual systems that don't necessarily share much common information among each other. A first step towards streamlining computing systems is to use an effective standard storage system.

Unfortunately, these systems are not yet well enough developed to be able to say much about them here. The only good comprehensive systems of this nature at this writing are expensive proprietary systems, well out of the budget of small businesses. Check the Web site for this book for more recent news at *http://opensourcesmall.biz/crm*, and in the meantime, you'll have to choose the best existing systems you can for each task, and synchronize them as necessary.

In this chapter, we've explored strategies for managing address books, contact lists, and sales calls. We looked at traditional systems, as well as the types of software people have developed. We looked at issues of keeping multiple address books synchronized, and tickler systems for reminding you when it's time to call a contact. Finally, we took a brief look at directory servers. For small business use, there isn't any open source client software that matches the features provided by ACT! and GoldMine, but there are a few good Web application options.

Next, we'll take a closer look at the other parts of Personal Information Management: calendars, appointments, and tasks.

CUSTOMER RELATIONSHIP MANAGEMENT REFERENCES

An updated list of resources for this chapter is on the Web site for the book at *http://opensourcesmall.biz/crm*.

Software

Intellisync, commercial synchronization software from Pumatech *http://www.pumatech.com/is_desktop_main.html*

Multisync, open source synchronization software for Linux *http://multisync.sourceforge.net*

Jpilot, open source PIM software for Linux *http://www.jpilot.org*

Rolodap, open source LDAP-based address book manager *http://rolodap.sourceforge.net/*

OpenLDAP, open source LDAP server *http://www.openldap.org*

Ximian Evolution, open source PIM software *http://www.ximian.com/products/evolution/*

ACT!, commercial CRM desktop software *http://www.act.com*

GoldMine, commercial CRM desktop software *http://www.frontrange.com/goldmine/*

Gnubis, open source Web-based CRM software *http://gnubis.sourceforge.net*

Customer-touch, open source Web-based CRM software *http://www.sourceforge.net/projects/customer-touch*

Guanxi CRM, open source Web-based CRM software *http://www.guanxicrm.com*

Retriever CRM, open source Web-based CRM software *http://opensourcesmall.biz/crm*

Web Sites

Palm, Inc. *http://www.palm.com*

Apple iPod *http://www.apple.com/ipod/*

PocketPC *http://www.microsoft.com/windowsmobile/products/pocketpc/default.mspx*

Zaurus handheld information *http://www.myzaurus.com/*

8 Calendar and Schedule Management

In This Chapter

- Introduction
- Using Calendars
- Calendar Tools
- Summary
- Calendaring References

INTRODUCTION

What do you do with your time? How do you know when to set an appointment? How do you schedule a project, or arrange a meeting? When do you have to pay your taxes, or get the payroll in? We use calendars for all kinds of activities every day. People use different types of calendars for different types of events. Calendars are the main ingredient in time management, and they're essential for any type of planning.

This chapter is not technical.

Using a computer-based calendar provides two primary benefits:

- Portability—depending on how you set up your calendar, it may be easier to access from multiple locations than a paper-based calendar.
- Communicating with others—by having your calendar online, others can see when you're available for appointments, or manage your calendar for you.

To address the first concern, many people carry a day planner containing all of their appointments. But like managing your addresses, more and more calendar information is being exchanged online, and keeping a separate paper appointment book takes more effort. Coordinating schedules is much easier when you can exchange information over the Web or email.

Closely related to a calendar is the task list. While a task list may seem quite different, tasks or to-do items are simply calendar events not associated with a specific time. Most software that allows you to create a calendar also provides a task list. The underlying computer standard for a calendar event describes task items as well.

People use calendars for four main reasons:

1. Personal time management
2. Scheduling appointments
3. Reserving resources
4. Managing projects

In this chapter, we'll take a closer look at these main functions of a calendar, discuss how to manage calendars on a computer, and examine some current calendaring tools.

Personal Time Management

Read any marketing case study and chances are, it will illustrate how much time you'll save by using the product it describes. Saving time is a key motivator, perhaps because we feel we never have enough of it. We go to time management seminars to learn how to get more done with our time. Meanwhile, we cram more stuff to do into our schedules.

The human brain isn't wired to remember all these things we need to do. We need help. We need tools like calendars and task lists, or we lose track of what needs to be done. We need a place to put this stuff so we'll remember to do them later. We need to know when our next dental appointment is, what time we set to meet the advertising sales rep for the local newspaper, and when we need to sign and mail the tax return.

Somehow we develop systems to keep track of these details, or else we wouldn't accomplish them. You can spend hundreds of dollars going to time management seminars, but all of them tell you the same basic thing: identify what your priorities are, make sure you get those things done, and don't worry about the rest.

Every task takes time to complete. Here's one time management strategy in a nutshell:

1. Use some sort of tool to capture everything you need to get done as soon as you think of them. Whether it's a small notebook, a voice recorder, or some other tool, carry it with you and record each task so you don't forget it later.

2. On a daily basis, move everything out of your capture tool or list, putting it either on your calendar to accomplish at a particular time, or onto a list of tasks you don't have time for now.
3. On a weekly basis, go through your task list to see what you can add to your calendar.
4. To achieve better piece of mind, keep another list of back-burner items—things you want to do someday, but don't foresee being able to schedule in the near term. Keep your main task list short enough to go through weekly, and move everything else to this *mañana* task list.

This is but one systematic approach to managing your tasks and time, one the author has found particularly effective.

The key to the effectiveness of any time management strategy is that you use it. The more complicated your system, the more difficult it will be to use, the less likely you'll stick with it. Inevitably you'll end up with multiple lists—each larger project will likely have a series of individual tasks to accomplish, and you won't necessarily clutter your personal agenda with these.

Carry Your Calendar with You

When you're a small business owner, you're always doing business development. Wherever you go, you usually have business on your mind. Before you can set up any appointments, you need to be sure you're not already booked. Carry your calendar with you, and you'll be able to make an appointment on the spot.

One of the killer features of a Personal Digital Assistant (PDA) is the ability to carry your calendar with you wherever you go, and synchronize it to a calendar on your desktop. If you keep all your appointments and tasks in a calendar application on your desktop, you can keep a synchronized copy on your PDA, giving you the ability to schedule a meeting on the fly, wherever you are. As long as you've recently synchronized, you can be confident that you don't have a conflict.

Of course, you can carry a paper calendar, too. The problem is, your paper calendar can only be in one place at a time. With some sort of online calendar, you can share your schedule—or at least the times you're available—with other people inside or outside of your company. This can make it easier for your colleagues to set up appointments or see when you're planning to accomplish particular tasks without having to interrupt you.

Subscribe to Event Calendars

Another benefit of keeping your calendar online is that you can more easily manage multiple calendars. Several calendar programs allow you to subscribe to an individual event calendar, to help you manage your personal schedule around other events. Most calendar programs can at least import events, meetings, and appointments. People using larger corporate systems have the infrastructure in place and use calendaring tools extensively to coordinate their efforts. Coordinating with external companies through the Internet is not yet widely done—but the standards are in place and programs are beginning to support it.

It's now possible with some calendar software to create and subscribe to a bunch of different calendars. You might have a different calendar for:

- Personal appointments and tasks
- Company events and meetings
- Booking the company's digital projector
- Company holidays
- Your daughter's soccer schedule
- Birthdays and anniversaries
- Your favorite baseball team's season schedule.

By organizing events into different calendars, you can share them more easily with people interested in those events.

Scheduling Appointments

One of the biggest reasons to put your schedule online is to simplify the task of creating appointments. It's much easier to see when somebody has free time on a calendar than to find out verbally. You can line up several calendars at once to find a time everyone has free for a meeting. You can publish company events where everyone can see them coming in their own schedules.

Free/Busy Information

Corporate calendaring systems have long made it possible to exchange information on your personal calendar with others within your organization. Some programs allow you to post your free/busy information to a Web site with public access. You can then add the URL for your free/busy information to a vCard, a standardized address format, and email it to your correspondents. If your contacts use software that recognizes free/busy information, they can see when you're available by attempting to set up an appointment with you.

Share Your Schedule

Beyond your free/busy information, you can also share the details of your calendar. In most cases, you probably don't want to share your calendar outside your company. But if you're always on the run, it may be helpful to have somebody at the office manage your schedule. You may want other people in your company to be able to see who you're meeting with when. Most calendar software allows you to mark particular events as private or confidential, so you can schedule your doctor appointments or ball games without it becoming public knowledge.

Reserving Resources

If you have some limited resource that many people want to use in your company, you can create a calendar for it. Most companies that have a meeting room use a calendar to manage it. You might use a calendar for a digital projector or a compressor or a company car. You might want to set up a resource calendar managed by a single person, or allow anyone in your company to reserve items first-come first-served.

Managing Projects

The other main use of a calendar is for project management. We're going to take a closer look at project management software in Chapter 11, but calendars are an important part. You will probably want to integrate your project schedule into your personal calendar. There are several different ways calendars are used in project management:

- Allocating people and resources to a project
- Scheduling shifts
- Creating a project timeline

Allocating People and Resources

Depending on the type of work your company does, you might find having a calendar for each person, or for each team, to be an effective way to schedule your work. The nature of your projects generally dictates the best way to manage them.

Is it better to manage a calendar for each employee, or for each project? If you have big projects and people with specialized roles, you're probably going to need to do both. Systems that provide unified scheduling but allow you to view schedules by project or by person are a bit more sophisticated than the types of calendars we discuss in this chapter.

On the other hand, if your projects are short, you may find it easiest to simply schedule each job on the appropriate person's calendar. You can then use some calendaring tools to pull up everybody's schedule at once, to see when you can fit a new job in.

Scheduling Shifts

Businesses that have a retail presence, or otherwise need to cover particular hours of operation with employees, have quite different needs than project-oriented businesses. To schedule shifts, you create a calendar and specify how many people of each role need to be scheduled for each time period. Then you go through your pool of employees and start assigning shifts to people. On paper, this is a time-consuming process, and it can be quite difficult to accommodate special requests of your employees.

Shift scheduling software eases this process enormously. You might set up an employee-only Web site and have people sign up for shifts themselves. As a schedule administrator, you can arbitrate and have the final say about who works when. But think of the time saved by the shift administrator, and the increase of satisfaction each employee has when they feel like they're choosing when they work. We discuss shift scheduling software in greater detail in Chapter 11.

Creating a Project Timeline

If your business has big projects, you'll need to create a timeline for them, with major milestones identified and people and resources allocated to each project. In this case, project management software provides the best set of tools for the job. But if you only manage one project at a time, you can still get by with a simple calendar for the job. Even if you use project management software to help schedule your project, you might want to create a project calendar to serve as a reminder for payment dates, meetings, and key milestones, especially if you find that you're already using calendar software for other tasks.

USING CALENDARS

Now that we've seen different reasons people use calendars, let's take a look at how you might actually use a computer-based calendar. Let's take a closer look at these tasks:

- Manage your tasks
- Set up a meeting
- Publish your free/busy information
- Publish an event calendar

Manage Your Schedule

For decades, people have used small appointment books such as the Filofax, or pocket calendars to help manage their days. Keeping everything in one place makes it possible to easily see what you need to get done any given day, who you need to meet, and where you need to be. Nearly all calendaring software helps you do the same thing. Whether you choose a Web calendar, a PIM program, or a special calendar application, you can add your own appointments, write down tasks you need to accomplish, and record upcoming events. Most calendar software also includes task lists not associated with any particular day.

Managing your schedule works the same way on a computer as it does on paper. If you're going to use an online calendar, choose one that fits the nature of your workday. If you travel often, use something that synchronizes to a PDA. If you find yourself in front of multiple computers connected to the Internet, a Web-based calendar may be the way to go. You can generally do anything on an online calendar that you can on paper—but it can be much easier to reschedule something online than have to rewrite the event on a different day. Other reasons to use a computer-based calendar are much more compelling.

Set Up a Meeting

You need to set up a meeting with a partner. You open up your personal information management (PIM) program and create a new meeting request. You add the people you need to meet with to the request, and go to the Scheduling tab to find a time that everybody is free. Figure 8.1 shows the Scheduling tab in a meeting request in Ximian Evolution.

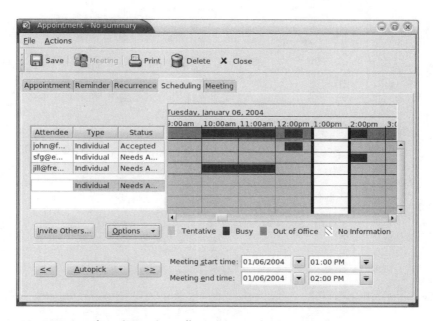

FIGURE 8.1 Choosing a time all participants have available.

Your contacts have already sent you their *vCard*, a virtual business card that includes a URL for their free/busy information. Your PIM program looks up everybody's free/busy information, and adds it to a graph. An Autopick button finds the next time slot that everyone is available. You type up a summary for the meeting request, click Save, and it's saved to your calendar and sent to the meeting participants.

When you receive a meeting request, you can choose how you want to respond. When you accept a meeting invitation, your PIM software automatically adds the meeting to your calendar and replies to the meeting organizer. Figure 8.2 shows a meeting request in Evolution.

Meeting requests use Internet standards, so they work between any two programs that support the standards. Only a handful of programs integrate calendars with email, however, so if meeting requests are something you do often, you'll want to use one of these programs. Programs that support meeting requests include: Ximian Evolution, Microsoft Outlook, Lotus Notes, and KDE Kontact.

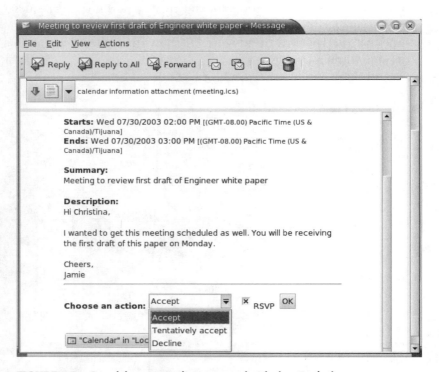

FIGURE 8.2 Receiving a meeting request in Ximian Evolution.

Publish Free/Busy Information

While scheduling a meeting, for other people to be able to see when you're free, you need to publish your free/busy information. If you use a corporate-style groupware server, everybody on the server automatically has access to your free/busy information. To allow people outside your company to see free/busy information, or if you don't run a calendar server, you can post a free/busy file on a WebDAV server anywhere.

We discussed setting up a WebDAV server in Chapter 6. WebDAV is a Web protocol supported by Apache and other Web servers. At this writing, only Microsoft Outlook can automatically post your free/busy server. By the time this book is in print, current versions of Ximian Evolution may be able to do the same. For now, Evolution and Korganizer can email free/busy files to people of your choosing—but most recipients can't do anything with them. It is possible to set up a special email address that runs a script to post your free/busy information to a Web server, if you're determined enough.

Once you have a Web location for your free/busy information, add it to your vCard, and distribute it to your colleagues. You create an address book entry for yourself using a PIM program that supports meeting requests. Somewhere on the card you'll find a place to put the URL for your free/busy information. It may be on a *collaboration* tab. You can usually configure your email software to automatically attach your vCard as a signature for the message.

Publish an Event Calendar

When you post your free/busy information, you're posting just that—when you're free, and when you're busy. The free/busy file contains no information about the events on your calendar. If your company works closely on projects, you may want to post your personal schedule somewhere where the rest of the company can see it. You probably don't want to publish your personal calendar to the general public. You might want to post an event calendar for your company, though, containing your business hours, your holidays, any speaking engagements you have, or other events of interest.

The procedure for posting any calendar is the same. If you want to post a private calendar for your company only, you put it on an internal server without public access, or use a password-protected directory. Public calendars you put on a public Web site somewhere.

Posting a calendar under the hood is exactly the same as posting your free/busy information—it's just that the file you post contains more details. Most existing PIM software supports posting either your free/busy information, or an event calendar—but not both. By the time this book is published, however, Ximian Evolution should be capable of both.

Apple Computers popularized the whole notion of calendar sharing with an application called iCal®, included in Mac OS X. With iCal, you can view multiple calendars, post new events to whichever calendar you have write access to, and share these calendars by posting to a public Web site. The Mozilla project has developed a program called Mozilla Calendar that does essentially the same thing, but is available for Windows, Linux, and the Mac.

Most Web calendars are also publicly viewable and available, and a few even use the same underlying file as iCal and Mozilla Calendar. Right now calendar sharing is only beginning to be discovered—by the time you read this, software support will probably be ubiquitous.

CALENDAR TOOLS

As you can probably tell from our discussion so far, there are many different calendar tools, and a wide range of features they support. Most have some capability for sharing particular events or entire calendars with your colleagues. We can group these generally into four different types of programs:

1. Calendar-only applications, client applications that run on your computer that can access multiple calendars.
2. Web Calendars, calendar-only applications that can be the easiest way to coordinate a group.
3. Personal Information Management (PIM) software, programs that integrate calendars with email and your address book. These programs handle meeting requests.
4. Groupware Servers, major server applications that make PIM functions available to your entire company. These servers generally provide Web access to all of their functionality, or can be used from PIM software.

Each of these categories has its own strengths. A few applications cross these boundaries, giving you all of the benefits of each type if you run the requisite software. Table 8.1 shows some of the features and benefits of some specific calendaring programs.

TABLE 8.1 Features of Different Calendar and Schedule Management Tools

Program	Synch to PDA	Share Calendar	Multiple Calendars	Send Meeting Requests	Look Up Free/Busy	Publish Free/Busy	Native Storage Format	Open Source	Platform
Calendar-Only Software									
Apple iCal	Yes	Yes	Yes	Yes	No	No	ICalendar files	No	Mac OS X
Mozilla Calendar	No	Yes	Yes	No	No	No	ICalendar files	Yes	Windows, Mac, Linux
Palm Desktop	Yes	No	No	No	No	No	Proprietary DB format—can import/export vCalendar	No	Windows, Mac
JPilot	Yes	No	No	No	No	No	Palm DB format	Yes	Linux
Web Calendars									
WebCalendar	One-way (download to Palm)	Yes	Yes	Yes (non-standard)	No	No	Database	Yes	ODBC/PHP/Apache, any Web browser
PhpICalendar	One-way (Upload to site)	Yes	Yes	No	No	No	ICalendar files	Yes	PHP/Apache, any Web browser
PHPGroupWare	No	Yes	No	Yes	Yes (within group)	Yes (within group)	Database	Yes	Apache/Mysql/PHP, any Web browser
Yahoo! Calendar	Yes (Windows only)	Yes	Yes	No	No	No	Proprietary	No	Any Web browser
Personal Information Management (PIM) Programs									
Microsoft Outlook	Yes	No	No	Yes	Yes	Yes	Proprietary database	No	Windows
Lotus Notes	Yes	No	No	Yes	Yes	Yes	Proprietary database	No	Windows/Mac
Kontact/Korganizer	Yes	No	No	Yes	No	No	ICalendar files	Yes	. Linux/KDE
Ximian Evolution	Yes	Version 2.0	Version 2.0	Yes	Yes	Version 2.0	ICalendar files	Yes	Linux/GNOME
Groupware Servers									
JiCal/WebDAV	No	Yes	Yes	No	No	Yes	ICalendar files	Yes	Java/Apache
Kolab Server	Yes	Yes	No	Yes	Yes	Yes	ICalendar files	Yes	Linux/KDE
Exchange	Yes	Yes	No	Yes	Yes	Yes	Proprietary database	No	Windows
OpenGroupware.org	Yes	Yes		Yes	Yes	Yes	Database	Yes	LInux

Calendar-Only Applications

Calendar-only applications run on your computer, not requiring any network connection to operate. They're all you need for basic time management and scheduling. The software services we discuss in this section do not necessarily integrate with email—while most of them can send meeting requests, few can receive them. These programs generally support sharing your calendar with others, but don't support the more private free/busy types of information. So you can publish your schedule, but not a generic outline of what times you have available.

Without an email component, meeting requests pose a particular challenge. It's relatively easy to have your calendar application attach a meeting request to an email in your default browser—but without integration to your address book, you have to figure out for yourself when the recipient is available. Receiving an invitation is also tricky—if your email client and calendar software isn't integrated, you need to manually transfer the message to your calendar. At best, you'll be able to open a meeting request and have the meeting imported to your calendar. You'll have to write your own mail to confirm that you'll be there. On the other hand, some of these programs excel at putting together group schedules and integrating calendars for different types of activities into one big-picture view.

Apple iCal and Mozilla Calendar

iCal, from Apple computer, is a new calendar management tool that brought easy calendar management to Mac OS X users. Its strength is managing and sharing multiple calendars. You can create separate calendars for anything you want, publish individual calendars to any WebDAV server you have available, and subscribe to other public calendars. As long as the calendar you want to view is in iCalendar format, you'll be able to open it in iCal and see its events.

You can also send meeting requests from iCal. While you can easily share calendars with iCal, it doesn't appear to have a concept of free/busy time. So while you can hide the nature of particular events by making them private, you can't necessarily just publish or view the time you have available.

While Apple iCal made multiple calendars popular, Mozilla Calendar brings almost exactly the same features and benefits to people running other platforms. Mozilla Calendar is an extension of the Mozilla platform, integrating into Mozilla 1.5 and later, or into Thunderbird and Firebird. At this writing, Apple iCal synchronizes with PDAs and can send meeting requests. While these features are planned for Mozilla Calendar, they are not yet available.

Palm Desktop and Jpilot

For carrying your calendar with you, nothing beats a PDA. Unfortunately, at this point most PDA software doesn't work well with multiple calendars. About the best you can do is import a calendar file from another program into a desktop PIM for your PDA.

For Palm-based PDAs, the Palm Desktop software is the standard PIM for Windows and Macs. For Linux, the open source Jpilot program fills the same role. These programs manipulate data in the native Palm database formats, providing a basic date book, address book, notes, and a task list. For managing your time, these programs are great. But they lack integration with email. You can't send or receive meeting requests, or work with multiple calendars.

Palm Desktop is one of the few calendar programs that doesn't support the iCalendar standard—it only supports the older vCalendar format, making it harder to share events between programs. However, you can export vCalendar files from many other calendars, and import them into the Palm software.

Jpilot supports both vCalendar and iCalendar, and has some great plug-ins for other Palm programs, providing access to an open source encrypted password manager called Keyring (*http://gnukeyring.sourceforge.net*), a secondary task list called Mañana by Bill Sexton (*http://bill.sexton.tripod.com/*), and synchronization to the AvantGo service to read stories syndicated on the Web.

You can, of course, synchronize your PDA to other applications, provided the application has support for the type of PDA you use. See the PIM section below for other applications commonly used with PDAs. Palm Desktop and Jpilot don't support email—they're basically desktop tools for a Palm-based PDA. And if your requirements are modest, they may be all you need.

Web Calendars

Like many applications in this book, calendars stored on the Web benefit from easy access from any networked computer, better ability to collaborate with other people in your group, and the promise of integration into other systems. There are dozens of Web calendar systems available, each with a different set of strengths and weaknesses. Some are compatible with the iCalendar standard, making it possible to view the same events on a Web site and in a calendar program. Others support vCalendar for easier importing to PDAs. Some focus on scheduling shifts to cover a retail floor, or helping a group work together to achieve a goal. A few are dedicated to scheduling resources such as classrooms or meeting areas.

Because of the plethora of open source Web calendars available for all sorts of different purposes, there's little need to even consider a proprietary solution. The Web calendars we consider here are good ones to meet each of these primary purposes. Shift scheduling and project management Web calendars are covered in Chapter 11.

WebCalendar

WebCalendar (*http://webcalendar.sourceforge.net*) is one of the best calendar applications available for managing group schedules. It runs on Apache/MySQL/PHP, so if you've set up a Web server as described in Chapter 6, installing WebCalendar is straightforward. For a team of office workers who need to have a common scheduling system, WebCalendar provides some powerful features in an easy-to-install package. It also might work well for people who mostly work away from computers, or have to share a workstation with others.

With WebCalendar, each user can have his own calendar. You can set it up so that people in your organization can see each other's calendars, overlaying multiple calendars over their own to find an available time to schedule a meeting. You can set up event calendars, schedule your resources, set up calendars for particular work crews, and delegate control over your personal calendar to an assistant. WebCalendar is a full-fledged, feature-packed calendaring system that anyone can access from any Web browser.

The downside is integration. While you can import and export to the iCalendar standard, and import and export to Palm devices, there is no easy way to synchronize and use your WebCalendar system with other devices.

PHPiCalendar

PHPiCalendar, on the other hand, works best in conjunction with another calendar program. PHPiCalendar provides easy-to-navigate views of standard iCalendar files. It doesn't provide any way to edit them, though. As we've already seen, you can make these using Apple iCal or Mozilla Calendar. You can also create iCalendar files in Ximian Evolution, and export them from a wide variety of calendar programs.

Rather than being a standalone application, PHPiCalendar is a viewer that makes your calendars available in any Web browser. It's a great complement to another standards-based calendaring system.

phpGroupWare

phpGroupWare is a Web-based "groupware" system that combines a Web calendar, email, address book, and task list in an extendable framework. You can plug in other modules to perform all kinds of other tasks, including accounting, project management, file sharing, content management, and a few others. The Web calendar functionality is derived directly from an older version of WebCalendar. If you want to set up a single Web site to manage all of your internal processes, php-GroupWare is a good project to check out. It's in fairly active development, and is quickly becoming a good overall system.

Its biggest drawback, like WebCalendar, is that it's a self-contained system that doesn't interact well with other software. It's possible, but cumbersome, to import and export data. You can't plug a standalone email client or calendar program into it and have it work well.

Yahoo!® Calendar

Another option is to use a hosted service such as Yahoo! You can host multiple calendars for you and your group, share them or keep them private, and do most of the things you can do with WebCalendar, without needing your own Web server.

The drawbacks to using Yahoo! include:

- Lack of interoperability with other calendar software
- Support by advertising—you either have to pay a subscription fee, or put up with ads
- Trusting a third party—as a public service, unknown people may have access to your schedule

On the other hand, you can set up a Yahoo! calendar for free, simply by signing up. Like the other Web applications, all you need to access your calendar is a Web browser.

PIM Applications

Another category of calendar applications is called Personal Information Management (PIM) programs. The goal of these programs is to provide all the information you need in one place, including calendars, task lists, notes, email, and address books.

Palm Desktop and Jpilot were discussed in the calendar-only section above, even though they're PIM software. What those programs lack is an email component. The main benefit of tying email software to a calendar application is the ease of scheduling meetings.

The PIM programs here can either be standalone PIM programs, or serve as the client applications for a groupware server. Groupware servers provide free/busy information for people in your organization along with a corporate address book. When you use these PIM programs by themselves, the available features differ substantially. PIM software seems to be very specific to the desktop management platform. Each of these full-featured PIM programs tends to be released for only one or two operating systems.

Microsoft Outlook

Microsoft Outlook, at the time of writing, is one of the most commonly used PIM applications in the world. By bundling it with the Office suite, Microsoft has made Outlook ubiquitous. It's considered by many to be the standard for integrating email, your calendar, tasks, address books, and notes in one place. It also includes a journaling feature for keeping track of how you spend your time. However, the ubiquitous nature of Outlook makes it a common target for many viruses and worms, which is perhaps the biggest drawback to using Outlook.

In 2003, Outlook is the only program in the bunch that can automatically publish free/busy information to your Web server. If you publish your free/busy information and send a vCard with the URL, others can schedule meetings around your existing free/busy information. Outlook also handles meeting requests well: adding them to your calendar, responding to requests, and keeping track of who has responded to your requests.

You cannot subscribe to multiple calendars with Outlook, though you can view other people's free/busy information. If you use a groupware server, you can also view other people's calendars by adding them to a meeting request. You can delegate management of your calendar to an assistant. Versions of Outlook before Outlook 2002 only understood the older vCalendar standard, not iCalendar. Outlook is available for Windows only. Microsoft sells a similar PIM program for the Mac called Entourage®.

Lotus Notes

Lotus Notes was perhaps the first widely used PIM program. You may still find companies using Lotus Notes, and if you already have it working for you, it may continue to be a compelling choice. The main thing Lotus Notes provides over the rest of the programs is integration with other documents. You can manage a fairly integrated view of everything, relating documents and email easily with calendar events.

By itself, Notes doesn't do much more than any other PIM, and with the number of other choices available, there isn't really a compelling reason to choose it over the other options. Lotus Notes is available for Windows and Mac.

A Loose Alliance of Small Programs: Kontact

Kontact is a brand new open source project by the KDE team. KDE is one of the two major desktop environments for Linux, and the KDE project includes a bunch of different programs that all begin with the letter "K." KOrganizer is the KDE calendar program, a full-featured calendar and task list application.

By itself, KOrganizer can only read one calendar at a time, but it can open calendars stored anywhere. KOrganizer can send meeting requests, but by itself doesn't receive them and cannot look up free/busy time. It can import and export several different calendar formats. It synchronizes with your PDA.

Kontact combines KOrganizer with Kmail, Kaddressbook, and Knotes to create an integrated PIM application. Some features, such as sharing free/busy information and properly handling meeting requests, only work if you use the Kolab groupware server in the back end.

Small Business Calendaring: Ximian Evolution

Ximian Evolution in its early versions looks very much like Microsoft Outlook, with a surprisingly similar feature set. At this writing, Evolution 2.0 is in development, and taking PIM applications in a new direction.

In version 1.4, Evolution provides very similar calendar features as Outlook, with two disadvantages:

- You can't easily create calendar events from tasks or emails.
- It doesn't automatically post your free/busy times to a Web server.

At this writing, the GNOME project has offered bounties on particular features for Evolution. Much like bounty hunters in the American Wild West, you can collect a bounty for being the one to deliver the requested feature. Open source projects use all sorts of motivations to get projects running—setting a bounty creates competition, provides monetary incentive, and gives the project a sense of fun.

In any case, if these bounties are collected, Evolution will have a lot more calendar features by the time this book is published. In Evolution 2.0, you should be able to manage multiple calendars, update, share, and subscribe to calendars published on a Web server, schedule meetings, delegate calendars, look up and publish free/busy information, and do just about everything you can do with any other software in this chapter. And you can do it without even needing a groupware server.

Evolution is a GNOME application, meaning it only runs in Linux. You can run Evolution using the KDE desktop manager, as long as you have the GNOME libraries installed. You'll be able to publish calendars to Web servers along with the PHPiCalendar application right from Evolution, and share specific calendars with Apple iCal and Mozilla Calendar users, and anybody else with a Web browser.

Calendar/Groupware Servers

Most large companies use some sort of groupware server to provide centralized administration for all of their employees. These groupware servers store email, interact with the corporate directory, and manage individual and resource calendars.

When you use a groupware server, all of your information is stored on the server. This means you can log in from multiple computers and see the same information. Instead of having everything in your PIM client, keeping it on the server means you can lose your laptop and not have to restore a backup. It makes setting up new users trivially easy. Finally, it makes scheduling meetings supported automatically throughout your company.

For small businesses, the administrative costs of a groupware server may outweigh the benefits you gain from them. If you find yourself supporting hundreds or thousands of users, you'll want to use a groupware server. For a smaller company, it's probably overkill, especially when you can use options like Ximian Evolution for active computer users, or WebCalendar to manage non-computerized teams. Still, let's take a brief look at some of the groupware servers.

Microsoft Exchange

Exchange is the groupware server for Outlook. It's primarily an email server, providing storage for calendar events, tasks, and other items using the same basic database as email. Exchange uses a proprietary protocol for access called MAPI, and only a handful of clients work with it:

- Microsoft Outlook, for Windows
- Microsoft Entourage, for Macintosh
- Ximian Evolution, with proprietary Exchange Connector, for Linux

You can access an Exchange server using IMAP, but this only provides access to email, not calendar events. You can also use a Web browser to log into the included Outlook Web Access interface. Exchange runs only on Windows servers.

Lotus Domino

Domino is a database server, and the back end for Lotus Notes. Domino can run on Windows servers and several flavors of Unix, including Linux. Domino has a reputation for stability and scalability, and together with Notes, provides an interesting way of storing and organizing all of your documents and personal information.

The downside is cost. With the open source groupware packages quickly developing, you may find the features you need at a fraction of the cost of Domino. Still, if you're looking for the most complete set of features, Domino with Notes is a strong contender.

Kolab Server

Like the client Kontact project, Kolab Server is a KDE project that combines a bunch of other programs under a single integrated package. Kolab combines an email server, a directory server, a Web server, and a common authentication framework into a single installation. For email, Kolab uses Postfix (discussed in Chapter 5) and the Cyrus IMAP server. Cyrus is a bit more difficult to administer than Courier-IMAP, but it can handle non-email items in its folders, and scales to tens of thousands of users.

Most of this book advocates putting together different pieces to get a whole that suits your business. Kolab is a project that does exactly that. When you use Kontact with Kolab Server, a few additional client features like free/busy information for other users become available. You can also connect Evolution to Kolab server, with a little more manual configuration. If you have enough users to demand streamlined administration, check out Kolab Server to see if it fits your needs.

OpenGroupware.org

Another open source groupware project, OpenGroupware.org, was spun out of a proprietary product by a German company called Skyrix. OpenGroupware.org provides better calendaring support than many other groupware servers. Instead of just storing an iCalendar file on the server somewhere, it uses iCalendar purely as a transmission format, parsing the events in it and inserting them individually in a database. By storing individual events instead of individual calendars, you can potentially put together custom calendars according to all sorts of different criteria.

The calendar part of OpenGroupware.org can be used by most of the calendar programs discussed in this chapter, including Apple iCal, Mozilla Calendar, Ximian Evolution, and Microsoft Outlook. For more complete groupware functions, you can use a proprietary plug-in for both Outlook and Evolution.

Like Kolab Server, OpenGroupware.org leverages the efforts of other open source projects. It also uses OpenLDAP and Cyrus IMAP, but puts everything together in a slightly different way. OpenGroupware.org provides most of the features of the proprietary groupware servers, and is a compelling solution for large and growing companies.

Free/Busy Server

At the other end of the scale, the simplest calendar server is an Apache Web server with a WebDAV-enabled directory. See Chapter 6 for hints about setting one up. You can set up different directories with different permissions: create one directory for public events calendars, another for public free/busy information, and another for private calendars requiring user logins for access.

Apple iCal, Mozilla Calendar, and Ximian Evolution 2.0 can automatically publish calendars to any WebDAV-enabled directory that the user has access to. Ximian Evolution 2.0 and Microsoft Outlook can automatically publish your free/busy information to the same directories, and read other people's free/busy information at the URL listed in their vCard. PhpICalendar can make posted calendars in any particular directory understandable using any Web browser.

SUMMARY

Calendars are one of the few business applications in this book that work primarily through desktop software, with minor benefits added by using a server. While there are a handful of full-blown proprietary calendar servers, they tend to be expensive and only offer benefits within your business.

In most cases, a simple WebDAV-enabled server is all you'll need to support a variety of different calendar programs. The key is to decide what you want to be public, what you want to be private, and what you want to be company-confidential. Then set up directories and access permissions to support your decisions.

An alternative solution is to set up WebCalendar and have your entire company use that instead of any other calendar system.

In this chapter, we discussed strategies for managing schedules, appointments, resources, and project calendars. We took a look at automatic appointment scheduling, posting free/busy information, and publishing event calendars. We examined some greatly differing types of calendaring software, including client calendar applications, Web applications, PIM software, and groupware systems.

In the next chapter, we're going to take a look at effective ways of tracking and managing your documents.

CALENDARING REFERENCES

An updated list of resources for this chapter is on the Web site for the book at *http://opensourcesmall.biz/calendar.*

Software

Apple iCal, commercial calendar application for Mac *http://www.apple.com/ical/*

Mozilla Calendar, open source calendar application *http://www.mozilla.org/projects/calendar/*

Ximian Evolution, open source PIM software *http://www.ximian.com/products/evolution/*

Palm Desktop, free commercial PIM software *http://www.palmone.com/us/software/desktop/*

Jpilot, open source PIM software for Linux *http://www.jpilot.org*

WebCalendar, open source calendar Web application *http://webcalendar.sourceforge.net*

PHP iCalendar, open source Web iCalendar file viewer *http://phpicalendar.sourceforge.net*

Microsoft Outlook, commercial PIM software *http://www.microsoft.com/outlook*

Lotus Notes, commercial PIM software *http://www.lotus.com*

Keyring, open source password manager for Palm OS *http://gnukeyring.sourceforge.net*

Mañana, free secondary task list for Palm OS *http://bill.sexton.tripod.com*

PHPGroupware, open source group management Web application *http://www.phpgroupware.org*

Yahoo! Calendar, free, hosted, ad-based calendar service *http://calendar.yahoo.com*

Kontact, open source PIM software for KDE *http://www.kontact.org/*

Jical, automatic posting of calendar information for groups *http://jical.sourceforge.net/*

Kolab Server, groupware server *http://kolab.kde.org/*

Microsoft Exchange, groupware and email server *http://www.microsoft.com/exchange*

OpenGroupware.org, groupware server *http://opengroupware.org*

Web Sites

GNOME Bounties *http://www.gnome.org/bounties/*

vCard and vCalendar standards *http://www.imc.org/pdi/*

9 Document Management

In This Chapter

- Introduction
- Keeping Track of Important Files
- Small Business Version Control: Subversion
- Summary
- Document Management References

INTRODUCTION

Your salesman, Joe, drafted up a contract for a new customer and sent it through email to you and your attorney, Linda. For once, you both got to working on it the same afternoon. Now there are three versions of the document floating around, and you have other matters that need attention. So you delegate the task of integrating everybody's changes to Josie, the intern. But she got mixed up and thought yours was the original, and so the result of her work was an adulterated draft of Linda's legal document with some key points missing.

The first part of this chapter discusses the business issues of managing documents, and is not technical. The proposed solution takes a good understanding of how the system works to be able to use it effectively, but if you take the time to train the employees in your business, you'll be amazed at how effective these tools can be. Actually installing the system is fairly technical.

Now your customer's on the phone wondering where the contract is, Linda wants to charge extra because her changes were mangled, and Joe's out meeting with the next prospect. There are six copies of the same document in different versions in your inbox, and who can say where to start? Sounds like it's time for a version control system.

KEEPING TRACK OF IMPORTANT FILES

All businesses need to keep track of documents. Contracts, meeting notes, incorporation documents, charters, bylaws, descriptions of your products, brochures, marketing collateral, business cards, logos, vendor lists, partner agreements, templates, deeds, licenses—the list goes on.

Before computers, you or an employee probably kept track of these in filing cabinets. As your documents became out of date, you need to clean out the old versions to make room for the current versions. You probably need to store back copies of just about everything, just in case something crops up later. If you're organizationally challenged, this can be a tremendous task. It generally requires some sort of system and a great deal of discipline to keep track of all of the important paper documents you need to do business.

Fast forward to the digital age. Clutter is still an issue, but the majority of the bulk of the documents you need can be stored electronically. Now you need to buy a big hard drive instead of more filing cabinets. Unless you maintain a similar high standard of discipline, it doesn't take long for your important documents to get lost in the vast organic jungle that is your hard drive.

You start out putting everything in My Documents, but quickly learn that you've used similar names for too many things, requiring you to open five documents to find the version you need. Then you made a folder for each project, but now you learn that it's constantly necessary to revise some documents and so you either add a number to the file name or maybe the date. Now you have multiple people working on the files on multiple computers, and no idea who worked on a document last. You have to go to each computer to hunt. You haven't been backing up these files very well, either, have you?

Approaches to Solving the Problem

Computers bring a suite of solutions to help you solve this problem, but the bottom line is that all of them require a certain amount of discipline, a certain amount of changing old habits and learning new ones. Let's break the overall problem down into more manageable parts. Ideally, the issues we need to address are:

1. Finding the document you're looking for
2. Always having the latest version of the document at hand, where everyone can access it
3. Knowing who has worked on the document over time, and what they've done to it
4. Being able to find and retrieve earlier versions, if the need arises

5. Providing some mechanism to ensure that only one person can change a document at a time, or provide an easy way to integrate changes if not
6. Backing up your important documents

The bad news is, no software package will do all of this for you. But there are some very good software packages that help you with these problems.

Problem #1—Finding the document you're looking for, is the main issue that doesn't quite fit in the solutions we're about to discuss. We'll cover searching for content in Chapter 13, in the section on Content Management.

Problem #6—Backing up your important documents, is a side benefit of implementing a content repository as we're about to review. Actually doing backups is covered in Chapter 18.

A revision control system is designed to specifically address the remaining four issues, and that's what we're going to talk about now.

Revision Control before Computers

The central problem we're discussing is not a new one. As long as businesses have needed documents, they've needed ways of managing these documents. What has changed with the advent of electronic copies is that suddenly you can have many different copies of the same document, and it has become very easy for multiple people to edit them at the same time. So let's take a look at some human solutions to the problem.

The Filing Cabinet

The most common way of managing documents is by keeping them in a filing cabinet somewhere, using some arbitrary system for organization. You might have one cabinet for contracts, organized alphabetically by name of the other party, perhaps subdivided by contract type first. Another cabinet contains the originals of your marketing collateral, organized by time. A third cabinet contains your accounting records, again organized by time.

When someone in your company needs to work on a file, they pull it out of the filing cabinet, take it to their desk, and work on it. They add their new work to the file, and when they're done, they put it back.

While a file is out of the cabinet, other people may not ever know that it exists, or who is working on the file. After the file is returned, you hope that whoever worked on it was organized enough to clearly date and signify what's new. If you don't understand how a cabinet is organized, or don't remember the name of the vendor you need to contact, finding the right file may be a challenge.

The Gatekeeper

To make it easier for others in your office to know where a file is, you might institute some sort of gatekeeping system. You might have a person doing this job—an administrative assistant who guards the files, only allowing a file to leave the cabinet after noting who took it and why. This person might enforce security, not allowing Josie to see the accounting filing cabinet or the sales contracts. If more than one person needs to use a file at the same time, the gatekeeper can assist by making a copy of it and telling you who is also working on it, to enable you to ascertain what they are changing.

Or, you might have a whiteboard on the filing cabinet, where everyone writes down the files they've removed, or adds a sticky-note attached to the empty file folder in the cabinet.

The Library

The library adds some more features to our document system. First, you have a *repository* of documents (the library itself). Next, you have a very formal gatekeeper (the librarian). Now, you also have an index (the card catalog).

Libraries are typically where you go for information. This part of the library (support for searching) we'll discuss more fully in Chapter 13 when we talk about Content Management Systems. For this chapter, let's turn the idea of the library around and imagine that we check things out of our library when we want to add to them, rather than just read them.

The librarian keeps an index of all documents in the repository and checks them out to people carrying a valid library card. While Linda has a contract checked out of the library, nobody else can edit it, but everyone can see that she has it checked out. In software terms, the document is *locked for editing*.

Now here comes the big added benefit of our pseudo-library: the librarian has a copy of every previous version of every document, and a record of every person who has checked it out, along with their changes. If you ever need to see what a document looked like at some particular time in the past, the librarian can retrieve that version for you.

One potential problem with a library is that if only one person can have a document at a time, what do you do if that person gets sick, leaves the company, or goes on a business trip, leaving an important document for which you are liable locked? Generally, the solution to this involves the librarian reporting you to the city, where they may actually put a lien on your house until you pay up. The librarian can also electronically restore the last version of the document and cancel the lock. This can naturally become inconvenient—it takes some time to resolve, and may result in duplicated efforts.

Software Configuration Management

Huh? What's that? Okay. We've run out of the human solutions. When we look at how computers can address this problem, we find one further layer of functionality. In our library example, let's change the role the librarian. Anybody can check a document out, and work on it without worrying about who else has it. When you go to check the document back into the repository, the librarian first tries to see if somebody else has changed it since you got your copy.

If so, the librarian checks to see if the changes you've made are in different enough parts of the document so that they don't overlap. If not, she sends you off to the desk in the corner to go through the conflicting changes, and only when you've resolved them all can you check your changes back in.

Meanwhile, the repository still contains all of the versions of each document, with a complete history of changes. But some of the restrictive nature of the library model has been eased—anyone can work on the files without checking them out first—but the last to check in has to handle any conflicts.

In large software companies, the practice of using these systems is called *software configuration management* (SCM), mainly because it was programmers who came up with the systems in the first place, so that they could collaborate effectively on large software applications. SCM also stands for *source code management*, if you ask programmers instead of managers.

Software Configuration Management Options

The different approaches to dealing with our version control problem have software counterparts. Which is right for your organization depends on how big you are, how many people need to work in the system on a daily basis, and many other factors that can be difficult to assess. In keeping with the rest of the book, we're going to choose one of these systems to implement, and describe how you might use it day to day. But first, let's see what's out there.

There are many other SCM packages out there. We chose those shown in Table 9.1 because of their ubiquity, or because of some differentiating features. Let's take a closer look at each one.

Email/Floppy disk

Pretty much everybody starts out with an ad hoc solution. You have one computer with everything on it, and then when somebody else needs to work on a file, you either email it, or copy it onto a floppy disk or CD and walk it over to them. This leads to the problems we outlined earlier in this chapter, with many different versions of the same file floating around your office.

TABLE 9.1 Feature Comparison of Selected SCM Software

Software Solution	Search Functionality	Document History	Access to Earlier Versions	Lock Files for Editing	Merge Changes on Check-In	Centralized Backup/Restore
Email/Floppy disk	Limited	Yes—if you don't delete	No	No	No	No
Network File Share (local server)	Yes—Windows Search	No	No (unless explicitly saved)	No	No	Yes
RCS (Revision Control System)	No	Yes	Yes	Yes	No	Yes
Microsoft Visual SourceSafe	No	Yes	Yes	Yes	No	Yes
CVS (Concurrent Versioning System)	No	Yes	Yes	Yes (Optional)	Yes	Yes
Perforce	Yes	Yes	Yes	No	Yes	Yes
Subversion	Limited—with search engine add-on	Yes	Yes	No	Yes	Yes

Network File Share

This is the simplest, most common method for keeping track of files: set up a file share on a server, and have everybody copy their files up there whenever they're done. To make this work requires a lot of communication among people working on the files—you have to establish some sort of coherent organization to be able to find what you're looking for.

Most people eventually come up with some sort of naming system to handle multiple versions of a file. You add the date and your initials to the end of the file-name, for example, or maybe just increment a number at the end, such as doc_v1, doc_v2, etc.

This method of version control has a couple of advantages:

1. Once you have your file share set up, there is no additional software to load.
2. You can use built-in operating system software to search for arbitrary text across all of the files. This works for file types the operating system under-stands—which in the case of Microsoft, includes Word, Excel, and the other Office software.

However, compared to more sophisticated SCM software, network file sharing has a number of drawbacks. First, there's no control. Anyone can overwrite an old file, often by mistake. Another common accident is for somebody to drag a file or an entire folder into some other folder without realizing it.

Other issues crop up when people attempt to open files directly on the file share, instead of copying it to their computer first. The person editing the file has to wait for delays across the network, nobody else can access the file, and if some-thing happens to the network connection or the client computer crashes, the file on the share may get corrupted.

Still, if you have a server set up, this is the first organized way to manage files, requiring no fancy software or people to maintain it.

Revision Control System (RCS)

RCS is the granddaddy of revision control systems still in current use. It's been around in active use among computer programmers for decades. It corresponds to the Library scenario we discussed earlier. RCS consists of a repository containing all of the files you're tracking, server software to handle access to the repository (the gatekeeper), and client software each person uses to check files in and out.

When one person checks out a file, their name is added to the repository, and the file is locked. Other people can get a read-only copy of any previous version of the file, but nobody else can work on it while it's checked out.

When used over a network, there is no built-in security—a malicious user might be able to gain access to the repository, and roll back changes or steal code. If you're on a secure network behind a firewall, this is not much of a concern.

RCS software is almost always already installed and available in Linux distributions, and other Unix environments. You can buy a Windows version from Component Software, called CS-RCS. The Windows client can communicate interchangeably with an RCS repository on a Linux computer.

Microsoft Visual Source Safe (VSS)

VSS is a revision control system that Microsoft ships with its developer environment, Visual Studio. It also sells the package separately. VSS adds some authentication structure to the repository, making it possible to delegate access for particular files to specific groups of people. It also has a familiar interface, similar to Windows Explorer.

You can set VSS up to automatically mirror to a Web site, making the latest copies available over the Web.

VSS uses an equivalent library system to RCS: only one person may have a particular file checked out at a time, and must check it back in before someone else can work on it.

Concurrent Versioning System (CVS)

Computers hooked up to networks have enabled collaboration on projects to a level simply not possible before. Open source projects proliferate now only because the Internet made it possible for programmers around the world to work together to solve a common problem. RCS and VSS do not work well when there are a lot of people working on the same files at the same time, so programmers developed a system that works better.

CVS is one of the oldest of the Software Configuration Management tools that allows multiple people to work on the same files at the same time. Instead of blocking access while one person is working on the file, CVS focuses its attention on resolving what happens when several people work on the same file.

In the case of plain text files, CVS is able to detect where two versions of a file have changed, and as long as these changes don't overlap, it can *merge* the changes automatically, without intervention. A case of overlap occurs when two people edited the same part of a file. CVS detects changes made by only the last person to *commit*, or change, the file.

Unfortunately, most of the files we're discussing in this chapter are things like Word documents, Excel spreadsheets, and graphics files. These are all considered binary files, and thus cannot be merged automatically. For binary files CVS provides both versions and lets the last person to commit the file resolve the changes manually.

CVS is actually built on top of RCS and uses it to store changes in its repository. Most of the open source projects of the world, including Linux itself, are managed in CVS repositories. One of the drawbacks of CVS is its security system—it can be configured to only allow valid users to write to the repository, but it almost always allows anyone to read from it, if they can access the repository at all. For open source code development, this limitation is not a problem. For your sensitive corporate documents, it might be.

Perforce

Perforce is a commercial "best of breed" SCM tool. It has all of the benefits of any of the packages we've looked at so far, and it has some enhancements to make it better.

VSS, RCS, and CVS store a single copy of each text file along with *deltas* describing how the file has changed over time. This saves a lot of disk space, and smarter client applications can use less network bandwidth by only sending the deltas back and forth to the repository. However, these systems are not capable of creating accurate deltas of binary files, so binary files are stored as a complete copy every single time. This means more disk space, more time to store the file to the repository, and, with most of the binary files you deal with in business, more headaches overall.

Perforce has been optimized to accurately generate deltas on binary files. That means for storage and network purposes, Perforce works as well for binary files as it does for text files. Perforce also includes some macros that install in Word, to show you changes whenever there's a conflict. (A similar feature is available in CS-RCS.) The main drawback to Perforce is price: at $750 per user, it's the most expensive solution on this list.

Subversion

Which leads us to the solution of this chapter: Subversion. Subversion is a very new open source entrant to the SCM field. The first working versions of Subversion were released in Fall 2001. The Subversion project has hosted its own code since September 2001, with no data loss.

Subversion aims to replace CVS as a better SCM tool. Like Perforce, it creates deltas on binary files as well as text, and sends only the deltas across the network when you commit your changes.

Subversion currently can access repositories through three different ways:

- Through the local file system
- Through a dedicated server process
- Through an Apache Web server

Back in Chapter 6, we set up an Apache Web server. Subversion can load as a module in Apache, and allow Apache to handle all of the authentication. It also means that anyone can download files without needing to install any client software beyond a Web browser.

Subversion is new enough that there aren't many client interfaces available for it. But because it's built into Apache, and uses an extension called WebDAV, most operating systems (Windows, Mac OS X, and Linux) can at least read and write to the repository with no additional software.

Subversion is in heavy development right now, and by the time you read this, may have many features it doesn't have at the time of this writing. Some of the features that aren't there yet include:

■ Being able to lock a document so others know you're working on it
■ Being able to search for text in binary documents
■ Automatic merging of binary documents

Of course, none of the other SCM packages provide all of this functionality, either. We will discuss searching for content more in Chapter 14, when we dig into content management. As for merging of binary documents, some of this trouble may be alleviated by moving to XML formats. By the time you read this, Subversion may be able to perform automatic merging of OpenOffice.org documents, since they use a compressed XML format. See Chapter 4 for more about OpenOffice.

Subversion is the newer, better CVS, and using it is what we cover in the rest of the chapter.

SMALL BUSINESS VERSION CONTROL: SUBVERSION

As mentioned earlier, perhaps the most important part of any version control system is the person doing the work. We're all human, and we're not necessarily consistent in how we categorize information. Our categories change over time, as do the people doing the categorizing.

So the first step is trying to come up with an appropriate organization for your documents. The easiest way is to just start using it for new documents. Create a few folders for your current projects, and put all the new documents in the correct place from the start. Then, later, when you have time, gradually move your older documents into the system.

Subversion Clients

Subversion can be used with three different types of clients: Web browsers, WebDAV clients, and native Subversion clients. Obviously, native clients provide more features, and are the best way to access your repositories, but in a pinch, the more generic interfaces work.

Subversion via Web Browser

Since access to your repositories is through an Apache Web server, you can simply point any Web browser to the URL of your repository and get a listing of the files and directories stored there. You can browse up and down the tree, and download any file stored there as in Figure 9.1. You can only get the most recent version of a file, but you know that's always what you'll get.

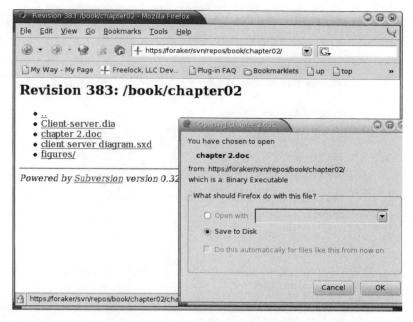

FIGURE 9.1 Checking out a Subversion repository in a Web browser.

You can use this feature to create links on your Web site for the most current copy of your document, and you won't have to worry about having old versions posted.

WebDAV

WebDAV is a newer Web protocol (DAV stands for Distributed Authoring and Versioning). WebDAV is built into many different software packages, including Internet Explorer, DreamWeaver, the Mac OS X Finder, Konqueror, and FrontPage.

In Internet Explorer, WebDAV is accessed through a feature called Web Folders (Figure 9.2). It basically allows you to mount the Web folder as a network share, and read and write copies of your files to and from the repository.

You generally can't edit a file in place on a WebDAV folder—the most reliable way to work on a file is to copy it from the Web folder to your computer, work on it there, and then copy it back up.

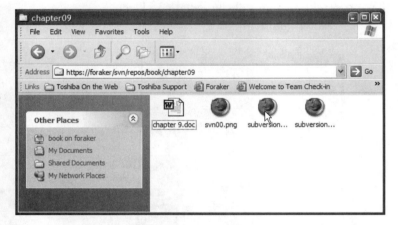

FIGURE 9.2 Accessing a Subversion repository using Windows Web folders.

WebDAV access to the repository is a unique feature of Subversion, one that makes it a compelling SCM tool simply for the ease of use, and the ability to not have to install any kind of client software, since most computers already have at least one WebDAV client available.

There are drawbacks to using WebDAV, however:

■ The whole file is copied back and forth to the server, instead of just the changes (the deltas).

- You do not get notified if someone edited the file after you copied it to your workstation, but before you copied it back—you lose the notification feature of SCM systems.

For these reasons you should install a real Subversion client on all the necessary computers, and only use WebDAV in a pinch.

Native Subversion Clients

Currently there are only a handful of Subversion clients available. By the time you read this, there will hopefully be many more. But the clients that exist are already very effective and useful.

The command line client, svn, needs to be run from a shell window. This is the most powerful client, allowing you to do anything in Subversion, but most people will prefer a graphical interface.

RapidSVN is a cross-platform GUI that provides access to most of the Subversion features. It can be difficult to get installed and working properly.

ViewCVS is a set of scripts that run on a Web server and provide SVN access. You can't write to Subversion repositories, but you can browse through the entire history of all the files in the repository, and retrieve any past or current version. If you need to access earlier versions without installing a full Subversion client, install this on your server.

Finally, TortoiseSVN (Figure 9.3) is a client for Windows, and gets installed right into Windows Explorer. This is a very handy place to have your version control—files in your repository have a little green checkmark on them when they're up to date, a red exclamation point when they're modified, and a yellow caution sign when they conflict. It provides most of the features you'll use on a day-to-day basis, allows you to browse through the history of a file or directory, and can even help you merge changes in text files.

ON THE CD

TortoiseSVN is on the CD-ROM included with this book, in the Windows directory.

NOTE

You can use TortoiseSVN in a standalone mode, without connecting it to a remote Subversion repository. After installing TortoiseSVN, read the daily use guide (available when you right-click in Windows Explorer). You can create a Subversion repository on your hard drive in Windows, and get many of the benefits of using revision control without the administrative efforts required to set up a fully shared repository.

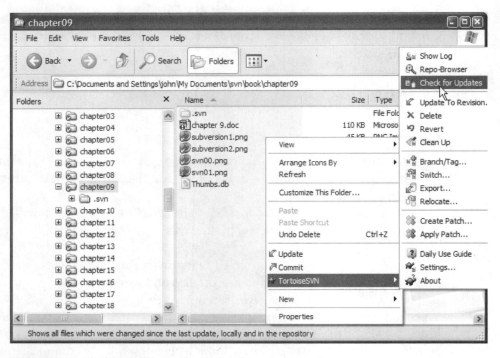

FIGURE 9.3   TortoiseSVN in action on a Subversion repository.

Repositories and Working Copies

When you work with an SCM tool, you download (`checkout` or `update`) a *working copy* of the files you need to your local hard drive, and work on them there. When you're done with your changes, you `commit` them back to the repository. This works as you'd expect, as long as you're working with files that already exist in the repository. But if you rename a file, or move it to a different sub-directory using Windows Explorer or a normal file management utility, the SCM tool has no way of knowing that the file in the new location or name is the same as the old one. That means if you then add the file to the repository, Subversion thinks it's a brand new file, with no history.

On the other hand, if you use the Subversion commands or tools to move, rename, or copy the file, you preserve the entire history of the file. Now you can browse through the log for the file, see all the previous filenames it used, and easily revert to a previous version.

Using Subversion

To illustrate how to use Subversion, we're going to install and use the TortoiseSVN package, but the basic process is the same no matter which client you use. You can find an installer for TortoiseSVN on the CD-ROM included with this book. Simply run the installer on any Windows-based computer and reboot to install TortoiseSVN.

TortoiseSVN is not a standalone software package—it simply adds some items to the right-click menu in Windows Explorer. These items are also available in Open or Save dialog boxes of many Windows programs.

A standalone software package, called RapidSVN, is available for Windows, Mac, and Linux. This software makes it easier to move, branch, or tag files within the repository, and browse or retrieve earlier versions. For day-to-day use in Windows, TortoiseSVN will do just about everything you need to do, however, and doesn't require starting up another program.

Import to the Repository

To get content into a repository, you *import* it. First, there must be a repository set up. Setting up a repository is an administrative task, which we cover at the end of the chapter. For now, we'll assume it's already there. You will have a URL for the repository, and you need to know this URL to get anything in or out of the repository.

You cannot import files into a repository and check them back out to the same directory. If you want to put a directory under version control, create an empty directory in the repository, check it out to the directory you want to import, add all the files to the repository, and commit your changes instead of following the directions in this section.

For this example, the administrator has set up a repository at *http://svn.company.com/clients*. You have organized the contracts for each client into a different directory on your hard drive, as follows:

```
C:\Documents and Settings\john\clients\
   client1\
     initial contract.doc
     signed copy.pdf
     work order 1.doc
     work order 2.doc
     project plan.sxw
```

```
client2\
  initial contract.doc
  signed contract.pdf
  work order 1.doc
client3\
  proposal 1.doc
client4\
  generic contract.doc
```

When importing, you can import any of these directories, or individual files. The import will put everything beneath a directory you specify into the repository, starting at the location you specify. For example, you could import only the files for client2 under a more specific name, as follows:

1. With TortoiseSVN installed, navigate to C:\Documents and Settings\ john\clients\ using Windows Explorer.
2. Right-click the client2 folder, and click Import...
3. For the Repository URL, type *http://svn.company.com/clients/cocacola.*
4. Click OK.

This action imports the three documents in the client2 directory into the repository as cocacola. If, on the other hand, you right-clicked the clients directory, and imported to *http://svn.company.com/clients*, Subversion would import all of the files and directories listed above into the repository.

Your files are now in the repository, but your originals are not yet under Subversion control. You probably want to back these files up to a CD or somewhere safe, and then proceed to check them out.

Check Out a Working Copy

When you check out files from the repository, Subversion actually puts two copies on your file system—one file to work on, and the other that Subversion uses to detect what has changed. These start out being identical.

Subversion tracks all changes while you're working by comparing the working copies to files in an administrative directory, named .svn. Whenever a directory has any files under Subversion control, you will find a hidden .svn directory in the file system. Never change anything in this administrative directory, or you'll risk breaking the revision.

The action of checking out from Subversion simply creates the appropriate administrative files and directories, and downloads the latest version of the appropriate files from the repository.

If there are files with the same name in both the repository and an existing directory you want to turn into a working copy, you won't be able to check out the working copy. The easiest way to get around this situation is to create a brand new directory to be your working copy.

So now that the files are in the repository, you can go to any workstation with TortoiseSVN installed, and get a working copy as follows:

1. Using Windows Explorer, browse to where you want to store your working copy and create a folder. For example:

   ```
   C:\Documents and settings\john\Desktop\clients
   ```

2. Right-click the blank space inside the folder, and click Check Out...
3. Type the repository URL: *http://svn.company.com/clients*
4. Click OK.

Subversion downloads all of the files to this directory. Press the F5 key to refresh the display, and they should all have green checkmarks on the files. You don't have to download the entire repository—you can download just the files for a single client by adding the client directory to the URL that you specify.

You can check out individual files, even from a different repository, to your working copy. Subversion keeps track of each file individually, and will update or commit changes to whatever repository each file belongs to.

You only need to check out files once, to correlate the files and directories between the working copy and the repository. Once you have a working copy, you will *update* to get the changes others have made.

Update Your Working Copy

Whenever you start working for the day, the first thing you should do is update your working copy. This gets the latest changes from the repository, downloading everything everyone has worked on.

Ideally, your working process goes like this:

1. Update your working copy from the repository.
2. Make your changes.
3. Commit your changes to the repository.

The less time between steps 1 and 3, the less chance there is that someone else has made changes to the same file while you're working on it—and therefore, the less chance you'll have to resolve conflicts.

The entire system works best if everyone updates and commits often. The more often, the less changes there are in each commit; the more history you have, the better your backups become, and the more current your repository.

While working on files, commit to the repository several times a day. Each time, also update the working copy, if there's anyone else working on the files.

To update your working copy with TortoiseSVN, simply open a Windows Explorer window to whatever directory you're working in, right-click in the empty space, and click Update. Subversion will download the latest version of any files that have changed since your last update.

Commit Your Changes

Once you have an updated working copy, you can edit whatever files you need to work on, move things around, add or remove files, or whatever you need to do. Any changes you make have no effect on the repository until you commit.

Subversion keeps a copy of everything you've checked out in its administrative directory. The version stored there is called the *BASE* revision, and files in your working copy are compared against the BASE revision to determine what has changed. When you commit to the repository, Subversion first generates a delta— a summary of exactly what has changed in each file. It then sends the deltas to the repository, instead of the entire file. This can save a substantial amount of bandwidth, making it much faster over a slow connection. It also saves disk space on the repository, since only one copy of each file is stored, along with a series of deltas.

Now here's where you will need to have some discipline: if you rename a file, delete it, or move it to a different directory, Subversion doesn't necessarily know what happened to it. Subversion doesn't sit over your shoulder, watching your every move. It simply compares the current directory contents with BASE to see what has changed. Whenever you change filenames, including adding, deleting, renaming, copying, or moving files, and you want the changes to be permanent in the repository, you need to use the corresponding Subversion command to do it.

With TortoiseSVN, this means right-clicking the item you want to change, and using the operation on the submenu to do the actual change.

You can use the Rename command to move files to another directory as well as rename them. Instead of using Windows Explorer to delete a file, use the TortoiseSVN Remove menu item. To make a second copy of a file, use the Branch command.

These commands only affect your working copy—nothing happens to the repository until you use the Commit command.

Finally, when you commit, get into the habit of typing a short note explaining what you've done. You'll thank yourself later when you need to find something you deleted.

Resolve Conflicts

If you have several people working on the same set of documents at the same time, sooner or later you'll have a conflict. As discussed earlier, there are basically two approaches to solving this issue: prevent them before they happen, or make them easy to resolve after they happen. Revision Control Systems are generally built around one or the other of these approaches.

Subversion uses the latter approach. For software developers, resolving conflicts is an easy task, mainly because nearly all the files they work with are plain text—there are no graphics, no formatting symbols, nothing to make the task difficult. Subversion simply attempts to merge the two deltas into the text file. If the deltas affect different parts of the file, it tells the user that it was able to successfully merge the changes.

On the other hand, if you attempt to commit a version of a text file, and changed the same line as somebody else who beat you to committing it, Subversion will give you a conflict message, and won't allow you to commit until you've resolved it.

To resolve it, first you need to update your copy from the repository. Subversion never overwrites your files without warning you first. You can always safely use the Update command on the TortoiseSVN menu, whether or not you've edited a file, to bring your working copy up to date. If someone else has edited the same file you've also changed, that's when Subversion attempts to merge it. If the merge fails, you have a conflict.

To help you resolve it, Subversion puts four different versions of the text file into your working copy:

- The BASE copy you originally checked out, with `.r` and the original repository revision number added to the filename
- Your version of the file, with `.mine` added to the filename
- The latest version of the file from the repository (the version somebody else checked in) with `.r` and the latest revision number from the repository
- Subversion's attempt to merge your changes, with the normal filename

This last version has the conflicting section(s) highlighted with easily recognizable marker lines of text at the beginning and end, along with both versions. You simply open up the merged file, delete the markers and the version you don't want to keep, make any further changes you want, and save it. Then, using TortoiseSVN, choose the Resolve action from the menu, and Subversion deletes the extra copies of the file. Again, nothing happens to the repository copy until you commit.

So what happens if the file is more than plain text? A Word document is considered a binary file, because it's full of style and formatting definitions, and may contain many other things that Subversion can't understand. Likewise, bit-mapped graphics files probably can never be successfully merged. If Subversion detects a conflict in a binary file, it doesn't even try to merge the versions. It simply puts the first three versions of the files in your working copy. You do whatever you need to do to resolve the changes, and save your final decision as the original filename. Then you click the Resolve action in TortoiseSVN, and you'll be able to commit your changes.

If the file you're working on is a Word or OpenOffice.org Writer document, you can probably open up your version of the document, and then use the Compare Documents feature from the menu items to see where your versions differ. Then you can just Accept or Reject each change one by one, and save and commit the final version.

OpenOffice.org uses a compressed XML file as its native format. XML is plain text, but there may be a filter available in the future that allows Subversion to uncompress it, automatically merge changes, and recompress it, bringing the benefits of automatic merging to Office documents. Here is one way where open source solutions may offer a compelling advantage over proprietary software.

Revert to an Earlier Version

Now we come to one of the key benefits of any revision control system: the ability to go back in time, and see your documents as they were at that time. The repository adds the time dimension to your files. You can back up to any point at which you committed changes. You do this by finding the version you want, and updating your working copy to that version. In TortoiseSVN, you can select a file and view the log to see all the times that file has changed over its entire history. Each log entry has the text typed in when that version was committed to the repository, the time, date, and person who committed the file, and a list of the other files that were changed at the same time.

Once you find a version you want to look at, right-click it in the list and you'll find an option to change to that revision. You can also save that version to a separate file, so you can compare the documents to see what has changed. If you want the old version to replace the current version, use the Merge option. The old version will replace your working copy, and become the current version when you commit your changes. You can undo this by repeating the process with the version you replaced. Revision Control is really a time machine.

Tag Official Versions

Programming teams set up their repositories to have multiple *branches*, and *tag* particular versions for release. The idea behind branches is to allow one or two developers to resolve a particular problem without affecting the main *trunk* branch. Once they have the problem solved, they merge their branches back into the trunk, using a process similar to resolving conflicts

In a small business, you probably don't need to do this. On the other hand, creating a tag can be useful so that you can quickly find a particular version of a document, even after it continues to change. Think of a tag as a snapshot of a file or directory in the repository.

In Subversion, a branch and a tag are really the same thing—they're just used differently. They're both just pointers to a particular version of another file in the repository. In practice, a branch continues to change because people check in new versions of the branch, but the overall file is still based on the old version of the original. A tag, on the other hand, never changes. It always points to the same version of the original file, and is never modified later.

In practice, you may have a standard description of services that you attach to each customer contract. Inevitably, this description changes over time, but you need to be able to see the version associated with any particular client. What you can do is have one directory as your generic contracts file, and then a separate directory for each customer. You use the Branch command on the TortoiseSVN menu to copy the description of services to the customer directory. Now, if you update the generic contracts file, the copy in the customer directory remains at the version you originally copied. It is now tagged to the version you started with.

Because Subversion runs within the Apache Web server, you can actually create a directory in the repository pointing to tagged versions of your literature. Depending on how you set up access, you can allow particular customers, or the general public, to get to the latest version, or any tagged version, of files in your repository without needing any more software than a Web browser.

Administer Subversion

Subversion is a very young software package, designed from the ground up to be a better CVS. Following the Unix tradition of having a single purpose for each software program, and then integrating many programs together to build up a system that exactly meets your needs, Subversion itself only manages repositories.

The rest of this chapter gets pretty technical. Installing and configuring a Subversion server can be a challenging task, and will require some technical know-how.

At this writing, there are three different interfaces to Subversion repositories:

- Local file system access directly in the client
- A native Subversion server that provides access over a dedicated TCP port
- A module that runs in Apache

Since other applications in this book work extensively in Apache, we're going to focus on the Apache module.

TortoiseSVN can create and manage a personal repository for you on your desktop, without needing to connect to a server. See its daily use guide for help doing this.

Installation

By far the easiest way to install Subversion is to use a package put together for your distribution. If you're using Mandrake Linux, and have the source media added to the search list (see Chapter 4 for instructions on setting up remote package media sources for Mandrake), simply type the following in a root shell:

```
# urpmi subversion-client-dav apache2-mod_dav_svn
```

Mandrake will download the latest version and all dependencies available for your system, and install them for you. Or go to the Subversion site, *http://subversion.tigris.org*, to download the latest version of the software.

To get Apache to load the Subversion module, edit the httpd2.conf file for your system and make sure you see the following line:

```
LoadModule dav_svn_module /usr/lib/apache2/mod_dav_svn.so
```

Make sure this is all on one line, and that the path to the *.so file is correct. Also, this line must appear later in the httpd2.conf file than the LoadModule dav_module directive, or Apache will generate unrecoverable errors when it starts.

Set Up a Repository

The svnadmin command is used to administer repositories. This program is part of the Subversion server installation.

To set up a repository, simply type:

```
$ svnadmin create /path/to/repository
```

The parent directories must exist, and the user account you're using must have permission to create files. If you're following the server layout discussed in Chapter 2, you might choose to create an svn directory in /var to contain all of the repositories on the server. To create a repository called contracts, for example, use this command:

```
$ svnadmin create /var/svn/contracts
```

The /var/svn directory must already exist and the current user account must have write access to this directory.

It's easiest to set up a different repository for different groups of users. It is possible to limit access by directory in the repository, but it's much easier to set up access individually per repository. So you might have one repository for sensitive Human Resources types of data, limiting access only to those who need it, a different repository for all sales-related material, and another for each project.

To use Subversion as an Apache module, the Apache user must have write access to the repository. So after creating the repository, change to the root user and set the ownership of all of its files to whatever user account Apache is running—if you're using Mandrake, Apache runs as user apache, group apache.

```
$ cd /var/svn
$ su
# chown apache:apache -R contracts
```

The repository is stored by default in a Berkeley Database format, in a db/ directory inside the repository. There are a number of other customizations you can make to the repository, such as adding custom scripts that execute on certain actions. See the Subversion documentation for more help.

Configure Access

Integration with Apache is what makes Subversion unique among SCM software. Once you set up the repository, all you have to do is tell Apache where it is, and then you can use any of the authentication methods available to Apache. You can even provide multiple URLs using <Location> blocks, all pointing to the same repository.

In the Apache configuration file (httpd.conf), set up a <Location> block for each URL you want to associate with a repository. Here's a brief example:

```
<Location /repository>
  DAV svn
  SVNPath /path/to/repository
</Location>
```

Restart the Web server with `apachectl graceful`, and the contracts repository becomes available at the URL *http://servername/repository/*. You can browse it with any Web browser, or provide this URL to a subversion client and begin importing or checking out files.

You can put the Location block inside a VirtualHost block to associate the repository with a particular host name. You can add access controls using Accept and Deny directives. You can add authentication using any of the authentication methods available to Apache—see Chapter 6 for more about setting up access and authentication in Apache.

If you want to make a repository read-only for particular users, you can add a Limit block and list only the appropriate methods. Here's the contract repository set up with different access for different groups:

```
<Location /contracts>
  DAV svn
  SVNPath /var/svn/contracts
  SVNAutoversioning on
  AuthType Basic
  AuthUserFile /var/www/conf/.htpasswd
  AuthGroupFile /var/www/conf/.htgroups
  AuthName "Contracts Repository"
  <LimitExcept GET PROPFIND OPTIONS REPORT>
    Require group managers
  </LimitExcept>
  <Limit GET PROPFIND OPTIONS REPORT>
    Require valid-user
  </Limit>
</Location>
```

This configuration allows any user with a valid password to check out or browse the repository, but only managers to make any changes. You can specify permissions on a more granular level using the `mod_authz_svn` module. See the Subversion documentation for help doing this.

Backup and Restore

Subversion provides two basic methods for backing up and restoring repositories—the `svnadmin hotcopy` command, script, and the `svnadmin dump` command. Both methods work directly from the command line, and you have to specify the path to the repository. If you don't use either of these tools and simply back up the existing repository directly in the file system, the backed up copy may get corrupted if a transaction is in progress. It's better to use the provided methods.

The svnadmin hotcopy command makes a complete working copy of the repository without requiring you to take it offline. You can drop this repository anywhere in the file system, point the Apache mod_dav_svn module to it, and be instantly back up and running. This command also does some housecleaning on the main repository, deleting log files that are no longer necessary. This command is appropriate to use when you do full system backups.

The svnadmin dump command exports all of the transactions of the repository to a *dump file*. You can designate a range of revisions to export, and specify whether the first revision of the range should be the complete file or just the delta from the previous version. This command is great for incremental backups, but it does not back up anything other than the data. If you have some custom hook scripts, these do not get backed up properly. The svnadmin load command loads the transactions from a dump file into an existing repository.

SUMMARY

Document Management is a major need for any business. There are always documents and files that must be managed. A traditional document management system provides a way to organize information in many different ways, making it easy to find. These systems are expensive, cumbersome, and can be overkill for most small businesses.

Revision Control systems provide an alternate method of archiving your files. The main purpose of these systems is to add the dimension of time to your filing system, making it possible to retrieve earlier versions of a file. Subversion is a brand new revision control system, completely written from scratch to make it work particularly well with the binary files that most business applications use.

The related problem of finding information can often be solved better with a content management system, which we'll discuss in Chapter 13. In a content management system, you store information, not files. You can then retrieve that information in a variety of formats.

In this chapter, we took a look at a few approaches to managing files and documents in your business. We examined different ways of distributing documents, and managing changes to them when they're edited by multiple persons. Finally, we went into detail about the use and administration of a powerful revision control system called Subversion.

In the next chapter, we continue our exploration of systems to manage your business, taking a look at accounting systems.

DOCUMENT MANAGEMENT REFERENCES

An updated list of resources for this chapter is on the Web site for the book at *http://opensourcesmall.biz/document*.

Software

Subversion, open source Apache-based revision control *http://subversion.tigris.org*

TortoiseSVN, Windows Explorer client for Subversion *http://tortoisesvn.tigris.org*

RapidSVN, cross-platform client for Subversion *http://rapidsvn.tigris.org*

ViewCVS, Web application for browsing Subversion and CVS repositories *http://viewcvs.sourceforge.net/*

RCS, open source file-based revision control *http://www.gnu.org/software/rcs/rcs.html*

CVS, open source project revision control system using RCS *http://www.cvshome.org/*

Microsoft VSS, commercial revision control system *http://msdn.microsoft.com/ssafe/*

Perforce, commercial revision control system *http://www.perforce.com*

Web Sites

The Subversion Book, Version Control With Subversion *http://svnbook.red-bean.com/*

10 Financial Management

In This Chapter

- Introduction
- What To Do with Your Accounting System
- Small Business Accounting: SQL Ledger
- Summary
- Accounting References

INTRODUCTION

At first glance, you might think accounting systems are the main type of software that keep you using Windows systems. QuickBooks®, Peachtree®, Microsoft Money®, and Quicken® all run on Windows, and not directly in Linux. These programs have certainly captured the market for financial software for small businesses.

Most of this chapter is non-technical, but may require some knowledge of accounting to fully understand. Some of the customizations involve some technical skills—installing the Web application and customizing templates.

Slightly larger businesses opt for expensive enterprise accounting systems such as Great Plains®, MAS 90®, and Lawson®. These programs require extensive customization to make them work for a particular business.

A few open source systems have emerged to provide compelling alternatives to proprietary accounting software. These systems are beginning to surpass the proprietary offerings in terms of features, customizability, and flexibility.

WHAT TO DO WITH YOUR ACCOUNTING SYSTEM

Different businesses have different accounting needs. Many businesses have an inventory. Manufacturers need to correlate parts in their inventories to the final assemblies. Service-based firms need to track billable hours. Businesses with employees have to keep a payroll system. All businesses need some system for billing, receiving payments, making payments, tracking their income, and reporting to tax authorities. Many businesses need to manage invoices and customer statements.

If your business is a small independent consultancy, your accounting needs are much different from those of your client, a medium-sized manufacturing firm. If you operate a retail store, you have much different accounting needs than your attorney's law firm. The best accounting package for your business depends completely on your needs.

Open source accounting packages have become compelling alternatives for all but the most consumer-oriented accounting programs. The single biggest advantage offered by open source accounting packages comes from the fact that they're open source—they're easy to customize to fit the exact needs of your organization.

In this section, we'll explore some of the common accounting tasks software can help you perform, along with some basic accounting concepts to help understand what makes for effective bookkeeping software.

Double-Entry Accounting

When you balance your checkbook, you probably keep a simple record of what check you wrote to whom for how much. Your personal financial records are probably not much more than a simple checkbook register for each account. Personal financial software, such as Quicken® and Microsoft Money, lets you categorize each purchase into standard categories, allowing you to reconcile statements, create budgets, and see where you spent your money.

What you can't do as easily is keep track of payments owed to you, or bills you owe but haven't paid. If you carry an inventory, the IRS requires you to report your business income on an accrual basis: you report what you have billed, not the cash you actually received. To account for the difference between when you generated an invoice and received the cash, bookkeepers use a system called *Double-entry accounting*. With double-entry accounting, every expense has its own account, and every transaction must appear on two different accounts: the *debit* account, and the *credit* account. Credits are amounts you owe, while debits are amounts owed to you. This is the reverse of what you hear from the bank teller—when a teller *credits* your account, the bank is adding to the amount it owes you. From your point of view, your account has been *debited*—the amount owed to you has increased.

Single-entry accounting systems work for personal finances and the tiniest of businesses. All business accounting packages use double-entry accounting. Almost all of the open source accounting packages are double-entry, making them more cost-effective and more compelling the larger your business is.

Cash versus Accrual Accounting

When it comes time to report your earnings to the IRS or your country's tax authority, you generally need to either use *cash*-based or *accrual*-based reporting. When you use cash as the basis for your accounting, you report exactly how much cash you have in your accounts. You don't report bills you've sent or received that aren't paid. With accrual-based accounting, you report income based on when you create or receive a bill.

If you have an inventory, in the United States the IRS requires you to use accrual-based accounting. Otherwise, it's up to you. To be able to do accrual-based accounting, you generally need to do double-entry accounting.

Handling Payroll

Payroll is a particularly difficult part of accounting, mainly because every location has different rules. Payroll taxes vary from state to state in the United States, and vary even more between countries. If your business has multiple locations, you may have to do more than one set of payroll calculations.

While there are a few payroll modules available for open source accounting packages, for the most part they require substantial customization for your location. For most small businesses, the best ways to manage payroll are to either outsource it to a firm specializing in handling payroll, or purchase regular payroll updates for your location for the proprietary accounting packages (such as Quick-Books and Peachtree). Lack of adequate payroll processing is perhaps the biggest shortcoming of the open source accounting packages.

On the other hand, if you have a payroll expert on staff, it's relatively easy to customize the open source software to set up the appropriate rules.

Managing Employee Hours

If you have hourly employees, you need to have some way of tracking the hours they actually work. If you bill customers on an hourly basis, you need to have some way of associating billable hours with the correct customer and project. Search the Internet for a time tracking solution, and you'll find hundreds, both proprietary and open source.

The simplest time tracking system is a spreadsheet or table. You can find many templates online for tracking hours. Figure 10.1 shows a simple timesheet you can have each employee fill out and submit at the end of a pay period.

As the number of employees increase, simple spreadsheets quickly become unmanageable. The next step up is hooking hours to a database. By having everyone report their hours in a single database, you eliminate the onerous task of having somebody manually moving hours from each employee's timesheet into your payroll and systems.

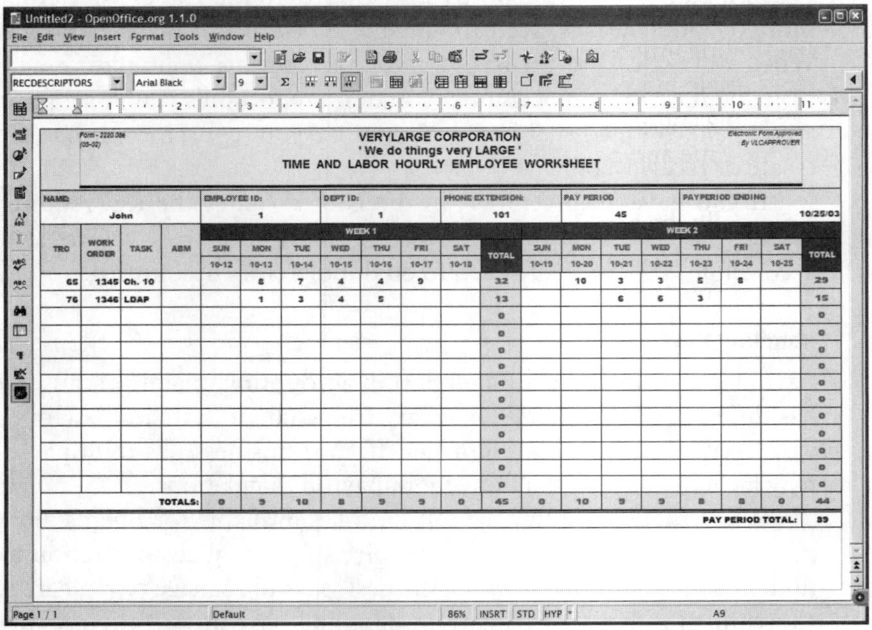

FIGURE 10.1 A template for a basic timesheet in OpenOffice.org.

Different types of businesses need to track hours for different reasons. The proliferation of timesheet software attests to the fact that no single timesheet system works for all businesses—and also that it may well be cheaper to develop your own system than modify somebody else's.

A retail operation may want employees to punch in and out of a system, recording the actual hours they're at work. Employees for service firms may not go online at all during the day, but simply record their own hours and report them to the company before the end of each pay and billing cycle. Many companies want a manager to approve hours before they become official.

Often, the best timesheet software is a database customized for your particular business. Building a Web application from scratch to serve as a timesheet program can take as little as a couple days of development for a competent Web developer. For an example, complete with working code, see *http://www.devshed.com/c/a/ PHP/Time-is-Money-part-1/*.

As a business grows more sophisticated, working with software packages that integrate time tracking with accounting systems start to become cost-effective. There are a number of Enterprise Resource Planning (ERP) systems that integrate time, billing, inventory, payroll, accounting, and project management components into a single place. We discuss these further in Chapter 11. The main drawback to using a big comprehensive system is that it needs to be customized to each business, and the time and cost involved usually outweigh the savings until you reach a certain size.

Usually the best way to manage time tracking and billing is to start with some spreadsheet-based solution, move to a database when the spreadsheet becomes cumbersome, and move to an ERP system only when you've determined that it can save you a substantial amount of employee time. Using this progression, not only do you delay the expense of implementing a complex system until you have the revenue to pay for it, you also have a chance to discover the quirks of your business as you grow. Trying to implement a big ERP system at the outset is usually a mistake until you have a lot of experience in your business.

Generating Invoices and Orders

Many businesses need to generate invoices or bills to get paid. Many customized timesheet programs have built-in invoicing capabilities. Many office applications include templates for invoices and receipts. What's the best way to generate invoices?

If you report earnings on an accrual basis, it's easiest to use accounting software to create your invoices. The instant you create your invoice, the amount is added to your Accounts Receivable account, which indicates the total amount owed to you. When you receive payment, the accounting software automatically credits the Accounts Receivable (deducts the amount) and debits your bank account (increasing the amount). Of course, if the payment is not electronic, you still have to take it to the bank.

Even if you report income on a cash basis, about the only reason you might not want to create invoices in your accounting software is if you already have another system that works well for you, or your accounting system isn't capable of generating invoices—or if you need to be able to generate an invoice without access to your accounting system.

Keeping Track of Inventory

A big part of accounting for manufacturers, distributors, and retailers is managing inventory. Inventory is simply a total count of each item a business has that it intends to sell to others. Tracking your inventory is no easy task. Exactly what you need to track varies by your location, but generally you need to be able to report on:

- Your cost of purchasing the items, or the parts that go into the items
- The number of items you have on hand
- The number of items converted to business use instead of being sold
- The number of items lost or damaged without being sold (called *shrinkage* in the retail industry)

As you purchase items, you need to add them to your inventory. As you sell them, you need to remove them. As you assemble items from parts, you need to know when you're running low to order more parts. Periodically, you need to perform a physical inventory to reconcile what's in your books with what's on your shelves.

Point-of-Sale Software

If you have retail sales, you also need to have a Point Of Sale (POS) system. The simplest POS is a tablet of receipts—you write a receipt to the customer when you receive payment. For most of the twentieth century, most retail stores used cash registers as their POS. A cash register generates a receipt for the customer, and keeps a running total of all sales during the day. At the end of the day, the cashier must balance the amount of sales with the amount of cash, checks, and credit card receipts left in the drawer.

With advances in technology, the POS has become more sophisticated. Bar code scanners instantly report exactly what items were sold, and can deduct them from the inventory. POS is basically software that runs your cash registers, updating both your accounting and your inventory systems while generating receipts and calculating change. You can buy commercial POS systems that integrate with common commercial accounting packages.

Most larger chain stores have created their own POS systems, often leveraging the efforts of open source packages. This is one area where the Java language has gained a strong foothold—the strength of Java is that a developer can write a program on one device (his computer) and trust that it will run correctly on another (the cash register). Generally, the bigger you are, the more of a custom solution you need—and the more a solution built on open source packages and technologies can save.

Online Transactions

More and more businesses are conducting transactions online. When you look at accounting software, some of the commercial packages mention the ability to do online banking. What this generally means is that you can download statements and transactions directly from your bank into the software, saving you the time of entering them manually. This type of feature is more about keeping your books reconciled with the actual balance in your accounts, and is most useful for the smallest businesses that do not have a bookkeeper.

A different type of online transaction involves processing a payment online. You might provide some sort of e-commerce facility to allow people to pay for your services through a Web site. These types of transactions are usually either a credit card charge through a merchant account, or an Automated Clearing House (ACH) transaction that deducts directly from a checking account. In either case, how you implement a solution depends largely on what your bank makes available to you. You almost always need to create customized code for your business, but most merchant accounts and ACH gateways provide simple interfaces, making it a task of a few hours for a savvy developer.

Taxes and Reporting

Whether or not you need to do anything else with your finances, the law requires you to report your income to the government and pay your taxes. Creating reports that tell you how much you've earned, how much you've spent, what you can deduct, and how much tax you need to pay is the bottom line of any accounting package. Almost any of the basic ledger packages can tell you the first part: what you've earned and where you've spent your money. What you owe to the government depends on what city, state, and country you do business in, where you're incorporated, what type of business you do—and not only that, it changes from year to year.

One of the tenets of open source software is that software is a service, rather than a product. There is hardly a better example of this concept than tax software. While there are several tax software products on the market, what you're really paying for when you buy one is the time and effort involved in keeping them up to date for each location the software vendor supports. You can't do your taxes with an outdated version of TurboTax®—you have to buy a new copy every year that contains the newest rates and rules.

To date, there isn't any open source tax software—all the packages are proprietary. The main reason for this situation is that open source projects develop by having a lot of programmers scattered around the world working together to solve a common problem, and while everyone shares the burden of paying taxes, each of our taxes are different enough that it's hard to create a single program that solves them all. That's why there's a different version of tax software for each state.

When a location reaches a critical mass of programmers available with an interest in solving the problem, we'll doubtlessly see open source tax software emerge, but for the near term, most of them are still solving the accounting problems that can be solved the same way everywhere. The bottom line is you're going to have to pay to figure out your taxes: you'll pay your accountant, or if you do the taxes yourself, you'll pay for software that has the specific accounting rules for your location and for the time spent in gaining expertise and staying up to date with your jurisdiction. Where open source comes into this discussion is that there's a huge opportunity for tax-savvy people with programming experience to provide services on a small scale to businesses in a particular location. If you're a programmer and know the business rules, it's relatively easy to create a custom solution. If you find somebody offering such a service, and they're willing to take responsibility for any accounting errors they might introduce, you may find a local service provider using open source technologies to be the most economical way to get your taxes done.

Choosing Accounting Software

Now that we've discussed the major types of accounting tasks computers can help you complete, let's take a look at some of the available software. There are thousands of software titles out there related to accounting, filling hundreds of niches. If you're a small company with no employees and no inventory, a simple spreadsheet in any office software is probably sufficient. Anything bigger, and you need more—but what is best for your business may be completely different from what's best for another business. The first thing to do is to think about your business requirements, as discussed earlier in the chapter, and then evaluate them against the features of a particular set of software.

If you're a small business in a particular profession, you might be able to find a custom software package designed specifically for your profession. If such a package uses a standard database, or has a good way of importing and exporting data in a standard format, it's probably worth moving to the top of the list of options to check out. Other colleagues in your profession may be able to point you to good software. The biggest caveat here is that if you can't easily move your data to something else, you may find that you become "locked in" to the product, stuck within its limitations, spending much more down the road when your business needs outgrow the product. If the data is all in a database or available in some sort of text-based standard, extracting it and moving to another system, while still costly, will be a fraction of the cost of implementing a new system.

TABLE 10.1 Comparison of Popular Business Accounting Packages

Software Package	Single- or Double-entry	Open Source?	Customizable?	Payroll	Invoices	Inventory	Online Banking	Print Checks	Access through Web Browser	Simultaneous Users
Quicken Home & Business	Single	No	No	No	Yes	No	Electronic Bank Reconciliation	Yes	No	No
GnuCash	Double	Yes	No	No	Yes	No	Electronic Bank Reconciliatoin	No	No	Yes (with special configuration)
QuickBooks	Double	No	No	Yes (recurring charge)	Yes	Yes (some versions)	Yes	Yes	Online version	Some versions
Aria	Double	Yes	Yes	Yes	Yes	Yes	No	No	Yes	Yes
SQL Ledger	Double	Yes	Yes	No	Yes	Yes	No	Yes	Yes	Yes
Peachtree	Double	No	No	Yes	Yes	Yes	Integrated Merchant Accounts	Yes	Some versions	Some versions
Great Plains	Double	No	Yes	Yes	Yes	Yes	Yes	Yes	Some installations	Yes

Table 10.1 lists some common business accounting packages. There are dozens of software packages available; these are a handful of ones commonly used by small businesses. There are also dozens of different features, and how they're implemented varies substantially among the different programs. This table illustrates some of the major differentiating features among the programs.

Let's take a closer look at these programs.

Intuit Quicken Home & Business

Quicken was one of the original accounting packages for personal computers. Quicken is geared primarily towards personal finance rather than business finance. The Home & Business version includes basic invoicing and business features.

Many sole proprietorships and independent contractors get their start using a personal accounting package, because they already are familiar with them, and already use them for their personal accounting. Generally this type of software lacks features needed by most businesses. As soon as you incorporate, hire employees, or keep an inventory, you will outgrow this type of software and need a real business accounting solution. Quicken is available from Intuit at *http://www.intuit.com*.

GnuCash

GnuCash® is an open source personal finance program that has recently added business features. It's a client program that runs on Linux and Mac OS X. Unlike Quicken, it uses double-entry accounting, making it much more suitable for business use. This program is a great choice for small businesses looking to move away from Windows. It's also good for personal finances, handling equity accounts and calculating loans. Figure 10.2 shows a report and a ledger in GnuCash.

GnuCash comes with the major Linux distributions, which is a good way to install it. It is possible, but difficult, to compile GnuCash to use a database back end, which allows multiple people to access the books at the same time. However, there is no mechanism for restricting access to particular functions for particular users, a feature highly recommended by most trained accountants.

Another benefit of GnuCash is that it uses a standard XML-based file format that any programmer can easily understand. This makes it possible to write scripts to extract or convert GnuCash data to other systems. Because GnuCash can import data from proprietary systems, it can work as an intermediary step in migrating a set of books from QuickBooks to a database-driven accounting system.

You can find out more about GnuCash at the project Web site, *http://www. gnucash.org*.

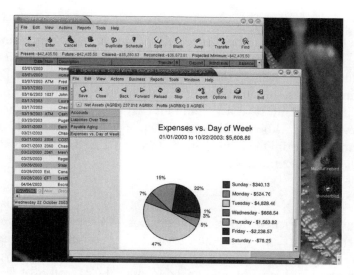

FIGURE 10.2   GnuCash is a personal finance program that can handle most sole proprietorship financial needs.

Intuit QuickBooks

QuickBooks is practically a small business standard. Many small businesses manage their books in QuickBooks, and perhaps more important for making a decision of accounting packages, many part-time bookkeepers are experienced in using Quick-Books.

GnuCash actually compares pretty favorably with QuickBooks. The main benefits of choosing QuickBooks, besides a plethora of people to help you implement it, are features like payroll modules that are regularly updated for your location, integration with tax software, and special-purpose customizations for small retailers, contractors, and non-profit organizations. If your bookkeeper does all of your payroll accounting in house, you may find QuickBooks and its payroll module worth the cost of the regular updates.

The other thing you get from QuickBooks is extensive help. For many open source accounting packages, the software is free but you have to purchase the documentation. If you don't have a bookkeeping or accounting background, you might find the wizards and help system included with QuickBooks worthwhile.

The biggest drawback to QuickBooks is that it's file-based—only one person can have the company ledger open at a time. When it comes time to do your taxes, you have to somehow get your QuickBooks file to your accountant. While there are secure ways of transferring files over the Internet, basic email isn't one of them. Many business owners write their data to a CD and have to physically carry it to their accountant. If your accountant changes anything, you need to physically retrieve the QuickBooks file with the changes—and you had better not make any changes in your QuickBooks in the meantime. QuickBooks is available from Intuit at *http://www.intuit.com*.

Aria

Now we've reached the first of the database-driven accounting packages. Aria® is an open source resurrected branch of an earlier accounting package called Nola. Aria offers most of the features small businesses need, including payroll, accounting, inventories, and receiving. You need to enter the payroll rules for your location, but it includes features such as the ability to designate birthdays for employees, generate a Bill Of Materials, create invoices, and conduct physical inventories. Figure 10.3 gives an idea of what Aria functions look like.

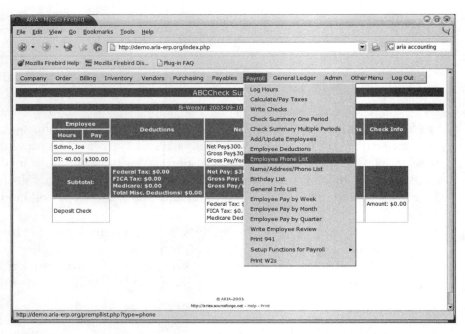

FIGURE 10.3 Payroll functions in Aria, an open source accounting package.

Aria is in active development at this writing, and has a small following. It uses PHP and MySQL, which is widely available on many Web hosts. Aria has built-in user administration, allowing you to provide access to particular areas of the software to particular people.

Aria has some great benefits for use in a business environment. Multiple people can use it at the same time. Your accountant can log in and make changes to your books that other users see the next time they run a report. You don't need to install any special software on your workstations—all you need is a Web browser capable of using JavaScript. It has all the basic functionality you'd find in much more expensive proprietary software environments.

With the data stored in a database, it's easy to extract for other purposes, or connect other systems to it. Many Web developers are experienced using PHP—you can easily find one to integrate other Web applications into your accounting system, connecting a time tracking program directly into the accounting system, for example.

The main drawbacks to Aria are related to security and reliability. While it's easy to post it to a Web host, the last thing you want to share on a generic server are the financial details of your company. On a shared host, other users may be able to connect to your database and see the financials for your company. The solutions are to either use a host that controls access to the server, or host it on your own server.

A slightly less obvious drawback is that if a connection or the script execution is interrupted, it's possible for only a part of your transaction to be added, not all of it. Since the software uses double-entry accounting, if there is some problem while the script is working, one ledger may get credited, while the other one never gets debited, leading to books that won't balance.

The chances of such an error happening are slim, and if it happens, it shouldn't be too hard to track down and correct. If you need features not offered by SQL Ledger, and are small enough that you don't need the most robust solution, Aria is a great accounting solution. You can test-drive Aria and download it at *http://www.aria-erp.org*.

SQL Ledger

SQL Ledger is quite similar to Aria, with many of the same features and benefits. It also runs on a Web server, stores its data in a database, requires nothing more than a Web browser to use, and solves the issue of allowing your accountant to view (and repair) your books without requiring an in-person visit. SQL Ledger differs in the technology it uses: Perl and PostgreSQL. The main benefit of SQL Ledger over Aria is that it's more robust.

SQL stands for Structured Query Language, a language developed by IBM to get results from and data into a database. SQL is used to interact with databases of all sizes and types. What PostgreSQL offers over MySQL (until recently) is support for transactions.

Let's take a quick look from a data point of view at what happens when you sell an item in your inventory. First of all, you must reduce your count of that item in your inventory, because you no longer have the item for sale. Then you need to increase the Accounts Receivable for the customer because they now owe you money for the item. Once all of the items have been entered, the customer needs to pay. You then reduce the amount in your Accounts Receivable, and increase the amount in your cash drawer. These are a whole sequence of events that affect several different parts of your database.

A *transaction*, in database terms, is the entire set of actions that occur during a complex process such as this. If the sale gets interrupted—the customer leaves without paying, you would need to reverse all of the previous actions—you have to put the items back in the inventory, making sure your Accounts Receivable is still correct. A transaction wraps all of these actions into a single, all-or-nothing action. If the final part of the action never occurs, none of the earlier actions are *committed* to the database.

Because SQL Ledger uses transactions, it's more reliable than Aria—if something interrupts its processing, no changes are made to the database. Your books need to be balanced before SQL Ledger even allows you to commit. In this respect, SQL Ledger is capable of handling much bigger, more intensive businesses more reliably.

SQL Ledger is great for keeping all of your ledgers, managing inventories, and generating and emailing invoices, orders, and statements. We'll take a closer look at SQL Ledger later in the chapter. SQL-Ledger is available at *http://sql-ledger.org*.

Peachtree

Peachtree is the other popular accounting package for small businesses. Much of its functionality overlaps QuickBooks, but it has its own set of strengths. Among its strengths is the ability to integrate with an ACT! contact database.

Like QuickBooks, Peachtree has a large following of independent bookkeepers. Also, there are different versions of the product, with successively more features. Generally, both Peachtree and QuickBooks do a great job of keeping track of your books, and if you have a bookkeeper already comfortable with one, it's often not worth switching to anything else. There is an online version of Peachtree that provides a very similar feature set to SQL Ledger on a subscription basis. Peachtree is available at *http://www.peachtree.com*.

Great Plains and Other Enterprise Software

Microsoft Great Plains is an accounting package designed for larger businesses. There are several enterprise accounting packages in the same category as Great Plains. You cannot buy software at this level off the shelf. To obtain it, you need to work with a *Value Added Reseller* (VAR), basically a consultant who specializes in the particular software package. The VAR sets up your system and the licensing arrangements.

At this level, open source solutions provide compelling cost advantages. When a company grows to a size that its accounting, Human Resources, and operations systems start consuming more time than they save, integrating them into a single, comprehensive, flexible system generally pays off over time.

All of these systems require custom installation. The problem with a big expensive system is that each of them was designed with one particular business in mind. Is it cheaper to customize it to meet your company's needs, or build a new one from the open source parts freely available? It depends on how closely your business compares to the mold the system was built around.

You can check out Great Plains at *http://www.greatplains.com*. Two open source projects are in development that promise to compete directly with this class of software: the Compiere project, at *http://compiere.org*, and GNU Enterprise, at *http://www.gnue.org*. At this writing, Compiere has many working modules but depends upon the proprietary Oracle database to store its data, while GNU Enterprise is mostly in the planning stage.

SMALL BUSINESS ACCOUNTING: SQL LEDGER

Let's take a closer look at SQL Ledger. We've already seen a few reasons why SQL Ledger is a good choice for a small business: it's reliable and easy to access from any computer, provides all the basic accounting features of any business package, and is inexpensive to extend to meet your needs.

The first question most bookkeepers ask about a system that can be accessed by many users is, can they be restricted from accessing the sensitive parts? You don't want unauthorized people adding a vendor to your system, creating a way to embezzle. You also may not want contract people who may interact with your competition to know the financial health of your company. In SQL Ledger, you can set up different login accounts, and for each account specify which menu items they're allowed to use. Only those items a user has permission to see appear in the menu. You can set up an account for your accountant, and he'll be able to run whatever reports he needs, or drill down to each transaction to find any details you've entered. Figure 10.4 shows some of the menu items available for granting or restricting user access.

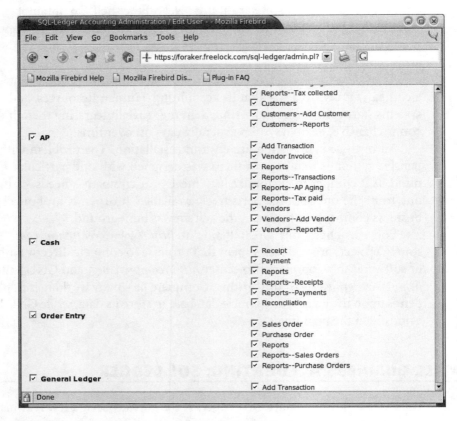

FIGURE 10.4 Setting user permissions in SQL Ledger.

Using SQL Ledger is as simple as browsing to the URL where SQL Ledger is installed, and entering your username and password. From there you get a menu of options in the left frame, and a welcome screen in the right frame.

Like other professional accounting packages, to find out anything you have to run a report. Since you may have hundreds of customers, you can find the one you're looking for by searching for specific characteristics: name, contact, email, etc. Figure 10.5 shows a report criteria page. If you don't add any criteria, the report returns a full list of items.

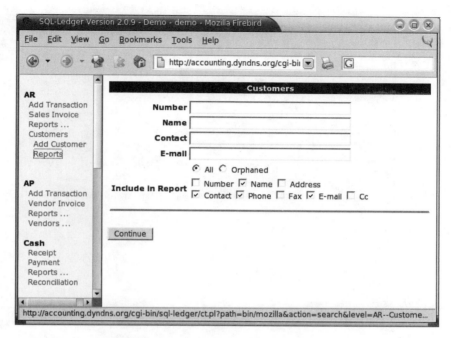

FIGURE 10.5 Report criteria for showing your customers.

SQL Ledger requires that your transactions balance. If you need to make an adjustment, you need to provide an account for the other side of the transaction—and the money needs to come from somewhere. This is true of inventory items, too. SQL Ledger keeps track of parts and assemblies, generates a Bill Of Materials, and handles all kinds of variations of taxes. It handles international transactions particularly well, including support for multiple currencies. You can create orders to use as a work order or estimate, and then convert it to an invoice for payment.

Customizing Invoices and Statements

One benefit SQL Ledger has over Aria is the ability to create PDF versions of forms. You can generate and email a PDF-based invoice directly from the Web site from any browser, without having to install any software on your desktop to generate the PDF. You can also send statements in plain HTML format if you're unsure about the technical capabilities of the person you're sending the form to.

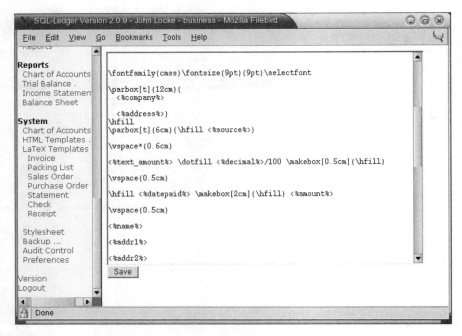

FIGURE 10.6 Editing a template for printing a check.

Each of the forms and reports can be customized. The reports are generated in HTML, checks and receipts are created using a text layout language called LaTeX (see Figure 10.6), and statements, invoices, and orders can be generated in either. Customizations in SQL Ledger involve generating the raw code that results in the appearance you want, and posting it into the site. To customize the HTML forms, you need to be able to understand and edit HTML code, inserting placeholders for names, addresses, items, and amounts. Likewise, for the LaTeX forms, you need to generate the markup by hand or use another program, and paste it into the Web form in SQL Ledger. Figure 10.6 illustrates the simple interface for customizing check printing.

While this system isn't user friendly, it provides a degree of control over the appearance and layout of each item—a professional Web designer and desktop publisher will be able to make the payee and dollar amount appear at a precise location on your checks.

Installing SQL Ledger

SQL Ledger has a great installation routine. You download a set-up script from the Web site, make it executable, and run it. The script checks for all of the software it relies on, warns you if something is missing, and downloads the latest version of all of the SQL Ledger files. It also configures and restarts Apache for you. If the script finishes without error, you should be able to browse to your server with any Web browser, and log into the admin page at *http://yourservername.com/sql-ledger/admin.pl*. Once you've set up a user account, you can log in at *http://yourserver-name.com/sql-ledger/login.pl*.

To make it easier for other users, it's helpful to add a redirection to the login page. In the `sql-ledger-httpd.conf` file, you'll find a <Directory> block for the main SQL-Ledger installation directory. Insert this line inside the block to redirect users to the login page:

```
DirectoryIndex login.pl
```

The other thing you need to do is create a user in PostgreSQL with access to the account database. The installation instructions in the new SQL Ledger directory tells you how to do this. The important thing to understand is that each regular user you create in PostgreSQL can only access databases it creates. If you are hosting account-ing data for multiple companies, you would set up a different database user account for each company. Then you could back up data for each user independently. Other-wise, you set up all of the SQL Ledger users to use the same database user account.

SUMMARY

The real value of a system like SQL Ledger is the ability to inexpensively customize the software to meet the needs of your business. Need to create a custom report? All you need is somebody who knows a bit of Perl to figure out where to add the mod-ule and write a short chunk of code. The source code is well documented, and the way it's designed makes it easy to add menu items and pages that do all kinds of tasks you might need.

Should your business use an open source accounting package? There are good reasons for and against this. If you want friendly interfaces with lots of built-in ad-vice provided by the software, you should probably stick with QuickBooks or Peachtree. If you plan to use bookkeepers who work outside your office, an online solution has some big advantages. As your business grows, inevitably your ac-counting systems will become more complex and outgrow the basic accounting packages. When your business reaches this level of complexity, the open source of-ferings start to become compelling for ease of customization and their cost.

In this chapter, we learned about the differences between single and double-entry accounting. We looked at some approaches to handling payroll, employee hours, invoices and orders, inventory, point-of-sale software, online transactions, and taxes. We examined a few popular proprietary accounting packages, and compared them to some open source alternatives. Finally, we discussed how to implement and use one of the leading open source accounting Web applications.

We'll take a closer look at some ERP tools, which usually include accounting modules, in Chapter 12. In the next chapter, we'll see how to use spreadsheets, databases, and project management tools to manage just about everything else in your business.

ACCOUNTING REFERENCES

An updated list of resources for this chapter is on the Web site for the book at *http://opensourcesmall.biz/finance.*

Articles

"Time is Money," by the Disenchanted Developer, article about writing your own timesheet Web application. Available online at *http://www.devshed. com/c/a/PHP/Time-is-Money-part-1/.*

Software

TurboTax, tax preparation software *http://www.turbotax.com/*
Gibbon, open source Point-Of-Sale software *http://gibbon.sourceforge.net*
jPOS, open source Java-based Point-Of-Sale software *http://jpos.org*
easyPOS, open source Point-Of-Sale software *http://easypos.sourceforge.net*
Intuit Quicken, commercial personal accounting software *http://www. quicken.com/*
GnuCash, open source desktop accounting software for Mac and Linux *http://www.gnucash.org/*
Peachtree, commercial desktop business accounting software *http://www. peachtree.com/*
QuickBooks, commercial desktop business accounting software *http:// quickbooks.intuit.com/*
Great Plains, enterprise-level commercial accounting system *http://www. greatplains.com*
Aria, open source accounting Web application *http://arias.sourceforge.net/*
SQL Ledger, open source accounting Web application *http://www.sql-ledger.com*

Web Sites

Free Software for Business accounting, summary of open source accounting software *http://cbbrowne.com/info/financefreesoft.html*

11 Managing Resources, Schedules, and Projects

In This Chapter

- Introduction
- Common Management Tools
- Finding Open Source Management Applications
- Managing Employee Schedules
- Managing Projects
- Summary
- Management System References

INTRODUCTION

The best management software is no substitute for a good manager. When it comes down to it, people manage. Computers provide tools to help you organize your tasks, but cannot do the job for you. Part II of this book is about tools that help any business. In this concluding chapter of Part II, we're going to look at a few different ways computers can help you manage specific things.

This chapter is the primary problem-solving chapter in the book, walking you through how to track down and evaluate open source projects, and use generic tools like spreadsheets and databases to solve all sorts of problems. There is a lot of detail in this chapter, but nothing extremely technical.

Any business with a public presence needs to schedule employees to be available for all of its open hours. Many other types of businesses also depend on assigning workers to cover each shift. The problem is, employees come with their own desires, needs, and constraints. When you try to juggle the schedules of a dozen employees, each with their own preferences, to cover all the available shifts you realize what a daunting task it can be.

Another common problem is managing reservations. As the Internet has grown in popularity, more and more people expect to be able to conduct their business online. If your business involves reserving a resource, such as a room, a table, or a seat, you may find yourself losing business to a competitor if you don't provide a computerized reservation system.

In a completely different vein, managing a project involves a different kind of scheduling. Large projects demand thinking through every step, identifying tasks and the critical path to get them done, scheduling, budgeting, and trying to use a crystal ball. Small projects require attention to detail, and if you're trying to juggle several of them, you need a system to make sure you've finished all of the associated tasks. Software isn't a crystal ball, but it can keep track of all those details and help you manage the actual project.

Let's take a look at some tools and techniques for managing schedules, resources, and projects.

COMMON MANAGEMENT TOOLS

When setting up a system to help you manage things, you have to consider ease of use. A system for managing schedules is useless if nobody uses it. If you keep your room reservations in several places, you're bound to have conflicting reservations. When tracking progress on a project, if you have to look in several different places to find out the status of each task, it's going to involve more effort than you'll want, leading inevitably to less accurate reports.

Choose your management system carefully, based on things you'll actually use. If your work involves being away from a computer, you have to bring your management system with you—either on a PDA, or in some sort of paperwork. Programmers have a saying: Garbage In, Garbage Out. If you and other people on your team don't consistently use a management system, it's worse than not having a system at all—you'll get systematically incorrect information out of it.

The best management systems grow organically with your needs. You can start out with a simple set of manila folders, labeled with each major task in a project, in a filing cabinet dedicated to that project. You can mirror that structure for electronic information in some file directories on your computer. You might also set up a corresponding email folder for the project, and move all related correspondence into it. When you're the primary person working on a project, three places to keep all project-related information may be sufficient.

But if you have to report your progress on a project to someone else, or work with other people to accomplish it, you'll probably find a need for having some sort of centralized repository for your documents, a database to track bookings, and some sort of summary accessible to everybody concerned. What sort of management tools you need depends entirely on the number of people who need to use them, and the size, nature, and complexity of what you're trying to manage.

In this chapter, we're going to take a look at a variety of management tools, ranging from paper to special-purpose programs. Some of this information may be basic, but perhaps you'll find a new use for an old tool. First, we'll take a look at common tools that can be applied to any management task. Then we'll explore a few special-purpose programs for particular management tasks.

Some common tools you can use to manage schedules, resources, and projects include:

- Paper systems
- Calendars
- Spreadsheets
- Relational databases

Tried and True: Paper Management Systems

Frank and Mary's Friendly Hotel uses a paper-based reservation system. There's a ledger book kept handy by the telephone. Each page represents a week. Each line represents a room, with the room number in the first column. Three columns in the grid represent each day.

During the day, Mary usually answers the telephone. When she gets a call for a room reservation, she opens to the appropriate week, marks the start and end columns of the reservation, draws a line between them, and writes the person's last name in pencil above the line. She then takes the name, contact details, reservation dates, and the room number for the person on a card and puts it in a file for the up-coming reservations. She now has the information indexed two ways: by date in the reservation book, and by name in the reservations file.

One of Mary's jobs is to schedule staff. She needs to make sure someone is always available at the front desk, and schedule the housekeeping staff, security guards, and the kitchen work. Each employee gets two days off a week, but most of these jobs need to be performed seven days a week. During the morning and evening rush, she needs extra front desk staff.

To solve the scheduling problem, Mary has identified some standard shifts. She has drawn a weekly schedule showing all 24 hours of seven days straight with a horizontal bar for each shift. She has found an arrangement of shifts that works well, week after week, and assigns the same people to the same shifts each week. But inevitably some of the staff have special requests for certain days off, sometimes at the last minute, and the schedule usually gets updated substantially through the week as people swap around. Also, she has a hard time finding people for the grave-yard shift, so she ends up dividing it up, giving it to each of her regular staff once a week. So when one of her front desk workers starts going to night school, the disruption to the schedule takes hours to figure out.

Meanwhile, Frank is having an annex built, which will eventually add another dozen rooms. Since he has a construction background, he's acting as the general contractor. He's been working with an architect to design the new structure, and now has to line up people to pour the foundation, frame the addition, provide wiring, plumbing, roofing, siding, insulation, dry-wall, and all the finish work. They have a limited budget to do the work, but want the work done to a quality that will hold up to heavy, daily use.

Some of the tasks have to happen in a particular sequence. Permits must be obtained before the work can be done. Plumbing and wiring must be done before the walls are closed up. None of the other construction can start until the foundation is done. But some of the work can be done simultaneously—roofers can be finishing the roof while the siding company installs and paints the exterior of the addition.

Frank needs to know what it's going to cost before starting. He'd like to have the addition finished and ready for guests by next summer, so he can benefit from the extra capacity during the high season. He starts by drawing up a project plan with the architect. They work out all the individual projects to be sub-contracted out. He hires a team of carpenters to do most of the labor, and maps out a schedule to keep them occupied through the length of the project. He identifies the critical path of tasks that must be accomplished in a particular sequence, and draws his timeline on paper.

Now that the project is underway, Frank has to go through his project plan on a weekly basis, evaluating the progress of the project against the plan. Inevitably he needs to adjust the plan as unforeseen obstacles appear. Perhaps he needs to fill some time for his carpenter team while waiting for an inspection. After photocopying his paper timeline and redrawing it several times, he realizes there may be a way his computer can help him with his project management.

Managing Intuitively with Calendars

We talked in depth about calendars and calendar software in Chapter 8. Different views in a calendar are useful for different types of tasks.

For a reservation system, the ledger notebook Mary uses is a form of calendar, with its information ordered by time into specific periods. If you only need to manage a few resources, you can set up an individual calendar for each one. Such a calendar can show you when a particular resource is available. Software that can show you multiple calendars side-by-side can help you find available resources for a specific time period. However, managing reservations for Frank and Mary's Friendly

Hotel is going to get a bit more difficult when that annex is done—there are only 48 lines on each page, and their room count is about to grow to 60. And none of the calendar software discussed in Chapter 8 can show you 60 calendars side-by-side, at least not in a way that's easy to use.

On the other hand, the work schedule fits on a weekly calendar for each department very nicely. Mary has a choice when setting up multiple calendars for scheduling each department: set up one calendar per employee, or one calendar per shift. With a shift calendar, it's hard for each employee to find their shifts at a glance, but easy to tell who is supposed to be on duty for any given shift. It's also easy to make mistakes and schedule somebody more than 40 hours, especially if they work on different shift calendars. With an employee calendar, you can ensure that each employee has the correct number of hours, but not easily ensure you have every shift covered.

For managing large projects such as Frank's annex, a calendar is but one essential tool. All the important milestones need to go on the calendar: the final completion date, inspections, and scheduled start and finish dates of each of the smaller projects. Because most of these interim milestones tend to move around a lot during the course of the project, using an electronic calendar helps a lot.

Here's how you might handle a project calendar:

1. Create a document repository for your project using Subversion, as described in Chapter 9. Set it up to allow WebDAV autoversioning.
2. Create an iCalendar-based calendar using one of the programs described in Chapter 8—Mozilla Calendar, for example.
3. Publish the calendar to the Subversion repository, and configure everybody's calendar application to use the Subversion URL for the project calendar.
4. Set up phpICalendar on the server to make your calendar viewable with any Web browser.

With this setup, everyone involved in the project can see the latest schedule using either a Web browser or a calendar program. As you update the calendar, Subversion automatically records each version. You can check out the calendar as it was at any time in the past, to see how your calendar has changed over the course of the project. The next time you plan a calendar for a similar project, you can see where your predictions were accurate, and how you needed to adjust them.

If your business does many small projects instead of few big ones, a calendar can be the most effective way to manage your time. Each of your workers can keep their calendar on a shared server. When you accept a new project, you can put everybody's calendar side-by-side to see who can take it, and when.

Easy Analysis with Spreadsheets

A spreadsheet can be a fantastic tool for figuring out how to manage things. A spreadsheet is like a sheet of paper with practically no limit to its height and width that arranges everything into horizontal *rows* and vertical *columns*. Everything you type goes into a *cell* that can be identified by its row and column. Rows are typically identified with a number, and columns by a letter.

Once you put items into a spreadsheet, you can perform calculations on the numbers, and sort, filter, or create graphs with the results. You don't have to use just numbers in a spreadsheet, however. Spreadsheets sort alphabetical lists as easily. Most regular spreadsheet users know a number of tricks that make using spreadsheets fast and powerful. We'll go through a few of these tricks shortly, but first let's take a look at how Frank and Mary might apply a spreadsheet to their management challenges.

A spreadsheet solves Mary's problem of running out of lines on her paper for the rooms. She can use one row for each room, and extend it as far down the page as necessary. It's relatively easy to manage up to hundreds of rooms in a spreadsheet. Mary then puts the dates across the top, one column per day. She can divide weeks with a thick border, and freeze the room numbers on the left side so they remain in view as the weeks go by and the spreadsheet scrolls to the right. Again, as she books rooms, she puts the name of the party into the spreadsheet in the cell that represents the room and the date. She can quickly drag the selection to the right and the spreadsheet automatically fills in subsequent days with the party's name. See Figure 11.1 for an example.

Mary still needs a separate system for managing the contact information and payment details for the party. And there's one fairly substantial drawback to this system, as the business grows: only one person can edit the spreadsheet at a single time. As long as there's only one person working the front desk and answering the phone at a time, this is acceptable. And it's practically instantaneous to set up. For scheduling staff, a spreadsheet works about as well as Mary's paper schedule, except that it's easier to edit and reprint as necessary.

For Frank's construction project, a spreadsheet can help in many different ways. For calculating the total cost of materials, a spreadsheet is ideal. A cost spreadsheet might have one column for listing an item, the next for containing the cost of the item, and a third column for the quantity needed. He can then create a calculation in the fourth column that multiplies the second and third columns together, to show the total cost of items. At the bottom of a list of all the materials needed for framing the annex, he can have a row of totals, including total cost. Because the calculations in the spreadsheet update whenever the contents of any of the cells change, Frank can see, for example, the effect on the bottom line of using different combinations of 8-foot long and 10-foot long lumber.

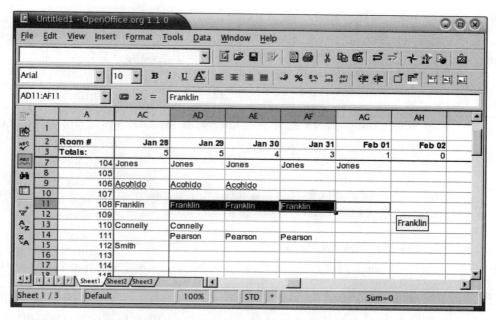

FIGURE 11.1 Auto-complete names by dragging the small black box in the lower right corner of a selected cell to the right. This fills in cells with values in the selected cell. If the selected cells contain a number, the spreadsheet attempts to follow whatever pattern you've set, or if there isn't a pattern, it increments the number. In this way, you can quickly create the date labels across the top and the room numbers down the side.

Spreadsheets are great for calculating costs and trying out different scenarios. You can try all sorts of combinations of figures to see what works out to be the most cost effective. Spreadsheets are great for manipulating text, calculating financial effects, creating statistical reports, and even doing the trigonometry to cut the braces and trusses to the right lengths.

Open Source Spreadsheets

So what do spreadsheets have to do with open source software? Nothing, directly—but there are some great open source spreadsheets you can use now. The most popular spreadsheet program is Microsoft Excel. The open source OpenOffice.org Calc provides pretty much the same features as Excel, including an equivalent to Excel's PivotTable feature called DataPilot, which allows you to analyze more than two dimensions of data.

ON THE CD OpenOffice.org is part of The Open CD, on the CD-ROM included with this book.

Of the open source spreadsheet programs, OpenOffice.org attempts to be as close to Microsoft Excel as possible. Each of the major open source desktops has its own streamlined spreadsheets. For GNOME, there's a project called Gnumeric (*http://www.gnome.org/projects/gnumeric/*). Gnumeric supports all of the functions in Excel, and adds its own set of functions that include complex numbers, different distributions of random numbers, and financial functions for working with stock options, among others. KDE's KOffice suite includes a program called, naturally, KSpread (*http://koffice.org/kspread/*). Both of these programs support scripting and embedding in other applications using their respective frameworks.

If you're unfamiliar with spreadsheets, you'll probably find Gnumeric on Linux to be friendly and powerful. If you're using Windows or Macintosh, or are already a power spreadsheet user, you'll probably prefer OpenOffice.

Spreadsheet Tips and Tricks

Here's a quick primer on using a spreadsheet. Most spreadsheet programs have a remarkably similar interface, and use very similar rules.

First of all, entering text. You select a cell anywhere on a spreadsheet using your mouse, the TAB key, the ENTER key, or the arrows. The actual contents of the selected cell appear in the *formula bar* at the top of the spreadsheet. If you start typing, you'll replace whatever is in the cell with what you type. If you want to edit the existing contents of a cell, you have to click in the formula bar and make your changes there—you won't see the cursor in the actual cell in the spreadsheet.

The value doesn't actually go into the cell until you move to another one. At that point, the formula you've typed is evaluated, the number is formatted, and the text is aligned according to your settings. You can cancel your changes to the cell by clicking the "X" icon next to the formula bar, or save it without leaving the cell by clicking the checkmark icon.

Secondly, the contents of a cell can be either a number, a formula, or text. You enter a formula by starting with an equals (=) character. A number must begin with, obviously, a digit, and contain only valid numerical characters. Anything else is considered text. You can force a number to be treated like text by starting a cell with a single quote character ('). The quote won't appear in the cell, but the number will be formatted according to the settings for text rather than numbers, which typically means it's aligned to the left edge of the cell instead of the right. Text is also ignored in calculations.

Thirdly, when you put a *cell reference* in a formula, the current value of that cell is used in the formula to evaluate it and come up with a result. A cell reference is a combination of the letter for the cell's column and the number of its row. Cell A1, for example, is the upper-left-most cell in the entire spreadsheet. Cell A2 is the one beneath it, and cell B1 is the cell to its right. If the value of the referenced cell changes, the formula is recalculated, and the result of the cell containing the formula is updated to contain the newly calculated value.

Some functions can calculate based on a range of cells. For example, you can use the SUM() function to get a total of all of the numbers in the cells you specify. You use a colon (:) to separate the cell references at either end of the range. If you type "=SUM(B1:B15)" in the cell B16, that cell will always have a total of all the cells above it in the same column. Most spreadsheets have function helpers you can access by clicking an equals icon (=) near the formula bar. This opens up a wizard that lists all of the available functions, organized by type, with help and a list of what that formula expects as an argument. You can often select other cells in the spreadsheet while you're using the wizard to have the formula use those cells in the calculation.

A formula can be as simple as just another cell reference: "=A1" will show whatever is in the upper left-most cell in the cell you put this formula. When the A1 cell is changed, this cell will automatically show the new value. You can use basic arithmetic in a formula: "=A1+1" adds one to the value of A1, and shows it as the result in the cell. "=A1*B1" multiplies the values in these two cells and shows the result.

Fourthly, you can have multiple *worksheets* within a *workbook*. You'll see tabs along the bottom left corner of the spreadsheet that take you to a different page. You can add, delete, and rename these pages, usually by right-clicking on the tab among other methods.

Auto-filling is another common spreadsheet feature. When you have one or more cells selected, notice that there's a little square box on the lower right corner of the selection. This is called a handle. Drag the handle up, down, left, or right for as many cells as you want. When you let go of the mouse button, the spreadsheet fills in values in the entire range you've dragged through.

Finally, cell references are relative unless otherwise specified. What that means is that if you copy cell B16 with the formula "SUM(B1:B15)" and paste it to cell D20, the spreadsheet will put in the formula "SUM(D5:D19)." Internally, the formula in a cell doesn't keep track of the exact cell references, but rather their position related to the current cell. So what you're actually copying is a formula that says "give me the sum of all the cells between the one 15 cells above me and the cell directly above me." This holds true no matter how far away the cell you're referencing is. This makes it possible to auto-fill formulas.

If you really want a formula to use an *absolute* reference to one particular cell no matter where the formula is, you use the dollar sign ($) in front of the absolute parts of the reference. To make a formula always refer to cell A1, you would put "=A1" in the reference. You can make the column relative and the row absolute, or vice versa, by putting the dollar sign in front of the part of the reference you want to remain constant: "=$A1" will always get a value from the "A" column no matter which column the formula is in, but the row will vary depending on where it was copied from and to.

These tips provide the barest introduction to how to use a spreadsheet. You can easily make charts based on data in a spreadsheet. You can filter a spreadsheet to quickly find rows containing specific values. You can sort spreadsheets based on the value of any particular column in several different ways. Spreadsheets are great for any mathematical calculation you can think of, especially if it involves working with large sets of numbers. Spreadsheets are also great for lists, and you can do a surprising amount of layout and design in one. If you don't already know how to use a spreadsheet, it's worth taking the time to get acquainted—you'll find all sorts of ways to put them to use.

Powerful Management with Databases

At a certain point, spreadsheets aren't enough. For a room booking system, when you reach a certain size, you need to allow multiple people to book rooms at the same time—but only one person can edit a spreadsheet at a time. You also need to manage customer information independently of the room bookings, and be able to retrieve that information by the customer's name. When scheduling people, you can organize your spreadsheet either by shift or by employee, but doing both requires double the effort.

A spreadsheet is a simple unstructured database. Each worksheet in a spreadsheet is a two-dimensional table, with rows and columns. You can do some clever things to analyze more dimensions of data, but it's hard to enter and organize this data, and you're limited to individual tables on different worksheets. It's extremely difficult to relate one table to another, to relate employees to shifts, to relate rooms to customers in a simple spreadsheet.

Enter the relational database. A relational database, like a spreadsheet, consists of tables with rows and columns. The difference is, each table has a specific predefined structure, and certain columns are used to relate one table to another. You can then run *queries* on the database to show the data you're looking for.

Let's take a closer look at a room reservation system. Mary has a few dozen rooms. Some of them have queen-sized beds, others twin beds. She needs one database table to keep track of the rooms. Each room becomes a row in this table, also called a *record*. The characteristics of the room go into the predefined columns: the room number, the number of queen-sized beds, the number of twin beds, the number of people who can sleep comfortably in the room, and whether it's equipped with a kitchenette. One of the columns in the table is designated as the *primary key*: a column that is guaranteed to be unique for each record in the table. Because each room has a unique room number, the room number is a good primary key.

She uses a different database table to keep track of her customers. In this table, she records the customer's first name, last name, address, phone number, the date she first talked with the customer, the most recent date she had interacted with the customer, and notes about the customer.

In database terms, a relationship can be one-to-one, one-to-many, or many-to-many. In a one-to-one relationship, each record in one table is related to only one record in another table, and the record in the other table isn't related to any other records. Much more common is a one-to-many relationship, where each record in one table can be related to multiple rows in another table. The purpose of the primary key is to identify a row in a table.

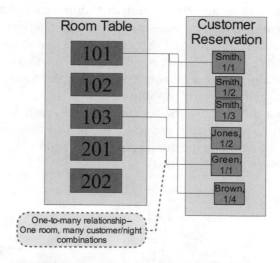

FIGURE 11.2 One-to-many relationship in a database. Note that this is not the best way to set up the table.

So Mary could set up a one-to-many relationship between her table of rooms and her table of customers, as shown in Figure 11.2: each room is related to multiple customers. By storing the date of a reservation and the room number in the customer table, she can keep track of her reservations. Here's where the power of a database starts to exceed what you can do in a spreadsheet or on paper.

Mary can now search for a reservation by customer, date, or room. She can look up any customer by name, and find the date of their reservation and the room number. By setting up a query that *joins* the room table to the customer table on the room number, she can find all the reservations for any particular night, and also identify the rooms that aren't currently booked.

But what if Frank & Mary's Hotel has repeat customers? For a new reservation for a repeat customer, Mary could just update the customer record with the new date and room number. But now the system has lost track of the previous reservation. If Mary had kept reservation data, she could use it to see how busy the hotel was on any particular night, data that might help them plan for the next season. And with this system, each customer could only have a single reservation at a time—if a customer wanted to book several different trips at a time, Mary would be unable to track it the way her database is set up.

The problem is, we set up the relationship to be one room to many customers. We also need to set up a relationship that allows one customer to have many rooms, in the form of reservations. A many-to-many relationship is really two different one-to-many relationships. On the "one" side of each relationship, we need a primary key. We already have a primary key for the room table. We need to create one for the customer table, assigning a unique number to each customer. So how do we set up the many-to-many relationship?

With a third table—the reservation table. Each row in the reservation table represents an individual reservation. It contains the room number, the customer number, the date, and the number of people. Figure 11.3 illustrates the idea behind a many-to-many relationships.

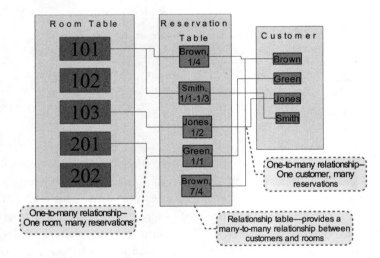

FIGURE 11.3 A many-to-many relationship suits the room reservation problem much better.

Now Mary can pull up a list of all the reservations for a customer, or all the reservations for a room. She can limit that list to reservations for a particular night, showing rooms reserved and rooms available. She can create a report counting all the room reservations for any particular month, and the total number of people staying any particular night—at least she could if the guests were honest. And she can send them all a holiday card, wishing them well and inviting them back, by setting up a mail merge in a word processor that pulls the addresses from the customer table.

That is the gist of how a relational database works. Every table represents a certain type of object. You define meaningful relationships between the tables, and the database transforms the raw data into useful information. Many of the applications in this book are simply a set of related database tables with a fancy graphical user interface. Many commercial applications are simply interfaces on top of a database.

Desktop Databases

Quite a few small businesses have figured out the basics of databases, and put together home-grown systems using them. Two proprietary database systems stand out in popularity among small businesses for their ease of creating solutions, and for their large number of database templates freely available on the Internet: Microsoft Access and FileMaker Pro. Both of these applications provide a structured graphical environment for setting up tables, putting together queries and views, and designing more user-friendly forms for entering data and reports for retrieving it.

These databases occupy a niche with few remaining competitors. They're simple to install and get working. Once you've identified what tables you need and how they relate, it's fairly easy to figure out how to make it work. Your actual data is stored in a single file that you can easily transfer to another computer—though you really don't want to try to juggle multiple copies of the same database. If you buy multiple copies of the database software, you can keep your actual database on one computer and access it from other computers.

These applications are easy to use, easy to install, and can provide many of the problem-solving characteristics of full fledged database servers. But they aren't database servers.

Database Servers

Compared to a desktop database, a database server is a program that runs continuously on a specific computer, accepting connections from other client database programs. With a desktop database, you can generally get up to about 10 people accessing the same database at the same time before you start running into problems. With a database server, the number of connections is only limited by the hardware that hosts it—you can have hundreds of concurrent users if you want. While Frank & Mary's Friendly Hotel is unlikely to ever have hundreds of front desk staff, if they put their booking system online, making it possible for customers to book their own reservations, it's possible to regularly have more than a dozen people accessing the database at once. If not now, hopefully when the annex is ready.

Proprietary database servers are expensive. Many big name companies in the computer industry have made their millions by selling database servers for thousands of dollars per installation, often more. Two database servers you have probably heard of are Oracle and Microsoft SQL Server. Table 11.1 lists some features of common database programs.

TABLE 11.1 Features of Common database programs

Database	Strengths	Built-in GUI	Transactions	Sub-queries	Stored Procedures
Oracle	Best reputation High stability High performance High data integrity Extra features	No	Yes	Yes	Yes
Microsoft SQL Server	Widely deployed Full-featured	Yes (MMC Snap-in)	Yes	Yes	Yes
MySQL	High performance High stability Widely available Open Source	No	Yes (with certain table types)	Version 5.0.0	Version 5.0.0
PostgreSQL	Full-featured High data integrity High stability Good performance	No	Yes	Yes	Yes
FileMaker Pro	Great graphical interface Cross Platform (Mac, Windows) No server needed	Yes	No	No	No
Microsoft Access	Good graphical interface Widely used	Yes	No	Yes	No

The reason there are no major open source desktop databases available is that there are already several extremely successful open source database servers. When you're a programmer and have a full-fledged database server, you have little need for a desktop database.

To interact with a database server, you build a query using a language called *Structured Query Language*, or SQL for short. (Some people pronounce it "see-kwil," others spell out the letters.) The database server returns a result. To find the available rooms in the hotel on July 4, 2004, a program might send a query that looks like this:

```
SELECT room.number, room.capacity, room.queens, room.twins FROM room
LEFT JOIN (SELECT reservation.room as roomid FROM reservation
WHERE reservation.date = '20040704') ON room.number=roomid
WHERE roomid IS NULL;
```

Now this is a fairly complicated query, but if you dissect it, it's not too hard to understand. The SELECT query asks the database to return a set of rows. The SELECT inside the parentheses asks for the room numbers in the reservation table for all rows (reservations) that have the date 2004-07-04. The outer SELECT statement asks for the room number, the room capacity, the number of queen beds, and the number of twin beds. It's asking the database to provide these records by combining the room table with the result of the SELECT query inside the parentheses. The LEFT JOIN statement means to include all the rows in the left table (the room table), but only the rows in the right table (the rows in the reservation table that have the date 2002-07-04) that have a matching room number. So now we have a list of all the rooms in a great big virtual table. The JOIN statement has added a column called roomid, which is the same as the room number if there is a reservation, or is undefined if there's no reservation. The WHERE clause then tells the database to only return the rows of this virtual table where the roomid column is undefined. While it may take some time to learn how to create a query like this, you can get a sense for why it's called structured query language: it's a limited set of keywords put together in a structured way to ask for data from a database. It's actually pretty easy to learn.

MySQL

The runaway success in the open source database world is MySQL. Many applications in this book use MySQL to store data in the back end. MySQL is extremely fast and stable, capable of going head-to-head on performance against any proprietary database on the highest traffic Web sites on the Internet. MySQL achieved this success by skimping on database features such as transactions, subqueries, and stored procedures. While the newest versions have started to add these features, MySQL is primarily used where speed is the driving factor.

The example SQL statement provided earlier is actually a subquery: it nests one SELECT query inside another. Until the latest versions of MySQL were available, you had to either get all of the data in a single SELECT query and filter out the results in your program, or you had to create a temporary table to put the results of one query, and use that temporary table in the next query.

A *transaction*, in database language, is a group of queries that insert data into the database or update existing rows in an all-or-nothing manner. When you buy something online, you're doing a transaction: you're exchanging dollars for a product. In the database, this might involve several different queries: reduce the inventory for the item, charge your credit card, add the item to the shipping queue. If one of these queries were to fail, the business would want the whole transaction to fail. If your credit card charge is not approved, the last thing the business wants to do is ship you the item. A transaction is a way of grouping these queries, testing to make sure they work and meet all the business rules. If everything is satisfied, the transaction is *committed* to the database. If not, the unfinished queries are *rolled back*.

The third major feature missing from MySQL until version 5.0.0 is support for stored procedures. A *stored procedure* is a program that runs within the database. It can do all sorts of data checking and special processing on the back end. A programmer can do everything a stored procedure can do using external programs, but those programs need to make additional queries to the database to accomplish the same tasks. A stored procedure can improve performance for database applications that involve a lot of data manipulation.

PostgreSQL

The other leading open source database is PostgreSQL. PostgreSQL is a much smaller project, but has been developed as an extremely reliable, full-featured database server. It has supported transactions and sub-selects since its beginning, making it a favorite for financial applications and other areas where transactions are important. In short, for applications where data is critical, it's going to be safer in PostgreSQL, and in complex applications, the database can do more of the work compared to MySQL.

For most small business operations, the bottom line is that some open source applications use MySQL and others use PostgreSQL. Both will perform fast enough for all your needs, and MySQL is perfectly sound for managing your custom applications.

Database Interfaces

Most Linux distributions come with several full-fledged database servers, usually including both MySQL and PostgreSQL. Without the easy graphical interface of the desktop databases, how can you easily set up a database in a database server?

You basically have five different ways to interact with a database on a server:

1. Through a graphical database management tool
2. Through a Web-based database management tool
3. By using an ODBC application
4. Through a command line client, using SQL
5. By writing programs that access the database through code

Graphical Database Administration

A number of projects provide management interfaces to open source databases. It's just a matter of finding one for your database and operating system. These tools can help you set up database user accounts, and create databases, tables, and queries. Some of them let you edit rows in the database.

Few of these applications are as easy to use as FileMaker Pro or Microsoft Access.

Web-Based Database Administration

The phpMyAdmin application shown in Figure 11.4 is an extremely popular way to manage a MySQL database. You can manage just about everything in your MySQL installation, from any Web browser. When you install it, make sure you set up Apache to require a login, or anybody could mess with your data.

Again, these administration interfaces require you to have some good idea about how your database is structured.

Using ODBC

Open DataBase Connectivity (ODBC) is an open standard way of communicating with databases. You can install special ODBC drivers and then connect to your database using any application that speaks ODBC.

The list of ODBC applications is lengthy. Most office software can connect to an ODBC data source and access the database. Microsoft Access uses ODBC as either a client or a server. OpenOffice.org can connect to any ODBC application, and use the data as the source of a mail merge.

ON THE CD
OpenOffice.org is part of The Open CD, on the CD-ROM included with this book.

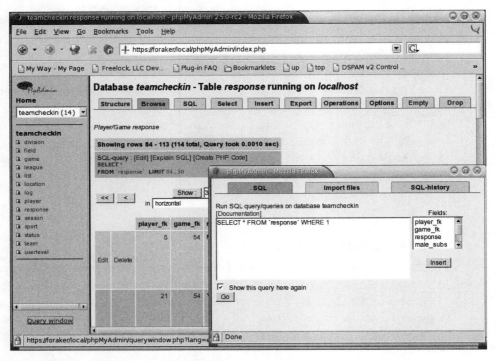

FIGURE 11.4 Using phpMyAdmin to manipulate a MySQL database.

OpenOffice.org can actually provide most of the desktop database features of Microsoft Access, when you hook it up to an ODBC back end. You can design convenient forms that insert data into the database. You can pull up custom reports based on data in the database. You can run mail merges using the data, define relationships between tables, and even edit the data directly.

The combination of OpenOffice.org, a MySQL database, and the MySQL ODBC driver can more than replace a desktop database in power, performance, and capabilities. It's just a little harder to get set up.

Command Line Database Clients

All databases provide a tool for sending plain SQL statements to the database. For MySQL, you can just type "mysql" in a command shell, and you'll go into the MySQL shell. From there, you can type your query and MySQL will print the results to the screen.

You can also use this interface to load data into the database from text files, or dump the contents of a database to a text file. If you take the time to learn SQL, this can be the fastest way to answer a question based on data in the database.

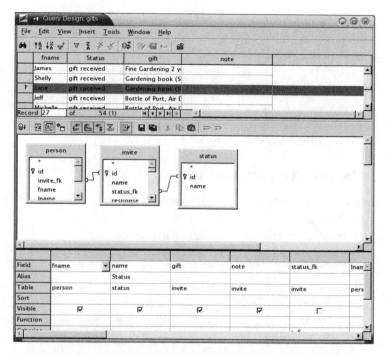

FIGURE 11.5 Using OpenOffice.org to set up relationships and queries in MySQL.

Programming Databases

Finally, the main reason to use a database server is so that you can create your own applications around it. Most computer languages have database functions built in or available through some sort of extension. Any programmer can use these functions to create an application. The combination of PHP and MySQL is especially effective for rapidly developing a sophisticated Web application.

FINDING OPEN SOURCE MANAGEMENT APPLICATIONS

Now that we have an understanding of how databases work, let's get back to Frank & Mary's Friendly Hotel. Frank and Mary can hire a programmer to create a special database application for their room bookings, managing their employee schedules, and creating some slick project management tools. However, as you might imagine, other businesses have similar needs, so there's a good chance somebody has already developed some open source software that already does what they need.

This thought process is key to successfully using open source to improve your business: first, understand what software is capable of. Then, look around to see if somebody has already done it. If they have, you now have a great solution at next to no cost. If someone has developed something close, but not quite, you can take their source code, turn it over to a developer, and get a system customized to meet your needs for minimal cost. And if you can't find an open source solution at all, your problem may be simple enough that you can hire a developer to create one for you for less than the cost of buying a proprietary program.

Choosing a Room Reservation Application

Mary doesn't want to go to the trouble of designing her own room-booking database. There are hundreds of thousands of hotels in the world; it's very likely somebody has already created a system that would meet her needs.

A search on Google for "open source hotel reservation application" returns over 90,000 results—but no major open source reservation applications appear in the first few pages of results (though there are a lot of results for booking rooms at open source events).

She next decides to search the major open source sites. Source Forge (*http://sourceforge.net*) is the largest, most popular site for coordinating small open source projects. A search for "hotel reservation" on the Source Forge site yields many pages of results. The first page has seven projects that might be suitable.

She visits each project and doesn't find a satisfactory one. The two projects that seem to be mostly complete are for reserving rooms and equipment on an hourly basis within a company or organization, not on a daily basis for guests. These include phpScheduleIt (*http://phpscheduleit.sourceforge.net/*) and eReserve (*http://ereserve.sourceforge.net/*). The other five projects are supposed to do exactly what she needs them to do, but none of them are finished yet. (If you're looking for hotel reservation software, try a Source Forge search now—some of these projects may be good alternatives for you.)

She continues the search on Source Forge, but the farther down the list she goes, the less active the software project is, and she doesn't find any other projects that fit her needs.

So she tries the next open source software site: Fresh Meat (*http://freshmeat.net*). Fresh Meat is basically a directory of Linux, Unix, and Palm software, and includes both proprietary and open source listings. Whereas Source Forge hosts thousands of open source projects, Fresh Meat merely provides listings, with a short description, links, contact URLs, and screenshots. A search on Fresh Meat returns a wider range of projects hosted at a variety of locations.

On Fresh Meat, a search for "hotel" returns four results. One of them is an open source project called php-residence (*http://www.digitaldruid.net/php-*

residence/en/), and it runs on a Linux Web server like the one Frank & Mary's Friendly Hotel set up using the ideas in Chapter 6.

Mary calls their Web developer up, who installs the software on their server. Within a day, their reservation system is online. The Web developer imported their room bookings from the spreadsheet Mary had been using. Now Mary can book rooms from any Web browser, and other front desk staff can make different reservations at the same time. Not only that, but the Web developer added a simple "check availability" form to the front page of the hotel's Web site, allowing potential guests to check availability for particular dates.

MANAGING EMPLOYEE SCHEDULES

Many different businesses share Frank & Mary's Friendly Hotel's need for an effective way to manage employee schedules. For only a handful of workers, setting up a system of calendars using a calendar application that supports multiple calendars can be the fastest way to get going. But as soon as you need to juggle the needs of more employees, creating a schedule can be one of the most time-consuming management tasks.

A database can certainly handle the task. But to try to design an effective database from scratch will take a considerable amount of analysis of the problem, and a fair bit of time. Once again, there's probably an open source solution to the problem.

This time, when Mary searches Source Forge, she finds two good solutions: Employee Scheduler (*http://empscheduler.sourceforge.net/*) and PhpSched (*http://sourceforge.net/projects/phpsched/*). Employee Scheduler is the newer program, designed to help a university schedule part-time student workers around their class schedules. Each student can specify their class schedule, and request particular shifts. The administrator can then assign work shifts and the system keeps track of conflicts. Employee Scheduler also integrates with a Content Management System called PostNuke, which is discussed in Chapter 13. This makes it work as part of an internal company Web site, where employees can get to the employee handbook, special notices about company events, and whatever else you want to post—it is essentially an online bulletin board.

PhpSched, on the other hand, appears to be an abandoned project. The demo of the application works great. Employees can request to work or not work particular shifts. When the administrator creates the schedule, the application tells her who has asked for each particular shift, and automatically notifies her when somebody has a full schedule. After the schedule is created, employees can offer their shift to others, if they want to change their schedule. The system automatically notifies the administrator and people looking to pick up shifts. It's quite powerful—but according to messages on the bulletin board for the project, some people have had trouble getting it to work on current Web servers.

Mary nevertheless decides to go with PhpSched because it offers better support for different departments. She hires a programmer with PHP skills to go through the application and update it to work with their Web server. Because the basic application was already written and working on an older version of PHP, the developer was able to get it working in a couple of hours.

After getting it working, the developer posted his changes back to the project, where everyone else could benefit. Mary got a full-fledged, powerful employee scheduling program for a fraction of the cost of hiring a developer to write one from scratch or buying one off the shelf. The open source community got an improved product. The programmer got paid. That's how open source projects grow and thrive.

MANAGING PROJECTS

Project management differs quite a bit from other types of management. With most management, your goals are open-ended, related to lowering costs, improving processes, motivating people, and generally maintaining things while making minor improvements. The very definition of a project implies that it has a specific end. A project begins, is executed according to some sort of plan, and is finished. Your goal is to finish the project however the end point of the project is defined.

There are several proprietary software packages designed to help you manage a project. Most of these tend to be oriented around managing big projects involving a lot of people. If your projects tend to be small, but you do more of them, you probably won't find project management software to be much help, mainly because more of your time will be spent trying to get projects in the first place, rather than managing them to get them done. For keeping track of small projects, you'll probably find calendars, spreadsheets, and database solutions to be more effective than specialized project management software.

The annex Frank is building qualifies as a big project: it's going to take several months to complete, it involves a bunch of smaller projects, each with a series of tasks, and Frank needs to manage the activities of several different groups of workers. For this type of project, specialized software can help you keep track of all the smaller details, help you identify the critical path, and let you play around with different scenarios to optimize the project plan.

Classical project management involves specifying the goal of the project, and identifying three constraints: budget, quality, and time. One of these constraints is likely to be the driver of the project, the one that must be met. The other constraints probably have a bit more give, and can be adjusted if necessary to complete the project. In Frank's case, the goal is to build an annex on his hotel. The budget is limited to his current savings, and the amount he can borrow from the bank. The quality constraint is to add a dozen rooms and bring them to a condition that they're attractive, functional, and pleasing to his guests. The time constraint is to finish the project before the busy season starts. Which is the driving constraint?

It's really up to Frank. Because you inevitably discover unexpected obstacles in the course of doing a big project, you have to be able to adjust your plan to accommodate them, or the project will fail. If time is the driving factor, and the project is running late, Frank has two choices: he can add more contractors, increasing the budget; or he can lower the quality of the project, either building a smaller annex or doing less finish work. If budget is the driving factor, Frank can lower the quality of the project, or spread the work out over a longer period of time. If quality is the driving factor, he can add more contractors or add more time.

The hard part is quantifying all of this. The reality is, people are not interchangeable. Some people work faster than others on particular tasks. The real art of management is matching the talents of the workers to the particular tasks that need to be done.

Very large projects bring statistical calculations to their planning process. They require an estimate of how much time, resources, and effort it will take to accomplish a certain task. By evaluating a best case, a worst case, and a most likely case, project managers can apply statistical calculations to arrive at a probability that a project will be completed in a certain amount of time and within budget. High end project management software packages handle these calculations for you when you provide the corresponding data. One common analysis technique is called Program Evaluation and Review Technique (PERT).

If you don't have a background in project management, these features probably do more harm than good—you'll spend more time trying to figure out how to use the software than actually planning your project. If you do have a project management background, you'll be able to assess software packages to support the methodologies you choose to use.

Project Management Tools

Most of the tools we've talked about in this chapter can be useful for managing projects. Perhaps the most commonly used tools are:

- Spreadsheets
- Gantt charts
- Hierarchical task lists
- Change management tools

Specialized project management software applications combine all of these tools. At this writing, the best known project management tool right now is probably Microsoft Project. Microsoft Project combines all of the above functions, and includes sophisticated resource management, PERT analysis, and many other functions. If you've been trained in project management, Microsoft Project can be a very powerful tool. If you attempt to learn project management from Microsoft Project, you'll inevitably stumble into many pitfalls. It's probably better to use separate tools to manage your projects, because you can see everything going on. Adjusting the amount of time a particular resource has available in Microsoft Project can manifest all sorts of unexpected results.

Let's take a quick look at these individual tools.

Examining Scenarios with a Spreadsheet

When planning a project, a spreadsheet is a great place to play with numbers. You can use it like scratch paper to jot out different scenarios, trying to determine the optimum number of laborers to hire to complete the project on time, adding up the cost of materials, and comparing the cost of bidding out different parts of the project.

Planning a Timeline with a Gantt Chart

A Gantt chart is a timeline that illustrates the dependency of tasks. A Gantt chart can help you figure out the critical path for a project. You find the critical path by considering each task, identifying which ones must be completed before the next task can start. You generally set up a schedule to show the shortest possible time for completing a project, with the dependencies between particular tasks accounted for.

In Frank's annex, the foundation must be done before framing can start. The framing must be done before the roofing, wiring, siding, and drywall are set. The wiring and plumbing should be done before the drywall is installed. The finish work can only be done after everything else is over. The plumbing and the electrical work can happen simultaneously. When you arrange all the tasks into the shortest time schedule, overlapping tasks that don't depend on each other, you'll find that some tasks can be delayed without impacting the schedule, while others directly affect the end date. Tasks that affect the end date of the project are said to be on the critical path of the project.

When managing the project, you pay particular attention to tasks on the critical path. Other tasks can often be shuffled around, earlier or later, to take advantage of your workforce availability. A Gantt chart illustrates all of these tasks and the critical path. You can track your progress on the chart, filling in the timeline as you go. You'll generally need to update the Gantt chart as the project progresses, changing the plan to fit the situation and obtain new corrected estimates. This can help you determine whether you're ahead or behind schedule.

After breaking the project down into tasks, and estimating the amount of work each task will take, you assign resources (in this case, people) to the tasks to generate your final timeline. You usually try to add a bit of padding to your critical path, to allow some room for the critical path tasks to adjust.

Here are three open source project management programs that primarily provide Gantt charts:

1. MR Project (*http://mrproject.codefactory.se/*), a GNOME-based project management tool that runs primarily in Linux
2. Gantt Project (*http://ganttproject.sourceforge.net/*), a Java-based client application, runs on any platform with a Java Runtime Environment installed
3. Ganttlet (*http://ganttlet.sourceforge.net/*), another Java-based client application

Tracking Your Progress With Hierarchical Task Lists

Most large projects can be broken down into smaller projects. Frank's annex project has many smaller projects: framing, roofing, plumbing, wiring, dry-walling, carpeting, and several others. Each of these projects involves a series of tasks, and often can be broken down into smaller projects.

Many project-oriented groupware applications keep track of the status of tasks and sub-projects related to a project. You can often use these to assign particular tasks to particular people. If your entire team uses the computer system regularly, this can be an effective way of tracking progress on a project.

Examples of these groupware suites include:

- PhpCollab (*http://www.php-collab.com/*)
- Tutos (*http://www.tutos.org*)
- WebCollab (*http://webcollab.sourceforge.net/*)
- dotProject (*http://www.dotproject.net/*)

If your team never touches computers, you might find it better to carry your task list with you. The open source Project program (*http://sourceforge.net/projects/progect/*) runs on a Palm PDA, and allows you to carry a hierarchical project task list with you. It synchronizes to an open source desktop program called Pdesk (*http://sourceforge.net/projects/pdesk/*), which is available for Windows, Linux, or Mac.

Change Management

Inevitably, the original scope of a project gets modified as the project progresses. In the planning phases, you create a written specification for the work. In the case of the hotel annex, the specification primarily takes the form of architectural drawings and lists of specific building materials. In other projects, the specification becomes part of the contract, detailing exactly what the end goal of the project is.

If, part way through construction, Frank decides to install top-of-the line windows in each room, it may affect the overall cost of the project. On larger projects that involve more than one stakeholder, it's essential that there be some process to manage these changes.

As we discussed in Chapter 1, software is essentially a concrete expression of a specific idea—clear thinking in code. Programmers have to break a problem down to its barest parts, and write step-by-step instructions to tell the computer how to work through the problem. When you're programming, you can't overlook any step—you have to work through every detail of the problem. Computing problems are rarely straightforward: you need to provide what seems like an endless list of instructions. Programmers create shortcuts, functions, and loops to make a program do more work with fewer lines of code. As you increase the complexity of a program, bugs creep in.

Computer bugs originally got their name from an actual bug found in an early vacuum-tube based computer. This bug caused the program to behave in an unexpected way. Ever since, programmers have called unexpected behaviors in their programs *bugs*. Programmers spend far more time trying to find the cause of bugs in their code than coding in the first place.

Every software project uses a bug tracking program of one sort or another to keep track of flaws in the program. The simplest bug tracking systems are spreadsheets or lists of tasks remaining to do—but most projects of any complexity, and all projects with multiple programmers, use some sort of database system. There are a good number of powerful open source bug tracking programs, developed to manage open source projects themselves, that make extremely effective change management tools.

With a bug tracking database, you encourage anybody involved in the project to add a new bug to the list whenever they notice something that should be addressed. The bug could be an enhancement to the project, a flaw in the implementation, a note to be added to the project plan, or an idea to use for future projects or later additional projects. Bug tracking software provides valuable feedback to whoever is doing the project management, and can make a tremendous difference on the outcome of the project.

When a new bug is added to the database, whoever is responsible for change management needs to review it. Large projects have a change management board, consisting of both the stakeholders and project management, that meets regularly to review bugs. The board decides which bugs should be addressed within the scope of the project, which ones should be added to the scope, affecting the budget or timeline, and which bugs should be recorded and left unfinished. The board also decides how to prioritize the bug, and who to assign it to.

If you have a complex, risky project with a lot of stakeholders, you should strongly consider establishing a change control process right from the beginning, and investigate a bug tracking tool to help you collect information about the changes.

Several of the groupware-based project management tools mentioned earlier include bug tracking systems. They're also known as trouble tickets, or help desk systems—basically a database that keeps track of incidents, issues, change requests, problems, etc.

Some popular standalone bug systems include:

■ Bugzilla (*http://www.bugzilla.org/*), from the Mozilla project
■ Mantis (*http://mantisbt.sourceforge.net/*)
■ Track+ Defect Tracking (*http://www.trackplus.de/*)

SUMMARY

In this chapter, we've learned how to find existing open source projects that help you manage people, resources, schedules, and projects. We've also spent time learning some useful ways to use spreadsheets and databases to solve business problems. These are fundamental skills for getting around in the open source world. We've compared several different database systems, and checked out a variety of open source project management and change management tools.

As your business needs get more complex, being able to customize software to meet them becomes more important. In Part III of the book, we'll take a look at software designed to help solve more complicated problems.

MANAGEMENT SYSTEM REFERENCES

An updated list of resources for this chapter is on the Web site for the book at *http://opensourcesmall.biz/management*.

Software

Microsoft Excel, commercial spreadsheet software *http://www.microsoft.com/excel*
Gnumeric, open source spreadsheet software *http://www.gnome.org/projects/gnumeric*
Kspread, open source spreadsheet software for KDE *http://koffice.org/kspread*
OpenOffice, *http://www.openoffice.org*
Microsoft Access, commercial desktop database *http://www.microsoft.com/access*
FileMaker Pro, commercial desktop database *http://www.filemaker.com*
Oracle, commercial database server *http://www.oracle.com*
Microsoft SQL Server, commercial database server *http://www.microsoft.com/sql*
MySQL, open source database server *http://www.mysql.com*
PostgreSQL, open source database server *http://www.postgresql.org/*

UnixODBC, open source ODBC connection software for Unix and Linux *http://www.unixodbc.org/*

phpScheduleIt, open source resource schedule Web application *http://phpscheduleit.sourceforge.net*

eReserve, open source resource schedule Web application *http://ereserve.sourceforge.net*

php-residence, open source room booking Web application *http://www.digitaldruid.net/php-residence/en/*

Employee Scheduler, open source Web application *http://empscheduler.sourceforge.net*

PhpSched, open source employee scheduling Web application *http://phpsched.sourceforge.net*

MR Project, open source desktop project management application *http://mrproject.codefactory.se*

Gantt Project, open source Java-based desktop application *http://ganttproject.sourceforge.net*

Ganttlet, another open source Java-based desktop application *http://ganttlet.sourceforge.net*

PhpCollab, open source project management Web application *http://www.phpcollab.com*

Tutos, open source project management Web application *http://www.tutos.org*

WebCollab, open source project management Web application *http://webcollab.sourceforge.net*

dotProject, open source project management Web application *http://www.dotproject.net*

Progect, open source project task list manager for Palm OS *http://sourceforge.net/projects/progect*

Pdesk, companion desktop program for project *http://sourceforge.net/projects/pdesk*

Bugzilla, open source change management web application *http://www.bugzilla.org*

Mantis, open source change management web application *http://mantisbt.sourceforge.net*

Track+ Defect tracking, change management web application *http://www.trackplus.de*

Web Sites

Source Forge, site for hosting open source projects *http://www.sourceforge.net*

Fresh Meat, directory of software for Unix and Palm OS *http://www.freshmeat.net*

Open and Free Project Management Tools *http://proj.chbs.dk*

Extending Your Business with Open Source

We've looked at some software that helps you manage your business. Now let's shift our focus to take a look at how computers can help you interact with your customers, partners, the general public, and roaming employees. Web services are revolutionizing businesses in a supply chain. Enterprise Resource Planning software can bring all the information services in a medium-sized business together in one place. Content management systems make it possible to share information across your team, or make it easy to keep your Web site updated. Remote access allows you to work securely over the Internet. Encrypted email can satisfy the privacy needs of legal and medical professionals.

This part of the book contains solutions that help you interact with people outside your office network. Not all businesses will need these solutions, but you're likely to need at least one. Read this part to see what's possible with expanded IT services, and to figure out how to get started.

Chapter 12 describes how Enterprise Resource Planning software can coordinate your systems with your partners, and what you can do with a programmer and some Web services.

Chapter 13 covers all kinds of tools to help you market your business and manage content on the Web, over email, and in print.

Chapter 14 provides a thorough discussion of providing remote access to your internal network, including Virtual Private Networking.

Chapter 15 explains how to manage your own certificate authority, so that you can provide encrypted email and authenticated connections.

12 Sharing Information with Your Partners

In This Chapter

- Introduction
- Integration Systems
- Sharing Information with Your Partners
- Integrating Systems with Your Partners
- Cooperate with Your Partners to Compete Effectively
- Summary
- ERP And Web Services References

INTRODUCTION

No business exists in a vacuum. All businesses have customers and suppliers. Most businesses have competitors. Many businesses form partnerships with other businesses in various ways.

This chapter is all about strategy and giving you an idea about the possibilities with enterprise software. Everything in this chapter needs implementation by experienced IT administrators or programmers. The middle part of the chapter, Setting Up A Client Extranet, provides some specific technical tips for beginning Web application developers. The rest of the chapter, before and after, is non-technical.

The software programs described in this chapter are frameworks for your data, but you have to provide a model to actually make a working system. Later in the chapter we discuss technologies that need to be implemented by a programmer. These solutions can be expensive to implement, but offer tremendous potential for building a competitive coalition with your key partners.

What makes for a good business partner? Basically a sense that you and your partner are working together with a common goal, satisfying some other customer. You might have a supplier or vendor as a partner, who provides the raw materials you need to deliver a final product to your customer. You might partner with a customer to help your customer deliver a big order to their customer. You might even partner with a competitor to gain the capacity you both need to deliver to a big, common customer.

A much greater flow of information between you and your partners distinguishes this type of business relationship. If your supplier is the main big-box warehouse store, it's not really a partner. If your customer is the general public, through a retail storefront, your customers are not usually your partners. You meet with your partners, strategize with them, align your business goals and processes, and end up with a product that can be greater than the sum of its parts.

At least that's the reason most businesses form partnership relationships with other businesses. In some ways, a more common partnership for small business is with a larger customer business.

In an attempt to save money, many large businesses have invested heavily in a category of software called *Enterprise Resource Planning* (ERP). These expensive systems integrate many different parts of their business: accounting, customer relationship management, inventory, project management, document management, and often others. While these ERP systems can save a lot of costs by automating menial and error-prone reconciliation between the internal systems of the business, they don't always end up saving the company money overall. They're extremely expensive to implement, because they always need extensive customization. They force businesses into specific processes that fit the ERP model. Often employees resist the changes imposed by a new ERP system. Overall, ERP systems can be a disaster.

But the lack of one can also be expensive. With ad hoc, separate systems, you might have a list of customers in your accounting database and another list of the same customers in a CRM system; and then a list of contacts in the shipping and receiving department and another list of the same the same contacts in the personal address books of account managers. When the contact information changes for a customer, unless you have a good process in place it can lead to, among other things, invoices being sent to the wrong places and sales calls to the wrong people. This in turn leads to a perception of your company as not being organized or coherent. Integrating business systems inside your business is a major challenge of small companies who are growing quickly.

Integrating disparate business systems within a company is only the first goal of an ERP system. Often the next goal is to manage the supply chain. Here's where small businesses may have already had a taste of the future, especially if you've been a supplier to a major retailer or manufacturer.

In the 1970s and 1980s, many large retailers, government organizations, and manufacturers invested heavily in technology called Electronic Data Interchange (EDI). These were systems for exchanging inventory, purchasing, and billing information automatically between partners in a supply chain. For the large company implementing these systems, the cost savings could be large. For the small suppliers who had to implement them or lose their major customer, these systems were painfully expensive, without saving them much money. In theory, EDI systems eliminate clerical overhead by automating purchasing transactions. In practice, each EDI implementation was different from others—if you were a supplier to two major businesses that each had their own EDI system, you had to invest in two different EDI systems to support them.

Today EDI is being replaced by Web Services, exchanging data in a language called XML. The advantage of using XML is that it's simple to translate from one form into another. No matter what internal system you use, you can write a program that will extract the necessary information and put it into a standard data structure defined by your industry. You can then share the same basic information in an XML standard with all of your partners, instead of building individual EDI systems for each one. Web Services provide the infrastructure for your ERP systems to talk directly with your partners' ERP systems, allowing you to see everything about your supply chain in one place. At least that's the promise.

E-commerce is a popular example of a Web Service. With e-commerce, your partner is a financial institution or a company specializing in payment processing—a supplier you work with closely to conduct your business. We'll take a brief look at e-commerce systems when we talk about Web Services.

For businesses that aren't part of a supply chain, you still might need to exchange specific information with particular partners. One way to do this is to build an extranet, a special Web site that provides access to particular information to your partners.

The Costs of EDI

As various industries define standard types of information to share, Web Services have begun to become essential ways of integrating with your partners. It's very difficult to figure out the return on your investment when you build systems for sharing information with your partners. In most cases, these systems so far have been spectacular failures for most of the businesses who implement them. One particular factor has led to this situation: the closed, proprietary nature of EDI systems.

When you're a proprietary software company, making a profit from your software is the primary goal of your business. Like any other product-oriented business, you want to differentiate yourself from the competition, usually by providing better features, more compelling advantages, and other incentives to make your potential customer choose your solution.

However, if you're a business trying to integrate with your partners, the interests of proprietary software companies directly stand in your way. Computers communicate using standards. Anything that deviates from the standard creates a communication problem. If you choose a different EDI provider than your customer, and your customer's EDI provider won't disclose the communications standard they use, you can't possibly integrate effectively. The only way you can effectively integrate your systems with all of your partners is if you all agree openly on the same standard. And Web Services, with XML, makes it easy to exchange information to a defined standard.

Furthermore, it's in your company's best interests to freely share information about your data standards with your partners, because it makes it less expensive and more desirable for your partners to do the work to integrate with you. The more businesses that share a standard way of exchanging information, the less expensive it becomes for everyone and the more value the shared standard gives to your business. This whole situation screams open source.

Why Integrate with Your Partners?

It's about customer service. Big consultant companies may try to sell an ERP package to you by telling you it'll save you money. It won't. ERP systems, supply chain integration, and customer extranets all cost a substantial amount to put together. You have to hire business process analysts to evaluate and determine the areas most ripe for improvement, programmers to build the systems, and trainers to teach your employees how to make the new systems work as they were designed. If everybody gets it right the first time, you may eventually save some costs, but you need to have quite a bit of disposable cash in the first place to get such a system implemented well.

The real benefit is that you can build a product customized to order, and know exactly when you can deliver.

Let's say you're a small manufacturer of a brand new kind of car. Your company designs and builds the actual cars—and you create them to order. Your cars are a unibody monocoque design, basically a fiberglass shell strengthened with space-age carbon fibers and Kevlar® strands. The interior is lined with several inches of reinforced styrofoam for safety, much like the inside of a bike helmet, but covered with leather for a comfortable feel. You have a number of designers who work to make the cars attractive, comfortable, and functional. Your crack engineers work with the designers to make the cars virtually indestructible, safe, and energy efficient.

You work with a number of partners: several independent dealerships, a company that makes fuel cells, a chemical distributor that provides the epoxies and raw materials that go into your car body, and other manufacturers who provide you with motors, special batteries, and wheels.

As a small business, you can't afford to make thousands of cars a year and have them sit in dealers' inventories around the country. But because your car construction doesn't need the expensive tooling required by steel manufacturing, you can make a profit on every car. And because you don't have to buy the motors, batteries, and wheels until you already have an order, you have minimal amounts of capital tied up in inventory. You don't need large warehouses to stockpile parts and finished cars. You don't have huge inventories of cars that turned out to be unpopular, because you can get all the parts and build to order in a matter of days. Business systems that integrate directly with your suppliers and your dealers make this just-in-time delivery possible.

EDI was originally developed in the name of efficiency, to reduce the bureaucracy of managing huge businesses, and make them more nimble. Large businesses have been successful because of the economies of scale they bring to bear on a particular problem. We live in a society built by large businesses, dominated by chains like McDonalds®, Wal-Mart®, and Time-Warner™.

But large companies with their economies of scale, churning out thousands of identical products, have a big problem when they reach a customer who wants a personalized, customized product. As soon as you have to spend time customizing something, all the benefit you've gained from making a bunch of things the same disappears. Large businesses can't always compete with small businesses when it comes to personalization and customer service. When you only have a few customers, each one is vitally important to you. When you have millions of customers, the concerns of any one are often irrelevant.

With ERP systems, the ability to integrate supply chain transactions with your partners, and the ability to instantly share data with your partners, can allow small businesses to compete head to head with the largest enterprises. Or to fulfill orders from them.

INTEGRATION SYSTEMS

Let's take a look at three ways software can help you streamline integration of your systems, and share them with your partners:

- Implementing an ERP system
- Providing custom extranets for your partners
- Using and providing Web Services

Implementing an ERP System

In Part II, we implemented a whole host of different business systems: Customer Relationship Management, shared calendaring, document management, billing and accounting systems, and project management systems. While we've mentioned programs that integrate some of these systems, for the most part small businesses implement each one independently. There's not necessarily a single place you can access all of the business information of your company. Add an inventory system, a point of sale, an e-commerce system, and partner integration, and you end up with a lot of overlapping data about your customers, suppliers, and partners in a lot of different, unrelated systems.

ERP is about bringing these systems together into one single place. ERP systems are designed to empower everyone in your company by putting appropriate information about the status of an order at their fingertips. It's about updating an order, or information about a contact, in one place and having that information instantly available throughout the systems of your company.

These are not small programs. A few years ago, only the Fortune 1000 companies were implementing ERP systems—but as they have done so, all of the ERP firms have been lowering their prices and trying to sell to medium-sized businesses. As recently as 1999, the minimum licensing charge for a base ERP package was around $250,000 USD [Niccolai03]. With a minimum installation cost of around $1 million, you needed to be a company with about $200 million of yearly revenue to even consider such a system. Leading ERP vendors included SAP AG, Oracle, Peoplesoft, and JD Edwards [Koch02].

Open source projects have blown the floor out from under these ERP systems. A hallmark of these programs is that they require substantial customization. When you have the source code for the software, you can more easily customize anything in the system. Nowhere in the software world are the cost savings so great as in ERP.

But if you rush out and implement a sophisticated ERP system before your company is ready, you'll likely sink so much cash into the project it can sink your business. For growing companies, it's essential to have an overall Information Technology strategy. Eventually you will need some integrated system; it's best to use systems that store data in some sort of database or file standard that you can easily import into an ERP system down the road.

The best approach for the smallest companies is to implement systems as you need them, choosing systems that allow for future integration. There are generally huge costs involved in implementing an ERP solution. You have to know a lot about your business needs before you can customize it appropriately. If your ERP solution doesn't fit your business, people won't use it, and you'll end up with a bunch of different solutions. Once your business has reached the volume that employees are spending a lot of time repeating the same tasks that could easily be automated, it's time to look for a better system.

We're going to take a look at three ERP systems that fall into the budgets of small businesses, each with a slightly different set of advantages:

1. Compiere
2. OpenMFG
3. GNU Enterprise

Small Enterprise Resource Planning with Compiere

Compiere (*http://compiere.org*) is taking the ERP world by storm. The open source Compiere project specifically targets businesses between $2 million and $200 million in yearly revenues. It has all the major modules of the proprietary ERP packages, it's easy to extend, customize, and integrate with existing systems, and it's open source.

Compiere provides an extendable set of interrelated modules, including accounting, inventory, supply chain management, CRM, payroll, and just about any other thing you want to design an entity for. It supports multiple currencies, multiple languages, and even multiple companies.

One way that a Compiere installation really makes sense is for integrating your partners. A small IT company might host a Compiere system for several different companies. The boutique car manufacturer might share a system with the fuel cell manufacturer, a number of independent dealerships, and the other partner manufacturing firms. When a car is ordered, the inventory on all the parts necessary to assemble it across all the small companies is automatically adjusted, and each company knows it needs to get its parts to the car manufacturer so the order can be delivered on time. With such a system, a group of small companies can coordinate to provide a product that competes directly with the offerings of much bigger companies, without the bureaucratic overhead.

It's not completely free, however. At this writing, it requires an Oracle database. Much of the business logic is written in an Oracle-specific language called PL/SQL. The original creator of Compiere, Jorg Janke, used to work for Oracle, and chose it as the base of the system so that he could get a working program faster. Efforts are underway to make Compiere work with an open source database, probably PostgreSQL, but they have been slow and uncertain.

Right now, if you don't already have an Oracle license, you need to buy at least an embedded license to use Compiere. You can buy a basic self-support contract from the company that backs Compiere (ComPiere, Inc.), including all the licensing fees for the embedded Oracle and PDF libraries at a 2003 cost of $1,500 for 10 users. Other than that, the Compiere system itself is free of licensing charges, released under the Mozilla Public License.

For Enterprise-level software, this is an amazing bargain. It's so much a bargain that this project, at the end of 2003, was one of the top 10 downloads of all 70,000-odd open source projects at Source Forge, with nearly 600,000 individual downloads.

Compiere uses a Java client/server architecture. You generally set up one server to be a dedicated database server, and a separate computer as an *application server*, running a Java system called JBoss. Any computer with Java installed can run the client software. Or you can connect to the application server and use the Web application from any Web browser.

Manufacturing Success with OpenMFG

OpenMFG is another very successful ERP program worthy of consideration, optimized specifically for small manufacturers. OpenMFG has created a sort of hybrid license—they freely share the source code for the application, but do not allow you to redistribute it and you must pay for a license to actually use it. OpenMFG builds on several open source projects: the PostgreSQL database, the QT toolkit (a graphical toolkit that is the base of KDE), and a variety of modules to make a powerful system at minimum cost.

OpenMFG has built around industry-recognized standards, making it work well with a variety of external systems, and providing built-in future-proofing. OpenMFG targets slightly smaller firms than Compiere, in the $1 million to $50 million USD yearly revenue range. If you're a small manufacturer, OpenMFG may turn out to be a compelling option. OpenMFG licenses in 2003 start at $10,000 yearly for 10 users.

Growing Your Business with GNU Enterprise

The only completely open source ERP system at this writing is GNU Enterprise (*http://www.gnuenterprise.org/project/what.html*). At this writing, only the basic framework is complete. It's got a long way to go before it can compete with Compiere or OpenMFG.

GNU Enterprise is meant to be a full-featured ERP solution for any size business. There is a small business sub-project called, appropriately enough, GNUe/ Small Business (*http://www.gnu.org/software/gnue-sb*). Again, this application is not available at this writing.

SHARING INFORMATION WITH YOUR PARTNERS

In Chapter 13, we're going to discuss setting up Web sites and providing marketing material to your potential customers. Some businesses may have a need to share confidential information with their partners, without revealing this information to the general public. The boutique auto manufacturer may want to provide an easy place for each dealer to find their commission structure. The manufacturer may need to provide different information to different partners.

You may also want to provide personalized information to your customers. Our auto maker might have a Web page dedicated to each individual car, containing the full specifications of each part of the car, along with service records, maintenance recommendations, and serial numbers of various components.

These are two different scenarios that can be fulfilled by a custom Web site that authenticates a user, and provides content appropriate to that user.

Setting Up a Client Extranet

A Web site that provides internal company information to particular external users is often called an *extranet*. There are several different ways you might implement such a Web site. If you're trying to provide a semi-confidential area on a Web site, allowing a particular group of people to access it, you might check out some of the content management systems in Chapter 13. With these systems, users can sign up on your site to become a registered user. You can then add particular users to a group that has access permission to different content within the system. This is definitely the most cost-effective way to set up a portal for your customers.

But it can be a cumbersome system. You might find it a management chore to identify your customers from among the guests who choose to register on your site—and many of your customers may not bother to sign up. It's still worthwhile to search the open source sites for solutions that address your needs, but you might find that the best solution is to create your own solution.

In 2002, the author of this book created a sophisticated client extranet for a medium-sized software company that sells telecommunications software. Because there aren't all that many telecommunications companies, this company wanted to provide a customized Web site for each of their clients, reflecting the different set of enterprise-level software they had purchased. Each client company might have dozens or hundreds of people who would access the extranet site for updated information about the options and service agreements. Essentially the extranet site provided some content customized for the client, including their logo in a banner, the service agreements, and contact information for the account manager, and other content shared by some or all of the different client sites.

This was a custom-developed Web site that used open source tools and technologies and provided authentication and per-user customization written from the ground up. In the late 1990s, such a site could easily run over $100,000 USD in development charges. By 2002, such a site could be easily developed for under $20,000 with open source technologies.

Let's take a closer look at the two key parts to such a client extranet: managing extranet users, and managing many customized versions of a site.

User Management and Authentication

The first problem to solve when designing an extranet is identifying the users. In the case of the telecommunications software company, that was relatively simple: any user who had an email that used one of their customers' domains could sign up for an account. If you already have your customer's email address associated with a specific contract that might dictate the content you want to make available, you can probably use whatever database in which you have the customer's contact details.

The next step is choosing a technology to allow the user to log in. If you're using Apache to host your application, you have a couple of options: use some form of Apache authentication, or handle authentication in your application. The advantage of Apache authentication is that it's extremely easy to set up, and Apache enforces whatever you tell it to enforce. You don't need to write much authentication code—your code just takes the username that Apache has validated, and uses that to generate your content.

The drawback is the user experience: when Apache asks for basic authentication, a password box pops up demanding a username and password. There's no way to add links to this password dialog—no way for new users to sign up, or help for people who have forgotten their password.

You can still provide sign-up and forgotten password links to your users, but they'll appear either on a launch page before the user enters the extranet, or after the authentication fails. This isn't the most friendly way to treat your users, and you'll find that most consumer-oriented sites don't use Apache authentication for this very reason.

Creating your own authentication system using a language such as PHP allows you to set up elegant, inviting forms for customers to use to log in, with all sorts of help available if they don't remember their password. The drawback to rolling your own authentication system is that there are many pitfalls and possible ways for people to spoof credentials, and crack into your system. The Web developer implementing an authentication scheme should be fully familiar with the source code for the authentication scheme, thinking through all its weaknesses. And, once the user has authenticated, you can't pass the credentials back to Apache—you have to verify that the user has the correct credentials before sending any content for every page on your site.

Apache Authentication Modules

Apache comes with several modules for authenticating users, and more are freely available on the Internet. By far the most common module employed for authenticating users is the mod_auth module.

There are two types of authentication: *basic* and *digest*. Basic authentication is supported by nearly all browsers. It sends passwords through the Internet in plain text. Digest authentication encrypts the passwords in the client Web browser before sending, but not very many browsers support digest authentication, and not many authentication modules support it on the receiving end. The easiest solution is to set up Apache with SSL and encrypt all traffic to and from the server, especially if you're trying to keep the information confidential anyway.

All of the authentication modules for Apache simply provide a different place to verify user and password credentials. Table 12.1 lists some useful authentication modules.

It's also possible to automatically authenticate users with a client certificate issued by a recognized Certificate Authority, or Internet Explorer users on a Windows domain against their user account in Active Directory. Setting up a Certificate Authority is discussed in Chapter 15. These authentications are a bit more complex, and are not discussed in this book, but you can find them in the Apache documentation.

TABLE 12.1   Apache Authentication Modules

Module	Authenticates Against	Notes	Available at
mod_auth	Flat file	Maintained by htpasswd program Easy to set up and start using Starts to slow down with more than a hundred or so users	Included with Apache
mod_auth_dbm	DBM database file	Much better performance for hundreds or thousands of users	Included with Apache
mod_auth_ldap	LDAP directory	Looks up users in an LDAP directory	Included with Apache
mod_auth_mysql	MySQL database	Looks up users in a MySQL database	*http://modauthmysql.sourceforge.net/*
mod_auth_pgsql	PostgreSQL database	Looks up users in a PostgreSQL database	*http://www.giuseppetanzilli.it/mod%5Fauth%5Fpgsql2/*
mod_auth_anonymous	Any	Allows users to successfully log in as "anonymous"	Included with Apache

Authentication with Apache is easy, and relatively secure if you use an SSL-encrypted connection. The authenticated user login name is available to scripts written in PHP or other scripting languages, allowing you to customize the content returned to a particular user.

Apache authentication works by specifying a file, location, or directory that requires authentication. Most commonly, you will do this by putting a special file named .htaccess in a directory you want to protect. In this file, you add directives corresponding to the authentication module you want to use, and specify a list of users to whom you allow access. You can allow access to any valid user, to specific users, or to specific groups. Each authentication module provides a way of putting users into different groups.

You can also use several different authentication modules within the same directory. In this case, each user login is looked up in each module, in the order the modules were loaded in the Apache configuration file. Each module has a directive specifying whether the module should be considered authoritative. Only one module may be authoritative—if a user account is not found in a module that thinks it's authoritative, the authentication fails.

Here's a sample set of directives that look up user account information in both a MySQL database, and a flat file generated by htaccess:

```
AuthName "DSPAM Quarantine Area"
AuthType Basic
AuthMySQLUser mailman
AuthMySQLPassword password
AuthMySQLDB maildb2
AuthMySQLUserTable users
AuthMySQLNameField id
AuthMySQLPasswordField crypt
AuthMySQLAuthoritative on
AuthAuthoritative off
AuthUserFile /var/www/conf/dspam.htaccess
require valid-user
```

In this case, because mod_auth was loaded by the main Apache configuration file before mod_auth_mysql, usernames are first looked up in the file /var/www/conf/dspam.htaccess. If the username isn't found there, it's looked up in the MySQL database named maildb2 on the local server, in the table named users. Apache looks for the username in a column called id, and the password in a column named crypt. Finally, because MySQL is the authoritative authentication method, if the username and password are not found in the MySQL database, authentication fails.

Web Application Authentication

When you set up different Web applications, you'll find some that depend on Apache authentication, but many that have come up with their own authentication schemes. If you're going to create your own, it's important to make sure you check every request for proper credentials. Otherwise, determined hackers might guess the name of your Web pages, and load them directly, bypassing your security. You also need to be careful that your credential-checking is done on the server—when programming authentication, you should never trust anything sent by a user's browser. It is extremely easy to spoof any requests from a browser.

Creating your own authentication system, if you have a good idea of what you're doing, can greatly improve the security of a system. If you use canned scripts for authentication, people may figure out a way to exploit the script. This can lead to your site being compromised. It's much easier to exploit a flaw in a script when you have the source code—if you create your own authentication system, you are the only one with the source code.

On the other hand, if you don't create your authentication system properly, you may have an easily exploitable security system, with no knowledge of its flaws. If you use an open source system, and stay aware of its flaws, you'll get the benefit of improvements from a community of people interested in the script's security.

Two open source authentication projects for PHP are UMA (*http://uma.neverwillbes.com/*) and PHP-Auth (*http://sourceforge.net/projects/auth/*).

Adding New Users

Whether you use Apache authentication or a Web application sign-up system, you need to have a good way to get passwords to your users. If your users sign up with their email accounts, you can send them some sort of confirmation code or password. This is an excellent way to verify that a user is who they say they are—if they don't provide a valid email address, they won't receive the information they need to log into your site.

For the telecommunications software company, anyone from one of the client companies could enter their work email address. The Web application checked to see if the email address used a recognized domain for one of the client companies, and if so, generated an activation code, sent it to the user, and created a user account associated with the client company. The user entered the activation code, and could then create a password for his account. If the user forgot his password, a new activation code was sent to the email address, allowing him to reset his password.

If your extranet users don't come from recognizable domains, you'll have to come up with some scheme for determining whether they should have access or not. Authenticating against an existing customer database or directory is a convenient way of doing this. You'll just need to make sure you have a password column in your database for this purpose, and decide on some way of getting the password or an activation code to the user.

Customizing Content for Particular Users

The next issue is providing custom content depending on which user logged in. Almost certainly you will use some sort of database for this purpose, looking up what the user should be able to access before assembling the page.

At its simplest, you will have a consistent page containing the individual details for the particular customer. With this sort of arrangement, you can keep your site navigation consistent, and simply load the data for the customer on particular pages. This type of solution is extremely easy to implement using a language like PHP that provides support for databases.

More complicated arrangements are limited only by your ability to define the behavior you want to see. For the telecommunications software company, not only were certain pages different, but the entire navigation for the site might be different. All pages had the client logo right next to the software company's logo at the top of the page. There was a bar of navigation buttons also at the top, but exactly what buttons appeared varied among the different versions of the site. One section described the company's products—but only those products bought by the client. When a product was updated, however, the administrators wanted to be able to easily update these product pages for all clients who used the product.

The solution was to create a many-to-many relationship between pages and clients. See Chapter 12 for a description of how many-to-many relationships work within a database. In short, for each client site, a sitemap of all the pages in the site could be loaded by a single query. A series of functions built the navigation for the site based on these pages. A set of administrative pages allowed site administrators to add and remove pages from a particular client site, using either already existing pages or creating new ones.

Every page in this site had a corresponding file on the Web server. This file, based on a simple template, contained the body text for the page and little else. All of the navigation, and a brief customizable abstract of the page that could be customized for each client, was stored in a database.

This is just an example of one way to approach the problem. This hybrid approach turned out to be an elegant solution for this particular problem. You might find that your needs would be better met keeping all of the content in a database, or by keeping all of it in specific files in a directory hierarchy, and applying access permissions to the directories.

INTEGRATING SYSTEMS WITH YOUR PARTNERS

Extranet Web sites are a great way to provide specific information to your customers and partners. However, your partners need to visit your Web site to get information from it. The next level of integration is allowing your data to appear in their systems.

Let's go back to the car manufacturer. If each of your partners has their own ERP system and a client extranet that provides inventory information for the appropriate partners, you can see what parts are available, and foresee any potential delays in getting a car built. But you might have to visit several different Web sites, one for each of your suppliers, to find out if indeed everybody has the necessary parts available.

If you're sharing an ERP system, like Compiere, you may have direct ability to see the necessary inventory in your own system—but what if a key supplier doesn't use the same host? This is where the brand new area of Web Services steps in. Just like a client extranet, a Web Service provides a customized view of data to particular users. Unlike a client extranet, you don't have to use a Web browser to get the data—you can request it from any program that can talk to the Web Service.

At the beginning of the chapter, we talked about EDI, which integrates supply chains, allowing large organizations to see the inventory of their suppliers, and automatically create transactions and have them fulfilled. Web Services are a new, standardized way of doing the same thing.

When EDI was developed, sending data between companies was excruciatingly slow and expensive. People implementing these systems created tiny packets to a specific standard, and exchanged these between systems. There were several problems with this. If the packet was slightly different than expected, the receiving system had no way of telling if the problem was an error in transmission, or whether it should attempt to fulfill it anyway. It was extremely difficult to track down these types of problems. There were no standardized packets—each system had its own set of expectations. If you wanted to add some type of data, it meant revamping much of the system, at great risk and expense.

The combination of Web Services and a new language called XML solves all of these problems, delivering the original promise of EDI in an extendable, flexible, powerful way. One of the most common applications for Web Services is e-commerce.

Web Services Provide the Medium

One of the big problems with EDI was that it depended on dedicated telecommunications connections between the partners. These were expensive and slow. Now that every company is on the Internet, it's much cheaper to send messages electronically through the Web. The Internet brings its own set of problems, however, security being one of the main ones.

Web Services are essentially Web sites meant to be used by other computers instead of people, and supply chain integration is one of their most compelling uses. You can create a Web Service using pretty much any server language available. By far the two most common at this writing are Java and .NET.

Java, made by Sun Microsystems, Inc., is designed to be a cross-platform, object-oriented language. There are a variety of ways that Java can be used on a server, but generally it will run under some sort of server application framework such as JBoss or the Apache Tomcat project. Java is available for just about every operating system available.

.NET (dot-NET) is a Microsoft competitor to Java that has quickly taken over the Web Services world because of its simplicity. While the primary language .NET employs is a new one called C# (C Sharp), the .NET framework provides a standard way of creating Web Services using a variety of languages. .NET itself only runs on Windows servers, but the open source Mono project is quickly providing a compatible open source alternative for Linux servers. You can also use PHP to create a Web Service. All you need to do is handle the request and return an appropriate response.

Many packages are starting to appear that provide or consume Web Services. Documentation is crucial for a Web Service: each one is expecting some sort of data in the request, and returns specific data in response, based on the function that was specified. The functions, input, and output are specified in what is called an *Application Programmer Interface* (API). Often the published APIs, documentation, tutorials, and examples are included in something called a *Software Developer's Kit* (SDK). By obtaining the SDK for a service you want to use, you can quickly design a Web application to use it.

The ERP programs we discussed earlier, and some of the groupware programs described in Chapter 8 and Chapter 11 include Web Services that allow you to create custom applications to access data in the systems.

Most Web Services use an online, Web-based format, where the response comes immediately after a request. Another type of Web Service provides a *disconnected* API, sometimes called a *messaging* interface. These Web Services work more like email than a Web site—messages are queued up at the Web Service, processed in order, and a response is sent out some time in the future. These are not yet very widely implemented, but it is possible to set up an email server to process messages for a Web Service.

XML Bears the Message

The other major innovation that solves the problems of EDI is *eXtensible Markup Language* (XML). XML is a way of defining data structures. Unlike the small EDI packets that only included raw data, XML includes the structure along with the data. It can also provide a definition of what data it contains, providing a built-in way that the receiving Web Service can determine if any given XML file is valid. Because an XML file contains both the data itself and the semantics, you can send whatever data you have to a Web Service, and the Web Service will use the data it recognizes, ignoring the rest. You can also very easily transform one XML document into another, quickly translating one type of XML document to a completely different type, leaving out some data, manipulating others.

Web Services speak XML. When you send a request, it's in XML format. When you receive a response, it's also XML. A number of tools called *parsers* allow your programs to quickly extract the important information, to do with as you want.

E-Commerce in Your Business

E-commerce is basically using Web Services to conduct financial transactions, a very common need for small businesses. For retail operations, e-commerce is becoming an essential offering, supplementing customers who come to your store with an online presence.

You basically have four approaches you can take to implement an e-commerce storefront:

1. Redirect customers to a payment processing company who handles all of the payment aspects for you.
2. Use an online hosted service that provides e-commerce.
3. Add a pre-built e-commerce package to your Web site.
4. Write your own custom e-commerce package.

Let's take a quick look at these options.

Use a Payment Processing Company

If you already have a Web site set up, this is probably the easiest way to get started. PayPal® (*http://paypal.com*) is one of the most well-known of these. You simply add a few lines of code to your Web site, so that when a user submits a form ordering an item, they are sent to PayPal, with all of your information and the purchase details all filled out. PayPal handles the payment, and notifies you when it has been processed. A similar service is 2CO (*http://www.2checkout.com*).

If you already have a merchant account with a bank, these services are probably redundant, costing you more in transaction costs than adding an equivalent ability through your bank. Your bank might provide similar payment processing over the Web, if you choose an e-commerce account with them. On the other hand, if you don't have enough transactions to justify a merchant account, these services have no monthly charges, perhaps saving you quite a lot of money in the long run.

Another downside to these services is that your customers obviously leave your Web site to go to the payment company. If your customers think you're a huge company, and then visit a third party payment processing site, it may cause a bit of confusion, or lack of confidence in your company. If your customers know you're a small company, using these services is fine. See Chapter 13 for more about setting brand expectations.

Have Your Online Store Hosted

Another option is to use a special hosting company that provides an online store-front, allowing you to customize the look and feel and create your own product list. The storefront then handles payment processing directly. There are dozens of these services. Perhaps the biggest are eBay (*http://www.ebay.com*) and Yahoo! Stores (*http://smallbusiness.yahoo.com/merchant*). A good smaller one to try is Kagi (*http://www.kagi.com*). These services allow you to build a Web site they host, and they provide all of the shopping cart functionality and payment processing.

Like using a payment processing company, these services give the impression that you're a small business. The biggest advantage of going with these types of storefronts is that you're automatically listed in their directory, and so you get some built-in advertising. eBay is particularly good exposure, especially if you auction a few of your products regularly.

Using E-commerce Software Packages

There are dozens of shopping cart scripts, and quite a few payment processing applications you can install on your server, hosting your own e-commerce. If you already have a merchant account, and you don't want your company to have the brand connotations you'll get by hosting at eBay, this is the way to go.

On the other hand, if you take credit card information over the Web, you have to take strong measures to protect that data. You automatically become a much bigger target, as soon as you do your own e-commerce—crackers have a financial incentive to break into your system. Before setting up any kind of e-commerce solution where you are collecting and storing credit card data, read Chapters 16 and 17, and be sure you take appropriate security measures.

Also, you should never host an e-commerce program that collects credit card data on a shared server—unless you can get some sort of guarantee from the provider that nobody else has access to your data. E-commerce demands having full, exclusive control over your server. If your provider isn't in the business of handling e-commerce, either set up your own server to handle the actual credit card transactions, or hand the payment processing off to a payment processing service.

A popular proprietary e-commerce system is Miva Merchant, available at *http://www.miva.com.*

For open source e-commerce packages, the osCommerce package (*http://os-commerce.org/*) is fast becoming the leader. Written using PHP and MySQL, os-Commerce has a thriving developer community, and at this writing, over 1,400 installed locations.

Creating Your Own E-commerce Solution

If one of the e-commerce packages already does what you need, use it. Unless your business is very unusual, either an e-commerce package or an ERP solution will likely meet your needs.

If you choose to write your own, try to leverage existing projects and code. PHP includes classes and functions for working directly with payment gateways. Using these functions, a Web application developer can easily conduct transactions with Verisign (*http://www.verisign.com/products/payment.html*) through their Payflow Pro extension, or with Mainstreet Softworks (*http://www.mainstreetsoftworks.com/*) using the MVCE extensions. Check with your merchant account provider for the various options you can use to make transactions.

Also, read the previous section for the warning about keeping your customer data secure.

COOPERATE WITH YOUR PARTNERS TO COMPETE EFFECTIVELY

This chapter is merely a starting point to introduce some of the basic concepts and technologies used to integrate your business information with other businesses. While much of it may seem abstract, and irrelevant to very small businesses, it has some very real applications and you're sure to see a lot more of these technologies in coming years. The technologies described in this chapter will allow a group of small businesses to partner with each other and compete very effectively against large enterprises.

Most of these technologies were developed by and for large companies in an effort to reduce costs, primarily to reduce bureaucratic overhead. Many large businesses, as a result, are becoming a coalition of smaller business groups within an enterprise, sharing a company name and infrastructure. Open source technologies, open standards, and open protocols are quickly falling into the budget of small businesses.

The ironic thing is that small businesses don't have these overhead cost inefficiencies in the first place—they're still small enough to not have that burden. So the real effect of bringing these technologies to a small business range is extending what a small business, or coalition of small businesses, can accomplish with limited resources. Especially if your business involves a supply chain, investigate these technologies, and include an IT firm in your group of companies to partner with.

SUMMARY

In this chapter, we've covered some broad territory, basically covering a wide range of systems for exchanging data among your business, your partners, your customers, and your suppliers. We looked at ERP systems that integrate a bunch of business systems into cohesive views. We examined client extranets, Web Services, and e-commerce. The systems in these chapters are still expensive, and people are still learning the best ways to perform these tasks, but hopefully you have gained a better understanding of what it takes to put these systems together.

In the next chapter, we'll take a look at software that can help you execute a coherent marketing plan, with Web, email, and print tools.

ERP AND WEB SERVICES REFERENCES

An updated list of resources for this chapter is on the Web site for the book at *http://opensourcesmall.biz/extranet.*

Books

The XML Handbook, by Charles Goldfarb and Paul Prescod, Prentice Hall, 3rd edition 2000

XML in a Nutshell, by Elliotte Rusty Harold and W. Scott Means, O'Reilly and Associates Inc., 2nd edition 2002

Articles

"Oracle lowers entry price for E-business Suite," by Jame Niccolai, March 25, 2003. Available online at *http://www.infoworld.com/article/03/03/25/HNorapricing_1.html.*

"The ABCs of ERP," by Christopher Koch, CIO.com, March 7, 2002. Available online at *http://www.cio.com/research/erp/edit/erpbasics.html*

"Open source ecommerce lights candlemaker's fire," by Robin Miller, Newsforge, December 1, 2003, available online at *http://www.newsforge.com/software/03/11/30/1352250.shtml*

Software

Compiere, an open source ERP application *http://compiere.org*

OpenMFG, not open source but source code provided *http://www.openmfg.com/*

GNU Enterprise, an open source ERP system *http://www.gnuenterprise.org*

GNUe Small Business, small business version of GNU enterprise *http://www.gnu.org/software/gnue-sb*

mod_auth_mysql, authentication module for MySQL *http://modauthmysql.sourceforge.net*

mod_auth_pgsql, authentication module for Postgresql *http://www.giuseppetanzilli.it/mod%5Fauth%5Fpgsql2*

Uma, open source authentication framework for PHP *http://uma.neverwillbes.com*

PHP-Auth, open source authentication framework for PHP *http://sourceforge.net/projects/auth*

Miva Merchant, commercial e-commerce suite *http://www.miva.com*

osCommerce, open source e-commerce suite *http://oscommerce.org*

Symphero, an open source Perl-based e-commerce suite, *http://sourceforge.net/projects/opensymphero/*

Web Sites

2CO, online payment processing service *http://www.2checkout.com*

Paypal, online payment processing service *http://www.paypal.com*

eBay, hosting for online stores *http://stores.ebay.com*

Yahoo! Stores, hosting for online stores *http://smallbusiness.yahoo.com/merchant*

Kagi, hosting for online stores *http://www.kagi.com*

13 Marketing Your Message

In This Chapter

- Introduction
- Your Online Business Presence
- Email Marketing
- Print Media
- Summary
- Content Management and Design References

INTRODUCTION

Branding is a current favorite buzzword among marketing people. A brand is a set of emotional associations people have with your business. Branding specialists suggest that you treat every contact with a customer or potential customer as something that reinforces the positive elements of your brand image, whatever it is. Positive brand associations include things like "quality customer service," "cares about its customers," "best bang for the buck," and similar statements. If you're not careful, it's easy to develop negative branding: "doesn't trust its customers," "poor quality control," "always shows up late."

This chapter is completely non-technical.

Marketing is all about promoting your business. It's more than just taking out an ad in the yellow pages—it's about being visible to your potential customers, with a message that fits your brand. You can't directly control your brand, but you can influence it with a marketing message.

Before the Internet, businesses used all kinds of ways of getting noticed. Besides the yellow pages ad, there's newspaper, television, and radio advertising. Businesses send letters, cards, and brochures to prospects. Having a contact refer your business is a particularly effective form of marketing. Telemarketing, door-to-door sales, and fax marketing, while distasteful to many, may still be an important part of your marketing plan.

The Internet has added two brand new mediums to the mix: email and the Web. They're as different as a brochure and a yellow pages ad. In this chapter, we're going to take a look at Web sites, email newsletters, and print media in the context of marketing your business to potential customers.

YOUR ONLINE BUSINESS PRESENCE

If you don't have a Web site now, get one. Fifteen years ago, if you didn't have a yellow pages ad, you didn't exist. Today, if you don't have a Web site, you don't exist. You probably need both. The question is, how much of a Web site do you need? At an absolute minimum, you need a one-page site that lists your primary products and services, your business name, and how to reach you. More or less like an online business card.

With a little more investment, your Web site can do more for you. If you provide a service, show an online portfolio of your work, or testimonials of your customers to help persuade potential customers to give you a try. If you sell products, you might want to set up an online store—or at least showcase a few feature products. Press releases can be a good way to generate publicity for your business. Having a regularly updated news section helps your Web site get closer to the top of search engine listings.

One of the best brand associations you can have is being an expert in your field. If you make your Web site rich with content about your business specialty, you'll likely make your bank account rich with proceeds from customers who seek out your services. Incidentally, developing a reputation as an expert in some area of software development is one of the biggest motivations for developers of open source software.

Another Web site strategy that can help your business is hosting an online community around your area of expertise. If you can spark conversations on your Web site related to your topic, the number of regular visitors to your site will snowball—and all of them see your company brand every time they visit. A tenet of advertising is that it can take seeing an ad around 10 times before people start to recognize the company being advertised. Any way you can keep your visitors coming back to your Web site helps to advertise your business. When one of your regular visitors needs your product or service, they'll call you first.

How do you create and maintain a Web site? We discussed setting up a Web server and hosting issues in Chapter 6. In this section, we'll take a look at traditional Web sites, Web logs or *blogs*, content management systems, and wikis.

Traditional Web Sites

There are two types of Web sites:

- Static Web sites
- Dynamic Web sites

A static Web site is a collection of Web pages connected with hyperlinks. Its pages only change when you upload new pages to the server. Creating a static Web site is relatively easy, and if you keep the graphic design simple, it can be very inexpensive. You can get a basic one-page Web site put together by a professional for a few hundred dollars, and with graphic design, about the cost of making a brochure. For slightly bigger portfolio sites, there are a few more design and usability issues to work out, but your cost is still in the range of a few hundred dollars per Web page.

HTML, the language Web sites are written in, is very easy to learn, and there are plenty of tools available to help you, if you have a desire and some design sensibility. Usually, though, like any other area of business, you're better off hiring a professional to get it done well and quickly, and focusing on your core business.

The problem with a static Web site is that you need to have some knowledge of HTML to add content to the site. Some Web tools hide the HTML from you, making adding and editing content easier, but you still need to have a pretty good understanding of the whole process, or you're bound to make mistakes that can make your site unusable for your visitors.

Dynamic Web sites, on the other hand, provide built-in tools for adding new content and editing existing content. Dynamic Web sites are often called Web applications, because they do things other than just showing canned content. Most dynamic Web sites use some sort of database to actually hold the content so it can be reused on different pages, more easily searched, and used in a multitude of ways not possible with a static site. Once a dynamic system is set up, you don't need any other tools to add or change content—the system itself provides you all the necessary tools. Many dynamic systems allow you to add pages and content without knowing a thing about HTML or how Web sites work.

There are several different types of dynamic Web sites that can fill the marketing needs of your business. By setting up some sort of dynamic site, you can update it regularly without having to keep a Web developer available for every little change. Most of these systems can be installed and customized by Web developers who don't necessarily have a lot of experience doing server side programming.

Here are some different types of dynamic Web applications you might find useful for a business Web site:

- Blogging software
- Bulletin boards

- Wiki Webs
- Content management systems

Let's take a closer look at how you might use each of these. After discussing each of these systems, we'll take a look at Web editing and development tools to provide you with a customized Web site or a more specialized Web application than these pre-built systems provide.

Blogging for More Than Belly-Button Lint

Web logs, a.k.a. Blogs, have become mainstream. People write blogs about every subject imaginable. Blogging has become a new form of journalism, with everyone from bored teenagers to New York Times writers and retirees writing them. Blogs are starting to become a new form of mass communication.

Blogs fulfill the original promise of the Web—the ability for anybody to publish anything, without needing to learn any technical details. You log into your blog, upload a new picture, write an entry, click the Post button, and your missive becomes available to the entire world.

So how does this help your business? There are several ways to work a blog into your marketing strategy. At a minimum, it's a simple framework for posting press releases for your company. You might have a Web designer put together a good Web site for you, and include one page of press releases that you can then easily update whenever you want. You might advertise special prices for a product, a new service you offer, or some item of interest related to your company's area of expertise that your customers would find interesting.

Search engines regularly crawl your site, searching for changes. Sites with fresh content tend to get higher rankings, meaning your Web page will be closer to the top. If you publish new stories often enough, you may get readers to visit your site regularly.

One feature common to most current blogging software is something called Really Simple Syndication (RSS), which is a news feed anybody can subscribe to with special software called a news aggregator. When you add a new entry to a blog, the RSS feed gets updated automatically. People don't even have to visit your site to see your new headline, and often they can read the opening paragraph or two in their news reader. Write compelling content and you just might gain some new customers.

Another use for blogging is to provide a central place for you to keep interesting links. Some blogging software provides little add-ons for your Web browser, so that if you stumble across a page you want to see again, you can instantly add it to your blog. Soon you can put together a repository of links for a given topic, useful for you, your employees, and anyone interested in the topic you're highlighting. This, too, can drive more traffic to your site.

There are dozens of blogging software systems. Some of them, such as Blogger.com and Radio Userland, are hosted services—you write your entry on their server, and then post it from there either to your own Web site, or to a special account on their server. There are a bunch of proprietary blogging packages, perhaps the most popular being Movable Type (*http://www.movabletype.org*). Movable Type is not an open source package—there is a charge for commercial use, and you cannot redistribute it.There are now some solid open source alternatives. Two to check out are Serendipity and WordPress.

Serendipity (*http://www.s9y.org/*) is a simple, clean, elegant blogging system. It's very easy to install on a Web server with a MySQL database. It can handle multiple users, allows guests to post comments to stories, and supports all the latest blogging technology. The best thing about Serendipity is its ability to easily embed a blog into your main site. If all you're after is an easy-to-update news page, your Web developer will be able to easily add this system to your site.

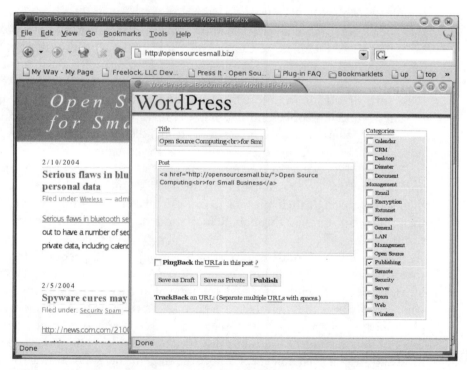

FIGURE 13.1   Easy Web publishing with Word Press.

WordPress (*http://www.wordpress.org/*) has more features, but still uses a clean, accessible design (Figure 13.1). With WordPress, it's easier to manage different users, and there are more extensions, bells and whistles to add to your blog without adding much clutter.

Host a Virtual Bulletin Board

Another popular dynamic Web application is a message or bulletin board. Our boutique car manufacturer in Chapter 12 might want to host an online message board where enthusiasts could talk about their cars, arrange events, compare notes about particular features of the car, or whatever else they care to discuss. If you have a unique product that proves to be popular among a group of people, somebody will most likely start some sort of community Web site around it. Why not you?

Hosting an online discussion can be a great way to promote your brand, and get direct feedback about your product from people who actually use it. People tend to be much less inhibited online, and you're likely to get incredibly valuable insight into what people like about your product, as well as what they don't like.

The biggest problem with providing any type of online forum open to the public is that there's a small percentage of troublemakers on the Internet. You will have to devote some time to maintaining your community, deleting profane responses, keeping conversations civil, and blocking persistent troublemakers. Doing these sorts of tasks is an unfortunate cost of having a public forum. Even worse is the latest trend of people sending spam to bulletin boards and blog comments. At this writing, there really aren't any tools to handle this problem, and it has made several places remove pubic forums entirely from their sites.

One solution is to provide a moderated forum, basically requiring somebody to approve the first few posts from any new user. Once users have demonstrated themselves through their messages, you can make them unmoderated, allowing their posts to go straight through. Being a moderator of a forum can be a time-consuming task.

One problem of moderating any online group is that if people start to feel censored, they won't participate. The best forums are an open, honest exchange of ideas. If the ideas being expressed are unfavorable to your company or products, you certainly have the right to censor them—it's your forum. But if you allow people to post criticisms, do your best to respond to them, and don't try to hide the flaws of your products through censorship, you'll likely engender a much more loyal and supportive audience. Finding the fine line between cutting off an obnoxious, unreasonable person trying to provoke an angry response and suppressing valid criticism can be a challenging task.

Bulletin boards, online forums, message boards, whatever you choose to call them, have been around a lot longer than blogs. There are hundreds of different systems. Here are two open source projects that will likely cover your needs: PhpBB and MiniBB.

PhpBB (*http://www.phpbb.com*) is a full-blown bulletin board system, providing just about every feature imaginable. It stores its messages in a variety of different databases, offers many different templates and management options, and can do a great job for a big bulletin board system.

As you might guess, MiniBB (*http://www.minibb.net/*) is a stripped-down, fast, effective bulletin board system. It forgoes features such as private messaging, message threading, and HTML in messages, but still provides plenty of customizability and power in a smaller package.

Web Sites Managed by Your Customers: Wiki Webs

An opposite approach to solving the problem of policing posts to your Web site is to allow anyone to change it. This surprising concept is embodied in a technology originally called a *Wiki Wiki Web*, or just *Wiki*. A project chose the name *Wiki wiki*, which in Hawaiian means "quickly." A wiki provides a system that allows anybody to quickly modify the content of the page, while keeping track of all previous versions. It may sound risky, but it works because reasonable people far outnumber troublemakers. If somebody defaces a page, the next person who comes along can undo the damage.

A wiki is a platform for open source content development. A programmer named Ward Cunningham brought the ideas behind a wiki together, named it, and popularized the first wiki Web in 1995. It's called the Portland Pattern Repository, and is still available at *http://c2.com/cgi/wiki*. The most famous individual wiki project is Wikipedia (*http://www.wikipedia.org*), a free online encyclopedia written and maintained by the general public (Figure 13.2)—basically an open source encyclopedia. It's been so popular that by the middle of 2003, it was suffering from its own success—its servers were unable to keep up with the number of visitors it was getting, making the site slow down and become unresponsive. The original creators of the site started a non-profit corporation, the Wikimedia Foundation, to raise money to support the project. As of January 2004, Wikimedia had raised most of the cash necessary to upgrade their servers and connections to meet the demand. Wikipedia has reached nearly 200,000 entries in English.

Wikis are a powerful way of distributing the authoring of a Web site. It's particularly useful for Frequently Asked Questions (FAQs), or new employee orientation Web sites. There are all kinds of ways you can put a wiki to use, wherever you want to encourage people who have knowledge to share it—it's so easy for people to make changes once they get the hang of it.

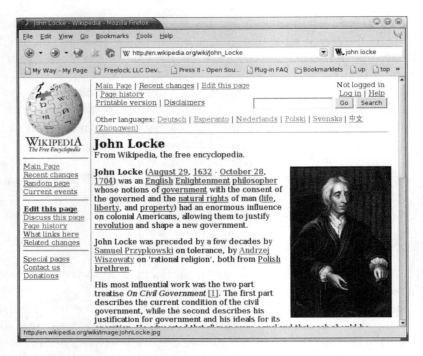

FIGURE 13.2   Wikipedia entry for the other John Locke.

What makes a wiki Web so easy? The main thing is that everything is done through the Web, including the creation of new pages. Each wiki engine has its own semantics for how to do this, but creating a new topic is often as simple as combining two capitalized words. For example, to create a topic about content management systems in a wiki Web, first you edit an existing page and collapse the words to use as the title: ContentManagementSystems. When you view your edited page, there will be a link next to this text you can follow to create a page for the content. The wiki Web handles all of the linking and page creation for you. That's what makes it so fast—you can create links for topics as you write, and anybody can come back and fill out the topic for them at any later time.

A company intranet is a natural place to put a wiki. One of the hallmarks of a wiki is that it's never finished—there's always room for improvement, and at any one point you may find a page that is inaccurate or misleading. On the whole, wikis capture certain types of knowledge better than most other forms.

For external systems, you'll have to decide whether a wiki fits your company brand image. Wikis, like message boards, provide feedback directly from your customers. The main difference is that message boards are organized by time and date of the posting, while wikis are organized by contents and hyperlinks. So with a wiki, all the related items end up together, either on one page or on a set of linked pages. Message boards often end up with the same questions posted multiple times, usually requiring more participation from your company.

There are hundreds of wiki Web systems you can implement. Some of the most popular are Twiki (*http://twiki.org*), MediaWiki (*http://wikipedia.sourceforge.net*), and PhpWiki (*http://phpwiki.sourceforge.net*). They vary substantially in the implementation languages, features, and how you specify links. The original wiki has a long page listing most wiki engines at *http://c2.com/cgi/wiki?WikiEngines*.

Content Management Systems

Ask for a content management system, and you'll find that the term means entirely different things to different people. *Content* might refer to a paragraph on a Web site, the serial number of a desktop computer, or a 600-page manual for an airplane. *Content Management* might refer to a system that enforces an editorial workflow for publishing an article on a Web site, communicates information within a company or to its customers, or makes it possible to find an important document. You can easily come up with a list of 40 different features provided by various content management systems. If you need something very sophisticated, you'll probably find something that comes close to meeting your needs, but no compelling package stands out.

Most content management software packages are designed to manage content on a Web site. Both wikis and blogs fall into this basic category. When you get a more sophisticated content management system, it might add more of a publishing workflow, routing a story back and forth among writers, developmental editors, copy editors, and proofreaders.

Another major type of content management system can be called a *Web portal*—a Web page that pulls information from many different sources and puts it on one page. These are sometimes called a digital dashboard.

Another class of systems is centered around making a paperless office: providing an online searchable filing cabinet of documents. These systems provide revision control as we discussed in Chapter 10, along with the ability to find documents a myriad of ways. With paper, when you store a document in a filing cabinet, you need to choose one organization system. When setting up the organization system, you need to forecast how you're going to find each document later. This may involve setting up some sort of indexing system.

With a content management system, the content is stored in a database, and each bit of content has a set of metadata associated with it. You can later find the document by searching on any of the metadata.

This last type of content management system is expensive to implement, and there aren't any compelling open source solutions yet. By all accounts there is a lot more to be done to make a system people actually like enough to use. There are accounts of people printing their emails, and then scanning them into their content management system where they can be associated with a project.

Let's take a quick look at two open source content management systems: Postnuke and Zope.

Small Business Portal: Postnuke

We've looked at blogging systems and wikis. Postnuke (*http://www.postnuke.org*) is a slightly more sophisticated combination of the two, providing a set of modules, a user and group authorization system, and a framework for developing custom modules to what is basically a multi-user blogging engine.

Postnuke is a fork of the earlier PhpNuke project (*http://www.phpnuke.org*), one of the first open source projects to provide a basic approval process for publishing stories on the Web, without requiring HTML or FTP experience of the writers. Due to political reasons, the PhpNuke project splintered into many different competing projects, collectively called "the Nukes." Other successful Nukes include Envolution (*http://www.envolution.org*), MyPhpNuke (*http://www.myphpnuke.org*), and Xoops (*http://www.xoops.org*). Each of these has a slightly different feature set, and has taken the basic concept in different directions.

Postnuke has developed two areas in particular: a system for setting up different groups of user accounts with very granular permissions, and an Application Programmer Interface (API) for developing individual modules containing different types of content, as shown in Figure 13.3. This makes it relatively easy to add custom-built modules to your Web site, or choose from among a wide range of existing modules. There are modules for photo galleries, classified ads, weather forecasts, and message boards. There's a calendar module that is compatible with the iCalendar standard described in Chapter 8.

All of the nukes work well for a public Web site. While you can restrict access to particular areas to particular groups, it's not very conducive to sharing documents, and it doesn't integrate very well with other internal systems like email or directory servers. But it's possible to get a Postnuke site up and running in half an hour, and begin working on content immediately.

Full Application Framework: Zope and Plone

If you need content management for your internal documents, Plone (*http://www.plone.org*) is the place to start. Plone is a powerful content management system that runs on the open source Zope application server (*http://www.zope.org*).

These tools can scale to the largest enterprises. NASA, Lufthansa, NATO, CBS New York, the AARP, and the government of Austria are among the largest of the many Zope installations. Plone has become one of the most successful content management systems in short order.

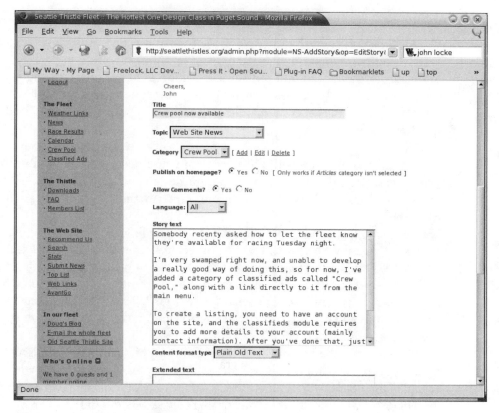

FIGURE 13.3   Editing a story in Postnuke.

Zope provides a consistent authentication system that can connect to any centralized LDAP directory or other system already set up on your intranet. It provides the building blocks to be able to put together a wide range of Web applications. By itself, Zope provides a set of tools, but nothing you can use out of the box, without programming.

Plone is a content management application that runs on the Zope server. You can download and install Plone, complete with Zope, with a single installation package. The Plone project provides installation packages for Windows, Mac, and Linux. With Plone, you can author pages in OpenOffice.org, and post them straight to the site. Plone converts them to appropriate pages automatically, making it a great platform for commenting and collaborating on documents. You can open up individual documents to comment, and you can create wiki-like pages that anyone can edit. These features compare quite well to proprietary solutions, such as Microsoft SharePoint™.

Web Development Tools

Content management tools mainly exist to separate content from graphic design. With a content management system, blog, or wiki, you either use a canned set of templates or themes, or you put some development time into creating your own. Once you have the basic design of your site, these systems free up your Web developers from working on content, allowing anyone in your company to update and maintain the stories.

The alternative, if your Web designer is to be responsible for updating your Web sites, is to just supply the content to him and make it his job to update static Web pages. In either case, you need graphic design and Web development tools to make your Web site support your brand, rather than looking like a generic template.

There are a wide range of Web site tools. Many different programs can help you create individual Web pages, including office programs like Microsoft Excel, Word, and PowerPoint, or OpenOffice.org Writer, Calc, and Impress. A Web site editor differs by providing tools for managing the entire site—updating links between pages, helping you upload your changes to your Web server, and usually adding special features like rollover scripts (a script that makes a link change when you move your mouse over it).

To make a Web site, you also need a good graphics editor. We'll discuss graphics editors in the print media section of this chapter. Finally, for anything more complex than basic HTML, there are a wide variety of tools that can make it easier for a developer to use a more sophisticated technology. All of these can be replaced by a text editor, but there are some helpful tools for working with Flash, PHP, ASP, Java, Perl, Python, and other Web languages. We don't cover these more specialized tools in this book.

Basic Web site editors fall into two primary camps: WYSIWYG, or code-based. What-You-See-Is-What-You-Get editors (WYSIWYG, pronounced "whizzy wig") hide the underlying code from you, allowing you to click and type wherever you want to add text to a page. You use tools similar to those in a word processor to insert graphics, align text, create tables, and add links. You build your Web pages graphically, moving things around where you want them and typing only your text. Because you will need to edit the source code of a Web page to solve certain design problems, WYSIWYG editors include a code view, though usually it's not very well developed. The better ones color-code HTML tags to make it easier to spot typos like missing quotation marks.

When using a code-based editor, you're working in the source code for a Web page. You need to know HTML, because instead of dragging things around graphically, you need to add the appropriate attribute to the correct tag. Code-based editors provide better syntax highlighting, color-coding text according to the rules of HTML or whatever language you're working in. They also provide macros, shortcuts that can add a group of tags automatically to achieve a desired effect.

For beginners creating a static Web site, a WYSIWYG editor is usually the easiest way to go, although depending on the editor, there may be some hidden pitfalls such as pages that look completely different in browsers on other operating systems. In general, the easiest programs to use generate the worst HTML, and lack features professional Web designers use daily. Some professional designers use the better WYSIWYG editors daily—for a static Web site, they can be faster than working in code.

You almost always get better code when you work with a code-based editor. Creating a dynamic Web site is usually a programming task, much better suited to code-based editors. WYSIWYG editors use a brute-force approach to code, adding a lot of unnecessary tags to get graphics to line up the way you dragged them. These tags lead to mixed results on different browsers, because of differences in the underlying browser engine. This means that a page that looks great in Internet Explorer in Windows may be practically unreadable in Safari, the new standard browser for Macs. If you don't have a Mac, you might not ever know that your customers who use Macs can't read your Web site. Writing and validating your own code in a code-based editor can greatly reduce this problem.

People creating dynamic Web sites use code-based editors almost exclusively. Because creating a dynamic Web site involves more programming than layout, you're generally able to develop and debug a Web application much quicker, with fewer quirks, if you can see exactly what's going on.

Because open source software was primarily developed by programmers, there are a great many excellent open source code editors, but very few open source WYSIWYG editors. Let's take a look at a few good choices for Web editing tools. Table 13.1 summarizes some of the key Web editing options.

Macromedia Dreamweaver

Macromedia Dreamweaver (*http://www.macromedia.com/software/dreamweaver/*) is among the most popular WYSIWYG editor among professional Web developers, mainly because it includes a lot of tools that make site navigation, rollover graphics, and other fairly sophisticated tasks very simple. And, it implements these features in a way that works well for most browsers.

Like many professional tools, it has a bit of a learning curve, and you do need to know a bit about how Web sites work to be able to use Dreamweaver effectively.

TABLE 13.1   Overview of Popular Web Editors

Program	WYSIWYG?	Key Benefits	Open Source?	Platforms
Macromedia Dreamweaver	Yes	Full-featured, favorite among professional Web developers	No	Windows, Mac
Microsoft FrontPage	Yes	Easy to use	No	Windows
Adobe GoLive!	Yes	Bundled with other popular graphic design tools	No	Windows, Mac
Mozilla Composer	Yes	Cross-platform, free	Yes	Windows, Mac, Linux
NVU	Yes	Free, open source	Yes	Linux
BBEdit	No	Popular among Mac professionals	No	Mac
Quanta Plus Screem Bluefish	No	Good code-based editors	Yes	Linux
ActiveState Komodo Nusphere PHPEd	No	IDE and Debugger for popular server languages, cross platform	No	Windows, Linux
PHPEdit	No	IDE and Debugger for PHP and Regular Expressions	Yes	Windows

Microsoft FrontPage

Microsoft FrontPage is probably the easiest full-featured Web editor available, especially for people who work with Microsoft products regularly. One problem with it is that it doesn't work well with non-Microsoft products. Most of its scripts and extras work great if you view the site in Microsoft Internet Explorer, but if you open the same page in another browser, like Opera, many of the scripts don't work correctly.

The worst thing about FrontPage is that if you use it, you can't easily work with other people who are using other Web site editors. FrontPage uploads files to Web sites using a proprietary set of FrontPage Extensions. These must be properly installed on the Web server. If you hire a Web developer to update the look of your site in Dreamweaver, the extensions get out of sync with the site, and you end up having to go through all sorts of hoops to rebuild the site.

If you use FrontPage, you're pretty much stuck with it—it's a pain to edit with any other editor and FrontPage on the same site.

Adobe GoLive!

GoLive! has a growing following, thanks largely to Adobe bundling it in packages with its other popular graphics and desktop publishing tools. Adobe Photoshop is the premium photo-editing program among graphic designers. Adobe Illustrator is a top-notch illustration tool. Adobe InDesign is a great desktop publishing package. Adobe has provided GoLive in special packages with these extremely popular products, and it's been very well received. It has quickly become a contender for a solid proprietary WYSIWYG editor.

Mozilla Composer

Mozilla Composer (*http://www.mozilla.org*) is perhaps the oldest open source WYSIWYG Web editor. It was originally developed in an early version of Netscape Communicator, and dates back to the early days of the World Wide Web. Unlike the other WYSIWYG editors we've discussed so far, Composer edits individual pages—it doesn't provide any site management tools, or extra script functionality. In this respect, it's a very basic tool.

NVU

At this writing, NVU (*http://www.nvu.com*) doesn't have a working release. It's a branch of the Mozilla Composer program that adds most of the site management tools provided by Dreamweaver and GoLive. It's on a fast development track, so it should be available by the time this book is published. NVU is backed by Linspire, a Linux distribution that is trying to make Linux as easy to use as possible for non-computer users.

NVU appears to be the only major project aiming to provide an open source full WYSIWYG Web editor with site management tools.

BBEdit

BBEdit (*http://www.barebones.com/products/bbedit/index.shtml*) is a popular code-based editor for the Mac. Because the Mac is especially popular among graphic designers, you'll find quite a few professional Web developers using this software to develop Web sites. It provides many features to help Web developers code Web sites in many different languages in a snap. You can download the software at *http://www.apple.com/downloads/macosx/productivity_tools/bbedit.html*.

Quanta Plus, Screem, and Bluefish

These are three different open source code-based editors for Linux. They differ primarily in the graphical toolkit they're based on. For the most part, they seem to offer quite similar functionality. Quanta Plus uses KDE, while Bluefish and Screem use the GNOME libraries.

These programs are quite comparable to BBEdit, providing automatic tag completion, site-wide link management, file uploads, integration with revision control systems, and many other features.

Komodo, PHPEd, and PHPEdit

These programs take the code-based editors one step further, adding debugging support. A debugger allows you to step through programs one line at a time, and see the state of all the variables at any point. These are programming tools that support PHP, one of the most popular server-side programming languages.

Of these three, only PHPEdit is open source—and it runs only on Windows. Komodo® and PHPEd™ have both Windows and Linux versions, but they're both proprietary. Komodo also provides debugging for Perl, Python, and XSLT.

Debugging support makes these types of editors much better for Web application development. You don't need a debugger for static HTML pages, but if you're programming something sophisticated, a debugger will save you many hours.

Other Editors

These only skim the surface. There are hundreds of editors out there, most with quite similar features. Editors come and go. If you find one you're happy with, stick with it. If you find one lacking, there are plenty of others to choose from.

EMAIL MARKETING

Aside from using email as a communication medium as we discussed in Chapter 7, there are three good ways you can use email to market your business: set up an autoresponder, host a mailing list, or publish an email newsletter.

The danger of sending email to large numbers of people is getting labeled as a spammer. There's a big difference between sending a newsletter to an existing customer or contact you've made, and sending an unsolicited email to someone you don't know. While direct mail advertising has been an effective way for some businesses to advertise their products or services, spam has made direct email something that may tarnish your brand a lot more than bringing in business.

We'll discuss the problem of spam in Chapter 19, but as a general guideline, you should always get permission from somebody before adding them to any sort of email list. If you're going to send an unsolicited email to someone you haven't already talked with, do your homework and make it personal. Never mass-email people without their consent.

Autoresponders

Before the Web, email was an even more dominant form of media. Autoresponders were the simplest way to get information about a company or product. Basically, an autoresponder sends a pre-written response to anybody who sends it mail. The most common autoresponder address is info@example.com.

For the most part, detailing your products and services on your Web site is more than enough. If you set an autoresponder up, very few people will actually use it. On the other hand, they are easy to set up if you're running a mail server, and provide one more way for potential customers to find out about your company.

An open source program called Reply-O-Matic (*http://sourceforge.net/projects/reply-o-matic/*) provides all the options you might want for creating autoresponses, including choosing different responses to different addresses, preventing multiple responses to the same address, and a number of security features.

Managing Mailing Lists

Mailing lists can be another way to host an online community, very much like a Web-based message board. Some people prefer a Web-based forum, others an email-based forum. Most email users set up simple lists in their client software so that they can mail a group of people all at once. This requires the sender to manage those addresses. Inevitably people change their email address, breaking the list. Sometimes this results in the mail not getting delivered at all. Other times, your mail gets to some of the recipients but not all. When you resend, some people get the message twice.

Also, with this style of mailing, everybody can see everyone else on your list, raising privacy concerns. You can prevent this by using a blind carbon copy (BCC), but this prevents conversations among your recipients, because nobody knows who has received the message.

Mailing list software moves control into the recipient's hands. As a recipient, you can choose to subscribe or unsubscribe to a mailing list. You can choose to receive each message as it's sent, or have the mailing list send you messages grouped into a *digest*, a single email containing all the messages sent during a specific period—a day, a week, for example—or by the number of emails.

As a list administrator, you can set up the software to maintain a Web-based archive, and make the archive public, or restrict it to the list members. You can also configure a mailing list to reflect a Usenet news group, so that people can use a news reader instead of an email reader. You can designate whether the mailing list accepts mail from anyone, or only subscribers. In moderated mode, the mailing list software holds messages for approval by a moderator. As a moderator, you can approve or reject individual messages.

Like hosting a message board, hosting a mailing list can be a great way to market your business. You can put a small ad at the bottom of every message, directing people to your Web site. If your list becomes successful, you'll find a built-in, core audience of people who think of your business with high regard, especially if you put some effort into moderating new posts and keeping the conversations civil. Online communities left to their own devices can quickly degenerate into hostile places—for some reason, when people communicate over networks, civility sometimes suffers. If you're going to run a mailing list, make sure you have a good list moderator, somebody who will calm people down when conversations become heated, kick unreasonable people off the list, and maintain a friendly atmosphere for newcomers.

Don't try to set up a mailing list that competes with an established, active list. Find a subject area related to your business that people want to talk about, advertise it on your Web site, make a press release to news sources in your industry, and start some conversations.

If a list has a public archive, it will most likely turn up in a search using Google. Search on terms related to your topic, and go several pages into the results to find out if a related list already exists. If the topics you want to discuss are already covered by an existing mailing list, you might consider joining the discussion, and become an active participant instead of setting up a new list. On most lists, outright advertisements are frowned upon, but you're free to attach a *signature*, a few lines of text advertising your business, below a message related to the topic being discussed. Whether you host a list or not, participating in one can give you direct communication with your customers.

There are quite a few proprietary mailing list software packages, but only a couple open source ones. The reason there are few open source mailing list projects is because one of them grabbed an early, solid lead: the Mailman project (*http://list.org*). Mailman is excellent. It's easy to administer, it matches every other list management software feature for feature, and it's becoming very widely used.

Creating Email Newsletters

While you may or may not host or participate in an email list, sending a frequent email newsletter can provide very effective marketing for your business, especially if it depends upon repeat business. Almost any business can benefit from an email newsletter. What makes a newsletter effective is providing good content, relevant to your audience.

If you're the manufacturer of an expensive product, or provide services for complicated products, your customers would appreciate maintenance tips or ways to make their investment last longer. If you're a small retail outlet, you might combine a light-hearted joke of the week, along with a coupon to encourage customers to come to your store.

Again, some people consider newsletters to be spam. You have to respect the wishes of each recipient, removing them from your mailing list if they ask. Make sure people have given you permission to mail to them before sending any generic newsletter to them, and you should avoid most problems.

You have two choices of ways to manage your newsletter: using a mailing list, or sending individual messages through a Customer Relationship Management (CRM) solution. See Chapter 7 for more about using a CRM system.

The Mailman list manager discussed above works great for managing newsletter subscriptions. At this writing, it doesn't integrate with a CRM system, and you cannot customize the content of your newsletter to say different things to different people, but it's very easy to add and remove subscribers, and the recipients can control whether or not they receive your messages. Plus, your newsletters are automatically archived, so people can read through past issues. And if they get indexed by a search engine, you may even gain new customers that may not otherwise find your Web site.

To set up a newsletter style mailing list, you set up the list software to make new list members moderated, reject posts from moderated members, and discard posts from non-members. Then make your account unmoderated.

You can post to a mailing list using any email software. If you want to make a fancy newsletter using color and graphics, you can send HTML email (though you'll need to change some of the list settings to allow the HTML through). Many technical computer users dislike HTML mail for a few reasons:

- HTML mail can carry viruses in the form of Javascript.
- Images loaded from Web servers can be used to identify that a particular user has received a message, using a technique called a "Web bug."
- Garish designs can make HTML mail virtually unreadable.

For these reasons, if you want to create HTML newsletters, you should consider either maintaining a separate email list that provides plain-text versions of your newsletter, or putting the fancy HTML newsletter on your Web site and mailing out a link to it.

Many email clients allow you to create well-formatted, elegant HTML emails. To make a newsletter with a consistent design using open source software, here are two options:

1. Use the Save As Template option in Mozilla Mail/Mozilla Thunderbird to save a copy of a newsletter after you've made it look the way you want it to

look. You can then easily reopen the template the next time you want to send a newsletter.

2. Create an HTML page using OpenOffice.org, or another Web editor. In Ximian Evolution, open up a new message and choose Insert | HTML File.

When inserting an external HTML file into Evolution or other email programs, make sure you post all images on a Web server, and set the images to load from the Web server.

However you create your newsletter, be sure to test it on several different email clients. Send it to a few friends that you know use a variety of email clients, and have them let you know if there are any problems before sending it out to a big list.

PRINT MEDIA

The addition of email and Web to the potential outlets for marketing have not made more traditional paper-based marketing disappear. Businesses still use business cards, brochures, catalogs, flyers, and print advertising. Graphic design is as important as ever, in both digital and print media. And creating personalized mass mailings is one of the first things small businesses did with personal computers. Let's see what open source software can do to help in these areas.

Brochures and Desktop Publishing

Desktop publishing provides the ability to print professional, creative designs. Like content management, there's a broad range of different types of software that can be called desktop publishing tools. Let's break these tools down into three basic categories:

- Professional desktop publishing tools for brochures, cards, and flyers
- Long document publishing tools
- Other publishing tools

Professional Desktop Publishing Tools for Brochures, Cards, and Flyers

Two companies lead the market in desktop publishing tools for everything from small print advertisements and business cards to newsletters, magazines, and small catalogs: Adobe and Quark. Adobe InDesign and QuarkXPress both provide a tremendous number of features for integrating text with graphics, and creating consistent layout templates for a few dozen pages.

Both of these programs are available for Windows and Mac. QuarkXPress seems to have the lead in small magazines, while InDesign has replaced the older PageMaker to fill most other print publishing needs.

There's one new open source entry to this category: the Scribus project (*http://www.scribus.net*), as shown in Figure 13.4. Scribus lacks many of the bells and whistles of the other projects, currently focusing on features that professional publishers appreciate, such as sophisticated color and font management—kerning, leading, and other fine-tuning controls. Scribus at this writing is only available for Linux, though by the time this is published it may well compile and run on Macs.

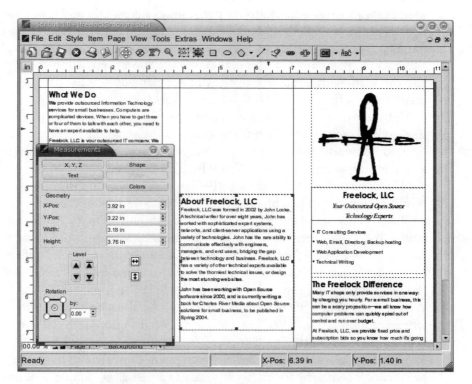

FIGURE 13.4   Desktop publishing with the open source Scribus software.

In short, the professional layout features of Scribus will allow you to do everything you can do with the proprietary programs, but many of the time-saving features the other programs provide will make them favored for years to come. Microsoft Publisher is a tool that aims to fill this same niche, but it lacks the color management and degree of control over fonts the others have, and is not a serious contender.

Long Document Publishing Tools

A leading publishing tool for books right now is another Adobe product, Adobe FrameMaker. FrameMaker is designed to make the pages in a long document consistent, and comes with good cross-referencing functions, support for generating formulas and tables, bullets, numbering, and many other things you might want to print. While FrameMaker can handle color, its strengths are in managing structure in a long document.

Another strength of FrameMaker is its support for XML, and more specifically, the Docbook XML schema. Docbook is a schema that defines all sorts of types of containers you might use in a document, everything from individual formatting specifications to paragraphs to chapters, index items, and tables of content. Docbook is used as an open standard for documentation of many large projects, and internally in several publishers. FrameMaker is one of the few graphical editors that allow you to edit native Docbook files in a WYSIWYG environment. FrameMaker also can work with just about any XML document, as long as you provide a Document Type Definition (DTD) that defines how to validate it.

For heavy duty publishing tasks, another language called LaTeX provides very fine-grained control over layout and macros for assembling pages and books. In the open source world, there isn't really a program that provides the same level of WYSIWYG editing as FrameMaker. What you'll find instead are quite a few people that use Docbook or LaTeX in a plain text editor equipped with macros to gain the same results. A favorite editor for this type of work is Emacs, an open source program available on just about every Unix and Linux computer. Emacs provides not just text editing but a whole environment that can be endlessly customized and tweaked to make a knowledgeable user extremely effective at creating all sorts of unique designs.

Emacs is quite similar to the code editors we discussed in the Web development tools section earlier in this chapter. Many people also use it for editing HTML and Web scripts. While it's extremely powerful, it's also quite difficult to learn, and when you publish with raw languages, you need to do a test print whenever you want to see the results of your work.

The big advantage of working with an open, standardized language like LaTeX or Docbook comes when you want to put together a big catalog, a phone book, or similar publications that pull together an enormous number of small bits of content from a database or other source. You can write a program to extract the data and transform it into your publication. This is a very specialized type of print production, but it's an area where open source and open standards is unmatched.

Other Publishing Tools

Microsoft Word and OpenOffice.org are both used for publishing, both for brochures and long documents. Neither has the advanced fine-tuning controls such as the ability to export color separations or to kern fonts. But both can do a reasonable job of creating anything we've discussed.

OpenOffice.org is part of The Open CD, on the CD-ROM included with this book.

Both of them have a number of helpful features such as built-in drawing tools and the ability to put text inside text frames, use multiple columns on a page, and maintain cross-references that automatically provide an updated page number to a marked bit of text. Both provide a master document feature, though master documents need to be used with care, because it's easy to lose documents entirely if you use them incorrectly.

In general, OpenOffice.org provides somewhat better support for templates and styles than Word. An OpenOffice.org style can inherit from another style, and you can define numbering, frame, page, and table styles, all features missing from Word. These features make it easier to keep long documents consistent. Word is easier to use if you're going to ignore these styles, making it perhaps a little easier to get exactly the layout you're looking for in a small document.

For most items you're going to develop in house, OpenOffice.org can probably do what you need it to do. If you use professional desktop publishers or designers, they're going to have their own preferences in design tools. If you like the work of a designer, let her use the tools of her choice—though you should make sure you'll be able to use the source files for the project in the future.

Graphic Design

For creating advertisements, brochures, and Web sites, you will need graphic design tools. There are a number of open source graphic design tools becoming more and more ready for production use.

The Gnu Image Manipulation Program (The GIMP, *http://www.gimp.org*) is one of the most popular, most mature open source projects around. It provides most of the functionality of Adobe Photoshop. The GIMP is available for Windows and Mac as well as Linux. At this writing, support for the CMYK color model is not quite finished, but it should be available by the time this book is published.

The GIMP for Windows is part of The Open CD, on the CD-ROM included with this book.

For vector drawing, open source projects aren't quite as close to the leading proprietary programs such as Adobe Illustrator and Macromedia Freehand. Two open source projects are working to provide comprehensive vector drawing programs, with slightly different aims: Sodipodi (*http://www.sodipodi.com/*) is trying to provide a premier vector drawing program; and Inkscape (*http://www.inkscape.org/*) is specifically devoted to completely implementing a newer standard called Scalable Vector Graphics (SVG).

Mail Merge

Finally, let's take a quick look at a common business tool: the mail merge. A mail merge allows you to send the same letter to many different people, customizing it slightly for each one. There are two parts to a mail merge: the data source and the template document. The process is similar in Microsoft Word and OpenOffice.org.

In OpenOffice.org, you can define many different data sources to use in a mail merge, including spreadsheets, a Windows address book, an Evolution or Mozilla address book (Figure 13.5), an LDAP directory, a text file, or any database that can be accessed through an Open Database Connectivity (ODBC) connection.

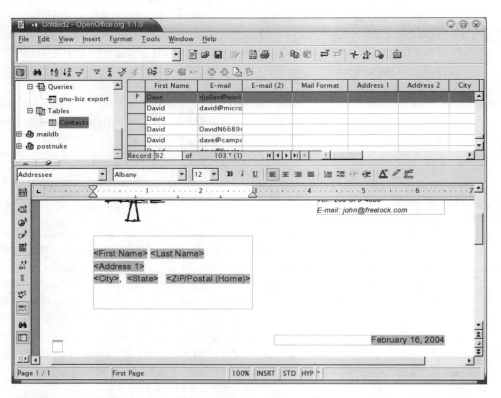

FIGURE 13.5 Setting up a mail merge in OpenOffice, using an Evolution address book.

The most common use of a mail merge is to merge names and addressed into a letter to personalize it. You can also use mail merging to create a page of labels, print unique addresses on envelopes, or create a catalog-style listing of anything in a database. Mail merging is a great time-saving feature of word processors, and well worth learning how to use.

SUMMARY

The tools discussed in this chapter are quite the mixed bag of tricks. The capabilities of a content management system make it easy to update your Web site without needing help from a developer. Open source graphical tools are quickly becoming equivalent to the best commercial offerings, and if you're going to do any automation, open source is the way to go. For the best interfaces for making professional designs, commercial desktop publishing tools and Web development tools still have a dominant lead—but if you're not a full-time designer, you're probably better off hiring a professional to create the graphical design for you.

In this chapter, we looked at a variety of ways of publishing content. For the Web, we looked at several different ways of creating Web sites that not only act as an online advertisement for your business, but also provide opportunities for interacting with your customers. These systems include blogs, bulletin boards, content management systems, and dynamic Web sites. We discussed using email for marketing, making newsletters, hosting email lists, and using automatic email responders. Finally, we looked at open source tools for creating marketing material in print: desktop publishing, graphic design, and mail merge.

In the next chapter, we'll cover all aspects of connecting to your business systems securely from remote locations.

CONTENT MANAGEMENT AND DESIGN REFERENCES

An updated list of resources for this chapter is on the Web site for the book at *http://opensourcesmall.biz/publishing*.

Software

Movable Type, free but not for commercial sites blogging software *http://www.movabletype.org*
Serendipity, open source blogging software *http://www.s9y.org*
Word Press, open source blogging software *http://www.wordpress.org*
PhpBB, open source message board forum software *http://www.phpbb.com*
MiniBB, stripped down open source forum software *http://www.minibb.net*
Twiki, open source wiki software *http://twiki.org*
Media Wiki, open source wiki software *http://wikipedia.sourceforge.net*
Postnuke, PHP-based Web portal/CMS software *http://www.postnuke.org*
PhpNuke, PHP-based Web portal/CMS software *http://www.phpnuke.org*
Envolution, PHP-based Web portal/CMS software *http://www.envolution.org*
MyPhpNuke, PHP-based Web portal/CMS software *http://www.myphpnuke.org*

Xoops, PHP-based Web portal/CMS software *http://www.xoops.org*

Plone, full-fledged CMS software for Zope *http://www.plone.org*

Zope, application server *http://www.zope.org*

Macromedia Dreamweaver, commercial Web development software *http://www.macromedia.com/software/dreamweaver/*

Microsoft Frontpage, commercial Web development software *http://www.microsoft.com/frontpage*

Adobe GoLive!, commercial Web development software *http://www.adobe.com/products/golive/main.html*

Mozilla Composer, open source Web development software *http://www.mozilla.org*

NVU, open source Web development software *http://www.nvu.com*

Quanta Plus, open source HTML editor *http://quanta.sourceforge.net/*

Bluefish, open source HTML editor *http://bluefish.openoffice.nl/*

Screem, open source HTML editor *http://www.screem.org/*

Activestate Komodo, commercial Web development IDE *http://www.active-state.com/Products/Komodo/*

NuSphere PHPEd, commercial Web development IDE *http://www.nusphere.com/*

PHPEdit, open source Web development IDE for Windows *http://www.phpedit.com/*

Reply-O-Matic, open source auto-responder software *http://sourceforge.net/projects/reply-o-matic*

Mailman, open source mailing list manager *http://list.org*

Scribus, open source desktop publishing tool *http://web2.altmuehlnet.de/fschmid/*

LaTeX, document publishing language *http://www.latex-project.org/*

Docbook, document publishing language *http://docbook.sourceforge.net/*

Quark Xpress, desktop publication *http://www.quark.com*

Adobe FrameMaker and InDesign, premier desktop publication *http://www.adobe.com*

The GIMP, open source graphic editor similar to Photoshop *http://www.gimp.org*

Web Sites

Portland Pattern Repository, the original Wiki Web *http://c2.com/cgi/wiki*

List of Wiki software *http://c2.com/cgi/wiki?WikiEngines*

Wikipedia, online wiki-based encyclopedia *http://www.wikipedia.org*

Open Source CMS, PHP-based CMS demo site for many different programs *http://www.opensourcecms.com*

Review of through-the-Web HTML editors, *http://www.bris.ac.uk/is/projects/cms/ttw/ttw.html*

14 Connect from Offsite

INTRODUCTION

The age of telecommuting is here. With the ubiquity of the Internet, and always-on, high-speed connections, if your work can be done on a computer you can do it from just about anywhere.

This chapter provides a comprehensive overview of different types of software that provide remote access. The first part, Web-enabled applications, is non-technical. The second part, Accessing Your Computer Remotely, needs a bit of comfort at the command line, and some familiarity with the principles of networking, to be able to figure out. The last part, about setting up a VPN, covers the very difficult set up, but easy of use.

As a small business, you might think remote access isn't that big a deal. Many small businesses don't see the need for allowing workers to access systems from anywhere other than the office. But if you look at remote access as a way of saving costs, you might change your mind. Providing remote access might mean that you don't need to pay for special office space for your bookkeeper. You can hire people who don't want to come to an office, such as stay-at-home parents looking for part-time work, or outsource various business functions to other businesses that already have their own offices set up. You may well be able to save office expenses, or attract more motivated employees by providing remote access.

Remote access becomes critical to your business when you have multiple business locations. When you open a branch location, it needs to have some secure way to exchange information with your headquarters. Remote access provides secure ways of exchanging data privately across your business locations.

You may find you prefer to do your business support work, such as answering email or reviewing marketing material, away from your storefront or office. Sometimes doing different tasks in different environments can be a good way to stay focused on each task. Remote access gives you the ability to look up something you forgot on your desktop computer, while you're at a client or partner's work site. Remote access lets you respond to important emails while you're traveling for business (or pleasure, if you can't afford to take the time completely off). Remote access blurs the lines between work and non-work—whether this is a good thing depends on how you look at it.

While many people want to leave work at work, and resent the encroachment of work on personal time, being able to work together remotely is a fundamental change in the nature of work. One of the main factors making open source software viable is that the Internet has allowed people to form "virtual" teams, working together on projects even while they're continents apart. You might find remote access opens opportunities for your business that were unimaginable a few years ago.

REMOTE ACCESS CONCERNS

For some organizations, transparency and openness is a good thing. Open source software projects work by allowing everyone to see what is going on with a project, providing opportunities for individuals to do something if they don't agree with a decision. Non-profits, churches, and public entities among others may find being completely open with their information engenders trust and higher returns.

But most businesses need to keep much of their corporate information private. You don't want to violate your customers' privacy by allowing everyone to browse your address book—depending on your industry, allowing customer information to appear anywhere public may even violate the law. Most legal discussions must remain confidential. The finances of your business should generally be protected, often from your employees, but always from your competitors. You probably don't want your competition to see your business plan, or find out your strategic direction.

The Internet is an inherently insecure medium. We will discuss security issues in much greater detail in Chapters 16 and 17—what's important to know now is that anything you do that involves data traveling over the Internet, without specific encryption methods applied, can be easily intercepted by anyone motivated enough to try. Any system you want to access remotely that contains any sensitive company data should be secured using some reliable form of authentication and encryption. These systems might include:

- Email
- Files stored on servers
- Customer databases, contact relationship management systems
- Contracts, other data exchanged with partners, vendors, and customers
- Credit card and payment information
- Marketing material, before you release it
- Business plans
- Employee contact information
- Accounting systems
- Project plans

So how do you make remote access possible? There are many ways. We're going to group them into three basic types of remote access:

1. Web-enabled applications
2. Accessing your computer from afar
3. Connecting remote computers to your LAN

Think of these as levels of remote access: you will almost always use the first level, Web-enabled applications. As your needs increase, you may set up your computer to be available when you're traveling. The third level involves shrinking the distance between you and your LAN, so that you can do everything as if you were plugged into it directly.

WEB-ENABLED APPLICATIONS

A majority of the solutions in this book are Web-enabled. Many business applications can now be accessed using a Web browser—which by definition is Web-enabled. Other applications use networking protocols that work over the Internet, with varying degrees of privacy.

Generally, most client-server applications work over the Internet, with varying degrees of security and usability. Obviously, if a program has to send a lot of data through the network, it's going to work best if you have a lot of bandwidth. Your LAN is probably much higher bandwidth than your connection to the Internet.

Most Web applications are considered to use a *thin client*—in other words, most of the sophisticated processing is done on the server. This means that your Web browser only has to transfer the text and pictures, not necessarily all of the data. Thin clients work great over slow Internet connections. By far the most common Web-enabled applications are Web sites and email. Other systems can be Web-enabled, but are much less common. Let's take a closer look at Web-enabled applications.

Web Applications

Web applications are applications that run behind a Web server. The SQL-Ledger accounting system we set up in Chapter 10, Subversion we set up in Chapter 9, and groupware and contact relationship management systems all use the Apache Web server to provide content to Web browsers. By using a single Web server for multiple functions, you create the easiest-to-administer type of remote access.

You can also install a Web email package, a content management system, and many other applications. Two huge advantages are that Apache includes support for encrypted SSL connections using a package called OpenSSL, and Apache has built-in authentication methods that can hook into all sorts of systems. The main remaining thing your application needs to do is to authorize users—determine which users can access which parts of the application.

The list of Web applications is growing longer every day. You can find Web applications to do nearly anything you need them to do, as we've seen throughout this book.

The main drawbacks to Web applications are:

1. There's only so much you can do in a Web browser.
2. Web applications take a lot of server power, and almost no client power.

The first issue has to do with usability. It's the down side of the biggest benefit of using Web applications—having software that runs on any Web browser makes it only work with the lowest common denominator. Browsers don't support drag-and-drop. To support most browsers, you can't do anything more sophisticated than provide a simple form and generate pages based on the results.

If you target specific browsers with more capabilities, you can make more usable Web applications. Newer browsers can load additional data directly from the server without loading a new Web page. Using dynamic technologies like Flash or Java can take away the usability implications, at the expense of requiring more in your Web browser.

The second limitation can be addressed with the same solution—doing more of the processing work on the client side. If all of your processing happens on the server, you don't need anything special in your workstation—but each user of the application multiplies the amount of power you need on your server. By distributing some of the processing load out to the clients, you can often get better performance out of your server.

The best thing about Web applications is the simplicity in extending them to the Internet. All you need to do is forward the appropriate port on your router to your Web server, and provide some sort of authentication method. Apache comes with modules for authenticating against a flat file on the server, different kinds of databases, company directories, or Windows domains.

Email Applications

In contrast to Web applications, email is a disconnected Internet application. It's designed to work over the Internet. As we saw in Chapter 5, running an email server is no easy feat—which is why the vast majority of people use somebody else's mail server and connect to it through the Internet. When you travel with a laptop, it's easy to download your mail anywhere you can connect to the Internet. It can be a bit more tricky to send mail.

Generally, you will be able to connect to whatever server is hosting your email from anywhere on the Internet, using an email client that speaks POP or IMAP. Your email software logs into your account using a username and password. We covered the issues of setting up an IMAP server in Chapter 5. If you're running a mail server, you might consider providing encrypted connections to it. The Courier-IMAP server described in Chapter 5 is very easy to set up for encrypted connections—you simply provide signed certificates and configure the encrypted daemons to start.

The problem with sending mail is that due to spam, you can't just set up a mail server to accept mail from any computer. Mail servers are set up to accept mail for particular domains (presumably the domains hosted by the server), and to relay mail to the correct receiving server for particular users. You can't just connect to any mail server and send your mail, because most server administrators block anonymous users in an effort to prevent spam.

The one reliable server you can use to send mail is one provided for you by your ISP. The problem is, if you travel somewhere else, you may well use a different ISP to connect to the Internet. This means you need to find out the correct server to send through, and change your mail settings, any time you use a different connection.

Computer people are a lazy bunch. The whole point of vast amounts of software is to reduce work and make the computer do the work for you. So you can be sure that countless people have gone to extensive trouble to avoid having to change their mail settings when they travel.

There are three main approaches people have taken to provide outgoing mail for remote users, regardless of what ISP the remote user uses:

1. Allow connections that have successfully logged in to check their mail access to the mail server for a fixed amount of time.
2. Require remote users to log into the sending server with a username and password.
3. Provide a Webmail system to bypass the issue.

The first solution, called Pop-Before-SMTP, or SMTP-After-POP, relies on the assumption that only one computer can have a single IP address at a time. An open source project called, naturally, Pop-Before-SMTP, watches the mail server log for successful logins to the POP or IMAP server. When it finds one, it adds the IP address to a database that the mail server uses to allow access to the sender. You can find a Perl script called Pop-Before-SMTP at *http://popbsmtp.sourceforge.net/*.

The second solution, setting up password authentication for people who want to send mail, sounds like the way to go. It's called SMTP Authentication. Unfortunately, it's very difficult to set up. Just to add password authentication, you need to install and configure two additional services, and get your mail server to use them. And if you want to avoid users sending their passwords in clear text across the Internet, you also need to install and configure encryption. Due to a complete lack of authentication and authorization in the basic SMTP protocol, providing SMTP authentication is one of the trickiest administration tasks around.

The other solution, setting up a Web application that provides access to email, is actually the easiest. It reduces the problem of remote access to your email down to the same elegance of any other Web application. Your users don't need to install or configure anything—all they need to do is log into the Web site with any Web browser. The drawback is that you're limited to the capabilities of the Web browser and can't drag and drop messages into different mail folders. You have to wait for each new message to load (rather than downloading all your messages at once) and don't necessarily have integrated access to other things on your computer, such as address books or HTML editors.

Other Web-Enabled Applications

Most people use Web applications and email daily. There are many other applications that run over the Internet that don't fall into these categories. Most are special purpose. Some pre-date Web applications. Some are brand new ways of exchanging information. Here are a few that are still in use:

- File Transfer Protocol (FTP)
- Remote backup software

- Streaming media
- Messaging
- Directory services
- Peer-to-peer file sharing
- Distributed computing

All of these applications are designed with the Internet in mind. Allowing remote users access to these services is generally just a matter of configuring your firewall to route traffic to the appropriate server—and figuring out how to authorize access for particular users, if there's a need.

File Transfer

One of the most common needs for small businesses is the ability to transfer files to and from their customers. File Transfer Protocol (FTP) is the standard way to transfer files, pre-dating Web applications. FTP is the standard way to post your Web site to a hosted service.

However, there are some real security issues with FTP, the biggest of which is that there is no way to encrypt your username and password. Anybody sniffing traffic between a valid remote user and your FTP server can use the login credentials to impersonate that user. FTP was designed around the same time as SMTP, and shares its open, trusting nature.

Better ways of transferring files include setting up an SSL-encrypted WebDAV server, or creating a Web application that accepts uploads from particular users. See Chapter 6 for more about transferring files over the Internet.

Remote Backup Software

Several companies provide a custom remote backup service. A special client runs on your computer, collects all of the files to back up, archives them and encrypts them, and then transfers them to a remote location. To run these securely over the Internet, they need to be designed around some form of encryption. None of these are standardized—they're almost all proprietary services. Search the Web for "Remote Backup Services" to find one, if you need such a service.

If you want to provide remote backups for your users, one possible scheme is to set up a system that synchronizes particular directories on your remote users' computers through an encrypted tunnel to their home directories on a server. These, too, will need to be custom-developed solutions for your particular business. Rsync over SSH is one way of doing this—search the Web to find examples of this type of operation. A software program called Unison provides synchronization capabilities across computers with different operating systems. See Chapter 18 for more about backing up data, or Chapter 9 for a better way to manage business documents securely over the Internet.

Streaming Media

Other than broadcasters, few small businesses need to provide remote access to streaming media. For the most part, if you have some audio/visual presentation you want to provide to remote users, you can simply post a media file on a secured Web server. Unlike media downloaded from a Web server, streaming media can be viewed and listened to while it's being downloaded. This requires servers designed specifically for the task.

In 2002, Real Networks released their multimedia server and player technology under an open source license as the Helix project (*http://www.helixcommunity.org*). If you have employees that never visit your offices, you might be able to use a streaming media format to provide training videos or broadcasts of internal lectures.

Instant Messaging and Chats

Instant messaging is a cross between email and a telephone conversation. You write something and the person you're corresponding with sees what you type immediately. People can dash quick notes to each other in real time, making short conversations much easier.

When you expand the conversation to more than two people, you have something called a "chat," a real time conversation that takes place in a "room" or on a "channel." Online conferencing adds presentations and application sharing to a broadcast or chat.

Many businesses with remote users subscribe to an instant messaging service such as Yahoo!, AOL Instant Messenger, or MSN Messenger so that employees can immediately communicate with each other. Chat rooms can be useful for obtaining a group consensus on a decision to be made, providing a virtual conference room.

All of these technologies rely on a server somewhere to connect people. Exactly where the server is depends on the service you're using. In general, if you use somebody else's service, you cannot expect anything that goes through the service to remain confidential.

Once again, setting up a Web application is one of the easiest ways of securely managing remote users. There are many scripts that provide chat room functionality that can run on a Web server. Put it on your SSL-encrypted Web server and require people to log in, and you can have a simple, secure chat with others on your team. A Web search for "PHP Chat scripts" returns dozens of choices you can install on your server.

If you want to run your own private instant messaging service, check out Jabber at *http://www.jabber.org*. Jabber is an open standard implemented by many different server and client software. Implementing a Jabber server is not a simple task, and not covered in this book.

Messaging is undergoing tremendous change at this writing. Not only are there competing incompatible services providing instant messaging, there are different standards being implemented on cell phones. At this writing, it's hard to tell what will come out to be the dominant solutions. Chat and instant messaging provide inexpensive, quick communications with your remote users, and bring their own set of problems to the remote access challenge.

Directory Services

As we discussed in Chapter 7, directories can fulfill two different functions: provide contact details for people you are trying to reach, and provide authorization services for your systems.

A protocol called Lightweight Directory Access Protocol (LDAP) describes how to interact directly with a directory service. Most larger corporate systems provide a company directory using LDAP. By connecting your email client's address book to an LDAP server, you can look up other employees to find their email address, phone number, manager, and whatever other details your organization stores there.

There are also public directories such as BigFoot and Verisign, where you can look up people who have chosen to be listed. If you don't want to grant public access to your company directory, you can set up encrypted, authenticated access to your LDAP service over the Internet.

Peer-To-Peer File Sharing

Peer-to-peer file sharing is a way of making files on your computer available to Internet users at large. There have been many different services making peer-to-peer file sharing possible, most of them made popular by college students and the general public exchanging music files: Napster, Kazaa, Morpheus, and several other services come to mind.

A newer peer-to-peer technology, called BitTorrent, is being used for distributing large files such as CD-ROM images of Linux distributions.

Unless you freely distribute large files as part of your business, peer-to-peer technologies are not likely to be important for your network. In fact, the copyright and legal issues surrounding file sharing should dissuade you from participating in most kinds of file sharing—the risk to your business is probably not justified, unless you clearly own the copyright to the material you are distributing.

On the other hand, BitTorrent is a remarkable technology for obtaining software distributed as open source. To use it, you may need to open particular ports on your firewall.

Distributed Computing

The main idea behind distributed computing is that most computers being used in an office for word processing, email, and Web surfing have a lot of computing power going unused. If you could tap that unused processing power on thousands or millions of individual computers, you could do amazing things.

By far the most popular distributed computing application is the SETI @ Home project (*http://setiathome.ssl.berkeley.edu/*), which harnesses the computing power of millions of unused computers to search through radio-telescope-collected data for signs of extra-terrestrial life. Other projects have been used to crack encryption algorithms, determine factors related to the effectiveness of chemotherapy, and predict the climate in 50 years. A good summary of current projects is at *http://www.aspenleaf.com/distributed/*.

Each distributed computing project has its own custom client software, and you generally don't need to do anything to allow your users to participate in somebody else's project. If you want to host a project, you'll need to have some crack programmers who can work out the access details—probably the simplest part of any such software.

Drawbacks Of Web-Enabled Applications

Perhaps the biggest drawback to Web-enabled applications is that each one must be secured independently. It's a relatively easy task to password-protect and encrypt a corner of your Web site. It's a bit tougher to secure your email system. When you start adding other Web-enabled applications, each one needs to be thoroughly evaluated for security holes, authentication, and proper encryption. Obviously the more services you run, the bigger this problem becomes.

There are several parts to this problem:

1. If you run each service independently, every user has a different password for each one. If they change a password in one service, it doesn't necessarily change it for any other service.
2. Even if you hook all your services up to a central password authority, such as an LDAP service, some of the services may not have sufficient encryption. If a user's password is compromised through one service, the attacker can gain access as that user to the rest of the services.
3. The more services that are directly available over the Internet, the more doors you provide to potential crackers. If any vulnerability is discovered in any one of these services, your entire network could be compromised.

Another problem is that there are some things you can't do on the Web. File sharing is the prime example. While there are Internet-capable alternatives to LAN-based file sharing, most of these are not as convenient as simply opening a window or mounting a network share and copying files directly. Unless you build some custom system, you can't browse your internal LAN over the Internet.

Finally, the more services you run, the more complex your firewall rules have to become. Complexity almost always leads to mistakes, and mistakes lead to vulnerabilities.

Making individual services available over the Internet is generally the easiest way to provide remote access, and for many businesses, all that is necessary. In many cases, it's insufficient, however. Let's take a look at the next level of remote connection.

ACCESS YOUR COMPUTER REMOTELY

None of the services we've discussed so far allow you to log into your work computer from home and access the contents of its hard drive. There are a whole host of other services that provide remote access to a particular computer.

Unix-based computers have several layers of applications. Most programs and files can be accessed from a command shell, using text-based commands. Because the graphical interface used by Unix systems has a client-server model, you can run an application on a remote computer but have its window open up on your desktop. Finally, there is software that allows you to see the whole desktop of another computer, safely nestled in an ordinary application window.

Most of this section discusses connecting to a remote Unix or Linux computer. For the most part, logging into a remote computer is a more advanced technique, requiring a bit more technical savvy than simply using a service remotely or logging into a Virtual Private Network. Logging into a remote computer generally provides access to data on that computer, and possibly access to the LAN that computer is connected to. Unlike the rest of this chapter, for this discussion the remote computer is the one connected to your LAN, and you are the remote user.

Log into Your Remote Computer with Secure Shell

Secure Shell (SSH) is the most basic secure way to connect to a remote computer. It actually provides several benefits:

- Secure access to a command shell on a remote computer
- Secure file transfer
- Secure tunneling of network traffic over specific ports

Secure Access to Command Shell

SSH is most useful for people administering servers. As an administrator, you can log into a Unix-based server and do just about anything as if you were sitting in front of it, even from the other side of the world. All traffic between your computer and the remote computer is encrypted, and SSH can even compress the data to make the encryption faster. In this capacity, SSH is a replacement for older programs called Telnet and RSH (Remote Shell).

ON THE CD

PuTTY is a Windows SSH client and part of The Open CD, on the CD-ROM included with this book.

Whenever you make an SSH connection, all traffic is encrypted. SSH uses several different encryption algorithms. Overall, it works in a similar way to SSL in that a symmetrical key is exchanged using an asymmetrical encryption algorithm. The client encrypts a session key to the public key provided by the server. If the encrypted key can be decrypted, the server then attempts to authenticate the connection.

You can provide a username and password for the simplest authentication, but if you want better security, you can use a client certificate instead and disable password logins. SSH software always includes the tools necessary to generate a certificate key pair. Once you generate the key pair, you transfer the public key to the server. Then when you log in, the server encrypts a token to your public key. Your client must decrypt it and re-encrypt it to the server's public key to verify your identity. Public key encryption is discussed more fully in Chapter 15.

Secure File Transfer

Even if you're not an administrator, SSH provides some useful abilities. Being able to securely transfer files back and forth is very handy—you can retrieve any file from the remote computer if you have read permissions for the file. From a Windows computer, the WinSCP program (*http://winscp.sourceforge.net/eng/*) provides a GUI that works pretty much the same as most FTP programs. Some FTP programs do Secure File Copy over SSH, too. See *http://filezilla.sourceforge.net/* for a file transfer program that can use secure FTP over SSH.

ON THE CD

FileZilla is part of The Open CD, on the CD-ROM included with this book.

Secure Tunneling

SSH can also forward network connections through the encrypted connection. Any of the Web applications we mentioned in the previous section can be secured using SSH to connect to a computer inside your network. When you make the SSH connection, you can specify any number of TCP ports to forward to any particular computer on the other side of the connection. You can piggyback several different applications through the SSH tunnel, requiring only the single SSH port to be open through the firewall.

Using SSH for remote access allows you to run less secure systems on your LAN, and set up SSH scripts that provide you with remote access. Any application that uses TCP to connect to specific ports on a server can be configured to connect through an SSH tunnel. In Windows, you can use the open source PuTTY program from *http://www.chiark.greenend.org.uk/~sgtatham/putty/*, or install the copy included on the CD-ROM for the book.

ON THE CD

On the Tunnels panel, you can specify particular ports to forward through the tunnel. Then you configure your client software to connect to the local computer on that port, instead of the remote computer.

For example, if you wanted to connect to a POP email server that has no encryption and is running behind a firewall, you could forward port 110 to the specific server name or IP address on the LAN. Then, when you make the connection, you would configure your email client to connect to the Pop server on `localhost`. As long as the tunnel is running, any connections to the `localhost` POP port get forwarded through the SSH tunnel to the server at the other end.

If you need to provide secure access through a firewall to a specific server, look at SSH tunneling as a solution. As long as you have a Linux server to connect to, you can easily forward connections to and from computers using any operating system.

Run Remote X Applications

X11 is the foundation of graphical interfaces for Unix systems. Also called X Windows, X11 uses a client-server model like many other Web-enabled applications. The server actually runs on your desktop, and accepts connections from X client applications. The X client applications do not have to be on the same computer as the server.

What this means is that you can open up an application on a remote computer and have its window appear on the computer in front of you. Everything in the window you open is on the remote computer—if you save to the file system, it saves on the remote computer, not on your local computer.

You can cut and paste text or objects in and out of the window like any other window. You can do pretty much anything through this window—though you have to open each application individually from a remote shell, on the command line.

SSH supports forwarding X windows through the encrypted tunnel, making this a very easy thing to implement, as long as you run an X server on your local computer. If you're running Linux, you have an X server running already. In Windows, you can get an open source X server and environment (along with many other Unix tools) from the Cygwin project at *http://cygwin.com/xfree/*.

The ability to easily run an application remotely is one of the advantages of using Linux on your desktop. To use it, here are the basic steps:

1. Start your X server, either on a local Linux computer or a special X server for Windows.
2. Make an SSH connection to the remote computer.
3. In the secure shell window, type the command to start the application you want to run.

That's it. SSH and X Windows handles everything for you pretty much automatically. If it doesn't work, you may need to check the tunneling section in PuTTY (if you're using Windows) or the default SSH settings in Linux to make sure it's allowing forwarded X sessions.

ACCESS YOUR ENTIRE DESKTOP REMOTELY

Finally, there's a whole class of software that provides a graphical view of a remote desktop. Setting up this remote access software to run securely may be slightly more involved than SSH or running remote X applications, but the end result is much more intuitive to use, and different software makes it easy to see remote desktops running any operating system.

Terminal Services

There are many different software applications that provide remote desktop services. Microsoft has included a slimmed down version, called Terminal Services, in several generations of their server operating systems. Windows XP Professional (and later) includes a desktop version of terminal services called Remote Desktop. Rdesktop (*http://www.rdesktop.org*) is an open source Linux client for Windows remote desktop and terminal services, and there's also a Unix-based terminal server.

Proprietary Remote Desktop Solutions

There are several popular proprietary remote desktop-type software programs. Two of the most popular are PC Anywhere from Symantec and GoToMyPC from ExpertCity. PCAnywhere (*http://www.symantec.com/pcanywhere/Consumer/*) provides remote control over a remote Windows PC, and can use a variety of types of connections. GoToMyPC (*http://www.gotomypc.com*) is perhaps the easiest of the remote access programs to configure over the Internet, but it works as a subscription service, so you have to pay a monthly fee. With GoToMyPC, the remote computer must be running Windows, but it works with any Java-capable client computer.

VNC

Finally, we reach the original open source remote solution: Virtual Network Computing (VNC). VNC was originally developed in 1994 by Olivetti Research Labs in Cambridge, England, which was later bought by AT&T. VNC provides an extremely efficient way of viewing the entire graphical contents of your desktop from a remote computer.

VNC is small, fast, and cross-platform—there are viewers and servers for most platforms. With VNC, you can view your Linux desktop from Windows, your Mac from Linux, or any other combination. Unlike terminal services, with VNC, the desktop display can be active on multiple machines, making it a good way to demonstrate how to perform certain tasks to remote users.

If you have a specialty Unix-based application that some employees in your company need to use, but they want to continue to use their Windows or Mac computers, you can set up an individual VNC server on a different virtual display for each user on a Linux computer. There can be dozens of virtual displays running on the Linux computer, each dedicated to a single user who connects to it as necessary using VNC.

VNC does not provide any authentication or encryption. When you connect to a VNC server, you're prompted to type a password set for the session—anyone with the password can connect. Unless you're connecting to another computer on the LAN, VNC doesn't provide the necessary level of privacy. What's the solution?

Tunnel the VNC connection through SSH. The VNC ports start at 5900, and go up for each additional "virtual display." When you run a VNC server on a Unix computer, it opens up a new virtual display for each server, incrementing the port number. So the first display would be at port 5901, the second at 5902, etc. Display number zero is the root display for an X server, and normally won't be used by VNC, though if your purpose is to see your Linux desktop from another computer, you'll need to use a special version of VNC to show the original desktop.

ON THE CD
TightVNC for Windows is part of The Open CD, on the CD-ROM included with this book.

There are many different versions of VNC. The original one is maintained at *http://www.realvnc.org*. Most of the other versions add features—one of the most popular versions is TightVNC (*http://www.tightvnc.org*) which adds better compression over remote connections. There are other versions available for Mac OS 9 and OS X. The x0rfbserver and KVNC versions make the root X window available over VNC.

CONNECT REMOTE COMPUTERS TO YOUR LAN

Besides providing remote connections to specific Web-enabled applications and accessing a specific computer remotely, the other way to solve the remote access problem is using something called a *virtual private network* (VPN). A VPN is essentially the opposite of connecting to a remote computer: when you connect to a remote computer, you get to directly use a computer that is behind a firewall, whereas with a VPN, you're bringing a remote computer into the LAN.

When you connect a computer to a LAN over a VPN, it can do anything any other computer on your LAN can do. It's as if you're physically plugged into the network, even though you could be on another continent. The only difference from a user standpoint is that depending on how the VPN was set up, the remote computer might be on a slightly different subnet, preventing some non-TCP/IP services from working.

Using a VPN has a couple of implications:

- If your network is properly secured, you can run insecure applications behind the firewall and have them completely available to remote computers with no additional configuration.
- If the remote computer is infected with a virus or compromised by a cracker, it can infect computers on your LAN because it's inside the firewall.

The main reason to run a VPN is to provide file sharing. Windows file sharing, AppleTalk, and NFS are all different file sharing schemes in common use in local networks. All of them should be strictly firewalled from the Internet, as they all have security issues. It's possible to provide SSH tunnels and do other tricks to enable remote file sharing. It's also possible to use WebDAV or another file sharing protocol that is designed for Internet use.

But these file sharing systems are integrated deep in the operating systems, and are in common use. It's much easier to turn these systems on and set up a VPN than to think through other ways of transferring files and figuring out the other necessary issues.

There are many different VPN systems, and they differ greatly in how convenient they are to set up, how easy they are to use, and what level of security they provide. VPNs are big business—there are many large software companies that exist primarily to provide VPNs to enterprises. There are also a great many open source VPN systems, though a lot of them have major security flaws. There's no point implementing a VPN that can be compromised.

Let's take a look at the best options for implementing a VPN with freely available software. The VPNs we discuss here are all available in open source versions—many interoperate with proprietary VPN programs. Table 14.1 lists the best available open source options. If you're considering an open source VPN that isn't listed here, check carefully for vulnerabilities and think again.

TABLE 14.1 Comparison of VPN Technologies

Configuration	Advantages	Drawbacks	Clients	Ease of Implementation
PPP or VTUN over SSH	Easy to set up Good security	Very poor performance Doesn't scale well Difficult to use from Windows Manual routing	Linux Mac OS X	Easy
PPTP	Very easy to use Client software built into most operating systems Connect from anywhere	Questionable security Problems with some firewalls	Windows 98/ME/2000/XP Mac Linux Many firewalls	Easy
OpenVPN	Excellent security Connect from anywhere No firewall issues Provides bridged routing Great performance	Macs require manual routing Few clients available	Command-line tool for most platforms	Easy, except for certificate management
IPSec	Fairly easy to set up Very good security	Requires static IP address for remote users Problems with firewalls Manual routing	Linux Mac Windows 2000/XP Some firewalls	Fairly easy to install site-to-site. Difficult to set up for roaming users.
IPSec with X509 Certificates	Best Security Already installed on many commercial firewalls Supported by many commercial clients Scales to large enterprises	Very difficult to manage Manual routing Problems with firewalls	Linux Mac Windows 2000/XP Some firewalls	Very difficult to install and administer

Let's take a look at some common difficulties with VPNs. First of all is the routing issue. Anytime you have computers set up on physically separate network connections, you need to figure out how to route traffic between them. A VPN is essentially an encrypted tunnel between two computers, one at each end. Each of these computers is called a *VPN Gateway*. If you're just trying to set up remote access to individual users, their computer is one of the gateways, and your VPN server is the other. Another common use of a VPN is to securely connect two local area networks, in which case both gateways need to route traffic for the network it's connected to.

For most VPN solutions, you need to add network routes to both of the gateways that send traffic bound for the other side through the encrypted tunnel. That allows computers to talk to computers through the encrypted tunnel using routable protocols such as TCP/IP. Unfortunately, often the reason you want to use a VPN is to provide access to non-routable protocols such as NetBeui, Windows networking, or other services that don't necessarily run over the Internet.

Once you have the routing set up, you still need to deal with getting network names to resolve. If all the computers are on the same subnet, Windows networking allows them to discover each other through a feature called the *master browser* service. Linux supports this if you install and run the Samba file sharing feature. However, your remote computers are most likely on a different subnet, so you won't necessarily be able to find the computer you want to connect to.

There are two basic approaches to solving these problems:

1. Create a virtual interface for the remote computer on the local network.
2. Run services on the network that resolve names across subnets.

With Windows and Linux, you can create a virtual interface called a *tap device*, and *bridge* your main network device to it. Only some VPN solutions support doing this, and it obviously doesn't work if you want to connect two networks. If you can configure the VPN to provide this, your remote computer gets an IP address on the network, and it can act exactly as if it were plugged into the switch in your office, other than the delay of going through your Internet connection. Unfortunately, at this writing, Mac OS X and BSD flavors of Unix do not support tap devices.

If you need to support remote Mac users, or are connecting remote networks to your LAN, you'll need to set up the second option. For most TCP/IP applications, the solution is to run a DNS server on your intranet. For Windows networking, you need to run a WINS server. You can find some basic network management hints in Chapter 3, but setting up a DNS and WINS server is beyond the scope of this book.

Let's take a closer look at the major VPN systems, and why you would choose one over another.

PPP over SSH

We've already looked at SSH. If you're running SSH, it's not too difficult to set up a PPP tunnel through an SSH connection. A package called Vtun is designed to be a simple VPN system—but its security system is not well implemented. But if you use Vtun to create a virtual unencrypted tunnel, you can route it straight through an encrypted SSH tunnel.

The downside is it's very slow and difficult to set up in Windows. Performance is the real issue, though. There are several layers of encapsulation going on, and so there's a lot more overhead piled on top of your data. It's definitely secure, and you can easily configure it to use Public Key Encryption with certificates, making it pretty much as secure as IPSec. But while in use, it can have slower connections and be subject to long delays to recover from lost data packets. It also requires a fairly deep understanding of networking.

PPTP

Point-to-Point Tunneling Protocol (PPTP) is an encryption scheme developed by Microsoft and supported in Windows operating systems back to Windows 98. Apple has included a PPTP client in Mac OS 9 and later, making it a contender for connecting older operating systems. Because of broad support, with many built-in clients and freely available servers, PPTP is perhaps the easiest type of VPN to install and use.

But PPTP has a spotty security record, especially in early versions. And the current version still uses password authentication, making your network as secure as the weakest password on the entire system. See *http://www.schneier.com/pptp.html* for more details about PPTP security issues.

If you want to implement PPTP on your network, you can try the open source Poptop server for Linux, available at *http://www.poptop.org/*. Windows has a PPTP client built into most versions. For Unix-based clients, try pptpclient from *http://pptpclient.sourceforge.net/*.

OpenVPN

OpenVPN is a newer system that provides a robust, lightweight virtual private network. For a small business, it's probably the best system in terms of cost, ease of installation and configuration, and security. It's entirely open source, and there are clients available for Mac, Windows 2000/XP, and Unix platforms.

OpenVPN leverages several other open source projects to offer a complete solution, while distributing the work of implementation. It uses OpenSSL for encryption, which is the same encryption library used by the Apache Web server and a great majority of encrypted services. It uses the Vtun project mentioned earlier for tunneling all network traffic through the connection.

Two features differentiate OpenVPN from the other VPNs:

1. OpenVPN can use a Tap device to forward Ethernet connections through the tunnel, not just TCP/IP. This makes it easy to support all sorts of LAN activity that doesn't go through other VPNs.
2. It uses UDP instead of TCP for its connections, making it faster.

OpenVPN works very well through firewalls. You need to open the appropriate ports for each OpenVPN connection, but otherwise, both ends of the tunnel can be forwarded through NAT routers without any problems.

OpenVPN has two ways of authenticating the remote connection: a private shared key, or public key encryption with X509 certificates. A private shared key is easier to set up, but if it falls into the wrong hands, anyone with the key can log into your network. For this reason, you should set up public key encryption, especially for laptops that are easily (and often) stolen.

The main drawback to using OpenVPN is that it's relatively new, there aren't many commercial devices that support or interoperate with OpenVPN. We'll take a closer look at OpenVPN shortly.

The Industry Standard: IPSec

The vast majority of large enterprise-level commercial VPNs use an implementation of IPSec. IPSec is an open standard that defines a way of encrypting TCP/IP connections. It uses a special protocol that encodes the IP addresses of each end inside the encrypted traffic in an effort to be able to detect tampering of the data stream. Unfortunately, common home broadband gateways may interfere with these addresses.

IPSec is clearly the industry standard, but it's difficult to administer and get to work, especially if the remote users don't have a static IP address. It requires special code in the kernel, the core of the operating system. These kernel modifications are available for current Linux and BSD kernels, and Microsoft includes them in Windows XP.

For small businesses, IPSec is most useful for connecting different sites that have permanent Internet connections. If both ends of the connection have static IP addresses, it's fairly easy to create a permanent VPN connection between the two sites using IPSec. Many firewalls and routers have IPSec capabilities built in. If you already have a commercial VPN appliance, you'll almost certainly use IPSec to connect to it.

The main open source implementation of IPSec is FreeS/WAN, at *http://www.freeswan.org/*. It can be configured or patched to do all sorts of connections, but doing so is a specialized task for a security expert.

 Since this chapter was written, the FreeS/WAN Project shut down. Most of the active developers moved to a new fork of this project, called OpenS/WAN at http://www.openswan.org.

There are a number of vendors of network appliances that support IPSec-based VPNs. If you need to support hundreds of remote users, at this point it's much more cost-effective to purchase the technology from one of these vendors—they have taken the time to figure out how to easily manage so many connections. While it's certainly possible to set up thousands of remote users with FreeS/WAN, it's going to take a lot of time to figure out how to manage them. IPSec vendors include WatchGuard, Cisco, SonicWall, and dozens of others.

For most small business situations, there are some open source firewall/router projects that include IPSec VPNs. These firewalls can be installed on older computers you're otherwise going to retire. Drop a couple network cards into them and set them up as your main gateway to the Internet.

Smoothwall is an excellent, easy-to-configure firewall available at *http://www.smoothwall.org*. It includes a simple IPSec VPN for setting up site-to-site tunnels. It only supports using a pre-shared key for encryption, and you must know the IP address of both ends of the tunnel.

Slightly more powerful is the Mandrake Multi-Network Firewall (MNF). This firewall also includes IPSec VPNs, but it uses client certificates for authentication. You can generate and manage client certificates for remote users, and set the MNF up to accept VPN connections from any computer with a recognized certificate.

Both of these firewalls use IPSec for their VPNs, but they're not compatible with each other, because of their differing authentication mechanisms. For connecting multiple sites, the Smoothwall is the easiest way to go. MNF provides more features to support roaming users on multiple platforms, or to set up more sophisticated routing rules.

SMALL BUSINESS VPN: OPENVPN

Being able to log directly into your LAN from the other side of the world and have everything just work is an amazing thing. Out of all the VPN solutions available in 2003, OpenVPN is the best combination of easy administration, easy use, and strong security. Even so, setting up OpenVPN takes a good understanding of networking and hardware. There are some great tutorials available at the OpenVPN Web site, at *http://openvpn.sourceforge.net*.

The general process of setting up OpenVPN is:

1. Install the required software: OpenVPN, bridge-utils, OpenSSL.
2. Install the OpenVPN software on each client computer.
3. Generate a certificate for each client computer and securely transfer it to the client.
4. Modify the template OpenVPN configuration for your subnet.
5. Make a copy of the configuration, setting a unique port, IP address, and tap device for each client.
6. Adjust your firewall to allow the appropriate traffic.
7. Set up each client to connect to the correct port with the correct configuration.

Once it's set up, you connect by running the script or configuration on the client, and everything starts to work.

SUMMARY

In this chapter, we've looked at three different ways to access data over the Internet. We checked out the wide variety of individual services that can be used over the Internet. Then we learned how to log into a remote computer, both through a command line, and through a remote graphical interface. Finally, we checked out the major Virtual Private Network technologies, taking a close look at OpenVPN.

Setting up and administering VPNs is not for the faint of heart. But once you have one running properly, you and your employees can be in the office virtually anywhere in the world. If all you need is to access something stored on your workstation, remote control software like VNC will let you do it with ease. Easiest of all is to simply make a few key services available on the Internet, with proper encryption and authentication.

Speaking of encryption and authentication, we're going to dig deep into the topic in the next chapter, where we'll discuss the use of encrypted email.

REMOTE ACCESS REFERENCES

An updated list of resources for this chapter is on the Web site for the book at *http://opensourcesmall.biz/remote*.

Software

Pop-before-SMTP, authentication for outgoing email *http://popbsmtp.source-forge.net*

Helix, an open source media player and server from Real Networks, *http://www.helixcommunity.org*

OpenSSH, Secure Shell client and server *http://www.openssh.com/*

PuTTY, open source Windows SSH client *http://www.chiark.greenend.org.uk/~sgtatham/putty/*

Filezilla, SFTP client for Windows *http://filezilla.sourceforge.net/*

PCAnywhere, commercial remote desktop software for Windows *http://www.symantec.com/pcanywhere/Consumer*

GoToMyPC, commercial remote desktop software for Windows *http://www.gotomypc.com*

VNC, open source cross platform remote desktop software *http://www.realvnc.com/*

TightVNC, open source extended version of VNC *http://www.tightvnc.com*

PopTOP, open source PPTP server for Linux *http://www.poptop.org*

Pptpclient, open source PPTP client for Linux *http://pptpclient.sourceforge.net*

OpenVPN, open source SSL-based VPN *http://www.openvpn.org*

FreeS/WAN, open source IPSec implementation *http://www.freeswan.org*

Smoothwall Firewall *http://www.smoothwall.org*

Web Sites

Distributed Computing Sites *http://www.aspenleaf.com/distributed*

15

Providing Private Communications

In This Chapter

- Introduction
- What Is Authentication, Authorization, and Encryption?
- Public Key Encryption
- Public Key Infrastructure
- Encrypted Email
- Summary
- Encryption References

INTRODUCTION

For all its power, the Internet is not a very friendly place. Sending an email is about as private as sending a postcard—anyone who handles it in transit can read your message. Your service provider can track every Web site you visit, and see unencrypted pages any time they choose to watch your traffic.

Worse, there really is no guarantee that the unencrypted Web site you visit belongs to who you think it belongs to. It's theoretically possible for someone to hijack the name server you're using, and replace otherwise legitimate Web sites with bogus ones of their own creation. Without some careful digging, you would be unable to tell the difference, if it wasn't for public key encryption and digital certificates.

This chapter gets very detailed and technical. If you need to guarantee the privacy of your email, you should read this chapter to understand how encrypted email works—and more importantly, what its weaknesses are. You can skip the parts about managing a Certificate Authority. This is vital content for anyone who needs to run an SSL-enabled Web server or set up a public key infrastructure for secure email, secure client authentication, or a VPN.

NOTE

339

Digital certificates serve two purposes: privacy and authentication. The privacy part uses complex encryption algorithms to obscure the contents of messages passing through the Internet. The authentication part of it gives you some assurance that the Web site you're visiting to pay your credit card really belongs to your bank, and not some scammer who's found a way to intercept your transactions.

Fortunately for commerce, Web servers have developed a reliable, universal system of public key encryption that supports privacy and authentication for Web sites. It's implemented in a system called Secure Sockets Layer (SSL), and you use it any time you visit an encrypted site. As we saw in Chapter 14, there are other services that use SSL and similar schemes to provide Virtual Private Networks (VPNs) and the like.

Unfortunately, there is no similar universal system for providing encrypted or authenticated email. There are systems, they work, and people use them, but they're awkward, hard to set up, and not in widespread use.

So why do we have reliable, encrypted Web connections, but not email? The gist of the problem is that Web browsing is a connected activity—there can be several exchanges between the server and the client—but email is a disconnected system, with no mechanism built in for end-to-end encryption.

While there are many different secure protocols, the strong ones all use a similar mechanism called *Public Key Encryption*. We've mentioned it in several chapters already. In this chapter, we'll see the gist of how it works, why (and when) you should trust it, and what its limitations are.

Certificate Authorities (CAs), as you'll see, are an important part of the public key infrastructure. While a CA may sounds like some big complicated thing, running one is actually really easy. By running your own CA, you can make remote connections to your network more secure and easier to use, and provide completely private, encrypted email between you and your clients. This chapter is heavy on theory, because if you don't understand basically how public key encryption works, you can expose some major security holes. Finally, we'll go through the two major systems for signing and encrypting email.

WHAT IS AUTHENTICATION, AUTHORIZATION, AND ENCRYPTION?

The Internet is an inherently insecure medium. We will discuss security issues in much greater detail in Chapters 16 and 17. What's important to know now is that anything you do that involves data traveling over the Internet or over a wireless network, without specific strong encryption methods applied, can be easily intercepted by anyone motivated enough to try.

To understand the critical parts of secure remote connections, let's take a look at a related example in the physical world. You go to a store, buy something, and write a personal check. The merchant looks at the check, asks to see some personal identification, and then compares your signature to the signature on your identification to see if it's authentic. If it matches, the merchant next calls the bank to make sure you have sufficient funds in your account. After your bank has authorized the transaction, the merchant accepts your check for payment. At the end of the day, an armored car comes to the merchant and takes all the checks and extra cash to the bank.

A secure remote transaction changes the order of these actions slightly, but consists of the same three basic processes:

1. Authentication
2. Authorization
3. Secure Transport

Authentication is the process of identifying a user, and verifying that you are who you say you are. If you're unknown to the system, it won't let you in. Authorization is the process of determining whether you, as an authenticated user, have the right permission to do whatever you're trying to do. And whatever you do from afar needs to happen using some sort of secure transport—either a private telephone line, or some sort of encryption that protects your data from prying eyes.

They don't release funds on authentication alone. First, they check your bank balance to determine if you have enough money to cover the check—whether you're authorized to make a transaction of that size. You might think of encryption as the armored car that carries all the checks, cash, and deposits between banks.

PUBLIC KEY ENCRYPTION

Cryptography is an extremely sophisticated practice. We won't go into all of the different ways of encrypting data—but there are some basic principles that are fairly easy to understand, along with the alphabet soup of different protocols.

At the most basic level, encryption is a highly sophisticated version of the little word games you find in the Sunday paper. In the puzzles, each letter has been replaced by a different letter in the alphabet. Find what the replacement letters are, and decoding the message is trivial.

The *key* is the table of replacement letters you use to find the solution to an encrypted puzzle. The problem with simple letter-for-letter replacement is that a speaker of the language can eventually figure out the key through a process of trial and error. This is possible because some letters, such as "e" and "t" occur more frequently than other letters. With the sheer power of computers, it becomes easy to use pure statistical frequency of these letters to begin to crack the message, exactly the same way you solve the word game. The longer the message is, the easier it is to decrypt.

Ken Follet, an author of spy novels, wrote one called *The Key to Rebecca*, which described an encryption method that is much more difficult to crack. In this encryption scheme, each letter was associated with a number: *a* is 1, *b* is 2, *c* is 3, right up to *z* being 26. To encrypt a message, you take the letter from the key, add its value to the letter of the message, and if the result is over 26, subtract 26 so you only have letters. The key? Pre-determined pages in a particular paperback novel (named *Rebecca* in the story). To decrypt the message, the spy went to the correct page in the novel, and subtracted the values from each letter of the text of the novel from the encrypted message. Since the key was tremendously long (the length of the novel), and secret (only known by the sender and receiver), it was impossible for the spies on the other side to decrypt the message.

With the help of computers, however, it is possible to decrypt these messages without the secret key—the key itself has a higher frequency of the common letters of the alphabet, providing some starting places for a *brute force* attack on the encrypted message. In a brute force attack, the attacker simply tries every possible combination of keys until he gets a readable message. Once a few characters have been cracked, it becomes easier to guess the remaining ones. So the actual method used to encrypt computer transmissions is quite a bit more sophisticated, but the gist of the technique is the same. This is called *Symmetrical Encryption*, because people use the same key to encrypt and decrypt the message. The Data Encryption Standard (DES) and the newer Advanced Encrypted Standard (AES) are two of the most widely used symmetrical encryption schemes.

There's a problem, though. In *The Key to Rebecca*, the encryption scheme worked because the people at each end knew the key. When you're on the Internet, how do you find out the secret key to decrypt a message, without anyone else getting it?

The answer is by using a completely different type of encryption, called *Asymmetrical Encryption*, in a scheme that has become known as Public Key encryption. In an asymmetrical encryption scheme, one key is used to encrypt a message, and a different key to decrypt. It was a theoretical possibility only, until 1977 when Ron Rivest, Adi Shamir, and Leonard Adleman figured out how to make it work.

One of the toughest mathematical problems to solve is trying to factor a product of prime numbers. If you remember your high school math, factors are numbers that can be multiplied together to generate the number you started with. For example, the number twelve can be factored as one times twelve, two times six, or three times four. A prime number is a number whose only factors are one and itself, such as the numbers five, seven, and eleven. When you multiply two prime numbers, you get a number that only has two sets of factors: the number one and the number itself, and the two prime numbers.

Remember your primary school math class, when you learned how to divide? Division is much harder than multiplication—it's basically a process of trial and error. You start with the number to divide, and the second number you want to divide by. You have to guess some arbitrary number, multiply it with the second number, and then subtract the result from the original number. If the remainder is bigger than the second number, you have to try again, with a bigger arbitrary number. The problem with factoring is that you don't have the second number, either. You have to try every possible combination of smaller numbers to find out if they are factors of the original number.

Computers have to do the same thing, but they can do it many millions of times faster than you. If you start with two enormous prime numbers, say with over 100 digits, and multiply them together, you still get a very large number with only the two prime factors. But trying to discover these factors takes, as Carl Sagan might have said, "billions and billions" of calculations, requiring several hundred years of processing time of the fastest of today's computers. On the other hand, if one of the factors is known, dividing it into the number, while still harder than multiplication, is something that can be done while you're waiting.

Rivest, Shamir, and Adleman came up with a way of using very large prime numbers to develop an asymmetrical encryption method now called RSA, based on the initials of their last names. Using some sophisticated but fairly straightforward calculations with very large, randomly selected prime numbers, they figured out a way to generate two different keys that work together to provide reliable one-way encryption.

The result is a pair of keys that have some useful properties. One key is called the public key, because it gets freely distributed, while the other key is the private or secret key. When you encrypt a message with the public key, it can only be decrypted with the private key—the ingenious algorithm they used makes it exceedingly difficult to decrypt, even with the public key that encrypted it. The public key cannot be used to decrypt the message, which makes it safe to distribute.

A second property of the system is that the private key can be used to *digitally sign* a message, and the signature can be verified by the public key. Using a different calculation, sort of an inverse of the encryption method, the private key can produce a fingerprint summary of the contents of a message. The public key cannot generate this fingerprint, but it can verify that it was generated by the private key from the exact message. If the message is changed, or a different private key was used to sign the message, the public key cannot verify the fingerprint, and the signature test fails.

These are true one-way calculations, as surprising as that idea may seem. As long as factoring very large numbers remains a difficult problem, the RSA scheme works. When the scheme was initially publicized in the August 1977 issue of *Scientific American*, Ron Rivest encrypted a simple phrase using a 129-digit public key, and offered a $100 reward to anyone who cracked it. Through some major advances in computing power, and some newer statistics-based algorithms for doing factoring, the phrase was eventually decrypted—in 1992, 15 years after the initial challenge, by the combined efforts of over 1,600 computers working the better part of a year.

Computing power has increased since then, but even with a full industrial strength key, still has little chance of breaking the encryption by brute force. A 129-digit public key is 425 bits long (remember that a bit is a zero or one, the basic number used by a computer). Most RSA keys are created with a 1,024-bit key, and you can create them as long as 2,048 bits with current encryption software. A 1,024-bit key is not merely two and a half times stronger than a 425 bit key—every time you add a bit, you double the number of calculations you must perform to crack it. So a 1,024-bit key would take two to the five hundred ninety ninth power—roughly the number two with 180 zeros after it—times as much processing power to crack. Processors have gotten more powerful since 1992—but not that much more powerful.

Problems with RSA

It's certainly possible that RSA will be cracked within our lifetime—if somebody figures out a faster way to factor large numbers. It's also possible that computer power will increase to the point that 1024-bit RSA keys can be cracked—but it's unlikely that the growth of computing power can keep up with increasing key lengths.

There are a few problems with using RSA:

1. Doing the calculations necessary for RSA encryption takes a lot of processing power, and is not practical for encrypting long (or even moderately long) messages.
2. You can either verify that a message was sent only to you, or that it was unchanged since the sender sent it—but not both.
3. If someone gets a copy of your private key, they can read messages encrypted to you, and sign messages as you. Keeping your private key private is crucial to the effectiveness of this system.
4. RSA by itself doesn't provide any mechanism to ensure that you have the correct public key for the person you're trying to communicate with.

To solve the first problem, encryption systems combine RSA with a symmetrical encryption system. The second problem is a subtle limitation of the encryption scheme that may be important in a legal context—we will discuss the implications later in this chapter. To solve the other problems, you need to have some sort of Public Key Infrastructure—a system of verifying public keys and revoking them if they become compromised.

Symmetrical keys take much less processing power to encrypt and decrypt messages. While most simple symmetrical encryption schemes can be cracked using a statistical analysis, modern encryption systems such as AES are extremely difficult to crack without the key. The problem with symmetric keys is getting the key to the recipient without anyone else intercepting it. So, to make it possible to send large encrypted messages, public key encryption systems first generate a completely random symmetrical key, then encrypt the message using a symmetrical encryption scheme with the key, and finally encrypt the key with RSA.

When you read about 40, 56, or 128 bit encryption for SSL-enabled browsers, it refers to the length of this symmetrical *session key*. Each transmission uses a new session key to encrypt the message, and then encrypts the session key to the public key of the receiver. This scheme also makes it possible to encrypt a message to multiple recipients—you encrypt the message once with the session key, and then encrypt the session key to the public keys of each of the recipients.

Of course, now your encryption scheme uses two different algorithms, and if either is compromised, so is your message. While the sophistication of the encryption schemes may make a brute-force attack impractical, there may be other shortcuts or vulnerabilities in the encryption code. Creative individuals have cracked many encryption standards thought to be invulnerable by their creators.

One weakness of all computer-based encryption schemes is the fact that computers aren't very good at generating random numbers. If your key is based on a number that isn't truly random, the possible number of keys an attacker needs to try may be a lot smaller than the size of the key might suggest. So a lot of attacks are on the code used to generate the key, rather than trying all possible combinations of keys in the first place. Flaws like these were in the first Netscape implementations of SSL, and the ill-fated Wired Equivalent Privacy (WEP) used to encrypt Wi-Fi connections.

To get around this, most computers use a *seed* value for their random number generator. The seed comes from some external stimulus—the exact movements of a computer mouse, for example, or the exact number of micro-seconds between two key strokes.

The encryption and authentication schemes used in current SSL-enabled Web browsers and servers, VPNs, SSH, and most other systems are considered secure. Expect a lot of press if any widely used encryption protocol is cracked.

PUBLIC KEY INFRASTRUCTURE

How encryption works is only one part of the public key infrastructure. You still need to manage keys in some way that you can trust that you have the correct public key for the server or person you're communicating with. There are basically two systems for doing this: by using a third party *Certificate Authority* trusted by both parties, or by specifically adding the public key verified through a *keychain*. In either case, someone you trust uses their private key to digitally sign the public key in question. Because you already have the public key of the person you trust, you can verify that this person has signed the public key, and is vouching for the authenticity of the public key. Remember that a digital signature is verified by a public key, and if the contents of the message have been changed, the signature does not validate.

The difference between using a certificate authority system and a keychain system is that a certificate authority signs and vouches for a public key, whereas in a keychain system, other users vouch for the authenticity of a key. It's a difference of being a centralized system, or authentication by peers.

A certificate is a public key that has been signed by a Certificate Authority (CA). A CA is simply an entity that uses exactly the same public key encryption algorithm to sign public keys of other people. So if you obtain the public key for the CA, you can use it to verify anything the CA has digitally signed—the certificate. Your Web browser comes with a set of public keys for major commercial CAs. When you visit an SSL-encrypted Web site, the Web server sends you its public certificate. If your browser recognizes the CA that signed the certificate, it can verify the signature, and thereby trust the certificate.

Getting a Server Certificate

As you might guess, running a Certificate Authority that the whole world seems to trust can be expensive, and requires the utmost of security—but that is exactly what has been done for SSL-enabled Web sites. To run a public SSL-encrypted Web site, you need to get one of these certificate authorities to sign a certificate for your Web server. This involves generating a certificate signing request for your server, submitting it to one of the trusted root authorities, and paying a fee ranging from US $120 to around $900 per year. VeriSign® is the most widely recognized company providing this service, but at this writing, other services such as TRUSTe, Thawte, and Entrust were substantially less expensive.

The OpenSSL software package is software that handles several aspects of creating and managing keys and certificates. It's generally installed in server installations of Linux. If you don't have it installed, in Mandrake Linux you can use URPMI or the Mandrake Control Center. The mod_ssl module for Apache handles encrypted Web server connections.

You can use OpenSSL to generate a private key and a certificate signing request at the same time. Remember that a certificate signing request includes your public key. The command to generate both is:

```
$ openssl req -new -nodes -keyout server.key -out server.csr
```

In this example, `server.key` will be the name of the file OpenSSL generates containing the private key for your server, and `server.csr` will contain the certificate signing request. Again, it's important to keep the private key private—if somebody else gets hold of it, they can impersonate your server. The certificate signing request, on the other hand, contains no confidential information, but nobody will trust it until it's actually signed by a trusted Certificate Authority.

The `openssl` command will ask a bunch of questions, such as the name of your organization, your location, country, and other details. Many of the fields are optional, but the certificate authority may require them to be filled out completely before signing it. The Common Name (CN) field must be the full host and domain name for your server, as you want the public to see it. You might use secure.example.com, www.example.com, or just example.com—but if someone visits an encrypted site using a different name, it won't match the certificate, and their browser will give them an authentication warning. So you must choose a single canonical name for this server. It also must be the only SSL certificate that is used on a particular IP address and port combination.

After you've generated the key and certificate signing request, you send the certificate signing request to the certificate authority. Most of them have a Web form where you can cut and paste the contents of the `server.csr` file straight into the Web page, and submit. You may have to provide other documentation and proof of your identity via fax or mail, to satisfy the Certificate Authority. You pay the fee, the Certificate Authority signs your certificate and returns it to you.

Finally, you install the signed certificate and private key in your Web browser. Put them in a private directory somewhere on the server, and configure Apache with these directives:

```
SSLCertificateFile /path/to/server.crt
SSLCertificateKeyFile /path/to/server.key
```

You can generally use the same key pair for other server programs on the same computer.

Running Your Own Certificate Authority

A Certificate Authority is nothing more than an entity that uses public key encryption to digitally sign other certificates. The OpenSSL software provides everything you need to become your own certificate authority.

In a business context, this has two purposes:

1. It can save the cost of buying a certificate for every server from a commercial CA.
2. It allows you to explicitly manage certificates and control who can connect to services on your network.

The problem with using your own CA is that nobody will trust certificates from it, until they specifically add its certificate to their list of trusted authorities. This works fine for providing a secure Web site for your employees, or some trusted business partners. The encryption is the same level of protection, and if you vouch for the authenticity of your own services, someone who knows you can choose whether or not to trust you.

You also might need a certificate authority to sign user certificates. A user certificate is exactly like a server certificate, except that it identifies a user instead of a server. The user needs to have the private key on whatever computer they are using, or on another security device such as a smart card or secure USB drive. Just like a server certificate, the user creates a certificate request, and you use the certificate authority to sign the certificate and return it to the user. This process can be automated on a Web server, and the major browsers are capable of generating user certificates.

User certificates signed by your private certificate authority can be used to encrypt and authenticate email using S/MIME, add security to Virtual Private Networks, provide authentication to wireless networks, or where it doesn't really matter if the rest of the world can verify the signature.

To set up a certificate authority, first configure the openssl.cnf file to choose a good location for the private key for the certificate authority, the index and database of signed keys, and the default values for things like your company name and location. In Mandrake, you'll find the file in /usr/lib/ssl. In other distributions, it might be in /etc, /etc/ssl, /usr/share/ssl, or /usr/local/ssl. Check the value of dir, and make sure this directory exists. You might set it to /etc/ssl/ca, or something like that. Here are some example settings for this file:

```
[ CA_default ]
dir            = /etc/ssl/ca           # Where everything is kept
certificate    = $dir/cacert.pem       # The CA certificate
database       = $dir/index.txt        # database index file
new_certs_dir  = $dir/certs            # default place for new certs
private_key    = $dir/private/ca.key   # The private key
certs          = $dir/certs            # Where the issued certs are kept
serial         = $dir/serial           # The current serial number
crl_dir        = $dir/crl              # Where the issued crl are kept
```

Next, create the basic files and directories to store your Certificate Authority:

```
# mkdir /etc/ssl/ca
# cd /etc/ssl/ca
# touch index.txt
# mkdir certs; mkdir private; mkdir crl
# chmod 700 private
# echo '01' > serial
```

Finally, create your self-signed certificate authority certificate with this command:

```
# openssl req -x509 -new -days 3650 -keyout private/ca.key -out
cacert.pem
```

A certificate authority certificate is simply a normal certificate signed by itself. This command generates a keypair, putting the private key in the ca.key file in a directory we set so that only root can access it, and the public certificate in cacert.pem. Make sure you use a good passphrase to encrypt the private key. For the Common Name, use the name of your organization.

Once you have a certificate authority set up, you can use it to sign certificate requests for any other certificates. For example, to sign the certificate request for your Web server, use this command:

```
# cd /etc/ssl/apache     #or wherever the certificate request is
# openssl ca -in server.csr -out server.crt
```

After typing the passphrase for the certificate authority's private key, you can verify the details in the certificate request and confirm that you want to sign it. When you're done, the signed certificate will be in the server.crt file. You can delete the server.csr file. Signing any other certificate with your certificate authority works the same way.

Installing the Certificate Authority Certificate

For any client to trust the signatures you've signed, they first have to trust your Certificate Authority. Most software that supports SSL/TLS provides some import mechanism. Most Microsoft products use a certificate store kept within Windows itself, so if you install a certificate authority certificate in Windows, it will be trusted by Internet Explorer, Outlook, and Outlook Express.

To make the certificate for the certificate authority available for your clients to download, copy the /etc/ssl/ca/cacert.pem file to somewhere on your Web server where everyone can download it. You might change the filename to have a .crt extension, and then Apache should automatically send the file with a header indicating that it's a certificate. If it doesn't, you might need to add the following Apache directive:

```
AddType application/x-x509-ca-cert .crt
```

Netscape and Mozilla browsers will install this file automatically when you click a link to it. Some later versions of Internet Explorer will automatically open the Certificate Import wizard, but with older versions users may need to save the file and open it directly from Windows. Some versions of Windows do not accept pem encoded certificates (the type we generated with this command). You can use OpenSSL to convert pem certificates to der, the encoding used natively in Windows, by using this command:

```
# openssl x509 -in cacert.pem -out cacert.der -outform DER
```

If you still have some ancient Windows machines, provide the cacert.der as a separate link on your Web site, and they can install the certificate authority certificate using it.

Revoking a Certificate

OpenSSL, and the standards it supports, provide a mechanism for revoking a certificate. Both a certificate itself and the signature by the Certificate Authority have an expiration date, and if either of these dates has passed, browsers will warn the user before using the certificate. Your Certificate Authority can revoke a certificate it has signed if it falls into the wrong hands. The commands are:

```
# openssl ca -revoke cert.pem
# openssl ca -gencrl -out /etc/ssl/ca/crl/crl.pem
```

The first command revokes the specified certificate, and the second generates a new *Certificate Revocation List* (CRL). You then post this CRL to your Web site for download.

The problem with the entire system is that nothing pushes the CRLs out to your browser—you have to get them yourself. If a certificate authority publishes a CRL on a Web site, you can install it in some browsers, but for others (such as Internet Explorer) you have to download the CRL and import it. It's basically the same procedure as installing a certificate for a certificate authority.

What this means is that if even one of the big public certificate authorities revokes a certificate, you have no way of knowing unless you go look. At least one public certificate authority doesn't publish the CRL as a file—you have to type in the serial number of a certificate they've signed into a Web form to verify whether it has been revoked or not.

With your internal Certificate Authority, you can manage this much better. Just make sure that any servers authenticating user certificates get the new CRL whenever you revoke a certificate.

Client Certificates

You can also create and use client certificates. While a server certificate provides authentication that a server is what it claims to be, a client server identifies a particular user. OpenSSL can create client certificates—all certificates are basically the same thing, used in a different way. SSL-enabled Web browsers can also create them, using some hidden features.

When you use client certificates in your business, you should have the user create them and keep the private key, and submit a Certificate Signing Request to your certificate authority. After you've verified that the request really came from the correct user, you can then sign the certificate and return it to the user. The user can then install the certificate in their browser, and use it for S/MIME email. We'll discuss encrypted email later in this chapter. The references at the end of this chapter can help you set up a system for generating client certificates.

Private Key Passphrases

If you've followed any of the directions in this chapter to create a certificate of any kind, you were probably asked for a passphrase to encrypt the private key. Because private keys are so sensitive, and can be used to impersonate you if they fall into the wrong hands, they are usually encrypted using a symmetrical encryption method. Unlike a normal password, the passphrase you type is an encryption key. The longer you make this phrase, the better. Try some simple sentence with several words in it—something you'll find easy to remember.

See Chapter 16 for some tips about generating a good passphrase.

Whenever you use your secret key, you'll have to type your passphrase to decrypt it. For the Certificate Authority, you definitely want to use the passphrase. Generally for personal certificates, if you have the ability to type in a passphrase, it's always best to keep one on your private key. The reality of running a server generally dictates leaving the private key for the server certificate unencrypted—if the physical server restarts for some reason, the server programs using encrypted private keys won't be able to start.

Using the -nodes option when you create a key or certificate request skips the passphrase encryption. If you already have a passphrase encrypting a key, you can remove it with this command:

```
# openssl rsa -in server.key -out new.key
```

How SSL/TLS Works

Secure Sockets Layer (SSL) is the name of the first couple versions of the system used to encrypt Web servers. Transport Layer Security (TLS) is the current correct name, but most people still call it SSL. It's the same basic thing—just a newer version.

First, the client browser makes a connection to the Web server and requests a certificate. The server returns the certificate. The client verifies the Common Name (CN) in the certificate to make sure it matches the server, and retrieves its built-in copy of the certificate for whichever Certificate Authority signed the certificate. It uses the public key in this second certificate to verify the signature on the server certificate. It also checks to see whether the certificate, or the signature, have expired.

If any of these steps fail, the browser warns the user that there was a problem authenticating the Web server. The user can usually choose to continue anyway, but now they know there could be a problem. If you see this warning, it means you're visiting an untrusted Web site.

Whether or not authentication succeeds, the browser has a public key for the server. It generates a random session key, using one of the symmetrical encryption techniques. It encrypts the session key using the public key in the server certificate, and sends it back to the server. Only the server has the private key to decrypt this session key.

Now both the server and the browser have the same secret session key, and they encrypt all of the traffic going in both directions with it. That's the essence of how SSL/TLS works.

ENCRYPTED EMAIL

Most traffic on the Internet can be easily encrypted by using TLS. Email presents a different problem, however, for one simple reason: it's entirely one-way. With TLS, the client initiates a connection, verifies the authenticity of the server, and then generates a symmetrical key and encrypts it to the server's public key. From then on, both sides can communicate using the symmetrical key with confidence that nobody else can intercept the message—all they can see is an apparently random stream of numbers.

With email, a message may traverse several different computers before reaching the user, and if the user is not online, you can't exchange keys during the message transmission. To encrypt a message to somebody, you must have his public key before you send the message.

Public Key Encryption still provides the same benefits of authentication and encryption; however, you can only do one at a time. To encrypt a message, your email software generates a random symmetrical key, encrypts the message with it, and then uses RSA to encrypt the key. If you're sending to multiple recipients, your software simply encrypts the key to the public keys of each recipient. When the recipient receives the message, the email client decrypts the key using the user's private key, and can then decrypt the message.

To authenticate a message, you simply sign it with your private key. What actually happens is that something called a *hash* is applied to your message, and the hash is signed by your private key. A hash is a one-way calculation that cannot be reversed. However, if you apply the same hashing algorithm to the same message, you get the same hash. If a message has been changed even by one character, the resulting hash is completely different. This provides an easy way to verify whether the contents of a message have been altered. To verify a signed email, the recipient email software checks to see what type of hashing was used, creates a hash, encrypts the result with the public key, and compares it to the attached digital signature. If the signature matches, it's considered valid. Notice that the message itself is not encrypted—anybody can read a digitally signed message. All the signature does is guarantee that the message came from the sender, and that it was not altered since the moment it was signed.

Digital signatures are not widely accepted in the business world, mainly because they're difficult to use. Many people are trying to get a Public Key Infrastructure as robust and widespread as TLS, but the problem is, there are many more email addresses than there are Web servers. As we've seen, maintaining a public certificate authority requires the utmost in security, especially since revoking certificates is not very reliable. It boils down to cost—how many people are willing to pay to maintain a public certificate authority, when they can get an email address for free? Such a centralized system would require even better security, and be able to handle a couple orders of magnitude more certificates. Still, the Secure Mail Internet Message Extensions (S/MIME) specification has been developed to provide a Public Key Infrastructure for email certificates.

An alternative, the grass roots system is in fairly widespread use. Originally called Pretty Good Privacy (PGP™), this system of exchanging keys was released to the world in 1991 when a relatively small community of people became concerned about some upcoming legislation that threatened to make owning tools for strong cryptography illegal. This system beat S/MIME into the world by nearly five years.

But there were some patent issues surrounding some of the algorithms, and the author of the software, Phil Zimmerman, had to stop distributing the software under court order. The open source Gnu Privacy Guard™ (GPG) software has emerged to take its place, eliminating the algorithms that had patent conflicts.

Both of these systems provide the same benefits: strong encryption and verifiable digital signatures. The difference is in how you verify that you have the correct public key for your correspondent. With S/MIME, you use a trusted certificate authority to vouch for the validity of a certificate. With GPG, you must install each individual public key and decide whether or not to trust it, based on how you obtained it. People sign each other's keys, essentially providing the same role as a certificate authority. If someone you trust, already in your keyring, vouches for the public key of someone unknown to you by signing it, then you can probably trust that public key.

The biggest problem is that these two schemes are completely incompatible. S/MIME adheres to a standard called X.509, which specifies all of the characteristics of a signature. X.509 certificates are the same format used by OpenSSL, certificate authorities, and Web servers. GPG keys are not certificates—they are simply a public key associated with an email address. The GPG software is completely self-contained, and OpenSSL cannot do anything with GPG keys.

Encrypted email and digital signatures promise to bring a whole new level of commerce to the Internet. Imagine being able to pay for services through email, sign official documents, notarize or approve items, and all sorts of things that email right now does not provide. Email, without one of these schemes, is a purely anonymous, public way of sending messages. Anyone can forge an email to make it appear to come from you—but only you can digitally sign your message. As these systems become more widespread, expect to see digital signatures start to hold up in court. Encrypted emails promise to provide a level of privacy people may falsely assume is already present in email. With encrypted email, you will be able to send a confidential message to your attorney, or to your bank, without risking it being compromised along the way.

Earlier we mentioned that public key encryption provides authentication or encryption, but not both at the same time. It is possible to sign a message and then encrypt it to your recipient. However, there is one detail that may never be a practical issue, but might cause a problem in a legal context: the recipient can't prove who sent the message to him. If you sign a message, you prove your identity, and that the message hasn't been changed. But you could have sent it to somebody else, who encrypted it to the recipient's public key and sent it to them. You may be confident that you signed and sent the message only to him, but your recipient can't prove that nobody else saw it. You, as the sender, can be verified, but the recipient can't be.

You could do it the other way around—encrypt first and then sign. The problem with this scenario is that anybody could strip your signature, and take credit for your message. Only the correct recipient is certain—the sender can't be verified.

This situation shows a fundamental flaw in all the current email encryption schemes. Whichever layer is on the outside, the encryption or the signature, is subject to one or the other vulnerability. The easiest solution to this is to always include both the name of your intended recipient and your own name in the body of your email. If you sign and then encrypt, the recipient address is inside your signature, so it's clear who the real recipient is. If you encrypt and then sign, your name is inside the encrypted message, and the recipient can easily tell there's a problem if somebody else has signed the encrypted message.

Let's now take a closer look at the two leading systems for handling encrypted email.

GPG

GNU Privacy Guard (GPG), for all its popularity, takes some motivation to use. Managing keys is a big part of it—you need to install keys for the people you want to send encrypted mail to, or verify signatures from, and assign them a trust rating. Quite often, even as a user, you have to drop to a command line to manage keys. Still, you can use GPG to encrypt files as well as mail, and if you want a good basic system without the overhead of running a certificate authority, you'll probably find more people you need to correspond with using GPG.

There is another catch—there are two ways of encoding a message using GPG. PGP originally used a format called Armored ASCII, which essentially encrypted the message directly, adding a signature at the end. The current implementation is called OpenPGP, which is now an Internet standard. It puts the body of a message in Mail Internet Message Extensions (MIME) attachments, and encrypts the attachment. The signature goes in another attachment. This is similar (but not compatible) to S/MIME.

Evolution, a leading email and personal information management program in Linux, only supports OpenPGP. Outlook Express only supports Armored ASCII, through a third party plug-in. So you'll need to choose an email client that supports the same form of encoding a GPG message as your correspondents, or you'll be reduced to saving messages and using the GPG command line.

A list of email clients supporting GPG, along with links to plug-ins if necessary, is at *http://www.openpgp.fr.st/courrier_en.html*.

Windows Privacy Tools, a set of Windows-based GPG tools, is part of The

ON THE CD Open CD, on the CD-ROM included with this book.

GPG is installed in most Linux distributions, and is used to verify signatures on downloadable software packages, among other things. Generally, if you need to use it for a specific purpose, follow the instructions provided. If you're starting from scratch, you're probably better going with S/MIME.

S/MIME

S/MIME is the growing standard in encrypted email. All of the major corporations have been using S/MIME exclusively for years. If you request a digital certificate in Microsoft Outlook, you'll get an S/MIME one.

If you're getting a server certificate for SSL from a public certificate authority, shop around to find one that will certify your own certificate authority for signing certificates used in email. Then you can sign certificates for your users, who can send them anywhere on the Internet. The recipient can then follow the chain of trust up to a root certificate authority they already trust.

If getting such a certification is beyond your budget, you can use your own root certificate authority, the same one you used to certify your SSL server. Again, each user (sender and recipient) needs to add the public certificate for your certificate authority into their list of trusted root authorities.

For encryption, you still need to get the public key of the recipient. You can do this the same way as GPG, by exchanging public keys ahead of time. Or you can use an LDAP directory server that provides the public keys of your employees and contacts, and configure your email software to use it. See the references at the end of the chapter to find out how to set this up, though it's a fairly difficult task.

Most of the major email clients support S/MIME, including Microsoft Outlook, Outlook Express, Netscape Communicator, Mozilla Mail and Thunderbird, Kmail (with a plug-in from Aegypten), Pegasus, Eudora (with a plug-in), and many others.

SUMMARY

The biggest problem with actually using encryption and authentication in your business is the number of competing incompatible standards. With a bit of effort, you can set up a Certificate Authority and use it to greatly increase security on your network. Persuading your customers to use it is a completely different challenge, because every single client needs to be manually configured to use it.

But it's absolutely essential in many situations. Attorneys know the need for confidential communication. The entire health-care industry is required to keep patient data confidential—something encrypted email can do, if properly deployed. Financial transactions must be kept secret.

The systems described in this chapter work just as well for authenticating computers to other computers for Web Services as they do for people. This will be useful for many transactions with your business partners.

Encrypted and authenticated email is not widely used, but it is here, it does work, and you can use it if you have the need.

In this chapter, we defined the different parts of secure connections: authentication, authorization, and encryption. We discussed public key encryption and public key infrastructure. Finally, we looked at the two major competing systems for encrypted email.

In the next part of the book, we get deeper into security issues, starting with how to prevent your sensitive data from being compromised if your computer is stolen.

ENCRYPTION REFERENCES

An updated list of resources for this chapter is on the Web site for the book at *http://opensourcesmall.biz/encryption.*

Books

The Key To Rebecca, by Ken Follet, William Morrow, 1985.
Crypto: How the Code Rebels Beat the Government—Saving Privacy in the Digital Age, by Steven Levy, Penguin Group, 2001.
Network Security with OpenSSL, by John Viega, Matt Messier, and Pravir Chandra, O'Reilly, June 15, 2002

Articles

"Securing Certificate Revocation List Infrastructures," by Eddie Turkaly. Available online at *http://www.sans.org/rr/paper.php?id=748*, 2001

Software

OpenSSL, open source encryption libraries *http://www.openssl.org*
GPG, open source encryption for files and email *http://www.gnupg.org/*
kgpg, open source graphical interface for GPG in KDE *http://devel-home. kde.org/~kgpg/*
Windows Privacy Tools, open source GPG interface for Windows *http://winpt. sourceforge.net/en/*

Web Sites

Verisign, a public certificate authority *http://www.verisign.com*
TRUSTe, a public certificate authority *http://www.truste.org*
Thawte, a public certificate authority *http://www.thawte.com*
Entrust, a public certificate authority *http://www.entrust.com/*
List of email clients supporting GPG *http://www.openpgp.fr.st/courrier_en.html*

PART

IV | Keeping Your Network Secure and Intact

Computers are supposed to save time, but they come with hidden costs. The more you rely on computers, the more effort you have to put into making them reliable. In this part of the book, we look at the pitfalls and costs of having a highly computerized business, and how to mitigate those costs through good planning.

Read this part of the book before someone cracks your network, before the next killer virus comes along and wipes your hard drives clean, before you open your digital doors and leak personal information out to the world where the next identity thief can find it.

Chapter 16 is a treatise about security, focusing on physical security and some measures you can take to minimize the risk of stolen data falling into the wrong hands.

Chapter 17 covers network security in the brand new context of widespread wireless networks. It also discusses how to deploy a Wi-Fi network, and what to watch for in the future.

Chapter 18 provides strategic guidance for developing a plan to recover from a data disaster. It's not backups that matter—it's the ability to recover from a disaster.

Chapter 19 covers the twin scourges of the Internet: viruses and spam.

16 Securing Business Data

INTRODUCTION

So far in this book we've discussed how computers and open source software can help you in your business. All the good stuff is over—the remainder of this book covers what you need to do to protect yourself online. Everything left is pure cost. It's hard to gauge any return on investment in the remaining chapters, because each chapter attempts to help you learn enough to deal with the downsides of computer systems.

This chapter provides perspective on how to keep your business data secure, and should be read by everyone who accesses or needs to protect sensitive data, such as confidential client information, credit cards, employee files, etc.

In the movie *Conspiracy Theory*, the character played by Mel Gibson keeps a toothpick in the crack near the top of the door to his apartment so he can tell whether it was opened or not while he was gone. Once inside, he locks half a dozen separate deadbolts, and then balances a beer bottle on the doorknob to act as an alarm if anyone tries to intrude.

If someone is really out to get you, you probably need to take a similar number of precautions—but be just as diligent about your windows, vents, and walls. Security is only as good as the strength of the weakest entrance. If nobody's out to get you, locking your doors and windows is probably sufficient. But talk to a security professional, and you'll hear all sorts of scary stories. The important thing to understand is that there's no such thing as completely secure data on a computer, unless it's locked in a lead-walled room with no network attached. Any realistic security assessment will discuss the weaknesses of your current system. The stronger your security, the more steps you have to take to maintain it—at which point you become the weak point. You can't possibly remember dozens of unique strong passwords, for example—you'll have to write them down somewhere, creating a security risk.

SECURITY IS A PROCESS, NOT A CONDITION

First of all, let's take a look at data security. We'll save all discussion of network security for the next chapter. Network security is all about locking the front door, preventing people from gaining access to your computer over the Internet or a wireless network. Before getting into network security, let's see what people can do when they already have access.

Why tackle data security first? Because it's almost entirely overlooked in most small business settings, and it provides a context for determining what to protect in your network. Why protect your data at all? Here are a few reasons:

- Identity theft
- Fraud
- Theft
- Embezzlement
- Illegal distribution using your computers
- Your business reputation/brand
- Competitive advantage
- Trade secrets
- Business plans
- Long-term strategy
- Business contracts

If your computers are compromised, your business, employees, or customers may fall victim to any of these, putting confidential information in your competitors' hands or costing you your business. Most security measures are designed to keep secret data secret, and prevent unauthorized use of your systems.

So how much do you need to worry about this stuff? Do you really need to worry about somebody breaking into your systems? If you have a small, innocuous business, who would bother? Isn't it enough to go about your business, and ignore security issues?

Perhaps. The number of system compromises may be low, compared to the number of people using computers. But you don't leave a cash register unattended, or your office unlocked at night. Taking basic precautions keeps honest people honest. A completely unsecured system invites violations. A completely secure system is practically unusable. The trick is to find a good balance between security and ease of use—secure enough to discourage would-be attackers, while not so secure you spend more time dealing with your security mechanisms than doing your job.

Let's get practical here. Security is a process of identifying where the weaknesses in your systems are, who is most likely to compromise your system, and what the consequences of a breach will be. Then plan accordingly.

Where Are the Weaknesses?

We'll discuss network security in much greater detail in Chapter 17, but obviously, your connection to the Internet is probably the biggest door to your network. But every person who can log in is already inside the apartment.

Application Logins

The first door to check out is anywhere people can log in. That includes Web applications, file sharing protocols, email systems, and remote access systems. These systems can usually be compromised in one of two ways: cracking the password, or cracking the system. For just about any of these systems, if they're available on the Internet, they're only as secure as the weakest password. Passwords on unencrypted connections can be sniffed, and then used to log in as the user. Passwords can be guessed. Crackers can write scripts to try thousands of different passwords out of a custom dictionary until one works—all they have to do is run it, and check back hours later to find out which one worked.

Systems are designed to expect certain input from the user. Due to programmer errors, sometimes not in the program but in the compiler used to generate the code, it turns out that many network applications have flaws that may be exploited to crash the application. The most famous type of exploit is called a buffer overflow, which basically involves sending more data than the program expects. If that data is crafted in a particular way, it may cause the application to crash, leaving the connection open and accepting commands from the cracker. Or the extra data may actually overwrite part of the program, allowing the cracker to substitute specific commands to further compromise the system. The end result, in either case, is that the attacker successfully logs into the server.

Gaining Administrative Rights

All modern server operating systems are designed to be multiuser: through the use of user accounts, you can limit what an individual user can do on the computer, and the damage an attacker can do if he logs in as that user. One of the big problems with security on Windows computers is that regular user accounts have full administrator rights, unless you specifically lower your privilege level. This means that if an attacker manages to log in as an administrative user, they can do anything on the computer. The downside of having an unprivileged user account is that it becomes much less convenient to install new software, change system settings, and perform other common administrative tasks.

Most services install and run under less-privileged system accounts on Windows, which can help to contain an attacker. Under Unix systems, only the superuser, the root account, can access everything—everyone and all services run under non-administrative accounts. You usually do not allow remote logins to the root account.

However, if an attacker can gain any login access that allows him to use commands, he can do anything the compromised user account can do. From there, a whole class of weaknesses provide *privilege elevation exploits*. Basically, a flaw in any program that automatically runs as a privileged user can be exploited to gain access to the root account on a Unix, Linux, or Mac, or an administrative account in Windows.

Social Engineering

One of the most common ways people gain access to your systems is by being given a password. Most companies do not take security that seriously. In many businesses, people can walk right into the office, act as if they belonged there, and plug a laptop or other device directly into your network, behind your firewall. Or they can sit down in front of a workstation that's already logged in. When questioned, these people may make up a story that sounds perfectly plausible, using photos and other things on a desk as clues to create fictional details. Perhaps they're the brother of an employee, just checking their email while they wait. Perhaps they're a cable technician, here to repair a non-existent problem.

Similar techniques work over the telephone. There are many perfectly innocent requests for information about your employees—but almost all attempts to surreptitiously gather information appear to be innocent requests. The hard part is telling the difference.

In the security world, the practice of making up a story to appear innocent while gathering information for an attack is called *Social Engineering*. The techniques can be very imaginative—think of how often James Bond talked his way through getting caught where he wasn't supposed to be. Furthermore, social engineering works. People leave their passwords written on scraps of paper, stuck to the side of their monitors. Most people use their pet's name, their children's names, or important dates like anniversaries and birthdays for passwords—gathering just a tiny bit of information about a person may give an attacker everything he needs to guess one of these passwords. A couple minutes on a logged-in computer is all that's necessary to create a new user account with administrative rights, or install a program that logs keystrokes and sends everything you type back to the attacker, or a back-door program that provides remote access to the computer.

Physical Access Exploits

If a would-be attacker has physical access to your computer, it's very difficult to prevent them from accessing anything on the box. Obviously, if somebody is logged in, the attacker can do anything that user has permission to do. If there's a root vulnerability on the computer, or the user is running with administrative rights, the attacker can bypass all permissions to get at whatever data is on the computer. Even without administrative rights, the user can access the password database in both Windows and Unix—and on both systems, the default encryption on passwords has been broken through brute force attacks in a matter of hours. All the user needs to do is copy the password database to a floppy, then go home and run the attacks to have a complete list of all login passwords on that machine. He can then use these passwords to infiltrate any system open to the Internet at his leisure. So your employees should always lock their workstations before leaving them if there's any chance someone could sit down at their desk while they're gone.

Given a little more time, a locked workstation won't stop an attacker for long. Even with secure passwords on your system, the attacker can boot with a recovery disk and change the root or administrator password, and then gain access to the entire system. If you manage to disable or password-protect this administrative login, the attacker can boot into a CD-ROM-based operating system, mount your hard drives, and access any data stored on them. If you disable booting from floppies and CD-ROMs, the attacker can go into your BIOS and enable them. If you password-protect the computer startup and the BIOS, the attacker can open the cover of your computer and reset the BIOS using a failsafe dip-switch on the motherboard, or remove the battery that keeps the BIOS settings. Or remove the hard drive completely and install it in another computer where it can be searched at leisure. If you put a lock on the cover of the computer, there's always a drill—or the key in your desk drawer. Put your server in a locked closet, and there's bound to be some way to break in. But notice how every additional step you take to protect your computer makes it take a little longer, a little more effort to gain access to the machine.

The goal of security is to make it take so much effort to break into your machine, that the eventual payoff doesn't end up being worth it. Make the attacker look for easier prey. A key point here is that if you have something your attacker wants, he may go to great effort to get it. The flip side is that if your security is lax, you may be compromised even though you have nothing of value to protect.

Who Owns Your Servers? Hackers, Crackers, and Script Kiddies

So that leads us to the question: who would compromise your system? We can group them into a few different categories:

■ People who don't care one way or the other about you, but want to use your computers for their own purposes
■ People who bear you some sort of grudge
■ People who stand to gain something from your data

While we're here, let's talk a bit about terminology. In the mainstream media, a *hacker* is often (wrongly) described as somebody who illegally breaks into computers. In the computer world, especially in open source, you'll find a lot of programmers who call themselves hackers, but they mean something quite a bit different by the word. A hacker is somebody who systematically tries to solve some problem with computers. The problem might be breaking some security mechanism—but more often it's something much more mundane, like making a gaming console run on a normal Web browser. Calling someone a hacker is usually a sign of respect of that person's skill, and has no negative connotation whatsoever. Implying that they're criminal for doing so will not win you any friends.

In computer circles, the term *cracker* is what most mainstream media should be using, instead of *hacker*. A cracker is a hacker who specifically breaks into computer systems, or writes code that does so. A *script kiddie* is somebody who takes a program made by a cracker and actually uses it to break into systems.

Cracking because It's There

If your security is lax, you'll inevitably become the target of an incidental attack. Plug an unsecured computer into a DSL connection without any type of firewall, and it will be compromised. The Internet is a wild, lawless place. People will break into your computer because they can, and generally not get penalized in any way for it.

These are the exploits of the script kiddies. Many of them are not that technical—they just download cracking programs and set them to work scanning network addresses, looking for a vulnerable computer.

Once they find one and successfully break in, they do all sorts of different things. Sometimes they'll vandalize your Web pages, the digital equivalent of marking territory. Sometimes they'll plant a file server for swapping copyrighted material, trading illegal files. Sometimes they'll use your computer to attack another, either as a way of hiding their tracks or as one of several hundred or thousand *zombie* computers in a distributed denial of service attack. Often they'll snoop around, look for anything of interest, and see what opportunities present themselves.

Fortunately, blocking this type of attack is relatively easy. Keep all of your systems that are connected to the Internet up to date and virus-free. Keep abreast of newly discovered security issues. Make it hard enough to break into your system that the script kiddies will look for easier targets.

Cracking for Spite

If an attacker is motivated enough, they will be able to compromise your system. The most common story behind a spiteful crack attempt is a disgruntled employee. A fired employee, or even a current one who is particularly angry, makes for a big security risk. As we discussed earlier, basic user accounts generally have limits on the damage they can do—but it's one step closer to a complete compromise of an administrative account.

Employees can generally log on to your systems, enter your buildings, and even install remote access on their office workstations. If you have an employee leave on bad terms, you'll need to immediately block access to all systems that user had access to. And make sure all your security systems are updated with new credentials.

The best way to prevent these sorts of problems is to treat people well. If you don't trust your employees, they won't trust you, and you'll waste more time and energy creating obstructions, extra procedures, and an environment of distrust. You're much better off being open and honest in most situations—but you have to be aware of the risks, you have to realize that granting root access to a user puts anything on that system under the user's control.

Not all people attacking your company for spiteful reasons are your employees. You might have business enemies, or people who choose to attack you for personal reasons. In most cases, you'll know pretty quickly if you have this sort of enemy. If you do, you need to harden your systems appropriately. The script kiddies are turned away by a locked door. The spiteful attackers will break your door down, if they're angry enough.

A good disaster recovery plan can help you recover from these types of attacks, and you can find security experts to help mitigate their effects. See Chapter 18 for more about making a disaster recovery plan.

Cracking for Reward

The other motivation for breaking into your systems is to get something out of it. This type of security exploit is much more rare—but the consequences can be much more dire. Quite often, the worst part about these attacks is that you might not know you were compromised until it's too late. Unlike the other attacks, crackers with these motives will often try to cover their tracks and leave no evidence that a computer has been compromised.

This sort of attack can lead to all sorts of terrible problems. If you accept credit cards online, and your customer's credit card numbers are somewhere in your database, you've got a tantalizing target for a cracker. If a dishonest employee feels underpaid and has access to your financial system, he might try to embezzle little chunks of cash, hidden in overlooked line items. If you're working on a high-profile project, with less than ethical competitors, you might even become a victim of the spy-versus-spy style of social engineering tactics.

These are perhaps the most difficult attacks to prevent. The main thing security helps you with is identifying the risks and trying to minimize them.

Consequences of Compromises

Obviously, the consequences of a compromise is directly related to what is compromised. The most common consequence is mainly inconvenience. Your data is destroyed. Your systems go offline, potentially causing lost customers who wonder if you've gone out of business. You waste a day or two recovering your data and hardening your systems, and then you're back in business.

If a script kiddie infiltrates your computer and uses it to distribute music, movies, or cracking software, your network might slow to a crawl as it consumes all your bandwidth. If your computer is used to relay spam, you might also find that your email starts getting rejected as other network administrators cut off all mail from your server. If your computer is used to attack other computers, you may get a knock on the door from the FBI. All of this adds up to more time spent doing things other than your business.

Worst of all, if your customer's financial data gets stolen, you may end up out of business if you get a reputation for not taking appropriate measures to protect that data. In several industries, you may be violating the law and subject to a huge fine if your customer's data falls into the wrong hands. Personal details about your employees in personnel files may be enough for a thief to steal an employee's identity, apply for credit in her name, and stick her with the bill. And if your competitors get hold of your business plans, or the plans of your new invention, they may be able to beat you in the marketplace, or register a patent or trademark that threatens your livelihood.

SECURITY POLICY

If your company is big enough to have its own office, you need to have some sort of security policy that covers physical access to the premises, who has access to the servers, and how desktop computers are to be used. Even more importantly, you need guidelines for company data stored on laptops, PDAs, and home computers. These remote computers, if they have sensitive data, can create a huge security hole that's much harder to protect. In general, any computer that has company data on it should at least require a valid username and password before logging in—never use the auto-login features on company computers.

If you're going to allow guests to use a computer, it should be on a physically separate network from the rest of your LAN. You shouldn't allow the general public to casually use your computers. Somebody must verify the credentials of anyone you don't know who comes into your private offices, especially if you have data that might prove valuable to anybody else.

Large companies need to think of all kinds of stipulations to go into their security policies. Industry regulations, such as the HIPAA act in health care, may define a certain set of minimum security criteria you must meet. In general, anything employees do with an employer's computer is the responsibility of the company, and the company can be liable for these actions. Because of this situation, you'll find in most large companies that the IT department locks all kinds of services, Web sites, file sharing, streaming media, and other things that aren't strictly work-related. Often these restrictions hamper the ability of employees to get their job done, setting up an inevitable conflict between the IT department and the users. This mirrors the inherent conflict between security and usability.

As a small company, you're still liable for these issues, but you may get away with a lot more. If only a handful of people use streaming media to listen to an online broadcast through your company DSL connection, it's not likely to cause any problems. A few dozen people listening to streaming media, however, can grind a T1 connection to a halt.

Your business needs to have a security policy that specifies:

- Who can be in the office after hours
- How employees should protect their home computers and laptops
- What data is allowed on a PDA
- How to handle guests
- How strong passwords need to be, and how often they are changed
- What software employees are allowed to run on company equipment
- Anything else you can think of related to security

People tend to think of their work computers as something they have a right to use for personal tasks. Whether you allow this or not is up to your business, but remember that anything your employees do using company equipment or services could make your company liable. Setting some good, reasonable expectations early can save you trouble down the road.

The Risks of Outsourcing

If you haven't thought about it before, it's important to note that everything discussed above applies to contractors as well as employees. Especially IT consultants, because they might have access to anything on your computers. If you're outsourcing computer work for your LAN to some sort of vendor, check their references, talk with them, get a sense of who they are before handing over the company jewels. You have far less control over an IT contractor than you do over your own employees. Find people you can trust.

Let's take a look at some things you can do to improve overall security on your network, discover system compromises, and encrypt particularly sensitive documents.

Creating and Managing Strong Passwords

The weakest point of most computer systems is the password. People choose all sorts of mundane, easily guessable things for passwords:

- Their dog or cat's name
- Their mother's maiden name
- Their children's name, birthday, or a combination of them
- Their anniversary
- The word "Password"
- Their favorite holiday destination

These are horrible passwords. If an attacker gets hold of an encrypted password database, he can run a program on an average desktop machine that can try millions of passwords in an hour. They can literally try every word in the dictionary, and have put together their own dictionaries of common pet and human names. With a little social engineering, these passwords can be easily guessed.

It doesn't take much to improve these passwords. When checking for a strong password, both Unix and Windows can require you to choose a mix of characters from different sets: capital letters, lower case letters, numbers, and punctuation/symbols. If you make your password using characters from at least three of these four sets, it's bound to be much stronger than a single word password. Take two words and stick a symbol between them, and you dramatically multiply the number of possible passwords an attacker needs to try.

There are two ways passwords can be discovered: brute force, or by an educated guess. The English language has somewhere around 200,000 words. With brute force, a computer can try 200,000 passwords in a matter of minutes. But stick any two random words together, and the number of possibilities multiplies dramatically, making 40,000,000,000 possible combinations, taking 200,000 times as long to crack. You get a similar number of possible passwords if you make it out of six totally random characters. But such random passwords are hard to create, and hard to remember.

Most people are afraid that if they make a random password, they won't remember it. Worse, a strong, randomly generated, difficult-to-remember password will inevitably get written down somewhere, often on a sticky note attached to the computer monitor or office wall. Writing down a password can entirely defeat the security of a strong password.

Creating Memorable Strong Passwords

There are many ways to come up with strong passwords, but remembering them and typing them consistently is an entirely different issue. If it's a password you've used frequently, you will learn to type it quickly—but being able to pronounce it can help you remember it. A random sequence of characters can be more secure, but it's very inconvenient if you have to glance at wherever you've stored your password three times just to get all the characters in the right order.

Let's take a look at two password creation strategies: a mnemonic acronym approach, and a completely random approach.

Mnemonic Acronyms

With this approach, you make up some phrase, and then pick characters corresponding to each word. Mix up the case of the letters, and use symbols and numbers wherever possible. For example, you might shorten the phrase "My crazy dog loves to chase cats in the park" to M*dL2ccItp. This is a good strong password—difficult to guess, not based on any dictionary words, using a mnemonic phrase to remember an otherwise nonsensical password. The important thing is to use things not necessarily associated with you. Notice that the phrase itself isn't as secure as the nonsense you turn it into.

Randomly Generated Passwords

Another good way is to choose some random system for generating a password. For a free, extremely effective way of doing this, try Diceware (*http://www.diceware. com*). One of the fundamental problems with computers is generating a truly random number. Computers do one calculation after another, in a direct sequence. Random number generators on a computer essentially combine a very long sequence of numbers with some physical interaction, such as the exact microsecond the computer was powered up, the position and direction of movement of the mouse, or other things that are difficult to predict. However, for the ultra-paranoid, that's not random enough. The reasoning behind Diceware is that you can rely on something completely separate from the computer to generate a much less predictable random number: a roll of a set of dice.

Diceware is simply a list of words, each word associated with a particular roll of five dice. To make a strong password, scrounge through your board games until you have five dice. Roll them twice, writing down the numbers you get. Then roll two dice once, to get a separating character. Look up the words in the Diceware list, and the characters in the Special Character list. Your password consists of the first word, the special character, and the second word. An example might be waldo~mire. Mix up the case of a few of the letters, and you have a good strong password, wAldO~mire, that isn't that difficult to remember.

It is a strong password, and furthermore, it's pronounceable. The best part of all is that it's fun.

The Diceware word list only contains 7,776 words, by itself trivial for a password cracker to scan. But with two words, you're at over 60 million words. Add a random separator character and mix up the case of the resulting words, and you're at somewhere near 70 billion different passwords.

Reusing Passwords across Systems

We all have far too many places for which we need a password. If we use a unique password for each Web site we sign up on, we have to somehow manage to remember what can quickly grow to be hundreds of passwords. Is it really that important to use a unique password on every site, on every Web application, on every computer?

The problem is, nobody can possibly remember all their passwords if they don't reuse them. If you write down your passwords somewhere, your list of passwords becomes an extreme security vulnerability. Anybody who gets their hands on it could access anything you've signed up for. But if you don't write them down, you'll inevitably forget which password you used where, type in the wrong password for the wrong site, potentially compromising every password you mistakenly enter. It's quite the conundrum, and there's no easy solution.

Most people end up using the same password over and over again. It's a security risk to do so, but the extra hassle it takes to find and track all those passwords is usually too much for the extra security gained. But here are some tips for minimizing the risks of reusing your passwords.

1. Never, ever, reuse an administrative or root password. These passwords are the skeleton keys to your system, and can be used to reset any password on the system. These passwords should be kept entirely confidential, given

only to highly trusted individuals who absolutely need them. On Unix-based systems, you can provide root privileges without revealing the root password using the sudo program.

2. Use a strong password for your system user accounts. It's fine to reuse these passwords within your network, synchronizing all of your internal systems to use the same password. However, you should change this password regularly, every three months or so. And you should never use this password on any Web site you don't control, or through an unencrypted connection.

3. For Web sites that remember your credit card number, social security number, or any other sensitive information, use a strong password and make sure the site uses an encrypted connection whenever you sign in. You should always log into these sites, and don't let the browser remember your password. It's best to create a unique password for each site, but if you trust a site enough to hand over your personal information, you can probably trust them to not impersonate you on other Web sites. If a site with your sensitive information logs you in automatically or over an unencrypted connection, don't use it—your information can be compromised. Complain to the site owner, and use a different medium to do business with them.

For sites that don't encrypt connections but require a username and password, there's really no need for a strong password, and there's very little need for creating unique passwords. The most damage somebody can do by impersonating you on these sites is sign you up for spam, write fake messages pretending to be you, or other annoying, nuisance things. In most cases, these sites don't have much security, and you should not trust them. If you're running your own Web application without encryption, don't put any sensitive data up there, and treat the entire system as already compromised—or put it behind a firewall, accessible only on your LAN. If you're not a system administrator, you can get by reasonably securely with a minimum of three passwords.

Storing and Managing Passwords

Most system administrators use some sort of password management software. A good password manager uses an encrypted database to store account names and passwords, indexed by the system. It's a huge mistake to put these in plain text files, Word documents, Outlook notes, or other unencrypted spots—these provide no security whatsoever. Whatever system you use, it should be encrypted except when you're actually using it.

Password managers essentially protect all of your passwords with one single strong password. Make sure you use a strong password for this master password, and don't reveal it to anyone. You might write it on a slip of paper, put it in a sealed envelope, and store it in a safe deposit box so that your next of kin can take over should something happen to you, but otherwise this password should be kept secret from everyone, and different from every other password you use.

Most password managers encrypt the entire database, but generally they use a relatively short password to generate a key—you're not going to write a 50-character passphrase in Palm Graffiti to look up a password. This makes the encryption not as strong. Decrypting can be a lot slower than testing a password hash, however, making it take a bit longer. So you should take steps to protect your password database, even though it's encrypted. Do not distribute it, or put it anywhere public. If you think it's been copied, treat it like a stolen wallet—change all your passwords, report compromised bank numbers to the banks, and treat it as a serious problem. The encryption on these databases will definitely slow down the compromise—you have at least a few days before they can be revealed—but change everything at your earliest opportunity.

One good system is to use an encrypted password manager on a PDA. The open source Keyring program (*http://gnukeyring.sourceforge.net*) is a good one to use on a Palm OS PDA. You can use it with companion programs to unencrypt and access your password database from your desktop. Jpilot (*http://www.jpilot.org*) includes a plug-in for Keyring that allows you to view and edit your password database in Linux. Projects are under way to provide a viewer for Windows and Mac; see the Keyring home page for links.

For an open source Windows-based password manager, try Oubliette, available at *http://sourceforge.net/projects/oubliette/*.

Finally, another alternative is to use a plain text file, and be diligent about encrypting it when it's not in use. This is not as good a method, because it's too easy to get distracted and forget to encrypt the file. File encryption is discussed later in this chapter.

What's a Passphrase?

A passphrase is essentially a long password. Instead of six to twelve characters long, most passphrases require 20 or more characters. Symmetrical encryption software often uses a passphrase as the encryption key, sometimes applying a hashing algorithm first. What this means is that any time you deal with strong encryption software, you'll probably need to generate a passphrase.

If you've already visited Diceware (*http://www.diceware.com*), you've probably discovered that its primary purpose is generating a passphrase, not a password. You take your five dice, roll them four or more times, and generate a phrase from the result.

Like password generation, if you use the first thing that comes to mind, it will be guessed. Never use a cliché or any common quotation as a passphrase. Pick three words randomly from the diceware list, and there are some 470 billion possible combinations. Add more words, mix up the case, and insert some random symbols and you'll have a passphrase that could not be cracked by brute force by all the computing power in the world before the sun goes nova in five billion years.

It's still important to keep aware of security algorithms—like any other security situations, if one entrance is heavily barricaded, the attacker will look for another way in. If your passphrase can't be cracked, it's still possible that someone will find a flaw in the encryption algorithm.

Monitoring for System Compromises

Given that security is a process, and that there's really no such thing as a secure system, part of your security strategy must include detecting when you've been compromised. In many cases, it will be immediately apparent—your Web site will be defaced, your hard drive erased, or you'll notice many other obvious symptoms. However, if the attacker hides his tracks, you might not ever know you've been compromised unless you look hard. Let's take a look at a few ways to find traces of such an attack.

System Logs

The first tool you have in your arsenal are the system logs. Nearly all server software programs log many different kinds of events to a system log of some sort. In Unix-based systems, most use a program called syslog to provide centralized management of these logs. The /etc/syslog.conf file specifies where syslog will write messages, based on the categorization of the message. These categories are called *facilities*. You can generally configure server programs to log to a particular facility, at a certain threshold message level.

For example, you can set syslog to log anything sent to the mail facility to the file /var/log/maillog, and then configure all of the different mail servers to send messages to the mail facility. This way you can get Postfix, Courier-IMAP, Dspam, and any other mail-related software to log everything to one easy-to-monitor file. You can also send log messages to another server. This allows you to set up a central logging server that all the other servers in your network send messages to.

Somebody should regularly review logs, scanning for anomalous events. Most attacks will get logged somewhere, and if your logs are intact, you may be able to figure out what the attacker did, and how he got in.

One major pitfall is that most savvy crackers know full well their actions are being logged, so one of the first things they will do upon breaking into your machine is to delete the evidence from the logs. This is one of the biggest reasons for running a separate logging server—if the logs aren't on the compromised machine, they can't be tampered with. If you happen to be monitoring a log when you're attacked, you will see the attack as it happens, before the attacker can hide the traces.

To monitor log files, use the `tail` command. For example, `tail -f /var/log/maillog` will print the contents of the mail log to the terminal as they happen.

On Windows, instead of logging to files, computers log to the central Event Log. You can find the Event Log in the Computer Management administrative tool applet.

Tripwire

Another tactic you should use is to set up a file monitoring program. Tripwire (*http://www.tripwire.org*) maintains a database of critical files on a Unix system, and notifies you of any changes to those files. So why can't the Tripwire database be tampered with? Because it uses strong encryption to manage updates.

Basically, Tripwire keeps track of data about every file in particular system directories you specify. It uses a hash function to create a checksum value for the file, records the ownership, permissions, and the internal filesystem location of the file (the inode number), and the modification and creation dates attached to the file. If any of these differ from the previous time Tripwire checked, it emails a report detailing the changes. You can then go in, verify that the changes are legitimate, and update the database with the proper passphrase.

Tripwire is designed to warn you of Trojan horses. A common technique among crackers is to replace otherwise innocent programs with special versions that hide the cracker's presence. For example, by replacing the `who` command, the cracker can substitute a special version that lists everybody currently logged into the system other than him.

The downside of Tripwire is that it catches compromises after they've occurred. You generally schedule Tripwire to run once a day, usually overnight when the server load is light. So it won't detect a compromise until up to 24 hours after the fact. It also doesn't do anything to stop an attack—it mainly lets you know if your system has been tampered with. You can set up policies to have Tripwire monitor sensitive documents as well as system files.

Tripwire is freely available for Linux with an open source license. You can purchase a commercial license to get it for Windows from *http://www.tripwire.com*.

Root Kits

Most script kiddies use software downloaded from the Web to attack computers. These programs hide in specific places, and execute a sequence of steps to gain root access, install back doors that allow them to connect later, and cover their tracks. Programs that take advantage of software flaws to gain administrative privileges are called *Root Kits*.

Because many of these programs are available on the Web, a different group of hackers makes it their mission to develop software that detects these root kits, and removes them from your system. These programs are often called spyware removal programs, and many of them are available for free or low cost.

These programs work like virus scanners. You tell them to run, and they search your system looking for specific root kits or spyware. If they find them, they give you the option of removing them. Like virus software, spyware detection programs need to get updated to be able to detect new root kits. These are handy tools to have in your arsenal.

For Linux, there's an open source tool called `chkrootkit` available from *http://www.chkrootkit.org/*. For Windows, there are no open source spyware removal tools, but several closed-source products that release free versions. Check out Spybot Search and Destroy (*http://www.safer-networking.org/*), and Ad-Aware from Lavasoft (*http://www.lavasoftusa.com/*).

Verifying Software Signatures before Installing

Much better than detecting a security breach is preventing it in the first place. In most cases, this is done by preventing physical access to your computers, setting up good security on your network (Chapter 17), and preventing viruses (Chapter 19). But it's possible for your users to install software that compromises their systems, opening a back door without anyone actually attacking your system.

Whenever you run a program, it can access anything on your computer that your user account can access. If a program is installed to run as an administrative user, it can do anything at all. You have to trust the developer of a program every bit as much as every employee who can log into your computer.

That is the reason software packages come with digital signatures. Whenever you download a program over the Web, you should verify that you got the software from a trustworthy source. How do you do this? It depends on the software.

Most Unix- and Linux-based programs use something called an MD5 checksum for verifying a download. MD5 is a hashing algorithm, a program that takes a file, crunches all the bytes in it, and comes up with a fingerprint identifying that program. If a single byte has been changed, you'll end up with a completely different MD5 sum.

After you download a program, you can verify it with the `md5sum` program. Simply type `md5sum <package_name.tar.gz>` to get the fingerprint, or checksum. It can take a while to generate this value. Then compare it to the source where you got the file. If you got it from an SSL-encrypted Web site, the SSL certificate provides authentication that the Web site belongs to who claims to own it. You can verify the digital signature by clicking on the encryption icon in your Web browser. Then verify that the `md5sum` you generated matches the one provided on the Web site. Alternatively, many open source projects sign their binaries or checksums with GPG. Get the GPG key from a keyserver by following the instructions on the site, and then you can verify the source.

Reading Security News Bulletins

In general, be choosy about software you install. One of the huge advantages of open source software is that anyone can look in the code to see if there's a back door. If you find a project with a lot of active developers, you can probably trust that there are no back doors, because they would have been discovered and publicized. In general, any software that gets a lot of press or public exposure can usually be trusted, because the people releasing the code would quickly go out of business or ruin their reputation if they did anything sketchy. Search on Google for programs you've never heard of, and get some third-party opinions before installing any programs. Make sure you get the programs from the correct source. Also watch for news about system compromises.

In the fall of 2003, the servers of two major open source projects were compromised, and somebody even attempted to insert a back door into the Linux kernel. Commercial software companies have also had their software infiltrated, and several have even accidentally shipped viruses, so this is hardly a problem limited to open source. These attempts were quickly caught and rectified, but it's possible to download a compromised package from an otherwise trustworthy source. For this reason, another part of your security strategy demands that you read security bulletins and be aware of newly discovered compromises.

There are several technology-related Web sites that publish security alerts whenever they come out. One good way of keeping abreast of these is by using some sort of news syndication reader, and subscribing to the news feeds from particular sites. See the references for more places to find these.

ENCRYPTING DATA

For computers that you can't physically secure, encryption can provide another layer of protection for extremely sensitive data, such as passwords, contracts, personnel data, or design plans. It's best to store these things on computers that have been properly secured, and access them through encrypted networks. But people use laptops because they're convenient. If you allow employees to connect from home, you should provide some way to lessen the chance of your sensitive data being compromised. If you have any files from customers or partners you've agreed to not disclose to anyone, you may be liable for damages if your computer is stolen and these files aren't protected.

For these sensitive files, use some sort of encrypted data storage to add a solid layer of protection.

There are many different systems for providing file encryption. There are a handful of trusted encryption algorithms, some of which we discussed in Chapter 15. Let's discuss a few easy-to-use encryption systems, appropriate for what we're discussing. Table 16.1 shows a matrix of the encryption types we're discussing. In this table, symmetrical encryption uses the same key to encrypt and decrypt, meaning anybody with the passphrase can decrypt the contents. Asymmetrical encryption uses public key encryption to encrypt a session key, potentially making it easier to share the file with other users without sharing a secret key—but also requiring your private key to decrypt the file.

TABLE 16.1   Grid of Encryption Types

	Symmetrical	*Asymmetrical*
Individual Files	Ccrypt	GPG/Windows Privacy Tools
File System/Directory	Linux Loopback Encryption/mountloop	Windows Encrypted File System

Encrypt Files with GPG

Gnu Privacy Guard (GPG, available at *http://www.gnupg.org/*) is an extremely popular and effective way to encrypt files. As the successor to Pretty Good Privacy (PGP), there's support built into many email programs, as we discussed in Chapter 15. It's also great for encrypting files.

GPG itself is a command line tool, but there are lots of graphical interfaces you can use to manage your keys, encrypt and decrypt files, and sign items you want to authenticate as coming from you. Your secret key is itself encrypted, requiring you to type a passphrase to decrypt and use it. Like a password manager, you should make every attempt to keep your secret key private, in spite of the encryption on it.

With GPG, you use an asymmetrical keypair consisting of a private key and a public key. You spread your public key far and wide, add it to your Web site, put it on a key server, email it to your contacts. Your public key can be used to encrypt anything, and make it so that only your private key can decrypt it. Your private key can decrypt files encrypted by the public key. Your private key can also sign a file or email, and anyone can verify your signature with your public key.

Using GPG, you can encrypt and decrypt individual files. You can back up encrypted files just as you do other files. You can safely store them on backup media.

The drawback is, it's all manual—you have to decrypt a file to use it, and re-encrypt it when you're done. During the time it's unencrypted, it's not protected from anyone else who might log into your computer. You have to remember to re-encrypt it. You can also encrypt a file to somebody else using GPG, and securely send it to them without needing to transfer any kind of secret key or passphrase.

GPG is available for most operating systems. To get a nice graphical interface for Windows, check out Windows Privacy Tools (*http://winpt.sourceforge.net/en/*). For Linux, try kgpg, provided in the basic KDE utilities package since version 3.2.

Windows Privacy Tools is part of The Open CD, on the CD-ROM included with this book.

Symmetrical Encryption with Ccrypt

Ccrypt (*http://sourceforge.net/projects/ccrypt*) is a simple symmetrical encryption tool that uses the current accepted standard for strong encryption, the Advanced Encryption Standard (AES). The Web site says that it is not symmetrical, but their definition is misleading. It's symmetrical in that you use the same passphrase to decrypt the file as you used to encrypt it. Obviously the key here is to use a strong passphrase.

Ccrypt is a command line tool for Unix-based systems. You can use Ccrypt in Windows if you install the Cygwin library, a big set of programs that bring Unix functionality to Windows.

Microsoft Encrypted File System

Microsoft Windows 2000, XP Professional, and later provide encryption at a file system level. What this means is that you can designate a directory to be encrypted, and its entire contents are automatically encrypted by the operating system, transparently. Copy a file into the encrypted part of the file system, and it automatically gets encrypted. You can use your normal programs on encrypted files, without having to manually decrypt them. Everything happens behind the scenes, and best of all, happens automatically. If somebody else logs into the computer, they cannot access your encrypted files because they're scrambled.

The Microsoft Encrypted File System uses public key encryption the same way as the others: it encrypts the files with a secret session key, and then encrypts the key with your public key. Only your secret key can decrypt it. Your secret key is further encrypted by your login password. If you change your password, your secret key is decrypted with your old password and encrypted with the new one. If an administrator changes your password, the secret key can't be decrypted, so you lose access to all your encrypted files.

Microsoft provides a system for making a password recovery disk. If you use Microsoft encryption, make one of these and put it somewhere safe. The password recovery disk is essentially an unencrypted copy of your secret key. You can also set up recovery agents, which use a separate keypair to encrypt the session key, providing access to the file.

The weak part of this system is your login password: if someone guesses that and logs into your computer as you, that process will decrypt all your files and give access. So make your login password strong, change it frequently, and rest assured that if your laptop is stolen, your sensitive data will remain safely encrypted.

Encrypted Linux Loopback File Systems

With encryption, Linux users are hardly left in the cold. There are many different encryption systems out there, and there's been a cryptographic module available for the operating system kernel for several years. Patent issues and cryptography export laws have kept these systems out of many distributions, but the code is all freely available on the Internet. Mandrake Linux, because it's based in France, includes a simple, effective encryption package on their installation CDs, in a package called `mountloop`. This package is basically a few programs that make it easy for you to set up an encrypted directory that is automatically decrypted and mounted when you log in. The techniques for doing this without the `mountloop` package are documented in many places on the Web.

The way it works is by taking advantage of Linux's ability to mount a single file as if it were a file system, called a *Loopback* file system. You create a container file of a fixed size that represents a hard drive partition. You use the cryptography interface to create an encrypted loop device out of the file. Then you mount the loop device as a file system and format it. This sounds technical, but it's really only a few brief commands. If you install the `mountloop` package, you'll find the DrakLoop program in the archiving section of the menu. This interface allows you to choose a location for an encrypted directory, creates the directory, creates the encrypted file inside it, mounts it so that its contents are encrypted with the passphrase, and sets it up to automatically remount when you log in. When you log in, you'll get a dialog asking you to type the passphrase. Get it wrong three times, and the file system won't be decrypted. Figure 16.1 shows DrakLoop.

Like the Microsoft Encrypted File System, this loopback encryption is completely transparent while you're using it. Encryption happens automatically, in the background. Unlike Microsoft encryption, you don't need to back up any private key—all you need is your passphrase to decrypt it, and you can decrypt it using any user account (as long as you have the right permissions for the file). On the other hand, if you want your backed up version to be encrypted, you have to unmount the loopback file system before you can copy the encrypted file—or the files will be decrypted when you move them out of the directory. Mounting and unmounting actions use shell commands—if you installed the `mountloop` package, you can use the `mountloop` and `unmountloop` programs as a normal user to do this. The other catch is that if other people can access your computer while you have the loopback file system mounted, they can access your decrypted files, if the file permissions allow them to.

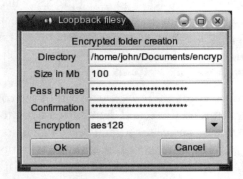

FIGURE 16.1   Creating an encrypted directory using Drakloop in Mandrake.

SUMMARY

Encryption tools take a little time to figure out, but in use they're extremely easy. If you carry around sensitive data on a laptop, use these tools to prevent losing them if your laptop gets stolen. Create a security policy specifying what employees may do with company equipment, specifying examples of risky activity they should not do—and communicate this policy to everyone in your company. Make people aware of the problem of data security, and more importantly, make them responsible for watching out for the company's interests.

Physical access to your network is often overlooked when people think about security. Plenty of sensitive data leaks into the wrong hands when a laptop containing sensitive data is stolen. Most people think that if they have a good firewall and virus filter, their network is secure—but as we've seen, there's a lot more to security than that.

In this chapter, we discussed the process of improving security, taking a holistic look at your information systems to identify the biggest weaknesses. We looked at motivations behind attackers, and what different motivations can mean to your security policy. We identified a few different ways to generate strong, memorable passwords and passphrases. We explored a few ways of detecting a system compromise. We discussed verifying software before installing, and monitoring security updates. Finally, we talked about encrypting sensitive data stored on portable computers.

In the next chapter, we take a closer look at network security, firewalls, and the additional precautions you need to take when you use a wireless network.

DATA SECURITY REFERENCES

An updated list of resources for this chapter is on the Web site for the book at *http://opensourcesmall.biz/security*.

Books

Stealing the Network: How to Own the Box, by Ryan Russell, Ido Dubrawsky, FX, Joe Grand, and Tim Mullen, Syngress 2003

Web Security, Privacy, and Commerce, by Simson Garfinkel and Gene Spafford, O'Reilly and Associates Inc., 2nd edition 2002

Articles

"Encrypted Root Filesystem HOWTO," by Christophe Devine. Available online at *http://tldp.org/HOWTO/Encrypted-Root-Filesystem-HOWTO/* .

Passphrase FAQ at Vanish.org. Available online at *http://www.vanish.org/security/ppfaq.htm*.

Software

Keyring, open source encrypted password storage for Palm OS *http://gnukeyring.sourceforge.net*

Jpilot, open source PIM software for Linux *http://www.jpilot.org*

Oubliette, open source encrypted password storage for Windows *http://sourcforge.net/projects/oubliette*

Tripwire, open source file monitoring program for Linux (commercial for Windows) *http://www.tripwire.org*

Chkrootkit, software for detecting rootkits in Unix-based systems, *http://www.chkrootkit.org*

Spybot Search and Destroy, free proprietary software for detecting spyware in Windows, *http://www.safer-networking.org*

Ad-Aware, commercial software for detecting spyware in Windows *http://www.lavasoftusa.com*

X-Cleaner, commercial software for detecting spyware in Windows, *http://www.xblock.com*

GPG, open source encryption for files and email *http://www.gnupg.org/*

kgpg, open source graphical interface for GPG in KDE *http://devel-home.kde.org/~kgpg/*

Windows Privacy Tools, open source GPG interface for Windows *http://winpt.sourceforge.net/en/*

Ccrypt, open source symmetrical encryption *http://sourceforge.net/projects/ccrypt*

Web Sites

Diceware, a system for generating random passphrases and passwords *http://www.diceware.com*

Security and Network Policy, an example security policy *http://www.linux-sec.net/Policy/*

SANS Institute Security Newsletters *http://www.sans.org/newsletters/*

Security Focus, regular security newsletters *http://www.securityfocus.com/newsletters*

Linux Security Network newsletters *http://www.linuxsecurity.com/general/newsletter.html*

17 Network Security in a Wireless World

In This Chapter

- Introduction
- Wireless Networking
- Network Security
- Setting Up A WLAN
- Mesh Networking—The Future of Wireless?
- Summary
- Wireless and Network Security References

INTRODUCTION

In Chapter 3, we discussed firewalls and routers, and detailed the basics of how networks work. Wireless is fast changing the rules. With a normal LAN, a firewall effectively separates it from the rest of the Internet. By setting strict rules about what traffic can pass in and out of your network, you can limit your exposure and thus your security risk.

This chapter is essential reading for anyone who sets up or manages wireless networks, especially if they connect to a business network. It's also essential reading for people who connect computers with sensitive data to an untrusted network, including home users.

TLA alert: if you think this book has used too many acronyms, you might think about skipping this chapter. Perhaps the only industry that relies on more obscure, impenetrable acronyms than open source computing is the telecommunications industry, and we're about to go on a short guided tour of it. If you get lost along the way, be sure to keep a bookmark in the glossary section—most of the acronyms are spelled out and defined there.

Wireless networks throw a monkey wrench into your firewall configuration: when you have a wireless network behind your firewall, rogue people can essentially connect directly to your network, behind your firewall, often without your knowledge. Furthermore, your employees who have wireless may want to connect to your LAN while they're at a public wireless hotspot, or at home.

We've already discussed all the pieces you need to help you address this problem. Chapter 3 explains networking in detail. Chapter 14 discusses specific remote access issues, along with perhaps the best solution: setting up a Virtual Private Network (VPN). Chapter 16 discussed the security implications of people gaining physical access to your computers. Let's take a look at how you put all of this together, in the context of wireless networking.

WIRELESS NETWORKING

The term *wireless* means something entirely different in 2004 than it did in 1994. What wireless is, what wireless does, changes every year as people think up new ways of using the technology. New security systems are developed, existing security systems are found to be flawed, and the whole landscape changes every year.

With this in mind, the content of this chapter may be obsolete within a couple of years. Nothing else in this book is changing quite as fast as the wireless landscape. In the time the book has been written, whole new standards have been approved, and new technology promises to change everything yet again.

But at this writing there are somewhere around 30 million Wi-Fi cards and access points in the world, and more wireless phones in the world than phones plugged into a wall. Wireless access is cheap and ubiquitous. It's likely that even if new systems are developed, much of this information will remain the same. We'll do our best to forecast the future of wireless.

What Is Wireless?

Good question. Even the experts provide conflicting definitions. You have a wireless phone, a cordless phone, Wi-Fi networks, remote controls, infrared, and something called Bluetooth, that all consider themselves to be wireless. The one thing that ties all of these devices together is that they somehow allow you to communicate data without being plugged into a wall.

Computers use several of these wireless technologies, for various purposes, in various capacities. At this writing, the wireless revolution is only at the beginning. Of all of the topics in this book, this one is changing the fastest, and by the time you read this, there may already be brand new technologies not publicized now.

So now let's get our bearings. We'll ignore your cordless telephone, but discuss the other wireless technologies as they relate to computers:

- Wireless networking with Wi-Fi
- Roaming access with cellular networks
- Small device synchronization with Bluetooth and infrared

Wireless Networking with Wi-Fi

When most people talk about a wireless network, they're referring to one of several specific systems that transfer high-speed network data over two-way radios. Apple was the first company to release Wi-Fi to general consumers in a technology they called AirPort in 1999. Since then, Wi-Fi has exploded. In 2003 alone, there were more than 22 million Wi-Fi devices sold. But when we talk about Wi-Fi, we're talking about several different standards, each with slightly different speeds and compatibilities.

The standards are determined by a group called the Institute for Electrical and Electronic Engineers, an international organization more commonly called the IEEE, pronounced "the I Triple-E." The IEEE has set up a number of committees with volunteer representative engineers from member companies. These committees set networking, telephony, and general communication standards for all kinds of electrical devices. Each committee has a number assigned to it, and most of the committees have smaller working groups that work on general types of standards. Each working group uses task groups to create individual standards. The standards then take the name of the task group.

The IEEE 802 committee defines standards for Local Area Networks (LANs) and Metropolitan Area Networks (MANs), including Ethernet (802.3), the no-longer-used token ring networking (802.5), and the Wi-Fi working group, 802.11. 802.11 includes a number of task groups that have set up the actual standards, 802.11b, 802.11a, and 802.11g. Other task groups are working on different aspects of Wi-Fi, most notably 802.11i, which should have a ratified standard for wireless authentication and encryption in place soon after this book is published.

It's easy to get confused about all these numbers, but unfortunately, there are no easier terms to describe the different standards. And it's important to be aware of which is which, because if you mix hardware that supports different standards, you may not be able to get a wireless network to work. So let's take a quick tour through the standards relevant to wireless networking in a small business.

First, let's take a look at the standards that relate to different types of cards. These standards specify a frequency range, speed, and the way the signal is digitized to travel across the radio waves. Later in this chapter we'll go over encryption and authentication issues, and the different configurations you can deploy Wi-Fi.

The Original Wi-Fi: 802.11b

Apple came out with the first consumer-oriented Wi-Fi system in 1999, calling it AirPort. It uses the 802.11b standard, which supports a theoretical 11 megabits per second (Mbps) transfer, using a specific type of spread-spectrum data transfer over 11 different, overlapping channels in the 2.4 GHz network band. That's a mouthful, isn't it? Let's break this down into what it means on a practical level.

Eleven Mbps is pretty fast, compared to your Internet connection. Cable connections in early 2004 are capable of 1.5 to 3.0 Mbps transfer, so this Wi-Fi standard appears to be much faster. However, a lot of that data transfer is overhead involved in managing the actual wireless connection, so the best data transfer speed you can actually expect is more like 5–6 Mbps. As you get further away from the base station, the signal isn't as clear so the speed goes down. The maximum range for most Wi-Fi setups is around a hundred feet, though people have managed to extend this through the use of improved antennae.

Each base station is set to use a specific channel, and you can choose among 11 of them. But because of the signal overlap, in practical use there are only three channels you can use to any effect—the highest, the lowest, and the middle. So when you set up a base station, choose channel 1, 6, or 11. If you set your station to use channel 3, it will interfere with neighboring stations that use both channel 1 and channel 6.

The 2.4 GHz spectrum is considered unlicensed in the United States, meaning that device manufacturers are free to make devices that use this spectrum, without needing a special license. As a result, there are many home devices that use this range—cordless phones and remote controls for cars. These devices can interfere with 802.11b networking.

To understand what this refers to, let's take a quick look at a more familiar type of radio—FM and AM commercial radio. Each of these is called a *radio band*, also known as a *spectrum*, and includes a range of individual frequencies. The commercial FM band uses an analog frequency modulation technique to transmit sound across radio waves, using frequencies from 88.5 MHz through 108 MHz. AM uses amplitude modulation to transmit sound in a band of frequencies from 520 KHz through 1710 KHz (or 1.710 MHz). The entire radio spectrum is divided up into different ranges, each devoted to particular purposes such as police, fire, aviation, marine, and military communications, in addition to commercial, amateur, and unlicensed bands.

Because it was the first to reach the market, 802.11b is by far the most widely implemented Wi-Fi standard. The term *Wi-Fi* was originally a marketing term for early 802.11b equipment, but now the term has been extended to include all of the related wireless technologies.

Chances are, if you have an 802.11b networking card, you'll be able to connect in any public *hotspot*, meaning a location that provides an access point for Wi-Fi users.

Faster and Less Interference: 802.11a

The next standard to reach the computer store shelves was the faster 802.11a. While 802.11b is plenty faster than most Internet connections, in practice it's much slower than wired Ethernet. Older Ethernet equipment runs at 10 Mbps, but the cost difference to put in a 100 Mbps LAN is tiny. At an effective speed of 5 or 6 Mbps, 802.11b feels very slow if you transfer a lot of big files within your LAN.

802.11a has a stated speed of up to 54 Mbps, in the 5 GHz range, with real-world data speeds of 20–24 Mbps. It gets the higher speed by sending data in parallel across several individual frequencies at the same time. The 5 GHz spectrum has been released as unlicensed bandwidth much more recently than the 2.4 GHz range, so a lot fewer devices interfere with 802.11a.

Because different network bands require different-sized antennae, very few network cards work on both 802.11a and 802.11b. So if you set up 802.11a, you'll probably need to provide network cards to go with any computers you want to use it with.

802.11a was expected to quickly eclipse 802.11b when it was released in late 2002, but it didn't, mainly because 802.11b had already sold millions of units, and was fast enough. Right now, about the only reason to get 802.11a is if you transfer a lot of multimedia streams over a wireless LAN (WLAN), and you can't get a reliable enough connection with 802.11g.

Backwards Compatibility and Speed: 802.11g

802.11a didn't become a runaway hit because 802.11g reached the market only a few months later. 802.11g offers the same network speeds as 802.11a, but it uses the same 2.4 GHz spectrum as 802.11b, making it easy for manufacturers to provide b and g with the same equipment. As a part of the new standard, all 802.11g equipment is supposed to work with 802.11b, at the slower 11 Mbps speed. Apple calls their version of 802.11g AirPort Extreme, and has added it to their new products.

One catch with the backwards compatibility is that if any device connects to an access point with 802.11b, it forces that entire network segment to use the slower speed. For this reason, in most office settings you can turn off the 802.11b compatibility and get higher speeds. You can buy an 802.11g card and use it on any public hotspot, as well as your faster office network.

Wireless for Gigabit Networks: 802.11n

At this writing, the "bleeding edge" standard of 802.11n is still on the drafting table. No devices currently support it. When the standard is finished, you'll begin to see wireless networking capable of real-world data transmission speeds of at least 100 Mbps, the speed of most Ethernet installations. It's designed to either replace Ethernet in small offices, providing even better performance, or to work with the relatively new Gigabit Ethernet, which provides around 1,000 Mbps of transfer.

Gigabit Ethernet is still more expensive than is warranted by most small businesses, and 802.11n will likely fall into this higher, premium price range.

802.11n is supposed to be ratified by the end of 2005, and be backwards compatible with all of the standards discussed above, including 802.11a in the 5 GHz band.

Roaming Access with Cellular Networks

The biggest issue with Wi-Fi is your dependence on being near an access point or hotspot. You lose your connection as soon as you get a hundred feet or so away.

For most of the 1990s, wireless meant cellular networks. Your cell phone uses remarkably similar technology to connect to cell towers placed at specific locations within and around cities, and across the countryside. There are, of course, several differences between Wi-Fi and wireless telephony—but as both technologies develop, the key differences are disappearing. The main differences are that cellular networks use much more power to cover distances of miles, rather than dozens of feet, and that because of this higher power, it uses licensed spectrum—each carrier has an exclusive license to use a particular set of frequencies for their service. In the United States, the Federal Communications Commission (FCC) is the agency that licenses this spectrum.

The term *cellular* is somewhat outdated—it technically refers to the first generation analog cell phones. A whole host of digital transmission technologies replaced the original cellular services, allowing a single cell tower to support many more handsets. These second generation digital technologies include acronyms like CDMA, PCS, TDMA, and GSM—if you really want to know what these acronyms stand for, see the glossary. These second generation technologies were the first to make wireless communications with a computer possible, though limited to speeds a lot slower than plain old telephone service (POTS to the telecommunications industry).

In the late 1990s, the telecommunications industry was all abuzz with the newest digital technologies, collectively called *3G* for "third generation." 3G technologies promise to bring broadband speeds to cellular-type wireless networks, though these speeds so far have ended up in the 200–300 Kbps range—less than 1/10th the speed of 802.11b.

So what do cellular networks have to do with computers? First of all, you could connect a laptop to a cell phone and dial up to the Internet several years before Wi-Fi was available, and on many phones and services, this is still available. Secondly, you can get cellular modems, essentially cell phones for your computer that connect you to the wireless grid, providing you with much better coverage (at least in the near term). Finally, cell phones themselves are becoming more and more like small computers, as many of the functions of PDAs get added to them, along with the ability to send pictures and text messages.

Wi-Fi networking in many ways is the opposite of cellular. Right now Wi-Fi networks are basically tiny hotspots scattered around cities, owned and maintained by individuals and businesses, connected to the Internet through cable or phone lines. Cellular networks, on the other hand, are big, centralized systems managed by wireless companies, that provide limited bandwidth to limited devices but with much broader coverage. The interesting point of convergence involves companies like T-Mobile, who now provides both cellular service and a network of Wi-Fi hotspots.

Every cellular network provider provides its own hardware and software to access its service. Because of the strict licensing of these networks, you can't just buy a generic card and expect it to work with a major carrier. If you need the ability to connect your computer at moderately high speeds anywhere your cell phone works, check out these services.

Related to cellular technologies are satellite connections. Outside the range of cell towers, cable connections, and DSL, you may find your only option for reasonably high-speed access is to use a satellite service. These, too, require special hardware and software to be able to access the service.

For most small businesses, Wi-Fi is a much better value than satellite or cellular. You buy the equipment once, and add it to a less expensive broadband Internet connection you already need for your business. You can then share the service among all your employees, and also access the Internet and your LAN from any of the rapidly increasing number of public hotspots.

Small Device Synchronization

A completely different type of wireless works more like your TV and car remote controls. There are actually two different standards we're going to discuss here that are completely unrelated other than in their use.

The first is infrared. The Infrared Data Association (IRDA) specifies how to use infrared light to communicate data between devices. This is exactly the technology used by most TV remotes. Infrared falls between radio waves and visible light in the electromagnetic spectrum. Because it's so close to light in the electromagnetic spectrum, it doesn't travel through walls or clothing, and it depends on a line of sight between both ends of the connection.

IRDA is perhaps the oldest form of wireless computing to reach the mainstream market, making its first appearance in the early 1990s. Microsoft Windows 95 included support for IRDA. Many laptops had built-in IRDA ports, and some still do. Most PDAs use IRDA to "beam" information to another PDA, and if you have an IRDA port on your computer, you can usually get your PDA to synchronize using it. You can even get software for a PDA to turn it into a universal remote control for your TV, VCR, DVD player, or stereo.

It's possible to set up point-to-point networking between two computers using IRDA, but due to the fact that you need to keep the devices aimed at each other, it isn't the most conducive technology for providing networks. At best, it's useful for transferring files between two computers without needing to set up a network. IRDA seems to have stalled—while most operating systems support it, very few new projects do much with it.

Bluetooth is the other short range wireless computing technology. Like 802.11b and g, it operates in the 2.4 GHz range. Bluetooth is specifically designed to replace cords that connect devices. You can get Bluetooth-enabled cell phones, PDAs, mice, keyboards, computers, digital cameras, printers, scanners, mp3 players, even earphones. These devices communicate over a variety of different Bluetooth standards at extremely low power, with a range of under 30 feet. Bluetooth essentially combines the security and wireless aspects of IRDA with the plug-and-play nature of USB hardware.

Using Bluetooth, you can set up a PDA to automatically synchronize its contacts and appointments when you walk into range of your PC. You can set your cell phone down next to your laptop, and use Bluetooth to synchronize phone numbers—or to have your laptop use your cell phone to connect to the Internet. You can listen to music on Bluetooth headphones that don't even have a cord connecting them to your mp3 player, and transfer music wirelessly between the mp3 player and your computer.

Bluetooth has had a lot of hype surrounding it since around 1999, but Wi-Fi beat it to the market. Wi-Fi only provides wireless networking, using Ethernet, but it does it much faster and at greater ranges. In 2003, Bluetooth devices finally started gaining moderate use.

IRDA and Bluetooth are both supported in Windows, Mac, and Linux. With the proper drivers set up, these devices should "just work." Most applications don't really know whether a device is connected by USB, serial port, or Bluetooth.

Wireless Insecurity

The ability to connect to networks and devices wirelessly, bypassing what might otherwise become a massive tangle of wires, is an amazing revolution. It's also a security nightmare. When all data traffic in and out of a computer goes through copper wires, it's easy to put a firewall in between your LAN and the rest of the world, and be confident that you'll at least detect compromises. With wireless, you can never be sure. Somebody can easily put in some sort of receiver and intercept all of the traffic within your network. Your neighbors might eavesdrop on your network activity, and you would never know the difference.

It's not quite that simple. All of the radio-based wireless systems use multiple frequencies, breaking up packets of the data and sending each message spread across the band. But because these devices all need to interoperate, it's easy to obtain hardware that's compatible with whichever system you're using.

In Bluetooth and IRDA, this is less a problem because the range is so short, and you need to tell each device to connect to the other one. Bluetooth has some built-in encryption to make sure data can only be understood by the other end of the connection. Cellular systems have their own systems for security, tightly controlled and managed by the carrier. No major exploits have been publicized for these systems. Because of these factors, for the rest of this chapter we will focus on Wi-Fi.

The Weakness of WEP

Wi-Fi has had encryption right from the beginning. The original form of wireless encryption was called Wired-Equivalent Privacy, or WEP. Right from the beginning, WEP was considered to be flawed, but it was successfully compromised very shortly after Wi-Fi products hit the market. Since 1999, WEP has been strengthened by using longer keys, but the basic problem is that the keys do not change frequently enough. Each packet uses a key derived from the original key, and after a certain number of packets, the original key is repeated. You can download free software for cracking WEP encryption, and collect enough data to reveal the key in an hour of eavesdropping on a busy network, or in a few days on a lightly used network. And once you have the key, you can connect to a WEP-protected network easily.

The other access control provided with WEP is called MAC address control. A MAC address is a unique hardware Ethernet address, much like a serial number, built into every network device. The problem is, it's easy to make a network card "spoof" a different MAC address, and if you've already cracked the WEP key, it's easy to see what MAC addresses are in use.

In short, WEP provides perhaps around five hours of protection every time you change the key. Long enough to discourage the drive-by snooper, but way too short to keep your neighbors out of your network, or to stop a determined attacker parked in a neighboring lot.

WPA Wars

To provide better security, several manufacturers worked together to create a new encryption standard called Wi-Fi Protected Access (WPA) at the end of 2002. WPA makes use of yet another 802 standard, 802.1X, which specifies a way to authenticate a user before a network connection is completed. The simplest type of authentication from a user point of view works the same as WEP—everybody uses a shared secret key as a passphrase for authentication. However, in WEP this key is used directly to encrypt the data. In WPA, the key is only used for authentication, and then a new key is generated and exchanged. This new key is different for each client, and expires after a short period of time, replaced by a new randomly generated one.

The 802.1X standard allows many different authentication methods. In larger enterprises, you can set up an authentication server somewhere behind the access point and use public key encryption, as we discussed in Chapter 15. Your computer signs and encrypts a message using the public key of the authentication server. The access point forwards this message to the access point, which decrypts it, verifies your signature, and encrypts a secret key to your public key. Once the entire authentication sequence happens, the access point connects your computer to the network.

In either case, the actual encryption of each packet uses an older symmetrical encryption algorithm. This algorithm isn't the strongest, but because the keys rotate frequently, WPA is considered moderately secure. Furthermore, it's designed to work on original 802.11b hardware, as well as g and a, through firmware upgrades.

The problem is, even though WPA was developed and released in December 2002, in January 2004 it was not widely supported. Microsoft developed WPA one way, Cisco and most of the rest of the companies involved in its creation developed it a different way. The Microsoft and Cisco implementations are not compatible. So while WPA has been deployed in several enterprise companies, the largest of which being Microsoft itself, it has not seen widespread adoption. And very few people using Wi-Fi have even heard of it, more than a year after its release. Most manufacturers of Wi-Fi hardware have only released updates for their newer 802.11g equipment, and support is spotty.

Integrating with 802.11i

At the time of this book's publication, yet another wireless encryption standard is right around the corner. The 802.11i task group is due to make its standard official in June 2004. It's related to WPA in that it uses the 802.1X authentication algorithm, but to encrypt the actual data, it uses the Advanced Encryption Standard (AES), the current premier encryption algorithm. AES is believed to be the most secure symmetrical encryption algorithm available, and it takes less processing power than the older, weaker 3DES. But it takes more computing power than is available on most current Wi-Fi cards, so it's going to require new hardware.

Which Encryption Should I Use?

So as you can see, there are problems with all of these wireless encryption standards. WEP can be easily cracked. WPA is implemented inconsistently, and you may have a hard time getting your systems to work together. And 802.11i will require new hardware, leaving old hardware vulnerable and obsolete. Given that there is somewhere around 30 million Wi-Fi network devices already sold, it's not likely that this situation will change anytime soon. You could shell out enough money to buy hardware that supports WPA or 802.11i (whenever it becomes available). Or you could do what security-conscious businesses have done since WEP was broken:

treat the wireless network as untrusted, and put a firewall between it and your critical systems. Then you can use remote access software as described in Chapter 14 to access the services you need. A VPN can work particularly well to secure your traffic from a wireless laptop to your LAN. Then if the WEP encryption is cracked, the actual data you're passing is still encrypted.

NETWORK SECURITY

We'll come back to Wi-Fi networks shortly. First, let's discuss some of the basics of network security. If your Wi-Fi network has the same trustworthiness as the general Internet, we can apply the same approaches to network security for both. In Chapter 16, we covered security of physical access to your computers. In this section, we'll take a look at some network security strategies.

Segmenting Your Network

One of the principles of security is granting least access—you disable everything, and then only enable what you need to do your job. In the same way, you can block access to services that do not need to be public. That's the basic purpose of a firewall. But if you run a Web server or an email server, you generally need to make these available to the Internet, or the outside world can't reach them. And if your Web server somehow gets compromised, the attacker gains a foothold behind your firewall, where he could then potentially jump to more sensitive file servers, accounting systems, and other things you'd rather keep private.

So how do you lessen the risk? You create a separate network segment for your public servers, isolated from the private servers and the rest of your LAN. In this case, the segment containing these servers is called a De-Militarized Zone (DMZ), named after the no man's land between North and South Korea. The idea behind a DMZ is that it's technically part of your network, but may be compromised by the enemy.

Firewalls often come with three network adapters for this purpose. The open source Smoothwall firewall (*http://www.smoothwall.org*) can automatically configure these network adapters, using color coding to represent the networks. The red network adapter is connected to the public Internet. The orange zone is the DMZ. The green zone is your trusted LAN. You can then configure the firewall to block traffic according to sensible rules. You can allow all traffic from the green zone, but drop all traffic going to it. You can allow traffic from the orange zone to the red zone, but not the green zone. You can allow traffic from the red zone to the specific services in the orange zone, but not to other services, or the green zone. You put the green LAN zone on one private network space, and the orange DMZ zone on a different subnet.

Using this same technique, you could create another zone for a wireless segment, separating it from your private LAN. You would then set up a VPN connection to allow remote machines to connect to the green zone, either from a remote Internet machine or from a computer on the wireless zone.

With this arrangement, your entire network can use a single public IP address, corresponding to the red interface on your firewall. You might set up your green LAN to use the 192.168.1.* private network, your DMZ to be on the 192.168.2.* subnet, and then add a wireless card to the firewall and have it provide addresses to wireless clients on the 192.168.3.* network. This arrangement is illustrated in Figure 17.1.

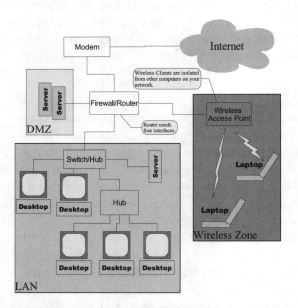

FIGURE 17.1 Segmenting your network with LAN, DMZ, and Wireless zones.

If you have a dedicated wireless access point, you could hook it up so that the public side is connected to the DMZ. See Figure 17.2 for this arrangement. In this case, wireless clients can connect to all the services on the DMZ, not just the ones forwarded by the firewall. If you copy files to your Web server over Windows Networking (Samba), this opens another potential security weakness.

Figure 17.3 illustrates one more possible way to configure your network. In this arrangement, you need to have a second public IP address—one for your wireless network, the other for your regular firewall, protecting the DMZ and LAN.

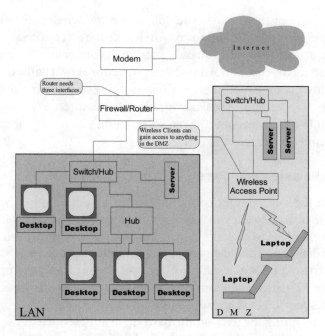

FIGURE 17.2   Wireless segment attached to the DMZ.

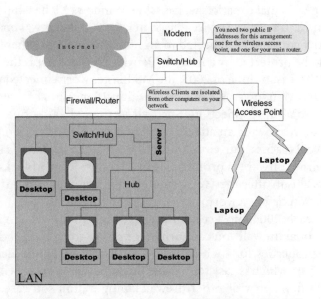

FIGURE 17.3   Wireless segment outside your firewall.

In any of these cases, you can set up the wireless network completely unencrypted, because the only way wireless computers access your private services is through a VPN or other already encrypted connection. Using WEP or WPA can be additional overhead, slowing down your connection without adding much value. If you don't encrypt your connections, nothing stops your neighbors from using your connection, so you're basically providing free Internet access within a hundred feet or so of your access point. Even so, you don't have any more security risk running it completely unprotected.

Secure Your Remote Computers

When the core servers containing sensitive data have been isolated from public servers by a firewall, you have significantly increased the security of those servers. The next place to look is at any other computer that might have a copy of that sensitive data. You should consider any computer that connects to any network besides your trusted LAN as a remote extension of your LAN, and protect it appropriately. If it has sensitive data and uses wireless, or connects directly to the Internet, it should be protected appropriately.

Encrypting the data on the hard drive as described at the end of Chapter 16 reduces the risks associated with physical theft of the computer. But while you're logged on, in most cases the files are decrypted, and potentially vulnerable to an attack over the network. These remote computers represent a huge hole in the security of your network. To make matters worse, while Windows XP has shipped with a built-in firewall, it wasn't until a service release in late 2003 that it was enabled by default.

Any computer connected to an untrusted network that has sensitive data on it should be protected by a firewall. Period. The Internet is the biggest untrusted network there is. In June of 2003, the MS Blaster worm infected unprotected Windows 2000 and Windows XP computers within 15 minutes of them being connected to a regular dial-up connection. Such viruses could easily open a back door to your computer, allowing an attacker to download files of his choice.

We'll discuss anti-virus software in Chapter 19, but it's important to note that anti-virus software is protection of last resort: it only blocks viruses and worms it knows about, after they've attempted to infect your computer. A firewall provides protection before a worm can infect your computer.

In early 2004, most computers have built-in firewalls. Windows XP has a built-in personal firewall you can turn on or off by going to the advanced tab of the network properties for each connection. Mandrake Linux includes a firewall called Shorewall, which is easy to manage through Webmin (see Chapter 2). Other Linux distributions provide other firewall configuration software, all of which basically manage rules for IP tables, the firewall built into the Linux kernel. Mac OS X added a personal firewall based on the Unix firewall.

What Does a Firewall Do?

We discussed the basics of networking in Chapter 3, and talked about firewalls towards the end of that chapter. A firewall blocks TCP/IP traffic based on the contents of individual packets. You configure a firewall using rules that specify what to do with packets that match a particular profile. The firewall works with a concept of zones, and on a personal firewall, these zones will include the Internet or untrusted zone, and the computer or trusted zone. Most commonly, when you turn on a personal firewall, it will use a rule set that specifies something like this:

1. If the packet is coming from the untrusted zone, and is a response to an earlier outgoing packet, allow it.
2. If the packet is coming from the untrusted zone, and is an ICMP ping, respond to it.
3. If the packet is coming from the trusted zone, allow it.
4. Don't respond to everything else—just drop the packet.

If you're configuring a firewall for your LAN, you will likely add quite a few more rules, forwarding traffic for specific ports to the appropriate server on the other side, specifying behavior between a trusted zone and a DMZ, and perhaps restricting outgoing traffic, channeling it through specific ports or through a proxy server.

It's important to note that these firewalls only block traffic through a network adapter—they do nothing to interfere with Bluetooth or other types of wireless. It's also important to notice that these firewalls operate at the TCP/IP level, which is above the Ethernet layer. It's possible for traffic that uses other protocols, such as NetBEUI or SPX/IPX, to bypass a TCP/IP protocol. These protocols cannot travel over the Internet, but if you connect to an Ethernet network in some public location, you should make sure these protocols are disabled or not installed.

Restricting Outgoing Traffic

Blocking incoming traffic is the main function of a firewall, but many larger companies also block outgoing traffic. If people behind the firewall use a relatively limited set of services, this is quite easy to do. You set up rules on the firewall that allow traffic from the trusted zone to the ports corresponding to the services you want to allow, and then block all other traffic. If you host your own email servers, and provide everything your employees actually need to use internally on your LAN, you could restrict all outgoing traffic, and allow only Web connections to port 80, or port 443 for SSL-encrypted Web sites. Then allow particular computers, such as your official mail server, to make outgoing connections on the proper ports.

There are a few benefits you might gain by doing this:

- Cut down on traffic through your Internet connection, saving bandwidth for specific purposes
- Stymie crackers and viruses that manage to compromise an internal machine—your firewall would block back doors in internal machines
- Filter out undesirable content, through the use of a proxy server that blocks connections to particular Web sites, or only allows connections to particular Web sites
- Prevent poorly configured machines from "leaking" information to neighboring networks

For most small businesses, these measures are overkill, causing more nuisance for your users than the extra security they provide. Quite often in larger organizations you'll find what amounts to a battle between the IT departments, who are trying to lock down access, and the general users who want to listen to streaming media while they work, conduct research on sites that have been intentionally or accidentally blocked, or simply access a service they need to do their job.

If your company is at the limits of its bandwidth, a proxy server may be the solution. Proxy servers cache frequently requested pages, eliminating the need to get the same unchanging page multiple times, greatly saving bandwidth on your Internet connection. It's also good to block outgoing packets on ports for particularly vulnerable services, such as Windows Networking, Universal Plug-and-Play, and RPC services. These services work very well in a LAN environment, but should not be broadcasting data to the Internet. Blocking everything else should only be done as a last resort, if you find that you have a security problem you can't solve any other way. Squid (*http://www.squid-cache.org/*) is an open source proxy server that runs on Linux servers.

Firewalls on Wireless Computers

Your wired LAN should have a firewall protecting it from the outside world, both from wireless networks and the Internet. Remote computers that access sensitive data on your LAN should always have a firewall protecting it from other computers on the Internet, or on a wireless LAN. When the remote computer is a desktop in somebody's home, it's relatively easy and inexpensive to set up a broadband router/firewall that protects the home computer from the Internet. If it's a computer with a wireless card, you need to turn on the firewall directly on the computer, protecting all traffic on the wireless connection.

With most firewalls, you can choose which network interface to protect with the firewall. You can protect as many interfaces, or connections, as you want. You should have the firewall protect all dial-up connections, all wireless connections, and any Ethernet connections you might plug into an untrusted network. To access your LAN through any of these connections, you can use a VPN as discussed in Chapter 14. A VPN connection might appear as a separate network interface, or as a dial-up connection for PPTP VPNs. You will need to make sure the firewall is disabled on the VPN connection (the virtual connection for the VPN, not the connection you're using to connect to the Internet!), or you won't be able to connect to services on your LAN. You can also disable the firewall for Ethernet connections you only use to plug into a trusted LAN.

Intrusion Detection

In Chapter 16, we discussed monitoring critical files as a way to detect a system compromise. A similar approach can be used to monitor network connections for suspicious activity. Programs that monitor the network for penetration attempts are called Intrusion Detection Systems (IDS). One of the best known, most effective IDS packages is the open source Snort™ program (*http://www.snort.org/*). Snort can be used to monitor network traffic, log network activity, or to set up a full-blown IDS using a flexible language for creating rules.

While the principles of using an IDS are fairly straightforward, using one takes time and attention. You can set up rules to automatically notify you of certain types of network events, but staying on top of these is a full-time job. Inevitably the automatic rules you set up give you too many false alarms, or fail to detect real problems. An IDS in the hands of an experienced security professional is a powerful tool, but if it's not monitored, and if nobody reviews the rules and the logs, an IDS doesn't do much to protect your network.

Another related open source IDS project is Prelude (*http://www.prelude-ids.org*). Prelude provides a more sophisticated framework, allowing you to deploy "sensors," programs installed on computers in different segments of your LAN, and combining all of the data from multiple sources. Prelude can be configured to gather data from your entire network, not just one particular machine. On the other hand, deploying and using it successfully depends on the experience and attention given by a security administrator.

These are a couple of the tools used by security professionals. By themselves, these tools do not provide security. If you're a high-profile company, or are a target for attackers for some reason, the best thing to do is hire a savvy security professional to help keep your data secure. At this level, you see crackers pitted against security professionals, each trying to outsmart the other in a game with your sensitive data as the prize. Don't take these measures lightly.

Types of Attacks

Let's take a look at common ways people attack networks and services.

Buffer Overflows

Read the security bulletins, and you'll find a large number of vulnerabilities that take advantage of *buffer overflows*. So what's a buffer overflow?

Whenever a program accepts data, it puts the data in a section of memory called a buffer. If the program accepts more data than the amount of memory allocated to the buffer, it needs to do something with that extra data. Most scripting languages and higher-level languages simply ignore the extra data. But for low-level languages that integrate tightly with the operating system, the programmer has to be careful to specifically stop accepting data before the buffer overflows. The problem is, buffers are used extensively throughout the code, and sometimes in ways that bypass the checks a programmer has put in. Buffer overflows are particularly prevalent in programs written in the C or C++ languages—high-performance, low-level languages used for operating systems, drivers, and most programs that need maximum speed.

What happens with a buffer overflow is that the extra data actually overwrites some of the program in memory. Crafty attackers figure out an exact sequence of data to send that rewrites the parts of the program that happen to be in memory just above the buffer, allowing them to do things like start a remote shell, or open up some back door.

To protect against buffer overflows, it helps to run server software under unprivileged user accounts on the system, confining the damage to whatever that user account can access. Installing patches that fix buffer overflow vulnerabilities is crucial—somebody in your organization needs to monitor security lists, staying abreast of new vulnerabilities as they're discovered.

A new tactic to reduce buffer overflows is to add protective code in the compiler, the program that turns the source code into executable code. By building in protection from buffer overflows in the compiler logic, it will hopefully improve the overall security of programs, protecting vulnerabilities that haven't yet been discovered.

As you might guess, buffer overflows tend to be more of a problem in large, complicated, monolithic software than in small modular programs.

Web Application Vulnerabilities

Higher-level languages, such as those used on Web servers to make Web applications, don't have to worry about allocating buffers and keeping track of where things are in memory. The individual languages keep track of these types of details for you.

Higher-level languages can be vulnerable to different types of exploits, however. These are usually a result of accepting input from the user without verifying its contents well enough, and can be especially common in PHP-based applications.

Here are three common types of problems:

Cross-site scripting: entering code instead of data into a Web site. This type of vulnerability is common on guest book-types of sites. The attacker puts what looks like an innocent link into a post. When somebody clicks this link, the attacker can "hijack" the user's session, revealing the contents of a cookie, allowing them to impersonate the user. This is especially dangerous on a site that does e-commerce.

SQL Injection: providing malformed data that has unintended results in a database. Many PHP applications use an SQL database to store data behind the scenes. By passing a special SQL request, the attacker can piggyback an additional SQL query to the request, potentially changing data already in the database.

Remote Code Execution: running code provided by a remote server. This is by far the most dangerous type of vulnerability. It's possible to include files from other servers and execute them as if they were on the original Web server. The attacker fools the site into loading a script from a server controlled by the attacker, and from there, can execute just about any command he wants.

These vulnerabilities are all easy to fix by simply checking everything a user provides before trusting it, through a process called validation. With good software application design, these vulnerabilities should never be an issue. But due to how easy it is to create a Web application in languages like PHP, many people develop them without paying much attention to security. The inevitable results are vulnerable applications.

If you use Web applications developed by someone else, keep aware of vulnerabilities in them. For major software packages, these are all announced on security mailing lists, as are the buffer overflows. If you've developed your own, design them carefully to validate any information coming from client software on the server—do not trust client-side validation scripts, as they can be easily bypassed.

Denial of Service

So far in our network security discussion, we've mostly focused on attacks that result in a compromise of your network. These are rare, especially if you take basic precautions like using a firewall, segmenting your networks, and keeping your software up to date. Much more common is the Denial Of Service (DOS) attack. The purpose of a denial of service attack is not to compromise your network so much as to make your network or particular services unavailable. This is much more a nuisance factor than a security risk.

On the other hand, if your business depends upon providing a service over a network, being prevented from providing that service may have a direct impact on your business. Online companies such as Amazon, eBay, and Yahoo! have much more at stake if their Web site becomes unavailable, compared to the situation if the corner hardware store's network goes down.

Denial Of Service is a result of, rather than a specific type of attack. There are many different ways to attack a network to cause a denial of service:

- Cut power to a key network device
- Overload the weakest part of a network, such as an authentication server, with more traffic than it can handle
- Make the server crash

Recovering from a denial of service is easy, but preventing one can be very difficult. One common technique for overloading a server involves compromising computers scattered all over the Internet, and coordinating them to attack one particular target at the same time. Several recent viruses, including Code Red and MS Blaster, have attempted to do this—Code Red by attacking the White House Web site, MS Blaster by attacking the Microsoft Windows Update site. Both of these attempts failed, but other more limited ones have succeeded, taking out Web sites for hours. This type of attack is called a Distributed Denial Of Service attack.

Wireless networks have other denial of service vulnerabilities. It's possible to disrupt wireless signals with a strong transmitter that broadcasts signals that interfere with your Wi-Fi connection. Cellular networks can be vulnerable to a completely non-human threat, such as large solar flares that bombard the Earth with strong signals at the height of the sunspot cycle. The newer WPA encryption system can be jammed by several computers submitting bogus authentication requests, blocking access to legitimate users.

For all the nuisance of denial of service attacks, in most cases you can locate the source and block their access. Wi-Fi units are small radios, and can be located with special receivers. Distributed DOS attacks can be identified and dropped by higher capacity routers upstream of your network location, with the help of your service provider. For natural interference you just have to wait for it to end, or use alternative systems.

SETTING UP A WLAN

Enough with the security issues. Let's take a look at how you set up and use a Wi-Fi network. As you might guess by now, there are many different ways to set it up. If you have no particular security concerns, you can simply get a wireless router, plug the wide area network port into your broadband connection, and you're set up. At a minimum, change the password on the wireless router to something other than the default, and set the SSID for the router to a single word identifier. You can use whatever word you want as the SSID—it's just a way of identifying this access point. If you want to prevent others from using your connection, set up encryption and access control based on the instructions for the unit, and turn off broadcasting of the SSID.

This wireless router becomes the access point for your wireless network, in what is called a managed connection, or infrastructure mode. If you keep encryption off, wireless clients should automatically discover the access point, and start using it. All you need is a wireless network card using compatible standards. Windows, Mac, and Linux will automatically find and start using unencrypted, broadcast networks.

Getting WEP to Work

If you turn on WEP encryption, you'll need to configure the network card with the appropriate encryption key. If you have trouble connecting, you may need to set the wireless card to connect to your specific SSID. Another thing that might cause issues with WEP is key sharing. Most wireless cards allow you to store up to four different WEP keys, selecting one to use at a time. There are a couple different modes of using WEP keys, and different manufacturers name them different ways. One mode is usually called Open System or just Open; the other is called Shared Key or Restricted. To get WEP to work, you need to use the same key settings on all devices.

Another confusing issue with WEP is the key itself. There are three different key lengths for WEP: 64, 128, and 256 bits. Each manufacturer of WEP-compatible equipment seems to support key generation using either hexadecimal keys or ASCII text—but some manufacturers use the ASCII text to generate a key, and for other manufacturers the ASCII text is the key. To make matters more confusing, there's a bit of overhead in the key, so some manufacturers list the key length including the overhead, while others exclude it. 64-bit encryption in WEP is the same thing as 40-bit encryption, and 128-bit encryption is the same thing as 104-bit encryption.

With that explanation understood, you need to provide a key of the correct length. For a 64-bit key, you need to provide five characters, or hexadecimal bytes. For a 128-bit key, you need to provide 13 characters or hexadecimal bytes. For a

256-bit key, provide 29 characters or bytes. See *http://www.digitwebsites.net/ wepkeys.php* for a handy tool to generate WEP keys, and links to explain how to get WEP working with different brands of equipment.

For WPA to work, you need to have firmware that supports it on both the access point and the wireless card. For current equipment, this means a firmware upgrade. You may be able to buy newer equipment to get it to work. WPA also depends on new drivers, and new client software. At this writing, there is no open source support for WPA, though it's now available with Apple Airport Extreme equipment, and Microsoft is providing the software to support it in a Windows XP service pack.

At this writing, there is no support for the 802.11i standard, as it hasn't yet been ratified.

Creating Your Own Access Points

Wi-Fi supports two basic modes of operation: Infrastructure and Ad Hoc. Infrastructure mode, also called Managed mode, is set up so that several wireless clients communicate with an access point that acts as a gateway to the rest of the Internet. Aside from just buying an access point appliance, with Linux and some other open source software you can set up your own access points, programming them to do all sorts of things.

For example, you could put a wireless card in your firewall, and set it up to run as an access point, automatically providing a DMZ for the wireless segment of your network. You can also reuse old computers for the purpose, extending the range of your wireless network.

Consumer wireless access points often have buggy firmware, leading to frequent disconnects and reboots. Running a Linux box as an access point often leads to better stability, and can give you the ability to better manage the whole system. You also may be able to put together a system to support newer standards like 802.11i as they get released, without having to upgrade your hardware.

Wireless Bridge

A network bridge is a way of making two different Ethernet or TCP/IP subnets act like one. You start with two or more network interfaces, and bridge them together. Traffic can then flow freely between the networks on either side. The bridge itself has a single IP address, representing the device hosting the bridge.

A wireless bridge is a way to connect two wired networks that have no physical connection between them. For example, you might have one network running in your main office, with a broadband connection and a wireless access point. You have a separate network in your shop, across a parking lot from the office. There are no network wires running to the shop, but you want computers in the shop to be connected. By setting up a wireless bridge in the shop, you can connect that secondary network to the primary office network, without running a cable.

One interface of the wireless bridge is the wireless part. The other interface is a network card, attached to a switch that connects to the other shop computers. The bridge connects the wireless to the wired network, transparently bridging the whole thing to your office network.

You can buy special wireless bridge devices that do this, or you can set up a computer to act as the bridge. Bridging is supported in Windows XP Professional, but not Windows 2000 or earlier. Bridging is also supported in Linux. However, there are some technical challenges to getting bridging to work with 802.11. Check out *http://bridge.sourceforge.net* for more information, or buy a network bridge device.

Multiple Access Points

When you need to cover a wide area with wireless coverage, you'll probably end up installing multiple access points. Generally, all you have to do is put them on non-overlapping frequencies, and use the same SSID. For example, you can set up three wireless access points, using channels 1, 6, and 11. Connect each to the same network segment, and your wireless clients should be able to get a strong signal anywhere in the area.

There can be problems with the connection handing off from access point to access point if the wireless client is moving. Some of the client software attempts to maintain a connection as long as possible, even when there's a stronger connection available. If you read the documentation for the driver software on the client, you can find out how to get it to automatically choose the strongest signal.

Ad Hoc Mode

The other mode you can use in Wi-Fi, besides infrastructure, is ad hoc mode. With ad hoc mode, you don't need any access point. You can connect directly to any other compatible Wi-Fi device in range. This is called peer-to-peer networking. To set it up, you configure all of the Wi-Fi computers to use the same SSID. You may also need to configure IP addresses manually to get networking fully working, if none of the computers are providing a DHCP service.

Ad hoc mode is very rarely used at this writing, but it holds great potential for community networks, or sharing services spontaneously.

MESH NETWORKING—THE FUTURE OF WIRELESS?

The hidden potential provided by wireless networks is the ability to do away completely with wired networks. Several companies are working on ways to provide high bandwidth through ad hoc networking. Called mesh networks, the basic idea is that wireless data hops from computer to computer through the air until it reaches its final destination, without ever needing to go through the phone lines. As more computers join and leave the network, it automatically adjusts, figuring out the best paths for data to travel. The more people that join the network, the more bandwidth everybody can use.

It's a very intriguing idea, and technically possible, but in practice nobody has quite gotten it to work. Hybrid systems work very well, however. In the UK, there are plans to install Wi-Fi units in lamp posts throughout the country, with a stated purpose of providing a way to track speeding. But these lamp posts communicate with each other in a massive grid, and some of them will be connected (by wire) directly to the Internet, providing nearly ubiquitous Wi-Fi access in Britain.

Another movement springing up in all sorts of corners in the world is the idea of community wireless networks. These networks are put together by volunteers who install access points in their homes and various locations, providing free access to anyone who wants to use them. In many cases, these networks don't provide Internet access—some are being built purely to provide an alternative. Inevitably these will grow to include Internet access, or die out.

Mesh networking and community Wi-Fi networks promise to totally change the way we connect to the Internet, and even how we make a phone call. Only time will tell how these technologies work out.

SUMMARY

In this chapter, we started out by looking at wireless networking. We learned about the different types of wireless available at the beginning of 2004, and various attempts to encrypt data over wireless connections. We then focused on network security, discussing the role of firewalls and intrusion detection in protecting your network. We examined the most common types of network attacks. Then we gave some practical advice for setting up a secure wireless network for your business. Finally, we attempted to identify some future trends in wireless.

In the next chapter, we take a look at how to recover from a network compromise and other disasters.

WIRELESS AND NETWORK SECURITY REFERENCES

An updated list of resources for this chapter is on the Web site for the book at *http://opensourcesmall.biz/wireless.*

Articles

"Wireless lamp posts take over world!" by Guy Kewney. Available online at *http://theregister.co.uk/content/69/34894.html*

"Radio Spectrum Chart." Available online at *http://www.ntia.doc.gov/os-mhome/allochrt.html*

"Bluetooth And Linux." Available online at *http://www.holtmann.org/linux/bluetooth/*

"Linux wireless how-to." Available online at *http://www.hpl.hp.com/personal/Jean_Tourrilhes/Linux/Wireless.html*

Software

Linux WLAN-NG drivers *http://www.linux-wlan.com/linux-wlan/*
Smoothwall Firewall *http://www.smoothwall.org*
Shorewall Firewall *http://www.shorewall.net*
Squid, open source caching proxy server *http://www.squid-cache.org*
Snort, open source intrusion detection system *http://www.snort.org*
Prelude Intrusion Detection System *http://www.prelude-ids.org*
Linux bridge tools *http://bridge.sourceforge.net*

Web Sites

Infrared Data Association *http://www.irda.org*
IEEE *http://www.ieee.org*
802.11 Working Group *http://grouper.ieee.org/groups/802/11/*
WEP key generator *http://www.digitwebsites.net/wepkeys.php*

18 | Disaster Recovery

In This Chapter

- Introduction
- Strategies for Disaster Recovery
- Backup Procedures
- Summary
- Disaster Recovery References

INTRODUCTION

Everybody knows you're supposed to back up your computer, but most businesses who don't have a dedicated IT staff never do. Ask a small business owner the last time he backed up his computer, and chances are he'll squirm and have to think for a while.

This chapter is meant for whoever is responsible for making sure your data is properly backed up. If you run any database applications, Subversion repositories, or other applications that store data in anything other than a normal file, be sure to pay attention to the special notes for these types of applications to back them up properly. This may take some shell scripting to do right, because it is fairly technical.

But an even worse situation is when somebody does regular backups, but never checks to see if they work or learns how to recover from a backup. Backups by themselves are useless. What's important is that you have a strategy to recover from whatever caused you to lose your information in the first place.

Why Do Backups?

The biggest reason people don't do backups is because they're inconvenient. They're inconvenient because generally the media you use to store the backups

411

(floppies, zip drives), generally have a lot less capacity than the hard drive you're trying to back up. To make the job easier, you could get progressively bigger media: CD-ROM, DVD-RW, tape drives, additional hard drives. Doing so costs money, however, and doesn't necessarily make recovery much easier.

As hard drives have become cheaper, the simplest way to do a backup is to simply copy your documents to multiple computers. As we saw in Chapter 9, though, having multiple copies of a document can make finding the most recent one a challenge. Implementing a revision control system offers a few benefits—you can get the same duplication of data by having a working copy checked out to several different computers, with a fairly easy way to update those working copies.

We've been talking about backups only a short while, but already you can see that there are many different ways of making backups, and some of the systems we've set up in this book make the problem even more complex. If we attempt to answer the question "How do you back up your computer?" we discover that the number of choices quickly becomes overwhelming.

However, if we re-frame the question to be "How do we recover our computer systems from a disaster?" the answer becomes "depends upon the disaster." The key point here is that you need to think about strategies for dealing with different types of disasters first, and then decide how best to go about recovering from them.

Disaster Recovery is a field full of experts, theories, and methodologies. It all boils down to assessing what the chances are of a particular type of disaster, what the consequences are, how expensive it is not to prepare for it, and what you can do to reduce the cost if the disaster befalls you. The most important tool you can use for disaster recovery is your brain. Take a few hours to think about the consequences of various types of disasters, and plan strategies ahead of time to help you deal with them if one happens to you. The time you spend planning for disasters could well make them a mere inconvenience, rather than a business-ending catastrophe.

Of course, you can never know the exact disaster fate has in store for you. With computers, however, you can group them into a handful of types of disasters, each with a corresponding set of strategies for dealing with them. Table 18.1 lists the major types of computer disasters for which you can develop a recovery strategy.

Let's take a closer look at these types of disasters.

Loss of Equipment

This is the most obvious type of disaster. Your office burns down. Somebody breaks in and steals your equipment. A tornado hits your office. These are the big disasters that everybody thinks about when hearing the term Disaster Recovery. Luckily, the chance of this type of disaster happening to you is very small, compared to other disaster types—but the consequences are large. And usually, the loss of the information on your computers is the least of your worries at the time—you may have many more important losses to deal with.

TABLE 18.1 Recoverable Computer Disasters

Type	Examples	Chance of Happening	Consequences	Strategies
Loss of Equipment	Fire, theft	Low	Total loss of all data—can put you out of business	Store data offsite, either on a remote server, or backup media removed from your office daily
Hardware failure	Hard drive fails, Network card fails	High	Partial data loss, loss of use of any systems depending on the hardware	Redundant hardware systems, backups
Compromised systems	Viruses, worms, malicious hacking, accidental deletions	Medium-High	If discovered early, loss of service while restoring backups. If undiscovered, potentially expensive data recovery and downtime	Revision control systems, disconnected mirrors, long-term backups
Loss of service	Power outage, service provider goes out of business, Denial of Service attack, connection outage	Medium	Loss of use of a system	Redundant systems, important data available in printed form
Lost passwords	Employee leaves the company, human memory	High	Loss of use of a system, can't access particular services/documents	Secure system for storing passwords

Still, the IRS expects you to pay your taxes, employees need to get paid, and if you're going to have any chance of continuing your business, you need to have an intact set of company records. Fortunately, it's relatively simple to make a total loss of your computer systems a recoverable problem: create offsite backups.

It's not enough to make a backup, and keep it in the same building—you have to put that backup somewhere else. And in light of the security considerations discussed in Chapter 16, you need to be confident that your backups are secure, or all of the security measures you've taken may as well be for nothing.

One way of doing offsite backups is to create backups on tape or optical media (DVD or CD), and physically remove them from the premises. Store them in a safe deposit box, put them in a safe at home, store them in a separate business location, or with a trusted partner. This type of arrangement can be onerous, but it's probably the most secure way to store backups if you have a lot of sensitive data, depending on where you put them, of course.

Another way is to replicate all your data through the Internet to some sort of data warehousing service. You might have a server hosted in a data center somewhere, or use a dedicated backup service. If you go this route, be sure you're working with a reputable firm—never use a free service to store confidential information. Also, make sure any data transfer is encrypted and authenticated. The advantage of this type of arrangement is that backups can happen automatically, as frequently as you want, and if you have a dedicated server, you may be able to eliminate downtime entirely.

Hardware Failure

If you've never seen the inside of a computer, take the cover off one sometime and look around. If you look closely, you'll find that the only moving parts are a couple of fans, and the disk drives. Moving parts eventually break down.

One of the statistics hard drive manufacturers use to sell their drives is Mean Time Between Failures (MTBF). You'll find hard drives with MTBFs of at least a few hundred thousand hours, up into a million hours. 300,000 hours is over 35 years, but in truth hard drives don't last anywhere near that long—while you may get ten years out of a hard drive, it's much more likely you'll get five to seven years out of a drive before it fails. MTBF actually corresponds to the number of failures of hard drives during the middle of their service life, not the actual length of their service life. There's also a high number of drives that fail in the first few months of use, so the time to implement a backup routine is right from the start.

Backups and redundant hardware are the strategies for dealing with a hardware failure. Having a backup is much cheaper than doing data recovery on a broken hard drive—if the drive head breaks, it can cost you thousands of dollars to get a data recovery company to retrieve what was on the drive. To deal with a failed hard drive, a simple backup works fine.

Redundant hardware basically means having more than one. You can set up a Redundant Array of Inexpensive Disks (RAID) system by purchasing a special controller and a bunch of hard drives. For an extra cost of a thousand dollars or so, you can get a system of three or four drives that provide fault tolerance—the ability to have a hard drive go bad with no data loss whatsoever. There are several different ways of setting up RAID, but perhaps the best one for small services is called RAID 5. It requires at least three hard drives, and uses an algorithm called parity to get more storage out of the whole set of drives—with three 40 GB drives, you'll get about 80 GB of total storage, the other 40 GB containing the parity data. RAID 5 also improves the performance of reading from the hard drive, especially for reading large files.

For other redundant hardware, you might just buy a second computer, duplicate the entire contents of the hard drive, and then disconnect it and put it in a closet. Then, when you have a hardware failure, you have a duplicate setup, and can restore the latest backups and be back up and running quickly.

Hard drives aren't the only hardware that fails, though they're certainly the most common, and because they hold all your data, the most important. If anything else on your computer fails, the quick solution is to put your hard drive in another computer. Then you can determine what other component has failed, and repair the original.

Compromised Systems

A system is compromised when an essential file or component has either been deleted or changed in an undesirable way. This can range from accidentally deleting folders containing files you still need, to being infected by a virus, to having a cracker break into your computer. (In the open source world, *hackers* refer to anybody who likes to play around with code and computer systems; *crackers* are hackers that illegally break into systems.) A compromised system might also occur if there's a power outage while a program is writing to the hard drive, resulting in a corrupted file.

The biggest issue with compromised systems is that you may not detect the problem right away. Imagine this situation: you back up your systems weekly, and keep the last four weeks of backups, but because you have a limited number of tapes, and they're expensive, you rotate them through your system. Then you discover a system compromise that actually happened two months ago, and you no longer have a backup that goes back to a known good state.

So what do you do? Viruses and worms sometimes infect documents, requiring risky recovery procedures. Accidentally deleted and corrupted documents are gone forever. Cracker programs running on your computer can be removed, but only with a full reinstallation of your system.

A RAID array or copies spread around multiple computers are useless to protect against system compromises. Corrupt data can be copied without your realizing it is corrupt. Worms crawl through your network and can potentially infect your entire LAN.

A disconnected system that is periodically updated with known good data is one strategy. Generally, the best strategy involves setting up a backup plan that ensures you have historical copies of important documents in a revision control system, and that everything backed up to permanent media like CD-ROMs.

Another type of compromised system is a laptop, desktop, or Personal Digital Assistant (PDA) that falls into the wrong hands. Laptops and PDAs in particular can be a gold mine of information about your company. Are your company's books in a spreadsheet on a laptop, or in the Web browser cache? Is your marketing strategy outlined in an email on your PDA? There are ways of breaking into any computer or PDA, given enough time. If a malicious user has your device, it won't take long for them to gain access to the data on it.

There's only so much you can do to prevent theft, especially as devices get smaller and easier to snatch. It's important to always encrypt any sensitive data you might have on these devices.

Loss of Service

Temporary losses of service happen all the time. Servers need to get updated periodically to close newly discovered security holes. Power outages happen. The time spent recovering from other disasters is itself a loss of service.

The impact of a loss of service is completely variable, depending on what type of service you've lost. If your public Web site goes down, you may lose potential customers who happen to be looking for your product while it's down. If your Internet connection goes down, it may or may not be a big problem for you, depending on the nature of your business. If your ISP changes hands, or your Web host goes out of business, it may take some time to get your systems back up and running. Only the individual business owner can determine how big an impact these outages are on the overall business, and how much time and energy should be devoted to lessening the impact.

In the discussion of each of the services in this book, we've covered the ramifications of different choices, whether you choose to host a service with an external provider or do it yourself. You always have at least one provider—you can't connect to the Internet without an ISP. If you host all your services yourself, and your connection goes out, you lose your Web site, email, and name service. Name service is particularly important—if your email server goes down, but your domain name resolves, most mail servers will simply queue messages to you and try again later.

However, if your name servers all go down, your mail will bounce immediately. For this reason, you should always have a backup mail server on a different network.

These are the three public services that affect your customers—email, Web, and name services. Most ISPs will provide backup name service for you for a small fee, or there are DNS services that can provide primary and secondary name services. For email, a backup mail server can collect mail when your primary server or connection goes down, and then you can immediately download the mail when it comes back up. This sounds like an important feature, but as long as your domain name resolves, mail servers will keep trying to send mail until it goes through, generally for up to five days.

For a public Web site, if it goes down you lose customers. If you don't have an extremely reliable connection with a stable provider, it's often better to host it somewhere else, especially if it has to share a server that has other services on it.

Aside from power outages or technical glitches, your service providers might go out of business. Worse, you might become the target of a Denial of Service attack—a type of malicious hacking, where a service (usually a Web site) gets bombarded with more traffic than it can possibly handle. The Slashdot effect isn't a Denial of Service attack per se, but it has the same effect—if millions of people decide to visit your Web site at the same time, it may not bring down the Web site, but it might make it impossible for anybody to get to the Web site. A basic Web server with static pages can easily handle hundreds of hits per minute, but unless you have some powerful hardware and the server optimized for high traffic, a few hundred thousand hits per minute simply can't be accommodated.

In August 2003, the University of Wisconsin was hit by an inadvertent denial of service attack. It turns out that Netgear, a manufacturer of consumer routers, had hard-coded the IP address of a time server located at the University of Wisconsin into the software running on a few of their routers. A bug in this software caused it to query the server every second when it was first turned on, and far more frequently than necessary after an hour or so. The University of Wisconsin recorded about 500,000 unique routers contacting their site in a single day, over and over again. You never know where you're going to have a problem.

There's not a whole lot you can do to reduce the impact of these types of problems, because they're pretty unpredictable. You never know what service you might lose. If your server gets cracked into and you no longer have access to the address book, do you have the phone numbers of your employees printed on paper somewhere accessible? Do you have the numbers of backup service providers? Preparing for an unknown loss of service requires thinking flexibly, having critical information in more than one format, and being ready to use another service at a moment's notice.

Lost Password

Losing a password is a special case of loss of service, mainly because it's such a common problem. You practically need a different password for every site. If you use the same password everywhere, you create a huge privacy risk—it's hard to know if any particular third party site stores your password encrypted, or in plain text. If you use the same password on some random Web site for other services, you open a huge security hole, potentially granting a malicious person access to any other place you've used that password. Yet if you use a different password for every Web site, network, and service you log into, you can't possibly remember them all, and if you write them down, suddenly you've created a new security risk. Anyone that gets a glimpse of wherever you've written down your passwords can potentially gain access.

Besides forgetting an important password, there's also a problem when an employee leaves the company, or somehow gets incapacitated—you have to consider both the security implications, and the loss of service if that employee was the only one with access to a particular system.

A popular solution among security-minded IT professionals is to use a small encrypted database of passwords on a Palm device. If you search for password storage palm software, you'll find dozens of programs, some commercial, some shareware, and a few free. The open source Keyring program, available at *http:// gnukeyring.sourceforge.net*, works very well and integrates with JPilot, a Linux-based Personal Information Management tool very much like the Palm Desktop software. It can generate strong passwords for you and store them in an encrypted database. You need to remember one master password to open the database; it remembers the rest of your passwords for you.

For systems under your control, administrative passwords are crucial to keep private, but also available to a very limited set of people. Administrative passwords, such as the root password on a server, have the ability to reset or change any password on the system, lessening the impact if a user forgets his password.

Private or secret keys are yet another type of authentication detail that needs to be accounted for in any type of recovery plan. You need to know what to do if a secret key falls into the wrong hands—can you revoke the certificate, or is the pass phrase strong enough to make the key useless?

Multiple Types of Disasters

From this discussion, you begin to see that any disaster generally falls into more than one of our categories. A loss of service is often the result of any disaster, and a hardware failure often results in a compromised system. Breaking out the types of disasters is a useful exercise to help analyze how to respond to different situations. When you actually have some sort of disaster, the first thing to do is assess which categories are at stake. Then you can decide what to do about it. Most medium-sized to large businesses create a formal Disaster Recovery plan. Very few small ones do. Creating such a plan is similar to creating a will—who wants to dwell on their potential demise? Yet creating a disaster recovery plan can well be the difference between recovering from some sort of digital disaster, or going out of business. It's as critical as an insurance policy—and better in that it helps you analyze what's crucial to your business, perhaps even providing focus.

STRATEGIES FOR DISASTER RECOVERY

We've explored most of the types of disasters as they affect computer systems. Your disaster recovery plan should include all aspects of your business. The information systems part of your plan should be as big a part of it as your computer systems are to your business. If you only use computers for a Web site and email, you probably don't need to develop a big plan. However, if many of your business transactions take place over the Internet, you had better have contingency plans describing what to do if your office burns down, your provider goes out of business, or any other outage. Furthermore, your plan needs to be redundant—what if you're on vacation during an emergency? Does the person in charge know what to do?

From Table 18.1 and the previous section, we've discussed several specific ways of dealing with particular situations. Here's a list of the key tactics:

1. Store copies of data in multiple physical locations.
2. Have additional hardware available to replace hardware that goes bad, and some easy way to restore backups to that hardware.
3. Keep an inventory of all of the computers and PDAs in your organization, and use a system to encrypt the most sensitive data, detect intrusions, and block viruses.
4. Use revision control systems to store critical documents.
5. Keep a list of important phone numbers for employees, service providers, business partners, and emergency personnel in printed form at multiple locations.
6. Make sure at least two people have administrative access to critical systems, and store all passwords securely.

The Disaster Recovery Plan

If you store any kind of data on a computer, you should have some sort of plan to deal with what to do in case there's a problem. So let's take a look at the kind of information you need to have in a disaster recovery plan.

Our plan needs to cover the following areas:

- Disaster types, and where in the plan they're addressed
- Key personnel, suppliers, and partners; specifically identify people with administrative access
- Current inventory of equipment: servers, types and sizes of hard drives, workstations, routers, laptops, and PDAs
- Software systems, versions, and locations; URLs or the location of installation CDs. Proprietary software licenses
- Server restoration procedure; location of backups
- Backup policies: what is backed up, and how often
- Backup procedures

A little planning goes a long way to helping you deal with not only big disasters, but also little disasters: finding the phone number of your ISP when the connection goes down, identifying the software you need to install on a brand new computer, and reminding you of a spare switch sitting in your closet when you've added three new employees to your company.

Take the time to create a disaster recovery plan, and you'll find it to be well spent. Print copies and distribute them to key people in your company, and consider making an abridged version to distribute to everyone. Keep a copy with your offsite backup disks, in case something as terrible as a fire takes out your primary office, and have an up-to-date copy in easy reach at your desk. You'll probably find you use it more than you might expect.

Disaster Types

As we've already discussed, there are several different types of disasters (Figure 18.1), each with different ramifications on your computer systems. A comprehensive disaster recovery plan should have a quick outline of steps to follow for each type of disaster. When something goes wrong, you want to be able to pick up the plan, look at the major categories, make a decision about what type(s) of disaster this is, and read a check-list of steps to take.

Key Contacts

You need to have contact information in printed form for all of the decision-makers in your company, as well as your suppliers. You should definitely list your ISP here, with the name and phone number of your account manager, if you have one. You should also have contact information for all your other service providers: Web hosts, name service providers, email providers, or anyone else who provides you with some service critical to running your business. It's a lot easier if you have this information in one place, than having to track it down when you need it.

Disaster Types

Loss of equipment

1. If server, switch to redundant systems if possible.
2. Obtain replacement equipment.
3. Determine software to restore from Software systems.
4. Follow restoration procedure.
5. Notify customers/partners.

Hardware failure

1. If server, switch to redundant systems if possible.
2. Obtain replacement equipment.
3. Determine software to restore from Software systems.
4. Follow restoration procedure.
5. Notify customers/partners.

Compromised systems

1. Immediately take system offline and determine extent of compromise.
2. Notify affected customers/partners.
3. If there's an exploit over the network, block ports and take appropriate action.
4. If limited to individual files, restore backups from earlier versions.
5. If limited to single machine, switch to redundant system if possible.
6. If systems continue to be vulnerable, take them offline and find solution with an unaffected system.
7. Follow procedures to clean systems. If necessary, reinstall systems and close vulnerabilities.
8. When all systems are clean and protected, restore data and reconnect.

Loss of service

1. Determine cause of service outage.
2. Contact service provider to determine course of action.
3. Switch to new provider if necessary.
4. Notify customers/partners.

Lost passwords

1. Contact administrator to reset necessary passwords.
2. Change all passwords of related systems, if compromised.

FIGURE 18.1 Example disaster types section of plan.

If your customers would be inconvenienced by a disaster on your part, you also need to have a way to reach them. Keep a list of current key customers in your disaster plan, if that's a reasonably small list, so you can provide superior customer service by being able to notify them when you have a problem that impacts them.

Finally, administrative passwords are the skeleton keys of your computer systems. You should not write them down anywhere—but everyone needs to know who to contact if their password is forgotten or compromised. Some people recommend never giving administrative access to anyone else—but then what happens if somebody needs to change a password, and you're on an airplane or otherwise out of communication? For your organization, you should have two or three trusted individuals (and no more) who have root access to your machines, and everybody should know who these people are. List these administrators in your plan, along with contact information.

Current Hardware Inventory

Having a list of the current hardware you're using in your business can come in very handy. If something happens to your main server, you can look down your list of workstations to possibly find one that can stand in until you can afford a replacement. Perusing this list before making any buying decisions can help you identify who needs an upgrade the most, and where you might have extra hardware you can move around to better meet your needs.

For each computer, you should list the network name, IP address (for static IP addresses), MAC addresses of all of the network cards, and the basic hardware specifications and peripherals. Also, list any software that requires an individual license, along with the keys you need to install the software.

For laptops, you especially need to consider the security implications of having private company information stored on them. Strong passwords aren't enough—an attacker can easily remove the hard drive and mount it in a different computer running an operating system of their choice. If the files or filesystems are not encrypted, there is little to prevent someone from getting all your data from a stolen computer. In this part of the plan, you should provide an assessment of how well sensitive data is protected on laptops and PDAs, perhaps as a roadmap for strengthening the security of the use of these devices in your network.

Finally, while you're doing an inventory of computer equipment, you may as well list all of your printers, along with connection details, and any other networked hardware or PDAs used in your company. A hardware inventory supports purchasing decisions, replacement of stolen or destroyed equipment, and the security of your systems. It's well worth having in a disaster recovery plan, because the more you use it, the better you'll keep the plan up to date.

Software Systems

Now here's where the disaster recovery plan starts containing crucial information. You should list all of your server systems: email, dns, Web sites, ldap servers, certificates and fingerprints, document repositories, accounting systems, and mailing lists. For each system, you should list all relevant configuration details.

This information becomes incredibly useful when you need to update software, especially if your system has been compromised. If you can't trust the settings on your server, having a printed copy of the basics will help you get a new version of the server up and running.

Inevitably, you're running some proprietary, non-open source applications. Keeping a list of all the software for which you've bought licenses, along with information about the computer its installed on and the license key or serial number you need to reinstall, helps greatly if somebody needs to migrate from one workstation to a new one. It also helps in the case of a visit from the Business Software Alliance.

Server Restoration Procedure

For each server, you should create a checklist of all the steps necessary to restore it from a backup. What systems are running on this server, where is the backup media stored, what settings do you need to specifically install for this server? You might include details for setting up time synchronization, and online media sources for Mandrake software. List all of the standard software packages to select when installing the operating system, the custom software compiled from sources, specific configuration files, certificates, databases, repositories, Web sites, mail, and home directories. List the sequence to start services. Make sure you update this list whenever adding new software to your system.

Backup Policies

Create a backup policy and stick to it. Make sure everyone in the company is aware of the policy, along with any partners or customers who may be affected by the systems. Your backup policy should specify what is backed up and how often, and how to manage offsite copies of your backups.

Offsite Backups

Backups are time consuming, hard to set up, and can be large security risks. If your backups fall into the wrong hands, you may as well give the burglars a key to your front door and welcome them in. As we discussed earlier in this chapter, though, keeping a backup set away from your premises is one of the key strategies that can make the difference in being able to recover from a major disaster.

You might keep a full backup of your systems in a safety deposit box at a bank, or hire a bonded security company to store them for you. For the smallest of businesses, you might work out a reciprocal arrangement with a partner business to keep a set of backups for each other. A lot of people simply bring a set of backups home, so that they're in two locations. The drawback to this is primarily security.

Another option is to do online backups and store them with a company on the Internet. This route can be very easy to automate, but has two drawbacks: first, you're dealing with an unknown company, so make sure it's one you can trust. Secondly, restoring over a network, especially if you don't have a fast connection, can add hours to the amount of time it takes to get your server back up and running.

A third option is to use a dedicated server in a data center, where someone else is responsible for doing backups. You can then back up the remote server to your office to have multiple physical locations for your data. This solution is very elegant, but again, you have to trust your provider, and have the additional trouble of making sure all your connections and data are secured as they cross the Internet.

Types of Backups

Next, you need to determine what type of backup to do. There are several types of backups:

1. Disk images
2. Full backups
3. Partial backups
4. Incremental backups
5. Differential backups

Your backup policy needs to identify how often your company does each different type of backup. Also, you need to specify what computers are backed up. If you have a server, and most important documents are already on the server, there is often no compelling need to back up everybody's workstations. Create a private share for each of your employees on a file server, and then do regular backups on the server. If your email is all stored in IMAP folders on the server, and important documents are in revision-controlled repositories, it is much easier to back the whole lot up on the server. Just make it a formal policy that "if it's not on the server, it's not backed up," and encourage everyone to keep anything important on the server in one place or another.

Let's take a closer look at these different types of backups.

Disk Images

One technique is to take a snapshot of the entire hard drive, and save it somewhere else. Disk images work great for workstations, when you've set up a configuration that many people can use without modification. Restoring from a disk image involves booting into some sort of emergency restore disk, and copying the disk image to the hard drive. It's much quicker than installing an entire operating system, because nothing gets configured. It also works for all operating systems—it just copies the whole disk byte for byte, and doesn't have to understand any of the file system or semantics of what it's doing.

On the downside, disk images don't necessarily work well for disaster recovery. If your system was compromised, your image may reinstall the vulnerability that led to the system compromise. Still, if you need to install the same basic stuff on a bunch of computers, disk images are the way to go. Norton Ghost™ is a proprietary Windows-based program that provides disk imaging. In Unix systems, the dd command copies raw blocks from the disk to another device or file.

Full Backups

A full backup copies every file on a computer to some backup medium. Full backups are time consuming, and work best with large media like a tape drive or DVD set. Making a full backup can be tricky—you can't just copy the entire directory tree. Files in use, special file types like sockets, devices, and pipes, and the Master Boot Record on your hard drives must be accounted for when doing a backup.

Generally, to do a full backup, you'll use some special software that accounts for all of these things. In the Unix world, try Mondo, a backup system available at *http://www.mondorescue.org*. You can install it in Mandrake using urpmi mondo, if you have set up the contrib media source as described in Chapter 2. Mondo not only backs up your entire file system, it also creates bootable rescue disks or CDs, and a very comprehensive restore procedure. You can omit directories from your backup, and selectively or completely restore files.

If you don't have a large backup media device, using a full backup solution is probably more effort than it's worth. A backup of a medium size server can take 25 or more CDs, if there's much data on there, or if you accidentally include files that don't need to be backed up. However, if you've made extensive changes to the configuration of a system, or installed a lot of custom software, a full backup of at least the basic operating system and software can be a good way to go.

The advantage of a solution like this is that if you lose your entire system, restoring is simply a matter of going through the restore script. You generally don't even need to make any decisions—your system is restored to exactly the way it was when you made the backup.

Partial Backups

With a partial backup, you only archive your data, and rely on the operating system installation disks to recover a system. After installing all software on a server, you simply restore the data files and configurations from your partial backup.

If you make relatively few changes to the operating system, and don't run very much custom software, reinstalling the operating system and then recovering your partial backups is often as easy as doing a recovery from a full backup. One advantage of using this style of backup is that you can easily upgrade your operating system and other software before restoring your data, ensuring that your systems are up to date.

Another advantage of partial backups is that you can use smaller or fewer media to store the backups. A system of partial backups can be reasonable to do with CD-Rs, though bigger media like tape drives and writeable DVDs are still easier and more likely to hold your entire backup.

The biggest drawback to partial backups is determining what to back up. You need to identify particular directories, generate archives of the files, and write them to a backup medium. You can use the same programs you use to make a full backup, and just specify a more limited set of directories to back up.

Quite often, the best way to set up a partial backup system is to create a script that does the backups for you, using basic Unix archiving commands like `tar` and `cpio`. There are many such scripts available on the Internet, if you do a Web search.

Synchronized Backups (Mirrors)

If you use a hard drive or network storage for your backups, some software allows you to update the backups with the changes you've made to the original hard drive. This type of backup arrangement is easy to make, and works great if your original hardware fails. However, if your system is compromised, or files corrupted, you may overwrite your backup with the compromised or corrupted files.

Keeping a mirror of your server provides the best *failover protection*—if something happens to the original system, you can replace it with the backup in a matter of a few minutes. If keeping your services available is important, having a mirror of your data can minimize the time spent restoring your systems. However, you still need other backup systems that can't be overwritten with bad data to cover other types of disasters.

Incremental Backups

Incremental backups are backups that only archive files that have changed since the previous backup. You scan the computer for new or updated files, and put them in the archive. They work in conjunction with a full or partial backup, adding a sequence of changes as you go. They're easy to make, take a minimum of space on your backup media, and better than no backups at all.

But incremental backups are terribly inconvenient to restore. First, you have to restore full backup, or the operating system and a partial backup. Then, you need to restore each increment in the correct sequence—if you don't, you run the risk of overwriting files with outdated versions as you restore. Incremental backups are the most difficult type of backup to restore.

Differential Backups

Differential backups are very similar to incremental backups, the difference being that you back up the difference between the current state of the system and a specific previous backup. For example, with a weekly differential backup, you start with a full or partial backup. After a week, you create a backup with all the changed files since the original backup. At week two, instead of archiving the changes since week one, you archive all the changes since the original backup.

When you go to restore a differential backup, you don't need the intervening backups—you restore the full or partial backup, and then the latest differential and you're done. The drawback, compared to incremental backups, is that the archive gets bigger and bigger and may eventually exceed the size of your backup media. When you reach that point, it's best to do another full or partial backup and start over.

Creating a Backup Policy

There is no best backup policy. Business needs and equipment vary far too much to make any one system the way to go. Variables include the media you have available to store backups, the size of your typical backups, how often you change equipment, and how important it is to restore a particular system immediately.

For small businesses with modest needs, a backup system using rewritable CDs can be perfectly adequate. Your backup policy might specify:

1. Partial backups of data and configuration directories only, initially and whenever weekly differential backups grow to be larger than a single CD. Make an additional copy for offsite storage. Create all partial backups on permanent (record-only) media.
2. Weekly differential backups archiving everything that's changed since the previous partial backup on rewriteable media.
3. Daily differential backups archiving everything that's changed since the last weekly backup on rewritable media.
4. What to do when a new weekly backup is made: take the old weekly backup and the last daily backup away for offsite storage.

With this arrangement, you can create a system that runs automatically every night, requiring you to only change the CD when you start in the morning. Your onsite backups are never more than a day old, and even if you lose your entire office, your offsite backups are current to the end of the previous week. Finally, restoring in this scheme involves installing the operating system, restoring the last partial backup, restoring the last weekly backup, and then restoring the last daily backup, a maximum of four sets of media for minimal daily effort. If your differential backups start exceeding the size of your media, you either need to change them to an incremental style, make the next higher level of backups more frequent, or purchase a backup media system with greater capacity.

There are three general trade-offs with backups: the time and effort it takes to make the backup, the time and effort it takes to restore the backup, and the size and cost of the backup media. You have to choose a policy that achieves the best balance for your needs.

BACKUP PROCEDURES

How you actually do the backups varies by the type of backup and the media you're using. Let's take a look at backup media now.

Backup Media

As of 2003, there are three general types of backup media:

1. Optical media, such as recordable DVDs and CDs
2. Magnetic media
3. Networked backups

Within these types, there are many different options of varying capacities and qualities. A comprehensive disaster recovery strategy may use all of these types of backups, but for most small businesses, you're limited by your budget.

Table18.2 lists some examples of various backup media.

Optical Media

Optical media, such as CD-ROMs and DVDs, have become a compelling way to create backups. The individual media is very inexpensive, making it reasonable to create extra full backups to store offsite. It also doubles as a permanent way of storing data you no longer need available—burn it to a DVD and store it in your files with completed projects so it is available if you ever need it, but not taking up space on your servers.

Some types of optical media have the additional advantage of only being able to write once. You cannot accidentally overwrite or erase an important backup. This type of media provides the best way to find an intact version of a file, if it becomes corrupt at some known point long before the corruption is discovered. Write-once optical media include CD-R, DVD-R, and DVD+R. These types of media are easy to store, inexpensive, easy to move offsite, almost universally readable on other computers, and can even be used to boot most computers into a recovery mode.

TABLE 18.2 Backup Media Options

Media	Type	Capacity	Typical Media Price	Notes
CD-R	Optical	650–700 MB	As low as US $0.20 each, or lower	Extremely cheap media for backing up. Able to restore on nearly any other computer. Storage life of about 10 years. Only writable once.
CD-RW	Optical	650 MB	US $0.50–US $1.00	Can be reused, unlike CDRs. Not always readable in standard CD-ROM drives, but still very widespread.
DVD	Optical	4.7 GB–9.4 GB	US $2.00–US $4.00	Larger, more permanent than recordable CDs Watch out for competing standards—not all media work with all drives
Tape systems	Magnetic	6 GB–100 GB	US $20–US $200	The only choice if you must do frequent full backups More software choices Much more expensive than optical media
Extra hard drives	Magnetic	Any size	Varies	Very fast, expensive Good for synchronized backups, and quick recovery Should be complemented with other backup devices
Remote file system	Network	Any size	Varies	Great way to create offsite backups Can back up multiple computers, saving more data Complex to set up, expensive, still requires other media for actual storage

Rewritable optical media, such as CD-RW, DVD-RW, DVD+RW, and DVD-RAM are great for incremental and differential backups. They're slightly more expensive and slightly less compatible—but for day-to-day backups that you don't need to keep permanently or distribute to other people, they work well.

CD technology has stabilized to the point that there are only the two choices: CD-R and CD-RW. DVDs, at the time of writing, are in a much different situation with five different competing standards. DVD-R and DVD+R are both write-once media types, and generally readable in other DVD drives—but you need to choose the media that goes with your drive to successfully record. DVD-RW and DVD+RW are two competing standards for creating rewritable DVDs. Again, you have to get the correct media to go with your drive. Rewritable DVDs may not work in normal DVD-ROM drives. The final type of DVD media is DVD-RAM. DVD-RAM again has its own special media, and can store quite a bit more data on a single disk—up to 9.4 GB, instead of 4.7 GB. But only other DVD-RAM drives can read from these disks.

At the time of writing, several manufacturers are producing drives that can write to all the different types of DVDs, as well as writing to CDs. These drives are more expensive, however.

Magnetic Media

Before optical media was widespread, backups were done to magnetic media: tapes, hard drives, or floppy disks. Magnetic media still comes in much bigger sizes than optical media, making it simple to back up your entire hard drive without having to split it up into small enough chunks to fit on your media. Most backup software is designed to back up to either another hard drive or a tape.

Tapes used to be the backup system of choice for large organizations. While they're more expensive than optical media, you simply set your backup software to dump the whole hard drive, either disk images or full backups, to tape. You can then run a special recovery disk to restore your hard drive from the tape. Most well-developed backup systems are built around tape drives.

The price of hard drives has dropped considerably since the early 1990s. Now you can buy enormous hard drives for not much more than the cost of a new tape. Hard drives are much faster than tape, and usually faster than optical media. You can maintain synchronized or mirrored copies of your main server, and not have to think a whole lot about backups.

Floppies, zip disks, and other types of magnetic media are pretty much obsolete, made so by inexpensive CD-R/RW drives. One CD holds more data than nearly any of the smaller removable disk systems, and costs far less.

The main drawback to magnetic media is that it's relatively easy to overwrite good data with bad, or to lose it completely if it's put near a strong magnet. Hard drives are the most common thing to fail in a computer, not just because of their moving parts, but also because the information on them is stored magnetically, and other devices with strong electronic currents can affect the data stored on them. Store a tape in an attic near an old ceiling fan, and you might be surprised when you go to restore the data on it.

Still, for ease of recovery, nothing beats having a single storage media bigger than your total data, easy to drop into place when you need it.

Networked Backups

A network backup location still uses some type of media to store the backups, usually magnetic. However, if you have an extra computer you can use as a backup server, all the other computers on your network can send their backups to that computer, making for an easy-to-use backup system.

With this type of system, you offload the pain of doing backups on each of your servers to a single computer—where the problem gets magnified. This type of solution is generally more expensive, requiring constant attention by dedicated IT personnel, and is usually only necessary when you have a lot of computers that need to be backed up.

Backup Software

We're down to the nitty-gritty details of doing backups. Unfortunately, there is no single solution that does it all, for all types of businesses. At the smallest level, you may be better off creating a script that provides the features you need. Unix provides a number of built-in archiving tools you can use to ease the task.

There are hundreds of different backup software programs available, each designed to solve the problem in a specific scenario. Table 18.3 lists a few open source backup projects that run on a Linux server. If you need the capabilities they provide, check them out.

Backing Up Databases

One big issue to consider while setting up a backup solution is that databases generally cannot be safely archived from their files, especially while they're in use. If you attempt to copy database files to an archive, when you recover the files the result may be unusable. Your backup procedure should perform database backups as specified by the databases you use.

TABLE 18.3 Backup Software

Software	Type	Media	Backup Type	Scenarios	Notes
Amanda http://www.amanda.org	Network backup system, client and server	Tape	Full, incremental	Providing automatic regular backups to all computers on a network.	Hard to retrieve individual files from a backup. Needs substantial hardware investment to get a system that works.
Mondo Archive and Restore http://mondorescue.org	Full backup and recovery solution	Tape, file, optical media	Full, partial, image	Focus on easy recovery of single computers, built-in tools for restoring individual parts of the file system, and bringing back a system to an identical state as it was before.	Slow, consumes a lot of backup media space. Can image other filesystem types (not just Linux-based).
tar cpio pax afio	Command line tool	File, tape	Partial, incremental, differential	Great for selecting particular files and directories to back up. Universal access to resulting files—tar archives can be opened with common Windows tools.	All of these programs provide basic archiving operations, and in conjunction with find, can archive files modified after a certain date. These programs work great for scripting custom solutions.
dump	Command line tool	File, tape	Image, incremental	Backs up an entire file system to a single location. Automatically handles incremental backups.	Another old backup mechanism, designed to work with restore to restore the backup.
dd	Command line tool	File, raw disk	Image	Copies a hard drive or partition byte by byte. No ability to select files.	Available on all Linux systems. Handles backing up and restoring boot records, and can make a single (big) image of a partition or entire drive.
yacdbak	Scripted solution	CD, file	Full, partial, differential	Uses tar to create archives, and splits the output into CD-sized chunks. Can only be automated if the data is less than one CD.	http://yacdbak.sourceforge.net/ Simple solution to get up and running
cdbkup	Perl solution	CD, file	Partial, differential	Similar to yacdbak, but also supports multi-session CDs, GPG encryption	http://cdbkup.sourceforge.net/ More comprehensive solution

In general, there are three ways to back up a database:

1. Shut down the database, copy the database files, and then start it up again.
2. Use tools provided by the database system to "dump" its entire contents.
3. Use the exact procedure specified by the database creators to do a "hot backup."

Shutting down a database before copying it results in a loss of service, but on a Unix-based system, is generally a safe way to copy the files.

Dumping the contents of the database is usually the best way to go, because you get all of the data in a format that can be easily loaded into other databases. However, this procedure may not back up everything related to a database, such as stored procedures, table optimizations, permissions files, or hook scripts.

Most databases provide a hot backup script that creates a full duplicate of a running database. You should create at least one backup in this manner, but often there's a lot of overhead in using this technique, and there is no way to do any kind of incremental or differential backup. Your backup is the same size as the full database, which may not be practical in many situations.

For small databases, keeping one full copy of the database created by the hot backup script is sufficient. Then you can generate database dumps and store those with your weekly and daily backups. You might be able to save some disk space by comparing a database dump against one you stored previously, to generate a differential dump of the database. The `diff` command can do this easily:

```
# diff weekly-db.dump daily-db.dump > daily-db.diff
```

When you need to restore your database, the `patch` command merges your changes. For a three-tier system, you might store the full database dump with your full file system backup, and then store a weekly differential and a daily differential. To restore a database file, you would use the following commands:

```
# patch full-db.dump weekly-db.diff
# patch full-db.dump daily-db.diff
```

Then you can load the `full-db.dump` into a newly created database to have your data fully restored.

Backing Up Subversion Repositories

Subversion is a revision control system discussed in Chapter 9. It stores its files in a Berkeley database, which is subject to the same problems as ordinary databases.

Subversion has the same basic solutions for creating a backup, but provides commands to make the job easier. There is a command to make a hot backup of your repository, including all the hook scripts and any authentication files you've included in the database, and the svnadmin dump command dumps all of the revisions in a repository. You can specify a range of revisions for an incremental (really a differential) backup of a repository.

Simple Backup Script for Files, MySQL, and Subversion

There is no tool that can handle all the varieties of servers described in this book. You can still set up automated scripts to handle backups for you—you just need to identify exactly what you want the script to do.

Listing 18.1 lists a simple sample script that generates a full backup and weekly and daily incremental backups, for all MySQL databases on the local server; a set of Subversion repositories; and a set of files. It also attempts to burn a CD, but if the total data is more than will fit on a CD, the script will fail if you attempt to run it automatically. If you're there and run the script from a shell, you'll be prompted to insert additional CDs as the archive progresses. Also, this script assumes you're making full backups to CD-Rs, but using CD-RWs for the differential backups.

LISTING 18.1   Simple Backup Script for Subversion, MySQL, PostgreSQL, and Files

```
#!/bin/bash

DATE=$(date +%y%m%d)
BACKUPDIR=/opt/backup
MYSQLDIR=mysqlbackup
SVNBAKDIR=svnbackup
SVNDIR=/var/svn
EMAIL=john@freelock.com

INPUTFILES=$BACKUPDIR/backup.list
SVNFILES=$(ls -d $SVNDIR/*)

tmpdir=burn
tmpfilelist=$BACKUPDIR/tmp.list

##############################
# Determine type of backup:
# - full (default) backs up all
#     files, dbs, and repos
# - weekly backs up changed
```

```
#     files, db diffs, and repos
#     compared to full
# - daily backs up changed
#     files, db diffs, and repos
#     compared to weekly
#############################

echo > $tmpfilelist
cd $BACKUPDIR
rm -Rf $tmpdir
mkdir $tmpdir
    LASTFULLDBDATE=$(< db.full.date)
    LASTWEEKLYDBDATE=$(< db.weekly.date)
    LASTFULLDATE=$(< files.full.date)
    LASTWEEKLYDATE=$(< files.weekly.date)

if  [ $1 == "nodbs" ]
then
  echo "db backup skipped"
  shift
else
case "$1" in
weekly)
    rm -f $MYSQLDIR/*.weekly.mysql
    ;;

daily)
    rm -f $MYSQLDIR/*.daily.mysql
    ;;
full)
  ;;
*)
  echo "Usage: backup [nodbs] (full|weekly|daily) [nofiles] [burn]"
  exit
  ;;
esac

# first, we do the database dumps
cd $MYSQLDIR
echo "Retrieving DB Dumps"
mysqldump --opt -u root -pPASSWORD --all-databases > server.$1.mysql
pg_dumpall -U postgres > server.$1.pgsql

# used relative paths in $MYSQLDIR so archive restores relatively
cd $BACKUPDIR
```

```
# Now we get the Subversion repos
cd $SVNBAKDIR
echo
echo "Dumping Subversion repositories"
for FILE in $SVNFILES
do
  base=$(echo $FILE | sed "s%$SVNDIR/\(.*\)\$%\1%")
  echo "dumping: $base"
  youngest=$(/usr/local/bin/svnlook youngest $FILE)
  case $1 in
    full)
      rm -f $base*.dump
      svnadmin dump $FILE > $base.$youngest.dump
      echo $youngest > $base.full; cp $base.full $base.weekly
      echo $SVNBAKDIR/$base.$youngest.dump > $tmpfilelist
    ;;
    weekly)
      full=$(< $base.full)
      [ $full = $youngest ] && continue
      rm -f $base.$full.*.dump
      ((full++))
      svnadmin dump $FILE -r $full:$youngest --incremental > \
          $base.$full.$youngest.dump
      echo $youngest > $base.weekly
      echo $SVNBAKDIR/$base.$full.$youngest.dump > $tmpfilelist
    ;;
    daily)
      weekly=$(< $base.weekly)
      [ $weekly = $youngest ] && continue
      rm -f $base.$weekly.*.dump
      ((weekly++))
      svnadmin dump $FILE -r $weekly:$youngest --incremental > \
          $base.$weekly.$youngest.dump
      echo $SVNBAKDIR/$base.$weekly.$youngest.dump > $tmpfilelist
    ;;
  esac
done

# Generate archive
cd $BACKUPDIR
# do this after successful dump of database/subversion
case $1 in
  full)
    echo $DATE > db.full.date
```

```
        cp -f db.full.date db.weekly.date
        ;;
    weekly)
        echo $DATE > db.weekly.date
        ln db.full.date $tmpdir
        ;;
    daily)
        ln db.full.date $tmpdir
        ln db.weekly.date $tmpdir
        ;;
esac
# nodbs end
fi

if [[ $# -gt 1 && $2 == "nofiles" ]]
then
    echo "file backup skipped"
else
case "$1" in
full)
        touch full.mark
        ;;
weekly)
        touch weekly.mark
        findargs="-newer full.mark"
        ;;

daily)
        findargs="-newer weekly.mark"
        ;;

    *)
    echo "Usage: backup [nodbs] (full|weekly|daily) [nofiles] [burn]"
    exit
    ;;
esac

echo "Searching for files and generating archive"
for findpath in `cat $INPUTFILES`
do
    find $findpath $findargs -depth -mount -print > $tmpfilelist
done
echo "Filelist generated."
```

```
freq=$1
case $1 in
  full)
        echo $DATE > files.full.date
        cp -f files.full.date files.weekly.date
        ;;
  weekly)
        echo $DATE > files.weekly.date
        ln files.full.date $tmpdir
        ;;
  daily)
        ln files.full.date $tmpdir
        ln files.weekly.date $tmpdir
        ;;
esac
### end of nofiles
fi

if [ $# -gt 1 ]
then
  shift
  if [ $1 == "nofiles" ]
  then
        shift
  fi

  if [ $1 == "burn" ]
  then
        echo
# If the data is more than one CD long, the rotate script
# changes the name of the image so it can be burned later by hand.
        afioargs='-H "/opt/backup/rotate.sh"'
  fi
fi
# Now create the archive(s):
echo "Creating Archive..."
cat $tmpfilelist | afio -ovZM 64m -s 600m -@ $EMAIL     $afioargs
$tmpdir/$freq.$DATE.afio > afio.log 2>&1

# now copy the log and list to the burn dir, and burn!
echo "copying log and file list to tmp dir"
ln afio.log $tmpdir
ln $tmpfilelist $tmpdir
```

```
echo "burning CD"
if [ $1 == "burn" ]
then
  /usr/local/bin/mkcd.sh $tmpdir $blank
fi
```

LISTING 18.2 /opt/backup/rotate.sh: A Script Used by Afio in the Backup Script to Move CD Images Out of the Way, If the Backup Is More Than One CD Long

```
#!/bin/bash
mv $2 $2.$1
```

LISTING 18.3 /usr/local/bin/mkcd.sh: A Simple Script That Makes a CD Image and Records It to a CDRW, Given a Path to a Directory

```
#!/bin/bash
nice -18 mkisofs -R -quiet $1 | cdrecord -eject speed=8 dev=0,0,0 \
blank=fast - || exit "CD record failed."
```

For the script to work, you'll need to have the afio and cdrecord packages installed, and have a CD or DVD burner, of course. To automate it, you can add an entry to the crontab for root. Cron is the Linux scheduler, and runs commands in the crontab for each user at the specified schedule. Adding these two lines set up this script to run:

```
3 2 * * 2-6 /opt/backup/backup.sh daily
3 2 * * 1 /opt/backup/backup.sh weekly
```

This schedule runs the weekly backup at 2:03 A.M. on every Monday morning, and the daily backup at 2:03 A.M. every Tuesday through Saturday. The burning command is set up for CD-RWs, and if you forget to change a CD, it just gets written over the next time it runs. So by setting up this schedule, you'll have a fresh new weekly backup when you arrive at work on Monday.

These are very basic scripts, hacked together to suit the needs of the author. You are free to use them for your own backup purposes, but the author takes no responsibility for their quality. You can download the latest version of these scripts from the backup section of the Web site accompanying the book at *http://opensourcesmall.biz/disaster*.

SUMMARY

At some point, you will lose data. No matter how secure your systems are, new vulnerabilities are discovered all the time. Whether you become compromised is a matter of whether the bad guys discover the vulnerability first. But plenty of other things can go wrong, including fires, theft, and other natural disasters. Regular business insurance can pay for the cost of replacing your equipment, but can you replace your data?

In this chapter, we've discussed how to plan for a data disaster to make sure that if it ever happens to you, the answer to the question is yes. We looked at reasons for doing backups, strategies for disaster recoveries, recovery plans, backup policies, procedures, media, and software.

In the last chapter of the book, we'll take a look at the two major annoyances of the Internet: viruses and spam.

DISASTER RECOVERY REFERENCES

An updated list of resources for this chapter is on the Web site for the book at *http://opensourcesmall.biz/disaster*.

Articles

"MTBF FAQ." Available online at *http://www.hardwaregroup.com/faq/gen_mtbf.htm*

"Flawed Routers Flood University of Wisconsin Internet Time Server," by Dave Plonka. Available online at *http://www.cs.wisc.edu/~plonka/netgear-sntp/*

Software

Mondo Rescue, complete open source disaster recovery system *http://www.mondorescue.org*

Amanda, open source network backup system *http://www.amanda.org*

cpio, open source archiving tool *http://www.gnu.org/software/cpio/cpio.html*

afio, open source archiving tool *http://www.gnu.org/directory/All_Packages_in_Directory/afio.html*

Yacdbak, open source backup to CD *http://yacdbak.sourceforge.net/*

Cdbkup, open source backup to CD *http://cdbkup.sourceforge.net/*

Drak Backup, built-in backup software in Mandrake Linux, *http://www.mandrakesoft.com*

19 Viruses and Spam

In This Chapter

- Introduction
- What Is A Virus?
- Diversity: The Open Source Advantage
- What Is Spam?
- Summary
- Spam and Virus References

INTRODUCTION

In many ways, the Internet is a brand new market, reaching hundreds of millions of people who never had the ability to communicate with others with the same level of freedom. Unlike all previous markets, this one crosses every national border and many social classes, creating many new rules and possibilities that we haven't discovered yet. This brings tremendous opportunity, but also creates hazards for the careless.

Spam and viruses are the early hazards of the Internet, and merit special consideration in our discussion about security.

This chapter is for anyone concerned about viruses, spyware, or spam. Rather than discussing technical solutions, we cover strategies to reduce the problems overall, and talk about how you can deal with the flood of unwanted messages. There is nothing technical in this chapter.

WHAT IS A VIRUS?

Computer viruses are called that because they act very much like physical viruses: they spread from computer to computer using various transmission means, they make the infected computer "sick," they can be prevented using various inoculations, and they vary in how badly they impair their host.

There is one substantial difference between computer viruses and physical viruses that many people don't realize: all computer viruses are programs written by people. Somebody has taken time and effort to think up a vulnerability in some computer system, and figured out how to make a program exploit that vulnerability to replicate itself and spread to other computers.

Who creates these dastardly programs, and what possible motives do they have? This is sheer speculation, but perhaps they get a rush out of being able to topple large institutions with a tiny, well-crafted program. Perhaps it's the thrill of being bad, doing something nasty and not getting caught. Perhaps it's a way of lashing out at the world, exhibiting superior intelligence by bringing the Internet to its knees. Many virus writers who have been caught are adolescents; several have been caught only after they bragged about the feat to their friends. Many viruses are a delivery mechanism for remote control software—infected machines can be controlled and used to attack other targets, such as government Web sites, unpopular businesses, or whatever arbitrary target the virus author chooses.

In any case, regardless of who wrote them and why, the threat posed by viruses is real. In August 2003, the Blaster worm attacked Microsoft operating systems by exploiting a vulnerability that had been patched by Microsoft a month earlier. This particular worm was designed to bring down the Microsoft site that distributes the patch for the very hole the worm exploited. Fortunately for Microsoft, it attacked the wrong address—otherwise the Windows Update site would have surely been unreachable for a few days. The Blaster worm may have even been a factor in the severity of the August 2003 power outage in the eastern United States.

A week later, a different programmer modified the Blaster worm in an apparent attempt to create a "good" virus. Called the Nachi virus, it used exactly the same exploit to install itself, delete the Blaster worm, download the patches from Microsoft to fix the vulnerability, and spread itself to other vulnerable computers before eventually deleting itself. The Nachi worm, in spite of its good intentions, did even more damage than the original Blaster worm: because of all the download traffic, it flooded many corporate networks, including airline reservation systems, resulting in delayed and canceled flights.

To make matters worse, many individual personal computers are still infected, without their owners' even realizing. The Code Red viruses and Nimda viruses infected Windows Web servers originally in the spring and summer of 2002. In fall 2003, you can still find attempts by infected computers to spread these viruses in any Web server log—some computers have been infected for years without their owners taking any action.

If your computer is infected, you might not even realize it. Viruses vary in noticeable effects: some make your computer slower, some make it crash, many fill up your network bandwidth, and some may go undetected for months. Just because you don't notice the presence of a virus doesn't mean it's harmless. A virus might install software that monitors your keystrokes and sends information back to somebody on the other end. Your network connection might slow down to the point that you invest in a faster, more expensive connection. And if your computer is used to flood some arbitrary site in an attempt by the virus distributor to shut it down, you may find yourself cut off from the Internet entirely when the affected site complains to your ISP.

Anatomy of a Virus

To prevent viruses from spreading, it's important to understand how they work. It's not enough to install an anti virus program and forget about it—keeping your system clean is a matter of taking basic precautions, regularly checking for infection, and keeping informed about what new dangers are out there. Let's take a closer look at how viruses work, so we can better understand how to defend against them.

A virus consists of several parts. One part of the virus replicates the virus so it can be transmitted somewhere else. Another part handles the actual transmission. A third part is called the *payload*, which is what the virus does once it has been transmitted. Different viruses have carried different payloads, but to date none of the payloads of common viruses have been destructive. There is no technical reason the next major virus won't carry a payload capable of destroying data—thus the importance of offsite backups of your critical data, as we discussed in Chapter 18.

As of fall 2003, the payload of viruses has been relatively harmless. The worst payloads have been key-loggers, which capture everything you type, including credit card numbers and passwords; and remote control devices, programs that make it possible to control your computer without your permission or knowledge to conduct attacks on other computers. Basically, if the rest of the virus works correctly, the payload is only limited by the overall size of the virus, and the intent of the virus author.

Copying a program is a simple task, so the techniques viruses use for replication is unremarkable. But the true creativity of a virus is exhibited in how it transmits itself. Anti-virus experts group viruses into a few broad categories, based on how they are transmitted:

- Worms
- Trojan Horses

- Email Viruses
- Other Viruses

Crawling from Computer to Computer: Worms

A worm is a type of virus that propagates with no help from humans. These viruses exploit vulnerabilities in software running on existing computers to install themselves and propagate to other vulnerable computers. Many of the fastest spreading viruses are worms, including Slapper, Slammer, Blaster, Nachi, Code Red, and Nimda.

The best defense against a worm is a good firewall, blocking all network traffic from the Internet that isn't absolutely necessary. A good firewall would have stopped the Slammer worm, as well as Blaster and Nachi.

The Slammer worm, also known as Sapphire, infected an estimated 75,000 computers within the first 10 minutes of its release on January 25, 2003. This worm exploited a vulnerability in Microsoft SQL Server, an enterprise database server, that had been discovered and patched some seven months before the worm appeared. Why were so many computers infected? Because the vulnerable database engine was included in many Microsoft office-related products unbeknownst to the users. Blaster and Nachi, both of which spread in August 2003, exploited the Windows implementation of a protocol called RPC over HTTP, which was turned on by default in many Windows machines even though it wasn't used for anything. Both the RPC and the SQL Server exploits were blockable by any firewall or consumer router, including the firewall built into Windows XP (which was disabled by default).

Other worms exploit vulnerabilities in essential server software. The Slapper worm infected just under 14,000 computers running the open source Apache Web server with a vulnerability in the SSL code libraries in September 2002. Code Red and Nimda both targeted Microsoft Internet Information Services (IIS), the Microsoft Web server. Code Red and its derivatives infected over 350,000 Web servers in July 2001. Blocking these worms is more difficult, mainly because most businesses need to run a Web server.

Sneaking into Your System: Trojan Horses

Another type of virus relies upon a gimmick to trick you into running it. Named after the wooden horse filled with Greeks given to the city of Troy, Trojan horses often appear to be something benign when they are not. Trojan horses have been hidden in online greeting cards, pop-up messages, peer-to-peer file sharing services, and many otherwise innocent-looking programs.

The best defense against Trojan horses is mild paranoia—never open anything if it's not from a trusted source, and even if it is, use caution. If you're sent a "cool program" from a friend, it might be worth searching the Web, especially antivirus sites, for information about the program before you open it. If you don't find any information about it, wait a few days and try again. Update your antivirus signatures, and scan the file before running it, because once you run it, it can infect your system.

Sometimes paranoia isn't enough. In 1995, Microsoft accidentally shipped a Word Macro virus on an installation CD. Novell and several other software companies have included viruses on other CDs.

A favorite trick of crackers trying to compromise your system is to put a Trojan horse version of a common program somewhere where it will get run by an administrator instead of the real program. The Trojan horse program can open up a back door, or elevate the privileges for an account, and then call the real program so the administrator never knows the difference.

Email Viruses

Because so many people use email, it has become a medium of choice for distributing viruses. Many email viruses share characteristics with worms and Trojan horses. Trojan horses abound in email. A common tactic of email-borne viruses is to use a double file extension to mask the nature of the virus. Windows uses file extensions to determine what a file is, and how to open it. An extension is usually three letters at the end of the filename, after a period. Windows by default hides the file extensions of files it knows about. By adding a second, real extension that Windows hides by default, users can be tricked into opening what appears to be an innocent file.

To make matters worse, many of the most virulent email viruses take advantage of flaws in the most common email software that allow scripts or programs to run without even requiring any action from the user—having the message appear in a preview pane, or even expanded to show the first few lines with no preview pane, was enough to allow the malicious code to execute.

When these programs run, they search for other email addresses and mail copies of themselves to other unsuspecting victims. The Sobig group of viruses sent copies of itself with both forged to and from addresses, so the recipient of the virus might think it came from a completely innocent, uninfected person.

There are a couple of simple tactics for avoiding email viruses: never open attachments without verifying their contents, and don't use email software that runs any kind of script automatically.

Other Viruses

Virus writers are arguably the most creative software developers out there, in a highly destructive way. They find flaws in software, and figure out novel ways of exploiting them in a self-replicating way. The original computer viruses infected files on floppy disks. Some viruses are spread by instant messaging programs. Several take advantage of flaws in Web browsers, infecting surfers when they visit a carefully designed Web page.

The Nimda virus combined several methods of infection: it was an email virus, a worm, and a Trojan horse. It infected files on file servers, infected Web servers using the same vulnerability Code Red exploited, sent copies of itself via email to large numbers of people posing as lurid content, and also infected people simply browsing Web pages on already-infected servers.

The Sobig virus appears to be developing as a spam delivery mechanism, spewing spam in all possible directions and adding a back door on infected systems, paving the way for future releases of the virus. What the next virus will do, and how it will spread, is only known to the virus developers.

Defending against Viruses

The common advice for defending against viruses is to get a good antivirus program, scan your system regularly, and keep the virus signature database up to date. The limitation of antivirus software, however, is that it's all reactive—it takes the antivirus companies some time to develop a way of detecting and blocking each new virus only after it's been released into the wild. That's small consolation if you get infected before there's adequate inoculation available.

Defending against computer viruses is very much like defending against physical viruses. Antivirus software inoculates you against known viruses, but is mostly useless against new ones. By taking basic precautions—don't drink from infected waters, limit your contact with unknown people, stay out of areas known to contain epidemics—you should be fine. In addition, get regular checkups to make sure you're healthy and that there isn't some infection slowly growing in your system that will cause you problems down the road.

There are basically three parts to a successful virus defense strategy:

1. Monitor your system for signs of infection, and keep aware of new viruses.
2. Shut down as many possible avenues of infection, to prevent people infecting you.
3. Practice "safe computing" by being cautious and aware of your actions that could lead to infection.

Monitor for Infections

Antivirus software is a good place to start. It's useless if you don't keep it updated, though. Many antivirus vendors have attempted to add *heuristic* virus detection to their programs, but there is no real evidence that this works. Heuristic virus detection attempts to identify a virus based on the actions it takes on a computer, modifying key system settings or accessing an address book. The problem is, virus writers evaluate and test their viruses against the antivirus software, and come up with an imaginative way to defeat the heuristic scanning. Or people turn it off because it interferes too much with their everyday use of the computer. Basically, antivirus software can identify known viruses on your system and help you clean your system. For many viruses, the antivirus software detects the virus before the system gets infected—but you shouldn't rely on this, and should take other precautions.

There are no open source antivirus programs. Keeping the virus signatures up to date takes a lot of time and effort. There are about a dozen antivirus software companies, and most of them have turned to a subscription pricing model, charging you for regular updates.

At this writing, the vast majority of viruses infect and spread through Windows systems. If you have any Windows computers, it's essential that you run antivirus software and regularly update it.

Several vendors make antivirus modules that plug into mail servers. The open source Amavis project provides a plug-in framework for antivirus modules in Linux, allowing you to filter email passing through a mail server, deleting viruses before they can ever reach your Windows computers. Amavis works well with the email server setup we discussed in Chapter 5, but it does nothing by itself—you still need to get a proprietary virus scanning system from one of the antivirus vendors. Check out the Amavis project at *http://www.amavis.org*.

Viruses are rare in Linux, but Trojan horses are not. We discussed the Tripwire program in Chapter 16. This program monitors critical files and systems on a Linux/Unix computer, and sends email notification if any of them are changed. Tripwire is available at *http://www.tripwire.org/*.

The other part of monitoring for infection is to prevent a possible infection from being a disaster. As we discussed in Chapter 18, your disaster recovery plan should include a contingency for restoring your data in the event of a virus infection. The worst-case scenario, if you have good offline backups, is that your service goes down until the antivirus makers determine how to clean an infected system. This is usually hours or days, not weeks. Once your system is patched and the virus removed, you can restore your data from your offline backups and continue where you left off.

Block Avenues of Infection

In the physical world, cesspools, places with rotten meat, and sewer systems that feed into drinking water sources are all things that can contribute to an epidemic. Restricting the means of transmission can go a long way to preventing an outbreak of a virus. To do that, you need to understand the means of transmission.

As we've already seen, viruses travel a variety of ways. They can be attached to an email. They have traveled between database engines. They worm through Web servers, file servers, and directories. They spread through chat rooms. You can even get a virus through a floppy disk or CD.

The obvious precaution to take is to block all access to services you don't need, and monitor the ones you do need. As we discussed in Chapter 17, a firewall is an essential part of your basic network security. Shutting down all unnecessary ports helps slow down an epidemic, and prevents you from being infected by many new viruses. A simple firewall that blocked RPC over HTTP and the SQL Server control ports would have blocked several epidemics in 2003—the SQL Slammer worm, Blaster, and Nachi.

The main problem with a firewall is that it sits between your internal network and the Internet. If an infected computer somehow gets behind your firewall, the firewall does no good. If an employee of your company takes a laptop home, connects directly to the Internet and gets infected with a virus, he is likely to infect the rest of your network when he comes back into your office. A firewall alone is not enough.

The second part to this strategy is closing all the vulnerabilities on your systems. Programming is a human endeavor. Inevitably, in all software, humans make mistakes when programming. These mistakes, if they go undetected, provide ways for hackers and viruses to do things the software programmer never intended. New vulnerabilities are discovered all the time. Most of the time they are discovered by "good" hackers, who notify the software vendors of the problem, and give them an opportunity to patch the software before making the flaw public. In the case of an open source project, the flaws are usually made public immediately, so the entire group of developers on a project can concentrate on fixing the flaw before a cracker can develop a virus to exploit it.

No matter what software you're running, you need to be aware of significant flaws when they're made public. At a minimum, get on announcement mailing lists for any server software you use. If you don't subscribe, make it somebody's job to monitor these lists and security bulletin sites for issues related to the software you use.

Many viruses that have become epidemic, infecting more than a few thousand computers, exploited known publicized vulnerabilities for which patches already existed. The exploit used by the SQL Slammer worm was patched seven months before the virus appeared. Many of the email viruses spread by Microsoft Outlook and Outlook Express exploit vulnerabilities Microsoft patched years earlier. Blaster and Nachi infected machines that didn't have a patch that had been available for a full month.

Use a firewall. Shut down unnecessary services. Keep your system up to date, especially if there's a security warning.

Practice Safe Computing

The Black Plague in the Dark Ages of Europe spread through the proliferation of rats. Epidemics happen when people don't understand how a virus spreads, or when it spreads faster than preventative methods can be deployed.

Before the Internet was widespread, viruses were mainly spread with pirated software copied from disk to disk and distributed from person to person. Now that everybody is connected to the network, the vast majority of viruses are spread through the Internet over one service or another. The key point is, infections only happen when one computer exchanges data with another. If the only contact is through the Internet, that's the only way you can get infected.

Some transmission methods are essential to our Internet lives in varying degrees—we cannot simply turn them off. We can disinfect our drinking water, though, and likewise, we can try to kill everything dangerous that lives in our email. We can choose to avoid areas that are known to have virus infections, and take extra precautions if we must visit them.

Email, by itself, is harmless. At its base, email is simply a plain text message. Some companies have taken the vision of Web pages and tried to bring the color, interactivity, and functionality to email. Unfortunately, the people who have taken the most advantage of this are the virus writers.

If you use a text-only email program, you won't be infected by an email-borne virus—unless you save an attachment and explicitly run it. It is theoretically possible for a specially crafted email message to exploit a flaw in your text-based email reader—but since such a tiny percentage of people use text-based email readers, there is no incentive for a virus writer to attempt the feat. But plain text is . . . boring. Color and pictures can add something to email. While purists may argue that the writing in the email is what's important, try telling that to the new parents sending a photo of their baby.

So most of us use email readers that are capable of sending and receiving mail that uses HTML formatting. If you prefer to use an HTML-capable mail reader (which includes the vast majority of mail programs in use), use one that doesn't allow any scripts or programs to run. Web pages use Javascript to make buttons appear more active, process forms, and do all kinds of other things. While you could make an argument that having a button that changes color when you mouse over it is a good thing in email, you'd be hard pressed to find anyone who thinks it's worth the price of allowing viruses to run.

Turn off all scripting functionality, all automatic execution of anything in email. Period. The fact that the two email programs in most widespread use in 1999–2003, Microsoft Outlook and Outlook Express, allowed scripts to run when an email is opened led directly to a long list of virus epidemics: Melissa, Bubbleboy, I Love You, Sircam, Klez, and Sobig.

Public peer-to-peer downloading systems are prime places for catching viruses. Recognize the risks you take if you choose to use these types of services. Likewise, instant messaging and chat systems are well known for the proliferation of viruses. If you choose to use these services, be very cautious before running any files, especially if you don't know where they came from.

Installing software is a particularly dangerous thing to do. Many freeware and shareware programs include "adware" or "spyware," third-party programs that snoop on what you do and try to report your actions back to some central source. While many of these may not be viruses, at a minimum they violate your privacy.

Pornographic sites are another place to pick up a computer virus. It's quite interesting to notice how the computer world mirrors the physical world—the same types of seedy places exist in both, with similar risks. But even apparently wholesome Web sites can transmit viruses.

As we saw earlier, there have been cases where software installation CDs have been infected right from the manufacturer. The best defense for this type of infection? Don't be the first person to install a new software package. Wait a week or two, at least, and check the Web site of the software provider to see if anybody has had any issues with it. Let somebody else be the person to discover the virus.

DIVERSITY: THE OPEN SOURCE ADVANTAGE

In nature, diversity strengthens immunity. Physical viruses infect some populations and not others. Many individuals are immune. Inbreeding often leads to more vulnerability to disease.

In the computer world, copies of software can be identical from machine to machine—whether a particular program will be infected by a virus or not is not a question of chance. If the program is vulnerable, and if it's exposed to the virus using its chosen method of infection, the computer will be infected. The dominance of the personal computer world by Microsoft Windows has led to a very homogeneous environment, extremely susceptible to infection by imaginative virus writers.

Simply choosing software that isn't mainstream almost eliminates your risk. One of the big drawbacks of open source software, too many choices, can be its greatest strength in regard to virus infection. The drawback of having too many choices of software for every imaginable task means it's harder for managers to decide what's best, harder for users to figure out the specific software used in your business—but also harder for virus writers to write something that will infect your system.

There are dozens of email programs available for all operating systems. An analysis of Microsoft Outlook and Exchange by the Radicati group estimated that at the end of 2003, there are 323 million installations of Microsoft Outlook in use. An August 1999 study by Veritest discovered that 63% of respondents used Outlook or Outlook Express. No other email program accounted for more than 15% [RRWeb03]. Using a different email program, especially if that email program doesn't execute scripts, is a great way to lower your risk of catching and spreading email viruses. The open source Thunderbird email program is a great choice, available for Windows, Linux, and Macintosh at *http://www.mozilla.org/*. Or you can use Mozilla Mail.

ON THE CD

Mozilla Mail is part of the Mozilla browser, and is included on The Open CD included with this book. Mozilla Thunderbird is also included on the CD-ROM for the book.

Likewise, using the number two or number three Web browser instead of the dominant one lowers the risk of malicious Web sites exploiting a browser flaw and infecting your computer. Using a different operating system entirely is even better.

Software monoculture has led to crippling virus epidemics. Choosing to use software outside the mainstream nearly eliminates your risk, and there are some great open source programs to choose from.

WHAT IS SPAM?

If you have an email account with any major provider, you've probably received spam. Everybody knows what spam is, right? Well, it turns out that people have quite different definitions of exactly what spam is. Most people consider unsolicited commercial email from an unknown sender to be spam. Some people consider any commercial mailing to be spam, even if they've done business with the company who sent the email. Some people think unsolicited mail from a charity or political group is spam. Some people even classify joke messages from their friends as spam. Obviously, people have different ideas of what spam is.

Most anti-spam groups define spam as Unsolicited Commercial Email, often referring to it as UCE. Spam gets its name from a Monty Python sketch where a chorus of Vikings chant the breakfast menu of a restaurant that has spam as part of every dish. The chorus of "spam, spam, spam, spam" eventually drowns out everything else in the sketch. The effect of spam on the Internet is similar—it threatens to drown the messages you really want to receive in a flood of UCE.

As a small business, you probably don't want to ban all unsolicited commercial email. Businesses depend on marketing to gain new customers and build brand images. All businesses need to engage in marketing, whether it's word of mouth, postcards mailed to prospective clients, cold calls, or advertising in various media. How is email different? Shouldn't email be a valid way to reach potential customers?

As we discussed in Chapter 13, an email newsletter to your customers and potential customers is a great way to build your brand image. There is such an extreme backlash against spam, however, that your message may get lumped with other

UCE and deleted unread. If some of the current legislation pending in the US Congress gets approved, you may also be required by law to obtain explicit permission before adding someone to your email list.

Email and the Web are opening up brand new markets, but scattered among the messages from legitimate businesses are get-rich-quick schemes, pyramid scams, organ enhancement businesses, porn, and all kinds of fringe products. The worst thing about this type of spam is the utter unscrupulousness of its senders. These people use fake return email addresses, route their mail through overseas servers in an attempt to conceal their true origin, and often engage in outright fraud. The problem with attempts to legislate spam is that the legislation is likely to have more of an impact on you, the small business, than these unscrupulous spammers who already dodge the law and evoke the fury of irate email activists.

Why Is Spam a Problem?

We can answer this in two different ways: why we need to treat spam as a problem, and what factors have allowed spam to become a problem.

Spam consumes resources. The Spamnet software estimates that it takes a person 13 hours to delete 40,000 spam messages, a figure some people receive in a few months. But the time you spend deleting it is only part of the problem. Every email sent through your system consumes bandwidth. If your company is receiving thousands of spams per day, that directly consumes bandwidth, server storage, administrator time, and other resources that could otherwise be doing something more productive. Many a small company has upgraded to a faster connection, not realizing that the reason their connection had gotten slow was that a spammer had hijacked their mail server and was using it to relay millions of messages all over the Internet.

Unsuspecting companies who have compromised mail servers eventually find themselves cut off from business partners and potential customers if their server becomes blacklisted. Completely innocent people can have their email addresses hijacked to use as the return address for a spam—and then suffer a backlash of thousands to hundreds of thousands of bounce messages and complaints from angry recipients.

And, of course, there's the problem of overlooking important email that arrives in a flood of spam.

These are the annoyances spam causes. There is still a worse side—the content of the spam. There are anecdotes of people who have been terminated from jobs for receiving "inappropriate" emails. In England in 2003, a man was arrested for distributing child pornography, who didn't know his computer had been compromised and used to send the files [BBC03]. Many families have begun to limit their children's access to email, screening out the pornography and inappropriate material.

Some spam messages are really viruses, carefully written to infect your email client and make it contribute to the problem. Many spam messages promise great riches, if you agree to be a conduit for a fortune to be transferred to your account. Others conceal the true product the spammer is trafficking in: your personal identity. Many spams are scams designed to get you to reveal your credit card numbers, your social security number, or to obtain a copy of your passport. Identity theft is perhaps the worst problem spread by spam.

There's a real difference between all of these nasty, fraudulent spams and commercial email from legitimate companies. If you're a legitimate company, the last thing you want to do is annoy your customers. Most legitimate companies honor requests to be removed from a mailing list. Most spammers use removal requests to verify that an email address works, if the removal address works at all.

So what makes spam such a problem? Why not ban it outright, or simply block fraudulent email? Why do you get spam that has links that don't even work, and no way to contact the business being advertised?

There are both technical and social factors that have contributed to the rise of spam. The technical factors include:

- It costs practically nothing to send one email or a million emails.
- It is trivially easy to forge the original source of an email.
- The Internet is a worldwide place—any attempt to shut down a source of spam simply makes the spammer move his virtual operations somewhere else.

The heart of the technical problem is that there's nothing in the current email system that prevents you from forging your return address. Email was designed as an open system, trusting its users to be honest about who they are and where a message comes from. Some early email users even advocated the open system as a way of guaranteeing privacy. Many people have valued the ability to make email completely anonymous, pointing to examples like politically oppressed groups in totalitarian countries being able to communicate without fear of retribution. Unfortunately, this ability of email to be anonymous or faked has been used by pornographers and spammers to the point that few people argue for this degree of privacy anymore. Many of the services that made your email anonymous have been shut down because they've been used by people with something to hide. But the infrastructure doesn't enforce the authenticity of messages, and so spam remains a problem.

The social factors contributing to spam boils down to this: spam is profitable. As amazing as it may sound, somebody responds to these messages, in enough numbers to make it worthwhile for the spammers. A 2003 study by the Pew Internet and American Life Project found that 7% of the survey participants had ordered a product or service from a spam message, and 12% of the participants had responded to an email offer that turned out to be fraudulent[PEW03].

Of course, neither of these figures reflect the number of people who respond to an individual spam, or even which definition of spam the participant used. But the cost to the spammer of sending an individual message is so tiny, a response rate of 0.001% can be the break-even point.

Solving the Spam Problem

As noted earlier, there are both technical and social factors contributing to the problem of spam. Effectively addressing the spam problem will need some fundamental changes to these factors. The hard part is that hundreds of millions of people, if not billions, already use the current email system. Replacing or overhauling it affects everybody who currently uses email.

Here are some things you can do on a small scale that contribute to solving the spam problem:

- Digitally sign your messages.
- Use mailing lists responsibly.
- Secure your email server, and set it up according to email specifications.
- Report spammers to their ISP.
- Never, under any circumstances, reveal your private information or purchase anything from a spam.

These are recommendations along the lines of "clean up your neighborhood," clearly falling into the cliché, "if you're not part of the solution, you're part of the problem." If everybody follows these guidelines, spam will cease to be a viable business and will be relegated to a nuisance of the 1990s and early 2000s.

Digitally Sign Your Messages

This is the most difficult recommendation to implement, as of 2003. Chapter 15 discusses encrypted email, how to do it, and what the issues are. The biggest issue is that there are competing systems for authenticating your messages.

The best thing to do is choose an authentication system you'll use in your business, and start using it. The more people digitally sign messages, the easier it will be to identify faked messages, and the stronger the infrastructure to support public key encryption and authentication will become.

Use Mailing Lists Responsibly

Chapter 13 discusses how to set up and manage an email list. An email list is a great way to communicate with your customers and market your business to potential customers. But the phenomenon of spam has made people particularly sensitive to receiving unsolicited email. If you're not careful, your messages may get categorized as spam and never read. Worse, if people start thinking of you as a company that deals in spam, your brand image will suffer.

Always ask for permission before adding somebody to a mailing list. Always honor requests from people who want to be removed from your list. Even though email has been around for decades, it's still a new medium for communication. Common manners are often ignored in email communications—you may well receive nasty, rude missives from people who gave you permission to send them mail, complaining about being on your list. Try to ignore the insults, and honor even these requests with courtesy—like any other way of communicating, courtesy defuses anger. Remember that it takes ten happy customers to balance one angry one.

Secure Your Email Server

Chapter 5 discusses how to properly set up a mail server. Chapter 14 discusses how to provide remote access to your email server using SMTP Authentication. It's critically important to prevent anonymous users from relaying email through your server. If your email server is slightly misconfigured, spammers will discover it, and they will use it to relay spam. This leads to effects we've already discussed: consuming your bandwidth, others blacklisting your server so you can't send or receive legitimate mail, and other dire consequences. If you don't have the resources to monitor and manage your email server, hire someone who does. Either put a mail server expert on retainer to manage your email server (among other duties), or outsource your mail to an email provider.

The next step is to provide a digital identity for your mail server. Just as you can digitally sign your messages to verify your identity, your email server can certify its identity with a digital signature. The more servers use digital certificates to transmit messages, the easier it will be to identify falsified email messages.

Setting up a digital certificate for outgoing connections on your mail server is beyond the scope of this book, but you can find instructions by searching the Web for "MTA Client SMTP Auth."

Report Spammers to Their ISP

Most ISPs want nothing to do with spam. In the United States, most ISPs have clearly stated terms of service prohibiting people from sending spam, and are actively implementing ways of blocking it. Identifying the true source of spam is not easy for the casual user. You can trace the path of an email through its `Received:` headers from server to server—but these, too, can be forged.

This is a task for an email administrator, not a user. If you find a large number of spams coming from a particular block of IP addresses, look up that block, contact the owner of the block, and report the problem. The more complaints an ISP gets, the more likely they are to take action to cut off the spammer's access to their network. As more and more email servers start using authentication, it becomes easier to stop accepting mail from ISPs who don't police their spammers.

Never Do Business with Spammers

This is perhaps the most obvious thing you can do to stop the spam problem—don't support their business. Spam is a business, after all. If nobody buys from spam, it will go away. The problem is, people do buy from it. There are enough people out there willing to respond to spam that it remains a profitable activity.

Educate your neighbors, your employees, your children about spam. Spam has not brought wondrous deals, unimaginable riches, or cheaper drugs to your doorstep—it has just provided a brand new way for snake oil dealers and scammers to reach you. Sooner or later, everyone will wise up and spam will disappear.

Coping with Spam Now

"Great! Wonderful! We won't have spam forever!" you may be thinking, "but I have 200 spams in my inbox right now. How am I supposed to get anything done?" There are several strategies you can employ to reclaim your inbox, and keep email as a useful means of communication rather than a repository of junk mail.

First of all, you can choose to simply delete the messages as they come in, doing nothing special. If you're lucky enough not to have been discovered by spammers, spam may be only a mild annoyance. Keeping an attitude of mild annoyance instead of outrage helps no matter what other strategies you choose to use.

Sooner or later, your mailbox will be discovered. So here are a few strategies you can put to work right now:

- Take steps to prevent spammers from obtaining your email address
- Use spam filters to identify spam and remove it from your inbox
- Only accept email from known or verified users

These strategies gradually escalate in effectiveness of blocking spam. The problem is, depending on how you implement the strategies, you may make it harder for potential customers to communicate with you. Let's take a closer look at these strategies.

Keep Your Email Address Out of Spammers' Hands

The first line of defense is to protect your email address from spammers. There are several tactics for doing this:

- Avoid using domains with lots of email users
- Use separate email addresses for public and private correspondence
- Never post your email address on any Web site
- Use unintelligible email addresses
- Use caution when reading your mail

These tactics vary in effectiveness. In general, the more discoverable your email address is, the more spam you'll receive. Email addresses on large, well-known ISPs receive more spam than private domains. Email addresses that are widely publicized, especially on Web pages, receive more spam than those that are kept private.

Some of these steps are becoming common sense in computing circles, while others are a bit extreme. As a small business, here's what you should do.

Get Your Own Domain Name

You need one for your business—your email address should advertise your business, not somebody else's. If you have an email address on another domain, you have no control over it. Countless businesses with cable connections had to change their business cards and marketing material when Excite@Home™ was bought by AT&T Broadband™ in December 2001 and their email address changed. Less than two years later, the same thing happened again when AT&T Broadband was sold to regional cable companies. Getting a new domain usually gives you a great reprieve on spam, mainly because spammers haven't discovered it yet.

Use Two Email Accounts

Set up one account for personal, priority mail, and a second one for commercial mail. Use your personal email account on your business cards, with friends, co-workers, partners, customers, and clients. Use your commercial mail account for mailing lists, newsletters, Web sites that ask you to provide an email address, or any situation where it might end up on a list somewhere. You will get spam on your personal account, but much less than you'll get on the commercial account. Plus, you can ignore the commercial account and read mail in it at your leisure, while still getting notified when a message comes into your personal account. You can set up the commercial mail account to deliver into a sub-folder in your main email box.

Don't Post Your Email Address on the Web

A Center For Democracy and Technology (CDT) study tested the amount of spam collected by email addresses released in different ways. Email addresses posted on Web sites ended up with far more spam than other email addresses, including those used to post to email lists, those used to sign up for products and services, and addresses that weren't used at all [CDT03].

Spammers use programs called *spiders* that crawl the Web looking for email addresses. This appears, in 2003, to be the single biggest way email addresses are collected. The study found that if an email address was removed from a Web site, the amount of spam it received decreased compared to other email addresses that were still there. The study also found that encoding email addresses by writing them out, using the word "at" instead of the "@" symbol, or doing other things to obfuscate the email addresses resulted in far less spam. Still, the software spammers use is developing over time, and it's not unlikely that spam spiders will soon get smart enough to decode these tricks.

Perhaps the best way to hide your email address but still allow potential customers to contact you is to provide a form on your Web site. Creating a form that is emailed to you without revealing your email address is an easy task, but beyond the capability of basic HTML. You will need to use a server-side scripting language such as PHP, Perl, Python, Cold Fusion, or ASP. You can find a plethora of scripts online that will do this, or any competent Web developer with server side scripting experience can create one for you in minutes.

Create Unguessable Email Addresses

Despite your best efforts, you will receive some spam. In the CDT study, even addresses that had never been used, posted, or revealed received a couple spam emails. Spammers use something called a *Dictionary attack*, employing a program that connects to your mail server and attempts to find valid email addresses by brute force. You can find these attempts in the mail server logs, where a server connects and checks to see if it can deliver to a whole list of similar names, usually in alphabetical order. Your server may be under attack for days.

The best thing to do is to stop these attempts by either blocking the connection at the firewall, or setting up rules on the mail server that make it disconnect after a certain number of delivery errors. But if you're not watching your maillogs, you may not detect the attack while it's in progress.

Having an obscure, unpronounceable email address may hinder this type of attack—but it also leads to your potential customers mistyping your address, or forgetting it completely. For a small business, it's usually better to have a memorable email address—the easier it is for someone to reach you, the more likely they will.

Use Caution When Reading HTML Mail

For the spammer, knowing which email addresses work is a great benefit. One trick many marketing firms use to verify a valid email address is to include a *Web bug* in the message. A Web bug is simply an image with a special code that identifies your email address. HTML messages include images quite frequently. These images can either be attached to the actual message, or be loaded from a particular Web server in exactly the same way a normal Web page loads images. Since Web servers keep logs of every file downloaded from a Web site, if you add a special code to an image in an email, the Web server will log that special code when the recipient opens the message in an HTML-capable email reader.

The ethics of including a Web bug in a marketing message is debatable. The simple presence of a Web bug is a slight violation of your privacy—the sender can determine your email address, and also associate it with your IP address, making it possible to track your movement through their Web site. On the other hand, including a Web bug can give you a hint on what percentage of recipients actually open and read your marketing messages. Used responsibly, Web bugs can be a very useful tool. But due to their misuse by spammers, it's probably better for your business reputation to avoid using Web bugs.

To avoid being bitten by a Web bug, set your email reader to either only show you plain text, or to not load images from the Internet. Exactly what you can choose to do, and how easy it is to change your mind, varies substantially among email clients. If you don't like the options you have in your email reader, consider choosing another one—the open source Mozilla Thunderbird allows you to mark an email as junk before you open it, and then it won't load images in that email.

Use Technology to Filter Out Spam

The next main strategy for dealing with spam is to try to filter it out so you don't have to read it. Before your domain is discovered, you may not need to take these steps—but sooner or later, you will. Most companies large enough to have a full-time IT staff have invested time and energy towards keeping spam out of their employees' inboxes.

The first filter to put in place is with your mail server. For years, most companies kept a catch-all email address: anything sent to the company domain name that wasn't addressed to a correct account would be directed to a separate account where somebody could review and forward it appropriately. These days it's much better to reject messages with typos in the recipient email address—you'd never find it in the catch-all address anyway. One small travel company forgot to check their catch-all address for a few months, and when they finally did, found some 120,000 messages in it. The vast majority of this mail was spam, but there were surely a handful of innocent messages sent to the wrong address, potentially customers who never got a response and took their business elsewhere.

Email filters have been around since the beginning of email. With any reasonably sophisticated email program, you can automatically move messages that meet particular criteria to separate mail folders. The problem is figuring out how to identify spam. Spam filters use one or more of four basic types:

- Blacklists
- Rules-based, heuristic
- Statistical token analysis, Bayesian
- Shared Spam flagging

Blacklists

The simplest spam filters block email coming from particular email addresses or domains. This type of filter is called a blacklist. For combating spam, a blacklist is useless—you rarely see mail coming from the same domain twice, unless it's from a major domain that also has legitimate users.

Blacklists can be useful for blocking specific people, though it's usually easier to simply delete the incoming mail.

When you read about email software that has spam filtering, often all it means is it has a simple way of adding a sender to a blacklist. Most email software comes with a blacklist feature.

Spam has become a battleground between spammers and spamfighters. To defeat simple blacklists, spammers started forging their "From" addresses, rendering these spam filters useless.

A more powerful form of blacklist is called a *Real-time Blackhole List* (RBL), which is basically a service that identifies domains and servers that have sent spam. Different RBLs have different criteria for adding sites to the list—some block all email coming from known dial-up addresses, others only list places that have actually sent them spam.

To use an RBL, you configure your mail server to look up the address or server name that is attempting to send a message before accepting the message. If the remote server is on an RBL, your mail server refuses to accept the message. RBLs are crude tools that often block innocent messages, without necessarily blocking spam. They are also controversial, and some have been shut down by court order.

Spam Filtering Rules

Spam-fighters next came up with rules-based filtering. The spam filters look for particular words or combinations of words to identify whether or not a message is spam.

The problem with a simple rule system is that it catches far too many innocent messages. Sometimes bad words happen in good mail—and a simple rules-based spam filter doesn't know the difference. The most sophisticated rules-based systems are called *heuristic* filters. These filters, instead of blocking or allowing mail based on the presence of particular words, applies many rules that each have a particular weight. If the result of these rules reaches a particular threshold value, the message is determined to be spam.

SpamAssassin is the runaway success of the open source heuristic spam filters. It provides a rules engine, allowing you to define your own rules and change the weight associated with particular rules. It comes with a few hundred starter rules, and does a fairly good job of separating the spam from the ham. But it still catches more innocent messages than you would like. Other drawbacks include having to update the rule sets as spammers change their tactics, making it an administrative burden to keep updated.

Remember that people have different definitions of spam. If you want to treat all commercial mail as spam, you might have to adjust the rules individually to block them. Likewise, if you only consider forged or fraudulent messages as spam, you may find yourself spending as much time tweaking the spam rules as you did deleting the spam.

To combat SpamAssassin and its siblings, spammers have begun doing tricks with their messages. Text in an email message can be encoded in a system called base-64, which obscures it when you look at the message source. HTML messages can have comments embedded in particular words, making the words perfectly readable to humans but not to spam filters. Spammers can also encode individual letters in HTML messages using a technique called URL encoding. These techniques result in the words in a message easily readable by humans but hard to recognize for computers.

As spammers add new tricks to their repertoire, spam-fighting programs have to compensate. The best heuristic spam filters de-obfuscate these messages and can then apply their rules. The very presence of these obfuscations can be detected by some rules; however, the variety is great, and adds to the administrative burden of maintaining your anti-spam solution.

The human brain is capable of some amazing things. You can easily decipher messages with misspelled words, with spaces in the wrong places, and many other errors that trip up a spam filter. Spam filters have a problem with catching too many innocent messages. You can counter this by keeping a *whitelist*, the opposite of a blacklist—a list of email addresses that bypass the spam filter.

Bayesian Spam Filters

In 2001, Paul Graham published an essay on his Web site called "A Plan For Spam." Graham, a mathematician, had come up with a way to use something called *Bayesian Analysis* to identify spam based on a statistical analysis of both spam and innocent messages, which Graham refers to as ham.

Thomas Bayes was a 17th century preacher and mathematician who came up with a way of predicting the probability of an event based on an analysis of the statistics related to prior events. Bayes's Theory is the basis of many expert systems implemented in various computing fields. For years people in different places have tried to figure out how to apply Bayesian technology to the problem of spam. Paul Graham was the first to spread the idea among open source enthusiasts.

There are now dozens of open source spam filters based on Graham's ideas. Spam-Assassin has added Bayesian filtering to its heuristic engine, making it even more effective over time. Popfile uses Bayesian filtering not only to identify messages, but also to create a relatively easy way to sort incoming mail into different folders of the user's choosing. Bayesian filtering is behind the Junk Mail feature in Mozilla Mail and Thunderbird. It's becoming the ubiquitous spam filtering technology for one main reason: it catches far fewer innocent messages than the rules-based filters.

Bayesian filtering depends upon training by its users. It has no rules, generally meaning it's a much easier system to administer. It also means that it takes some time before it becomes effective at identifying spam. Out of everything we've discussed in this book, Bayesian filtering is the closest thing to artificial intelligence in one respect: your computer actually learns from its mistakes.

The way a Bayesian filter works is:

1. It breaks each incoming message up into *tokens*. Each token is a word, a header, or some chunk of text.
2. Out of all of the tokens in a message, it chooses a set of the most interesting tokens—the 15 to 30 tokens that seem most unusual.
3. For each of the most interesting tokens, it queries a database to find out how often the token has appeared in spam messages and in ham messages.
4. It uses a Bayesian calculation of these figures to come up with an overall score for the message.
5. If the score exceeds a particular threshold, the message is classified as spam; otherwise, it's classified as ham.
6. It updates the database, increasing the count of each of the interesting tokens for the classification the message received.

It's up to the user to verify whether the classification was accurate. If a mail was improperly classified, the user has some way to reclassify it—it's either a missed spam, or a *false positive*.

One advantage of Bayesian filters is that they automatically learn according to the user's preference. It doesn't matter how the user defines spam—the filter adjusts accordingly. It also doesn't matter what techniques the spammers come up with—as spam changes, the filter learns the new most interesting tokens.

We'll take a closer look at some Bayesian spam filters shortly.

Shared Spam Tagging

Another way to filter spam is similar to the RBLs we discussed earlier in that you're checking an external source in real time, when you receive the message. Instead of checking for whether spam has been sent through the remote server, software you run in the email client creates a fingerprint from the message and checks with a service to see if others have already marked the message as spam. It's kind of a mass-distributed effort to identify each spam message. The first few hundred people receive a spam, mark it as such, and then the software blocks it for the remaining million or so. At least, that's the idea.

The problem with shared spam tagging is that you have to accept the majority opinion on what a spam is. The software doesn't mark a message as spam the first time it's reported—it waits to get a few hundred reports from reliable people before automatically blocking it. But there's no way to really customize the service to make it match your definition of spam; if you want to block newsletters or joke emails from an acquaintance who won't take a hint, shared spam tagging won't do it for you.

The other problem with shared spam tagging is technical—there's no standard way to mark or exchange information about spam. The only existing systems at this writing are proprietary, charge a monthly subscription fee, and only work with Microsoft Outlook and Outlook Express.

Only Accept Mail from Known Senders

An entirely different strategy for dealing with spam is simply rejecting messages from unknown senders—filtering good mail in, instead of filtering bad mail out. A system called *Tagged Message Delivery Agent (TMDA)* is the prime example of this type of system. TMDA is a whitelist system that runs on your mail server. You add your entire address book to the whitelist. Anybody not already on your whitelist that attempts to send you a message gets a friendly response from the system asking them to confirm their identity and email address. If the person responds, you get a message, and have the choice of adding the sender to the whitelist or permanently blacklisting them.

For a small business, this is generally a bad idea—you don't want to make potential customers have to jump through hoops to reach you. It's an easy way to lose a sale. But if you have non-business email addresses being overwhelmed with spam, TMDA may be an option to consider.

One likely solution to the spam problem is simply the use of digital signatures. If enough people begin signing their email, eventually you'll be able to filter out email that isn't signed. A digital signature, just like a physical one, adds authenticity to a message. Digital signatures can be traced, verified, and accounted for. The biggest problem with spam is the unaccountability of it. The worst spam messages are those with forged sender addresses, misleading content, and statements of outright fraud. Simply making senders accountable for their email will go a long way towards solving the problem.

An Overview of Spam Filters

There are dozens of spam filters available. Table 19.1 lists a few. They all seem to work slightly differently. Depending on how you get your email, and whether you want spam filtering for yourself or for the entire company, it's fairly easy to identify a good solution for your business.

TABLE 19.1 Comparison of Popular Open Source Spam Filters

Filter	Type	Where Runs	Notes	Available at
SpamAssassin	Primarily Heuristic, Bayesian	From individual server-side mail delivery agent	Extremely popular, fairly effective, difficult to administer and use.	http://spamassassin.org
Popfile	Bayesian	Mail server	Used for intelligent mail sorting, not just spam. Requires training.	http://popfile. sourceforge.net/
SpamBayes	Bayesian	Email clients	One of the more effective spam filters, must be installed by individual users.	http://spambayes. sourceforge.net/
Dspam	Bayesian	Site installation on mail server	Very easy to use, once it's set up. Very effective. Flexible configuration options. Requires a lot of disk space.	http://nuclearelephant. com/projects/dspam
Bogofilter	Bayesian	From individual server-side mail delivery agent	Simple, effective, but needs supporting scripts for retraining.	http://bogofilter. sourceforge.net
SpamNet	Shared Spam Tagging	Email clients (Outlook and Outlook Express Only)	Very effective. Individual subscriptions and installations.	http://spamnet.com
TMDA	Verified Sender Filter	Mail Server	Uses a challenge/response model for unknown senders—people trying to send you mail must confirm their identity.	http://tmda.net

When evaluating a spam filter, first determine how easy it is to use. Bayesian filters must be trained—if training is a hassle, people won't do it, and the filter becomes worthless. What do you need to do to train a Bayesian filter if it misses a spam? How easy is it to untrain it when it catches a false positive?

Small Business Spam Filter: Dspam

When it comes to spam filters, easier is better. What's easiest depends a lot on the personality of the person having to administer the spam filter. For most small businesses, it's best to get a solution that works for the entire company, not needing to be configured individually. It should be easy to correct problems. One spam filter that fits these criteria is Dspam.

Dspam plugs into a Unix-based mail server, like the one described in Chapter 5. Basically all you need to do is configure a spam address in your mail server, and set up a simple Web application that provides access to the quarantine.

When your mail server receives a mail and verifies the recipient's user account, it passes it to Dspam. Dspam evaluates the message against the existing token database. If it decides the message is innocent, it adds a signature to the message and delivers it to the recipient's mailbox. If Dspam decides the message is spam, it sends it to the quarantine.

Using Dspam

As a user, you simply check your email. If you receive a spam, you send it to your spam email address, and then delete it. That's about all you have to do.

Periodically, you should check your quarantine to make sure Dspam didn't catch any innocent messages by mistake. At first, it will probably catch a few. Checking the quarantine involves simply logging into a Web page. On the Web page are statistics about the amount of email and spam Dspam has processed. Follow a link and you'll see everything in the quarantine, listed with the sender's name and email address, and the subject of the message. If it looks innocent, you can safely click on it to check it out, and if it is innocent, click one other button and Dspam will unlearn it and deliver it to your mailbox. Otherwise, a single click deletes everything held in your quarantine.

Figure 19.1 shows some messages in a Dspam quarantine. The quarantine only contains mail Dspam has caught—messages you send to the spam address are trained and deleted. You can set Dspam up to have a single quarantine for your entire company, assigning one person to check it regularly. Or you can give each employee their own personal dictionary, allowing them to train Dspam with their own preferences (by forwarding messages they consider to be spam).

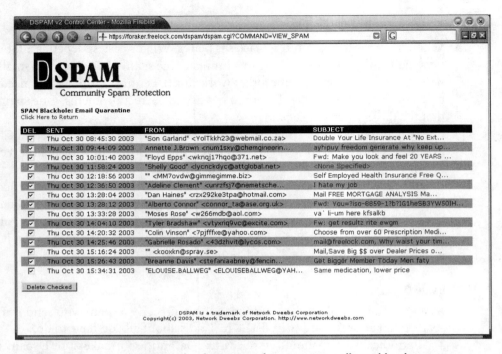

FIGURE 19.1   A Spam Quarantine in Dspam shows spams collected by the system, allowing you to correct any mistakes made by the software.

Installing Dspam

Dspam is perhaps the easiest to use, most powerful, and most flexible spam filter available. Unfortunately, it's not the easiest to set up. Dspam needs to be integrated into both your email system and your Web server, and it works best if you have it use a MySQL database to contain the token database. So before attempting to install Dspam, you must get these other systems working properly.

Further instructions for setting up Dspam for your business are online at the Web site for this book, at *http://opensourcesmall.biz/spam*.

SUMMARY

Viruses and spam consume a lot of bandwidth and network administrator time, on top of the great inconvenience they cause everybody else. Everybody thinks you need a good antivirus program to catch viruses. However, antivirus software on your desktop is software of last resort—your computer has already received the virus before it ever gets detected, and antivirus software does nothing to prevent new viruses it doesn't yet recognize.

The best defense against viruses is diversity. Using email programs that aren't targeted by virus writers will save you a lot of headaches. Using alternative operating systems, like Mac or Linux, make you invulnerable to the very numerous Windows viruses that inhabit the Internet.

Some of the best spam filters are open source. While deploying them may not be the easiest task, the end result can be a huge relief if the spammers have discovered your mailbox.

In this last chapter, we took a close look at viruses and spam. We dissected the different types of viruses, examined strategies for defending against them, and proposed a diverse computing environment as the best long-term defense. Then we turned to spam, identifying why it's a problem, and how we may be able to eventually solve it. We looked at a variety of spam prevention strategies, and compared different filtering techniques. Finally, we discussed using an open source spam filter called Dspam, which has easy administration and user friendliness.

SPAM AND VIRUS REFERENCES

An updated list of resources for this chapter is on the Web site for the book at *http://opensourcesmall.biz/spam.*

Articles

"Blaster worm linked to severity of blackout," by Dan Verton, *http://www.computerworld.com/securitytopics/security/recovery/story/0,10801,84510,00.html*

"Computer virus infects Air Canada check-in system," Reuters, *http://www.usatoday.com/travel/news/2003/08/20-aca-virus.htm*

"The Spread of the Sapphire/Slammer Worm," by David Moore, Vern Paxson, Stefan Savage, Colleen Shannon, Stuart Staniford, and Nicholas Weaver, *http://www.cs.berkeley.edu/~nweaver/sapphire/*

"Man cleared over porn 'may sue'," by The BBC News, 31 July 2003. Available online at *http://news.bbc.co.uk/1/hi/england/devon/3114815.stm*

"Spam: How it is hurting email and degrading life on the Internet," by Pew Internet & American Life Project, October 22, 2003. Available online at *http://www.pewinternet.org/reports/toc.asp?Report=102*

"Why Am I Getting All This Spam?" Center for Democracy & Technology (CDT) report on the origins of spam, March 19, 2003. Available online at *http://www.cdt.org/speech/spam/030319spamreport.pdf.*

"Virulent worm calls into doubt our ability to protect the Net," by Rob Lemos. Available online at *http://news.com.com/2009-1001-270471.html?legacy=cnet.*

"There will be an estimated 302 million corporate mailboxes worldwide by year end 2003 and Microsoft Exchange is estimated to power 35% of these." Analysis by Research And Markets, PRWeb. Available on line at *http://www.prweb.com/releases/2003/9/prweb79039.htm*

"A Plan for Spam," by Paul Graham, *http://www.paulgraham.com/spam.html*

Software

Amavis, open source framework for email virus scanning *http://www.amavis.org*

Tripwire, open source file monitoring program for Linux (commercial for Windows) *http://www.tripwire.org*

SpamAssassin, open source heuristic spam filter with Bayesian component *http://www.spamassassin.org*

Popfile, open source spam filter *http://popfile.sourceforge.net*

SpamBayes, open source spam filter *http://spambayes.sourceforge.net*

Dspam, open source spam filter *http://nuclearelephant.com/projects/dspam*

Bogofilter, open source spam filter *http://bogofilter.sourceforge.net*

SpamNet, shared spam tagging server *http://spamnet.com*

TMDA, open source verified sender filter *http://tmda.net*

Maia Mailguard, Web application for managing Amavis and SpamAssassin *http://www.renaissoft.com/projects/maia/*

A The Open Source Definition

The Open Source Initiative (OSI) is a non-profit company that certifies open source licenses. They maintain a definition of what makes a license open source. We have used the OSI definition throughout this book to identify whether particular software is open source. The current Open Source Definition is available at http://opensource.org/docs/definition.php. Version 1.9 is reproduced here, under the Open Software License version 2.0.

INTRODUCTION

Open source doesn't just mean access to the source code. The distribution terms of open source software must comply with the following criteria:

1. Free Redistribution

The license shall not restrict any party from selling or giving away the software as a component of an aggregate software distribution containing programs from several different sources. The license shall not require a royalty or other fee for such sale.

2. Source Code

The program must include source code, and must allow distribution in source code as well as compiled form. Where some form of a product is not distributed with source code, there must be a well-publicized means of obtaining the source code for no more than a reasonable reproduction cost preferably, downloading via the Internet without charge. The source code must be the preferred form in which a programmer would modify the program. Deliberately obfuscated source code is not allowed. Intermediate forms such as the output of a preprocessor or translator are not allowed.

3. Derived Works

The license must allow modifications and derived works, and must allow them to be distributed under the same terms as the license of the original software.

469

4. Integrity of the Author's Source Code

The license may restrict source-code from being distributed in modified form *only* if the license allows the distribution of "patch files" with the source code for the purpose of modifying the program at build time. The license must explicitly permit distribution of software built from modified source code. The license may require derived works to carry a different name or version number from the original software.

5. No Discrimination against Persons or Groups

The license must not discriminate against any person or group of persons.

6. No Discrimination against Fields of Endeavor

The license must not restrict anyone from making use of the program in a specific field of endeavor. For example, it may not restrict the program from being used in a business, or from being used for genetic research.

7. Distribution of License

The rights attached to the program must apply to all to whom the program is redistributed without the need for execution of an additional license by those parties.

8. License Must Not Be Specific to a Product

The rights attached to the program must not depend on the program's being part of a particular software distribution. If the program is extracted from that distribution and used or distributed within the terms of the program's license, all parties to whom the program is redistributed should have the same rights as those that are granted in conjunction with the original software distribution.

9. License Must Not Restrict Other Software

The license must not place restrictions on other software that is distributed along with the licensed software. For example, the license must not insist that all other programs distributed on the same medium must be open source software.

10. License Must Be Technology-Neutral

No provision of the license may be predicated on any individual technology or style of interface.

B ❚ Basics of Networking

Inside This Chapter

- What You Need To Know about Ethernet
- Internet Protocol
- TCP and UDP
- Domain Name System (DNS)
- URLs and Individual Services

Networking involves many different layers of protocols. These protocols build on each other to eventually provide the meat of the information being transmitted. To send a single email involves an astonishing number of transactions between servers, complex lookups, shredding of the message at one end and recombining it at the other. We're going to simplify our discussion to highlight five basic parts.

WHAT YOU NEED TO KNOW ABOUT ETHERNET

Ethernet is a basic protocol that specifies the format of signals on the cables between network devices, and prevents them from interfering with each other. There's not much you need to know about Ethernet—generally, you just make sure you have an Ethernet card in each computer (also called a Network Interface Card, or NIC), and run the appropriate cables between them. The important thing to know at this level is that every NIC has a unique identifier, much like a serial number, called a Media Access Control (MAC) address. Devices are often identified by their MAC addresses. When a computer is first turned on or connected to the network, you can use the MAC address to decide what segment of your LAN to put it in, or choose to grant or deny access. This is one common way to secure your network, especially in a wireless network. It works reasonably well, though it is possible to spoof a MAC address and hijack a network session by a nefarious wireless user. Consumer routers almost always come with the ability to spoof the MAC address of the computer you originally signed onto a broadband account with, so that you can start using these routers without your ISP knowing.

One alternative to Ethernet is Token Ring, but there are very few people still using it.

INTERNET PROTOCOL

You've heard the acronym TCP/IP, right? It stands for Transmission Control Protocol/Internet Protocol, and it's the fundamental way data travels across the Internet. We'll get to TCP next, but first let's discuss IP. The important thing to know about IP is that it defines network addresses for any computer on the Internet, much like your street address. The Internet currently uses version 4 of this protocol (IPv4), but because there are now so many devices connected to the Internet, there is a slow migration being made to IPv6, which has many more valid addresses.

An IPv4 address uses what's called a *dotted decimal* location, consisting of four bytes. A byte is eight bits, and a bit is either a zero or a one. The net result is that a byte is a standard unit of computing that can contain a number between zero and 255. So an IPv4 address is a series of four numbers between zero and 255, separated by dots (periods to English types).

Every network device that uses TCP/IP has a set of routing tables that tell it where to send packets of information bound to any IP address. If the IP address is nearby, the network card can attempt to deliver it directly. But if the address is outside the local *subnet*, the packet is delivered to the *gateway*.

The gateway analyzes the packet to see which of the routing rules to apply to send the packet to the next router. This process repeats until the packet eventually arrives at the destination IP address.

The general rule is that there can only be one computer for each IP address. Simple math tells us that there are 4,294,967,296 possible IP addresses—less than the number of people in the world, but probably far more than the number of computers. But due to the fact that many of these addresses have special meanings (such as to identify a subnet, or to broadcast to an entire subnet), and many other large blocks are reserved, in practice there are far fewer IP addresses available than you might initially expect.

The rules for IP addresses have been overhauled into a new version, called IPv6. An IPv6 address is made up of 16 bytes, instead of 4. This isn't just four times as many addresses—if you do the math, it works out to be something like 6.5×10^{23} addresses for every square meter on earth. An IPv6 address uses a hexadecimal format of eight two-byte sections separated by colons. Hexadecimal is a way of expressing numbers in base 16 (meaning each digit can have a value between zero and

15, expressed by the numbers 0–9 and the letters A–F) instead of decimal, which is base 10. With IPv6 addresses, since there are so many possible addresses, there is a convention that allows you to omit one or more sections that have a value of zero and replace them with a double-colon. Here's an example IPv6 address, expressed in two different ways:

```
1080:0:0:0:8:800:200C:417A
1080::8:800:200C:417A
```

It's also possible to represent the last four bytes in decimal format, which will eventually be how existing IPv4 addresses are migrated to IPv6.

The problem with IPv6 is that it isn't in wide use yet. It will take several years before it is fully in place. When it is, it will be possible for all devices on Earth to have a unique IP address.

Meanwhile, there are a couple of tricks people use to make the available IPv4 addresses go around. First off, they share the IP addresses among multiple domains. A single public IP address is associated with exactly one computer (called a host), but many services provide the ability for the same computer to handle other host and domain names using a technique called *virtual hosting*. The effect is that many domains can be handled by a single computer.

The other trick to ensure that there are enough IP addresses to go around is called Network Address Translation (NAT). The gist of NAT is that it allows a whole network of machines on a private LAN to share a single public IP address. What makes this possible is that in IPv4, there are three address spaces reserved for private networks. One of the principles behind IP addresses is that no two computers can use the same IP address at the same time. When you make a dial-up connection, the computer you connect to assigns you an IP address from a pool of addresses controlled by the ISP. You usually get a different IP address every time you connect. Packets of data travel from one IP address to another, hopping from one router to the next. Each router knows where to send a packet next, based on the IP destination. Quite often, each packet goes through a dozen routers on its way from one IP address to the other.

There are three sets of IP addresses that have been set aside for use by private networks. If any packet has one of these three sets of IP addresses as it crosses the Internet, routers simply drop it—these addresses essentially don't exist. The reason they don't exist is so you can use them in your private networks, and be guaranteed that no other computer on the Internet duplicates it.

A NAT router is a special type of router that translates anything coming from the private network going to the Internet by rewriting the packets to make them come from the public IP address assigned to the router. It keeps track of which private IP address sent the packet, so that when a response comes back, it can again rewrite the packet, this time to send it to the private IP address.

The three private IP address ranges are:

```
10.0.0.1 to 10.255.255.254
172.16.0.1 to 172.31.255.254
192.168.0.1 to 192.168.255.254
```

You can set your LAN to use any subnet in any of these ranges.

The other part of IP has to do with *subnets*. Subnets are used to define how to route packets. A computer on a subnet can send a packet directly to another computer on the same subnet. The last address in the range is a broadcast address, which sends packets to all computers on the subnet. To communicate with computers anywhere outside the subnet, a computer sends the packet to the address designated as the gateway. A *gateway* is a computer that has more than one NIC, and so can be part of multiple subnets.

So when you set up your network, you want to choose a particular subnet to put all of your computers on, and set up your router to be the gateway for all the computers for that subnet. If you have another location and want all of your locations to be able to network together, set it up on a different subnet, and then you can create a special route between the subnets through an encrypted tunnel. We discuss this more in Chapter 14.

TCP AND UDP

The next layer up in networking is Transmission Control Protocol (TCP), and Uniform Datagram Protocol (UDP). Both of these protocols build on IP by defining the structure of packets and how to send them. Both of these protocols use IP addresses to define the source and destination of a packet. They also specify a *port* at each end.

For each IP address, there are 65,535 different numbered ports that can be specified as the source or destination of a packet. Some of these port numbers are associated with particular services. For example, the standard port for World Wide Web pages is TCP port 80. The standard port for Simple Mail Transport Protocol (SMTP, the protocol that handles the routing of email) is TCP port 25. Each of the Internet services you might want to support uses a specific port by default—though you can usually change the configuration to run a service on a non-standard port.

Ports under 1,024 are reserved for privileged services (generally services that need to run as root). Ports over 32,768 are used for outgoing packets.

When you open your Web browser and point it to *http://www.yahoo.com*, your computer first looks up the IP address for the Web site. For the actual Web page, it finds a high-numbered port that isn't already in use, and sends a request to TCP port 80 on whatever IP address handles yahoo.com, asking for the main Web page, and putting the high-numbered port and its own IP address as the source. The Yahoo server sends the response back to your computer's IP address, to the high-numbered port your computer specified.

An understanding of ports is essential to configure a firewall, especially if you plan to host particular public services on a computer in your LAN. With a NAT router, for example, if you want to host your company's Web site on your server, you need to tell the router to forward packets destined for TCP port 80 to the IP address of your server.

TCP is a connection-based protocol. Before any data is transferred, the connection must be established. Your client software initiates the connection, the server at the other end acknowledges it, your client sends the request, the server returns a response, and finally, the client acknowledges the response.

In contrast, UDP is a connectionless protocol. The client puts together its request and sends it. At some later point, the server composes a response and sends it back. UDP is often used to stream data, such as streaming media. It's also used to look up domain names, and to discover computers on a Windows network.

TCP is more common, but you will see UDP here and there, and need to configure your firewall rules to accommodate it.

TCP/IP is fundamental to networking with Unix-based computers. Since the Internet itself is largely built on Unix-based computers, TCP/IP is how all traffic on the Internet is handled. However, there are a couple of other competing networking protocols that have been popular for LANs. These include IPX/SPX (from NetWare) and NetBUEI (from Microsoft). If you currently use these protocols, it's best if you change over to TCP/IP to prevent problems interacting with your server.

DOMAIN NAME SYSTEM (DNS)

The Domain Name System is a complex system that translates human-friendly names into IP addresses. It has nothing to do with Windows domains—Windows domains are a completely different, unrelated topic.

DNS is a service provided by special servers called *name servers*. There are two types of name servers: *authoritative name servers*, which definitively define what IP address is associated with a host; and *caching name servers*, that handle requests from clients, tracking down the appropriate authoritative name server to get the correct IP address. On a small network, you can set up a name server to perform both functions. Root name servers are authoritative name servers that handle the Top Level Domains, and there are 13 of them scattered around the Internet.

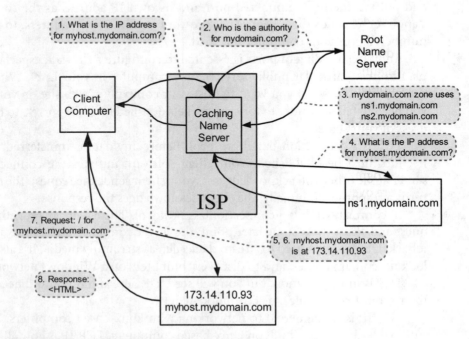

FIGURE B.1 Anatomy of a DNS request.

Figure B.1 illustrates what happens when you pull up a Web page in a browser. The first thing that happens is your computer contacts the caching name server specified in its network settings, asking for the host record, the full domain name in the URL. The caching name server checks to see if it happens to know it, from a previous request. If it has, it simply returns the value from its cache. If it doesn't know anything about the domain, it contacts one of the Root name servers to get the address of an authoritative name server for the domain. Then it contacts the name server to get the IP address of the host. The caching name server then stores this value in its cache, and returns it to your computer. Finally, your computer connects to the host and asks for the Web page.

Your ISP provides caching name servers for you to use. When you set up your Internet connection, you may have to add the IP addresses of these caching name servers in a setting labeled "DNS Servers." If you want your Linux computers to be able to see other computers on your LAN without having to add each machine manually, you'll need to set up your own name server.

Authoritative name servers are a bit more complex. Let's take a closer look at a domain name:

```
some.domain.example.com
```

A domain name is composed of a hierarchy of parts separated by dots. The more significant parts are at the right end of the name—the least significant parts of the domain name are at the left end. The part to the right of the last dot, in this case, com, is called the Top Level Domain (TLD). The next part to the left, example, is the second level domain. The other parts are the third (domain) and fourth (some) level domains.

DNS defines domain names that are universal on the Internet. To get your domain recognized on the Internet, you need to register it with one of the *Registrars*. There are over a hundred official domain registrars to choose from. The registrars are gatekeepers who add and remove domains from the Internet Registry, and are associated with particular TLDs. The root name servers use the Internet Registry to locate the name servers for a domain.

To get your own domain, you need to choose one that's not already in use, and register it with a registrar. In 2003, registrars charged between $5 and $35 per year for a domain.

The registry lists the second level domains, and for each domain, identifies at least two authoritative name servers that handle the domain. Changes to the registry can take from 48 to 72 hours to propagate through the root name servers for the Internet. For third, fourth, and lower level domain names, the same authoritative name servers can handle all the name service, or they can delegate authority for a zone to yet another name server. A zone corresponds to some specific domain name and all domains underneath it in the hierarchy.

URLS AND INDIVIDUAL SERVICES

To tie everything back together, let's take a look at individual services. We saw earlier how Windows Networking uses UNC paths. An email address has its own format. Most other services use a URL scheme to locate the appropriate port on the correct server. Table 3.1 lists some common services, the ports they use by default, and the name of the protocol. You can find a more complete list on a Linux system in the /etc/services file.

TABLE 3.1   Default Ports and Protocols for Common Services

Service	Port	Protocol
Web	80	http
Web (SSL-encrypted)	443	https
Email (outgoing, server to server)	25	SMTP
Email (Post Office Protocol)	110	POP
Email (Encrypted POP)	995	POPS
Email (IMAP)	443	IMAP
Email (Encrypted IMAP)	993	IMAPS
DNS	53 (both UDP & TCP)	DNS
Windows networking	137-139 (both UDP & TCP)	smb
Secure Shell (Remote access)	22	ssh
Telnet (Remote Access)	23	telnet
File Transfer Protocol	21	ftp
Internet Printing Protocol	631	ipp
MySQL database	3306	mysql
Virtual Network Computing	5900-59xx	vnc
X Windows	6000-60xx	x

These are only the default ports for the service. When a service starts, it *binds* itself to the port and waits for a client to connect. It is usually possible to configure a server to bind to any arbitrary port of your choosing, subject to two points:

■ Only one service can be actively listening on any single port—you cannot run two different services on the same port at the same time.
■ Clients of the service need to connect to the port you chose.

How do you connect to a different port? You specify it in the URL. There's actually a bit more to a URL than you usually see. Take, for example, a URL pointing to Charles River Media:

http://www.charlesriver.com/titles/opensourcebusiness.html

The part before the colon is the protocol. In this case, it's http, short for Hypertext Transport Protocol, the standard protocol for Web pages. It's also used to transfer data between all kinds of services. But if this address is entered into a Web browser, the browser assumes that it's a Web page, and uses the standard port 80 for the connection. It looks up the address for www.charlesriver.com (209.15.176.206), opens a connection to port 80 at that IP address, and requests whatever data is associated with `/titles/opensourcebusiness.html`, passing www.charlesriver.com in an additional header as the host name.

To indicate a non-standard port, insert a colon and the port number immediately after the domain name, before the first forward slash of the path:

http://www.charlesriver.com:8080/titles/opensourcebusiness.html

If there is no service running on port 8080, the browser will time out. But you could run a second instance of a Web server with completely different content, especially if you want to put a somewhat more secret Web site up.

The basic point of this discussion is that every Internet service is a separate thing. You can run all of them on a single server, if the server is powerful enough to support the number of users and amount of load. Or you can dedicate a different server to each service, spreading the load out among different computers to optimize performance and improve security. You can even host some services on appropriately secured servers outside your LAN, on the public Internet. For high-maintenance services like email and Web servers, it may be desirable to have someone else responsible for making sure they're always available. Windows file and printer sharing, on the other hand, is much less secure and should be isolated from the Internet using a good firewall, and never hosted somewhere else.

C Common Open Source Licenses

*T*here are dozens of licenses that meet the OSI definition of Open Source, and new ones appearing all the time. You can write your own, if you like. The Open Source Initiative certifies licenses that meet the definition (as listed in Appendix A). Here are a few of the most common licenses.

THE GNU GENERAL PUBLIC LICENSE (GPL)

The GPL is perhaps the most common Open Source license, mainly because it was the original license promoted by the Free Software Foundation. Linus Torvalds chose to release the Linux kernel under the GPL. It's one of the more extreme licenses, compelling companies who release object code based on other GPL software to also provide source code. In this respect, it's also called "viral" or "copyleft." It's important to note that the GPL doesn't require you to release source code that you only use internally, or source code that interacts with GPL software—only software derived from or added to GPL software that you actually distribute to somebody must make source code available.

GNU GENERAL PUBLIC LICENSE
Version 2, June 1991

Copyright (C) 1989, 1991 Free Software Foundation, Inc.
59 Temple Place, Suite 330, Boston, MA 02111-1307 USA

Everyone is permitted to copy and distribute verbatim copies of this license document, but changing it is not allowed.

Preamble

The licenses for most software are designed to take away your freedom to share and change it. By contrast, the GNU General Public License is intended to guarantee your freedom to share and change free software—to make sure the software is free for all its users. This General Public License applies to most of the Free Software Foundation's software and to any other program whose authors commit to using it. (Some other Free Software Foundation software is covered by the GNU Library General Public License instead.) You can apply it to your programs, too.

When we speak of free software, we are referring to freedom, not price. Our General Public Licenses are designed to make sure that you have the freedom to distribute copies of free software (and charge for this service if you wish), that you receive source code or can get it if you want it, that you can change the software or use pieces of it in new free programs; and that you know you can do these things.

To protect your rights, we need to make restrictions that forbid anyone to deny you these rights or to ask you to surrender the rights. These restrictions translate to certain responsibilities for you if you distribute copies of the software, or if you modify it.

For example, if you distribute copies of such a program, whether gratis or for a fee, you must give the recipients all the rights that you have. You must make sure that they, too, receive or can get the source code. And you must show them these terms so they know their rights.

We protect your rights with two steps: (1) copyright the software, and (2) offer you this license which gives you legal permission to copy, distribute and/or modify the software.

Also, for each author's protection and ours, we want to make certain that everyone understands that there is no warranty for this free software. If the software is modified by someone else and passed on, we want its recipients to know that what they have is not the original, so that any problems introduced by others will not reflect on the original authors' reputations.

Finally, any free program is threatened constantly by software patents. We wish to avoid the danger that redistributors of a free program will individually obtain patent licenses, in effect making the program proprietary. To prevent this, we have made it clear that any patent must be licensed for everyone's free use or not licensed at all.

The precise terms and conditions for copying, distribution and modification follow.

GNU GENERAL PUBLIC LICENSE
TERMS AND CONDITIONS FOR COPYING, DISTRIBUTION AND
MODIFICATION

0. This License applies to any program or other work which contains a notice placed by the copyright holder saying it may be distributed under the terms of this General Public License. The "Program", below, refers to any such program or work, and a "work based on the Program" means either the Program or any derivative work under copyright law: that is to say, a work containing the Program or a portion of it, either verbatim or with modifications and/or translated into another language. (Hereinafter, translation is included without limitation in the term "modification".) Each licensee is addressed as "you".

Activities other than copying, distribution and modification are not covered by this License; they are outside its scope. The act of running the Program is not restricted, and the output from the Program is covered only if its contents constitute a work based on the Program (independent of having been made by running the Program). Whether that is true depends on what the Program does.

1. You may copy and distribute verbatim copies of the Program's source code as you receive it, in any medium, provided that you conspicuously and appropriately publish on each copy an appropriate copyright notice and disclaimer of warranty; keep intact all the notices that refer to this License and to the absence of any warranty; and give any other recipients of the Program a copy of this License along with the Program.

You may charge a fee for the physical act of transferring a copy, and you may at your option offer warranty protection in exchange for a fee.

2. You may modify your copy or copies of the Program or any portion of it, thus forming a work based on the Program, and copy and distribute such modifications or work under the terms of Section 1 above, provided that you also meet all of these conditions:

a) You must cause the modified files to carry prominent notices stating that you changed the files and the date of any change.

b) You must cause any work that you distribute or publish, that in whole or in part contains or is derived from the Program or any part thereof, to be licensed as a whole at no charge to all third parties under the terms of this License.

c) If the modified program normally reads commands interactively when run, you must cause it, when started running for such interactive use in the most ordinary way, to print or display an announcement including an appropriate copyright notice and a notice that there is no warranty (or else, saying that you provide a warranty) and that users may redistribute the program under these conditions, and telling the user how to view a copy of this License. (Exception: if the Program itself is interactive but does not normally print such an announcement, your work based on the Program is not required to print an announcement.)

These requirements apply to the modified work as a whole. If identifiable sections of that work are not derived from the Program, and can be reasonably considered independent and separate works in themselves, then this License, and its terms, do not apply to those sections when you distribute them as separate works. But when you distribute the same sections as part of a whole which is a work based on the Program, the distribution of the whole must be on the terms of this License, whose permissions for other licensees extend to the entire whole, and thus to each and every part regardless of who wrote it.

Thus, it is not the intent of this section to claim rights or contest your rights to work written entirely by you; rather, the intent is to exercise the right to control the distribution of derivative or collective works based on the Program.

In addition, mere aggregation of another work not based on the Program with the Program (or with a work based on the Program) on a volume of a storage or distribution medium does not bring the other work under the scope of this License.

3. You may copy and distribute the Program (or a work based on it, under Section 2) in object code or executable form under the terms of Sections 1 and 2 above provided that you also do one of the following:

a) Accompany it with the complete corresponding machine-readable source code, which must be distributed under the terms of Sections 1 and 2 above on a medium customarily used for software interchange; or,

b) Accompany it with a written offer, valid for at least three years, to give any third party, for a charge no more than your cost of physically performing source distribution, a complete machine-readable copy of the corresponding source code, to be distributed under the terms of Sections 1 and 2 above on a medium customarily used for software interchange; or,

c) Accompany it with the information you received as to the offer to distribute corresponding source code. (This alternative is allowed only for noncommercial distribution and only if you received the program in object code or executable form with such an offer, in accord with Subsection b above.)

The source code for a work means the preferred form of the work for making modifications to it. For an executable work, complete source code means all the source code for all modules it contains, plus any associated interface definition files, plus the scripts used to control compilation and installation of the executable. However, as a special exception, the source code distributed need not include anything that is normally distributed (in either source or binary form) with the major components (compiler, kernel, and so on) of the operating system on which the executable runs, unless that component itself accompanies the executable.

If distribution of executable or object code is made by offering access to copy from a designated place, then offering equivalent access to copy the source code from the same place counts as distribution of the source code, even though third parties are not compelled to copy the source along with the object code.

4. You may not copy, modify, sublicense, or distribute the Program except as expressly provided under this License. Any attempt otherwise to copy, modify, sublicense or distribute the Program is void, and will automatically terminate your rights under this License. However, parties who have received copies, or rights, from you under this License will not have their licenses terminated so long as such parties remain in full compliance.

5. You are not required to accept this License, since you have not signed it. However, nothing else grants you permission to modify or distribute the Program or its derivative works. These actions are prohibited by law if you do not accept this License. Therefore, by modifying or distributing the Program (or any work based on the Program), you indicate your acceptance of this License to do so, and all its terms and conditions for copying, distributing or modifying the Program or works based on it.

6. Each time you redistribute the Program (or any work based on the Program), the recipient automatically receives a license from the original licensor to copy, distribute or modify the Program subject to these terms and conditions. You may not impose any further restrictions on the recipients' exercise of the rights granted herein. You are not responsible for enforcing compliance by third parties to this License.

7. If, as a consequence of a court judgment or allegation of patent infringement or for any other reason (not limited to patent issues), conditions are imposed on you (whether by court order, agreement or otherwise) that contradict the conditions of this License, they do not excuse you from the conditions of this License. If you cannot distribute so as to satisfy simultaneously your obligations under this License and any other pertinent obligations, then as a consequence you may not distribute the Program at all. For example, if a patent license would not permit royalty-free redistribution of the Program by all those who receive copies directly or indirectly through you, then the only way you could satisfy both it and this License would be to refrain entirely from distribution of the Program.

If any portion of this section is held invalid or unenforceable under any particular circumstance, the balance of the section is intended to apply and the section as a whole is intended to apply in other circumstances.

It is not the purpose of this section to induce you to infringe any patents or other property right claims or to contest validity of any such claims; this section has the sole purpose of protecting the integrity of the free software distribution system, which is implemented by public license practices. Many people have made generous contributions to the wide range of software distributed through that system in reliance on consistent application of that system; it is up to the author/donor to decide if he or she is willing to distribute software through any other system and a licensee cannot impose that choice.

This section is intended to make thoroughly clear what is believed to be a consequence of the rest of this License.

8. If the distribution and/or use of the Program is restricted in certain countries either by patents or by copyrighted interfaces, the original copyright holder who places the Program under this License may add an explicit geographical distribution limitation excluding those countries, so that distribution is permitted only in or among countries not thus excluded. In such case, this License incorporates the limitation as if written in the body of this License.

9. The Free Software Foundation may publish revised and/or new versions of the General Public License from time to time. Such new versions will be similar in spirit to the present version, but may differ in detail to address new problems or concerns.

Each version is given a distinguishing version number. If the Program specifies a version number of this License which applies to it and "any later version", you have the option of following the terms and conditions either of that version or of any later version published by the Free Software Foundation. If the Program does not specify a version number of this License, you may choose any version ever published by the Free Software Foundation.

10. If you wish to incorporate parts of the Program into other free programs whose distribution conditions are different, write to the author to ask for permission. For software which is copyrighted by the Free Software Foundation, write to the Free Software Foundation; we sometimes make exceptions for this. Our decision will be guided by the two goals of preserving the free status of all derivatives of our free software and of promoting the sharing and reuse of software generally.

NO WARRANTY

11. BECAUSE THE PROGRAM IS LICENSED FREE OF CHARGE, THERE IS NO WARRANTY FOR THE PROGRAM, TO THE EXTENT PERMITTED BY APPLICABLE LAW. EXCEPT WHEN OTHERWISE STATED IN WRITING THE COPYRIGHT HOLDERS AND/OR OTHER PARTIES PROVIDE THE PROGRAM "AS IS" WITHOUT WARRANTY OF ANY KIND, EITHER EXPRESSED OR IMPLIED, INCLUDING, BUT NOT LIMITED TO, THE IMPLIED WARRANTIES OF MERCHANTABILITY AND FITNESS FOR A PARTICULAR PURPOSE. THE ENTIRE RISK AS TO THE QUALITY AND PERFORMANCE OF THE PROGRAM IS WITH YOU. SHOULD THE PROGRAM PROVE DEFECTIVE, YOU ASSUME THE COST OF ALL NECESSARY SERVICING, REPAIR OR CORRECTION.

12. IN NO EVENT UNLESS REQUIRED BY APPLICABLE LAW OR AGREED TO IN WRITING WILL ANY COPYRIGHT HOLDER, OR ANY OTHER PARTY WHO MAY MODIFY AND/OR REDISTRIBUTE THE PROGRAM AS PERMITTED ABOVE, BE LIABLE TO YOU FOR DAMAGES, INCLUDING ANY GENERAL, SPECIAL, INCIDENTAL OR CONSEQUENTIAL DAMAGES ARISING OUT OF THE USE OR INABILITY TO USE THE PROGRAM (INCLUDING BUT NOT LIMITED TO LOSS OF DATA OR DATA BEING RENDERED INACCURATE OR LOSSES SUSTAINED BY YOU OR THIRD PARTIES OR A FAILURE OF THE PROGRAM TO OPERATE WITH ANY OTHER PROGRAMS), EVEN IF SUCH HOLDER OR OTHER PARTY HAS BEEN ADVISED OF THE POSSIBILITY OF SUCH DAMAGES.

END OF TERMS AND CONDITIONS

How to Apply These Terms to Your New Programs

If you develop a new program, and you want it to be of the greatest possible use to the public, the best way to achieve this is to make it free software which everyone can redistribute and change under these terms.

To do so, attach the following notices to the program. It is safest to attach them to the start of each source file to most effectively convey the exclusion of warranty; and each file should have at least the "copyright" line and a pointer to where the full notice is found.

<one line to give the program's name and a brief idea of what it does.> Copyright (C) <year> <name of author>

This program is free software; you can redistribute it and/or modify it under the terms of the GNU General Public License as published by the Free Software Foundation; either version 2 of the License, or (at your option) any later version.

This program is distributed in the hope that it will be useful, but WITHOUT ANY WARRANTY; without even the implied warranty of MERCHANTABILITY or FITNESS FOR A PARTICULAR PURPOSE. See the GNU General Public License for more details.

You should have received a copy of the GNU General Public License along with this program; if not, write to the Free Software Foundation, Inc., 59 Temple Place, Suite 330, Boston, MA 02111-1307 USA

Also add information on how to contact you by electronic and paper mail.

If the program is interactive, make it output a short notice like this when it starts in an interactive mode:

Gnomovision version 69, Copyright (C) year name of author Gnomovision comes with ABSOLUTELY NO WARRANTY; for details type 'show w'. This is free software, and you are welcome to redistribute it under certain conditions; type 'show c' for details.

The hypothetical commands 'show w' and 'show c' should show the appropriate parts of the General Public License. Of course, the commands you use may be called something other than 'show w' and 'show c'; they could even be mouseclicks or menu items—whatever suits your program.

You should also get your employer (if you work as a programmer) or your school, if any, to sign a "copyright disclaimer" for the program, if necessary. Here is a sample; alter the names:

Yoyodyne, Inc., hereby disclaims all copyright interest in the program *Gnomovision* (which makes passes at compilers) written by James Hacker.

<signature of Ty Coon>, 1 April 1989
Ty Coon, President of Vice

This General Public License does not permit incorporating your program into proprietary programs. If your program is a subroutine library, you may consider it more useful to permit linking proprietary applications with the library. If this is what you want to do, use the GNU Library General Public License instead of this License.

THE LIBRARY GENERAL PUBLIC LICENSE (LGPL)

Also called the "Lesser General Public License," software programs licensed under the LGPL can be directly used in proprietary applications without providing the source code for the application.

GNU LESSER GENERAL PUBLIC LICENSE
Version 2.1, February 1999

Copyright (C) 1991, 1999 Free Software Foundation, Inc.
    59 Temple Place, Suite 330, Boston, MA 02111-1307 USA
Everyone is permitted to copy and distribute verbatim copies of this license document, but changing it is not allowed.

[This is the first released version of the Lesser GPL. It also counts as the successor of the GNU Library Public License, version 2, hence the version number 2.1.]

Preamble

The licenses for most software are designed to take away your freedom to share and change it. By contrast, the GNU General Public Licenses are intended to guarantee your freedom to share and change free software—to make sure the software is free for all its users.

This license, the Lesser General Public License, applies to some specially designated software packages—typically libraries—of the Free Software Foundation and other authors who decide to use it. You can use it too, but we suggest you first think carefully about whether this license or the ordinary General Public License is the better strategy to use in any particular case, based on the explanations below.

When we speak of free software, we are referring to freedom of use, not price. Our General Public Licenses are designed to make sure that you have the freedom to distribute copies of free software (and charge for this service if you wish); that you receive source code or can get it if you want it; that you can change the software and use pieces of it in new free programs; and that you are informed that you can do these things.

To protect your rights, we need to make restrictions that forbid distributors to deny you these rights or to ask you to surrender these rights. These restrictions translate to certain responsibilities for you if you distribute copies of the library or if you modify it.

For example, if you distribute copies of the library, whether gratis or for a fee, you must give the recipients all the rights that we gave you. You must make sure that they, too, receive or can get the source code. If you link other code with the library, you must provide complete object files to the recipients, so that they can relink them with the library after making changes to the library and recompiling it. And you must show them these terms so they know their rights.

We protect your rights with a two-step method: (1) we copyright the library, and (2) we offer you this license, which gives you legal permission to copy, distribute and/or modify the library.

To protect each distributor, we want to make it very clear that there is no warranty for the free library. Also, if the library is modified by someone else and passed on, the recipients should know that what they have is not the original version, so that the original author's reputation will not be affected by problems that might be introduced by others.

Finally, software patents pose a constant threat to the existence of any free program. We wish to make sure that a company cannot effectively restrict the users of a free program by obtaining a restrictive license from a patent holder. Therefore, we insist that any patent license obtained for a version of the library must be consistent with the full freedom of use specified in this license.

Most GNU software, including some libraries, is covered by the ordinary GNU General Public License. This license, the GNU Lesser General Public License, applies to certain designated libraries, and is quite different from the ordinary General Public License. We use this license for certain libraries in order to permit linking those libraries into non-free programs.

When a program is linked with a library, whether statically or using a shared library, the combination of the two is legally speaking a combined work, a derivative of the original library. The ordinary General Public License therefore permits such linking only if the entire combination fits its criteria of freedom. The Lesser General Public License permits more lax criteria for linking other code with the library.

We call this license the "Lesser" General Public License because it does Less to protect the user's freedom than the ordinary General Public License. It also provides other free software developers Less of an advantage over competing non-free programs. These disadvantages are the reason we use the ordinary General Public License for many libraries. However, the Lesser license provides advantages in certain special circumstances.

For example, on rare occasions, there may be a special need to encourage the widest possible use of a certain library, so that it becomes a de-facto standard. To achieve this, non-free programs must be allowed to use the library. A more frequent case is that a free library does the same job as widely used non-free libraries. In this case, there is little to gain by limiting the free library to free software only, so we use the Lesser General Public License.

In other cases, permission to use a particular library in non-free programs enables a greater number of people to use a large body of free software. For example, permission to use the GNU C Library in non-free programs enables many more people to use the whole GNU operating system, as well as its variant, the GNU/Linux operating system.

Although the Lesser General Public License is Less protective of the users' freedom, it does ensure that the user of a program that is linked with the Library has the freedom and the wherewithal to run that program using a modified version of the Library.

The precise terms and conditions for copying, distribution and modification follow. Pay close attention to the difference between a "work based on the library" and a "work that uses the library". The former contains code derived from the library, whereas the latter must be combined with the library in order to run.

GNU LESSER GENERAL PUBLIC LICENSE
TERMS AND CONDITIONS FOR COPYING, DISTRIBUTION AND MODIFICATION

0. This License Agreement applies to any software library or other program which contains a notice placed by the copyright holder or other authorized party saying it may be distributed under the terms of this Lesser General Public License (also called "this License"). Each licensee is addressed as "you".

A "library" means a collection of software functions and/or data prepared so as to be conveniently linked with application programs (which use some of those functions and data) to form executables.

The "Library", below, refers to any such software library or work which has been distributed under these terms. A "work based on the Library" means either the Library or any derivative work under copyright law: that is to say, a work containing the Library or a portion of it, either verbatim or with modifications and/or translated straightforwardly into another language. (Hereinafter, translation is included without limitation in the term "modification".)

"Source code" for a work means the preferred form of the work for making modifications to it. For a library, complete source code means all the source code for all modules it contains, plus any associated interface definition files, plus the scripts used to control compilation and installation of the library.

Activities other than copying, distribution and modification are not covered by this License; they are outside its scope. The act of running a program using the Library is not restricted, and output from such a program is covered only if its contents constitute a work based on the Library (independent of the use of the Library in a tool for writing it). Whether that is true depends on what the Library does and what the program that uses the Library does.

1. You may copy and distribute verbatim copies of the Library's complete source code as you receive it, in any medium, provided that you conspicuously and appropriately publish on each copy an appropriate copyright notice and disclaimer of warranty; keep intact all the notices that refer to this License and to the absence of any warranty; and distribute a copy of this License along with the Library.

You may charge a fee for the physical act of transferring a copy, and you may at your option offer warranty protection in exchange for a fee.

2. You may modify your copy or copies of the Library or any portion of it, thus forming a work based on the Library, and copy and distribute such modifications or work under the terms of Section 1 above, provided that you also meet all of these conditions:

a) The modified work must itself be a software library.

b) You must cause the files modified to carry prominent notices stating that you changed the files and the date of any change.

c) You must cause the whole of the work to be licensed at no charge to all third parties under the terms of this License.

d) If a facility in the modified Library refers to a function or a table of data to be supplied by an application program that uses the facility, other than as an argument passed when the facility is invoked, then you must make a good faith effort to ensure that, in the event an application does not supply such function or table, the facility still operates, and performs whatever part of its purpose remains meaningful.

(For example, a function in a library to compute square roots has a purpose that is entirely well-defined independent of the application. Therefore, Subsection 2d requires that any application-supplied function or table used by this function must be optional: if the application does not supply it, the square root function must still compute square roots.)

These requirements apply to the modified work as a whole. If identifiable sections of that work are not derived from the Library, and can be reasonably considered independent and separate works in themselves, then this License, and its terms, do not apply to those sections when you distribute them as separate works. But when you distribute the same sections as part of a whole which is a work based on the Library, the distribution of the whole must be on the terms of this License, whose permissions for other licensees extend to the entire whole, and thus to each and every part regardless of who wrote it.

Thus, it is not the intent of this section to claim rights or contest your rights to work written entirely by you; rather, the intent is to exercise the right to control the distribution of derivative or collective works based on the Library.

In addition, mere aggregation of another work not based on the Library with the Library (or with a work based on the Library) on a volume of a storage or distribution medium does not bring the other work under the scope of this License.

3. You may opt to apply the terms of the ordinary GNU General Public License instead of this License to a given copy of the Library. To do this, you must alter all the notices that refer to this License, so that they refer to the ordinary GNU General Public License, version 2, instead of to this License. (If a newer version than version 2 of the ordinary GNU General Public License has appeared, then you can specify that version instead if you wish.) Do not make any other change in these notices.

Once this change is made in a given copy, it is irreversible for that copy, so the ordinary GNU General Public License applies to all subsequent copies and derivative works made from that copy.

This option is useful when you wish to copy part of the code of the Library into a program that is not a library.

4. You may copy and distribute the Library (or a portion or derivative of it, under Section 2) in object code or executable form under the terms of Sections 1 and 2 above provided that you accompany it with the complete corresponding machine-readable source code, which must be distributed under the terms of Sections 1 and 2 above on a medium customarily used for software interchange.

If distribution of object code is made by offering access to copy from a designated place, then offering equivalent access to copy the source code from the same place satisfies the requirement to distribute the source code, even though third parties are not compelled to copy the source along with the object code.

5. A program that contains no derivative of any portion of the Library, but is designed to work with the Library by being compiled or linked with it, is called a "work that uses the Library". Such a work, in isolation, is not a derivative work of the Library, and therefore falls outside the scope of this License.

However, linking a "work that uses the Library" with the Library creates an executable that is a derivative of the Library (because it contains portions of the Library), rather than a "work that uses the library". The executable is therefore covered by this License. Section 6 states terms for distribution of such executables.

When a "work that uses the Library" uses material from a header file that is part of the Library, the object code for the work may be a derivative work of the Library even though the source code is not. Whether this is true is especially significant if the work can be linked without the Library, or if the work is itself a library. The threshold for this to be true is not precisely defined by law.

If such an object file uses only numerical parameters, data structure layouts and accessors, and small macros and small inline functions (ten lines or less in length), then the use of the object file is unrestricted, regardless of whether it is legally a derivative work. (Executables containing this object code plus portions of the Library will still fall under Section 6.)

Otherwise, if the work is a derivative of the Library, you may distribute the object code for the work under the terms of Section 6. Any executables containing that work also fall under Section 6, whether or not they are linked directly with the Library itself.

6. As an exception to the Sections above, you may also combine or link a "work that uses the Library" with the Library to produce a work containing portions of the Library, and distribute that work under terms of your choice,

provided that the terms permit modification of the work for the customer's own use and reverse engineering for debugging such modifications.

You must give prominent notice with each copy of the work that the Library is used in it and that the Library and its use are covered by this License. You must supply a copy of this License. If the work during execution displays copyright notices, you must include the copyright notice for the Library among them, as well as a reference directing the user to the copy of this License. Also, you must do one of these things:

a) Accompany the work with the complete corresponding machine-readable source code for the Library including whatever changes were used in the work (which must be distributed under Sections 1 and 2 above); and, if the work is an executable linked with the Library, with the complete machine-readable "work that uses the Library", as object code and/or source code, so that the user can modify the Library and then relink to produce a modified executable containing the modified Library. (It is understood that the user who changes the contents of definitions files in the Library will not necessarily be able to recompile the application to use the modified definitions.)

b) Use a suitable shared library mechanism for linking with the Library. A suitable mechanism is one that (1) uses at run time a copy of the library already present on the user's computer system, rather than copying library functions into the executable, and (2) will operate properly with a modified version of the library, if the user installs one, as long as the modified version is interface-compatible with the version that the work was made with.

c) Accompany the work with a written offer, valid for at least three years, to give the same user the materials specified in Subsection 6a, above, for a charge no more than the cost of performing this distribution.

d) If distribution of the work is made by offering access to copy from a designated place, offer equivalent access to copy the above specified materials from the same place.

e) Verify that the user has already received a copy of these materials or that you have already sent this user a copy.

For an executable, the required form of the "work that uses the Library" must include any data and utility programs needed for reproducing the executable from it. However, as a special exception, the materials to be distributed need not include anything that is normally distributed (in either source or binary form) with the major components (compiler, kernel, and so on) of the operating system on which the executable runs, unless that component itself accompanies the executable.

It may happen that this requirement contradicts the license restrictions of other proprietary libraries that do not normally accompany the operating system. Such a contradiction means you cannot use both them and the Library together in an executable that you distribute.

7. You may place library facilities that are a work based on the Library side-by-side in a single library together with other library facilities not covered by this License, and distribute such a combined library, provided that the separate distribution of the work based on the Library and of the other library facilities is otherwise permitted, and provided that you do these two things:

a) Accompany the combined library with a copy of the same work based on the Library, uncombined with any other library facilities. This must be distributed under the terms of the Sections above.

b) Give prominent notice with the combined library of the fact that part of it is a work based on the Library, and explaining where to find the accompanying uncombined form of the same work.

8. You may not copy, modify, sublicense, link with, or distribute the Library except as expressly provided under this License. Any attempt otherwise to copy, modify, sublicense, link with, or distribute the Library is void, and will automatically terminate your rights under this License. However, parties who have received copies, or rights, from you under this License will not have their licenses terminated so long as such parties remain in full compliance.

9. You are not required to accept this License, since you have not signed it. However, nothing else grants you permission to modify or distribute the Library or its derivative works. These actions are prohibited by law if you do not accept this License. Therefore, by modifying or distributing the Library (or any work based on the Library), you indicate your acceptance of this License to do so, and all its terms and conditions for copying, distributing or modifying the Library or works based on it.

10. Each time you redistribute the Library (or any work based on the Library), the recipient automatically receives a license from the original licensor to copy, distribute, link with or modify the Library subject to these terms and conditions. You may not impose any further restrictions on the recipients' exercise of the rights granted herein. You are not responsible for enforcing compliance by third parties with this License.

11. If, as a consequence of a court judgment or allegation of patent infringement or for any other reason (not limited to patent issues), conditions are imposed on you (whether by court order, agreement or otherwise) that contradict the conditions of this License, they do not excuse you from the conditions of this License. If you cannot distribute so as to satisfy simultaneously your obligations under this License and any other pertinent obligations, then as a consequence you may not distribute the Library at all. For example, if a patent license would not permit royalty-free redistribution of the Library by all those who receive copies directly or indirectly through you, then the only way you could satisfy both it and this License would be to refrain entirely from distribution of the Library.

If any portion of this section is held invalid or unenforceable under any particular circumstance, the balance of the section is intended to apply, and the section as a whole is intended to apply in other circumstances.

It is not the purpose of this section to induce you to infringe any patents or other property right claims or to contest validity of any such claims; this section has the sole purpose of protecting the integrity of the free software distribution system which is implemented by public license practices. Many people have made generous contributions to the wide range of software distributed through that system in reliance on consistent application of that system; it is up to the author/donor to decide if he or she is willing to distribute software through any other system and a licensee cannot impose that choice.

This section is intended to make thoroughly clear what is believed to be a consequence of the rest of this License.

12. If the distribution and/or use of the Library is restricted in certain countries either by patents or by copyrighted interfaces, the original copyright holder who places the Library under this License may add an explicit geographical distribution limitation excluding those countries, so that distribution is permitted only in or among countries not thus excluded. In such case, this License incorporates the limitation as if written in the body of this License.

13. The Free Software Foundation may publish revised and/or new versions of the Lesser General Public License from time to time. Such new versions will be similar in spirit to the present version, but may differ in detail to address new problems or concerns.

Each version is given a distinguishing version number. If the Library specifies a version number of this License which applies to it and "any later version", you have the option of following the terms and conditions either of that version or of any later version published by the Free Software Foundation. If the Library does not specify a license version number, you may choose any version ever published by the Free Software Foundation.

14. If you wish to incorporate parts of the Library into other free programs whose distribution conditions are incompatible with these, write to the author to ask for permission. For software which is copyrighted by the Free Software Foundation, write to the Free Software Foundation; we sometimes make exceptions for this. Our decision will be guided by the two goals of preserving the free status of all derivatives of our free software and of promoting the sharing and reuse of software generally.

NO WARRANTY

15. BECAUSE THE LIBRARY IS LICENSED FREE OF CHARGE, THERE IS NO WARRANTY FOR THE LIBRARY, TO THE EXTENT PERMITTED BY APPLICABLE LAW. EXCEPT WHEN OTHERWISE STATED IN WRITING THE COPYRIGHT HOLDERS AND/OR OTHER PARTIES PROVIDE THE LIBRARY "AS IS" WITHOUT WARRANTY OF ANY KIND, EITHER EXPRESSED OR IMPLIED, INCLUDING, BUT NOT LIMITED TO, THE IMPLIED WARRANTIES OF MERCHANTABILITY AND FITNESS FOR A PARTICULAR PURPOSE. THE ENTIRE RISK AS TO THE QUALITY AND PERFORMANCE OF THE LIBRARY IS WITH YOU. SHOULD THE LIBRARY PROVE DEFECTIVE, YOU ASSUME THE COST OF ALL NECESSARY SERVICING, REPAIR OR CORRECTION.

16. IN NO EVENT UNLESS REQUIRED BY APPLICABLE LAW OR AGREED TO IN WRITING WILL ANY COPYRIGHT HOLDER, OR ANY OTHER PARTY WHO MAY MODIFY AND/OR REDISTRIBUTE THE LIBRARY AS PERMITTED ABOVE, BE LIABLE TO YOU FOR DAMAGES, INCLUDING ANY GENERAL, SPECIAL, INCIDENTAL OR CONSEQUENTIAL DAMAGES ARISING OUT OF THE USE OR INABILITY TO USE THE LIBRARY (INCLUDING BUT NOT LIMITED TO LOSS OF DATA OR DATA BEING RENDERED INACCURATE OR LOSSES SUSTAINED BY YOU OR THIRD PARTIES OR A FAILURE OF THE LIBRARY TO OPERATE WITH ANY OTHER SOFTWARE), EVEN IF SUCH HOLDER OR OTHER PARTY HAS BEEN ADVISED OF THE POSSIBILITY OF SUCH DAMAGES.

END OF TERMS AND CONDITIONS

How to Apply These Terms to Your New Libraries

If you develop a new library, and you want it to be of the greatest possible use to the public, we recommend making it free software that everyone can redistribute and change. You can do so by permitting redistribution under these terms (or, alternatively, under the terms of the ordinary General Public License).

To apply these terms, attach the following notices to the library. It is safest to attach them to the start of each source file to most effectively convey the exclusion of warranty; and each file should have at least the "copyright" line and a pointer to where the full notice is found.

<one line to give the library's name and a brief idea of what it does.>
Copyright (C) <year> <name of author>

This library is free software; you can redistribute it and/or modify it under the terms of the GNU Lesser General Public License as published by the Free Software Foundation; either version 2.1 of the License, or (at your option) any later version.

This library is distributed in the hope that it will be useful, but WITHOUT ANY WARRANTY; without even the implied warranty of MERCHANTABILITY or FITNESS FOR A PARTICULAR PURPOSE. See the GNU Lesser General Public License for more details.

You should have received a copy of the GNU Lesser General Public License along with this library; if not, write to the Free Software Foundation, Inc., 59 Temple Place, Suite 330, Boston, MA 02111-1307 USA

Also add information on how to contact you by electronic and paper mail.

You should also get your employer (if you work as a programmer) or your school, if any, to sign a "copyright disclaimer" for the library, if necessary. Here is a sample; alter the names:

Yoyodyne, Inc., hereby disclaims all copyright interest in the library 'Frob' (a library for tweaking knobs) written by James Random Hacker.

<signature of Ty Coon>, 1 April 1990 Ty Coon, President of Vice

That's all there is to it!

MOZILLA PUBLIC LICENSE

The Mozilla Public License covers most Mozilla programs, including Firefox and Thunderbird which are on the CD-ROM. MOZILLA PUBLIC LICENSE Version 1.1

---

1. Definitions.

1.0.1. "Commercial Use" means distribution or otherwise making the Covered Code available to a third party.

1.1. "Contributor" means each entity that creates or contributes to the creation of Modifications.

1.2. "Contributor Version" means the combination of the Original Code, prior Modifications used by a Contributor, and the Modifications made by that particular Contributor.

1.3. "Covered Code" means the Original Code or Modifications or the combination of the Original Code and Modifications, in each case including portions thereof.

1.4. "Electronic Distribution Mechanism" means a mechanism generally accepted in the software development community for the electronic transfer of data.

1.5. "Executable" means Covered Code in any form other than Source Code.

1.6. "Initial Developer" means the individual or entity identified as the Initial Developer in the Source Code notice required by Exhibit A.

1.7. "Larger Work" means a work which combines Covered Code or portions thereof with code not governed by the terms of this License.

1.8. "License" means this document.

1.8.1. "Licensable" means having the right to grant, to the maximum extent possible, whether at the time of the initial grant or subsequently acquired, any and all of the rights conveyed herein.

1.9. "Modifications" means any addition to or deletion from the substance or structure of either the Original Code or any previous Modifications. When Covered Code is released as a series of files, a Modification is:

A. Any addition to or deletion from the contents of a file containing Original Code or previous Modifications.

B. Any new file that contains any part of the Original Code or previous Modifications.

1.10. "Original Code" means Source Code of computer software code which is described in the Source Code notice required by Exhibit A as Original Code, and which, at the time of its release under this License is not already Covered Code governed by this License.

1.10.1. "Patent Claims" means any patent claim(s), now owned or hereafter acquired, including without limitation, method, process, and apparatus claims, in any patent Licensable by grantor.

1.11. "Source Code" means the preferred form of the Covered Code for making modifications to it, including all modules it contains, plus any associated interface definition files, scripts used to control compilation and installation of an Executable, or source code differential comparisons against either the Original Code or another well known, available Covered Code of the Contributor's choice. The Source Code can be in a compressed or archival form, provided the appropriate decompression or de-archiving software is widely available for no charge.

1.12. "You" (or "Your") means an individual or a legal entity exercising rights under, and complying with all of the terms of, this License or a future version of this License issued under Section 6.1. For legal entities, "You" includes any entity which controls, is controlled by, or is under common control with You. For purposes of this definition, "control" means (a) the power, direct or indirect, to cause the direction or management of such entity, whether by contract or otherwise, or (b) ownership of more than fifty percent (50%) of the outstanding shares or beneficial ownership of such entity.

2. Source Code License.

2.1. The Initial Developer Grant.

The Initial Developer hereby grants You a world-wide, royalty-free, non-exclusive license, subject to third party intellectual property claims:

(a) under intellectual property rights (other than patent or trademark) Licensable by Initial Developer to use, reproduce, modify, display, perform, sublicense and distribute the Original Code (or portions thereof) with or without Modifications, and/or as part of a Larger Work; and

(b) under Patents Claims infringed by the making, using or selling of Original Code, to make, have made, use, practice, sell, and offer for sale, and/or otherwise dispose of the Original Code (or portions thereof).

(c) the licenses granted in this Section 2.1(a) and (b) are effective on the date Initial Developer first distributes Original Code under the terms of this License.

(d) Notwithstanding Section 2.1(b) above, no patent license is granted: 1) for code that You delete from the Original Code; 2) separate from the Original Code; or 3) for infringements caused by: i) the modification of the Original Code or ii) the combination of the Original Code with other software or devices.

2.2. Contributor Grant.

Subject to third party intellectual property claims, each Contributor hereby grants You a world-wide, royalty-free, non-exclusive license

(a) under intellectual property rights (other than patent or trademark) Licensable by Contributor, to use, reproduce, modify, display, perform, sublicense and distribute the Modifications created by such Contributor (or portions thereof) either on an unmodified basis, with other Modifications, as Covered Code and/or as part of a Larger Work; and

(b) under Patent Claims infringed by the making, using, or selling of Modifications made by that Contributor either alone and/or in combination with its Contributor Version (or portions of such combination), to make, use, sell, offer for sale, have made, and/or otherwise dispose of: 1) Modifications made by that Contributor (or portions thereof); and 2) the combination of Modifications made by that Contributor with its Contributor Version (or portions of such combination).

(c) the licenses granted in Sections 2.2(a) and 2.2(b) are effective on the date Contributor first makes Commercial Use of the Covered Code.

(d) Notwithstanding Section 2.2(b) above, no patent license is granted: 1) for any code that Contributor has deleted from the Contributor Version; 2) separate from the Contributor Version; 3) for infringements caused by: i) third party modifications of Contributor Version or ii) the combination of Modifications made by that Contributor with other software (except as part of the Contributor Version) or other devices; or 4) under Patent Claims infringed by Covered Code in the absence of Modifications made by that Contributor.

3. Distribution Obligations.

3.1. Application of License.

The Modifications which You create or to which You contribute are governed by the terms of this License, including without limitation Section 2.2. The Source Code version of Covered Code may be distributed only under the terms of this License or a future version of this License released under Section 6.1, and You must include a copy of this License with every copy of the Source Code You distribute. You may not offer or impose any terms on any Source Code version that alters or restricts the applicable version of this License or the recipients' rights hereunder. However, You may include an additional document offering the additional rights described in Section 3.5.

3.2. Availability of Source Code.

Any Modification which You create or to which You contribute must be made available in Source Code form under the terms of this License either on the same media as an Executable version or via an accepted Electronic Distribution Mechanism to anyone to whom you made an Executable version available; and if made available via Electronic Distribution Mechanism, must remain available for at least twelve (12) months after the date it initially became available, or at least six (6) months after a subsequent version of that particular Modification has been made available to such recipients. You are responsible for ensuring that the Source Code version remains available even if the Electronic Distribution Mechanism is maintained by a third party.

3.3. Description of Modifications.

You must cause all Covered Code to which You contribute to contain a file documenting the changes You made to create that Covered Code and the date of any change. You must include a prominent statement that the Modification is derived, directly or indirectly, from Original Code provided by the Initial Developer and including the name of the Initial Developer in (a) the Source Code, and (b) in any notice in an Executable version or related documentation in which You describe the origin or ownership of the Covered Code.

3.4. Intellectual Property Matters

(a) Third Party Claims.

If Contributor has knowledge that a license under a third party's intellectual property rights is required to exercise the rights granted by such Contributor under Sections 2.1 or 2.2, Contributor must include a text file with the Source Code distribution titled "LEGAL" which describes the claim and the party making the claim in sufficient detail that a recipient will know whom to contact. If Contributor obtains such knowledge after the Modification is made available as described in Section 3.2, Contributor shall promptly modify the LEGAL file in all copies Contributor makes available thereafter and shall take other steps (such as notifying appropriate mailing lists or newsgroups) reasonably calculated to inform those who received the Covered Code that new knowledge has been obtained.

(b) Contributor APIs.

If Contributor's Modifications include an application programming interface and Contributor has knowledge of patent licenses which are reasonably necessary to implement that API, Contributor must also include this information in the LEGAL file.

(c) Representations.

Contributor represents that, except as disclosed pursuant to Section 3.4(a) above, Contributor believes that Contributor's Modifications are Contributor's original creation(s) and/or Contributor has sufficient rights to grant the rights conveyed by this License.

3.5. Required Notices.

You must duplicate the notice in Exhibit A in each file of the Source Code. If it is not possible to put such notice in a particular Source Code file due to its structure, then You must include such notice in a location (such as a relevant directory) where a user would be likely to look for such a notice. If You created one or more Modification(s) You may add your name as a Contributor to the notice described in Exhibit A. You must also duplicate this License in any documentation for the Source Code where You describe recipients' rights or ownership rights relating to Covered Code. You may choose to offer, and to charge a fee for, warranty, support, indemnity or liability obligations to one or more recipients of Covered Code. However, You may do so only on Your own behalf, and not on behalf of the Initial Developer or any Contributor. You must make it absolutely clear than any such warranty, support, indemnity or liability obligation is offered by You alone, and You hereby agree to indemnify the Initial Developer and every Contributor for any liability incurred by the Initial Developer or such Contributor as a result of warranty, support, indemnity or liability terms You offer.

3.6. Distribution of Executable Versions.

You may distribute Covered Code in Executable form only if the requirements of Section 3.1–3.5 have been met for that Covered Code, and if You include a notice stating that the Source Code version of the Covered Code is available under the terms of this License, including a description of how and where You have fulfilled the obligations of Section 3.2. The notice must be conspicuously included in any notice in an Executable version, related documentation or collateral in which You describe recipients' rights relating to the Covered Code. You may distribute the Executable version of Covered Code or ownership rights under a license of Your choice, which may contain terms different from this License, provided that You are in compliance with the terms of this License and that the license for the Executable version does not attempt to limit or alter the recipient's rights in the Source Code version from the rights set forth in this License. If You distribute the Executable version under a different license You must make it absolutely clear that any terms which differ from this License are offered by You alone, not by the Initial Developer or any Contributor. You hereby agree to indemnify the Initial Developer and every Contributor for any liability incurred by the Initial Developer or such Contributor as a result of any such terms You offer.

3.7. Larger Works.

You may create a Larger Work by combining Covered Code with other code not governed by the terms of this License and distribute the Larger Work as a single product. In such a case, You must make sure the requirements of this License are fulfilled for the Covered Code.

4. Inability to Comply Due to Statute or Regulation.

If it is impossible for You to comply with any of the terms of this License with respect to some or all of the Covered Code due to statute, judicial order, or regulation then You must: (a) comply with the terms of this License to the maximum extent possible; and (b) describe the limitations and the code they affect. Such description must be included in the LEGAL file described in Section 3.4 and must be included with all distributions of the Source Code. Except to the extent prohibited by statute or regulation, such description must be sufficiently detailed for a recipient of ordinary skill to be able to understand it.

5. Application of this License.

This License applies to code to which the Initial Developer has attached the notice in Exhibit A and to related Covered Code.

6. Versions of the License.

6.1. New Versions.

Netscape Communications Corporation ("Netscape") may publish revised and/or new versions of the License from time to time. Each version will be given a distinguishing version number.

6.2. Effect of New Versions.

Once Covered Code has been published under a particular version of the License, You may always continue to use it under the terms of that version. You may also choose to use such Covered Code under the terms of any subsequent version of the License published by Netscape. No one other than Netscape has the right to modify the terms applicable to Covered Code created under this License.

6.3. Derivative Works.

If You create or use a modified version of this License (which you may only do in order to apply it to code which is not already Covered Code governed by this License), You must (a) rename Your license so that the phrases "Mozilla", "MOZILLAPL", "MOZPL", "Netscape", "MPL", "NPL" or any confusingly similar phrase do not appear in your license (except to note that your license differs from this License) and (b) otherwise make it clear that Your version of the license contains terms which differ from the Mozilla Public License and Netscape Public License. (Filling in the name of the Initial Developer, Original Code or Contributor in the notice described in Exhibit A shall not of themselves be deemed to be modifications of this License.)

7. DISCLAIMER OF WARRANTY.

COVERED CODE IS PROVIDED UNDER THIS LICENSE ON AN "AS IS" BASIS, WITHOUT WARRANTY OF ANY KIND, EITHER EXPRESSED OR IMPLIED, INCLUDING, WITHOUT LIMITATION, WARRANTIES THAT THE COVERED CODE IS FREE OF DEFECTS, MERCHANTABLE, FIT FOR A PARTICULAR PURPOSE OR NON-INFRINGING. THE ENTIRE RISK AS TO THE QUALITY AND PERFORMANCE OF THE COVERED CODE IS WITH YOU. SHOULD ANY COVERED CODE PROVE DEFECTIVE IN ANY RESPECT, YOU (NOT THE INITIAL DEVELOPER OR ANY OTHER CONTRIBUTOR) ASSUME THE

COST OF ANY NECESSARY SERVICING, REPAIR OR CORRECTION. THIS DISCLAIMER OF WARRANTY CONSTITUTES AN ESSENTIAL PART OF THIS LICENSE. NO USE OF ANY COVERED CODE IS AUTHORIZED HEREUNDER EXCEPT UNDER THIS DISCLAIMER.

8. TERMINATION.

8.1. This License and the rights granted hereunder will terminate automatically if You fail to comply with terms herein and fail to cure such breach within 30 days of becoming aware of the breach. All sublicenses to the Covered Code which are properly granted shall survive any termination of this License. Provisions which, by their nature, must remain in effect beyond the termination of this License shall survive.

8.2. If You initiate litigation by asserting a patent infringement claim (excluding declatory judgment actions) against Initial Developer or a Contributor (the Initial Developer or Contributor against whom You file such action is referred to as "Participant") alleging that:

(a) such Participant's Contributor Version directly or indirectly infringes any patent, then any and all rights granted by such Participant to You under Sections 2.1 and/or 2.2 of this License shall, upon 60 days notice from Participant terminate prospectively, unless if within 60 days after receipt of notice You either: (i) agree in writing to pay Participant a mutually agreeable reasonable royalty for Your past and future use of Modifications made by such Participant, or (ii) withdraw Your litigation claim with respect to the Contributor Version against such Participant. If within 60 days of notice, a reasonable royalty and payment arrangement are not mutually agreed upon in writing by the parties or the litigation claim is not withdrawn, the rights granted by Participant to You under Sections 2.1 and/or 2.2 automatically terminate at the expiration of the 60 day notice period specified above.

(b) any software, hardware, or device, other than such Participant's Contributor Version, directly or indirectly infringes any patent, then any rights granted to You by such Participant under Sections 2.1(b) and 2.2(b) are revoked effective as of the date You first made, used, sold, distributed, or had made, Modifications made by that Participant.

8.3. If You assert a patent infringement claim against Participant alleging that such Participant's Contributor Version directly or indirectly infringes any patent where such claim is resolved (such as by license or settlement) prior to the initiation of patent infringement litigation, then the reasonable value of the licenses granted by such Participant under Sections 2.1 or 2.2 shall be taken into account in determining the amount or value of any payment or license.

8.4. In the event of termination under Sections 8.1 or 8.2 above, all end user license agreements (excluding distributors and resellers) which have been validly granted by You or any distributor hereunder prior to termination shall survive termination.

9. LIMITATION OF LIABILITY.

UNDER NO CIRCUMSTANCES AND UNDER NO LEGAL THEORY, WHETHER TORT (INCLUDING NEGLIGENCE), CONTRACT, OR OTHERWISE, SHALL YOU, THE INITIAL DEVELOPER, ANY OTHER CONTRIBUTOR, OR ANY DISTRIBUTOR OF COVERED CODE, OR ANY SUPPLIER OF ANY OF SUCH PARTIES, BE LIABLE TO ANY PERSON FOR ANY INDIRECT, SPECIAL, INCIDENTAL, OR CONSEQUENTIAL DAMAGES OF ANY CHARACTER INCLUDING, WITHOUT LIMITATION, DAMAGES FOR LOSS OF GOODWILL, WORK STOPPAGE, COMPUTER FAILURE OR MALFUNCTION, OR ANY AND ALL OTHER COMMERCIAL DAMAGES OR LOSSES, EVEN IF SUCH PARTY SHALL HAVE BEEN INFORMED OF THE POSSIBILITY OF SUCH DAMAGES. THIS LIMITATION OF LIABILITY SHALL NOT APPLY TO LIABILITY FOR DEATH OR PERSONAL INJURY RESULTING FROM SUCH PARTY'S NEGLIGENCE TO THE EXTENT APPLICABLE LAW PROHIBITS SUCH LIMITATION. SOME JURISDICTIONS DO NOT ALLOW THE EXCLUSION OR LIMITATION OF INCIDENTAL OR CONSEQUENTIAL DAMAGES, SO THIS EXCLUSION AND LIMITATION MAY NOT APPLY TO YOU.

10. U.S. GOVERNMENT END USERS.

The Covered Code is a "commercial item," as that term is defined in 48 C.F.R. 2.101 (Oct. 1995), consisting of "commercial computer software" and "commercial computer software documentation," as such terms are used in 48 C.F.R. 12.212 (Sept. 1995). Consistent with 48 C.F.R. 12.212 and 48 C.F.R. 227.7202-1 through 227.7202-4 (June 1995), all U.S. Government End Users acquire Covered Code with only those rights set forth herein.

11. MISCELLANEOUS.

This License represents the complete agreement concerning subject matter hereof. If any provision of this License is held to be unenforceable, such provision shall be reformed only to the extent necessary to make it enforceable. This License shall be governed by California law provisions (except to the extent applicable law, if any, provides otherwise), excluding its conflict-of-law provisions. With respect to disputes in which at least one party is a citizen of, or an entity chartered or registered to do business in the United States of America, any litigation relating to this License shall be subject to the jurisdiction of the Federal Courts of the Northern District of California, with venue lying in Santa Clara County, California, with the losing party responsible for costs, including without limitation, court costs and reasonable attorneys' fees and expenses. The application of the United Nations Convention on Contracts for the International Sale of Goods is expressly excluded. Any law or regulation which provides that the language of a contract shall be construed against the drafter shall not apply to this License.

12. RESPONSIBILITY FOR CLAIMS.

As between Initial Developer and the Contributors, each party is responsible for claims and damages arising, directly or indirectly, out of its utilization of rights under this License and You agree to work with Initial Developer and Contributors to distribute such responsibility on an equitable basis. Nothing herein is intended or shall be deemed to constitute any admission of liability.

13. MULTIPLE-LICENSED CODE.

Initial Developer may designate portions of the Covered Code as "Multiple-Licensed". "Multiple-Licensed" means that the Initial Developer permits you to utilize portions of the Covered Code under Your choice of the NPL or the alternative licenses, if any, specified by the Initial Developer in the file described in Exhibit A.

EXHIBIT A -Mozilla Public License.

"The contents of this file are subject to the Mozilla Public License Version 1.1 (the "License"); you may not use this file except in compliance with the License. You may obtain a copy of the License at *http://www.mozilla.org/MPL/*

Software distributed under the License is distributed on an "AS IS" basis, WITHOUT WARRANTY OF ANY KIND, either express or implied. See the License for the specific language governing rights and limitations under the License.

The Original Code is _____.

The Initial Developer of the Original Code is _____.
Portions created by _____ are Copyright (C) _____
_____. All Rights Reserved.

Contributor(s): _____.

Alternatively, the contents of this file may be used under the terms of the _____ license (the "[___] License"), in which case the provisions of [_____] License are applicable instead of those above. If you wish to allow use of your version of this file only under the terms of the [____] License and not to allow others to use your version of this file under the MPL, indicate your decision by deleting the provisions above and replace them with the notice and other provisions required by the [___] License. If you do not delete the provisions above, a recipient may use your version of this file under either the MPL or the [___] License."

[NOTE: The text of this Exhibit A may differ slightly from the text of the notices in the Source Code files of the Original Code. You should use the text of this Exhibit A rather than the text found in the Original Code Source Code for Your Modifications.]

OPEN SOFTWARE LICENSE

The Open Software License is a more generic, less restrictive license than the GPL/LGPL. The Open Source Definition (Appendix A) is reprinted under the terms of the Open Software License.

Open Software License
v. 2.0

This Open Software License (the "License") applies to any original work of authorship (the "Original Work") whose owner (the "Licensor") has placed the following notice immediately following the copyright notice for the Original Work: Licensed under the Open Software License version 2.0

1) Grant of Copyright License. Licensor hereby grants You a world-wide, royalty-free, non-exclusive, perpetual, sublicenseable license to do the following: a) to reproduce the Original Work in copies;

b) to prepare derivative works ("Derivative Works") based upon the Original Work;

c) to distribute copies of the Original Work and Derivative Works to the public, with the proviso that copies of Original Work or Derivative Works that You distribute shall be licensed under the Open Software License;

d) to perform the Original Work publicly; and

e) to display the Original Work publicly.

2) Grant of Patent License. Licensor hereby grants You a world-wide, royalty-free, non-exclusive, perpetual, sublicenseable license, under patent claims owned or controlled by the Licensor that are embodied in the Original Work as furnished by the Licensor, to make, use, sell and offer for sale the Original Work and Derivative Works.

3) Grant of Source Code License. The term "Source Code" means the preferred form of the Original Work for making modifications to it and all available documentation describing how to modify the Original Work. Licensor hereby agrees to provide a machine-readable copy of the Source Code of the Original Work along with each copy of the Original Work that Licensor distributes. Licensor reserves the right to satisfy this obligation by placing a machine-readable copy of the Source Code in an information repository reasonably calculated to permit inexpensive and convenient access by You for as long as Licensor continues to distribute the Original Work, and by publishing the address of that information repository in a notice immediately following the copyright notice that applies to the Original Work.

4) Exclusions From License Grant. Neither the names of Licensor, nor the names of any contributors to the Original Work, nor any of their trademarks or service marks, may be used to endorse or promote products derived from this Original Work without express prior written permission of the Licensor. Nothing in this License shall be deemed to grant any rights to trademarks, copyrights, patents, trade secrets or any other intellectual property of Licensor except as expressly stated herein. No patent license is granted to make, use, sell or offer to sell embodiments of any patent claims other than the licensed claims defined in Section 2. No right is granted to the trademarks of Licensor even if such marks are included in the Original Work. Nothing in this License shall be interpreted to prohibit Licensor from licensing under different terms from this License any Original Work that Licensor otherwise would have a right to license.

5) External Deployment. The term "External Deployment" means the use or distribution of the Original Work or Derivative Works in any way such that the Original Work or Derivative Works may be used by anyone other than You, whether the Original Work or Derivative Works are distributed to those persons or made available as an application intended for use over a computer network. As an express condition for the grants of license here-

under, You agree that any External Deployment by You of a Derivative Work shall be deemed a distribution and shall be licensed to all under the terms of this License, as prescribed in section 1(c) herein.

6) Attribution Rights. You must retain, in the Source Code of any Derivative Works that You create, all copyright, patent or trademark notices from the Source Code of the Original Work, as well as any notices of licensing and any descriptive text identified therein as an "Attribution Notice." You must cause the Source Code for any Derivative Works that You create to carry a prominent Attribution Notice reasonably calculated to inform recipients that You have modified the Original Work.

7) Warranty of Provenance and Disclaimer of Warranty. Licensor warrants that the copyright in and to the Original Work and the patent rights granted herein by Licensor are owned by the Licensor or are sublicensed to You under the terms of this License with the permission of the contributor(s) of those copyrights and patent rights. Except as expressly stated in the immediately proceeding sentence, the Original Work is provided under this License on an "AS IS" BASIS and WITHOUT WARRANTY, either express or implied, including, without limitation, the warranties of NON-INFRINGEMENT, MERCHANTABILITY or FITNESS FOR A PARTICULAR PURPOSE. THE ENTIRE RISK AS TO THE QUALITY OF THE ORIGINAL WORK IS WITH YOU. This DISCLAIMER OF WARRANTY constitutes an essential part of this License. No license to Original Work is granted hereunder except under this disclaimer.

8) Limitation of Liability. Under no circumstances and under no legal theory, whether in tort (including negligence), contract, or otherwise, shall the Licensor be liable to any person for any direct, indirect, special, incidental, or consequential damages of any character arising as a result of this License or the use of the Original Work including, without limitation, damages for loss of goodwill, work stoppage, computer failure or malfunction, or any and all other commercial damages or losses. This limitation of liability shall not apply to liability for death or personal injury resulting from Licensor's negligence to the extent applicable law prohibits such limitation. Some jurisdictions do not allow the exclusion or limitation of incidental or consequential damages, so this exclusion and limitation may not apply to You.

9) Acceptance and Termination. If You distribute copies of the Original Work or a Derivative Work, You must make a reasonable effort under the circumstances to obtain the express assent of recipients to the terms of this License. Nothing else but this License (or another written agreement be-

tween Licensor and You) grants You permission to create Derivative Works based upon the Original Work or to exercise any of the rights granted in Section 1 herein, and any attempt to do so except under the terms of this License (or another written agreement between Licensor and You) is expressly prohibited by U.S. copyright law, the equivalent laws of other countries, and by international treaty. Therefore, by exercising any of the rights granted to You in Section 1 herein, You indicate Your acceptance of this License and all of its terms and conditions. This License shall terminate immediately and you may no longer exercise any of the rights granted to You by this License upon Your failure to honor the proviso in Section 1(c) herein.

10) Termination for Patent Action. This License shall terminate automatically and You may no longer exercise any of the rights granted to You by this License as of the date You commence an action, including a cross-claim or counterclaim, for patent infringement (i) against Licensor with respect to a patent applicable to software or (ii) against any entity with respect to a patent applicable to the Original Work (but excluding combinations of the Original Work with other software or hardware).

11) Jurisdiction, Venue and Governing Law. Any action or suit relating to this License may be brought only in the courts of a jurisdiction wherein the Licensor resides or in which Licensor conducts its primary business, and under the laws of that jurisdiction excluding its conflict-of-law provisions. The application of the United Nations Convention on Contracts for the International Sale of Goods is expressly excluded. Any use of the Original Work outside the scope of this License or after its termination shall be subject to the requirements and penalties of the U.S. Copyright Act, 17 U.S.C. 101 et seq., the equivalent laws of other countries, and international treaty. This section shall survive the termination of this License.

12) Attorneys Fees. In any action to enforce the terms of this License or seeking damages relating thereto, the prevailing party shall be entitled to recover its costs and expenses, including, without limitation, reasonable attorneys' fees and costs incurred in connection with such action, including any appeal of such action. This section shall survive the termination of this License.

13) Miscellaneous. This License represents the complete agreement concerning the subject matter hereof. If any provision of this License is held to be unenforceable, such provision shall be reformed only to the extent necessary to make it enforceable.

14) Definition of "You" in This License. "You" throughout this License, whether in upper or lower case, means an individual or a legal entity exercising rights under, and complying with all of the terms of, this License. For legal entities, "You" includes any entity that controls, is controlled by, or is under common control with you. For purposes of this definition, "control" means (i) the power, direct or indirect, to cause the direction or management of such entity, whether by contract or otherwise, or (ii) ownership of fifty percent (50%) or more of the outstanding shares, or (iii) beneficial ownership of such entity.

15) Right to Use. You may use the Original Work in all ways not otherwise restricted or conditioned by this License or by law, and Licensor promises not to interfere with or be responsible for such uses by You.

D   About the CD-ROM

The CD-ROM contains version 1.2 of The Open CD, itself an open source project that provides a number of high-quality Free and Open Source Software programs for Windows, along with essays and a short video about open source software. Many of the software projects on the CD-ROM are discussed in this book.

Software on The Open CD version 1.2 includes:

- OpenOffice.org 1.1.0, a complete office suite
- Mozilla 1.5, a full-featured web browser and email client suite
- AbiWord 2.0.1, an excellent word processor
- The GIMP 1.2.5, a professional-level graphics editor
- FileZilla 2.2.1b, a powerful FTP/SFTP client
- httrack 3.30, an offline web browser
- TightVNC 1.2.9, a remote access server and client
- PuTTY 0.53b, a Secure Shell (SSH) client
- Audacity 1.2.0-pre3, a full-featured sound editor
- CDex 1.5.1, software for making MP3s from CDs, and managing a music collection
- Crack Attack!, a Tetris-like game
- Sokoban YASC, 1.94, a puzzling game
- Celestia 1.3.0, an astronomy multimedia program
- Really Slick Screensavers
- 7-Zip 3.11, a file archiving utility that handles zip files, CAB files, tarballs, and its own special format
- NetTime 2b7, a time synchronization utility
- Scintilla Editor 1.56, a simple text editor with syntax highlighting
- Windows Privacy Tools 1.0rc2, a graphical toolset for Gnu Privacy Guard (GPG)
- A short video trailer for the movie *Revolution OS*

- "The Cathedral and the Bazaar," by Eric S. Raymond, one of the seminal essays describing why the open source development model is so effective
- *Free As In Freedom*, by Sam Williams, a biography of Richard M. Stallman, the founder of the Free Software Foundation
- *Open Sources: Voices from the Open Source Revolution*, a collection of essays about the history of Free and Open Source Software

You can find updated versions of The Open CD at their web site, *http://theopencd.sunsite.dk/*.

Also on the CD-ROM are some other Windows programs mentioned in the book. These programs are in the windows/ directory on the CD-ROM:

- Mozilla Thunderbird 0.5, a standalone email client
- Mozilla Firefox 0.8, a fast standalone web browser
- TortoiseSVN 1.0.3, a Subversion client that can provide a standalone repository

INSTALLATION INSTRUCTIONS

Most of the software can be installed using the menus in the Open CD. The additional programs: Mozilla Firefox, Mozilla Thunderbird, and TortoiseSVN must be installed individually. There are also specific notes below about Windows Privacy Tools (WinPT) and CDex.

The Open CD

The Open CD's menu should appear automatically after you insert the CD-ROM into your drive on a Windows computer. If it does not, browse to your CD-ROM drive in Windows Explorer and double-click the Start.exe file.

All of the programs on The Open CD part of the CD-ROM can be easily installed by following the instructions and menus in The Open CD program.

Windows Privacy Tools

When you install Windows Privacy tools, if you haven't already used GPG or another related encryption package, it will give you a dialog saying it couldn't find any keyrings. Choose the option to have WinPT create a keyring for you.

On some versions of Windows XP, Windows Privacy Tools doesn't always install correctly. If it doesn't work the first time, uninstall Windows Privacy Tools and reboot. You should then be able to successfully install the software and use it.

CDex

On Windows NT, Windows 2000, and Windows XP systems, the first time you run CDex it will give you an error message saying: Failed to load the wnaspi32.dll driver! Use the "Native NT SCSI library" driver option instead?

Answer Yes to this question and proceed. While the message may seem unfriendly, the program works fine.

Mozilla Firefox

To install Mozilla Firefox, browse to the windows folder on the CD-ROM, and double-click the FirefoxSetup-0.8.exe file.

Mozilla Thunderbird

Mozilla Thunderbird is still an early release, and does not have a normal Windows installer. To install Mozilla Thunderbird:

1. Start a program that can unpack zip files, such as 7-Zip (included on The Open CD part of the CD-ROM), WinZip, or Alladin Stuffit Expander.
2. Use the unzipping program to browse to the windows directory on the CD-ROM.
3. Extract the zip file named thunderbird-0.5-win32.zip to your C:\Program Files directory.
4. Create a shortcut on your desktop pointing to the C:\Program Files\thunderbird\thunderbird.exe file.
5. Use this shortcut to launch Mozilla Thunderbird.

TortoiseSVN

There are two different versions of the TortoiseSVN installer: one for Windows NT-based systems, including Windows 2000, Windows XP, and later; the other for Windows 98 and Me. Note that TortoiseSVN does not work well with Windows 95 or Windows NT 4.0.

To install TortoiseSVN in Windows 98/Me, browse to the Windows folder on the CD-ROM and double-click the TortoiseSVN-1.0.3-MBCS_svn-1.0.1.msi file.

To install TortoiseSVN in Windows 2000, Windows XP, and newer Windows operating systems, browse to the Windows folder on the CD-ROM and double-click the TortoiseSVN-1.0.3-UNICODE_svn-1.0.1.msi file.

In either case, you will have to log out and log back in again to fully activate TortoiseSVN.

TortoiseSVN is a Windows Explorer shell extension, rather than a standalone program. This means that you can't start it from any kind of shortcut or Windows menu item. You use it by right-clicking on files and directories in Windows Explorer. See Chapter 9 for more information.

SYSTEM REQUIREMENTS

The programs on the CD-ROM are all Windows versions of open source programs. The minimum system requirements for these programs are:

- Windows 98, Windows 2000, or later. Most applications will work in Windows NT 4.0.
- Pentium 233 MHz (Recommended 500 MHz or greater)
- At least 64 MB of RAM
- About 500 MB of hard drive space to install everything; some programs can be installed with less than 1 MB of drive space.

These requirements are minimal for the larger programs on the CD-ROM: OpenOffice.org, all of the Mozilla software, The GIMP, Celestia, and Audacity. These programs will run better with more memory and a faster processor. Most of the other software runs fine in systems as old as Windows 95, with even more minimal hardware specifications.

Glossary

3DES: Triple-DES. A stronger variation of the Data Encryption Standard (DES), a symmetrical encryption method that uses a 168-bit key. While considered more secure than DES, it's slow to encrypt and decrypt, and is not considered to be a leading cipher.

3G: Third Generation. Used to describe new wireless telecommunications infrastructure that supports broadband levels of data transfer. 3G supports features like camera phones and high-speed computer connections to cellular networks.

802.1X: An IEEE standard framework for authenticating remote users with a variety of methods, including smart cards, digital certificates, and passwords.

802.11: A family of standards related to wireless local area networks and metropolitan area networks, also called Wi-Fi.

802.11a: A specific standard for Wi-Fi networking that uses the 5 GHz radio band to transfer data at up to 54 Mbps.

802.11b: A specific standard for Wi-Fi networking that uses the 2.4 GHz radio band to transfer data at up to 11 Mbps.

802.11g: A specific standard for Wi-Fi networking that uses the 2.4 GHz radio band to transfer data at up to 54 Mbps, compatible with 802.11b.

802.11i: A standard framework for authorizing and encrypting data on a Wi-Fi network, due to be approved in June 2004. This standard will likely use AES for encryption, and 802.1X for authentication.

802.11n: A specific standard for Wi-Fi networking currently in development, due to be approved by the end of 2005. The requirements for this specification include at least 100 Mbps of actual data transfer, not including the wireless overhead, using both the 2.4 GHz and 5 GHz bands, backwards compatible to 802.11a, 802.11b, and 802.11g.

Absolute Path: In Web sites, an absolute path is a full URL starting with http. On a computer, an absolute path is the location of a file from the very root of the file system. In Windows, the root of the file system is a drive letter. In Linux and Macs, the root is "/."

Active Directory: An LDAP implementation by Microsoft. Active Directory describes users, computers, and business units within a LAN, providing centralized, distributed management of authentication.

AES: Advanced Encryption Standard. The U.S. government standard for strong encryption that replaced DES. The government chose an algorithm named *Rijndael* to use as the standard, from among a dozen proposed candidates.

API: Application Programmer Interface. A set of functions and properties provided by one program, allowing it to be used from another.

Application: A program that fulfills some purpose, that people interact with directly.

Apt-get: A program that makes installing other programs easier on certain Linux systems. Apt-get was developed for the Debian Linux distribution, but many other distributions use it as well. Apt-get downloads software packages, finds any other packages required for the installation, and installs them all together.

ASCII: American Standard Code for Information Interchange. ASCII is a standard that describes a set of text characters. The ASCII set includes upper and lower case letters, numbers, symbols, and special control characters. It does not include characters with accents, or other non-English characters.

Authentication: The process of identifying a user, and confirming his identity. The most common way to authenticate is by using a password. More secure methods of authentication can also be used.

Authoritative Name Server: A DNS name server that is recognized as being the final word for a particular domain. When looking up a domain name, a caching name server finds the authoritative name server for the requested domain from a root name server, and then asks the authoritative name server where to find the server it's looking for.

Authorization: The process of identifying what a particular user can do with a particular resource. After authenticating the identity and age of a young man by looking at his driver's license, a liquor store clerk can then authorize him to buy liquor.

Bandwidth: The amount of data that can pass through a connection. Usually measured in bits per second, or multiples thereof.

Bayesian Filtering: A statistical equation applied to a content problem. Bayesian filters are currently a popular solution for dealing with spam. They work by breaking each message up into tokens, identifying the most interesting tokens, and comparing these tokens against a big collection of previous messages to identify whether a particular message more resembles spam or nonspam. You train these filters by correcting any mistakes it makes, so it gradually learns.

BIND (name server): Berkeley Internet Name Daemon. The original program that provides domain name service. BIND is one of the earliest open source projects, and it's absolutely essential to the Internet. It finds the IP address of a Web site when you request it by name.

Bind (to a port): Server programs listen for requests on particular ports on a particular network address. The process of attaching a server to a port is called *binding*. Only one program may be bound to a particular port on a particular IP address. On Unix-based machines, only programs running as a root user may bind to a port under 1024.

BIOS: Basic Input Output System. A small program that runs on all IBM-compatible PCs. The BIOS controls how computer hardware appears to the operating system, and decides how to boot the computer. It loads the master boot record of a disk, which then loads the operating system.

Bit: The smallest numerical unit in a computer, either a zero or a one. At its lowest level, all computers deal with bits of data, combining them to be higher numbers, characters, and programs.

Blacklist: A list of addresses to ignore. These might be IP addresses, email addresses, or domains. If you find someone who is being particularly offensive, you can add them to a blacklist to prevent them from accessing particular systems.

Blog: Shortened version of *Web log*. Blogs are basically online diaries. Blogging is made possible through the rise of simple Web site content management tools that allow people with no Web development experience to easily post content. Blogging software can be great for maintaining a Web site without needing to hire a Web developer.

Block Device: A category of hardware that accesses data in large chunks, rather than one character at a time. Block devices include hard drives, floppy drives, CD-ROMs, DVDs, and most storage hardware.

Blowfish: A strong encryption algorithm that was a candidate for AES. While it wasn't chosen, it has no known vulnerabilities.

Bluetooth: A short-range wireless standard. Bluetooth enables what the manufacturers like to call a *Personal Area Network*. With Bluetooth devices, you can eliminate cords and cables that connect devices like keyboards, mice, cameras, PDAs, cell phones, and printers to your computer.

Bridge (network): A way of making two network segments work as one. A network bridge takes an interface on each segment, and sends traffic transparently between them.

BSD: Berkeley Software Distribution. The first open source operating system. BSD was a branch of Unix developed at the University of California, Berkeley. It currently has several variations, one of which is the base of the Apple OS X operating system.

Boot Loader: A small program stored in the master boot record of a drive, used to load the kernel of an operating system. If you have multiple operating systems on a computer, the boot loader allows you to choose which one to load.

Buffer Overflow: A type of vulnerability where a stream of data goes past the end of computer memory allocated for it, causing the program itself to be rewritten with dire consequences.

Byte: Eight bits. The lowest level of memory you can actually manipulate with a program. A byte has a value between 0 and 255, and is often expressed in base-16, hexadecimal. A byte is two hexadecimal digits.

Caching Name Server: A server that is used to look up a domain name. Your client software requests a particular domain name from a caching name server. If the name server has recently looked up that name, it will have it cached, and return an answer immediately. If not, it finds the authoritative name server for the domain, and asks that name server where to find the requested domain.

Canonical Name: The domain name corresponding to an IP address. Every domain name has a corresponding IP address. Many domains can share the same IP address. An IP address can only have one domain name associated with a reverse lookup, so a canonical name is the domain name returned when you look up an IP address.

CDMA: Code Division Multiple Access. A second-generation algorithm for dividing digital cell phone calls up into little chunks, and interleaving the data from multiple conversations into the same radio frequencies. Competing algorithms include GSM and TDMA.

Cell (spreadsheet): The intersection of a row and a column. A cell in a spreadsheet is a location that can contain data, text, or a formula. Tables also have cells, used in the same way.

Central Processing Unit: A chip that makes a computer work.

Certificate: A little file used for authentication and public key encryption. A certificate is a public key that has been signed by a certificate authority. A certificate can be used to encrypt data to the certificate's owner, or to authenticate a message from the owner.

Certificate Authority (CA): An organization that signs public keys. By signing a public key, a certificate authority is essentially vouching that the public key really belongs to the individual presenting it. If you trust a certificate authority, you implicitly trust any public keys it has signed, because you can verify the signature of the CA. Commercial CAs charge money for signing keys. You can run your own CA.

Character Device: A type of hardware that feeds data to the computer one character at a time. Examples include keyboards, modems, infrared, and serial devices.

Chroot jail: A way to isolate a server program to a particular directory. Theoretically, if a chrooted program is compromised, attackers can't get out of the jail, thus limiting the damage they can do to the rest of the server.

Client: A program that is used to access a server. A Web browser is a client for a Web server. An email program is a client for an email server.

CMS: Content Management System.

CMYK: Cyan, Magenta, Yellow, and blacK. A color scheme used in professional printing, corresponding to the four ink colors that can be combined to create full color.

Column (database): A category of information in a table. In a spreadsheet, a column is a vertical group of cells. In a database, the results of queries are often presented in tabular form, with each column representing a field in the database. Examples might include: first name, last name, social security number, annual pay.

Commit (database): The completion of a transaction. In a database transaction, you use queries to insert or update data in the database. These changes are held in a buffer, waiting for everything to be added. Once all of the data has been added successfully, a *commit* makes the change permanent. You can roll back the transaction to its original state any time before the commit takes place.

Community Network: A volunteer network of computers that provides an alternative way to communicate data, without using the Internet. Wi-Fi community networks are springing up in many cities around the world, and could represent the beginning of a totally new infrastructure, outside the traditional telecommunications infrastructure.

Content Management System: An application used to manage content—text, pictures, etc.—on a Web site or in a repository.

Courier: An open source email server application.

CPU: Central Processing Unit.

Cracker: A hacker who breaks into computers and networks, or writes code specifically for breaking into computers and networks.

CRM: Customer Relationship Management.

Cross-Site Scripting: A type of vulnerability in a Web application that an attacker can use to trick Web users into visiting a different site without their knowledge.

CSV: Comma-Separated Values. A common text-based file format for storing tabular data. You can often export and import in CSV files to move data from one application to another.

Customer Relationship Management (CRM): A category of software that keeps track of contact names, telephone numbers, and addresses, along with your activities with that contact. A good CRM system reminds salespeople when it's time to do a follow-up call, and makes an entire customer history available to customer service staff.

Daemon: Synonym for server. A program that runs continuously, waiting for a request from a client.

Data: Raw, unfiltered information. Data is a generic term for the bits and bytes that make up files and other items you want to work with on a computer.

Denial of Service: A type of attack that makes a service unavailable for the period of the attack.

DES: Data Encryption Standard. The original U.S. government-approved standard for encrypting data for financial transactions. It was developed in the 1970s, and uses a 56-bit key for encryption. With the advances in computing power, DES is no longer considered secure—it can be cracked by a typical PC in a matter of hours. DES has been replaced with the much stronger AES.

Dictionary Attack: A type of attack that uses a long list of words to attempt to defeat a password or discover an email address. Dictionary attacks use not just words from an English dictionary, but lists of names, places, or anything else the attacker cares to try.

Differential Backups: A technique for backing up data that only saves files that have changed since the last full backup.

Digest (email): A group of mailing list messages combined into a single message. When you subscribe to a mailing list, you can often choose to get the messages delivered as a digest, containing all the messages in a day or week, or containing a count of messages, instead of receiving the individual messages as they are sent.

Digest (password): A method for encrypting a user name and password, without encrypting the rest of the message.

Distributed Denial of Service Attack: A coordinated flood of traffic from many different computers. If an attacker is motivated to bring down a Web site, this is one of the favorite techniques. He first gains control of a number of innocent computers, called zombies. Then he directs all the zombies to attack the same server at the same time, in an attempt to bring down the Web site. This type of attack has been successful on the largest Web sites, and is a frequent component of viruses.

Distribution: An individual compilation of an operating system with a bunch of programs. There is no standard Linux operating system—Linux is mostly just the kernel program. A distribution combines the Linux kernel with many of the GNU tools and a selection of other software in a single installable package. Popular Linux distributions include Red Hat, Mandrake, Suse, Fedora, Yellow Dog, Debian, and Knoppix, but there are hundreds of others. BSD is considered a Unix distribution, instead of a Linux distribution.

DMZ: De-Militarized Zone. A technique for isolating servers that face the public from your LAN, minimizing the risk of a system compromise.

Domain Name System (DNS): The system that finds the IP address associated with a name. It can also find the canonical name associated with an IP address.

Domain (Windows): A collection of computers that share an authentication and authorization scheme using a proprietary Microsoft standard. The open source Samba program can interoperate with Windows domains.

Duplex: A mode of sending data in both directions at the same time. Telephones are duplex devices, in that you can hear what the other party is saying while you talk.

Dynamic Web Site: A Web site that can be updated without posting new Web pages. Dynamic Web sites pull content from databases, self-updating Web pages, or other servers automatically, without requiring intervention by a Web developer. Dynamic Web sites are really programs that run on a Web server, and are also called Web applications.

Encryption: The process of scrambling data so that it can only be unscrambled by the intended person. A strong encryption algorithm defeats statistical analysis, dictionary attacks, and all known exploits, and requires so much processing power to defeat through brute force that there's not enough computing time in the world to crack it.

Enterprise Resource Planning (ERP): A class of software that combines all the operations of a company in one place, providing a set of unified views to the entire company. ERP keeps track of all data associated with customers, inventory, the supply chain, accounting, personnel, and management, allowing employees to access everything they need to do their job in a system that is always up to date.

Essid: Verbal pronunciation of SSID. Some Wi-Fi programs replace SSID with Essid in their user interface.

Ethernet: A low-level networking protocol. Ethernet provides a standard way for hardware devices to find each other and exchange data. Higher-level protocols like TCP/IP sit above Ethernet and communicate data between programs.

Extranet: A private Web site used by business partners. You set up an authenticated extranet to communicate somewhat confidential information to your customers, suppliers, or partners.

Failover Protection: A redundant system ready to take over immediately if a primary system goes down.

File System: Your hard drive. Actually, it refers to all of the files and directories you can access in your computer. It can also refer to an individual partition on a hard drive, or a type of formatting you use to create space on a disk to contain files and directories.

File Transfer Protocol (FTP): A method for transferring files from one computer to another. Requires an FTP client and a server.

`fish:/ protocol`: A KDE shortcut for accessing files over an SSH connection.

FreeS/WAN: A popular open source implementation of IPSec, used to create a VPN.

FTP: File Transfer Protocol.

FUD: Fear, Uncertainty, Doubt. A description of a very common type of rhetorical argument made against anything other than the status quo.

Gantt Chart: A timeline-style chart used in project management. A Gantt chart uses a separate row for each task within a project, and a horizontal bar representing the time spent on that task. You use a Gantt chart to help identify the critical path of a project, and the shortest amount of time it will take to complete a project when given a set of tasks that must be finished in a particular sequence.

Gateway: A computer that connects one network to another.

GNOME: A popular desktop environment for Linux. GNOME provides a set of libraries for programmers to easily create desktop programs. The other major desktop environment for Linux is KDE. GNOME is usually more comfortable for Mac users.

GPG: GNU Privacy Guard. A replacement for PGP, GPG is a popular program that securely encrypts and decrypts email and files.

GSM: Global System for Mobile communication. A second-generation algorithm for dividing digital cell phone calls up into little chunks, and interleaving the data from multiple conversations into the same radio frequencies. Competing algorithms include CDMA and TDMA.

Guanxi: Chinese word for connections and value. Guanxi is an important Chinese business concept, meaning roughly a system of assessing the intangible value of a person's connections and ability to get something done.

Hacker: A computer-savvy person who plays around with code and computers, finding unusual ways to solve a tough problem. The term *hacker* has little to do with breaking into computers illegally (*cracking*), and much to do with great technical ability.

Hash (lookup table): A simple file or database that efficiently associates one value with another. You call a function to get a value for a particular key. Hash tables are used to store thousands of values in a way that's easy to retrieve.

Hash (one-way function): A function that generates a unique, repeatable, single short value for a given set of data. Hash functions provide data integrity. You can apply a hash function to a large file, and provide the result to a recipient. The recipient can apply the same hash function to their copy of the file, and if the resulting hash value matches yours, it verifies that the files are identical. If somebody modifies just one byte in the file, the result is a completely different hash. A sum of MD5 values is a common way of generating a hash.

Heuristic Filtering: Filtering based on pre-defined rules. Many commercial spam filters, and the popular open source SpamAssassin, use a set of heuristic filters to identify spam. Each rule is compared to the message, and if the rule matches, a score is added or subtracted to the message. After all the rules have been run, if the score exceeds a certain threshold, it is considered spam.

Hexadecimal: Base-16 numbering system. We're used to base-10 numbers, also called decimal numbers, with digits from 0 to 9. Decimal numbers don't fit into an even number of bits. By using base-16, each digit can be converted to 4 bits. Hexadecimal digits are represented with a number from 0 to 9, and the letters A to F that represent values from 10 through 15.

Host: A single computer, when discussed in the context of networking.

HTML: HyperText Markup Language. A language of tags used to mark content on a Web page to make it appear in a particular way. HTML is the main language used to create Web pages.

HTTP: HyperText Transfer Protocol. A protocol defined by the IETF that describes how to request and receive documents over the Web.

Hub: A network device with multiple Ethernet ports. All traffic coming into any port is transmitted to all of the other ports. Less expensive than a switch.

ICalendar: Version 2 of the Vcalendar data format. A standard format for storing and exchanging calendar events, tasks, and free/busy information.

iCal: An Apple program for working with calendars. The first widely used program for managing multiple calendars.

IDE: Integrated Development Environment. An application that provides useful tools for programming in a particular language. These tools include editors, debuggers, and compilers.

IDEA: International Data Encryption Algorithm. A strong symmetrical encryption algorithm used in many different programs. IDEA is protected by patent in Europe, the United States, and Japan until around 2011. The patent holder allows anyone to use it for non-commercial use, but if you're using it in a business, you're obligated to pay a licensing fee.

IEEE: Institute of Electrical and Electronics Engineers, Inc. An international organization that creates standards used in telecommunications and networking equipment.

IETF: Internet Engineering Task Force. The IETF defines standards and protocols for exchanging data over the Internet. It is responsible for many networking protocols for applications and devices.

IMAP: Internet Message Access Protocol.

Incremental Backup: A type of backup that stores only files or data that have changed since the previous backup.

Information: Meaningful data. With enough information, you gain knowledge.

Internet Message Access Protocol (IMAP): A protocol for managing email on a server. An IMAP server provides corporate-style email service, keeping your email on the server in a series of mail folders. You can access the same mail folders and mail from multiple clients. IMAP is an alternative to POP, providing many more features.

Intranet: An internal corporate network, protected from the Internet by a firewall. Sometimes the term *intranet* is used to describe a Web site specifically for employees.

Intrusion Detection: The process of analyzing traffic on a network to identify and prevent it from being compromised.

IP Security (IPSec): A protocol and framework for tunneling encrypted data through an untrusted network. IPSec is the most popular standard for creating a VPN, but different vendors implement it in different ways, and it can be very difficult to set up and administer.

IRDA: InfraRed Data Association. An organization that sets the specifications for sending data over infrared devices, and the standard named after it.

IS (department): Information Systems. Common name for the technology division within a corporation or organization. Synonymous with IT.

ISP: Internet Service Provider. Usually the company you pay for your connection to the Internet. An ISP might also provide hosting services.

IT (consultant, department): Information Technology. Common name for computer experts and workers. Synonymous with IS.

ITU: International Telecommunications Union. The ITU has defined a number of telecommunications and information technology standards.

Java: A popular object-oriented language. Java programs run in a *virtual machine*, making them portable to a wide range of operating systems and devices.

KDE: A popular desktop environment for Linux. KDE provides a set of libraries for programmers to easily create desktop programs. The other major desktop environment for Linux is GNOME. KDE is usually more comfortable for Windows users.

Kernel: The main program in an operating system. The kernel manages the CPU and all of the hardware devices. It works like a traffic manager, directing input to the appropriate programs and allocating CPU time to each of the programs running on the system. Linus Torvalds wrote the original Linux kernel. The rest of the operating system—hardware drivers, utilities, shells, applications—are meant to be contributed by others.

Knowledge: A system of information. Knowledge is a framework of information that provides insight and understanding. Gain enough knowledge, and you reach wisdom.

LAN: Local Area Network. An Ethernet network running in an office, usually separated from the Internet by a firewall. Essentially a synonym for an intranet.

LaTeX: A macro and markup language for desktop publishing.

LDAP: Lightweight Directory Access Protocol. An IETF standard for managing objects, often used to provide centralized, distributed user authentication on a LAN. LDAP is a subset of the X.509 standard.

Library: A set of programs that provides standard functions to other programs. A code library isn't an application, but it allows other programs to call upon it to provide standard functionality.

Linux: The best-known open source program. Linux is a complete Unix-like operating system, designed to be able to use many of the same programs. Unlike BSD, Linux is a complete re-implementation, not directly derived from Unix. In this book, the term Unix generally is used as a whole category of software, including Linux.

Listserv: A popular mailing list manager program. Listserv is a proprietary program, but many long-time Internet users still call email lists using the name Listserv.

Local User: A user who can log directly into a computer, even if it were disconnected from the network. Local users have a home directory, mail account, and preferences on an individual computer.

MAC Address: Media Allocation Control address. The MAC address is a number built into the hardware, used to uniquely identify a network card.

MAPI: Messaging Application Programmer Interface. MAPI is a proprietary protocol for exchanging mail and other types of messages used by Microsoft Exchange and Outlook.

Maildir: A mailbox that stores each message in a file, and each mail folder as a directory.

Mailing List Manager: Software that manages a list of email addresses. A mailing list manager provides a single address to email a group of people, and allows each person to update their own accounts, unsubscribing at will.

Mail Merge: The process of personalizing a letter template to each of a large number of recipients.

Master Browser: In Windows networking, keeps track of all computers in a workgroup on an individual segment of a LAN. The master browser is a role that can change between computers, through a process called *forcing a browser election*. If the computer that happens to be the master browser gets disconnected, you can't browse the network for a few minutes until a new computer is elected as the master browser.

Master Boot Record (MBR): The very first sector of a drive. If a drive is bootable, it contains a program called a boot loader. It also contains the partition table for the drive. The BIOS loads the boot loader from the MBR as the first step of booting up.

Metadata: Data about data. Metadata describes attributes about something. For example, metadata for a word processing document might contain the document author, the title, the subject, and some notes about the document.

MIME: Multipurpose Internet Mail Extensions. MIME is an Internet standard for defining a type of file, used for transferring files over email and http.

Mono: An open source implementation of .NET.

MTA: Message Transport Agent, or Message Transfer Agent. A program that relays email between servers. An email client uses an MTA to send email. The MTA relays the mail to the destination MTA, which hands it off to a local delivery agent such as Procmail. Popular MTAs include Sendmail, Postfix, Exim, Qmail, and Microsoft Exchange.

Name Server: A server that responds to DNS requests. BIND is by far the most common software for name serving used by the root Internet name servers, and one of the oldest open source software projects.

.NET: A framework for developing Web applications. .NET is a Microsoft initiative, providing a set of standards and tools for developing programs that provide information to other programs over the Internet.

NFS: Network File Service. NFS is a Unix-based file sharing system for accessing files on a server in a LAN.

NIS: Network Information Services. A Unix-based system for centrally managing user accounts on a LAN.

Node: An individual item in a system. In a Linux file system, a node is an individual file. Using something called a hard link, a file may appear under multiple names or in different directories. In this case, a single node appears as multiple files.

Object (LDAP): An entry in an LDAP directory. An object usually has a set of attributes, and a parent object above it in a hierarchy.

Object Oriented: A method of programming that puts all of the code in a container representing an object of some kind. A class definition describes all of the properties and methods an object may have, and what it does. An object is a specific instance of a class. Classes may inherit properties and methods from other classes. Overall, it's a very effective way of designing modular programs that can be more easily debugged, sometimes at the expense of performance.

ODBC: Open DataBase Connectivity. An open standard for accessing a data source. ODBC provides a way to interchangeably load data from a variety of sources, including databases, spreadsheets, and plain text files.

Open Relay: A mail server that allows anybody to send mail through. Spammers use open relays to send massive amounts of mail in a way that obscures the real source.

OpenSSH: An open source implementation of an SSH client and server.

OpenSSL: An open source set of development libraries for implementing SSL or TLS.

OpenVPN: An easy-to-configure open source VPN project that uses OpenSSL to encrypt data over a UDP tunnel.

PAM: Portable Authentication Module. PAM is a Unix framework for providing authentication for specific services using a variety of mechanisms. Originally developed by Sun Microsystems.

Partition: A subdivision of a hard drive. In Windows, each partition appears as a separate drive.

Payload (virus): The part of a virus that executes after infection. As of December 2003, most viruses have carried a relatively harmless payload. Often there is no payload—the virus only contains code to replicate itself and infect other hosts. Common payloads are programs that open up a back door on a computer, allowing it to be remotely controlled, or programs that install a mail server that may be used to relay spam.

PCS: Personal Communication System. PCS is a range of the radio spectrum used for second generation cellular technology, and a generic term for that technology.

PDA: Personal Digital Assistant.

Permissions: Metadata that defines authorization. Permissions specify who may access a file or resource, and whether they have read-only or full writable permissions.

Personal Digital Assistant (PDA): A miniature, stripped down, portable computer. Popular PDAs include the Palm devices and Pocket PCs. PDAs are usually used as an extension of your PCs, providing portable access to your appointments, contact data, email, tasks, notes, and a variety of other information.

Personal Information Management (PIM): Programs that manage appointments, contacts, and tasks.

PERT Chart: Program Evaluation Review Technique. A project management methodology developed by the U.S. Navy in the 1950s. In a PERT chart, you put individual tasks in a little box, listing the time and cost of completing the task, and then draw arrows to other boxes to help determine the best way to execute a project.

PGP: Pretty Good Privacy. An extremely popular, early encryption program widely adopted to encrypt email and files. It infringed on the RSA patent, and was pulled from circulation. The open source GPG is mostly compatible with PGP, and has effectively replaced it.

PHP: PHP Hypertext Processor, or Personal Home Page. An extremely popular server scripting language for generating dynamic Web sites.

PIM: Personal Information Management.

Pipe: A Unix mechanism for passing data from one program to another. Also the name of the "|" character.

PKCS: Public Key Cryptography Standards. A set of implementation standards to support a public key infrastructure. The PKCS standards were developed by RSA Laboratories, in a consortium with a group of other interested companies.

PKI: Public Key Infrastructure.

POP: Post Office Protocol. A POP server provides access to email clients. Mail is stored on the mail server until the POP client connects and downloads it.

POTS: Plain Old Telephone Service. The telecommunication term for a normal phone line.

PPP: Point-to-point. A type of network connection that routes traffic between two IP addresses. PPP is used in most dial-up connections, and for several different tunneling systems.

PPTP: Point-to-Point Tunneling Protocol. A simple tunneling system designed by Microsoft to be used as a VPN. Considered less secure than some of the alternatives because it can be subjected to a password attack.

Port: The final part of a network address on a particular host. With TCP/IP, each host has a single IP address. Each IP address has 65,535 port addresses for

TCP and UDP. Specific services listen on certain standard ports. Higher numbered ports are used for outgoing connections. Ports are used to determine where a packet of data is sent, and where it came from.

Postfix: A popular open source SMTP mail server. Postfix is developed and maintained by Weitse Venema, a programmer who works for IBM. Postfix is designed to be an easier-to-maintain, highly secure replacement for Sendmail.

Primary Key: A value that uniquely identifies a row in a database.

Private Key: The part of a public key encryption key pair that must be kept private. Also called a secret key. A private key is used to sign a document or authenticate a user. It is also used to decrypt data that has been encrypted with the corresponding public key.

Privileged Account: A local user account that can change ownership and permissions on a file or directory.

Procmail: A local mail delivery agent. Procmail is a program that receives email from an MTA and delivers it to a mailbox.

Program: A file that executes. Programs perform actions on a computer.

Protocol: The definition of a format for data that allows multiple programs to communicate with each other.

Proxy Server: A server that provides data that really comes from a different server. A proxy server is often used to cache frequently requested Web pages on a LAN, conserving Internet bandwidth for more important or more frequently changing traffic.

Public Key Encryption: A type of encryption that uses asymmetrical keys. Public key encryption involves two keys to provide one-way encryption—one key, the public key, can encrypt but not decrypt. Data encrypted by the public key can only be decrypted with the private key. Public key encryption can also provide authentication by reversing the process. A private key can digitally sign data in a way that can be verified by the corresponding public key.

Public Key Infrastructure (PKI): A system for managing public keys. There are two different strategies for PKI. The PGP/GPG approach uses something called a key server to store public keys that anybody can request. People sign other people's keys, vouching that the public key belongs to the person it claims to belong to. If enough people sign enough keys, it creates a Web of trust you can use to verify the validity of a public key. The other approach is to use a centralized Certificate Authority (CA) that all people trust. The individual creates a Certificate Signing Request and sends it to the CA along with documentation to verify their identity. The CA signs the request, creating a certificate. This certificate can then be verified by anybody who trusts the CA, and used to encrypt data to the private key.

Publish (file sharing): In networking, to be able to access files and directories on another computer, the other computer must *publish* those directories to the network. Computers that publish directories in this manner are called file servers.

Qmail: A popular MTA by Dan Bernstein.

RADIUS: Remote Access Dial-In User Service. A centralized system for authenticating and tracking users logging into a network. Commonly used by ISPs and large enterprises that provide dial-up service. Also starting to be used to authenticate Wi-Fi users.

Random Access Memory (RAM): Memory in a computer used to hold programs and data while they are being used. RAM requires power—when you turn off a computer, everything in RAM is lost. RAM is very high-speed—the more RAM you have, the more programs you can run at the same time without the computer slowing down.

RDBMS: Relational Database Management System. Common acronym for a specific large relational database program and all its utilities.

Realm (Apache): A zone for authentication. When you protect directories using some sort of access control, everything on a single server that uses the same realm can use the same authentication credentials. By changing the realm in a different directory, you can force a new login.

Real-Time Black Hole List (RBL): An Internet-based database of servers known to send spam. People subscribe to an RBL, and their email server can use it to reject mail automatically, before even attempting to deliver it. The problem with black hole lists is that servers regularly change their addresses on the Internet, and RBLs quickly become out of date, blocking mail from what becomes an innocent server.

Recipe (procmail): A text-based rule that a local delivery agent uses to identify a message and perform a specific action with it. Very similar to an email rule or filter in email clients.

Record (database): A row of data in a table. In an address table, for example, a record represents one single address, and contains fields that hold the street address, city, state, country, and postal code.

Registrar: A service that manages domain names. You buy your domain name from a registrar, and tell it what name servers to use. The registrar adds your domain to the root name servers.

Relational Database (RDBMS): A database that enforces relationships between tables. You might have a table for addresses and another table for customers. A relational database allows you to specify multiple rows in the address table for a single row in the customer table. If you delete the row in the customer table, the relational database can automatically delete the corresponding rows in the address table.

RFC: Request For Comment. The written form of most standards defined by the W3C. Anybody can create an RFC and submit it for review. If the W3C ratifies it, it becomes an Internet standard.

RGB: Red, Green, Blue. The color model used by computers. By specifying different amounts of light of each of these colors, you can describe any of the many millions of colors your monitor is capable of displaying. In contrast, printed material deals with ink, and to get better quality a graphics program must convert the color to CMYK, corresponding to ink colors.

Rich Client: A client program that contains much of the functionality in a client/server application. A Web browser is a thin client, because you can usually interchange it with another Web browser. Many email programs, however, are rich clients because they can do a lot without connecting to the server.

Root File System: On a Unix-based computer, the root file system is the very top of the hierarchy on your disk, beginning with "/." You must mount some disk on the root file system, and everything under it is stored on that disk unless it's overridden by another file system. You can then mount other disks under particular directories. In Windows, each disk or partition is considered a root file system, and has a drive letter associated with it.

Root Name Servers: A small set of servers scattered around the world that resolve DNS queries to top level domains (.com, .net, .biz, .uk, etc.). At this writing, there are 13 root name servers that handle all domain name requests. Your caching name server contacts a root name server to find the authoritative name server for a domain.

Root User: The administrative account on a Unix-based computer. The root user is the only account that may change the ownership of a file, and generally has access to everything on the computer. The root user account should not be used except when absolutely necessary.

Router: A network device that connects two or more networks or subnets. A computer with multiple network cards can be set up as a router.

Row (database): Another name for a record. A row is an individual item in a database table, containing the data for a specific instance of something.

RPM: RedHat Package Manager. A system for packaging a program so that it may be distributed as a single file and more easily installed. Used by many popular Linux distributions, including Red Hat, Fedora, Mandrake, SuSE, and others.

RSA: Rivest, Shamir, and Adelman. The initials of the first people to come up with an effective scheme for public key encryption. The algorithm they invented is called RSA.

Samba: Server and client software that allows Unix-based computers to use Windows networking.

Schema: A specific model for representing objects. A database schema is the definition of tables, columns, and relationships between them. An XML schema describes what tags are allowed within a document, generally corresponding to some particular object.

SDK: Software Development Kit. A set of examples, instructions, and interfaces for the use of one software system by another. An SDK is used by software developers to build applications around a technology or application.

Secret Key: The side of a public key encryption key pair that must be kept secret. A secret key is used to digitally sign data, or decrypt data that has been encrypted by its corresponding public key. Also called a private key.

Secure Shell (SSH): A program that provides encrypted remote access to a command shell. SSH has replaced telnet as a standard way to remotely administer servers. SSH can also tunnel TCP/IP traffic to a specific port to the remote network.

Sendmail: The granddaddy of all email servers. Sendmail is a Message Transport Agent (MTA), and is responsible for relaying emails from server to server across the Internet.

Server: A program that provides a specific type of network service. Also a computer that hosts server programs. Also specific computer hardware optimized to be used as a server.

Service: A program that runs continuously on a server, waiting for requests from a client. When it gets a request, it performs whatever action it's designed to do, and returns a response. Also called a *Daemon*. The term *Service* is usually used in Windows, while *Daemon* is more often used in Unix-based systems.

Session Key: A unique identification number used by a Web application to identify a particular session with a user. This number is randomly generated using an algorithm that guarantees it to be unique, when a user logs into an application. The user's client (usually a Web browser) sends the session key with every request so the Web application can know which user it's working with.

SGML: Standard Generalized Markup Language. A general system for defining a markup language—a way of associating formatting or meaning with content. HTML is an SGML language. XML is based on SGML, but has changed some of its rules slightly, and has generally replaced SGML.

Simplex: Communication that can go only one direction at a time. Simplex network devices can both send and receive, but not at the same time. These devices must stop sending before they can receive. An example is a walkie-talkie, family radio, or push-to-talk systems. Duplex devices, like your telephone, can send and receive at the same time.

Slashdot: A very popular Web site among computer enthusiasts, with a strong open source slant. Its tagline is "News for Nerds. Stuff that matters."

Slashdotted: This is what happens when a Web site is unable to keep up with a sudden burst of traffic generated by a link from the Slashdot site. Also called "the Slashdot Effect," Web sites often succumb to the sheer number of clicks by millions of users who read about something on Slashdot, effectively leading to a Denial of Service.

S/MIME: Secure MIME. One of two competing systems for encrypting the contents of an email. S/MIME uses a public key infrastructure with certificate authorities to authenticate and encrypt email.

SMS: Short Message Service. A wireless system for sending text messages to telephones or pagers. Also called text messaging.

SMTP: Simple Mail Transport Protocol. The standard protocol for transferring email to another server.

Social Engineering: A term that describes the process of getting people to reveal passwords or system information by talking to them, misleading people into thinking the person asking about the information has an innocent or legitimate reason to get an answer. Commonly used by people trying to gain access to a specific network or computer.

Socket: One end of a data connection. TCP/IP sockets are associated with a port number. Unix sockets are associated with a file path. A socket connection passes data between two sockets.

Spider: A program that "crawls" the Internet, collecting information by following links in the page.

Spreadsheet: A program that allows you to put numerical values, formulas, and text into a tabular format. Popular spreadsheet programs are Microsoft Excel, Lotus 1-2-3, and OpenOffice.org Calc.

SQL: Structured Query Language. A simple language for interacting with a database.

SSH: Secure Shell.

SSID: Service Set Identifier. A name given to a wireless access point, used to distinguish it from other access points within range.

SSL: Secure Sockets Layer. A system for encrypting a connection, originally developed by Netscape for securing Web browsing. In its third major revision, it's now called Transport Layer Security (TLS).

Static Web Site: A Web site that uses HTML files stored on a server to contain content that doesn't change until it's replaced.

Stored Procedure: A program that runs inside a database.

String: A programming term for a sequence of characters. Strings are a type of variable used to hold text.

Subnet: A small group of related network addresses. Subnets are used to represent physical groupings of network devices. Usually a LAN uses a single subnet. In large organizations, networks may be divided into multiple subnets, mainly for routing purposes.

Subnet Mask: A set of numbers that is used to define the size of a subnet. A subnet mask uses binary arithmetic to find the base network address for any given IP address.

Superuser: Common name for an account with administrative permissions. In a Unix-based system, the Superuser is the `root` account.

Switch: A network device with multiple Ethernet ports. Traffic coming into a port is sent only to the port connected to the destination network device, unlike a hub.

Symmetrical Key: A key used in an encryption system where the same key is used to both encrypt and decrypt a message.

Tap Device: A virtual network adapter. Several VPN and tunneling programs create a tap device to tunnel Ethernet connections through some other network transport.

`tar`: Tape Archiver. A Unix program that combines multiple files into a single file, making it easy to back up or transfer to other computers.

Tarball: An archive file created with the `tar` program, often compressed. The Unix equivalent of a zip file.

TDMA: Time-Division Multiple Access. A way of slicing up wireless signals to allow multiple simultaneous telephone connections over the same frequencies.

Thin Client: A program that runs with very little resources on a computer, providing access to richer functionality on a server. A Web browser is a thin client for a Web application.

TLA: Three-Letter Acronym.

TLS: Transport Layer Security. Version 3 of SSL. TLS is a current standard for authenticating and encrypting connections over the Internet.

Transaction (database): A collection of queries that need to be treated as a single unit. A transaction describes several different interactions that all need to succeed before being committed to the database. If any of the interactions fail, the whole transaction is rolled back to the state it was at the beginning.

`urpmi`: A Mandrake program that locates software packages and dependencies, and handles downloading and installing them.

Value-Added Reseller (VAR): A consultant who sells, implements, and customizes Enterprise-level software.

vCalendar: A standard for exchanging and storing calendar data. Version 2 of vCalendar is called iCalendar.

vCard: A standard for exchanging contact data.

Views (BIND): A view is an interface that shows a limited set of data, sometimes transformed from its original format. In the BIND 9 domain name server, you can set up different views for different networks, allowing you to hide your private network names from the Internet, while using the same name server to run your public domain.

Virtual Host: A secondary domain name recognized by a server. Each server has a single canonical host name, but many daemons and services can handle any number of additional host names, called virtual hosts. The Apache Web server is perhaps the most common example of this—one Web server can host thousands of individual Web sites, each on its own virtual host.

Virtual Machine: A computer within a computer. Several software programs provide an environment that imitates a real computer, allowing you to install an operating system within it. Using a virtual machine, you can run programs in other operating systems without rebooting.

Virtual Network Computing (VNC): A system that makes the desktop environment of a remote computer accessible over a network.

Virtual Private Network (VPN): A system that encrypts generic network traffic over the Internet, allowing remote users to securely connect to a LAN.

Virtual User: A login in a server that does not have its own local user account. It's possible to set up an email server to have thousands of virtual users, each with their own mailbox, all sharing a single local Unix user account.

VPN Gateway: A computer that connects a remote computer or network to the local LAN using a Virtual Private Network (VPN).

W3C: World Wide Web Consortium. The W3C specifies standards for HTML, XML, and most information protocols on the Web through a series of documents called RFCs.

WAN: Wide Area Network. A network that covers multiple locations. The Internet is the biggest WAN in the world, but some corporations have private WANs set up to connect offices in remote locations.

Web Bug: An image embedded in an email that contains a code uniquely identifying the message. When you open an email containing a Web bug in an HTML-capable email client, your email client loads this image and in the process confirms to the sender that you read it.

WebDAV: Web-based Distributed Authoring and Versioning. An extension to the basic HTTP protocol that allows programs to copy files to a Web server, in addition to getting them from the server.

Web Service: A program that provides data to other programs, usually using XML, over the Internet.

WEP: Wired Equivalent Privacy. The original encryption system for Wi-Fi, WEP has some fundamental implementation flaws that make it relatively easy to crack with available computers and software.

Whitelist: A list of items you want to bypass a filter and get successfully delivered.

Wi-Fi: A friendlier term to describe wireless devices that use 802.11 standards. Wi-Fi originally only applied to 802.11b, but now is used for any of the related technologies.

Wiki Web (Wiki): A content management system that allows anybody to edit a page. A Wiki often provides a simplified way to format a page, automatically handles links, and allows people to easily create new pages.

Wireless: Technology that sends data without wires. The term wireless includes cellular technologies, infrared, remote controls, Wi-Fi, and a variety of other devices.

Wisdom: Enough knowledge to anticipate unexpected events.

WLAN: Wireless LAN. A local area network that uses Wi-Fi to connect a group of computers.

Workgroup: A Windows networking configuration that associates a group of machines in a peer-to-peer arrangement.

WPA: Wi-Fi Protected Access. An interim method for authenticating and encrypting wireless connections. WPA, at this writing, is used by large organizations to control wireless access before 802.11i gains widespread support.

WYSIWYG: What-You-See-Is-What-You-Get. A description of HTML editors and word processors that show you something that resembles the final result, instead of the code instructions that specify formatting. Pronounced "whizzy wig."

X.500: The original ITU standards describing online directories, including standards, servers, clients, and data structures. X.500 has never been fully implemented; LDAP provides a large subset of the X.500 standards, and has gained widespread use.

X.509: A standard describing digital certificates, authorities, and public key infrastructure.

XML: eXtensible Markup Language. A system for creating markup languages, which allows content to be labeled so it can be used in a particular way.

Zone of Authority: The part of a domain a particular name server controls.

Index